Power and Humility

Democracy urgently needs re-imagining if it is to address the dangers and opportunities posed by current global realities, argues leading political thinker John Keane. He offers an imaginative, radically new interpretation of the twenty-first century fate of democracy. The book shows why the current literature on democracy is failing to make sense of many intellectual puzzles and new political trends. It probes a wide range of themes, from the growth of cross-border institutions and capitalist market failures to the greening of democracy, the dignity of children and the anti-democratic effects of everyday fear, violence and bigotry. Keane develops the idea of 'monitory democracy' to show why periodic free and fair elections are losing their democratic centrality; and why the ongoing struggles by citizens and their representatives, in a multiplicity of global settings, to humble the high and mighty and deal with the dangers of arbitrary power, force us to rethink what we mean by democracy and why it remains a universal ideal.

JOHN KEANE is Professor of Politics at the University of Sydney and at the Wissenschaftszentrum Berlin and Distinguished Professor at Peking University. His many published works include *The Life and Death of Democracy* and *Democracy* (2009) and *Democracy and Media Decadence* (Cambridge, 2013) and *When Trees Fall, Monkeys Scatter: Rethinking Democracy in China* (2017).

Power, by Alfred Kubin (1903)
Image credit: Städtische Galerie im Lenbachhaus und Kunstbau Munich

Power and Humility

The Future of Monitory Democracy

JOHN KEANE
University of Sydney

CAMBRIDGE
UNIVERSITY PRESS

University Printing House, Cambridge CB2 8BS, United Kingdom

One Liberty Plaza, 20th Floor, New York, NY 10006, USA

477 Williamstown Road, Port Melbourne, VIC 3207, Australia

314–321, 3rd Floor, Plot 3, Splendor Forum, Jasola District Centre, New Delhi – 110025, India

79 Anson Road, #06-04/06, Singapore 079906

Cambridge University Press is part of the University of Cambridge.

It furthers the University's mission by disseminating knowledge in the pursuit of education, learning, and research at the highest international levels of excellence.

www.cambridge.org
Information on this title: www.cambridge.org/9781108425223
DOI: 10.1017/9781108348997

© John Keane 2018

This publication is in copyright. Subject to statutory exception and to the provisions of relevant collective licensing agreements, no reproduction of any part may take place without the written permission of Cambridge University Press.

First published 2018

Printed in the United States of America by Sheridan Books, Inc.

A catalogue record for this publication is available from the British Library.

ISBN 978-1-108-42522-3 Hardback
ISBN 978-1-108-44137-7 Paperback

Cambridge University Press has no responsibility for the persistence or accuracy of URLs for external or third-party internet websites referred to in this publication and does not guarantee that any content on such websites is, or will remain, accurate or appropriate.

Contents

	List of Figures	*page* ix
	Introduction	1
	PART I INDIGENISATION	
1	Asia's Orphan: Democracy in Taiwan, 1895–2000	61
2	Indigenous Peoples	75
	PART II COMMUNICATIONS REVOLUTION	
3	Monitory Democracy	103
4	Wild Thinking	133
5	Lying, Truth and Power	180
6	Silence, Early Warnings and Catastrophes	207
	PART III RE-IMAGINING EQUALITY	
7	Capitalism and Civil Society	225
8	The Greening of Democracy	249
9	Child Citizens	270
	PART IV DEMOCRACY ACROSS BORDERS?	
10	Quantum Metaphors	301
11	The European Citizen, 1970–2005	318
12	Antarctica: Democracy at the End of the World	347

PART V VIOLENCE, FEAR, WAR

13 Does Democracy Have a Violent Heart?   379
14 The Triangle of Fear   410

PART VI WHY MONITORY DEMOCRACY?

15 Is Democracy a Universal Ideal?   439

Index   471

Figures

3.1	Territorially bound representative democracy (by Giovanni Navarria)	*page* 111
3.2	Monitory democracy (by Giovanni Navarria)	112
4.1	Ratio of media supply to consumption in minutes per day per household in the United States, 1960–2005	138
4.2	Centralised, decentralised and distributed networks	162
5.1	A. Paul Weber, *Das Gerücht* (The Rumour) 1943	193
14.1	The Triangle of Fear	420

Introduction

The unorthodox perspectives on democracy sketched in this book are the product of deep dissatisfaction with much of the prevailing literature and commentary on the subject. Using various political trends, conflicts and puzzles as its raw material, the book draws inspiration from the conviction that good political writing both engages its readers with contemporary matters and forces them to rethink their cherished certainties: nudged this way and that, they come to question their convictions and prejudices and, generally, grow more wondrous and daring about the world which shapes who they presently are and how in future they might live their daily lives. The whole approach supposes that the subject of democracy urgently requires bold and creative thinking. It calls on those concerned about the future of democracy to abandon dead concepts and worn-out formulae, to become better attuned to the novelties, opportunities and grave dangers of our times. It argues that the option of clinging to the tried, tested and true is not an option, simply because the contemporary democratic imagination is failing in its efforts to name, explain and engage with many threats and opportunities posed by twenty-first century realities. The book sets out to show readers how and why things are happening that are unexpected, or stranger than was once thought possible, or probable. Its whole point is to demonstrate that many real-world things are happening that are far stranger than we can presently think.

Conceived and written and revised at various points during the past two decades, the book attempts to write democratically about democracy. It comes in the form of a set of integrated essays written in a 'pizzicato' style designed to encourage readers to see that the observations, conjectures and predictions offered in these pages are *interpretations*, not set-in-stone

'Truths'. The book does not suppose arrogantly its immunity from follow-up questioning, empirical investigation, critical amendment or savage rejection. It aims to mimic the complex rhythms of democratic life. Building upon the findings presented in *The Life and Death of Democracy*,[1] it probes a new range of research themes, each of them informed and bound together by the astute observation of the Japanese scholar Masao Maruyama (1914–1996) that democracy is a unique and highly contingent political form whose embrace of the principle of equality of power cannot in practice happen, and cannot survive the ravages of time, unless human actors minimally experience a quantum leap of imagination. Every political form, Maruyama insisted, has a 'fictional' or 'imaginary' quality. Democracy is no exception to this rule. There is nothing 'natural' or inevitable about it. Democracy's refusal to accept that some human beings are fit to rule the rest becomes possible only when there is an imaginary leap, a profound transformation of the linguistically structured mental horizons of people, who as a consequence become capable of rejecting what Maruyama called the 'psychology of the ruled'. When this transformation of their horizons happens, he concluded, they become capable of regarding each other as equals, as confident citizens who can govern themselves without recourse to the bossing and manipulation inevitably associated with other political forms.[2]

Not every reader will agree or be satisfied with the book's call for a radical stretching and refiguring of the imaginary horizons of democracy. Yet there can be no doubt that the whole idea of linguistic horizons that pre-form our thinking – an approach developed elsewhere, for instance in the philosophy of one of my former teachers Hans-Georg Gadamer[3] – is a most useful framing category in the analysis of democracy and its future. Of course, those who deal daily with horizons – airline pilots, astronauts, fishermen, coastguards, surveyors, landscape artists – know from experience just how deceptive and contestable they are. Intellectuals who think of themselves as indebted to the heliocentric revolution first proposed by Copernicus against Ptolemy, or who have pondered the astonishing Earthrise photograph taken during the Apollo 8 mission of 1968, also know that horizons are not fixed points or tangible places; they constantly

---

[1] John Keane, *The Life and Death of Democracy* (London and New York: Simon & Schuster, 2009).
[2] Masao Maruyama, *Thought and Behaviour in Modern Japanese Politics* (Tokyo: Oxford University Press, 1979), p. 251.
[3] Hans-Georg Gadamer, *Truth and Method* (New York: The Seabury Press, 1975).

play tricks on our senses, seduce us into believing that distances and destinations are tangible, that they can be defined, plotted and searched for with a fair measure of certainty. The elusiveness of horizons makes them a useful metaphor for what I am aiming to achieve in this book. To speak of refiguring the twenty-first-century horizons of democracy is to confront mainstream political science and its fetish for 'facts' and figures. It puts to the test its conviction that such democratic phenomena as elections, political parties and legislatures are best studied using empirical and statistical methods that put an end to future paradigm revolutions because they yield certain knowledge of our political world, in effect ensuring that in the field of democracy research findings are so 'firmly established' that 'future discoveries must be looked for in the sixth place of decimals'.[4] The approach of this book stands restlessly at right angles to such presumption. It calls for urgently needed 'thinking outside the box', for 'wild thinking' or what philosophers have called abductive reasoning; that is, new approaches that pay attention to the way modifying and stretching our linguistic horizons can help make better sense of our world, transforming our perceptions of democracy, and, in the process, altering research priorities and methods and generally upgrading the capacity of researchers to understand their subject better, as well as to communicate with each other, and with citizens and representatives, about matters that are of pressing importance to the present and future of democracy.

PRECEPTS

The contrarian but constructive perspectives developed below draw on several deep precepts; they are important to spell out because they divulge my biases and provide a 'feel' for the prickly distinctiveness of my analysis of the transformations, trials and tribulations of contemporary democracy. In what follows, the commonplace solipsist view that everyone has their own definition of democracy, and that each individual definition is as valid as any other, is called into question. The Humpty Dumpty Principle, the view that democracy can be made to mean anything powerful people want it to mean, is given an equally hard time. The approach of this book is altogether different. It supposes that publicly meaningful

---

[4] These are the oft-quoted words of the German–American physicist Albert Abraham Michelson, *Light Waves and Their Uses* (Chicago: University of Chicago Press, 1903), pp. 23–24.

analyses of democracy must find their bearings in *context-sensitive, evidence-enriched* re-descriptions of the languages, institutions and actors that comprise any given experiment with democracy. Note the word re-description: it serves as a reminder that 'reality' is a word, and that every description of 'reality' (including this one) is unavoidably from a particular point of view.

The book further supposes that democratic realities are always infused with ideals, so that *normative accounts of democracy* are not a theoretical distraction or unnecessary luxury, but a vital component of the study of democracy. This is another way of saying that in matters of research on democracy 'reality' is never straightforwardly 'real'; what counts as 'evidence', 'facts', 'objectivity' and 'reality' always and everywhere comes wrapped in language-structured perceptions of the way things are, and where supposedly they are heading, and ought to be heading. Although written more than a century ago, the remarks of Max Weber are surely still convincing on this point: 'There is no absolutely "objective" scientific analysis of ... "social phenomena" independent of ... "one-sided" viewpoints according to which – expressly or tacitly, consciously or unconsciously – they are selected, analysed and organized for expository purposes.'[5] The point was reiterated in Ludwig Wittgenstein's later reflections on the ways in which what counts as certain knowledge of 'empirical facts', and such matters as the difference between 'true' and 'false', are always shaped by more or less taken-for-granted presumptions harboured by the language 'scaffolding' (*Gerüst*) within which we think, interpret, judge and live our everyday lives. His point was that certainty takes refuge in the language games we play; but the presumptions that feed our certainties are themselves contingent; that is, time–space dependent, and therefore never fully insulated from doubt, uncertainty and rejection. 'What people consider reasonable or unreasonable changes', wrote Wittgenstein. 'At certain moments, people find reasonable what at other periods they found unreasonable.'[6]

Wittgenstein's insight remains important, for it underscores the point that considerations of the past, present and future of democracy are always infused with time–space imaginings. That is why, on every page of this book, emphasis is given to the strategic importance within democratic

---

[5] Max Weber, *The Methodology of the Social Sciences* (New York: The Free Press, 1949), p. 72.
[6] Ludwig Wittgenstein, *Über Gewissheit/On Certainty* (New York, London and Sydney: Arion Press, 1972), aphorism 336 (my translation).

theory of developing a much stronger sense of *historical awareness*, not just because nothing is ever forever, or because contemporary democratic theory is largely in the hands of amnesiacs whose neglect or ignorance of the past inevitably spawns misunderstandings of the present, but also (and much less obviously) because democracy is a *uniquely time-sensitive political form* that tends to cultivate a shared public sense of the contingency of power relations within human affairs.[7] The analysis in the pages below of the ways children are coming to be seen as potential citizens is just one instance of democracy in action. For when people's lives are infused with the spirit of democracy, their 'sense of possibility' (Robert Musil) grows strong. Their contrasting 'sense of reality' includes the realisation that things that are might well be otherwise. They push themselves to the known limits of human achievement. They do not privilege what is past or present over what is not yet. They know that reality is malleable; they are believers in metamorphosis. Their sense of possibility thus sharpens their conviction that power relations are never simply given, or forever.

Throughout this book, power relations are understood not just as synonymous with state or governing institutions but as a universal feature of all human life lived within non-human contexts. Of course, power is not a 'thing'. It is not a substance to be held or grabbed, but a relationship of enablement and disablement of people born into environments not of their own choosing, or their subsequent making. Power is the institutionally constrained capacity of people to act upon the world, to realise their chosen capacities, their strivings to live well with others, in multiple domains. Power is here, there and everywhere: from the bedroom and the homeless shelter to the boardroom and the backroom to the battlefield and beyond, to the biomes in which we dwell. So are the flipside dialectics: cunning, cheating, clever and brutish power moves, defensive and aggressive exercises of *arbitrary power* are equally universal features of human life lived within non-human contexts. This ubiquity of power principle leads this book to draw upon another precept, one emphasised by C.B. Macpherson (my doctoral supervisor), for whom democracy was much more than just a mode of electioneering or government. According to Macpherson, democracy must instead be understood expansively, as *a whole way of life*, as a vision of citizens equally entitled (his favourite words) to the 'use and enjoyment' of their capacities.[8] It follows from this

---

[7] This is among the key points made at length in Keane, *The Life and Death of Democracy*.
[8] C.B. Macpherson, *The Life and Times of Liberal Democracy* (Oxford, London and New York: Oxford University Press, 1977).

ubiquity of power principle that reflection on the subject of the past, present and future of democracy must spread its wings. It needs to engage themes as diverse as the colonisation of indigenous peoples, the labelling and treatment of children, the fate of our planetary biosphere, the failures and follies of capitalist markets, the political risks posed by megaprojects and the poisonous effects of fear, violence and bigotry in everyday life settings.

Finally, this book is motivated by dissatisfaction with the *unthinking habit of applying Western yardsticks* when studying democracy. For more than seven decades, the languages and institutions of democracy in representative form have been disseminated to all four corners of our Earth, on a scale never before witnessed. The whole world is making its mark on democracy, and this growing worldliness of democracy contrasts sharply with the unfortunate fact that the centre of gravity of research on democracy continues to be universities, think tanks and other institutions situated in the rather confined Atlantic region of our large planet. Research on democracy remains mostly an affair of the WEIRD world: societies that are by global standards Western, Educated, Industrialised, Rich and nominally Democratic.[9] Pushing beyond the first-go effort of *The Life and Death of Democracy* to try its hand at writing a global history of democracy, this book supposes that the hegemony of the WEIRD world has outlived its usefulness. Its grip has become untenable and now must be broken. What is urgently needed are more worldly wise approaches, bold and feisty research initiatives that acknowledge that the world is less and less America or Europe; that the imaginary homelands of democracy are changing; and that the analysis of democracy must open its horizons to a wide variety of global settings, global issues and global dynamics previously ignored by mainstream scholars of the Atlantic region.

INDIGENISATION

The sense of worldly adventure sewn into the pages of this book begins by noting that in 1945, following several decades that saw most experiments in democratisation fail, only a dozen parliamentary democracies were left on the face of our Earth. Since then, despite many ups and downs, the political form and way of life called democracy has bounced back from near oblivion to become a planetary phenomenon, for the

---

[9] Jared Diamond, *The World Until Yesterday: What Can We Learn from Traditional Societies?* (New York: Penguin Books, 2013).

first time in its history.¹⁰ Fresh research perspectives on this epochal change are urgently required. For the point has been reached where the spirit, language and institutions of democracy have taken root in so many different geographic contexts that several reigning presumptions of democratic theory have been invalidated. As democracy has spread through the world, the world has made its mark on democracy, even though the metamorphosis has remained largely unregistered in the literature on democracy. Two Anglo-centric examples of this lack immediately spring to mind: the effort of the English scholar John Dunn to write a history of the word democracy while ignoring its pre-Greek origins, its survival in the early Muslim world, its earliest modern redefinition in the Low Countries, its penetration of the countries of Spanish America during the nineteenth century, and its more recent metamorphosis in contexts as different as southern Africa, Taiwan, Indonesia and India;¹¹ and the influential textbook treatment by David Held of various 'models' of democracy, a fairly conventional narrative whose core normative 'principle of autonomy' has a nineteenth-century liberal individualist bias, and whose whole distinctively Anglo-centric approach precludes references to many anomalous cases and worrying trends, both past and present.¹²

The insularity lurking within these accounts has much deeper foundations. Well into the twentieth century, Atlantic-region analysts of democracy supposed that the functional prerequisites of democracy included (a) a 'sovereign' territorial state that guaranteed the physical security of a resident population of citizens living within a rule of law system; (b) a political culture favouring mechanisms that were widely supposed to be synonymous with democracy – parliamentary government based on competition among political parties and periodic 'free and fair' elections; (c) a more or less homogeneous social infrastructure or 'national identity' bound together by a common language, common customs and a common sense of shared history; and (d) a market economy capable of generating investment and wealth that lifted citizens out of poverty and guaranteed them a basic standard of living sufficient to enable them to take an interest in public affairs.

---

¹⁰ Larry Diamond, *The Spirit of Democracy: The Struggle to Build Free Societies Throughout the World* (New York: H. Holt, 2008); Keane, *The Life and Death of Democracy*, especially the final part.
¹¹ John Dunn, *Setting the People Free: The Story of Democracy* (London: Atlantic Books, 2005).
¹² David Held, *Models of Democracy*, 3rd edn (Cambridge: Polity Press, 2006).

The grip of each of these supposed prerequisites has been broken during the past generation. The thought-provoking case of Taiwan is discussed in the opening section of this book; elsewhere, I have analysed in some depth the novelty and global significance of India's experiment with 'banyan democracy'.[13] Together with South Africa, Botswana, Colombia, Nepal and the Tibetan Government in Exile, these two cases are just some of the anomalous cases that throw into disarray many presumptions about 'liberal democracy' in such disciplinary fields as political science, sociology, economics and international relations. In each case, the meaning of democracy and the ways in which it took root in local soils prompt new questions regarding what future research might call the *indigenisation of democracy*. In this book, drawing on the Asia Pacific examples of Taiwan and Australia, this phrase refers to the manifold complex ways in which the language and institutions and normative ideals of democracy undergo mutations when they are carried more or less successfully into unfamiliar environments, where previously they either did not exist or exercised little or no influence. Indigenisation is what happens when locals take the language, norms and institutions of democracy from the outside and make them their own. Democracy undergoes domestication; the domestic experiences democratisation.

Indigenisation is always a highly complex and contested set of processes.[14] So what is arguably needed is a new twenty-first century *political anthropology of democracy*: new approaches sustained by fresh perspectives, metaphors, theories and methods for making sense of the way in which democracy undergoes alterations when it takes root in strange new soils. For this purpose, translation and other literary similes drawn from linguistic philosophy have sometimes been utilised, most notably in Frederic Schaffer's remarkable study of the ways in which Wolof and French speakers in Senegal, the country with the oldest tradition of multi-party government in Africa, adopted and transformed ('vernacularised') the European donor language of *démocratie* to make new sense of the importance of electoral practices within a culturally divergent society that calls itself a *demokaraasi*.[15] Other scholars have adapted a different

---

[13] Keane, *The Life and Death of Democracy*, pp. 585–647.
[14] Marshall Sahlins, 'What is Anthropological Enlightenment? Some Lessons of the Twentieth Century', *Annual Review of Anthropology*, 28 (1999), i–xxiii.
[15] Frederic C. Schaffer, *Democracy in Translation: Understanding Politics in an Unfamiliar Culture* (Ithaca, NY: Cornell University Press, 1998). Subsequent accounts of the 'vernacularisation' of democracy, focused on India, include Akio Tanabe, 'Toward Vernacular Democracy: Moral Society and Post-Postcolonial Transformation in Rural Orissa, India',

approach, originally outlined by Michel de Certeau, to examine the ways in which the tactical adoption of a procedure, like the secret ballot, is always a creative 'theatrical' performance that results, unpredictably, in long-lasting changes in its functioning.[16]

Still other literature (*The Life and Death of Democracy* strives to be an example[17]) has borrowed the language of mutations, mutagens and other terms from evolutionary biology within the field of the bio-sciences. In contrast to political science approaches that emphasise aggregate trends guided either by teleology ('liberal democracy' as the 'end of history'[18]) or by maritime metaphors (most influential has been the 'third wave' approach[19]), this third alternative examines changes in the language, institutions and norms of democracy by drawing loose analogies with those sudden or more protracted mutations in the inherited characteristics of the cells of organisms deep down within the earth's biosphere. The reasoning of this approach is a direct challenge to mainstream searches for a general theory of democratisation with homogeneous qualities. It rather highlights the ways in which particular mutations may transcend unfitness and consequent death. Mutations can be beneficial. Sometimes they produce organisms much better adapted to their environment, in which case the process of competitive selection enables the altered gene to be passed on successfully to subsequent generations. These beneficial mutations turn out to be the raw material of evolution and adaptation to changing environments, as in the illuminating case, examined below, of Taiwan's adventure with a form of democracy that cannot be called 'liberal democracy' in any meaningful sense. Taiwan is not America. Taiwan is not the United Kingdom, or Germany. It is different: in the East Asia region, outside the secure framework of 'sovereign territoriality', its citizens and their representatives have managed to craft a new mutant form of 'dragon fruit' democracy guided by a mixed parliamentary/presidential form of government embedded in a media-saturated and

---

American Ethnologist, 34, 3 (2007), 558–574; and Lucia Michelutti, *The Vernacularisation of Democracy: Politics, Caste and Religion in Contemporary India* (London and New York: Routledge, 2008).

[16] Romain Bertrand, Jean-Louis Briquet and Peter Pels (eds.), *Cultures of Voting: The Hidden History of the Secret Ballot* (London: C. Hurst, 2007).

[17] Keane, *The Life and Death of Democracy*, pp. 673–686.

[18] Francis Fukuyama, *The End of History and the Last Man* (New York: The Free Press, 1992).

[19] Samuel P. Huntington, *The Third Wave: Democratization in the Late Twentieth Century* (Norman, OK: University of Oklahoma Press, 1991).

multi-cultural civil society. Taiwan is a distinctively non-liberal democracy, a mutant polity whose citizens are strongly aware of their own indigenous roots and strongly attached to the belief in multiple deities, the virtues of strong households and deep political suspicion of concentrated power in arbitrary form.

It should be obvious that analogies drawn from linguistics, theatre and evolutionary biology must be handled with great care, and with keen awareness of their limitations. But in pursuit of new ways of analysing and evaluating the global processes by which democratic languages and institutions become 'embedded'[20] and reinterpreted in particular contexts, one thing seems abundantly clear: the field of research centred on the global spread of democracy is wide open for creating novel metaphors, fresh interpretations and original case studies that add significance to the thesis of indigenisation and, in turn, force the redefinition and refinement of our understanding of democracy, past and present. Much arguably can be learned from the reinterpretation of efforts to nurture democracy on 'foreign soils', including Athenian efforts at what has come to be called 'democracy promotion' and the invention of the norms and institutions of representative democracy in France and their diffusion to the British colonies and Spanish America.[21] Of equal interest are the colonial sources of democratisation in China and Japan during the last great growth spurt of globalisation that lasted roughly from 1870 to 1930.[22] There is much scope as well for scholarly reinterpretation of the spread of new forms of democracy in the current round of globalisation,

---

[20] Wolfgang Merkel, 'Embedded and Defective Democracies', *Democratization*, 11 (2004), 33–58.
[21] John B. Hirst, *Australia's Democracy: A Short History* (Sydney: Allen & Unwin, 2002); Alexander Keyssar, *The Right to Vote: The Contested History of Democracy in the United States* (New York: Basic Books, 2000); Pierre Rosanvallon, *Le sacre du citoyen: Histoire du suffrage universel en France* (Paris: Gallimard, 1992); Pierre Rosanvallon, *Le peuple introuvable: Histoire de la représentation démocratique en France* (Paris: Gallimard, 1998); Pierre Rosanvallon, *La démocratie inachevée: Histoire de la souveraineté du peuple en France* (Paris: Gallimard, 2000); Pierre Rosanvallon, *Le modèle politique français: La société civile contre le jacobinisme de 1789 à nos jours* (Paris: Gallimard, 2004).
[22] Rwei-Ren Wu, *The Formosan Ideology: Oriental Colonialism and the Rise of Taiwanese Nationalism, 1895–1945* (Chicago, IL: University of Chicago Press, 2003); Hao Chang, *Liang Ch'i-chao and Intellectual Transition in China 1890–1907* (Cambridge, MA: Harvard University Press, 1971); Nobutaka Ike, *The Beginnings of Political Democracy in Japan* (Baltimore, MD: Johns Hopkins University Press, 1950); John W. Dower, *Embracing Defeat: Japan in the Aftermath of World War II* (Harmondsworth: Penguin, 2000).

including much-neglected cases that include Bhutan, Papua New Guinea, Tanzania and the world of predominantly Muslim societies, such as Tunisia and Indonesia.[23]

The conventional accounts of the implantation of federalist visions of representative democracy in so-called settler societies also seem ripe for reinterpretation along these lines. In the case of Australia, examined in the early pages of this book, the standard narrative is that the piecemeal colonisation of the continent propelled the conjoining of the various colonies into a new democratic federation, as if through an act of historical inevitability backed by imperial power. It turns out that the nineteenth-century push towards federation proved to be more complicated, and intensely conflicted. Parliamentary federalism was the contested resultant of many forces. Post-1776 reassessments of British views of empire certainly played a role, as did the militant resistance of both indigenous peoples and local colonists, visions inspired by the American 'compound republic' (Madison) and decentralist initiatives guided by the pre-colonial mental maps and patterns of movement of indigenous peoples.[24] Of special interest to the analysis sketched below is a contradiction that was deeply structured into the local form of representative democracy, a deep tension that in retrospect gives a brand new meaning to the word indigenisation. There is no doubt that local settler struggles for popular representation in *terra australis* had a positively democratic side: they threw into question the anti-democratic prejudices of power groups, rich and powerful, male landowners for instance, who supposed that inequalities among people were 'natural', or God-given. Especially during the decade after 1845, my analysis suggests, the white-skinned champions of democracy typically thought of themselves as free-born Britons. They sang God Save the Queen and professed their belief in the

---

[23] Examples of the new scholarly interest in the contemporary indigenisation of democracy include Nitasha Kaul, 'Bearing Witness in Bhutan', *Economic and Political Weekly*, 43, 37 (2008), 67–69; Ramachandra Guha, *India after Gandhi: The History of the World's Largest Democracy* (London: Pan, 2007); Benjamin Reilly, *Democracy in Divided Societies: Electoral Engineering for Conflict Management* (Cambridge: Cambridge University Press, 2001); Leo Scheps, 'The Native Roots of Papua New Guinea's Democracy', *Quadrant*, 44 (2000), 52–58; Keane, *The Life and Death of Democracy*; Larbi Sadiki, *Rethinking Arab Democratization: Elections without Democracy* (Oxford: Oxford University Press, 2009) and R. William Liddle, *Indonesia's Democratic Transition: Playing by the Rules* (Oxford: Oxford University Press, 2002).

[24] Alexander J. Brown, 'Constitutional Schizophrenia, Then and Now: Exploring Federalist, Regionalist and Unitary Strands in the Australian Political Tradition', *Papers on Parliament*, 42 (2004), 33–58.

monarchy. They were also fierce champions of what they variously called 'representative government', 'democracy', 'self-government' and 'responsible government' based on the will of 'the people'. Yet all this rhetoric stood at right angles to their murderously anti-democratic portrayal of local indigenous peoples as 'uncivilised', as ugly, dirty beasts miserably under-equipped for modern life. The white settlers' 'civilised' way of thinking came tinged with bigotry and violence. Since colonial control over land and resources was at stake, 'civilisation' implied, at a minimum, the physical subjugation of indigenous peoples and either their outright elimination (although colonial governors typically spoke against unrestrained frontier violence) or the transformation of these peoples – using such means as informal negotiations, land clearing, government reservations, adoption practices and religious education – into 'civilised' characters capable of acknowledging that representative democracy was a superior form of government.

For 'the Aborigines', such talk of 'civility' and 'civilisation' had a killing quality; my analysis suggests that the sad and well-documented truth is that the civilising process forced them to fight life-or-death battles against extinction. Facing frightening odds, their population numbers were reduced by an estimated five-sixths during the period of colonisation. Yet they managed to survive and more recently to multiply, with several important implications for the local form of representative democracy. Slowly but surely, my analysis concludes, indigenous peoples forced many white Australians to carve out a distinctive sense of national identity through the generous absorption of indigenous symbols. Indigenous citizens have begun to teach white people lessons about the need to 'blacken' their ways, for instance by swapping their reckless and profligate ways with the biosphere for a self-conscious understanding of their dependence upon its long-term sustainability. Indigenous peoples are today also engaged in experiments with self-government and making demands for political representation in the prevailing structures of power. Of greatest significance, perhaps, is that indigenous peoples have helped give birth to a new politics of restorative justice and 'irruptions of memory', of the kind that has emerged in other settler/coloniser democracies, such as Canada, Bolivia and Chile.[25] Thanks to their survivor

---

[25] See the treatments of Bashir Bashir and Will Kymlicka, 'Introduction: Struggles for Inclusion and Reconciliation in Modern Democracies', in Will Kymlicka and Bashir Bashir (eds.), *The Politics of Reconciliation in Multicultural Societies* (Oxford: Oxford University Press, 2008), pp. 1–24; Alexander Wilde, 'Irruptions of Memory: Expressive

qualities, indigenous peoples and their supporters in these settings have gradually forced onto the political agenda the whole issue of public memory of injustice. The new politics of remembering asks whether, and to what extent, the predominantly white citizens who are the offspring of a conquering democracy can come to feel shame. It calls on them to understand that if they forget the past, they are its guilty accomplices. The new politics implies the need for them to say more than sorry, and to strive for new democratic forms of representation and reconciliation that have no precedent in the history of their local democracy.

MONITORY DEMOCRACY AND THE COMMUNICATIONS REVOLUTION

New research on the indigenisation of democracy inevitably raises questions about how to construct meaningful time periods within the history of democracy. When historians look back on the early years of the twenty-first century, for instance, will they categorise existing forms of democracy differently than we currently do? We cannot by definition be sure. But among contemporary journalists, politicians, scholars and other analysts of democracy it is customary to speak of 'liberal democracy', 'Western democracy' and 'parliamentary democracy'. These and other epithets arguably function as living-dead 'zombie' categories that have the effect of suppressing the novel spacetime dynamics that are unfolding within actually existing democracies. Spacetime variations of the political form known as democracy are multiplying; ever more species of democracy are identifiable. At the same time, the genus of democracy itself is undergoing a major historical transformation. The family of democratic types is expanding. Slowly but surely, against formidable odds, a new historical type or genus of democracy unknown to our ancestors is being born.

The theory of monitory democracy presented here tries to grasp and re-describe these spacetime transformations. Guided by a strong sense of the historicity of things, and by the thought that the history closest to us is the most difficult to comprehend, it draws strength from the historical observation that since 1945 a major sea change has been taking place in the real world of democracy. The age of monitory democracy is a worldwide

---

Politics in Chile's Transition to Democracy', *Journal of Latin American Studies*, 31, 2 (1999), 473–500; and Nancy Grey Postero and Leon Zamosc (eds.), *The Struggle for Indigenous Rights in Latin America* (Brighton: Sussex Academic Press, 2006).

phenomenon born a generation ago.²⁶ A clue to its novelty is the invention of scores of power-scrutinising and power-checking mechanisms – truth tribunals, human rights organisations, summits, public forums, integrity commissions, digital whistle-blowing, earth watch networks, participatory budgeting schemes and citizens' assemblies are among the best known – whose combined effect has been gradually to alter the spirit, language, political geometry and everyday dynamics of democracy. From the monitory democracy perspective, democracy is coming to mean much more than the periodic election of representatives to a legislature – though nothing less. In the new age of monitory democracy, or so this line of thinking suggests, elections still count, but parties and parliaments now have to compete with a myriad of monitory organisations and networks geared to keeping arbitrary power on its toes, and to taming its excesses and evils.

'Elections, open, free and fair', wrote a past master in the field of political science, 'are the essence of democracy, the inescapable sine qua non'.²⁷ That is no longer true. In the age of monitory democracy, political parties and parliaments have lost their footing. They are finding it hard to track and tame the pulses of power, or to play the role of leading public representatives of citizens and their interests. The old meaning of democracy as 'the organisation of peaceful competition to hold the reins of power',²⁸ the periodic election of representatives, based on the rule of one person, one vote, is dying. It is being superseded by a type of democracy guided by a different and more complex rule: one person, many interests, many votes and chosen representatives, both at home and abroad. Democracy means not just free and fair elections held at periodic intervals. It is not to be equated with so-called 'deliberative democracy', in which individuals try to 'defend their moral and political arguments and claims with reasons' and 'deliberate with others about the reasons they provide'.²⁹ Nor is it to be confused with the originally Greek ideal of 'participatory democracy' and citizens' 'right to participate' in decision-making that 'affects their lives'. Monitory democracy is different. It means

---

[26] John Keane, 'The Origins of Monitory Democracy', *The Conversation* (24 September 2012), https://theconversation.com/the-origins-of-monitory-democracy-9752.
[27] Samuel Huntington, *The Third Wave: Democratization in the Late Twentieth Century* (Norman, OK and London: University of Oklahoma Press, 1991), p. 9.
[28] Raymond Aron, *Introduction à la philosophie politique: Démocratie et revolution* (Paris: Livre de Poche, 1977), p. 36.
[29] Carole Pateman, 'Participatory Democracy Revisited [APSA Presidential Address]', *Perspectives on Politics*, 10, 1 (2012), 1–19.

Def of monitory democracy [handwritten annotation]

something much richer: the ongoing struggle by citizens and their representatives, in a multiplicity of settings, to humble the high and mighty. Democracy is the unending, never-finished public business of scrutinising and restraining their power. It is the struggle against arbitrary power and the hubris it breeds by people and institutions skilled at using both the weapon of periodic elections and various monitory mechanisms positioned beneath and beyond parliamentary and state institutions.

The following pages offer many examples of the impressive resilience and creativity of monitory democracy in defining, handling and settling power disputes, outside of the rhythms and mechanisms of electoral politics. Often against daunting odds, courts and other monitory mechanisms backed by civil society organisations manage to achieve such victories as same-sex marriage laws and court rulings against the detention of military prisoners without trial.[30] The contemporary growth of monitory democracy nevertheless has no historical guarantees of political success. When rocked by economic or political crises, or confronted head-on by its enemies, this new historical form of democracy may not survive. And there are signs that monitory democracy suffers from auto-immune diseases. Think of the way present-day monitory democracies produce widespread disaffection with political parties, politicians and 'politics'. Then think of the way this disaffection is tapped by power-hungry populist leaders, Thaksin Shinawatra, Silvio Berlusconi, Marine Le Pen and Geert Wilders, for instance, who pride themselves on their plain-speaking 'bad manners' and rail against political establishments to convince their admirers that their own interests are identical with those of the leader, so turning flesh-and-blood people into the restless, swooning People that the leader says they are.[31] Such anti-democratic trends naturally prompt many difficult but highly intriguing research questions with political implications. For example: What have been the principal drivers of the growth of extra-parliamentary power-scrutiny bodies? How are the different types of monitory mechanisms best catalogued? How best to

---

[30] David Cole, *Engines of Liberty: The Power of Citizen Activists to Make Constitutional Law* (New York: Basic Books, 2016).

[31] Among the best contemporary analyses of populism is Benjamin Moffitt, *The Global Rise of Populism: Performance, Political Style, and Representation* (Stanford, CA: Stanford University Press, 2016). The Italian case is well analysed in Umberto Eco, 'On Mass Media Populism', in *Turning Back the Clock: Hot Wars and Media Populism* (London: Vintage, 2008), pp. 128–156; Paul Ginsborg, *Silvio Berlusconi: Television, Power and Patrimony* (London: Verso, 2005); and Giovanni Sartori, *Il sultanato* (Rome: Laterza, 2009).

construct a taxonomy that is capable of acknowledging, for instance, that auditors-general, anti-corruption commissions and public enquiries are adjuncts to parliamentary assemblies, while other mechanisms, such as environmental watchdogs, WikiLeaks-style platforms, crowd-sourced funding and human rights campaigns operate at a distance from, and often in tension with, elected representatives, parliaments and incumbent governments? Questions should be asked about the extent to which these various monitory mechanisms are presently compounding the political blind spots and weaknesses of contemporary political parties and parliaments, and whether, in effect, these extra-parliamentary monitors are forcing them further into marginality, or historical decline. Counter-questions arise, for instance: Can political parties, elected representatives and parliaments claw back some measure of their legitimate powers? Or are they fated (as seems probable) to share power with *unelected* representatives whose public legitimacy, as explained elsewhere in a study of the fate of leaders after leaving high office, stems from such *unelected* criteria as ethical probity, meritorious achievement, subscription membership, media outspokenness and resilience in suffering?[32]

Among the most basic propositions of this book is that the growth of power-contesting, public accountability institutions is functionally connected to the growth of new communication media. With just a few exceptions, the historical affinities between forms of democracy and modes of communication media are still poorly analysed in contemporary social science literature. The work presented below, as in previous books,[33] tries to combine these two fields, to think in imaginatively 'wild' ways about media and democracy. It thinks of the affinities along the following lines: ancient forms of assembly democracy belonged to an era dominated by the *spoken word*, backed up by laws written on stone or papyrus, and by messages despatched by foot, or donkey or horse. Early modern representative democracy in territorial state form (dating from the end of the eighteenth century) sprang up in the age of *print culture* – the era of the printing press, the book, pamphlet, newspaper and novel, and telegraphed and mailed messages – and fell into crisis during the advent of early mass communication media, especially radio and

---

[32] John Keane, 'Life after Political Death: The Fate of Leaders after Leaving High Office', in John Kane, Haig Patapan, and Paul 't Hart (eds.), *Dispersed Democratic Leadership: Origins, Dynamics, and Implications* (Oxford: Oxford University Press, 2009), pp. 279–298.
[33] John Keane, *The Media and Democracy* (Cambridge: Polity Press, 1990); and *Democracy and Media Decadence* (Cambridge and New York: Cambridge University Press, 2013).

television and cinema and (in its infancy) television. By contrast, or so the argument runs, backed by evidence, contemporary forms of monitory democracy are tied closely to the growth of *multi-media-saturated societies*: societies whose structures of power are continuously interrogated by monitory institutions operating within a new galaxy of media defined by the ethos of 'communicative abundance'.

The reasoning may be overdrawn, but there can be little doubt, as this book tries to make clear, that regardless of how the changing historical relationship between communication media and democracy is interpreted, the distinctive qualities of the emerging galaxy of new communication media require much new thinking and many new questions. The book argues that the new galaxy of communicative abundance is best described in terms of an historic shift: a transition towards the institutional and everyday use of overlapping and networked media devices that integrate texts, sounds and images and enable communication to happen through multiple user points, in chosen time, either real or delayed, within modularised networks that are affordable and accessible to many thousands of millions of people scattered across the globe. From this historical perspective, the book probes the several ways in which the unfinished communications revolution constructively feeds the spirit and institutions of monitory democracy. The positive instances of this feedback relationship include the irruption of publicity in zones of life once regarded as 'private'; the challenge of muckraking investigative journalism to cheap and nasty 'churnalism'; and the democratisation of information privileges once monopolised by elites thanks to the growth of new information banks and information-spreading; that is, the dramatic widening of access to published materials previously unavailable to publics, or formerly available only to restricted circles of users.

The analysis sticks to the coastline of current trends. It tries throughout to be sober, not starry-eyed, and it does so by paying attention to the darker sides of our new age of communicative abundance. It acknowledges the remarkable democratic potential of communicative abundance. Yet it also notes that the communications revolution of our time spawns public disappointments and harmful self-contradictions, for instance in the shape of concentrations of media capital, the erosion and commercialisation of public service media and the widening power gaps between communication-rich and communication-poor citizens. The book asks whether and to what extent the strongly generative qualities of digital media networks are vulnerable to degenerative trends (viruses and cyberattacks are examples) that fuel the growth of a 'splinternet' defined by new hierarchies and restricted public access 'gated communities' that weaken the richly democratic potential of communicative abundance. Other dysfunctions are discussed, including the threats to monitory democracy posed by red-blooded journalism concerned less with fact-based 'objectivity' (an ideal born of the age of representative democracy) and more with adversarial and 'gotcha' styles of commercial journalism driven by ratings, sales and hits.

The book notes the transformative effects of 'citizen journalists' who operate through hand-held cameras, mobile phones, weblogs, tweets and social networking platforms. It interprets their work as part of a much bigger transformation: the decline of gate-keeping media that once decided for millions of people what was newsworthy, and what was the truth, and the rise of networks of gate-watching platforms that make, discover, share and dispute news about our world.[34] The book acknowledges that democracies functionally require an 'unlovable press'.[35] It has an open mind about the extent to which media sensationalism adds substance to democracy by giving a voice to 'ordinary people' talking publicly about their private fears, fantasies, hopes and expectations. But the book also pinpoints some of the seriously perverse effects of the work of 'churnalists' who hunt in packs, feed upon unconfirmed sources, spin titillating sensations and concentrate much too much on personalities and 'breaking news' events, rather than time-bound contexts. Of special interest to the analysis are the dangerous dynamics of public silence (non-information) and 'post-truth' lying (dis-information, intentionally 'saying what is not so') that grip media-saturated societies. The phenomena of public silence and lying are used to illustrate the point that democratic theory can speak meaningfully and critically of 'media decadence' and 'media failures'.[36] These phrases are used to analyse those junctures when powerful actors and organisations are not subject to public scrutiny, or when journalists are responsible for circulating firestorms of dis-information before inaccuracies and outright lies are corrected. Drawing upon the writings of Alexandre Koyré and others, the book emphasises

---

[34] Axel Bruns, *Gatewatching: Collaborative Online News Production* (New York: Peter Lang, 2005) and *Gatewatching and News Caution: Journalism, Social media, and the Public Sphere* (New York: Peter Lang, 2017).
[35] Michael Schudson, *Why Democracies Need an Unlovable Press* (Cambridge: Polity Press, 2009).
[36] The concept of media decadence was first introduced in John Keane, 'Media Decadence and Democracy', *Senate Occasional Lecture* (Canberra, Australian Senate, 28 August 2009). It is refined in Keane, *Democracy and Media Decadence*.

the paradoxical quality of these dysfunctions: it shows why an age of multi-media saturation, that turns everything 'private' into raw material for 'publicity', in reality produces zones of arbitrary (publicly unaccountable) power camouflaged in veiled silence laced with lies. In opposition to this trend, the book sketches and defends a new understanding of public communication guided by the 'early warning principle'. It reminds readers that unaccountable power is prone to folly and hubris. Suspicious of those who gripe publicly against the modern 'addiction to believing the worst of everyone' (former British Prime Minister Tony Blair), this book warns that there are times when arbitrary rule results in great irreversible evils. Publicly unaccountable power is threatening and dangerous for democracy which is why, the book argues, crying foul, surprise 'leaks' and shocking public revelations become necessary and predictably commonplace in the age of monitory democracy.

MARKETS AND DEMOCRACY

The tensions between journalism, communications media and democracy are mired in a larger magnetic field: the fractious and often contradictory relationship between capitalist markets and monitory democracy. A new politics based on new analyses of the history of this embattled force field is vital for guaranteeing the future of democracy, as Wolfgang Streeck, Thomas Piketty and others have recently reminded us.[37] From the early years of the nineteenth century, and especially during periods of capital dis-investment and mass unemployment, the relationship between capitalism and democracy has been a source of great public disturbance, state violence and pressures for institutional reform. At various moments in its crisis-ridden history, capitalism has been charged with crushing the spirit and substance of representative self-government; as Thorstein Veblen famously formulated the equation, there are historical moments when 'democratic sovereignty' is converted into 'a cloak to cover the nakedness of a government that does business for the kept classes'.[38] The recent

---

[37] Wolfgang Streeck, *Buying Time: The Delayed Crisis of Democratic Capitalism* (London: Verso, 2014); Thomas Piketty, *Capital in the Twenty-First Century* (Cambridge, MA and London: Harvard University Press, 2014); Juergen Kocka, *Capitalism: A Short History* (Princeton, NJ: Princeton University Press, 2016).

[38] Thorstein Veblen, *The Vested Interests and the Common Man* (New York, 1919), p. 125; compare his earlier complaint that 'constitutional government is business government', a political arrangement that thrives on the 'popular metaphysics' that 'the material interests of the populace coincide with the pecuniary interests of those business men who live

period of global recession and stagnation has helped revive new versions of this old formula. The subject of capitalism versus democracy is back; market stasis has had the political effect of breathing new life into an old subject waiting for fresh research and a new democratic politics to happen.

The work on markets, civil society and the problem of inequality that is presented below is a modest contribution to larger efforts to fill the gap. It engages the emerging 'capitalism and democracy' debate in several ways. The discussion aims to be forward-looking, but it has eyes in the back of its head. Drawing strength from past thinkers and key historical cases, it shows why the standard 'no bourgeois, no democracy'[39] formula is implausible, and why viable democratic institutions, such as citizens assemblies, public juries, political parties and periodic elections, have always been contingently related to a wide repertoire of property forms. The early Greek assembly democracies, for instance, enjoyed a functional but tense relationship with commodity production and exchange; the life of (male) citizens was widely seen as standing in opposition to the production by women and slaves of the necessaries of life in the sphere of the *oikos*. The modern forms of representative democracy that first sprang up in the Low Countries, at the end of the sixteenth century, were by contrast intimately bound up with profit-driven commodity production and exchange. Modern capitalism and representative democracy were often warring twins. 'The further democratisation advanced', a distinguished historian notes, 'the more likely it was to find large parts of the bourgeoisie on the side of those who warned against, criticised or opposed further democratisation'.[40] From the beginning, capitalism seemed to be supportive of parliamentary government. Capitalist dynamics helped gradually erode older forms of unequal dependency of the feudal, monarchic and patriarchal kind. The spread of commodity production and exchange triggered tensions between state power and property-owning and creditor citizens jealous of their liberties provided by civil society. Modern capitalism also laid the foundations for the radicalisation of civil society, in the shape of powerful mass movements of workers protected

---

within the same set of government contrivances' (Thorstein Veblen, *The Theory of Business Enterprise* [New York: Macmillan, 1915], pp. 285–286).

[39] Barrington Moore, Jr., *Social Origins of Dictatorship and Democracy* (Boston, MA: Beacon Press, 1966), p. 418.

[40] Jürgen Kocka, *Capitalism Is Not Democratic and Democracy Not Capitalistic* (Florence: Firenze University Press, 2015), p. 24.

by trade unions, political parties and governments committed to widening the franchise and building welfare state institutions.

Since early modern times, and especially from 1945 onwards, capitalist markets have proven to be a mixed blessing for democracy in representative form. The dynamism, technical innovation and enhanced productivity of (unconstrained) markets have been impressive. Equally notable have been their rapaciousness, unequal (class-structured) outcomes, reckless exploitation of nature and their vulnerability to bubbles, whose inevitable bursting generates wild downturns. These typically bring manias, fear and misery to people's lives, in the process destabilising democratic institutions, as happened on a global scale during the 1920s and 1930s and is again happening in parts of the world today.[41]

My approach throughout this book is guided by an inexact but pithy formula: in these early years of the twenty-first century, monitory democracies can neither live with capitalist markets nor live without capitalist markets. The aporia is designed to provoke second thoughts and fresh thinking; along the way, it also helps to shed some light on the wildly divergent scholarly and political assessments of the future of markets and democracy. According to pro-market observers, more than a few of whom are dogmatic market fundamentalists, political democracy is an unwanted parasite on the body of economic growth. Democracy whips up unrealistic public passions and fantasies. It distorts and paralyses the spirit and substance of rational calculations upon which markets functionally depend; understood as government based on majority rule, democracy is profoundly at odds with free competition, individual liberty and the rule of law. What is therefore required is 'democratic pessimism'[42] and the restriction of majority-rule democracy in favour of 'austerity' (cutbacks and restructuring of state spending) and limited constitutional government ('demarchy'[43]) whose job is to protect and nurture 'free markets'. Other scholarly observers, political commentators, policy advocates and politicians forcefully stake out the contrary view. They maintain that since markets are never 'naturally' free but always, in one way or another, the creature of laws and governing institutions, market failures and market 'externalities' require correction by finely crafted political

---

[41] Charles P. Kindleberger and Robert Aliber, *Manias, Panics, and Crashes: A History of Financial Crises* (Hoboken, NJ: John Wiley & Sons, 2005).
[42] Bryan Caplan, *The Myth of the Rational Voter: Why Democracies Choose Bad Policies* (Princeton, NJ: Princeton University Press, 2007).
[43] Friedrich A. von Hayek, *Law, Legislation and Liberty: The Political Order of a Free People*, Vol. III (London: Routledge, 1979).

interventions. Drawing strength from popular consent, these democratic interventions can redistribute income and wealth, repair environmental damage caused by markets and, generally, serve in practice to reinforce the ideals of equality, freedom and solidarity among citizens.

Exactly what this general democratic formula means in practice has been hotly disputed since the earliest (nineteenth-century Chartist and co-operative movement[44]) public attacks on markets in the name of 'the people'. The democratisation of markets has meant different things at different times to different groups of people. For some analysts, democracy requires the replacement of markets by the principles of Humanity (Giuseppe Mazzini), or by communist visions of 'social individuality' (Karl Marx) and post-market individualism (C.B. Macpherson). For most avowed democrats of the past century, the democratisation of markets meant greater state intervention and control of markets. More recently, confronted with the collapse of the Soviet model of socialism, some analysts have tried to develop fruitful comparisons among contemporary Anglo-Saxon, Rhineland, Japanese, Indian, Chinese and other 'varieties of capitalism'. Recognising that parliamentary democracy is constantly vulnerable to corporate 'kidnapping', these analysts champion updated versions of the social democratic vision of liberating ('de-commodifying') areas of life currently in the grip of unregulated markets. What is needed, it is argued, are new state policies that 'socialise' the unjust effects of competition by 'embedding' markets within civil society institutions guaranteed by election victories, welfare mechanisms and government regulation. Whether such regulation can succeed without crossing borders and through state efforts alone remains an open question. Yet the broad vision is clear: in defence of the democratic principle of equality, government instruments are needed to limit 'predatory' forms of capitalism and to protect and extend social citizenship rights through such 'pre-distribution' strategies as raising the minimum wage and enforcing new contract law arrangements that empower workers and consumers.[45]

---

[44] Dorothy Thompson, *The Chartists: Popular Politics in the Industrial Revolution* (London: Pantheon, 1984); G.D.H. Cole and Raymond Postgate, *The Common People 1746–1938* (London: Methuen, 1938), pp. 267ff; and M. Sanders, *The Poetry of Chartism: Aesthetics, Politics, History* (Cambridge and New York: Cambridge University Press, 2009).

[45] Thomas H. Marshall, *Citizenship and Social Class and Other Essays* (Cambridge: Cambridge University Press, 1950); Karl Polanyi, *Origins of Our Time: The Great Transformation* (London: Victor Gollancz, 1945); Peter A. Hall and David Soskice (eds.), *Varieties of Capitalism: The Institutional Foundations of Comparative Advantage*

In broad sympathy with these proposals for a new politics of breaking the stranglehold of capitalist markets on people's lives, this book emphasises the urgency of bringing the subject of worsening economic and social inequality back into the heart of scholarly work on democracy. Pauperism mixed with plutocracy is today a feature of practically every democracy on our planet. For all democratically minded scholars, disparities between rich and poor ought to be intellectually and politically scandalous. 'Enough is enough' should be their declaration. The pages below remind readers that wide gaps between rich and poor have ruinous effects on civil society: citizens in unequal societies, researchers have shown, more likely end up sick, obese, unhappy, unsafe, or in jail. Such dysfunctions, in various ways, have a marked impact on the richest and wealthiest strata. Even they feel the effects; nobody is safe from the clutches of inequality. Inequality is strangely egalitarian. Market-generated inequalities also endanger the institutions and mechanisms of monitory democracy. Wealth likes secrecy, surveillance and law and order. It outvotes ballots; and wealth tilts public policy in favour of the rich, towards short-sighted rewards or special treatment (deregulation, tax breaks) and away from the public goods (education, infrastructure) so essential for future economic growth. Finally, in normative terms, market-generated inequality plainly contradicts the democratic spirit of equality. Historically speaking, democracy in every form has questioned and rejected the presumption that the wealthy are 'naturally' entitled to rule; like salt to the sea, the principle of equality is the heart and soul of the democratic ideal.[46]

(Oxford: Oxford University Press, 2001); Geoff Mulgan, *The Locust and the Bee: Predators and Creators in Capitalism's Future* (London: Princeton University Press, 2013); Robert B. Reich, *Saving Capitalism: For the Many, Not the Few* (New York: Knopf, 2015); and the classic work by Claus Offe, *Contradictions of the Welfare State*, edited by John Keane (London: Hutchinson, 1984).

[46] See Keane, *The Life and Death of Democracy*, p. xii: 'The exceptional thing about the type of government called democracy is that it demanded that people see that nothing which is human is carved in stone, that everything is built on the shifting sands of time and place, and that therefore they would be wise to build and maintain ways of living together as equals, openly and flexibly. Democracy required that people see through talk of gods and nature and claims to privilege based on superiority of brain or blood. Democracy meant the denaturing of power. It implied that the most important political problem is how to prevent rule by the few, or by the rich or powerful who claim to be supermen. Democracy solved this old problem by standing up for a political order that ensured that the matter of who gets what, when and how should be permanently an open question. Democracy recognised that although people were not angels or gods or goddesses, they were at least good enough to prevent some humans from thinking they were. Democracy was to be government of the humble, by the humble, for the humble. It meant self-government among equals, the lawful rule of an assembly of people whose sovereign

Guided by the equality principle, this book argues a fresh case for radical thinking about the vexed relationship between markets and monitory democracy. Elsewhere, in support of this aim, I have probed the ill-understood phenomenon of *democracy failure*[47] under market conditions dominated increasingly by banking and credit corporations. Economists conventionally speak about market failures, but there is plenty of evidence of moments when the absence of viable mechanisms of democratic scrutiny and restraint of reckless markets induces their breakdown. The communist-turned-conservative Austrian-American journalist Willi Schlamm famously quipped that 'the trouble with socialism is socialism. The trouble with capitalism is capitalists.'[48] The sentences require an important rider: 'And the trouble with capitalists is that without democracy they bring trouble to both capitalism and democracy.' Democracy failure breeds market failure; and market failure deepens democracy failure. A topical example of this harmful dynamic is to be found within the highly complex and arcane food production and distribution chains that span our planet. Every transaction in these supply chains doubles as an opportunity to cheat. For the moment, watchdog bodies such as the Aquaculture Stewardship Council and the Belfast-based Institute for Global Food Security are in short supply on the ground, and it therefore comes as no surprise that unmonitored food supply chains are highly vulnerable to scams and swindles led by fraudsters and organised crime. The modern history of banking and credit institutions is another topical case in point of democracy failure. During the past several decades, especially in the Atlantic heartlands of the global banking and credit sector, the willingness of unelected regulatory bodies, elected governments and self-regulation agencies (such as Standard and Poor's) to leave unchallenged the practice of dispersing credit risk by selling it to third-party investors produced the near-collapse of the whole system. Collateral debt obligations, mortgage-linked securities and other new-fangled

---

power to decide things was no longer to be given over to imaginary gods, the stentorian voices of tradition, to despots, to those in the know, or simply handed over to the everyday habit of laziness, unthinkingly allowing others to decide matters of importance.'

[47] John Keane, 'Democracy Failure', *WZB-Mitteilungen*, 24 (2009), 6–8; and 'A Short History of Banks and Democracy', *OpenDemocracy* (23 April 2013), www.opendemocracy.net/john-keane/short-history-of-banks-and-democracy. The concept of market failure is traceable to Francis M. Bator, 'The Anatomy of Market Failure', *Quarterly Journal of Economics*, 72, 3 (1958), 351–379.

[48] Cited in Linda Bridges and John R. Coyne, *Strictly Right: William F. Buckley, Jr. and the American Conservative Movement* (Hoboken, NJ: John Wiley & Sons, 2007), p. 51.

instruments encouraged investment firms, hedge fund operators and banks such as Lehmann Brothers and the Royal Bank of Scotland to pursue reckless adventures. Their swashbuckling eventually had destabilising effects on the whole global economy. The resulting damage has prompted financial regulators around the world to force big banks to raise their capital levels and improve the liquidity of their funding sources. New laws (such as the Dodd–Frank Wall Street Reform and Consumer Protection Act in the United States) have been passed. Yet big banks have mostly not been broken up; some risk-laden giants, including JPMorgan, have actually grown much bigger since the crisis. The people responsible for the serious social and political damage caused by the near-collapse of the financial sector have meanwhile remained largely untouched by courts of law. Hence the cascade of unanswered political questions: Are risk taking, recklessness and broken promises within the banking and credit sectors by definition neither fully predictable nor controllable by market forces? If so, does that mean that financial markets are never fully guided by rational calculations that keep things in permanent equilibrium?

A short answer to these questions is that there is plenty of evidence, both past and present, that periodic disequilibrium of financial markets is the normal pattern. Especially when left to their own devices, private banks and credit institutions typically fuel major market movements that assume lives of their own, entrap investors in foolish illusions (J.M. Keynes called them 'animal spirits') that have the effect of seducing other market participants into expecting permanent gains – until feedback signals driven by actual underlying trends puncture the foolish illusions, at which point a boom–bust sequence with anti-democratic effects takes hold. Assuming (therefore) the need for new early warning systems, the fundamental question is whether more democratic ways can be found for doing things that central banks, banking and finance companies, securities regulators and accounting standards bodies manifestly failed to do. In other words, is the democratic quest to extract folly and hubris from capital markets, to rein in the ruinous power of foolishly inflated expectations, as necessary as it is obvious? If so, as seems likely, why is it that monitory democracies are now witnessing so few attempts to build local, regional and global oversight structures in the fields of banking, insurance and securities? Why is there a shortage of credible forums capable of cracking down on fraud, discouraging excessive risk-taking, fostering best practice through open-minded counsel and providing means by which those hurt by this crisis may seek redress? Does the widespread failure to extend the early warning mechanisms of monitory democracy into the banking and credit sector reveal its crushing veto power? Are these democracy failures the prelude to the next round of market recklessness – and market catastrophes laced with anti-democratic outbursts?

These are challenging political questions. They should have sobering effects on every democrat. Their placement at the heart of political thinking about democracy is imperative, especially because in these early years of the twenty-first century, in the era of financial capitalism and its misadventures, the gap between rich and poor is almost everywhere widening so rapidly that actually existing monitory democracies feel as though they are sliding backwards, returning to the patterns of social injustice of eighteenth- and nineteenth-century Europe. In the pages below, building on my earliest writings, the decadent trend is explored using a radically reworked version of the old eighteenth-century category of civil society.[49] Although recent literature and public discussion of civil society has misleadingly treated civil society as a market-free zone, the pages below emphasise the way early modern discussions of civil society were in fact deeply preoccupied with the dysfunctions and pathologies of market power. Consider just one example: Adam Smith's famous *Lectures on Justice, Police, Revenue and Arms* (1763), which noted how commodity production and exchange – the forces and relations of production, mediated by nature – are both the dynamic motor of civil society and the key cause of social inequality, to the point where 'the people who clothe the whole world are in rags themselves'. His *Wealth of Nations* (1776) puts the same point even more forcefully. 'Wherever there is great property there is great inequality', he wrote. 'For one very rich man there must be at least five hundred poor, and the affluence of the few supposes the indigence of the many.' Living well before the advent of the universal franchise, Smith expected that market economies would generate political troubles. 'The affluence of the rich', he noted, 'excites the indignation of the poor, who are often both driven by want, and prompted by envy, to invade his possessions.'[50]

Much the same concern about market-generated inequality grips the work of contemporary political economists, including Thomas Piketty, who emphasises that market economies, when left to themselves, contain

---

[49] See John Keane, *Democracy and Civil Society* (London and New York: Verso, 1988) and *Civil Society and the State: New European Perspectives* (London and New York: Verso, 1988).

[50] Adam Smith, *Lectures on Justice, Police, Revenue and Arms: Delivered in the University of Glasgow* (Oxford: Clarendon Press, 1869 [1763]), part 2, section 17; Adam Smith, 'On the Expense of Justice', *Wealth of Nations* (1776), book 5, chapter 1, part 2.

'powerful forces of divergence'[51] that are potentially destructive of democracy and its ethic of equality. The roots of market instability are traceable to the historical fact that in all capitalist economies the private rate of return on capital (r) is typically higher than the rate of income and output (g). The inequality $r>g$ is another way of saying that there is a built-in tendency for wealth to accumulate more rapidly than output and wages. It took the catastrophes of the twentieth century to reverse this trend, and to reduce significantly the favourable returns to capital. For a time, Piketty argues, the Keynesian welfare state led many to believe that the structural inequality problem had been resolved by democracies. In practically every OECD country, however, growth is now modest and household and state debts are rising along with wealth and income gaps. Contrary to the prevailing consensus, enhanced GDP growth is no equalising solution, he shows. This is because technologically innovative economies typically cannot grow faster than 1–1.5 per cent in the long run (the historical record shows that only countries engaged in catch-up can grow at Chinese-style rates); and because even when growth rates are modest the $r>g$ inequality gap is never automatically reduced. Hence the sobering statistics for rich OECD countries such as the United States, where nearly 40 per cent of citizens between the ages of 25 and 60 will experience at least a year of poverty at some point; or the case of France, where the average disposable income (after transfers and taxes) of the wealthiest 0.01 per cent of the population now stands at seventy-five times that of the bottom 90 per cent.[52]

The troubling trends are clear, but much less definite are the answers to questions about how to think positively about equality, and what is to be done politically to combat its anti-democratic effects. This book notes that a striking feature of the age of monitory democracy is the way the equality principle is democratised. *Simple notions of equality*, understood as equal treatment and equal prospects of advancement for each individual citizen, within a socially undivided and homogeneous political community, become unworkable, and undesirable. In our age of monitory democracy, awareness is growing that there are many different kinds of equalities that in turn are entangled with many other different kinds of relationships. The simple word equality is transformed into a much more *complex grammar of equality*, or so it is argued below. What this implies

---

[51] Thomas Piketty, *Capital in the Twenty-First Century*, p. 571.
[52] Pierre Rosanvallon, *The Society of Equals* (Cambridge, MA and London: Harvard University Press, 2013), p. 303, note 2.

for the rough and tumble world of politics is another matter. There are signs of a developing consensus that social inequality is a poisonous fruit of capitalist accumulation, and that even for the sake of the future of capitalist accumulation – and for our biosphere and our democratic ways of life – something needs urgently to be done. But what can be done? Can new versions of the old ideal of numerical equality – the basic state pension; one person, one vote; a citizens' basic income – once more inspire public passions, as they did from the end of the eighteenth century? This book aims to raise questions about this question. In reply, it suggests that the old communist, socialist, anarchist and syndicalist visions of abolishing markets are dead, and for good reasons. The utopia of abolishing markets failed: either because it trusted blindly in the capacity of strong dictatorial states to monopolise the exchange with nature; or because it wrongly imagined that law and government could be replaced by forging social harmony (Proudhon called it 'social communion') based on individual consent, voluntary exchange and the 'natural' solidarity of the collective producers. In both scenarios, in the estimate of this book, civil society *sensu stricto* was to be abolished. So, in these early years of the twenty-first century, the key questions are tabled: Given the follies and cruelties associated with the past century's efforts to exterminate civil society, and given the need to stop market fundamentalism in its tracks, how can the normative vision of a self-organising and socially equal civil society find a new footing? Isn't the point not only to change the world, but also to interpret it in new democratic ways? If so, how in practical terms can the old political project of 'socialising' markets and making civil societies more equal and more open and more 'civil' be nurtured in the coming years? Which political forces will support the necessary radical reforms in areas such as basic income, affordable housing, health care and public amenities? How can they help re-embed capitalist markets in civil society, render business enterprises and business chains publicly accountable and generally bring greater freedom and solidarity and equality (understood in new and more complex ways) into our world, this time on a global scale?

These are pressing questions made more challenging and necessary by environmentalist objections to the treatment of 'nature' as an exploitable for-profit commodity. Among the unorthodox features of this book's efforts to stretch and widen the horizons of democratic thinking is its engagement with the 'greening' of contemporary politics. It does so initially by revisiting the old topic of political representation and the universal franchise; the analysis points towards a thorough rethinking of the human, all-too-human anthropocentrism built into inherited understandings of democracy.

It is commonly said that the bitter struggles to extend the vote to all classes and categories of people came to an end during the course of the twentieth century. Hence the belief of many political scientists and political commentators that the whole issue of the universal franchise is now settled. From this perspective, the matter of *who votes* has been replaced by questions concerning *where* people can or should vote.[53] Quite aside from the whole issue of votes rigged by dark money, gerrymandering and restrictive registration, one great exception to this handy formula is the emergence of new battlefronts on the political terrain of the biosphere.[54] Most democracies are nowadays preoccupied not merely with tough questions about the causes and effects of species destruction, industrial toxins, global warming and other changes within our biosphere. The matter of how democracies can reverse, modify or adapt to these changes produces moments of doubt about democracy's fitness for the job, but more than a few activists and policymakers have understandably decided that the world of nature should have political rights, in the sense that our biosphere is blessed with entitlements that require people to care for it by finding ways of respecting and representing it through new modes of governance that are mindful of the parameters of such criteria as 'sustainability' and 'intergenerational justice'.[55]

To speak as if the biosphere is in favour of its own inclusion in political affairs is, of course, only a way of speaking, but it functions as a stern reminder of the possibility that human labours will be in vain unless the complex powers and requirements of non-human nature are heeded. But how can this happen? Can it happen at all?

In the early years of the age of monitory democracy, arguably the boldest reply to this line of questioning was Martin Heidegger's critique of the human will to control our biosphere through measurement and mechanisation (what he termed *Machenschaft*). Heidegger was appalled by efforts to render everything 'makeable' (*machbar*). He instead appealed to the ethic of 'caring for others' (*Fürsorge*); he urged the

---

[53] Norberto Bobbio, *Democracy and Dictatorship: The Nature and Limits of State Power* (Cambridge: Polity Press, 1989).
[54] Sonia Alonso, John Keane and Wolfgang Merkel (eds.), *The Future of Representative Democracy* (Cambridge: Cambridge University Press, 2011), especially the contributions by Robyn Eckersley and Michael Saward.
[55] Richard P. Hiskes, *The Human Right to a Green Future: Environmental Rights and Intergenerational Justice* (Cambridge: Cambridge University Press, 2009).

counter-need to cultivate an abiding sense of 'dwelling poetically on the earth'.[56] Technological hubris, homelessness and their poisonous effects ('world-darkening', 'devastation', 'the flight of the gods') are not necessarily the destiny of the world, he argued. Through a combination of meditative reflection and a new 'openness to mystery', plus a disposition of 'releasement toward beings [*Gelassenheit*]', humans can come to dwell within our biosphere by acting as shepherds who refuse to lord over other beings by preserving them in their nearness to the truth of being – their sense of fruitfully being rooted within a world that must be respected, not dominated.

Researchers in the field of democracy can learn much from Heidegger, including the need for heightened awareness of the dangers posed by his vision of 'rootedness' or 'autochthony', or what he termed *Bodenständigkeit*. Heidegger's short-sighted rejection of democratic politics (which could not 'genuinely confront the technological world', he claimed) was bound up with his vision of 'rootedness in the soil'; his attachment to roots proved to be the flipside of his gushing embrace of Nazism. That is why the fundamental theoretical problem outlined by Heidegger must be resolved differently, inspired by cutting-edge research questions posed from a democratic perspective. Several lines of questioning are followed in the pages below, beginning with perhaps the toughest question of all: Is democracy, considered as an unfinished historical project, conceptually implicated in the trends that Heidegger spotted? Put in the frankest way: Isn't political thinking customarily guided by the principle of the supremacy of 'the people' and their indefeasible right to 'self-government' soaked in the bile of human arrogance, incorrigibly anthropocentric, an all-too-human way of life inherently at loggerheads with the biosphere and its supposedly lesser creatures?

Following the methodological rule of context-sensitive, evidence-enriched and time-sensitive re-description, outlined at the beginning of this introduction, this book charts a reply to these questions by examining the way monitory democracies transform the meaning and significance of democracy. They do so by fostering institutional innovations, such as bioregional assemblies, green political parties, environmental courts, protected zones with legal standing and other early warning eco-detector and eco-protection systems. These innovations do more than stimulate

---

[56] Martin Heidegger, *Holzwege*, 5th edn (Frankfurt am Main: Vittorio Klostermann, 1972 [1950]) and *Feldweg-Gespräche: 1944–1945*, in *Gesamtausgabe*, Vol. 76 (Frankfurt am Main: Vittorio Klostermann).

public awareness of our entanglement with the biosphere, in a wide range of matters, ranging from air and water quality to the decontamination of hazardous waste sites, climate change and the protection of bio-diversity. In effect, these innovations extend new democratic forms of representation to nature itself, despite the fact that it has no personality and no voice or 'subjectivity' in any straightforward sense.

These innovations prompt many challenging conceptual questions: Can democracy be radically redefined, to make room for the non-human, so that it comes to refer descriptively and normatively to the never-finished political project of taming, not just markets. but also the arrogance of humans, extending the equality principle to their relationship with nature, finding new and more equal human relations with the biomes upon which they depend? Can the mythical 'People' so loved by past democrats be brought back to Earth, encouraged to eat humble pie, regarded hereon as peoples capable of living their lives, as equals, entangled in complex biomes they know to be part of themselves, and for which they share profound respect? Then there are the tough strategic questions: Compared with other ways of making and taking decisions, is monitory democracy generally better equipped to handle the complex, intractable, open-ended and often 'wicked' problems connected with our compulsive market-driven quest to dominate nature? And another strategic consideration: Given that democratic mechanisms continue to be heavily encased within territorial state frameworks that are often dysfunctional when it comes to handling environmental problems, can regional and global institutional mechanisms subject to democratic control be developed?

DEMOCRACY BEYOND BORDERS?

Whether and to what extent regional and global institutions can be democratised, and what this might mean for our understanding of democracy, is among the great under-explored themes of contemporary democratic theory and democratic politics. As this book tries to show, drawing upon a range of different examples, the subject of cross-border democracy pushes democratic theory to its limits, beyond the boundaries of the present, towards uncharted horizons. It is not just that in cross-border settings many things are happening that are far stranger than our forebears would have thought unlikely, or impossible;[57] more pertinent

---

[57] Charles S. Maier, *Once within Borders: Territories of Power, Wealth, and Belonging since 1500* (Cambridge, MA and London: Belknap Press, 2016).

and challenging is the striking fact that there are things going on in cross-border settings that cannot currently be thought about intelligibly if we continue to rely upon the reigning terms provided by orthodox democratic thinking.

The illusions of orthodoxy, the conviction that we are who we are and that this normality is what it is, are today indulged by those analysts of democracy who downplay, or dismiss, the importance of the subject of cross-border democracy. They do so usually on the definitional ground that states are still the principal political actors in international relations, and that democracy in representative form functionally requires a sovereign territorial state framework. Robert A. Dahl and other analysts insist that because a 'nation-state or country' is indispensable for the political institutions of 'polyarchal democracy', that is 'a modern representative democracy with universal suffrage', the extension of democracy to 'international organisations' is highly improbable. Citizens are said to be too ill-informed to understand the complexity of the international sphere; and since there is no 'strong common identity' at the global level, no global public, no political parties and no system of party representation of majorities, 'to call the political practices of international systems "democratic" would be to rob the term of all meaning'.[58] Some commentators (and plenty of contemporary populists) twist this defence of territorial state democracy into a strong political critique of globalisation. They speak of the 'revolt of capital against the post-war mixed economy' and the neo-liberal push towards 'deregulation, privatisation and market expansion'. In consequence, given that 'democracy is tamed by markets instead of markets by democracy', the political priority, they say, is the refusal of the market 'sterilisation' of democracy and the restoration of 'democratic sovereignty'.[59]

The reasoning and conclusions are debateable. The flirtation with the forces of populism and nationalism is obvious; the failure of imagination disappointing. That is why some democratic thinkers are beginning to interrogate the conviction that democracy is ineluctably a domestic affair, a political way of life that is liveable only by means of elections within

---

[58] Robert A. Dahl, *On Democracy* (New Haven, CT: Yale University Press, 1998), chapters 8–9, and p. 117; compare his parallel reasoning about the way 'transnational institutions' force 'trade-offs between system effectiveness and citizen effectiveness', in 'A Democratic Dilemma: System Effectiveness versus Citizen Participation', *Political Science Quarterly*, 109, 1 (1994), 23–34.

[59] Wolfgang Streeck, *Buying Time: The Delayed Crisis of Democratic Capitalism* (London: Verso, 2014), pp. 2–5, 116.

territorial state boundaries. Some efforts at refuting the orthodoxy prove to be false starts. Consider the attempt by a leading political economist to define a proper balance between the 'world economy' and 'democracy'. 'If we want to push globalisation further', so runs the reasoning, 'we have to give up either the nation state or democratic politics. If we want to maintain and deepen democracy, we have to choose between the nation state and international economic integration.' Within this 'trilemma', says the political economist, the trade-offs should favour the principle of democratically elected governments operating within sovereign territorial states. 'Democracies have the right to protect their social arrangements, and when this right clashes with the requirements of the global economy, it is the latter that should give way.' The claim is that when national sovereignty in democratic form has primacy over supra-national forces and organisations; that is, when countries exercise 'their right to protect their own social arrangements, regulations, and institutions', the efficacy and legitimacy of both dimensions are strengthened. If this strengthening takes place, if a 'new globalisation' happened, then the future growth of 'international guidelines' and 'international coordination' would be bound by the democratic rule that they must always 'reinforce the integrity of the domestic democratic process rather than ... replace it'.[60]

The pages below point out that this line of thinking is ill-equipped to make sense of the growing volume and range of cross-border problems and challenges that cannot be dealt with by 'sovereign' states alone. The 'territorial mentality' of this understanding of democracy is oddly out of step with real-world trends that are deeply contradictory. There are more than a few forces afoot that greatly complicate and weaken the effectiveness of electoral democracy and public scrutiny mechanisms inside state boundaries: trends such as the concentration of arbitrary power in the hands of global firms and the hesitations of parliamentary mechanisms in the face of globalising markets; the disproportionate power of a few states within global bodies such as the United Nations and the G7/G8/G20; and the growth of 'assemblages' of supra-national institutions, agencies and 'governance' networks that are wholly unaccountable to citizens and their elected representatives.[61] Yet, in matters of monitory democracy, all is not

---

[60] Dani Rodrik, *The Globalization Paradox: Democracy and the Future of the World Economy* (New York: W.W. Norton, 2011), pp. xviii–xix, 240, 242.

[61] Mark Bevir, *Governance: A Short Introduction* (Oxford: Oxford University Press, 2012); Saskia Sassen, *Territory, Authority, Rights: From Medieval to Global Assemblages* (Princeton, NJ and Oxford: Princeton University Press, 2006).

lost. There are cross-border democratic counter-trends that are typically ignored or neglected by the textbooks of democracy. The Asia Pacific region is a critical case in point: during the past three decades, despite mounting regional military tensions, bilateral and multilateral cooperation by governments, market investment flows, supply chains and development corridors, ad hoc accountability and problem-solving bodies have combined to bring a greater sense of 'top-down' and 'bottom-up' interdependence of states and societies. Correspondingly, this stronger sense of common fates and 'connectivity' has heightened the need for new arguing and bargaining mechanisms, including cross-border civic initiatives, peer review panels, inter-city associations, cross-border parliaments and regional summits.[62]

Exactly how, for the first time on any scale in the history of democracy, the spread of power-scrutinising and power-restraining mechanisms, whose effects are felt across borders, can be included in a new democratic imaginary is no straightforward matter. Analysts of 'global power chains' and 'cosmocracy',[63] as well as advocates of 'cosmopolitan democracy' and 'demoicracy',[64] are generally agreed that democracy in territorial state form is today worryingly besieged by publicly unaccountable forces that stretch across borders. Their concern is well-placed: monitory democracy as we know it is feeling the pinch of these pressures, and may find it difficult in the long run to survive them – much less normative and political agreement follows from the shared diagnosis of the trends. For instance, some champions of 'global civil society' think of it as the best hope for protecting struggles for justice, freedom and solidarity across borders. Others give priority to the reform of the United Nations, for instance by convening a global constitutional convention, or by widening

---

[62] T. J. Pempel (ed.), *Remapping East Asia: The Construction of a Region* (Ithaca, NY: Cornell University Press, 2005); James Cotton, *Crossing Borders in the Asia-Pacific: Essays on the Domestic–Foreign Policy Divide* (New York: Nova Science Publishers, 2002); and the exaggerated but insightful thesis of the triumph of investment and supply chains over territory developed in Parag Khanna, *Connectography: Mapping the Future of Global Civilization* (New York: Random House, 2016).

[63] Robert Latham and Saskia Sassen (eds.), *Digital Formations: IT and New Architectures in the Global Realm* (Princeton, NJ: Princeton University Press, 2005); John Keane, *Global Civil Society?* (Cambridge and New York: Cambridge University Press, 2003).

[64] Daniele Archibugi, *The Global Commonwealth of Citizens: Toward Cosmopolitan Democracy* (Princeton, NJ: Princeton University Press, 2008); David Held, *Democracy and the Global Order: From the Modern State to Cosmopolitan Governance* (Cambridge: Polity Press, 1995); Francis Cheneval, Sandra Lavenex and Frank Schimmelfennig, '*Demoi*-cracy in the European Union: principles, institutions, policies', *Journal of European Public Policy*, 22, 1 (2015), 1–18.

the basis of representation of the General Assembly. Against considerable odds, still other democrats work for the general proliferation of power-chastening monitory mechanisms, including cross-border human rights networks, regional parliaments, summits, forums, enhanced public scrutiny of non-governmental organisations and the making and enforcement of laws by local, regional and global courts.

Each of these approaches has advantages and disadvantages; they are explored below, in search of a more worldly understanding of democracy and its rebellious spirit and dynamics in spacetime settings inside and outside the boundaries of territorial states. This book is especially concerned to question 'two-tier' thinking, of the kind found within the cosmopolitan democracy approach, its call for 'the creation of new political institutions which would co-exist with the system of states but which would override states in clearly defined spheres of activity where those activities have demonstrable transnational and international consequences'.[65] The two-tier approach seems too simple, too dependent upon architectural metaphors, and too close to conventional accounts of state-bound representative democracy, or so this book argues. Cosmopolitan democracy certainly counts as a brave and important effort to find a new language through which the lineaments of 'post-electoral' democracy are defined. But its vision of 'an intensive, participatory and deliberative democracy' certainly begs many questions about the meaning of both deliberation and democracy. Why (in the final analysis) in a globalising age should democracy depend functionally on territorial states and why, for instance, should democracy in cosmopolitan form require the supplementary but unworkable fiction of a 'global people' capable of participating and 'deliberating' in global decision-making mechanisms?

The research agenda sketched in this book aims to explore and exploit these weaknesses. It protests against the confinement of democracy to state barracks. The analysis is especially critical of the 'territorial mentality' of much present-day thinking about democracy, which is commonly supposed to require telluric qualities. By that I mean that place is supposedly the exclusive address where democracy lives; it is self-government through the medium of a defined, three-dimensional patch of land or sea. Democracy is said to require fixed-place settings, such as rural communities, urban neighbourhoods, provinces and territorial states. The reigning flat-earth view of democracy as grounded in a physical location,

---

[65] Held, *Models of Democracy*, pp. 305, 308–309.

this book argues, not only forestalls the hard work of re-imagining the dynamic architecture or 'political geography' of democracy, in ways that make new sense of twenty-first-century dynamics – more is at stake. Whether it knows it or not, the flat-earth understanding of democratic ideals and institutions is caught up in a slow-burn crisis rooted in the plain fact that every nation-state democracy is today *post-sovereign*, entangled in worldwide webs of interdependence backed by space- and time-shrinking flows of mediated communication. Within every actually existing monitory democracy, politics no longer unfolds in splendid isolation from the rest of the world. Albert Einstein doubted the reality of 'spooky action at a distance' (*spukhafte Fernwirkung*), but all representatives and citizens of local democratic states are today aware of their entanglement within far-away fields of power and action. Butterfly effects, spillover consequences and arbitrage pressures are the new norm; things that happen politically in one place have both positive and negative effects elsewhere, in far-away locations, and often simultaneously, within mediated local and global frameworks.

In the world of natural objects, particle physicists, cosmologists, quantum theorists and others refer to these spacetime dynamics using such terms as 'entanglement', 'quantum tunneling', 'non-locality' and 'extra dimensions'. This book makes every effort to absorb this language, in order to drive home the point that in the age of communicative abundance democracy needs to be reconceived kaleidoscopically: understood in quantum terms of multiple and inter-connected spacetime frameworks in which peoples, with the help of their representatives, govern themselves and their ecosystems in differently sized, media-saturated settings marked by different spacetime rhythms. The unorthodox approach squarely belongs to the age of monitory democracy. It helps make sense of many of its new spacetime dynamics, and, in so doing, it aims at nothing less than the 'de-territorialisation' of the spirit and language and politics of democracy. The point is to try to set democracy loose on the world, to think of it as an always unfinished political project centred on more open and just ways of deciding who gets what, when and how; to re-imagine it as a process featuring flesh-and-blood people and their representatives seeking public control over institutionalised power, wherever it is exercised, in a pluriverse of interconnected spacetime settings.

The art of rethinking democracy in multiple and interconnected spacetime settings is expressed in the pages below by way of several detailed case studies. Leading off is a genealogy of the language and mechanisms of the European citizen, the first-ever modern attempt to imagine and systematically institutionalise democratic citizenship by means of cross-border entitlements and duties. The genealogy describes how the democratic ideal formed an important part of the European integration process that took place during the years from 1970 to 2005. It shows why its new vision of a dynamic, multi-layered type of citizen was without precedent; and it probes the several ways it faced unresolved challenges even before the current round of European dis-integration.[66] The analysis notes how the whole idea of European citizenship, for instance as it appeared during this period in a string of judgements issued by the European Court of Justice, preserved in a way the conventional understanding of citizenship, dating back to Aristotle, as a form of self-reflexive civic allegiance in which being a citizen implied membership of a *political community of common laws* and the sharing of its *entitlements and duties equally with others*. The analysis also notes why, in striking contrast to previous state-centric definitions, European citizenship implied a unique form of *post-national citizenship*. Citizenship was once presumed to be possible only when nations could articulate their needs and determine their fates through territorially structured government. The new language of European citizenship posed a direct challenge to such thinking. Rejecting the long history of territorial rivalry and violence of the old European state system, which on balance proved disastrous for representative democracy,[67] the new language implied the right of self-governing citizens to be different, and it underscored one of the big challenges faced during this period by the emergent European polity: how institutionally to protect and nurture a multiplicity of complex, overlapping, hybrid, national identities, which for obvious reasons will not wither away into some

---

[66] The principal implosive trends are analysed by Jan Zielonka, *Is the EU Doomed?* (Cambridge: Polity Press, 2014).

[67] John Keane, 'Nations, Nationalism and European Citizens', in Sukumar Periwal (ed.), *Notions of Nationalism*, with an introduction by Ernest Gellner (Budapest, London and New York: Central European University Press, 1995), pp. 182–207. The bellicose qualities of the doctrine of national self-determination were spotted by many observers during the first decades of the twentieth century. A striking example is the remark of Denmark's leading composer, Carl Nielsen: 'The feeling of nation, which hitherto was considered something high and beautiful, has become like a spiritual syphilis which has devoured the brains and grins out through the empty eye sockets in senseless hate. What kind of bacillus is it that conquers the warring nations' best heads?' He added: 'One thing I would wish: that this war should not end until the whole civilized world lies in ruins! Now we must do it thoroughly! Now we must finally finish it off. This must never happen again, therefore it must now be done with a vengeance'; from a letter to Bror Beckman (27 October 1914), cited in Richard Taruskin's 'Introduction' to *repercussions* (Spring-Fall, 1996), p. 5.

common 'European' identity based upon a common language, ecological sensibility, sense of history and shared culture. Seen from the perspective presented below, the political project of European citizenship set out to accomplish several things never before achieved on a continental scale: to detach nationality and democratic citizenship; to guarantee and protect citizens' entitlements to their own national identities; and (the biggest challenge of all) to ensure that democracy would never again be bedevilled by its own demons by protecting the whole political order from politically dogmatic or violence-prone ideologies of national identity, expressed as extra-parliamentary 'take back our country' *populism* and *nationalism* that feeds upon mild, confused or mindless 'Euroscepticism'.

European citizenship was born of exceptional circumstances. The ideal sprang up from inside the structures of an emergent polity, loosely called 'Europe'. This polity was born more than half a century ago in conditions of total war, concentration camps, urban rubble and devastated economies. Underground visions of a 'united Europe', the early failures (during the 1940s) to institutionalise these grand visions, and American efforts (e.g. the Marshall Plan) to 'rescue' Europe from Soviet domination all combined to encourage the first modest efforts to develop European-wide initiatives in strictly limited policy areas, such as coal, iron and steel production, and agriculture and transportation.[68] These *petits pas* (as Jean Monnet called them) were supposed to have grander effects, eventually leading to the voluntary creation of a new form of multi-layered and multi-jurisdictional polity that was both rooted within and standing 'above' its member states. The pages below emphasise that there was no commonly agreed political science term for this polity. The main crucible of European citizenship, the European Union, was neither a federation nor a confederation nor an empire nor a territorial macro-state. It resembled a *condominio*[69] marked by the following features: multi-tiered structures of governance whose competence cut through and across the powers of its Member States and a polity defined by legal rules and processes and by compulsory acceptance of the *acquis communautaires*. During the period under review, the European polity lacked both a clearly defined supreme authority and a stable, contiguous territory. Europe had no

---

[68] Derek W. Urwin, *The Community of Europe: A History of European Integration Since 1945*, 2nd edn (London: Longman, 1995).

[69] Philippe Schmitter, *How to Democratize the European Union ... and Why Bother?* (Lanham, MD: Rowman & Littlefield, 2000); Philippe Schmitter and Alexander H. Trechsel, *The Future of Democracy in Europe: Trends, Analyses and Reforms* (Strasbourg: Council of Europe Publications, 2004).

effective monopoly over the legitimate means of coercion, no standing army, only a limited defence strategy and an uncertain identity in world affairs (despite the Lisbon Treaty provision for a new High Representative of the Union in foreign affairs and security policy).

Whatever the eventual fate in practice of the ideal and substance of the European citizen under mounting pressures of dis-integration,[70] the whole experiment suggests, in the age of monitory democracy, that the spirit and language and practices of democracy have no automatic or exclusive affinity with the territorial state and its fixed boundaries. It becomes possible to think democracy through multiple spacetime horizons. The pages below also show that in the field of monitory democracy, led by indigenous peoples, there are taking place bold spacetime transformations that have profound implications for the way democracy is imagined and practised. Consider the new experiments with what this book calls 'bio-democracy'. Even though not widely known or appreciated by scholars and publics alike, these experiments with indigenous self-government in the north-east Pacific archipelago Haida Gwaii (Islands of the People), the Whanganui River Te Awa Tupua framework agreement in New Zealand and Uluru-Kata Tjuta National Park in central Australia set trends.[71] In effect, these 'bio-democracies' are new modes of self-government that consider people, animals, trees, rocks and rivers as woven together in a common fabric and fate. These experiments reject the presumption that the land on which people dwell is simply definable 'territory', understood as a resource exploitable by citizens and representatives. The citizens involved in these democratic experiments think of themselves as embedded in living dynamic networks of human interactions that run 'deep' into the world of the non-human, and vice versa; drawing strict boundaries between 'local' and 'far-away' peoples and political institutions is deemed difficult. These bio-democracies have a strong sense of the dynamic and fragile complexity of the world, of its non-linear effects and, hence, the chronic indeterminacy and potential instability within human efforts to govern themselves within ecological settings. The entanglement and self-organising potential of all living and non-living elements within the political environment is supposed. There is deep respect for the non-human and its legitimate 'right of representation'

---

[70] Jan Zielonka, *Is the EU Doomed?* (Cambridge: Polity Press, 2014).
[71] See for example Director of National Parks, *Uluru–Kata Tjuta National Park: Tjukurpa Katutja Ngarantja Management Plan 2010–2020* (Canberra: Australian Government, 2010).

in human affairs, for instance through councils, legal standing arrangements, cultural heritage forums and other methods of political decision making that refuse arbitrary power.

Perhaps the largest-scale and politically boldest experiment in re-fashioning the spirit, language and institutions of democracy has happened on and around the continent of Antarctica. Knowledge of the government and politics of Antarctica is not widespread, but developments there force us to think again about how we think about democracy, or so this book proposes. Antarctica is a vast space at the bottom of our world where new methods of politically representing the biosphere have been invented, and where the nature/politics distinction makes little sense. It is also the first continent (well before similar things happened in Europe) to move beyond the modern doctrine of sovereign territorial statehood. The pages below describe the several ways in which post-sovereign Antarctica is a new type of compound government. Guided by the Antarctic Treaty system, it is a law-infused polity comprising many 'clumsy' power-sharing institutions designed to make and take decisions subject to public scrutiny and the exercise of voting rights. Its governing instruments are not tied to territory in any simple sense. Entangled in worldwide webs of commerce, media, law and government, Antarctica is viewed below as a species of monitory democracy defined by its reliance upon many public scrutiny mechanisms, a parliament in the making (the ATCM) and by citizen scientists whose role as 'watchdog' representatives of the biosphere require a new definition of expertise, or so it is contended in the pages below.

VIOLENCE, FEAR, WAR

In and around the continent of Antarctica, and within its governing institutions, as elsewhere on various parts of our planet, there are signs of intensifying state rivalries, which serve as a reminder that tough-talk brinkmanship, diplomatic jostling, mercenary violence, civil war and war-mongering among heavily armed states have been the constant companion of democracy throughout its long history. The historical point about war and democracy is sometimes forgotten, or its complexity suppressed, especially by journalists and scholars who compress it down to the pragmatic proposition of whether and to what extent democratic states (as in the un-ending 'war on terror') are capable of defending their ideals by using armed force to deal with their avowed enemies at home and abroad, or whether they are justified in deploying their military muscle into the affairs of countries trampled by tyrants.

The question of whether and why democracies are charged with the military duty to protect others, for instance people in far-away lands who are the victims of insufferable bullying or life-threatening violence, is no straightforward matter. Things are not made easier by the fact that the field of democratic ethics remains underdeveloped, and by the not unrelated fact that the subject of democracy only entered the disciplinary field of international relations belatedly, principally during the past several decades.[72] In recent years, in disciplines otherwise as unconnected as diplomatic studies, international relations, peace studies and classics, things have changed; a large body of literature has been produced on the subject of war, peace, terrorism and democracy promotion. Much emphasis has been given to a fundamental ethical dilemma confronting all democracies. The dilemma has deeply political implications: if, in the name of 'democracy', democratic states intervene in contexts riddled with violence using military and other means (as India did in Bangladesh in 1971, and the United States first did in Mexico, the Philippines and Cuba and has repeatedly done around the world during recent decades), then those democracies are readily accused of double standards, of violating the territorial 'sovereignty' and autonomy of peoples entitled to govern themselves. Democracies and their democrats are denounced as meddlers, conquerors, autocrats, colonisers and imperialists. On the other hand, if democratic states fiddle while people's lives are ruined, and choose by design or default not to intervene directly in these troubled contexts (recent cases include Ukraine, Syria, Rwanda, Palestine and Timor Leste), then democracies are easily accused of hypocrisy, of avoiding their responsibility to protect people by sitting back smugly with their arms folded, hence of turning a blind eye to cruelty that contradicts the democratic principle that all people should be treated as equals, with dignity and mutual respect.

Historical experience suggests, within any particular context, that in practice the general ethical dilemma is not easily handled, resolved or attenuated. Democracy promotion frequently fails to achieve its stated

[72] Christopher Hobson, *The Rise of Democracy: Revolution, War and Transformations in International Politics Since 1776* (Edinburgh: Edinburgh University Press, 2015); Anna Geis, Harald Müller and Niklas Schörnig (eds.), *The Militant Face of Democracy: Liberal Forces for Good* (Cambridge and New York: Cambridge University Press, 2013); and my review in *Ethics and International Affairs* (December 2016) of Christopher Kutz, *On War and Democracy* (Princeton, NJ and Oxford: Princeton University Press, 2016).

goals. Figures cited in the pages below suggest that around three-quarters of military interventions in the name of democracy end in failure. Why? There are many reasons. Strategic military difficulties, electoral backlashes, incompetent political leadership and budgetary concerns often stand in the way of military intervention and democratic victory by democratic states. There are other issues. The violent attacks on citizens living in cities during the past decade are signs that military intervention abroad risks 'blowback' revenge attacks at home. Far-away high-tech wars breed new forms of globally reported local violence.[73] And when democratic states resort to enhanced 'security measures' in order to protect 'democracy' against its avowed 'enemies', including 'terrorists' operating inside and across their borders, these states flirt with the devils of secretive, arbitrary power. When democratic states engage in top-secret data harvesting and total surveillance of their citizens, they stand accused of openly violating the accountability norms and procedures of monitory democracy.[74]

All these considerations help explain why armed intervention under the fluttering flag of democracy is always a tricky business, and why there are times (the American invasion of Iraq in early 2003 is a recent case in point) when intervention ends badly. True, the building of democracy from scratch in hostile contexts no longer remains an impossibly daunting 'leap in the dark', to recall the well-known words of Lord Derby when denouncing the electoral reform proposals of Prime Minister Benjamin Disraeli in the mid-1860s. The coming of democracy to Taiwan, the plaything of military power in the East Asia region, is a positive case in point. Yet the historical record suggests that successful 'democracy promotion' is always and everywhere subject to the most stringent preconditions, prerequisites that defy simple-minded presumptions that democratisation is a matter of will, firepower, policy, strategy, toolkits and implementation. For instance, in addition to the factors already considered, states that intervene militarily in the name of democracy need to think geopolitically, and to build a form of 'trusteeship' or 'shared sovereignty' managed by multilateral institutions that help produce a viable, wider regional settlement. Contrary to Fukuyama and others, democratisation is not synonymous with 'sovereign state'

---

[73] John Keane, 'War Comes Home', *The Conversation* (15 November 2015), https://theconversation.com/war-comes-home-50715.
[74] Michael P. Colaresi, *Democracy Declassified: The Secrecy Dilemma in National Security* (Oxford and London: Oxford University Press, 2014).

building.⁷⁵ Contemporary cases otherwise as different as Northern Ireland, the former Yugoslavia and the European Union suggest that successful democratisation cannot happen without prior or simultaneous regional pacification. Viable democratic states functionally require cross-border props. Much the same pattern was evident in the world of ancient Greek democracies, where (the pages below suggest) something like an 'Arcadian Law' was at work: the viability of any territorial city-state democracy was inversely proportional to the quantity of outside ('geopolitical') threats to its existence.

What is also clear is that military occupation, if it is to be successful, must in the planning stage ensure that 'all aspects of any intervention' are 'calculated, debated and challenged with the utmost rigour'.⁷⁶ Military occupation must also acknowledge its own limits, for instance by following a clearly defined timetable. Democracy requires military restraint. That means that occupation must aim to rebuild and nurture the institutions of a civil society, including functioning markets. To add to the challenges, the intruders must also make every effort to cultivate local trust, not just through respect for local ways of life but above all by sowing the seeds of monitory democracy, enabling the occupied population non-violently to speak against the occupiers and to hold them accountable for their misconceptions, mistakes, and their crimes.

Whether occupying powers are capable of such stringent self-restraint that leads to successful democracy building in contexts formerly racked by violence is a vital research matter made more complicated by the privatisation of military force. Self-government requires a functioning set of governmental institutions capable of making and executing policies, extracting and distributing revenue, producing laws and public goods and, of course, protecting citizens by wielding an effective monopoly over the existing means of violence. These functional requirements are made especially challenging in an age when private military forces and 'contract warfare' are resurgent, and gaining momentum.⁷⁷ The spread of private armies has been encouraged by the belief that free market principles ought to be extended to

---

⁷⁵ Francis Fukuyama, *Political Order and Political Decay: From the Industrial Revolution to the Globalization of Democracy* (New York and London: Farrar, Straus & Giroux, 2014); see my review 'Francis Fukuyama Sticks to His Guns on Liberal Democracy', *The Age* (Melbourne), 14 February 2015.
⁷⁶ Public statement by Sir John Chilcot (London, 6 July 2016), p. 12; the point is developed at length in *The Iraq Inquiry* (London, 2016).
⁷⁷ Sean McFate, *The Modern Mercenary: Private Armies and What They Mean for World Order* (Oxford and New York: Oxford University Press, 2014).

the field of armed force, the conviction that highly motivated and experienced mercenaries get results more effectively and efficiently and the concern of democratically elected politicians and governments to hide away the human costs of war by reducing casualties in their standing armies. The pace-setter has been the United States, a democracy that wants to project its force abroad but whose citizens no longer feel a burning desire to march to war. Military interventions in Afghanistan and Iraq were heavily dependent (around 50 per cent) on contractors provided by for-profit companies such as Blackwater (bad publicity forced it to change its name twice, first to Xe Services and then to Academi, whose current brand motto is 'Elite Training. Trusted Protection'). If the trend continues, championed by the world's most powerful democratic state, it is easy to imagine a near-future world in which all monitory democracies will be entrapped by state- and corporate-sponsored contract warfare fuelled by modern-day *condottieri* unhindered by the 'laws of war' that apply only to inter-state military conflicts.

The return of mercenary armies to the battlefield undoubtedly intensifies the contradiction between the promise of self-government and the harsh realities of forcible occupation by a power calling itself a democracy. Matters are further complicated by the problem of imperial power. This book shows why historical perspectives are needed so as to spotlight a phenomenon so far rather badly neglected in the scholarly research on democracy: *democratic empires*. The phrase sounds oxymoronic, but the striking fact is that the history of democracy has featured polities whose power radiates from an imperial centre, outwards over vast geographic distances, in the process compulsorily reorganising the lives of peoples, at times by using violence and often in violation of the democratic principles of self-government. In the history of democracy, this book notes, there have been three empires that did what they did in the name of 'the people', 'citizens' and 'democracy': classical Athens, revolutionary France, and the United States of America. All three had a mixed record in matters of war, peace and democracy promotion. During the fifth century BCE, for instance, there was a strongly symbiotic relationship between Athenian democracy and its war-making prowess. The power-sharing and power-constraining institutions of the *demokrātia* of Athens were deeply entangled in city-state rivalries, empire-building, war and rumours of war; democratic Athens was both famous and feared as a busybody (*polypragman*) driven by the desire for gain (*ktasthai*).[78] In the

---

[78] D. M. Pritchard, 'The Symbiosis between Democracy and War: The Case of Ancient Athens', in David M. Pritchard (ed.), *War, Democracy and Culture in Classical Athens* (Cambridge: Cambridge University Press, 2010), pp. 1–62.

decades after 1789, revolutionary France witnessed new forms of violence carried out at home and abroad in the name of the 'droits de l'homme et du citoyen'; while America's stated global commitment to 'make the world safe for democracy' (Woodrow Wilson) signed a long-term devil's pact with empire and war that has regularly embroiled its leaders and citizens in bitter accusations of double standards and ulterior motives.[79]

The reconsideration of the Greek, French and American empires spawns several insights, this book contends. It heaps doubt on the fashionable presumption that in the field of international relations democracies tend to be 'peaceful', or the claim that democracies do not go to war with other democracies. The analysis of democratic empires spotlights the connections between each major historical phase of democracy and radical alterations of the methods and means of war fighting. It raises tricky questions about the war-fighting capacities of imperial democracies and the way many of their 'fight them, beat them and make them democratic' wars have been fraught and bloody affairs, or outright failures. The diagnosis presented below also hints at a more radically unsettling implication: it reminds us that when democratic states transform themselves into big powers bent on expansion, they risk more than just the power-intoxicated hubris that comes with the militarisation of their domestic politics and social life. When entangled in interstate rivalries and cavorting with the demons of war, imperial democracies typically spawn rivals and enemies (who make every effort to protect themselves), along the way emphasising the double standards of a democracy that by its actions contradicts the language of equality and peaceful self-determination of citizens. The fate of the democratic empires of Athens and revolutionary France suggests not only that their instincts for political survival within a world bristling with arms make them highly prone to violent conflict, military adventurism, glorious victories and cheerless defeats. Insofar as democratic empires trigger the desire for resistance and revenge, their eventual demise and eventual downfall become a near certainty, in accordance with a simple but sobering rule: dominant democratic powers that live principally by their own swords ultimately die by the swords of their opponents. They fall victim to the cast-iron rule that democratic empires and states can never permanently control the dark forces of contingency. 'All the past history of the world', remarked the nineteenth-century German scholar Johann

---

[79] Tony Smith, *America's Mission: The United States and the Worldwide Struggle for Democracy in the Twentieth Century* (Princeton, NJ: Princeton University Press, 1994).

K. Bluntschli, 'testifies against the immortality of state power, and the earth is covered with the ruins of the fallen'.[80]

WHY MONITORY DEMOCRACY?

Imagine a world where monitory democracy was no longer protected militarily by the American empire, or by its allies, a world littered with the ruins of disgraced democrats, fallen democratic states, mortally wounded civil societies. If that happened, if in other words the political form known as democracy was crushed underfoot by political forces, what would be lost? Would anything be lost? Is democracy really worth defending, especially given that confusions about its meaning and significance are fortified everywhere by the fact that everyone seems to have their own definition of democracy? Given that the twenty-first century is already witnessing plenty of other ways of handling power, the questions are worth pursuing. Isn't democracy to be seen as just one – dispensable – ideal among many others? Is it really a universal norm, as many observers have claimed? Or, when all is said and done, is democracy actually just a fake universal norm (as the nineteenth-century German anti-philosopher Friedrich Nietzsche thought), just one of those pompous little Western values that jostles for people's attention, dazzles them with its promises and – for a time – seduces them into believing that it isn't a mask for power, a tool useful in the struggle by some for mastery over others?

These kinds of questions were last debated thoroughly, and often fiercely, during the 1940s, when economic collapse, totalitarian power and global war rendered parliamentary democracy an endangered political species.[81] The questions are again pertinent because of the rise of political forces and state regimes that mangle the spirit and substance of monitory democracy. Just several decades ago, scholars and journalists liked to remark that 'democracy' (by which they meant 'liberal democracy', free periodic elections) had become the dominant global norm, the 'only game in town'. The claim now seems other-worldly. These early decades of the twenty-first century have witnessed the rise of new types of criticism and organised resistance to monitory democracy, often, paradoxically, in the name of 'the people' and 'democracy' with 'non-Western'

---

[80] Johann Caspar Bluntschli, *The Theory of the State* (Oxford: Clarendon Press, 1885), p. 279.
[81] John Keane, 'The Origins of Monitory Democracy', *The Conversation* (24 September 2012), https://theconversation.com/the-origins-of-monitory-democracy-9752.

characteristics. It remains to be seen whether this latter-day 'democracy pushback'[82] is the prelude to something like a repeat of the widespread failures of democracy during the 1920s and 1930s. We do not yet know. For the moment, however, it seems clear that the manifold confusions, defects and pathologies of actually existing monitory democracies examined in this book are putting wind in the sails of the critics and foes of democracy. Their conviction that history is on their side, and that American-style 'liberal democracy' has become demoded and is not for them, is succoured by the rise of states whose rulers have no love of monitory democracy. Democracy is facing uphill battles in many contexts, including eastern-central Europe (e.g. Ukraine and Hungary), Southeast Asia (Thailand and Malaysia), Africa (Uganda), the Arab world (Egypt) and Latin America (Venezuela, Peru).[83] In Russia, for some time, the leadership of Vladimir Putin has been pushing for 'managed democracy' protected by a strong state, corrupted political parties, grave deficiencies in the rule of law, media manipulation and a general spirit of populist domination. Striking are the plebiscitary qualities of this 'managed democracy'. Intermediary institutions, such as parliaments, political parties and civic organisations, do not actively represent people's interests; it is rather the president, the leader of 'the people' that claims to represent the nation's will. The form of politics unleashed by 'managed democracy' bears more than a faint resemblance to the type of popular sovereignty proposed by Carl Schmitt in his critique of the emerging representative parliamentary democracies of the early twentieth century.[84] Under conditions of 'managed democracy', plebiscitary or populist politics is a form of pseudo-representation: based on claims that the direct and unfiltered will of the people is both honoured and implemented, such politics leads to the weakening and deinstitutionalisation of democracy in monitory, representative form. More than a few commentators are meanwhile projecting the coming triumph of 'Asia' over a declining West, especially at the hands of China, itself said to be a distinctive 'civilisation state' that cares little for monitory democracy and much for political order, locally made forms of democracy and

---

[82] Thomas Carothers, 'The Backlash against Democracy Promotion', *Foreign Affairs*, 85 (2006), 55–68.

[83] Fareed Zakaria, *The Future of Freedom: Illiberal Democracy at Home and Abroad*, rev. edn (New York: W.W. Norton, 2003).

[84] Carl Schmitt, *Die geistesgeschichtliche Lage des heutigen Parlamentarismus*, 7th edn (Berlin: Duncker & Humblot, 1991 [1923]).

economic growth, a new global dominant power that will overtake the United States in economic, cultural and political matters.[85]

In the face of these threatening developments, the question rebounds: What is so good about monitory democracy? The question is becoming urgent, for the reason spelled out in dark times a generation ago by Max Horkheimer. 'Once the philosophical foundation of democracy has collapsed', he noted, 'the statement that dictatorship is bad is rationally valid only for those who are not its beneficiaries, and there is no theoretical obstacle to the transformation of this statement into its opposite'.[86] A standard but unconvincing reply to the question is that since 'democracies do not fight wars with one another',[87] the virtues of democratic peace shine forth, as a universal standard, for all of humankind. The entanglement of democratic states in the grubby business of violent interventions, war and empire casts grave doubts on this democratic peace thesis, to the point where some scholars have been tempted to draw the opposite, scandalous conclusion that democracy functions in fact as a form of sublimated violence. Often influenced by René Girard's *La violence et le sacré* (1972), they say that 'violence is ineradicable' in human affairs because the quest for reciprocity breeds rivalry and blood-spilling antagonisms fed by democratic institutions.[88]

This book shows there is no scandal. It reasons a case against dragging the whole idea of democracy down into the dirt of timespace contingent violence that is falsely alleged to be ontological. The insistence that democracy has a violent heart correctly underscores the entanglement of democratic norms and procedures in the facts and fantasies of violence, and the fears it generates. Yet it fails to grasp the way its own concern

---

[85] Kishore Mahbubani, *The New Asian Hemisphere: The Irresistible Shift of Global Power to the East* (New York: PublicAffairs, 2008); Martin Jacques, *When China Rules the World: The Rise of the Middle Kingdom and the End of the Western World* (London: Allen Lane, 2009); and Weiwei Zhang, *The China Wave: Rise of a Civilizational State* (Hackensack, NJ: World Century Publishing Corporation, 2012). Compare my account of 'phantom democracy', in *When Trees Fall, Monkeys Scatter: Rethinking Democracy in China* (London and Singapore: World Scientific Europe, 2017).

[86] Max Horkheimer, *The Eclipse of Reason* (New York: Oxford University Press, 1947), p. 19.

[87] Dahl, *On Democracy*, p. 57; the democratic peace thesis was made popular by Bruce Russett, *Grasping the Democratic Peace: Principles for a Post-Cold War World* (Princeton, NJ: Princeton University Press, 1993).

[88] Chantal Mouffe, 'Foreword', in Pierre Saint-Amand, *The Laws of Hostility: Politics, Violence, and the Enlightenment* (Minneapolis, MN and London: University of Minnesota Press, 1996), pp. vii–xi. Compare my discussion of 'surplus violence' and extended reply to René Girard's *La violence et le sacré* (Paris, 1972) in John Keane, *Violence and Democracy* (Cambridge and New York: Cambridge University Press, 2004).

Introduction

with violence, fear and democracy is deeply implicated in the long-term historical tendency for democracies to render contingent or 'denature' war and other forms of violence. The pages below emphasise more than the obvious fact that unwanted wilful psycho-physical interference with people's bodies and personalities – violence – is ethically incompatible with the democratic principle that all people should be treated with respect and dignity. Robust democracies, it is argued, unleash a process of the democratisation of violence, and fear of violence. By this strange phrase I mean that violence and fear are rendered *problematic* and *unnecessary*. They are denatured. Violence and fear are no longer viewed as a *natura naturans* (nature doing what nature does), or as the will of gods or a God, or determined by historical fate, or traceable to wolfish 'human nature'. Violence and fear are understood as a *political* or *publicly treatable* problem. Non-violent methods of publicly naming and monitoring violence and fear take root in a wide variety of settings. The methods, meanings and effects of violence and fear are exposed on battlefields, at sites of murder, police brutality, disappearances and terrorist attacks. Violence and fear are probed in such fields as misogyny, the maltreatment of children, cruelty to animals and the remembrance of past efforts to exterminate indigenous peoples. In each and every case, the democratisation of violence and fear has the effect of rendering them publicly accountable, and, in the process, defining anew fear and violence as *alterable* and *preventable* through human will and effort.

Least obviously, democratisation even affects the semantics of words such as 'war' and 'violence' and 'fear'. Later in this book, it is shown that a key catalyst in the modern democratisation of fear was its categorisation: the development of taxonomies of different types of fear that raised basic questions about their aetiology and possible overcoming. In matters of violence, through time, much the same has happened. It is not often recognised that in the ancient Greek world of assembly democracy, the word *dēmokratia*, a compound noun formed from demos ('people') and kratos ('rule' or 'conquest'), was itself infected by the virus of war.[89] In our times, by contrast, the meaning of the words violence and war tend to develop negative connotations. The words themselves are applied to more and more areas of life (think of 'domestic violence', 'genocide' and other neologisms of our generation) and come to be controversial and contested in such fields as criminal law, journalism, government policy and (evident

---

[89] Keane, *The Life and Death of Democracy*, pp. 55–62.

in controversies about torture) even within the ranks of armies, whose ultimate job brief is to kill other human beings.

The propensity of democracies and efforts of democrats to name, shame and eradicate violence and fear from the world around us surely grant democracy some ethical high ground, at least compared to regimes of power that feed upon fear, violence and war. The words of Thomas Mann a generation ago still ring true. Compared to democratic ways of living, regimes laced with violence (he had in mind European fascism) dwell 'on different planets' simply because in the face of the 'injustice, malice, cruelty ... stupidity and blindness' perpetrated by some human beings against others, democracy is a 'form of government and of society which is inspired above every other with the feeling and consciousness of the dignity of man'.[90]

From a twenty-first-century perspective, of course, the reach for the ethical high ground by democrats and democratic states is weakened in practice by double standards (think of water-boarding and other forms of torture practised in the name of democracy), as well as by the temptations of imperial hubris and democracy promotion by muddled military means. There is also the inconvenient historical fact, analysed in the pages below, that in the ancient Greek world of assembly democracy, the orators, poets and playwrights of Athens, who tried for the first time to justify democracy as a good way of life, made the mistake of associating it with military virtues and military successes. Thick traces of that justification of democracy (evident in the bellicose speeches by President George W. Bush on the eve of the American invasion of Iraq) are still to be found in the thinking and pronouncements of democrats in these early years of the twenty-first century.

These complications and contradictions in matters of violence and the ethics of democracy force us to think again, and more imaginatively, about why democracy is a good thing, a worthwhile way of life worth living. Despite the global rise of the new populist despotisms, analysed in a forthcoming book,[91] some democrats try to avoid the option of fresh thinking by embracing the well-worn argument that democracy is the best form of handling power because it draws life from the principle that 'the people' are sovereign. Their reasoning borders on the tautological; and their trustfulness in the foundational signifier 'the people' is striking.

---

[90] Thomas Mann, *The Coming Victory of Democracy* (London: Secker & Warburg, 1938), pp. 22–23.
[91] John Keane, *The New Despotisms* (London: Harvard University Press, 2019).

When confronted with doubts about the precise meaning and justification of democracy, they reply by means of a syllogism: since 'democracy means government by the people'[92] and since 'the people' usually know what is in their own best interests, it follows that democracy is the best available political form for protecting and nurturing 'the people' on our planet. Those who reason in this way typically brush aside complications and nuances and doubts about the universality of democracy. When they hear the complaint (famously formulated a generation ago by T. S. Eliot) that 'when a term has become so universally sanctified as "democracy" now is, I begin to wonder whether it means anything, in meaning too many things',[93] they commonly reply that democracy, despite its many forms and multiple meanings, is, in essence, a political form that rests upon the principle that 'the people' are the right and proper foundation of political authority. The formula is a convenient shorthand way of summarising its distinctiveness. It is a synecdoche that highlights the commonality of its various different parts, but those who speak of democracy in this way, this book argues, fail to acknowledge the changing historical meaning, shifting public salience and political pitfalls of the sovereign people principle. What is needed in these early years of our century, this book holds, is the democratisation of the old democratic principle of the sovereign people.

What does this imply? Bringing greater democracy to the ideal of democracy means, in effect, to liberate it from previous dogmatic attachments to metaphysical First Principles by rendering it more humble, more open to the contingency and complexity of things in its egalitarian commitment to the public restraint of arbitrary power. The choice of the connected essay form in this book is designed to reinforce this need for democracy to 'dream of itself' again, to heighten readers' sense of the complexity and contingency of all matters pertaining to democracy. Note that the chosen literary form has no grand narrative or plot. The 'broken narrative' and pizzicato style of this book are purposeful. It is a cardinal quality of its philosophical strategy, a literary reminder that its core propositions are *reasoned evidence-enriched interpretations* and not hard-and-fast 'Truths' that stand beyond further questioning, and further empirical investigation. The book searches for a distinctively democratic style of writing. It favours

---

[92] G. Bingham Powell, Jr., 'Conclusion: Why Elections Matter', in Lawrence LeDuc, Richard Niemi and Pippa Norris (eds.), *Comparing Democracies 4: Elections and Voting in a Changing World* (London: Sage, 2014), p. 187.

[93] T. S. Eliot, *The Idea of a Christian Society* (New York: Harcourt, Brace & World, 1940), pp. 11–12.

the plural prose of life. Its separate sections and segments are reminders that the sum of the parts is not the whole story. The book supposes, to borrow from Nietzsche, that everything is an interpretation, including even this statement. In this sense, the proposed 'grand hypotheses' of the book have a strong inner sense of their own conjectural quality. So does the plea for 'wild thinking' and 'radical stretching and refiguring' of the imaginary horizons through which democracy is currently thought.

The thoughts outlined below on how best to democratise the democratic ideal also come steeped in a strong sense of historicity. The proposition to bring the sovereign people principle back to earth runs as follows: Athenian-style assembly democracy supposed, rather literally, that the ultimate source of power and authority is 'the people', a body that is capable of periodically assembling face-to-face in a public place to decide matters concerning the common good. The invention of representative democracy (a phrase coined only during the last quarter of the eighteenth century) had the long-term effect of reconfiguring the sense and function of 'the people'. Representative democracy cast doubt on the presumed homogeneity of 'the people'; it also proposed reasons why flesh-and-blood people were to be kept at arm's length from government; that is, transformed into part-time judges of how well or badly the representatives performed. Representative democracy meant a form of self-government guided by elected representatives of a people of many people, with diverse and divergent interests.[94] In our times, representative democracy in this sense triggers spirited political backlashes phrased in the name of an imagined collective subject called 'the people'. For instance, there are scholars and political activists nostalgic for the age of assembly democracy, and who agitate for forms of 'real' or 'deep' or 'participatory' democracy forms that are designed (they say) to recapture the energies and wisdom of the collective power of 'the people'.[95] Paradoxically, they speak much the same language as contemporary populists, who denounce

---

[94] Publius [James Madison] famously sketched the principle in 'The Structure of the Government Must Furnish the Proper Checks and Balances between the Different Departments': 'It is of great importance in a republic, not only to guard the society against the oppression of its rulers; but to guard one part of the society against the injustice of the other part. Different interests necessarily exist in different classes of citizens. If a majority be united by a common interest, the rights of the minority will be insecure' (*The Federalist: A Collection of Essays, Written in Favour of the New Constitution* [New York, 1788], number 51).

[95] Benjamin R. Barber, *Strong Democracy: Participatory Politics for a New Age* (Berkeley, CA: University of California Press, 1984); Sheldon S. Wolin, *Politics and Vision: Continuity and Innovation in Western Political Thought* (Princeton, NJ: Princeton University

political establishments in the name of a fictional 'people' capable of 'taking back' power safely, into their own steady hands.[96]

Both variants of nostalgia for an unadulterated 'sovereign people' are unconvincing, and not just because they court the political dangers of big-mouthed demagogy, a devil's pact with leaders who pretend to be the earthly avatars of 'the people'. Those who are nostalgic for the age of assembly democracy, with 'the people' centre stage, are ill-equipped to grasp the ways in which the dynamic and plural structures of monitory democracy are having transformative effects on the practical meaning and legitimacy of 'the people' principle. Put simply, monitory democracy exposes all talk of 'the people' as a politically dangerous fraud. It warns against its despotic potential. 'In a heterogeneous world', noted a prominent philosopher, Mao Tse-tung and Tito in mind, 'there is no possibility of meaningful political action except if sectorial identity is conceived as a nucleus and starting point in the constitution of a wider popular will'.[97] The champions of monitory democracy ask: In this process of constituting popular will, who decides who gets what, when and how? What counts as 'meaningful political action' and 'a wider popular will'? For whom is the political action meaningful and how do its champions deal with differences and disagreements about means and ends? Are they subject to institutional restraints?

Fuelled by such questions, monitory democracy is on bad terms with populism in all its variants. It champions unending struggles for the equalisation of peoples who are not the same, and cannot and should not be made homogenous. Monitory democracy stands against the theoretical fiction and practical phantasm of a unified 'sovereign people'. It asks 'Who is this people?' and 'Why refer to everybody, and nobody in particular?'[98] Monitory democracy demonstrates in action that the world is made up of many *demoi*, which is to say plainly that any particular polity comprises flesh-and-blood people who have different interests and do not necessarily see eye-to-eye. In the age of monitory democracy, references to 'the people' flourish, but monitory mechanisms have the

---

Press, 2004); Sheldon S. Wolin, *Democracy Incorporated: Managed Democracy and the Specter of Inverted Totalitarianism* (Princeton, NJ: Princeton University Press, 2008).

[96] Benjamin Moffitt, *The Global Rise of Populism: Performance, Political Style, and Representation* (Stanford, CA and London: Stanford University Press, 2016).

[97] Ernesto Laclau, 'Why Constructing a People Is the Main Task of Radical Politics', *Critical Inquiry*, 32, 4 (2006), 674–675.

[98] Compare similar questions posed by Ortega y Gasset, 'Suddenly, "People" Appear', in *Man and People* (London: George Allen & Unwin, 1957), p. 173.

effect of democratising (desacralising) literal-minded accounts of the principle of 'the sovereign people'. Monitory democracy publicly exposes and de-natures haughty talk of 'the people' as a potentially dangerous populist fiction; its mechanisms daily serve as barriers against the uncontrolled worship of 'the people', or what could better be dubbed demolatry.

Of course, the extent to which the sovereign people principle is democratised – transformed by citizens and their representatives into a handy signifier that most flesh-and-blood people know to be a political fiction that serves as a reminder that everybody counts in matters of politics – is an empirical question. It is an empirical question as well whether, or to what degree, the institutions of monitory democracy can practically tolerate divergent forms of 'peoplehood';[99] that is, conflicting understandings of who are 'the people'. Just one thing is clear. It might be called the paradox of monitory democracy: while the public scrutiny and restraint of the exercise of power practically requires a downgrading of the 'sovereign people' principle, it also requires its confinement to those exceptional moments when the resolution of sharp disagreements and savage contests of power requires the invocation of the fiction of an undivided people who are the ultimate source of authority. German constitutional lawyers like to say that 'the people' are a *'Zurechnungssubjekt'*, a putative legal subject to whom collectively binding powers are attributed, but a subject that is not itself capable of acting as a purposeful unified subject. The shift of meaning is significant. It reveals how, in the age of monitory democracy, talk of 'the people' is at best a fictional device vital for humbling the high and mighty, by reminding citizens and their representatives that those who make the laws are not the ultimate source of their own claimed legitimacy.

If the sovereign people principle is deconstructed, brought back to earth, stretched to include differences and cross-border trends, in the way proposed by this book, the question naturally arises as to why diverse peoples with diverse interests might favour monitory democracy as a way of life dedicated to the equalisation of power. Set against what it calls a 'great normative silence', this book surveys the history of justifications of democracy, and finds them all wanting. It shows how the history of democracy has been shaped and shadowed by a sequence of overlapping but conflicting First Principle justifications of why democracy is a universal norm. The single-mindedness of these so-called 'foundationalist'

[99] Rogers M. Smith, *Stories of Peoplehood: The Politics and Morals of Political Membership* (Cambridge: Cambridge University Press, 2003).

arguments today ought to feel strange to us. Some examples analysed below include the originally nineteenth-century Christian view that democracy is desirable because it draws strength from the inspiration of the Gospel; the belief that democracy rests upon the universality of Family and Nation, or upon History; or the claim that the universality of democracy stems from its institutional nurturing of public reason linked to the discovery of Truth. Philosophically speaking, when assembled in this way, these and other First Principle justifications of democracy are not just mutually contradictory. They are in their own way sententious, arrogant and potentially fanatical. Their magisterial quality contradicts the whole idea of democracy as a defender of equality amidst a diversity of ways of life. The point developed throughout the pages below is that the spirit and language of democracy, as many people still think of it today, harbours a great deal of inherited philosophical conceit that is plainly undemocratic. It follows that the justification of democracy is in need of humbling through fresh but rigorous 'weak' thinking that at the same time breaks with metaphysics and avoids pre-political 'anything goes' relativism, a form of 'weak' thinking that emphasises that democracy is a universal norm because it is the guardian of a plurality of lived interpretations of life.[100]

But what might this humbling move imply for the ethic of democracy? How could this ethic become more capacious, more universally tolerant of different and conflicting definitions of democracy, and more capable of making better sense of the vast complexity of our human and non-human worlds? The reasoning of this book is at odds with the arguments of scholars who have proposed that democracy should part company with the whole business of philosophical justification, conventionally understood as the search for unquestionable First Principles. Influenced by the pragmatism of Richard Rorty, these scholars have drawn the conclusion that a truce between philosophy and democracy should be declared, so that democracy sheds its old philosophical baggage and hereon travels light in the world, following the path of pragmatic calculation.[101] This book questions this pragmatic turn. It calls for more (albeit 'weak')

---

[100] Gianni Vattimo, *A Farewell to Truth* (New York: Columbia University Press, 2011); Stanley Fish, *The Trouble with Principle* (Cambridge, MA: Harvard University Press, 1999).

[101] Richard Rorty, 'The Priority of Democracy to Philosophy', in Richard Rorty, *Philosophical Papers: Objectivity, Relativism, and Truth*, Vol. I (Cambridge: Cambridge University Press, 1991), pp. 257–282; compare Keane, *The Life and Death of Democracy*, especially pp. 839–872.

thinking, not less reflection on why democracy can be considered a universal ideal. That is why the pages below emphasise that the fashionable resort to so-called consequentialist arguments for democracy is unconvincing, and needs to be set aside. Democracy is not straightforwardly a promoter of non-violent peace. It is not the natural precondition of market-generated wealth or sustained or sustainable 'economic growth'. To say that democracy fosters 'human development more fully than any feasible alternative' (Robert Dahl) is equally unconvincing. In each case, or so it is argued, the claimed practical consequences of adhering to democratic ways of handling power beg too many questions. The claimed positive consequences of democracy are unwarranted, and cannot therefore serve as the final court of appeal which establishes that democracy is a universal norm.

The pages below acknowledge that in the countryside villages and mega-cities of India, Thailand and other countries, the word democracy is not treated as a philosophical matter. When it is prized, it is prized for much less esoteric reasons, for instance those to do with uncorrupted, elected governments providing clean running water, electricity and decent schools and hospitals. Elsewhere, democracy is sometimes valued as a code of common sense belief. 'Have faith in democracy', said an outgoing American president. 'It's not always pretty, I know. I've been living it. But it's how, bit by bit, generation by generation, we have made progress.'[102] These points of good rhetoric are noted; but given that there are many moments in public contexts when normative arguments for democracy really count, by making a difference to the prevailing power dynamics, a new and supplementary case is made in these pages for thinking of democracy in terms of the *humbling* of arbitrary power. This approach rejects all previous efforts to ground democracy in the metaphysical arrogance of First Principles. 'Democracy is not figurable', writes Jean-Luc Nancy. It is a special form of the political that 'overthrows the assumption of the figuration of a destiny, of a truth of the common'. Democracy 'opens up the greatest possible proliferation of forms that the infinite can take, figures of our affirmations and declaration of our desires'.[103] It follows from this way of thinking, one that is developed

---

[102] Barack Obama, address to Rutgers University's 250th anniversary commencement ceremony (15 May, 2016), http://commencement.rutgers.edu/250th-anniverary-commencement-videos#ObamaAddress.

[103] Jean-Luc Nancy, *The Truth of Democracy* (New York: Fordham University Press, 2010), p. 27.

on every page of this book, that a core aim of the project of stretching the horizons of democracy is to build into the norm of democracy its own radical originality; its defiant insistence that people's lives are never simply given, that all things human are built on the shifting sands of spacetime, and that no person or group, no matter how much power they presently enjoy, can be trusted permanently, in any given context, to govern those people's lives.

The perspective developed below sees monitory democracy, the most power-sensitive form of self-government in the history of democracy, as the best weapon so far invented for guarding against the 'illusions of certainty'[104] and breaking up camouflaged monopolies of power, wherever they operate. This interpretation of democracy does not think of itself as a True and Right norm. Just the reverse: the norm of monitory democracy is aware of its own and others' limits, knows that it does not know everything, and understands that democracy has no meta-historical guarantees. It does not suffer fools gladly. Democracy worries that humans are toad-eating animals.[105] It warns against hubris; it takes a stand against the humiliation of people. It is committed to the public humbling of arbitrary power. Power on stilts is not its thing. It issues early warnings against those who abuse their power, questions the arrogant and takes the side of the powerless against the powerful. With the help of a plethora of power-humbling mechanisms, it supposes that a more equal world of greater openness and diversity is possible. Monitory democracy is the public champion of greater complex equality, but not because all women and men are created equal. It rather supposes that no man or woman is good enough to rule permanently over their fellows, and the terrestrial environments in which they dwell, and upon which they so profoundly depend.

---

[104] Daniel Kahnemann, *Thinking, Fast and Slow* (London and New York: Allen Lane, 2011), p. 418.
[105] William Hazlitt, 'On the Connexion between Toad-Eaters and Tyrants [1817]', *Political Essays, with Sketches of Public Characters* (London: William Hone, 1819), p. 163.

PART I

INDIGENISATION

I

Asia's Orphan: Democracy in Taiwan, 1895–2000

Among the most astonishing political developments of our times is the appearance of a proud and lively young democracy on a densely forested, densely populated archipelago in the East China Sea known as Taiwan. The archipelago is sometimes called Asia's orphan, and for a good reason.[1] Born of a region seemingly hostile to constitutional government, Taiwan is an important case of the indigenisation of democracy. It showed that monitory democracy with 'Asian' characteristics was possible, and even that this form of democracy had distinctively indigenous 'Asian' roots. The local pressures for democratisation proved that 'Asians' were not by nature deferential to superiors, or condemned by poverty to superstition, or bigoted in their association of the word 'democracy' (*mín zhǔ*) with Western conceit and gambling, prostitution, family breakdown and other forms of Western decadence. And Taiwan had another, larger significance. It turned out to be remarkable above all in its defiance of the modern textbook rule that democracy could only survive in a 'country' defined by a strong sense of homogeneous national unity and sovereign territorial borders.

---

[1] The description is drawn from the allegorical novel by the influential journalist and literary figure, Zhuoliu Wu, *The Orphan of Asia* (New York: Columbia University Press, 2006). Written under the Japanese occupation and completed in 1945, its central character is Hu Taiming, a man who was born in Japanese-occupied Taiwan, enrolled by his grandfather in the Ladder to the Clouds, a school that taught the Confucian classics, only to suffer disillusionment and a deep identity crisis after being forced to teach in the Japanese-run school in a Taiwanese village, where he not only found many of his students backward but was forced to realise that his own professional integrity was threatened by Japanese contempt for the colonised Taiwanese.

The Taiwanese population, a diverse people living on islands without an internationally recognised state, defied the gravity of so-called realist politics. They showed that the issue of official statehood did not first have to be resolved in order for democracy to be possible.[2] That is to say, they demonstrated that representative democracy and sovereign territorial statehood were conjoined twins that could be separated. During the six decades after 1945, Taiwan resembled a laboratory whose people embarked on a lonely search for new solutions to a problem that first appeared among the scores of self-governing city states that thrived for a time in the early years of assembly democracy: the problem of whether and how democracy can create and maintain a wider peaceful environment; that is, a 'security community' in which the scavengers of violence, fear and war are both unwelcome and kept at bay.

FROM COLONISATION TO WHITE TERROR

The Taiwanese experiment with democracy was born in a crucible of war, military conquest and colonial rule. It all started during the period of Japanese colonisation that lasted from 1895 (when the Qing Dynasty handed over the archipelago as a spoil of war) until 1945. Colonisation brought violence and bossing and the enforced assimilation of subjects usually associated with imperial rule. But from the point of view of democracy, Japanese rule also produced some ironic effects with long-lasting implications.[3] It had the unintended consequence of 'nationalising' local identities. A certain feeling among the local educated elites of being 'Taiwanese' (*dăi wăn láng*) was strengthened, along with some aspirations for self-rule. There was some talk of the nation (*min zoku*) and popular sovereignty (*min-pon shugi*) and self-rule (the Japanese term *jichi* was used for this) and the right of people to participate in politics (*sansei ken*). In 1920, a Movement for the Establishment of the Taiwan

---

[2] Compare the claim about the fundamental importance, in transitions to democracy, of solving the number-one problem of 'stateness', in Juan J. Linz and Alfred Stepan, '"Stateness", Nationalism and Democratization', in *Problems of Democratic Transition and Consolidation: Southern Europe, South America, and Post-communist Europe* (Baltimore, MD: The Johns Hopkins University Press, 1996), pp. 16–37.

[3] The following draws from my interview with Rwei-Ren Wu, Taipei (2 July 2005); and his excellent *The Formosan Ideology: Oriental Colonialism and the Rise of Taiwanese Nationalism, 1895–1945* (Chicago, IL: University of Chicago, 2003); and E. Patricia Tsurumi, *Japanese Colonial Education in Taiwan, 1895–1945* (Cambridge, MA: Harvard University Press, 1977).

Parliament was born; it dared even to petition the Imperial Diet in Tokyo, which had the effect of stimulating the strong growth of local associations and factions (some of which had antecedents in traditional Chinese associations, known locally as *huì guǎn* and *jishi gongye*).

Then came local elections, the first of which was held in 1935. While the bulk of the aboriginal and settler population had not been drawn fully into the resistance to Japanese imperial rule, it was plain that the seeds of non-violent, constitutional government were planted locally, by the efforts of the people of Formosa, as they were still called at the time. The sentiments stood them in good stead for the painful history that awaited their archipelago. With the crushing surrender of Japan after the atomic bombing of Hiroshima and Nagasaki in August 1945, the Formosans were handed over by the Allies to the Kuomintang government of Generalissimo Chiang Kai-Shek. The change was at first welcomed locally, but his rule quickly proved unpopular. On 28 February 1947, it sparked an island-wide uprising that was eventually crushed through a murderous campaign (the so-called 'Countryside Sweep') waged by Chiang Kai-shek's KMT troops. The wanton cruelty and violence, in which at least twenty to thirty thousand people died, prefigured something much worse: the arrival of between one and two million refugees (the local population was around six million) and Chiang Kai-shek's army of 600,000 troops after their defeat by the communist forces of Mao Zedong in the year of the ox, 1949.

So began nearly four decades of White Terror – the twentieth century's longest unbroken period of martial law. The Chinese nationalist government of Chiang Kai-shek resembled an oversized Leviathan, a garrison state apparatus that was permanently mobilised to root out and destroy all local resistance, in preparation for the day when it would return to the Chinese mainland, to replace the communists and govern an empire that would include 600 million Chinese people, plus Tibetans and Mongolians. These were of course times of Cold War, and dictators using totalitarian – communist and fascist – methods of rule were welcome in the world of freedom, so long as they did not call themselves communists or fascists. There was naturally a ticket required to enter the gates of freedom. Dictators had to be seen to be on the side of liberty, which meant signing up to the Universal Declaration of Human Rights and choosing a good name for the state – Formosa was blessed with the democratic-sounding Republic of China – as well as allowing a good measure of private property and market freedom, capped off by the staging of periodic – rigged – elections.

The colonised population proved to be no pushover; and the fact of elections, even though they were held only at the local level, kept alive memories of old struggles against the Japanese, as well as extending a hand of hope by encouraging people to imagine the day when the nationalist KMT dictatorship got its comeuppance. The military regime did its best to ensure that its day of reckoning was a long time coming. Protected from Mao's China by the US Seventh Fleet, the KMT constitution was used as if it were a book of instructions issued by the Generalissimo and his faithful officials. There was lifelong tenure for him and for some two thousand KMT parliamentarians, who claimed (following elections on the Chinese mainland in 1948) to represent the will of their constituents in support of the only 'legitimate government of China'. The death penalty was brought in for the designated crimes of rebellion and troublemaking. Local religious bodies, such as I Kuan Tao (*yí guàn dào*) and the popular Buddhist Nichiren sect, were treated as if they were worms in the guts of the body politic. A blanket ban on visits abroad, especially to visit relatives on mainland China, was enforced. Everyone aged fourteen or older was required to carry an ID card at all times, or otherwise risk being carted away as a 'communist agent'. Billboards were splattered with messages like 'Caution! A spy is by your side!'

Nets of suspicion were cast widely, so that imprisonment was sanctioned for 'knowing but not reporting bandits'. That commitment to detecting and eradicating enemies meant that virtually all friends and every household and workplace were placed under suspicion, especially because those who grassed on their fellows, or who made false accusations, were rewarded with thirty per cent of the assets of the convicted dissident (35 per cent was awarded as well to personnel handling the case, so increasing the chances that sycophants and other law-abiding subjects would strike it rich by proving that crime paid after all). Anyone suspected or accused of favouring local 'independence' from mainland China was treated harshly. Plainclothes police, telephone tapping, mail inspection, the fabrication of facts, and trumped-up accusations were their lot. Whole families and villages were rounded up, disappeared, tortured or murdered, then (if they were lucky) buried secretly in unmarked graves.

Christian missionaries were meanwhile banned from carrying on their work in local vernacular languages, such as Hoklo, Hakka and several aboriginal tongues. Communication media were heavily controlled, and in general the regime did everything it could to turn journalists into hierophants, guardians and enforcers of the mysteries of state. In the name of conserving paper, newspaper production runs were strictly controlled. Magazines and publishers suspected of disloyalty were closed down; in one year alone (1969), 4.23 million copies of 'bad publications' were burned, buried or shredded.[4] Private radio stations were banned; official radio stations were controlled with heavy hands; and all listeners were required to register for a user's licence and to pay a monthly fee. School textbooks and materials were vetted. Bans were slapped on so-called effeminate songs, local folk music and any tunes that were inclined to social realism. The KMT regime did everything it could to define and exterminate what it called 'red poison, yellow harm, and black crime' (communist, pornographic, and gangster influences). It even waged a war against bodily resistance to power. It tried to get under people's skin, beginning with young people at school. Men's hair could not be longer than one centimetre. Girl's hair that crept over their ears was not permitted. The regime was otherwise even-handed in matters of appearance: hirsute young men in bell-bottomed trousers and mini-skirted young women with funky hair were equally subject to arrest and imprisonment, or worse.

CIVIL RESISTANCE

There was a local saying that those who create enemies pay high prices, and so it was with the Kuomintang regime. Its moment of reckoning came with its enforced withdrawal in 1971 from a seat on the United Nations Security Council and, the following year, the historic visit of President Richard Nixon to Beijing for the purpose of negotiating an end to two decades of frosty relations between the United States and China. Opening the UN door to Communist China signalled the end of an era. Suddenly, from that moment, the regime of Chiang Kai-shek lost its raison d'être. It became the orphan of Asia. Its relations with the giant panda across the straits grew tense. Once more, the settlers of Taiwan found themselves playthings of big powers. The effect was to embolden many Taiwanese people, to make many of them see they were on their own, that taking things into their own hands was not just desirable, but imperative.

The resistance forms an important episode in the history of monitory democracy. Among the first group of citizens to protest publicly were

---

[4] From the figures cited in *The Road to Freedom: Taiwan's Postwar Human Rights Movement* (Taipei: Taiwan Foundation for Democracy, 2004), p. 28; see also the doctoral dissertation by Lihyun Lin, *The Transformation of Press – State Relationships in Taiwan 1945–1995* (London: University of Westminster, 1997).

local Presbyterians whose roots on the archipelago extended back several generations. True to their sixteenth-century invention in Scotland of the practice of constitutional conventions, they called upon the government several times to respect human rights, including freedom of religion and the entitlement to social justice; they proposed as well a full re-election of the national legislature and recognition of 'the right of the people' to determine their own future in 'a new and independent country'.[5] These were brave words that brought the secret police flocking to their chapels, but to no avail. Bit by bit, month by month, citizens' resistance began to cut the claws of the KMT state. A tattered string of open protests against election fraud led (in November 1977) to violent scenes at Chungli, where a flamboyant opposition candidate for county magistrate, Hsu Hsin-liang, was declared winner, denied victory by the government, then – after rioters wrecked a local police station – declared the winner. At Kaohsiung, a town on the southern coast of the main island, a large demonstration on International Human Rights Day (10 December 1979) produced martyrs when the city was shelled and its police rioted, killing and injuring scores of young civilian men and women. Troubles doubled and began to spread to the point where, by the mid-1980s, the KMT regime grew nervous, especially with the founding of the Democratic Progressive Party (DPP). It was soon to score the first of a string of electoral victories, by capturing the post of mayor of the capital city, Taipei. The party used well-targeted, sometimes witty, state-of-the-art campaigning methods. Others drew upon nativist themes (like 'patching the broken fishing net' or 'humble administration' or 'have confidence in Taiwan') that could mean different things to different voters, especially when expressed in Taiwanese dialect rather than the Mandarin used by the KMT authorities.[6]

---

[5] Further details are to be found in Christine L. Lin, 'The Presbyterian Church in Taiwan and the Advocacy of Local Autonomy', *Sino-Platonic Papers*, **92** (1999), 1–123.

[6] According to the DPP's campaign director during this period, the ex-student movement leader and student of theatre, Luo Wen-Chia, the electioneering methods that were used owed something to the Maoist understanding of 'politics as the art of locating and utilising socially meaningful points of contradiction for the purpose of forging alliances, making gains and winning the power to do things. Mao Zedong and the Chinese Communist Party were very good at these political arts, but when stripped of their communist qualities they can be used to good advantage in a democracy' (interview, Taipei, 31 May 2005). I am also grateful for the remarks on elections, media and the 'sanctification' of democracy in Taiwan provided by Felix Schöber (interview, London, 3 May 2005) and Lihyun Lin (Taipei, 3 June 2005).

The founding of Taiwan's first genuinely oppositional political party was inspired by the deepening sense among the population that public protests were now legitimate, and that they could win important gains. Their peaceful and self-disciplined qualities were remarkable. They had as well a deep respect for the rule of law and a strong experimental air about them, for instance in the way they made use of temples as places of refuge, as public spaces where citizens could gather in safety, to feel stronger by getting to know each other better. A memorable example in the mid-1980s was the staging of unofficial election rallies by supporters of the *'dǎng wài'* ('Outside the Party') opposition movement. In west Taipei, they chose as their venue the wonderfully ornate, early nineteenth-century Buddhist temple at Longshan. It was a safe haven where the riot police did not dare show their face, for fear of upsetting the calm routines of local people gently chanting from scripts and praying for the health and well-being of their children and their families and loved ones. No one knew what the local goddess Guan Yin (*guān yīn*) thought of the rallies that sheltered there in her presence, but one fact was plain: when ten thousand citizens at a time huddled in solidarity in the temple courtyard, protected from water cannon and tear gas by bright flowers and sweet fruits, gongs and drums, candles and smouldering incense, they rapidly learned the arts of politics by talking freely among themselves, and openly to journalists and others, about the need to create a 'civil society' (*gōng mín shè huì*) and a 'democracy' (*mín zhǔ*) that enabled citizens (*gōng mín*) to cast a free and fair vote – to throw a ticket (*tóu piào*) as the Taiwanese liked to say.

KOLONKO DEMOCRACY

These words proved to be the key terms in a new political language that the authorities did not understand, and certainly could never accept. The KMT state tried to stay tough, like a bully losing his grip, but state bullying served only to steel the resolve of many citizens, who were cheered by the growing visibility and numbers of supporters outside their archipelago. One very interesting thing about the democratic mutations that happened in Taiwan during this period was the way they could not have happened without long-distance, external support, by both governmental and civil society bodies. The active human rights diplomacy directed by the Carter administration against the regime was a good illustration of this point. So too was the non-governmental overseas rescue network, as it came to be called. Bound together across borders by information that travelled through disguised 'underground railroads', the rescue network included many hundreds of initiatives, such as church groups, university links, Amnesty International letters and reports, press and media coverage, visits by lawyers to monitor political trials, as well as efforts by groups of exiles like the Formosan Association for Human Rights (based in New York) and the Taiwan Political Prisoner Rescue Association (based in Tokyo). The long-lasting effectiveness of this hotchpotch of activity was to mark the new democracy of Taiwan indelibly with unusually strong cosmopolitan instincts, which served to strengthen local feelings that resistance was worthwhile, despite everything. That cosmopolitanism – the strong sense that what was happening inside Taiwan was being co-determined by outside developments – had one striking effect. It worked to neutralise attempts to popularise simple-minded beliefs in 'the nation' and its right to a 'sovereign state'.

What was especially remarkable about the push for democratisation was its avoidance of nationalist rhetoric. Perhaps that wasn't surprising, given that both the Japanese and Chinese conqueror regimes had taught locals to suspect or detest talk of Nations and Enemies of the Nation. There was also the historical fact that prior to the arrival of Japanese colonisers at the end of the nineteenth century, the 'Ilha Formosa' or 'Beautiful Island', as Europeans had called it, had been colonised successively by Dutch, Spanish and Chinese forces. The point was that by the middle of the twentieth century, given this complex history, much of the population felt and understood its own hybridity. People were not inclined to fall for easy definitions of the Nation.[7] They had lost the habit of dying for their Country. Questions about who belonged to the archipelago, and why, were felt to be open questions with no straightforward answers, and that in turn was felt to be a good thing. Doctrines of racial or ethnic 'purity' – like that promoted by KMT rule – were to be feared, and resisted. Equally repugnant were the communiqués – the hawkish squawking by birds sitting in nests of ready-to-fire missiles – that were issued constantly by Beijing about how there was only One China, and that anybody who challenged its 'sovereignty' and 'territorial integrity' would have to be punished.[8]

---

[7] A neologism, taken from Japanese at the end of the nineteenth century, nation, the word *guo jia*, combines two characters, *guó* meaning a bounded polity or kingdom and *jiā* meaning a family, the latter represented by the character of a pig in a barn (国家).

[8] See, for example, the official reaction of the Chinese Communist Party to President Chen Shui-bian's inauguration speech, 'One-China Principle Allows for No Evasion or Ambiguity: Commentary' (Beijing, 21 May 2000), members.tripod.com/~Ken_Davies/response.html: 'Anybody who dares insist on splitting Taiwan from China, in spite of the warning

From the standpoint of many within Taiwan's democratic opposition, there was to be no 'true' Taiwan, simply because 'Taiwan' and 'Taiwanese' were felt to be power-ridden rhetorical terms caught up in a life-and-death political process of continual inscription. More positively, 'Taiwan' was to be a place where many different ethno-national identities should freely live side by side. That point was courageously driven home, at the end of December 1984, during the last years of the KMT regime, by the formation of the Taiwan Association for the Promotion of Aboriginal Rights. It was a civil society network that agitated, with some measure of success, for the right of the descendants of Taiwan's earliest inhabitants to be publicly visible – and to have greater control over their lands and to be called by their tribal (non-Chinese) names. Respect for difference was also the theme of actions by the Malayo-Polynesian Tao people of Orchid Island, who on more than one occasion dressed up as 'radioactive people' to protest against the KMT decision to dump nuclear waste on an island famed for its natural scenery and butterfly orchids. The right to be different was also an explicit theme of protests by the Hakka people against the suppression of their language and culture – a right that was finally acknowledged in 2003, when the first television channel broadcasting in Hakka came on stream.

Like all other defenders of differences of language and culture, Hakka citizens were more or less prepared to identify politically with 'Taiwan' – the word itself was anathema to the KMT regime – but only on the condition that it was used as an open signifier. Its role as a symbol and vision and reality was to be kept incomplete, and not monopolised by any particular power group. The point is worth underscoring: the historic significance of the Taiwanese people's resistance to totalitarian rule was that it stood beyond the confines of narrow-minded nationalism. It was not a repeat performance of the old play called the Third World struggle for 'national independence'. The resistance to cruel arbitrary power in Taiwan was fuelled by a new form of ultra-modern or 'outward-looking' patriotism that favoured mutual respect and solidarity among the different settlers of the archipelago. Resistance sprang from a new alliance of Taiwanese based on principles of equal justice and

---

from the Chinese government and people, must bear responsibility for all the serious consequences arising therefrom. The principle concerns China's reunification, sovereignty and territorial integrity, and the Chinese government and people will make no concession on this major matter of principle.'

freedom and respect for all groups. The alliance both required and implied a civil society made up of many different senses of the meaning of being Taiwanese. It implied making room for new migrant workers from south-east Asia (well over a quarter of a million landed on the shores of Taiwan after the defeat of the KMT dictatorship). The right to be different was important. Taiwan was to be (let's call it) a colourful *kolonko* democracy: a self-organising archipelago whose civil society contained all the variety of the kolonko fruit – the fish-shaped melon with white flesh and black seeds and pink, green and yellow skin that grows in abundance on its soils.

In its commitment to social pluralism, the Taiwanese battle for *kolonko* democracy repeated, under very different circumstances, and in much quicker time, what the Congress Party had first attempted in India. In just over a decade, Taiwan started to build democratic structures that protected different lived views of how to define Taiwan. It managed to do what Europe – through a complicated and messy process of integration – took more than half a century to initiate. But the case of Taiwan was not only quick-paced and polymorphic, it was also something very special because it was the first-ever transition to democracy in which neither a single organised religion nor a strongly shared sense of common dependence upon the sacred played a significant role. Local democrats used methods – flowers, processions, even a smiling Mona Lisa on billboards – that had the effect of sanctifying democracy, certainly. There was also plenty of respect for people's different personal senses of the sacred (*shén shèng*). In search of the Way, many people visited temples and frequented worship circles (*jì sì yuán*) for the purpose of expiating their wrongdoings and nourishing their vital powers; politicians followed after them, in search of money and votes. Some people called on the gods and goddesses to help them out of a tight spot; demonstrators, especially those engaged in environmental politics, referred often to the sea goddess of mercy, Mazu (*mā zǔ*) and there were plenty of lingering beliefs in 'small ghosts' (*xiǎo guǐ*) and magic (*wū shù*). But the *kolonko* democracy was not tied tightly to these practices. All things considered, it dispensed with self-justificatory talk of trusting in God, or goddesses and gods. It proved that a thoroughly secular, this-worldly democracy – a *shì sú xìng* democracy – was possible. It was felt by millions of Taiwanese that their country was ideally to be bound together by something more tangible: suspicion and ridicule of unaccountable power and deep respect for the practice and principles of human rights.

1 Asia's Orphan: Democracy in Taiwan, 1895–2000

ASIA'S NEW DEMOCRACY

That was the language used by the politician Chen Shui-bian shortly after his successful presidential bid in mid-March 2000 – in a fierce but fair election that signalled the end of the KMT regime's fifty-five-year monopoly on governmental power. In his inauguration speech, the son of a poor tenant farmer and illiterate day labourer, dressed in a grey suit with a red tie, his wife Wu Shu-jen (disabled by an opposition assassination attempt in 1985) seated beside him in a wheelchair, pledged allegiance not to the flag, or to a God, but to the adherence of the Taiwanese government and its people to the 'third wave of democracy', to 'rule by the clean and upright', and to a peaceful way of life in which vote-buying, corrupt business and other 'black gold' practices would not be tolerated.[9] Taiwan would commit itself to the vision of a multi-cultural archipelago. 'We must open our hearts with tolerance and respect, so that our diverse ethnic groups and different regional cultures communicate with each other, and so that Taiwan's local cultures connect with the cultures of Chinese-speaking communities and other world cultures.' Chen Shui-bian went on to say that his country would rejoin the best global trends of the twenty-first-century ways of life. It would do so by adhering to the Universal Declaration of Human Rights, incorporating international human rights covenants into domestic law, and by establishing – with the help of Amnesty International and the International Commission of Jurists – a National Human Rights Commission.

Chen Shui-bian spoke of 'building a human rights nation' and so did many official documents and declarations.[10] Such talk would later skewer both his political career and second term as president, when he and his wife came under intense media and judicial scrutiny for their operation of a discretionary 'state affairs' fund used to conduct secret diplomacy. At the time, citizens' reactions to his talk of a 'human rights nation' were

---

[9] The full text of the speech (20 May 2000, Taipei) is found at www.taipei.org/chen/chen0520.html.
[10] See, for example, the statement that is reprinted from the 2002 Human Rights Policy White Paper, in 'National Human Rights Policy', *The Road to Freedom: Taiwan's Postwar Human Rights Movement*, p. 163: 'In the post-war "age of human rights", the rights to which humankind are entitled are no longer limited to those stipulated by and protected by national constitutions, but should include all universal rights prescribed in international human rights instruments ... Taiwan, despite being isolated internationally, is still a member of the global village and is willing to take action to shoulder her rightful responsibility in the protection and realization of universal rights.'

divided and suitably ambiguous – as one would have expected of a democratic country that was not a country in any conventional sense. The majority of voters seemed to accept the many anomalies associated with some loosely defined, de facto 'independent sovereignty'. They sided with the principles of human rights, and accepted (as Taiwan's leading campaign strategist put it) that 'although democracy [*mín zhŭ*] may not always be the most efficient way of making decisions, it is a way of dividing and controlling power that helpfully prevents mistakes from being made and positively encourages respect for human beings, their choices, beliefs and different ways of living, such as same-sex partnerships'.[11] The majority of voters embraced the fact that the shrinking army of Taiwan was dependent ultimately for its survival on American naval and air power. But they also expressed approval of another fact: that around 50 per cent of Taiwanese trade and investment was with China (according to local black humour, Taiwanese businessmen favouring unification with China supported the policy of 'one country, two wives'). Only around a quarter of the voting population (the figure depended on the wording of opinion poll questions) favoured an outright declaration of independence; that figure dropped to around one-sixth of voters when it came to a formal change of the name 'Republic of China'.[12]

Not everyone agreed with the tricky compromises required of the new democracy. Some high-minded critics likened Taiwanese democracy to an evening television soap series, with a scrambled script. Hard-core recidivists within the KMT, now forced to play the role of opposition party in what had become basically a two-party system divided between 'blues' (the KMT and a splinter party or two) and 'greens' (the DPP and the pro-independence party TSU, led by a former KMT president, Lee Teng-hui), called for the 'return' of Taiwan to its rightful owners, the regime run by the Chinese Communist Party. Reacting against such 'one-China' talk, some Taiwanese politicians, government officials, businesses and citizens chose to engage in a struggle for 'independence'. Faced down by the Beijing government and its talk of Taiwan as a 'province', some locals even dared to talk defiantly of 'sovereign independence'. The two apparently divergent views were in fact cut from the same cloth. Both the fans of a united China and independence for Taiwan indulged the originally European, early modern belief that democracy can only survive in territorial states that are 'sovereign' in the sense that those who govern have

---

[11] Interview with Luo Wen-Chia (Taipei, 31 May 2005).
[12] Interview with Professor Michael Hsiao (Taipei, 31 May 2005).

the ultimate say, backed up by their monopoly over guns, police and the army, over what goes on within the boundaries of the territorially bounded state.

Both the 'unification' and 'sovereign independence' positions arguably failed to grasp the historical novelty of what had been achieved in Taiwan during the past several decades: a post-nationalist, secular democracy blessed with a plurality of different identities, a polity that had managed to consolidate itself and to survive its transition, even within the field of force of governments hungry for territory and resources and a region bristling with arms and armies.

But what would protect democracy made in Taiwan from predators? It is important to recall – the point crops up frequently in the history of democracy – that democracies survive and best thrive within what has been called a 'security community'. In other words, they require for their support a like-minded group of democracies that share some sense of community and sets of overlapping institutions. These must be sufficiently strong to withstand internal and external 'shocks', so guaranteeing with a fair measure of probability over a fairly long period of time that peaceful co-ordination and change can take place among the members of the group, who can settle their differences short of war.[13] Only a handful of democracies have appeared to escape this rule. The new American republic managed to democratise itself during the first half of the nineteenth century, thanks to some loose and shifting military alliances and the protection afforded by two oceans in the age of muskets and wind-powered ships. Perhaps the newly independent republic of India counted as another case of a state that reshaped itself into a democracy, very often through its own efforts – and of course with some help from the Soviet Union.

The young democracy of Taiwan was almost certainly not describable in terms of either the American or Indian pathways to 'sovereignty'. It was an entirely new *indigenised* democracy with *post-sovereign* characteristics. Born of struggles to shake off two imperial powers – Japan and China – with long-term designs on its peoples and their resources, Taiwan

---

[13] The classic account of the idea and practice of security communities was that developed by Karl Deutsch *et al.*, *Political Community and the North Atlantic Area: International Organization in the Light of Historical Experiences* (Princeton, NJ: Princeton University Press, 1957), and Karl Deutsch, 'Security Communities', in James Rosenau (ed.), *International Politics and Foreign Policy* (New York: The Free Press, 1961). See also Emanuel Adler and Michael N. Barnett (eds.), *Security Communities* (Cambridge: Cambridge University Press, 1998).

was better described as a democratic orphan with diverse parents, as the *resultant* of many intersecting forces, both at the level of government and civil society. The strange, at times comical mixture of official and unofficial Chinese and English names given to the archipelago – province, nation, prefecture, China, Formosa, Free China, Nationalist China, Chinese Taipei, the Republic of China, and now Taiwan – was symptomatic of these hybrid origins and their polymorphous trajectory.[14] Its fast-track transition to democracy took place at the intersection of powerful forces that pulled it this way and that. Sometimes this helped protect it from the clutches of war and violence; sometimes it was pushed towards the nervousness and self-pity that came from being Asia's orphan democracy in the world of territorial states and regional alliances. That made both its survival and identity as a political unit permanently controversial. But by the early years of the new millennium, the governments and citizens of Asia's orphan achieved what many had thought to be impossible. Backed by the American 7th Fleet and helped along by 'Made in Taiwan' global trade, local civil 'protection strategies' designed to obstruct military occupation, diplomatic recognition by several handfuls of states and vigorous 'soft power' efforts to make its presence felt in the affairs of the world, the archipelago had managed to secure its hard-won democratic freedoms. Against all odds, Taiwan had become the 'cuckoo' in the nest of the People's Republic of China – a clear alternative to a political system of one-party rule.[15]

---

[14] See Mark Harrison, *Legitimacy, Meaning and Knowledge in the Making of Taiwanese Identity* (New York: Palgrave Macmillan, 2006), especially chapter 1.
[15] John Keane, *When Trees Fall, Monkeys Scatter: Rethinking Democracy In China* (London and Singapore: World Scientific Europe, 2017).

2

Indigenous Peoples

When thinking about the indigenisation of democracy, the duty to reconsider the historical relationship between indigenous peoples and popular self-government is important, for several reasons. In surprising ways, as the Asia Pacific case of Australia shows, such rethinking raises questions about the bigotry and violence encoded within the history of modern democracy in representative form. It also prompts new questions about what is meant by the indigenisation of democracy, and whether and to what extent local indigenous ways of handling and restraining the exercise of power helped shape, either positively or negatively, the institutions of representative democracy that were forcibly imported and subsequently developed under colonial and post-colonial conditions. The rethinking of representative democracy has yet another significance: it poses still-unanswered questions about how functioning monitory democracies can today best come to terms with their violent past, in effect by forcing onto the political agenda the unresolved matter of the need for predominantly white citizens who are the offspring of a conquering democracy to feel shame, to say sorry and to strive for new democratic forms of reconciliation and empowerment that have no precedent in the history of their local democracy in representative form.

GOVERNMENT DEMOCRATICAL, BUT REPRESENTATIVE

The case of Australia, a former British colony and today a wealthy Asia Pacific region democracy with a sizeable indigenous population, highlights the importance of tabling and addressing all these questions, initially by engaging the standard historical narratives through which the country has come to imagine itself as a proud multi-cultural democracy. Historians tell us that although the first Australian association of self-declared democrats was only formed in Sydney in 1848, the year of revolutions in Europe, the political tides flowing in their favour were anticipated several decades earlier, for instance in a short but salient commentary by the former President of the United States, Thomas Jefferson. Writing in the northern summer of 1816, Jefferson pondered the astonishing changes that had come over government and political thinking during his lifetime. Jefferson wasted no words: the arrival of self-government in democratic and representative form, he wrote, was fundamentally altering the dynamics of the modern world centred on the Atlantic region. He pointed out that the ancient Greeks knew nothing of the principles of representation. For them, *dēmokratia* meant 'direct democracy', the making of decisions by the whole body of (male) citizens gathered in one place. The ancient Greeks were unable to think, let alone act, outside a political framework that posed a stark choice between either 'democracy' or forms of oligarchy, such as aristocracy and tyranny. According to Jefferson, it did not occur to the Greeks 'that where the citizens cannot meet to transact their business in person, they alone have the right to choose the agents who shall transact it'. Greek citizens, political thinkers and orators alike did not see the possibility of breaking free from the false choice between self-government of the people and government based on rule by a few.

The defining novelty of the modern era, Jefferson continued, was its invention of a new type of self-governing polity based on the mechanics of popular representation. The experiment in combining 'government democratical, but representative, was and is still reserved for us', he concluded. Without historical precedent, the new representative system offered 'the people' a new method of protection 'against the selfishness of rulers not subject to their control at short periods'. In providing such protection, the experiment with representative democracy 'rendered useless almost everything written before on the structure of government'.[1]

Jefferson's letter proved prescient. Its bold words accurately signalled the birth of a new vision of handling power through a form of self-government in which people, understood as voters faced with a genuine choice between at least two alternatives, are free to elect others who then

---

[1] Thomas Jefferson to Isaac H. Tiffany, 26 August 1816, in Andrew A. Lipscomb and Albert E. Bergh (eds.), *The Writings of Thomas Jefferson*, Vol. XV (Washington, DC: Thomas Jefferson Memorial Association of the United States, 1903–1904), pp. 65–66.

act in defence of their interests; that is, *represent* them by deciding matters on their behalf. Lord Henry Brougham's widely read defence of the nineteenth-century struggle for representation captured its spirit: 'the essence of representation', he wrote, 'is that the power of the people should be parted with, and given over, for a limited time, to the deputy chosen by the people'. The job of the representative is to 'perform the part of the government which, but for the transfer, would have been performed by the people themselves'.[2]

The vision of government by the people through their chosen representatives was charged with radical potential. Wherever it took root, the struggle for representation threw into question the anti-democratic prejudices of those – rich and powerful men – who supposed that inequalities among people were 'natural'. New groups, like slaves, women and workers, demanded the franchise. Subjects of empires joined in, as in the Australian colonies, especially during the decade after 1845, when the struggle for self-government came laced in local variants of the principles of representative democracy. While its white-skinned champions often thought of themselves as free born Britons, sang God Save the Queen and professed their belief in monarchy, they were fierce champions of what they variously called 'representative government', 'democracy', 'self-government' and 'responsible government' based on the will of 'the people'.[3] The term 'representative democracy' was rarely used, but its substance and spirit commanded increasingly wide support, manifested in the refusal of 'tyranny' and 'corruption' and calls for adult male suffrage, periodic elections, the supremacy of parliament, a free press, trial by jury and the right of peaceful public assembly.

At first, the demand was for 'representative government', with the aim of limiting the power of the Governor, who was seen as a local autocrat responsible to the British government. Legislatures were created, with a blend of nominated and elected members, but the Crown still had a veto on legislation, and Westminster representatives retained ultimate control of public affairs in the colony because Parliament's powers were devolved to the colony, not surrendered. By the 1850s, demands increased for a more 'democratic' responsible government, where the legislature, not the

---

[2] Lord Henry Brougham, *The British Constitution: Its History, Structure and Working* (London: Richard Griffin & Co, 1861), p. 33.
[3] See Paul Pickering, 'The Oak of English Liberty: Popular Constitutionalism in New South Wales, 1848–1856', *Journal of Australian Colonial History*, 3 (2001), 1–27.

Governor, controlled the selection of the effective executive, the premier and the cabinet, which controlled both government policy and its implementation through advice to the Governor. The Crown, however, still appointed the Governor (who now played a largely ceremonial role) and, most importantly, could still veto legislation considered inimical to British imperial interests.[4]

With a whiff of popular empowerment through representation permanently in the air, the nineteenth century unleashed what the French writer and politician Alexis de Tocqueville famously called a 'great democratic revolution' in favour of political and social equality.[5] The principle of representation seemed inherently democratic, capable of being stretched to include the whole adult population. But the historical records show that such stretching, which often reached breaking point, happened with great difficulty, and against formidable odds. Throughout the nineteenth century, the ideals and institutions of representative democracy were permanently on trial. Whatever advance they enjoyed sparked great public excitement, tinged with sabotage and pandemonium. Sending shock waves outwards from the Atlantic region, all the way to the far-flung colonies founded and run by Europeans, the revolution in favour of 'government democratical, but representative' often suffered setbacks and reversals, especially in Europe, where in the early decades of the twentieth century it was to collapse into a swamp filled with political predators.[6] Elsewhere, including the United States, the reigning definition of representation was actually narrowed during the course of the nineteenth and early twentieth century by withdrawing the right to vote from certain groups, particularly black and poor people.[7] Not until the early decades of the twentieth century did the right of people to vote for their representatives come to be seen as a *universal* entitlement. That happened first for adult men and later – usually much later – for all adult women.

---

[4] Martin Wight, *British Colonial Constitutions 1947* (Oxford: Clarendon Press, 1952); Alan Ward, *Parliamentary Government in Australia* (Melbourne: ALS, 2013), chapter 3.
[5] Alexis de Tocqueville, *Democracy in America*, Vol. I, edited by J. P. Mayer (New York: Doubleday, 1969), p. 12.
[6] John Keane, *The Life and Death of Democracy* (London and New York: Simon & Schuster, 2009), pp. 455–581.
[7] Alexander Keyssar, *The Right to Vote: The Contested History of Democracy in the United States* (New York: Basic Books, 2000).

2 Indigenous Peoples

WHY POPULAR REPRESENTATION?

Organised resistance to the principles and practice of popular representation was widespread, and often effective.[8] It confirmed that there was nothing 'natural' about democratic self-government. 'Ever since the birth of modern societies', the nineteenth-century French liberal author and politician François Guizot told a Paris audience during a famous course of public lectures on the subject, 'the representative form of government ... has constantly loomed more or less distinctly in the distance, as the port at which they must at length arrive, in spite of the storms which scatter them, and the obstacles which confront and oppose their entrance'.[9] Only nineteenth-century believers in historical progress could have thought so optimistically about representative democracy. For the prickly truth is that its appearance was bitterly contested, subject to unforeseen consequences and constant setbacks. Its champions were dogged by double standards, especially when they excluded women, slaves and the labouring classes from the structures of government. Great controversies erupted over what exactly representation meant, who was entitled to represent whom and what had to be done when representatives snubbed or frustrated those whom they were supposed to represent. The advantages and disadvantages of 'government democratical, but representative' were hotly disputed. Its friends had to work hard to win over sceptics and hostile opponents.

Their reasoning proved complex and novel. Popular self-government in representative form was praised as a new type of polity distinguished by its respect for the principle that when electing their representatives people are entitled publicly to air their different social interests and political opinions. Representative government consequently exposed the fictional quality of talk of 'the people'. It underscored the point that 'the people' is in reality rarely a homogenous social body; and that political reality is therefore usually disputed and fractured. Representative government was further praised as a way of freeing citizens from the fear of leaders to whom power is entrusted, according to merit; the elected

---

[8] Compare Benjamin E. Lippincott, *Victorian Critics of Democracy: Carlyle, Ruskin, Arnold, Stephen, Maine, Lecky* (Minneapolis, MN: The University of Minnesota Press, 1938); and Jon Roper, *Democracy and Its Critics: Anglo-American Democratic Thought in the Nineteenth Century* (London: Unwin Hyman, 1989).

[9] François Guizot, *Histoire des origines du gouvernement représentatif, 1821–1822* (Paris: H.G. Bohn, 1821–1822), translated as *The History of the Origins of Representative Government in Europe*, Part 1 (London, 1861), Lectures 1, 12.

representative temporarily 'in office' was seen as a positive alternative to power personified in the body of tyrants, or unelected monarchs. Although, as in the colonies of Australia, more than a few champions of representative democracy expressed their loyalty to the Crown, they consistently thought in terms of 'the people' as the ultimate source of legitimate power. Popular government founded on responsible leadership guided by merit, in their view, cast grave doubts on the view that fine breeding and regal sperm were carriers of good government. Representative government was hailed as an effective way of ridding the world of hereditary stupidity, a new method of apportioning blame for poor political performance – a way of encouraging the peaceful rotation of leadership and, thus, of overcoming the unpalatable choice between the despotism of leaders who ignore the wishes of their subjects and the confusion and demagoguery of government based on the vicissitudes of a *dēmos*. In open defiance of talk, later associated with figures such as Thomas Carlyle and Friedrich Nietzsche, of hero-worship as rooted in the human condition, representative democracy was thought of as a useful weapon against pandering to the powerful. It was reckoned to be a new form of humble government, a way of creating space for dissenting political minorities and levelling competition for power, a method of enabling elected representatives to test their leadership skills in the presence of others equipped with the power to sack them. If representatives fail, then they are removed. The rotation of leaders, hence, was seen as a way of peacefully controlling the exercise of power by means of permanent competition that ensures that nobody has the last word.

Then there was a pragmatic justification of popular representative government. Many of its nineteenth-century champions saw it as the practical expression of a simple but challenging reality: that it was not feasible for all of the people to be involved all of the time, even if they were so inclined, in the business of government. Large populations living across vast swathes of territory were unbreakable barriers to democracy in its ancient assembly form. Given that reality, so the argument ran, the people must delegate the task of government to representatives who are chosen at regular elections. The job of these representatives is to keep tabs on the expenditure of public money. Representatives make representations on behalf of their constituents to the government and its bureaucracy. Representatives debate issues and make laws. They craft foreign policy. They decide who will govern and how – on behalf of the people, at a distance from them. Thomas Paine put the point forcefully. 'In its original state', he wrote, 'simple Democracy was no other than the commonhall of the ancients. As these democracies increased in population, and the territory extended, the simple democratical form became unwieldy and impracticable.'[10] The peculiarly modern political problem of handling large-scale societies with diverse identities could be solved through a new form of open and fair-minded government called representative democracy. 'By engrafting representation upon democracy', he concluded, 'we arrive at a system of government capable of embracing and confederating all the various interests, and every extent of territory and population.'

'THE NATIVES'

The bold spirit of universalism fostered by the earliest champions of representative democracy was impressive, but (as we are about to see) it was so deeply self-contradictory that it bequeathed problems that are still unresolved. The vision of a representative democracy did more than help unleash claims for inclusion in the body politic by unrepresented groups. The case for representative government also became entangled in the colonial problem of how its ideals and institutions could come to terms with indigenous peoples. Cold silence about their exclusion from the claimed benefits of democratic representation was one type of reaction; but those scholars who suppose indigenous peoples functioned as the 'absent centre'[11] of the colonisation project during the nineteenth century considerably understate the great volume of public outpourings on the need to combat the 'backwardness' of the peoples encountered by the colonisers.

Far from thinking in terms of occupying an uninhabited or thinly inhabited land that supposedly belonged to nobody, the colonisers treated indigenous peoples as a clearly *visible* problem. Democrats and anti-democrats alike rummaged around to find a political language that could recognise and assimilate these *visible* differences in order better to rank

---

[10] Thomas Paine, *Rights of Man*, Part 1 (New York: Thomas Paine National Historical Association, 1925 [1791]), pp. 272–274. See also Nadia Urbinati, *Representative Democracy: Principles and Genealogy* (Chicago, IL: University of Chicago Press, 2006).

[11] Stuart Macintyre, *A Colonial Liberalism: The Lost World of Three Victorian Visionaries* (Oxford: Oxford University Press, 1991), p. 211. The counterpoint to the 'absent centre' thesis is developed by Duncan Ivison, 'Locke, Liberalism and Empire', in P.R. Anstey (ed.), *The Philosophy of John Locke: New Perspectives* (London: Routledge, 2003), pp. 86–105, and Bruce Buchan, *The Empire of Political Thought: Indigenous Australians and the Language of Colonial Government* (London: Pickering & Chatto, 2008).

them as deficiencies. An initial theme, affirmed in the original 'secret instructions' given more than a generation earlier (in 1768) to Captain Cook before setting off for *Terra Australis Incognita*, was the importance of 'consent'. His brief was to 'observe the Genius, temper, Disposition and Number of the Natives, if there be any, and endeavour by all proper means to cultivate a Friendship and Alliance with them'. The appropriate means included 'such Trifles as they may Value' and 'every kind of Civility and Regard'. Cook was authorised 'with the Consent of the Natives to take possession of Convenient Situations in the Country in the Name of the King'. If the territory was found to be unoccupied, then the order was to 'take Possession for His Majesty by setting up Proper Marks and Inscriptions'.[12]

The principle that the governed must consent to their representatives was fundamental to the vision of representative democracy, but this mission to engage and control peoples deemed strange and inferior required that representation be understood in the old regressive sense once defended by Thomas Hobbes. In this earlier meaning, 'representation' was simply equivalent to the supposed prior authorisation of state power by its passive subjects; on the basis of that fiction, the rulers of the state were entitled to claim that they were 'personating' those subjects by acting on their behalf.[13] Top-down definitions of representation as the 'personation' of subjects by agents of the state may have had roots in the world of theatre, as Quentin Skinner has pointed out,[14] but they nevertheless made a mockery of the whole process of representing citizens considered as independent actors entitled to express and to defend their separate interests before their representatives. The colonisers claimed to be representative of those they subjugated by virtue of their superior power and civilisation. That understanding contained a difficulty for nineteenth-century definitions of self-government in representative form. In effect, it called into question the whole effort to restrain excesses of

---

[12] 'Secret. Additional Instructions for Lt James Cook, Appointed to Command His Majesty's Bark the Endeavour', in J.C. Beaglehole (ed.), *The Journals of Captain James Cook on His Voyages of Discovery: The Voyage of the Endeavour 1768–1771*, Vol. I (Cambridge: Published for the Hakluyt Society at the University Press, 1955), p. cclxxxii.

[13] Thomas Hobbes, *Leviathan or the Matter, Forme, and Power of a Commonwealth Ecclesiastical and Civil* [1651], M.S. Egerton (London: The British Library, 1910), Chapter 16 ('Of Persons, Authors and Things Personated').

[14] Quentin Skinner, *Visions of Politics: Hobbes and Civil Science*, Vol. III (Cambridge: Cambridge University Press, 2002), p. 181 ('Hobbes and the Purely Artificial Person of the State').

governmental power through the use of such inventions as written constitutions, adult male suffrage, periodic elections and the secret ballot. Representative democracy instead became a champion of tyranny over people who had given their 'virtual' consent to a form of popular self-government that treated them as unworthy and incapable of abiding by its rules.

The solution to the contradiction, which drew upon an earlier meaning of representation that it otherwise categorically rejected, led representative democrats towards an equally suspect family of phrases centred on terms like 'civility' and 'civilisation'. The ideals of representative democracy were rescued by portraying indigenous peoples as 'uncivilised', as ugly, dirty beasts miserably under-equipped for life. The linguistic pact was mooted in the additional 'Instructions' given to Cook before his departure. Bloodshed should be avoided. The 'voluntary consent' of 'the Natives' was mandatory, both because they were 'the natural ... legal possessors of the several Regions they inhabit' and, importantly, because these people were 'the work of the same omnipotent Author, equally under his care with the most polished European'.[15]

Talk of less 'polished' peoples readily fed claims about the 'savagery' of 'the natives', but great intellectual and political muddle was the consequence, especially considering that the formal acknowledgement of their status as 'British subjects' had existed for some time. But the invaders had other thoughts. For if the indigenous inhabitants were indeed British 'subjects', then, according to some colonial authorities, their 'savagery' required that they be fully subsumed under the strictures of British law. George Grey (who became Governor of South Australia in 1841) was among the chief proponents of the view that the laws of indigenous peoples should be treated as 'barbarous customs' and correspondingly replaced by British laws applied by colonial governors throughout the continent.[16] The recommendation won the support of Lord John Russell, chief architect of the Great Reform Act of 1832, but dissenting figures, such as Governor Hutt in Western Australia, maintained that there were practical and ethical

---

[15] 'Hints Offered to the Consideration of Captain Cooke, Mr Bankes, Doctor Solander, and the Other Gentleman Who Go upon the Expedition on Board the Endeavour', in *The Journals of Captain James Cook*, Vol. I, pp. 514–519.

[16] 'Captain Grey to Lord John Russell 4 June 1840', in F. Watson (ed.), *Historical Records of Australia*, Vol. XXI (Sydney: Library Committee of the Commonwealth Parliament, 1914–1925), pp. 34–35, cited in Bruce Buchan, *The Empire of Political Thought: Indigenous Australians and the Language of Colonial Government* (London: Pickering & Chatto, 1998), p. 97.

reasons why 'the aborigines are not in a position to be treated in all points as British subjects'. Reacting against the claim by Paine and others that representative government could be applied on any scale, Hutt acknowledged the special difficulty of subjugating by law nomadic hunting and gathering peoples. He pointed out 'we have not the means to supervise and control their dealings with one another in the bush and in the wild districts'. He went on to emphasise the ethical pointlessness of efforts 'to make them at all times and under all circumstances in their habits and customs amenable to our laws'. Not only would 'the aborigines' understandably resist the 'teasing and tiresome persecution' of being forced to live under the laws of the colonial authorities, such force would have the contradictory effect of hardening the attachment of 'the aborigines' to 'their own rude and barbarous observances'.[17]

Hutt's 'civilised' way of thinking came tinged with violence. It was profoundly anti-democratic in any meaningful sense of the word. Since colonial control over land and resources was at stake, it implied at a minimum the physical subjugation of indigenous peoples and either their outright elimination (although colonial governors typically spoke against outbreaks of frontier violence) or the transformation of these peoples, using such means as informal negotiations, government reservations and religious education, into 'civilised' characters capable of acknowledging that representative democracy was a superior form of government. Here was yet another case of the self-contradiction of representative democratic norms, this time by talk of 'civility' and 'civilisation'. The difficulty that some people could be robbed of their land, bossed and bullied and physically eliminated in the name of a political ethic founded on the equality of citizens seemed lost on Hutt, but it triggered a nineteenth-century alternative that seemed ethically preferable: indigenous peoples were to be regarded as 'dependent allies' or as 'nations' with whom some kind of agreement or treaty was desirable.

The option failed to gain traction, especially at the Colonial Office, although the Aboriginal Protection Society in London did support it.[18]

---

[17] 'Hutt to Lord John Russell 10 July 1841', in *Historical Records of Australia*, Vol. XXI, p. 312. See also Ann Hunter, 'The Boundaries of Colonial Criminal Law in Relation to Inter-Aboriginal Conflict ("Inter se Offences") in Western Australia in the 1830s–1840s', *Australian Journal of Legal History*, 10 (2004), 215–236; and Lisa Ford, *Settler Sovereignty: Jurisdiction and Indigenous People in America and Australia, 1788–1836* (Cambridge, MA: Harvard University Press, 2010).

[18] Standish Motte, *Outline of a System of Legislation for Securing Protection to the Aboriginal Inhabitants of All Countries Colonized by Great Britain* (London: John Murray, 1840), p. 14.

So did J.W. Willis, a loose cannon justice of the District Court at Port Phillip whose heterodox finding in the *Bonjon* case (1841) was that an indigenous man accused of murder could not be tried before a colonial court because the alleged act could only be judged in terms of the criteria of indigenous customary law.[19] It was a ruling with politically dangerous connotations. Although its reasoning remained, strictly speaking, within the confined universe of European 'civilisation', it stated explicitly that the indigenous tribes were 'neither a conquered people' nor that they had 'tacitly acquiesced in the supremacy of the settlers'. The conclusion (unsurprisingly) hastened the dismissal of Willis from the bench. By tabling the principle of competing sovereignties, he did more than call into question the legitimacy of British colonisation. Willis had also implied that indigenous peoples enjoyed their own legitimate form of law and government.

CAMPFIRE DEMOCRACY?

Among the most striking qualities of nineteenth-century thinking about 'government democratical, but representative' was its insistence that the methods used by indigenous peoples to handle the exercise of power within their communities did not count as a form of government. The judgement was not nurtured by lack of curiosity, or plain ignorance. As Buchan has pointed out, figures such as colonial explorer Edward John Eyre and George Grey (Governor of South Australia from 1841) were simultaneously fascinated and repulsed by 'savages' and 'hordes' who allegedly had no sense of 'social ties and connections', who bore the iron yoke of 'custom' that allowed no freedom of thought or action, and who therefore (as Colonial Secretary Edward Deas Thomson summarised the mantra) lacked 'possession of any Code of Laws intelligible to a Civilized People'.[20]

The claim that 'the Natives' had no regular 'intelligible' society, or government, made its mark on later ethnographic and anthropological

---

[19] *R. v. Bonjon*, Supreme Court of New South Wales, 16 September 1841, http://en.wikisource.org/wiki/Melbourne_Advertiser/Report_of_R_v_Bonjon, accessed 10 December 2011. See also Susanne Davies, 'Aborigines, Murder and the Criminal Law in Early Port Phillip, 1841–1851', *Historical Studies*, 22 (1987), 313–334.

[20] *Historical Records of Australia*, Vol. XXI, p. 655; Buchan, *The Empire of Political Thought*, Chapters 5–6; George W. Stocking, *Victorian Anthropology* (New York: The Free Press, 1987); and L. R. Hiatt, *Arguments about Aborigines: Australia and the Evolution of Social Anthropology* (Cambridge: Cambridge University Press, 1996).

studies of the customary habits of 'primitive societies'. As we shall see in some detail, the claim was false, yet among the factors that made it appear plausible was the contrast with the North American encounter with indigenous peoples, who had considerable bargaining power in the interstices of British imperial rivalries with Spanish and French and (later) United States forces. In the colonies of Australia, indigenous peoples stood alone, face-to-face with their invaders. Growing bodies of evidence show that they resisted, cleverly and on all fronts.[21] But the power imbalance they suffered fed the presumption, originally noted by Cook, that whereas the Tahitians, with their 'kings' and 'chiefs', or the Maori, who appeared to be 'united under one head or chief',[22] the indigenous peoples of Australia had no polity. Sovereign authority and regular government was foreign to them, or so it was said. They knew nothing of the arts of making fine clothing, or putting a cup to their lips. They had no houses, no agriculture, no farms, no sense of property rights, and no systems of law or government. 'It is the universal opinion of all who have seen them', concluded a Methodist missionary in the 1830s, 'that it is impossible to find men and women sunk lower in the scale of human society. With regard to their manners and customs, they are little better than the beasts.'[23]

For 'the Aborigines', such talk had a killing quality; it forced them into life-or-death struggles for survival. Little wonder that intellectuals who, during the twentieth century, tried to engage with indigenous peoples on their own terms, to right wrongs, were attracted by the thought that indigenous polities were examples of a 'crude' or 'primitive' or 'early' form of democracy. The possibility that indigenous peoples had their own form of 'democratic' self-government is implied by the research of anthropologists who claim that since democracy involves people getting together as equals, to decide things for themselves, it has in effect always been around, even in the earliest hunting-gathering societies. The claim has older provenance. Its roots stretch back to the 1940s, when the Polish–American anthropologist Bronislaw Malinowski first attempted to define these societies as examples of 'proto-democracy'. According to

---

[21] Henry Reynolds, *The Other Side of the Frontier: Aboriginal Resistance to the European Invasion of Australia* (Ringwood: Penguin, 1982), especially Chapters 3–4.

[22] Cook, *The Journals of Captain James Cook*, Vol. I, pp. 85, 121. On the background, see Julie Evans, Patricia Grimshaw, David Philips and Shurlee Swain, *Equal Subjects, Unequal Rights: Indigenous Peoples in British Settler Colonies, 1830–1910* (Manchester: Manchester University Press, 2003).

[23] Joseph Orton, *Aborigines of Australia* (London: Thoms, 1836), p. 3.

Malinowski, the propensity of people to form political communities is more or less a universal human quality. Equally human is the knack of developing independent, functionally autonomous institutions that both facilitate non-violent co-operation among divergent social interests and prevent the concentration of power in a few hands. In this respect, Malinowski argued, modern representative democracies are located on exactly the same continuum as hunting-gathering cultures, in which 'there is no ballot, no vote, yet a general public approval and acceptance. There is very little centralised power, which gives results as good if not better than when such power is placed in the hands of authorities elected and controlled by the people.'[24]

The thesis that all human beings yearn for democracy and that democracy is human, or that to be human is to be fit for democracy, is re-stated at length by more recent political anthropologists, such as Ronald Glassman. Aware that early kinship systems were riddled with hierarchies structured by criteria such as gender and age, he nevertheless thinks of our earliest hunting-gathering ancestors as practitioners of democracy as we experience it today. The propensity for democracy is among the 'unique species characteristics of human beings'. He adds: 'consciousness plus intelligence, plus language communication, produce the possibility of democracy'. But what is democracy? For Glassman, the term is synonymous with deliberative democracy. It refers to 'decision making through *discussion,* and *rational* processes of legitimation'. It is deliberation guided by such core principles as popular participation in the making of rules and the punishment of rule breakers; the application of strict limits upon the exercise of power and leadership; and the use of rules designed to preserve group order as debatable and amendable. In hunting-gathering societies, he continues, the felt need to co-ordinate both the search for food and defence against invasion spawned the growth of 'campfire democracy'. It was a form of self-government founded upon the 'popular assembly', the 'male council' and mechanisms for guaranteeing unanimity. Campfire democracy stimulated informal discussion of perceived problems: 'the men, the women, the old, the young – everyone discusses the problem informally. Everyone makes his or her opinion known.' Campfire democracy also depended upon formal procedures for reaching agreement, above all the practice of adult men sitting 'in a circle around a campfire in the center of the band'. Their job was to 'attain

---

[24] Bronislaw Malinowski, *Freedom and Civilization* (New York: Roy Publishers, 1944), pp. 228–229.

unanimity or unanimous approval of the political course finally emergent from the formal debate'. Campfire democracy minimised the use of 'physical dominance and fear'. It knew nothing of majority rule or minority rights, or the harsh punishment of deviants. 'Social pressure is brought to bear on all dissenters who continue to resist the decision reached', says Glassman. 'Women as well as men are talked to, persuaded, chided, cajoled into unanimity.'[25]

Is there substance in this way of thinking about 'proto-' or 'campfire' democracy? Much evidence speaks against the whole idea of a deep political connection between modern representative democracy and hunting-gathering peoples. The implied teleology lurking within the prefix 'proto-', the inference that campfire assemblies were the first of a kind, a prototype of what was to follow, begs tough questions about their historical links with latter-day democracies. The inference supposes, in other words, that in spite of all the differences there is an unbroken evolutionary chain that links the earliest forms of assembly with contemporary representative forms of democracy, as if the Pitjantjatjara or Kunai peoples were the original brothers and sisters of James Madison, Winston Churchill, Jawaharlal Nehru and Barack Obama. That is implausible. The free use of the term 'proto-democracy' risks falling into the trap of calling too many societies 'democratic', just because they lack centralised institutions and accumulated monopolies of power, or because they prohibit centres of violent oppression, blatantly illegal or camouflaged, against which people have no redress or appeal.

Matters are not helped by the anachronistic use of the word 'democracy'. The anthropological record shows quite clearly that neither the word (which in fact has roots in the Mycenaean civilisation) nor anything resembling it was ever used during campfire assemblies. But this point is minor compared with the least obvious but most consequential objection: by calling campfire gatherings 'democratic' there is a great danger of overlooking or understating the *strange originality* of democracy as a way of naming and handling and controlling power.

The experience of democracy, whether in representative or other institutionalised forms, requires and reinforces people's shared sense of the

---

[25] Ronald M. Glassman, *Democracy and Despotism in Primitive Societies* (Millwood, NY: Associated Faculty Press, 1986), pp. 45, 46–53; compare Larissa Behrendt, 'Aboriginal Australia and Democracy: Old Traditions, New Challenges', in Benjamin Isakhan and Stephen Stockwell (eds.), *The Secret History of Democracy* (London: Palgrave Macmillan, 2011), p. 149: 'Within traditional Aboriginal societies, notions of collective agreement-making that resonate with democracy were pervasive.'

2 Indigenous Peoples

contingency or mutability of the world – their rejection of claims that matters to do with who gets what, when and how in life are determined by 'natural' or God-given or deity-determined processes, or by mere chance.[26] Democracy is much more than citizens gathering together in public assemblies, joining or supporting political parties, voting in periodic elections, or keeping tabs on decisions taken by parliamentary representatives. These practices are surface symptoms of something that runs much deeper. Considered as a set of institutions and as a whole way of life, democracy stimulates people's awareness that as *equals* they do not need to be bossed about by powerful others; it teaches them that they have the ability to shape and structure their lives, as equals who are capable of living together and deciding in common how they are to live during their time on earth. Democracy thus supposes humans' release from pure determination by forces natural and supernatural, however they are conceived. Democracy does not necessarily demand the practical rejection of belief in transcendental or sacred standards (the history of democracy is full of examples of actors and customs and institutions which thrive on belief in the sacred[27]). But for a society to qualify as 'democratic' it must contain mechanisms that foster a measure of self-reflexivity among equals, their awareness that is and ought are not identical, that things do not have to be what they currently are, or seem to be.

It is true that those who speak of 'proto-democracy' have been guided by benign intentions. Malinowski himself explicitly acknowledged that the incorporation of hunting-gathering peoples in the analysis of democracy would help counter the prejudice that they were 'savages' with 'blind passions' and 'slaves to custom, warlike and cruel'.[28] He had a point. By favouring the inclusion of hunting-gathering societies in the history of democracy, he and other scholars have sought to overcome the long-standing prejudice that dismisses these people as 'backward', 'uncivilised' and generally inferior to us. It is also true that those who have spoken of 'proto-democracy' never intended to overlook the fundamental quality of democracy, its propensity to 'de-nature' power relationships and to resist bondage, in the name of equality. Yet that is exactly what they have done, by exaggerating the degree to which hunting-gathering societies cultivated the capacity to foreground and question the so-called nature of things.

---

[26] This is a core theme of Keane, *The Life and Death of Democracy*.
[27] Irfan Ahmad, 'In Conversation with John Keane: Gods, Power and Democracy', *Journal of Religious and Political Practice*, 1 (2015), 73–91.
[28] Malinowski, *Freedom and Civilization*, p. 241.

SOCIETIES AGAINST THE STATE

In a fine study of the Maori of New Zealand, Marshall Sahlins emphasises that hunting-gathering societies are typically in the powerful grip of cosmic myths that structure everyday life and adjust it to particular circumstances, in effect by interpreting, harnessing, controlling and concealing their contingency.[29] He makes the important point (against Evans-Pritchard and other anthropologists) that it is a mistake to see these societies as 'frozen', or as without 'history'. That condescending view needs to be replaced with an understanding of how different cultures have different senses of historicity. But even when hunting-gathering societies are seen in this fresh way, the evidence he presents strongly suggests that these societies are *different* from – not necessarily inferior to – political orders defined by institutional mechanisms that have the effect of making explicit people's felt sense of contingency of the power relations that shape their lives as equals.

Within the nineteenth-century world of Maori people, for instance, Sahlins shows that while many relationships were constructed by choice, desire and interest, the level of 'openness' to history was different than anything that democracies are used to. The ongoing, daily interaction between new and old ways of doing things was structured by communities of meaning that ensured that everything ultimately appeared to its members as if it were unfolding by means of an unending process of return to the way things have always been. In the absence of such means of communication as alphabets and writing that enabled past, present and future to be prised apart – Sahlins presumes their absence – the present and future were understood as recurrent manifestations of a past that was very much alive. Everyday life is a re-enactment and confirmation of the wider ways of the world; or, in the words of Sahlins: 'Ontogeny recapitulates cosmogony'.[30]

Much the same picture emerges from studies of indigenous societies in the neighbouring continent of Australia. As usual, generalisations are as risky as they are difficult: in 1788, when the British colonisers began to arrive in force, there was no single Aboriginal and Torres Strait Islanders 'nation'; and (unlike Maori) no shared language. There were at least two hundred and fifty different communities; each spoke a different language or dialect and typically occupied more or less geographically separate

---

[29] Marshall Sahlins, *Islands of History* (Chicago, IL: University of Chicago Press, 1985).
[30] Sahlins, *Islands of History*, p. 59.

areas. The diversity was the product of prior indigenisation across a vast territory, but also partly the effect of differential contact with non-Aboriginal and Torres Strait Island peoples, for instance Indonesian and Macassan traders and fishing peoples.[31] Yet what is clear is that these diverse indigenous societies and the multiple spaces they inhabited were not an 'Australian tribe' with a common language unblessed by a 'political authority'.[32] Contrary to the claims put by nineteenth-century believers in representative democracy, they were not 'primitive' societies 'lacking' a territorial state. Their modes of life and methods of handling power were *different*. The surviving evidence suggests that these societies had no system of government in any hierarchical sense; and that there was no single body that made laws and no hierarchy of courts or other enforcing authorities. These were most definitely 'societies against the state' (the famous formulation of Pierre Clastres).[33] Power was handled largely through informal and loosely organised means. Wherever there were hierarchies, power relations were understood in terms of 'looking after' others and acknowledgement of the importance of co-operation, help and interdependence. The 'boss' was duty-bound to assist and support others. Although these societies were infused with a strong sense of gerontocracy, in that older people were repositories of ancestral virtues and customs, they were always heavily dependent upon mechanisms of consensus and balance, not force. There were tribal elders (whether and how commonly they or councils of elders held sway is still disputed) but no chieftains and no organised political class of men. Marriage customs for women, along with their roles in ritual life, were typically defined by men, yet women generally regained control with age; they were not treated as objects of male consumption and typically they were protected by eminent women ancestors, who lived on in the form of birds, reptiles and other animals.[34]

In all matters, including sexuality and age, the interpretation and application of ancestral laws played a primary co-ordinating role. The

---

[31] The diversity and complexity of indigenous communities at the point of European invasion is examined at length in Ian Keen, *Aboriginal Economy and Society: Australia at the Threshold of Colonisation* (Oxford: Oxford University Press, 2004).

[32] Alfred R. Radcliffe-Brown, 'The Social Organisation of Australian Tribes, Part 1', *Oceania*, 1 (1930), 36–37.

[33] Pierre Clastres, *La Société contre l'État* (Paris: Éditions de minuit, 1974).

[34] Francesca Merlan, 'Gender in Aboriginal Social Life: A Review', in Ronald M. Berndt and Robert Tonkinson (eds.), *Social Anthropology and Australian Aboriginal Studies* (Canberra: Aboriginal Studies Press, 1988), pp. 15–76.

effect was to make it appear as if norms and rules were 'external' to the community, so that matters as varied as access to land and water, the performance of ceremonies and marriage arrangements were decided *for* the community by reference to totemic rules that were understood to be non-arbitrary because of their timelessness. Adherence to the 'proper ways' of ancestral laws, living within a totemic landscape infused with ancestral authority, meant that the Pitjantjatjara, the Pintupi and other indigenous communities had no need of legislators or legislatures; but, paradoxically, the communication of such laws by means of oral traditions scattered across wide geographic areas meant that considerable discretion in their interpretation and application was exercised by individuals, kin groups and whole communities; some of them overlapping.[35] More or less elaborate ceremonies, some requiring pain or privation, took care of the resulting tensions. The dramas of male initiation, bodily mutilation and female marriage, for instance, imbued ancestral laws with a 'uniquely realistic' quality.[36] If and when they failed, and power disputes erupted, as they often did, sophisticated mechanisms for mediating and resolving disputes and nurturing order then came into play.

These conflict resolution methods are intriguing, exactly because they underscore the strange originality of representative democracy as a political form, and as a whole way of life. Common to the indigenous communities of the Australian continent were different mechanisms that had a weighty effect: since ultimate authority was collectively understood to be external and prior to the foundation of the political community, its members' sense of openness to novelty was constrained. These were not 'frozen' societies in any simple sense. The ways and means of naming, handling and resolving disputes about who gets what, when and how within the community certainly depended heavily on manoeuvres by aggrieved parties to win support for their cause. Justice was contingent, and it was never blind revenge. Punishment was understood as reciprocity in exchange and its purpose was always to restore balance, even when sorcerers and 'feather-foot men' filled victims with fear or (as in the case of serious infringements of ritual secrecy) the verdict was death. The proceedings were infused with a powerful sense of the primacy of past events and living-dead characters. It was taken for granted that obedience

---

[35] See Fred R. Myers, *Pintupi Country, Pintupi Self: Sentiment, Place and Politics among Western Desert Aborigines* (Canberra: Australian Institute of Aboriginal Studies, 1986).

[36] Clifford Geertz, 'Religion as a Cultural System', in Michael Banton (ed.), *Anthropological Approaches to the Study of Religion* (London: Routledge, 1966), pp. 8–12.

of individuals and kin groups to their instructions was mandatory, and that dangerous consequences would otherwise follow, as surely as night follows day, or sun follows rain.

The presence of the past within these events and characters was powerfully reinforced by an unshakable sense of dependence upon their surroundings, to the point where the indigenous communities normally saw themselves as extensions of the sacred living landscape. Its spirits lived inside them, beyond and around them. The landscape was their 'spirit home'.[37] It conferred their names. It could smell their presence. Their own blood, flesh, hair, faeces and urine belonged to it. The landscape throbbed with life; it was the space of their ancestors, the medium through which they communicated with living people, offering them guidance, providing them with 'the proper way' (the *tjukurrpa* [dreaming] of the Pitjantjatjara and the *rom* [law] of the Yolngu are examples) and granting them powers to act, even to travel far and wide when they were asleep. At death, the individual rejoined the landscape as 'spirit' or (in some communities) in reincarnated form. This strong spiritual and physical dependence upon the biosphere was supervised by a host of mythical characters who belonged to the origins of the world, but who regularly reappeared among the living, as shadowy ghosts, or as animals or objects. The strong dependence of the living upon their landscape was structured by the performance of sacred rites and sacred songs and the possession of sacred objects (known among the Loritja, the Illpirra and other peoples as *tjurunga*) and it was mediated by sacred places and special knowledge, vested in a few men and women of the community.

There is much surviving evidence that although indigenous peoples were unfamiliar with such distinctions and terms as 'good' and 'bad', 'sin' and 'atonement' for wrongdoing – they were the terms used by their invaders – harsh penalties were applied to individuals or kin groups who violated the sacred rules of ancestral law. Various means were invoked. There were informal customs such as ridicule and gossip and the hearing of evidence and the meting out of punishment by meetings of older people or (as among the Ngarinyerri of South Australia) leaders of neighbouring groups.[38] Conflicts were resolved as well by forms of 'payback', such as thigh wounding,

---

[37] W.E.H. Stanner, 'Religion, Totemism and Symbolism', in Ronald M. Berndt and Catherine H. Berndt (eds.), *Aboriginal Man in Australia: Essays in Honour of Emeritus Professor A.P. Elkin* (Sydney: Angus & Robertson, 1965), pp. 207–237.

[38] George Taplin, *The Narrinyeri: An Account of the Tribes of South Australian Aborigines* (Adelaide: J.T. Shawyer, 1873).

death by spearing, and extended blood feuds, some of them lasting for many years. The means of justice encompassed the dispatch of avenging parties (such as the Aranda *atninga*, where the attackers fought mainly with words, not weapons). There was compensation in the form of goods; the use of sorcerers to inflict harm on offenders, supposedly by such means as removing their 'dream spirit' or inserting stones inside their bodies; and deprivation of mortuary rites. Secret meetings of ritual leaders were convened; and there was the ceremonial practice of running a gauntlet of blunted spears (an example was the *magarada* of northern Arnhem Land). Alleged offenders were also brought to trial before councils, such as the *tendi* of the Lower River Murray peoples, where different clans gathered in the presence of negotiators (*rupulle*) whose judgements and punishments were guided by the testimonies of the accused, the defendants and witnesses.

Ceremonies designed to repair the fabric of the social order, to structure the lived experience of time as the repetition of a living past, were typical. A pertinent example was the *bugalub* ceremony found in northeastern Arnhem Land.[39] It was not a case of 'campfire democracy', but a ritual washing ceremony that was believed to heal dissension and to produce mutual goodwill among the disputants, as well as provide entertainment for the rest of the community not directly involved in the dispute. People gathered around specially prepared ground in the main camp, outlined with mounds of sand, within which a hole had been dug to represent a sacred waterhole connected to the living-dead persons responsible for hosting the rite. Secret-sacred songs were sung, usually to the accompaniment of clapping sticks and didjeridu. During the singing, women jumped up and danced, in preparation for the moment of final healing, when the prime parties to the dispute (most often they were men) finally entered the 'waterhole' to be showered with water and invocations of the mythical beings connected with the ceremonial site.

RESTORATIVE JUSTICE

Why should the political practices of indigenous peoples be given closer attention by historians of colonialism, political thinkers and citizens

---

[39] Ronald Berndt and Catherine Berndt, *The World of the First Australians: Aboriginal Traditional Life – Past and Present* (Canberra: Aboriginal Studies Press for the Australian Institute of Aboriginal and Torres Strait Islander Studies, 1999), pp. 349ff; and Larissa Behrendt and Loretta Kelly, *Resolving Indigenous Disputes: Land Conflict and Beyond* (Leichhardt: The Federation Press, 2008), pp. 93ff.

interested in the history and present-day fate of representative democracy in Australia and elsewhere? There are several reasons.

Most obviously, ceremonies such as the *bugalub* are revealing of the complex patterns of power and conflict resolution that structured daily life within and among indigenous communities on the threshold and during the next century of European colonisation. They show that indigenous societies were not stone-age people caught in the unbreakable grip of 'kinship' obligations and 'nature worship'. Indigenous communities were neither instances of 'primitive society' nor examples of 'proto-democracy'; they were *different* societies, for which different categories are needed in order to comprehend their sophisticated rituals of what are now called power and politics.

Paying attention to the historical relationship between indigenous peoples and popular self-government is important for another reason: in surprising ways, it potentially alters our understanding of the history of democracy in representative form. It prompts questions about whether and to what extent indigenous ways of handling and restraining the exercise of power helped shape, either positively or negatively, the resulting institutions of representative democracy. Contemporary scholars presume that influence was all a one-way street, altogether negative, and that during the nineteenth century, indigenous forms of government were simply crushed alive. That belief (as Brown has pointed out in a critique of conventional accounts of the coming of federalist visions of democracy to Australia) probably understates the ways in which the nineteenth-century push towards a federated representative democracy was the contested resultant of many forces, including the calls by white settlers for decentralised regional institutions that were quite probably inspired by the mental maps and patterns of seasonal movement of indigenous peoples.[40] The calculated use of the petition by indigenous peoples to press their claims for compassion and compensation is another example of the same counter-trend. Their petitions not only helped give them a voice in public affairs, they also publicised the vital point that the emergent system of representative democracy suffered a fundamental defect: its dependence upon the Westminster principle of 'winner-takes-all' majority rule meant that some minorities, and certainly indigenous peoples, were fated

---

[40] Alexander J. Brown, 'Constitutional Schizophrenia Then and Now', *Papers on Parliament*, 42 (2004), 33–58.

mathematically to be permanent 'losers' in the political game of electoral competition.[41]

The broader implication here is that the 'indigenisation' of representative democracy is a subject worth exploring. There is plenty of evidence that some nineteenth-century Europeans learned to speak pidgin versions of indigenous languages, whose words (kangaroo, gibber, woomera, waddy) permanently entered the local English-language vernacular.[42] In the same vein, many white Australians have since carved out a distinctive sense of national identity through the generous absorption of indigenous symbols. Slowly but surely, indigenous peoples have meanwhile begun to teach white people lessons about the need to 'blacken' their ways with nature, to abandon their reckless and profligate ways with the biosphere, to understand and acknowledge their dependence upon its long-term sustainability. So the question, analogously, is whether the history of Australian democracy might be re-described, certainly so as to include the never-to-be-forgotten terrible bigotry and violence that it unloaded upon indigenous peoples and their polities, but also, more positively, re-written in terms of a new understanding of the creative impact of indigenous practices upon the transplantation of representative democracy into the soils of the Australian continent?

The whole point about indigenisation is admittedly speculative, but typically it is neglected within recent historical narratives, probably because the deep implication of representative democracy in the wanton destruction of indigenous polities seems more consequential, and more disturbing. Their point is well taken; to invert the meaning of a favourite term in the arsenal of its nineteenth-century champions, the 'barbarous' side of representative democracy should not be forgotten, and needs further investigation. More detailed analyses elsewhere have shown that there was nothing 'essentially' violent about either the spirit or structures of representative democracy.[43] Yet the hard fact remains that both the

---

[41] Mark McKenna, *This Country: A Reconciled Republic?* (Sydney: University of New South Wales Press, 2004), pp. 67ff; Ann Curthoys and Jessie Mitchell, '"Bring This Paper to the Good Governor": Indigenous Petitioning in Britain's Australian Colonies', in Saliha Belmessous (ed.), *Native Claims: Indigenous Law against Empire, 1500–1920* (Oxford: Oxford University Press, 2012), pp. 182–203; and the discussion of the early experiment with proportional representation in the colony of South Australia in Keane, *The Life and Death of Democracy*, 517–522.

[42] Reynolds, *The Other Side of the Frontier*, pp. 40ff.

[43] Claims about the intrinsically violent quality of representative democracy are traceable to the leading proto-fascist jurist of Weimar Germany, Carl Schmitt: 'A democracy demonstrates its political power', he wrote, 'by knowing how to eliminate or keep at bay something that is foreign and unequal and threatens its homogeneity.' He added: 'Does

2 Indigenous Peoples

colonial opponents and colonial champions of representative democracy indulged talk of 'the aborigines' and their 'uncivilised' ways.[44] As if to prove that representative democracy could sit comfortably at the table of tyranny, such talk fuelled the bigoted belief that a 'people' comprising proud adult male voters could do no wrong, that the majority was always right, certainly when confronted by 'savages' complaining of mistreatment.

From the point of view of indigenous peoples, the coming of representative democracy from over the horizons of Europe made things worse. Armed with strange ways of talking, weird institutions and lethal weapons, the invaders prided themselves on their commitments to popular self-government in representative and responsible form. The sad and well-documented truth is that the invaders refused to recognise and respect the fundamental difference between the hunting-gathering polities of the Australian continent and the conquering 'civilisation'. The refusal inflicted great misery and violence on indigenous peoples, who nevertheless fought back hard against their conquerors. Facing frightening odds, their population numbers were reduced by an estimated five-sixths during the period of colonisation. Yet they managed to survive and to multiply, even to experiment with new ways of living, including, as in our time, demands for political representation in the prevailing structures of power.

Such demands suggest another powerful reason for rethinking the relationship between indigenous peoples and nineteenth-century representative democracy: the unintended birth of a politics of restorative justice, of the kind that has emerged in other settler democracies, such as Canada, Chile and South Africa. Thanks to their survivor qualities, indigenous peoples and their supporters have gradually forced onto the political agenda the whole issue of whether and to what extent the predominantly white citizens who are the offspring of a conquering

---

the British Empire rest on universal and equal voting rights for all its inhabitants? It could not survive for a week on this basis; with their monstrous majority, the coloureds would outvote the whites. In spite of that, the British Empire is a democracy' (*Die geistesgeschichtliche Lage des heutigen Parlamentarismus* [Berlin: Duncker & Humblot, 1926], pp. 14, 15–16). See my extended replies in 'Dictatorship and the Decline of Parliament: Carl Schmitt's Theory of Political Sovereignty', in John Keane, *Democracy and Civil Society* (London and New York: Verso, 1988), pp. 153–189; and 'Does Democracy Have a Violent Heart?', talk delivered at the conference War, Culture and Democracy in Classical Athens, 4–6 July 2006, University of Sydney.

[44] An important iteration of this point is developed in Jessie Mitchell, '"Are We in Danger of a Hostile Visit from the Aborigines?" Dispossession and the Rise of Self-government in New South Wales', *Australian Historical Studies*, 40 (2009), 294–307.

democracy can come to feel shame, to say sorry and to strive for new democratic forms of reconciliation that have no precedent in the history of their local democracy.[45]

In the Australian context, this process of restorative justice has barely begun, but its political significance and strong sense of unfinished business should not be underestimated. Guided by the fundamental principle that in the twenty-first-century democracy is much more than elections, and that democracy means nothing unless it strengthens the diversity and influence of all citizens' voices and choices in the decisions that affect their lives – the unfinished politics of remembering refuses to let bygones be bygones. Its starting point is that elections and elected governments alone cannot handle the terrible injustices of the past. In effect, the politics of restorative justice seeks to extend a vote to an excluded constituency: the dead. With the help of sympathetic historians,[46] it supposes that democracy among the living requires democracy among the dead; on that basis, it points to the need publicly to remember not only the patterns of indigenous resistance, contribution, collaboration and adaptation, but also the injustices they suffered in the name of representative democracy, under the whip hand of methods ranging from murder, rape, dispersal and child removal to exclusion from elections, insult, amnesia and the silence of outright public and private denial.

The theory and politics of restorative justice keeps an open mind about whether and to what extent indigenous peoples can retain or 'go back' to at least some of their customary ways of handling power, but it certainly takes a hard-nosed view of forgetfulness. It warns of the dangers to democracy of amnesia, confabulation and political manipulation. At a more personal level, restorative justice supposes that victims and victimisers alike are vulnerable to these dangers, albeit in different ways. Convinced that memories of past injustices can be a corrective to present-day injustices, it therefore depends upon the encounter of all parties and

---

[45] See Jennifer Balint and Julie Evans, 'Transitional Justice and Settler States', in M. Lee, G. Mason and S. Milivojevic (eds.), *The Australian and New Zealand Critic Criminology Conference 2011*, http://ses.library.usyd.edu.au/bitstream/2123/7361/1/Balint%20and%20Evans%20ANZCCC2010.pdf (accessed 5 January 2012).

[46] Notable examples include Charles Rowley, *The Destruction of Aboriginal Society* (Canberra: ANU Press, 1970); Reynolds, *The Other Side of the Frontier*; Bain Attwood and John Arnold (eds.), *Power, Knowledge and Aborigines*, special edition of *Journal of Australian Studies*, 5 (1992); Anna Haebich, *Broken Circles: Fragmenting Indigenous Families 1800–2000* (Fremantle: Fremantle Arts Centre Press, 2000); and Ann Curthoys, Ann Genovese and Alexander Reilly, *Rights and Redemption: History, Law and Indigenous People* (Sydney: University of New South Wales Press, 2008).

requires apologies, bills of rights and treaties to protect the restitution of land and other forms of compensation for the victims.[47] The politics of restorative justice provides no quick fixes. It takes time. It is a form of slow politics. It calls on victims to take an active role in the restorative process, while offenders meanwhile are encouraged to take responsibility for their actions, to help repair the harms that were done long ago, but which can still be felt and observed. Restorative justice reckons that nobody is entitled straightforwardly to cast the first stone of accusation. It supposes in principle that there were and are no saints and sinners, and that all living citizens are in one way or another deeply implicated in the sordid past.

The work of remembering the past harnesses the principle that both victims and victimisers likely suffer from what analysts call 'dissociation', the painful and disabling repression of traumatic memories. Restorative justice therefore calls on whole societies to own up, to bear witness to past acts of injustice and violence. It recognises that the tricky process of setting the record straight, opening up and democratising memories of the past is not easy; it understands that the past is at least as complicated as the present. It calculates that memories are always constructed – reconstructed – and not just straightforward matters of recall and that, for that reason, it is always better to prevent the denial of incriminating memories or the implantation of false memories by having an open process of publicly checking and cross-checking claims about what actually happened in the past. Armed with these principles, the politics of restorative justice is willing to take on accusations of wearing indigenous armbands. It opposes cults of forgetfulness. The politics of restorative justice tries in practice to shatter public silences, to expose past abuses using unconventional narratives; it examines practical ways of restoring the dignity of both the dead and the living; and it supposes that the work of publicly monitoring and compensating for the evils committed in the name of representative self-government can eventually help to discharge political tensions.

Can the balm of public 'truth telling' have soothing effects, like helping symbolically to heal the wounds of indigenous peoples, or helping the offspring of the colonisers to hold their heads higher, and, less in shame? The new politics of restorative justice supposes that these effects are

---

[47] Roderic Pitty, 'The Political Aspects of Creating a Treaty', in Peter Read, Gary Meyers and Bob Reece (eds.), *What Good Condition? Reflections on an Australian Aboriginal Treaty 1986–2006* (Canberra: ANUE Press, 2006), pp. 51–69.

possible, so long as certain conditions are met. Restorative justice involves much more than positive initiatives by professional experts, the courts or by the government of the day. It operates according to the quite different premise that the standard machinery of electoral politics and constitutional protections cannot alone deliver restorative justice, which can take effect only when citizens themselves, and the whole civil society, pitches in and works hard to make amends in search of solutions that promote repair, reconciliation and the rebuilding of relationships, the better to promote a culture of mutual respect through the permanent remembrance of things past. The point of restorative justice is to keep alive what happened through public fact-finding, to promote public shaming and forgiveness so as better to enable the wider society to live together through a more durable monitory democracy – in effect, by granting a vote to the past for the sake of the future.

PART II

COMMUNICATIONS REVOLUTION

3

Monitory Democracy

Thinkers and practitioners often overlook a point of basic importance: every historical era of democracy is entangled with a specific mode of communication. Assembly-based democracy in the ancient Greek city states, for instance, belonged to an era dominated by the spoken word, backed up by laws written on papyrus and stone, and by messages dispatched by foot, by donkey and horse. Eighteenth-century representative democracy, a new historical form of democracy understood as the self-government of people by means of elected representatives, sprang up in the era of print culture, within the world of the book, pamphlet and newspaper, and telegraphed and mailed messages delivered by land and sea. Representative democracy in this sense stumbled and fell into crisis during the advent of early mass broadcasting media, especially radio and cinema and (in its infancy) television. By contrast, or so this line of thinking runs, democracy in our times is tied closely to the growth of multi-media-saturated societies whose structures of power are continuously questioned by a multitude of monitory or 'watchdog' mechanisms operating within a new media galaxy defined by the ethos of communicative abundance.

Thinking in this way about changing modes of communication requires a fundamental shift of perspective – a *Gestalt* switch – in the way contemporary democracies are understood. Compared with the era of representative democracy, when print culture and limited spectrum audio-visual media were much more closely aligned with political parties, elections and governments, contemporary democracies experience constant public scrutiny and spats about power, to the point where it seems as if no organisation or leader within the fields of government or business and social life is immune from political trouble. It is easy to see that prevailing ways of describing and analysing contemporary democracy – talk of the 'end of history' (Francis Fukuyama) and a 'third wave' of democracy (Samuel Huntington) – are either inadequate or downright misleading, too bound to the surface of things, too preoccupied with continuities and aggregate data to notice that political tides have begun to run in entirely new directions, to see that the world of actually existing democracy is experiencing an historic sea change that is taking us away from the assembly-based and representative models of democracy of past times towards a form of democracy with entirely different contours and dynamics.

It is much harder to find an elegant name for this new historical form of democracy, let alone to describe in just a few words its workings and political implications. Elsewhere, and at some length, the case has been made for introducing the strange-sounding term *monitory democracy* as the most exact for describing the big transformation that is taking hold in many regions of the world.[1] Monitory democracy is a new historical form

---

[1] See John Keane, *The Life and Death of Democracy* (London and New York: Simon & Schuster, 2009), pp. 648–747. The adjective 'monitory' derives from the mediaeval *monitoria* [from *monere*, to warn]. It entered Middle English in the shape of *monitorie* and from there it wended its way into the modern English language in the mid-fifteenth century to refer to the process of giving or conveying a warning of an impending danger, or an admonition to someone to refrain from a specified course of action considered offensive. It was first used within the Church to refer to a letter or letters (known as 'monitories') sent by a bishop or a pope or an ecclesiastical court who acted in the capacity of a 'monitor'. The family of words 'monitor', 'monition' and 'monitory' was soon used for more secular or this-worldly purposes. The monitor was one or that which admonishes others about their conduct. The word 'monitor' was also used in school settings to refer to a senior pupil expected to perform special duties, such as that of keeping order, or (if the pupil was particularly bright or gifted) acting as a teacher to a junior class. A monitor also came to mean an early warning device; it was said as well to be a species of African and Australian and New Guinean lizard that was friendly to humans because it gave warning of the whereabouts of crocodiles. Still later, the word 'monitor' came to be associated with communication devices. It referred to a receiver, such as a speaker or a television screen, that is used to check the quality or content of an electronic transmission; and in the world of computing and computer science, a 'monitor' either refers to a video display or to a programme that observes, or supervises or controls the activities of other programmes. In more recent years, not unconnected with the emergence of monitory democracy, 'to monitor' became a commonplace verb to describe the process of systematically checking the content or quality of something, as when a city authority monitors the local drinking water for impurities, or a group of scientific experts monitors the population of an endangered species. Such usages helped inspire the theory of 'monitorial democracy' developed by the American scholar, Michael Schudson (interview, New York City, 4 December 2006). See his 'Changing Concepts of Democracy', *MIT Communications Forum*, 8 May 1998, http://web.mit.edu/m-i-t/articles/index_schudson.html (accessed

of democracy, a variety of 'post-electoral' politics and government defined by the rapid growth of many different kinds of extra-parliamentary, power-scrutinising mechanisms. Supposing the existence of independent publics, to whom their messages are addressed, these monitory bodies take root within the 'domestic' fields of government and civil society, as well as in 'cross-border' settings once subject to the arbitrary power of empires, states and businesses. In consequence, the architecture and dynamics of self-government are changing. The central grip of elections, political parties and parliaments on citizens' lives is weakening. Democracy is coming to mean much more than free and fair elections, although nothing less. Within and outside states, independent monitors of power begin to have major tangible effects on the dynamics and meaning of democracy. By putting politicians, parties and elected governments permanently on their toes, monitory institutions complicate their lives and question their power and authority, often forcing them to chop and change their agendas – sometimes by smothering them in political disgrace.

Whether or not the trend towards this new kind of democracy is a sustainable, historically irreversible development remains to be seen; like its two previous historical antecedents, the assembly-based democracy of the ancient world and modern representative democracy in territorial form, monitory democracy is by no means inevitable, or historically guaranteed. It did not have to happen, but it nonetheless happened; the whole issue of whether it will live or fade away or die suddenly remains an open question, well beyond the scope of this book, a matter for the verdicts of future historians.[2] Yet when judged by its institutional contours and inner dynamics, monitory democracy is without doubt the most complex form of democracy known to us. Those with a taste for Latin would say that it is the *tertium quid*, the not fully formed successor of the earlier historical experiments with assembly-based and representative forms of democracy. In the name of 'people', 'the public', 'public accountability', 'the people', 'stakeholders' or 'citizens' – the terms are normally used interchangeably in the age of monitory democracy – power-scrutinising institutions spring up all over the place, both within the fields

---

5 July 2014) and the fuller version in *The Good Citizen: A History of American Civic* Life (New York: The Free Press, 1998), to which my use of the term monitory democracy is indebted.

[2] The subject of counter-trends and dysfunctions of monitory democracy is taken up in my *The Life and Death of Democracy*. A full range of related materials is to be found at www.thelifeanddeathofdemocracy.org.

of government and beyond, often stretching across borders. Elections, political parties and legislatures neither disappear nor decline in importance; but they most definitely lose their pivotal position in politics. Contrary to the orthodox claims of many political scientists, many of whom have unwittingly plunged themselves into deep seas of forgetfulness, democracy is no longer simply a way of handling the power of elected governments by electoral and parliamentary and constitutional means, and no longer a matter confined to territorial states.[3] Gone are the days when democracy could be described (and in the next breath attacked) as 'government by the unrestricted will of the majority' (Friedrich von Hayek). Whether in the field of local, national or supra-national government, or in the world of business and other non-governmental organisations and networks, some of them stretching down into the roots of everyday life and outwards, towards the four corners of the earth, people and organisations that exercise power are now routinely subject to public monitoring and humbling by an assortment of extra-parliamentary bodies.

MONITORY MECHANISMS

The historical shift is of major importance. Symptomatic is the appearance, during recent decades, of scores of new types of power-scrutinising and power-checking mechanisms unknown to previous democrats, or whole systems of democracy. These monitory mechanisms have appeared in many different global settings. They are not exclusively 'American' or 'European' or 'OECD' or 'Western' inventions, but have diffused around the globe, from all points on the globe. They operate in different ways, on many different fronts, including groups and networks (such as the Alberta Climate Dialogue, BirdLife International and the World Glacier Monitoring Service) dedicated to scrutinising and defending our biosphere against wanton destruction by humans. Some scrutinise power primarily at the level of *citizens' inputs* to government or civil society bodies; other monitory mechanisms are preoccupied with monitoring and contesting what are sometimes called *policy throughputs*; still others concentrate on

---

[3] Examples include Adam Przeworski, Susan C. Stokes and Bernard Manin (eds.), *Democracy, Accountability, and Representation* (Cambridge: Cambridge University Press, 1999); Adam Przeworski, *Democracy and the Limits of Self-Government* (Cambridge: Cambridge University Press, 2010); and the review essay by Gerardo L. Munck, 'Democratic Theory after Transitions from Authoritarian Rule', *Perspectives on Politics*, 9 (2011), 333–343.

scrutinising the *policy outputs* of governmental or non-governmental organisations. Quite a few of the inventions concentrate simultaneously upon all three dimensions, doing so in different rhythms and through different spatial settings. Monitory mechanisms are often long-haul institutions. Yet some of them are remarkably evanescent; in a fast-changing media world, like strong gusts of wind, they suddenly make their presence felt, stirring things up before dissolving into thin air, leaving things not quite as they were before. Power-monitoring mechanisms also assume different sizes and operate on various spatial scales; they range from 'just round the corner' bodies with quite local footprints to global networks aimed at keeping tabs on those who exercise power over great distances.

Given such variations, it should not be surprising that a quick short list of the inventions resembles, at first sight, to the untrained eye, a magpie's nest of randomly collected items. The list includes: citizen juries, bio-regional assemblies, participatory budgeting, advisory boards and focus groups. There are think tanks, consensus conferences, teach-ins, public memorials, local community consultation schemes, open houses (developed for instance in the field of architecture), animal ambassador schemes, indigenous tent embassies and professional networking forums. Citizens' assemblies, justice boats, democratic audits, brainstorming conferences, conflict of interest boards, global associations of parliamentarians against corruption and constitutional safaris (famously used by the drafters of the new South African constitution to examine best practice elsewhere) are on the list. Included as well are food testing agencies and consumer councils, online petitions and chat rooms, democracy clubs and democracy cafés, public vigils and peaceful sieges, summits, bridge doctors and protestivals (South Korean specialties) and global watchdog organisations set up to bring greater public accountability to business and other civil society bodies. The list of innovations extends to deliberative polls, independent religious courts, public 'scorecards' and consultation exercises, electronic civil disobedience and websites, weblogs and twitter feeds dedicated to monitoring the abuse of power. And the list of new inventions includes unofficial ballots (text-messaged straw polls, for instance), international criminal courts, truth and reconciliation commissions, global social forums and the tendency of increasing numbers of non-governmental organisations to adopt written constitutions, with an elected component.

Let us pause, if only because the inventory is disjointed, and potentially confusing. Clear-headed thinking is needed to spot the qualities that these inventions share in common. Monitory institutions play several roles.

Some monitors, electoral commissions, anti-corruption bodies and consumer protection agencies for instance, use their avowed neutrality as 'guide dog' institutions to protect the rules of the democratic game from predators and enemies. Other monitors are committed to providing publics with extra viewpoints and better information about the performance of various governmental and non-governmental bodies. Since they typically contest imbalances of power by appealing to publics, monitory institutions (to scotch a common misunderstanding) must not be confused with top-down surveillance mechanisms that operate in secret, for the privately defined purposes of those who are in charge of government or civil society organisations. The public monitoring of unequal power stands in opposition to internal audits, closed-circuit surveillance ('for quality and training purposes, your call may be monitored') and other managerial techniques of administrative power.[4]

Monitory mechanisms are geared as well to the definition, scrutiny and enforcement of public standards and ethical rules for preventing corruption, or the improper behaviour of those responsible for making decisions, not only in the field of elected government, but in a wide variety of power settings, banks and other business included. The new institutions of monitory democracy are sometimes geared to altering the time frame of official politics; in such fields as the environment, pensions and healthcare, they publicise long-term issues that are neglected, or dealt with badly, by the short-term mentality encouraged by election cycles. Monitory institutions are further defined by their overall commitment to strengthening the diversity and influence of citizens' voices and choices in decisions that affect their lives. Especially in times when substantial numbers of citizens believe that politicians are not easily trusted, and in

---

[4] There are clear differences in this respect between public monitors and the 'regulatory' agencies of the kind analysed by Frank Vibert, *The Rise of the Unelected: Democracy and the New Separation of Powers* (Cambridge and New York: Cambridge University Press, 2007). While monitory bodies are often unelected, their wide appeals for public attention mark them off from bodies, such as independent central banks, economic regulators, risk managers and auditors, whose principal function is to demarcate boundaries between the market and the state, and to resolve conflicts of interest and to allocate resources, even in sensitive ethical areas, such as those involving bio-technology. Vibert argues that such regulatory bodies, taken together, should be viewed as a new branch of government with its own sources of legitimacy and held to account through a new separation of powers. Vibert's belief that such unelected regulatory bodies help promote a more informed citizenry because they provide a more trustworthy and reliable source of information for decisions rather seriously understates their tendency to wilful blindness and hubris, of the kind that enveloped banking and credit sector institutions on the eve of the post-2007 great recession.

which governments are often accused of abusing their power or being out of touch with citizens, or simply unwilling to deal with their concerns and problems, monitory democracy serves as a brake upon majority-rule democracy and its worship of numbers. It proves (contrary to twentieth-century advocates of so-called free markets) that democracy does not necessarily crush minorities. Monitory democracy also defies descriptions of democracy as essentially a matter of elite-led party competition dressed up in the razzamatazz of elections.[5] Freed from the measured caution and double speak of political parties and official politics, monitory institutions in fact boost the chances of democracy with a small 'd', 'minoritarian' democracy. Regardless of the outcome of elections, and sometimes in direct opposition to the principle of majority rule, monitors give a voice to the losers and provide independent representation for minorities, for instance to indigenous and disabled and other peoples who cannot ever expect to lay claim to being or becoming a majority.

ONE PERSON, MANY REPRESENTATIVES

By making room for representations of ways of life that people feel strongly about, despite their neglect or suppression by parties, parliaments and governments, or by powerful organised private interests, the new monitory inventions have the combined effect of raising the level and quality of public awareness of power, including power relationships 'beneath' and 'beyond' the institutions of territorial states. It is little wonder that in many democracies the new power-monitoring inventions have changed the language of contemporary politics. They prompt much talk of 'empowerment', 'high energy democracy', 'stakeholders',

---

[5] Ludwig von Mises, for whom markets unfailingly cater for minority interests, strongly objected to representative democracy, seeing it as a recipe for the tyranny of the majority. 'In the political democracy', he wrote, 'only the votes cast for the majority candidate or the majority plan are effective in shaping the course of affairs. The votes polled by the minority do not directly influence policies. But on the market no vote is cast in vain. Every penny spent has the power to work upon the production processes. The publishers cater not only to the majority by publishing detective stories, but also to the minority reading lyrical poetry and philosophical tracts. The bakeries bake bread not only for healthy people, but also for the sick on special diets'; see Ludwig von Mises, *Human Action: A Treatise on Economics* (San Francisco, CA: Fox & Wilkes, 1963 [1949]), p. 271. The view that democracy in representative form in essence is oligopolistic rule by manipulative political party machines was famously defended by Joseph Schumpeter, *Capitalism, Socialism, and Democracy* (New York: HarperCollins, 1942), p. 283: 'The psycho-technics of party management and party advertising, slogans and marching tunes, are not accessories. They are the essence of politics. So is the political boss.'

'participatory governance', 'communicative democracy' and 'deliberative democracy'; and they help spread a culture of voting and representation into many walks of life where previously things were decided by less-than-democratic methods. Monitory democracy is the age of surveys, focus groups, deliberative polling, online petitions and audience and customer voting. There are even simulated elections, in which (the annual Eurovision competition is an example) television audiences granted a 'vote' by media companies are urged to lodge their preference for the star of their choice, by acclamation, cell phone or the Internet. Whether intended or not, the spreading culture of voting, backed by the new power-monitoring mechanisms, has the effect of interrupting and often silencing the soliloquies of parties, politicians and parliaments. With the help of new information banks, unelected representatives, muckraking and cross-border publics, the new power-scrutinising innovations tend to enfranchise many more citizens' voices. The number and range of monitory institutions have so greatly increased that they point to a world where the old rule of 'one person, one vote, one representative' – the central demand in the struggle for representative democracy – is replaced with the new principle of monitory democracy: 'one person, many interests, many voices, multiple votes, multiple representatives'.

A different way of putting the same point is to say that what is distinctive about monitory democracy is that potentially *all fields of social and political life* come to be publicly scrutinised, not just by the standard machinery of representative democracy, but by a whole host of *non-party, extra-parliamentary and often unelected bodies* operating within and underneath and beyond the boundaries of territorial states. In the era of monitory democracy, it is as if the principles of representative democracy – public openness, citizens' equality, selecting representatives – are superimposed on representative democracy itself. This has many practical consequences, but one especially striking effect is to alter the patterns of interaction – political geography – of democratic institutions.

We could put things in this way: once upon a time, in the brief heyday of representative democracy, say immediately after the First World War, the thing called democracy had a rather simple political geography (Figure 3.1). Within the confines of any given state, from the point of view of citizens, democracy principally meant taking an interest in an election campaign and, on the great day of reckoning, turning out to vote for a party or independent candidate. He – it was almost always men – was someone local, a figure known to the community, a local shopkeeper or professional or someone in business or a trade unionist, for instance.

3 Monitory Democracy

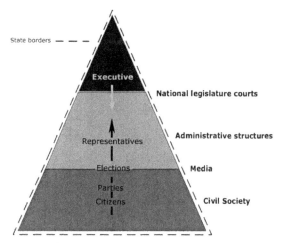

FIGURE 3.1 Territorially bound representative democracy (by Giovanni Navarria)

Their test was democracy's great ceremonial, the pause of deliberation, the calm of momentary reflection, the catharsis of ticking and crossing, before the storm of result. 'Universal peace is declared', was the sarcastic way the nineteenth-century English novelist George Eliot (1819–1880) put it, 'and the foxes have a sincere interest in prolonging the lives of the poultry'. Her American contemporary, Walt Whitman (1819–1892), spoke more positively of the pivotal function of polling day as the great 'choosing day', the 'powerfulest scene', a 'swordless conflict' mightier than Niagara Falls or the Mississippi River or the geysers of Yosemite, a 'still small voice vibrating', a time for 'the peaceful choice of all', a passing moment of suspended animation when 'the heart pants, life glows'.[6] If blessed with enough votes, the local representative joined a privileged small circle of legislators, whose job was to stay in line with party policy, support or oppose a government that used its majority in the legislature to pass laws and to scrutinise their implementation, hopefully with results that pleased as many of the represented as possible. At the end of a limited stint as legislator, buck passing stopped. Foxes and poultry fell quiet. It was again time for the 'swordless conflict' of the great

---

[6] George Eliot, *Felix Holt: The Radical* (Edinburgh: Blackwood, 1866), chapter 5, p. 127; Walt Whitman, 'Election Day, November 1884', in *Leaves of Grass* (New York, 1891–1892), p. 391.

112   Power and Humility

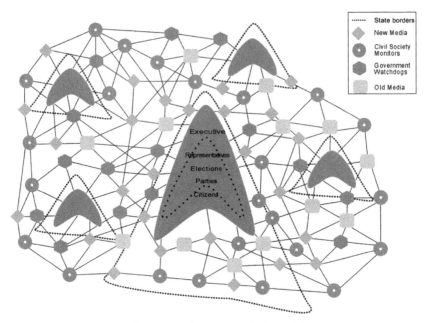

FIGURE 3.2 Monitory democracy (by Giovanni Navarria)

choosing day. The representative either stepped down, into retirement from political life, or faced the music of re-election.

This is obviously a simplified sketch of the role of elections, but it serves to highlight the different, much more complex political geography of monitory democracy (see Figure 3.2). There are historical continuities, of course. Just as modern representative democracies preserved the old custom of public assemblies of citizens, so monitory democracies keep alive and depend upon legislatures, political parties and elections, which continue to be bitterly fought and closely contested affairs. But such is the growing variety of interlaced, power-monitoring mechanisms that democrats from earlier times, if catapulted into the new world of monitory democracy, would find it hard to understand what is happening.

The new form of democracy demands a shift of perspective, a break with conventional thinking in order to understand its political geography. For this purpose, let us imagine for a moment, as if from a satellite orbiting our planet, the contours of the new democracy. We would spot that its power-scrutinising institutions are less centred on elections, parties and legislatures; no longer confined to the territorial state; and spatially arranged in ways much messier than textbooks on democracy typically suppose The vertical 'depth' and horizontal 'reach' of monitory institutions is striking. If the number of levels within any hierarchy of institutions is a measure of its 'depth', and if the number of units located within each of these levels is called its 'span' or 'width', then monitory democracy is the deepest and widest system of democracy ever known. The political geography of mechanisms like integrity commissions, citizens' assemblies, web-based message systems, children's parliaments, local action groups, regional summits and global watchdog organisations defies simple-minded descriptions. So too does the political geography of the wider constellation of power-checking and power-disputing mechanisms in which they are embedded – bodies like human rights networks, citizen juries, audit and integrity commissions and many other watchdog organisations set up to bring greater public accountability to business and other civil society bodies.

POSSIBLE MISUNDERSTANDINGS

New ways of thinking about the political world inevitably produce confusions and misunderstandings. The theory of monitory democracy is no exception. While it is often said, for instance, that the struggle to bring greater public accountability to government and non-government organisations that wield power over others is in effect a struggle for 'grassroots democracy' or 'participatory democracy' or 'popular empowerment', the metaphors rest on a misunderstanding of contemporary trends. The age of monitory democracy is not heading backwards; it is not motivated by efforts to recapture the (imagined) spirit of assembly-based democracy – 'power to the people' – as some supporters of groups like Students for a Democratic Society (SDS) liked to chant at political demonstrations during the 1960s. Many contemporary champions of 'deep' or 'direct' democracy still speak as if they are Greeks, as if what really counts for a democracy is 'the commitment and capacities of ordinary people to make sensible decisions through reasoned deliberation and empowered because they attempt to tie action to discussion'.[7] The reality of monitory democracy is otherwise, in that all of the new power-scrutinising experiments in the name of 'the people' or citizens' empowerment rely inevitably on *representation*; that is, public claims about some or other matter made

---

[7] Archon Fung and Erik Olin Wright, 'Thinking about Empowered Participatory Governance', in Archon Fung and Erik Olin Wright, *Deepening Democracy: Institutional Innovations in Empowered Participatory Governance* (London: Verso, 2003), p. 5.

by some actors on behalf and in defence of others. These experiments often draw their legitimacy from the imagined, politically crafted body known as 'the people';[8] but they are not understandable as efforts to abolish the gap between representatives and the represented, as if citizens could live without others acting on their behalf, find their true selves and express themselves as equals within a unified political community no longer burdened by miscommunication, or by misgovernment.

Monitory democracy in fact thrives on representation, as treatments of the much-discussed example of citizen assemblies show.[9] It thrives as well on elections, even though their changing status and significance prevents many people from spotting the novelty of monitory democracy. Since 1945, when there were only a dozen democracies left on the face of the earth, party-based democracy has made a big comeback, so much so that it tricked scholars like Francis Fukuyama and Samuel Huntington into thinking that nothing had changed, except for a large global leap in the number of representative democracies. Their mistake is understandable: following the widespread collapse and near extinction of democracy during the first half of the twentieth century, most parts of the world have since become familiar with the basic institutions of electoral democracy. Conventional party-centred forms of representation do not simply wither away. Millions of people have grown accustomed to competition among political parties, periodic elections, the limited-term holding of political office and the right of citizens to assemble in public to make their

---

[8] To rephrase this paradoxical idea, if the principles of representative democracy turned 'the people' of assembly democracy into a more distant judge of how well representatives performed, then monitory democracy exposes the fiction of a unified 'sovereign people'. The dynamic structures of monitory democracy serve as barriers against the uncontrolled worship of 'the people', or what might be dubbed demolatry. Monitory democracy demonstrates that the world is made up of many *demoi*, and that particular societies are made up of flesh-and-blood people who have different interests, and who therefore do not necessarily see eye to eye. It could be said that monitory democracy democratises – publicly exposes – the whole principle of 'the sovereign people' as a pompous fiction; at best, it turns it into a handy reference device that most people know to be just that: a useful political fiction. There are indeed times when the fiction of 'the people' serves as a monitoring principle, as a former Justice of the Federal Constitutional Court in Germany, Dieter Grimm has explained: 'The circumstances are rare in which the fiction of "the demos" is needed as a reminder that those who make the laws are not the source of their ultimate legitimacy. Democracies need public power; but they need as well to place limits on the exercise of public power by invoking "the people" as a fictional subject to whom collectively binding powers are attributed: a *"Zurechnungssubjekt"* that is not itself capable of acting, but which serves as a democratic necessity because it makes accountability meaningful' (interview, Berlin, 23 November 2006).

[9] Keane, *The Life and Death of Democracy*, pp. 699–701.

views known to their representatives in legislatures and executives that operate within the jurisdictional boundaries of territorial states. In contexts as different as Bangladesh, Nigeria, Trinidad and Tobago, Malta and Botswana, even among Tibetans living in exile, the mechanisms of electoral democracy have taken root for the first time. In other contexts, especially those where electoral democracy is well embedded, there are ongoing experiments to improve the rules of the electoral game, for instance by keeping tabs on elected representatives via electoral literacy and parliament watchdog initiatives (examples include innovative web platforms such as Parliament Watch [*Abgeordnetenwatch.de*] in Germany and Vote Compass in Canada). Still other experiments include the introduction of primary elections into political parties; tightened restrictions on campaign fund-raising and spending; improvements in voting facilities for disabled citizens; and the banning of elected representatives from party hopping (a decision taken by the Brazilian Supreme Court in 2007).

For all these reasons, it seemed perfectly reasonable for Huntington and other scholars to speak of the spectacular rebirth and extension of representative forms of democracy in recent decades as a 'third wave of democratisation'. Enter monitory democracy: a brand new historical type of democracy that operates in radically different ways from textbook accounts of 'representative' or 'parliamentary' or 'liberal' democracy, as it is still most often called. In the age of monitory democracy, democracy is practised in new ways. Where monitory democracy exists, institutions like periodic elections, multi-party competition and the right of citizens to voice their public approval or disapproval of legislation remain familiar fixtures. To repeat: under conditions of monitory democracy, the whole issue of who is entitled to vote, and under which conditions, continues to attract public attention, and to stir up troubles. Think of the legal and political controversies sparked by the question of who owns the software of unreliable electronic voting machines manufactured by companies such as Election Systems and Software. Or consider the disputes triggered by gerrymandering, or by the withdrawal of votes for people such as felons; or by claims that groups such as diasporas, minority language speakers, the disabled and people with low literacy and number skills are disadvantaged by the secret ballot; or the loud public complaints about how still other constituencies, such as women, young people and the biosphere, are either poorly represented, or are not properly represented at all.

Struggles to open up and improve the quality of electoral and legislative representation are by no means finished. But slowly and surely, the whole architecture of democracy has begun to change fundamentally. So too has the meaning of democracy. No longer synonymous with self-government by an assembly of privileged male citizens (as in the Greek city states), or with party-based government guided by the will of a legislative majority, democracy has come to mean a way of life and a mode of governing in which power is subject to checks and balances – at any time, in any place – such that nobody is entitled to rule arbitrarily, without the consent of the governed, or their representatives. An important symptom of the redefinition of democracy is the advent of election monitoring. During the 1980s, for the first time in the history of democracy, founding elections in new or strife-torn polities began to be monitored systematically by outside teams of observers.[10] 'Fair and open' methods – the elimination of violence, intimidation, ballot-rigging and other forms of political tomfoolery – are now expected of all countries, including the most powerful democracy on the face of the Earth, the United States, where the Organization for Security and Co-operation in Europe (OSCE) observers played a role for the first time in the presidential elections of November 2004.

In the era of monitory democracy, the franchise struggles which once tore whole societies apart have nevertheless lost their centrality. As the culture of voting spreads, and as unelected representatives multiply in many different contexts, a brand new issue begins to surface. The old question that racked the age of representative democracy – *who* is entitled to vote and *when* – is compounded and complicated by a question for which there are still no easy answers: *where* are people entitled to vote, *for whom* and *through which representatives*?

The intense public concern with publicly scrutinising matters once thought to be non-political is one symptom of this historical shift towards monitory democracy. The era of representative democracy (as Tocqueville first spotted) certainly saw the rise of self-organised pressure groups and schemes for 'socialising' the power of government, for instance through councils of soldiers, workers' control of industry and Guild Socialist proposals. Yet few of these schemes survived the violent upheavals of the first half of the twentieth century, which makes the contrast with monitory democracy all the more striking. The sea change in favour of extra-parliamentary monitors is also evident in the unprecedented level of interest in the old eighteenth-century European term 'civil society'; for the

---

[10] Eric C. Bjornlund, *Beyond Free and Fair: Monitoring Elections and Building Democracy* (Baltimore, MD: The Johns Hopkins University Press, 2004).

first time in the history of democracy, these two words are now routinely used by democrats around the world. The change is equally manifest in the strong trend towards the independent public scrutiny of all areas of government policy, ranging from public concern about the maltreatment and legal rights of children to the development of habitat protection plans and efforts to take democracy 'upstream', to ensure that the future development of quantum computers, nanotechnology, alternative energy sources and genetically modified food are governed publicly in the interests of the many, not the few. Experiments with fostering new forms of citizens' participation and elected representation have meanwhile begun to penetrate markets; a notable early example, an invention of the mid-1940s, is the German system of co-determination, known as *Mitbestimmung*, in which employees in firms of a given size are entitled to elect their own representatives onto the management boards of companies. More recent examples of efforts to constrain arbitrary power within markets include struggles of the poor in such fields as land rights, food production and literacy. The 'guerilla auditors' who made their presence felt during Paraguay's long transition to democracy are an interesting case in point: an activist movement that waged pitched legal battles in defence of Guaraní land and the right to literacy by winning public access to previously unobtainable written documents held in state archives.[11]

In the age of monitory democracy, there is rising awareness as well of the possibility and desirability of exercising new rights of criticism and casting a vote in previously off-limits areas such as health and social care design and patient choice. The experience of publicly voicing concerns and voting for representatives even extends into large-scale global organisations, such as the International Olympic Committee (IOC), which (thanks to its becoming a target of 'muckraking' investigative journalism in the 1980s) has been transformed from an exclusive private gentlemen's club into a global body where the rules of public scrutiny and representative government are applied to its inner workings, so that its co-opted governing members meet at least once a year in Session, an assembly open to journalists and charged with managing the common affairs of the IOC, including the recommendation of new IOC members, monitoring the codes of conduct of existing members and overall performance of the IOC itself.

---

[11] See Kregg Hetherington, *Guerrilla Auditors: The Politics of Transparency in Neoliberal Paraguay* (Durham, NC: Duke University Press, 2011).

The vital role played by civil societies in the invention of power-monitoring mechanisms seems to confirm what might be called James Madison's Law of Free Government: no government can be considered free unless it is capable of governing a society that is itself capable of controlling the government. The rule (sketched in the *Federalist Papers*, number 51) has tempted some people to conclude – mistakenly – that governments are quite incapable of scrutinising their own power. The truth is sometimes otherwise. In the era of monitory democracy, experience shows that governments, for the sake of their own efficiency and effectiveness, as well as for the good of their own citizens, can be encouraged to submit their own powers to independent public scrutiny.

Government 'watchdog' and 'integrity' or 'anti-corruption' institutions are a case in point. Their stated purpose is the public scrutiny of government by semi-independent government agencies (it is worth remembering that the word scrutiny originally meant 'to sort rubbish', from the Latin *scrutari*, meaning 'to search', and from *scruta*, 'rubbish'). Scrutiny mechanisms bring new eyes, ears and teeth to the public sector. In this way, they supplement the power-monitoring role of elected government representatives and judges, even though this is not always their avowed aim. While scrutiny mechanisms are often introduced and backed by the general authority of elected governments, for instance through the mechanism of ministerial responsibility, in practice things often turn out differently. Government scrutiny bodies tend to take on a life of their own, especially when they are protected by legislation, given adequate resources and managed well. Building on the much older precedents of royal commissions, public enquiries and independent auditors checking the financial probity of government agencies – inventions that had their roots in the age of representative democracy – the new scrutiny mechanisms add checks and balances to avoid possible abuses of power by elected representatives. The national policy conferences held periodically in Brazil are an example; so also are the offices of Inspector General in all cabinet-level agencies and most major federal government agencies in the United States.[12] The trend is confirmed by more recent web-based experiments

---

[12] Thamy Pogrebinschi, 'Participatory Policymaking and Political Experimentalism in Brazil', in Stefanie Kron, Sérgio Costa and Marianne Braig (eds.), *Democracia y reconfiguraciones contemporáneas del derecho en América Latina* (Madrid: Iberoamericana, 2012), pp. 111–136; Nadia Hillard, *The Accountability State: US Federal Inspectors General and the Pursuit of Democratic Integrity* (Lawrence, KS: University of Kansas Press, 2017); and Michael Schudson, 'Political Observatories, Databases and News in the Emerging Ecology of Public Information', *Daedalus* (Spring 2010), 100–109; *The Rise of*

such as the Open Government Platform (a joint initiative of the Indian and United States governments) and Recovery.gov. These government-initiated scrutiny mechanisms are justified in terms of enhancing the capacity to govern, for instance (say their champions) through improved decision making that has the added advantage of raising the level of public trust in political institutions among citizens considered as 'stakeholders' entitled to keep track of state-sector spending. The whole process displays a double paradox. Not only are government scrutiny mechanisms often established by governments that subsequently fail to control the workings of these same mechanisms, for instance in cases of fraud and corruption and the enforcement of legal standards. The new mechanisms also have democratic, power-checking effects, even though they are normally staffed by judges, professional experts and other un-elected officials who themselves operate at several arms' length from the rhythm of periodic elections.

It is worth noting, finally, that monitory democracy challenges the prejudices of those who are resistant to the whole idea of 'cross-border' or 'international' democracy. These prejudices have deep roots. As the pages below explain, they date from the era of territorially bound representative democracy, and in consequence almost all leading scholars of democracy today defend the supposed truth of such propositions as 'democracy requires statehood' and 'without a state there can be no democracy'. An interesting feature of monitory democracy is that it helps in practice to confront these prejudices head on. Agencies such as the Electoral Assistance Division of the United Nations, the Office for Democratic Institutions and Human Rights (part of the Organization for Security and Co-operation in Europe, or OSCE) as well as inventions such as cross-border parliaments, peer review panels, laws outlawing corporate bribery, regional and global courts and other latticed forms of power monitoring effectively scramble the distinction between 'domestic' and 'foreign', the 'local' and the 'global'. Like other types of institutions, including businesses and universities, democracy too is caught up in complex processes of 'glocalisation'. This is another way of saying that its monitory mechanisms are dynamically interconnected, to the point where each monitor functions simultaneously as both part and whole of

the Right to Know: Politics and the Culture of Transparency, 1945–1975 (Cambridge, MA and London: Belknap Press, 2015); and the discussion of monitory democracy in 'Walter Lippmann's Ghost: An Interview with Michael Schudson', *Mass Communication and Society*, 19, 3 (2016), 221–229.

the overall system. Innovations such as the US Foreign Corrupt Practices Act 1977 (the first legislation anywhere to make bribery payments by corporations to foreign government officials a criminal offence) and the follow-up OECD Anti-Bribery Convention (1999) spotlight the point that public resistance to arbitrary power is no longer 'housed' exclusively within 'sovereign' territorial states.[13] Under conditions of monitory democracy, parts (state-based monitors) and wholes (regional and global monitors) do not exist in a strict or absolute sense. The units of monitory democracy are better described as sub-wholes – 'holons' is the term famously coined by Arthur Koestler[14] – that function simultaneously as self-regarding and self-asserting entities that publicly chasten power without asking permission from higher authorities and push and pull each other in a multi-lateral system of monitoring in which all entities play a role, sometimes to the point where the part and the whole are blurred beyond recognition.

WHY MONITORY DEMOCRACY?

It is often said that the public business of power scrutiny changes very little, that states and big business are still the 'real' unchecked centres of power in deciding not only who gets what in the world, but also when, and how. Evidence that this is not necessarily so is suggested by the fact that all of the big public issues that have erupted around the world since 1945, including civil rights for women and minorities, opposition to nuclear weapons and American military intervention in Vietnam and Iraq, poverty reduction and the greening of politics, have been initiated not by political parties, elections, legislatures and governments, but principally by power-monitoring networks that run parallel to – and are often aligned against – the conventional mechanisms of party-based parliamentary representation. These monitoring networks have played a vital role in building and strengthening monitory democracy, but to say this is to raise a difficult question: have there been other forces at work in making monitory democracy possible? How can its unplanned birth and development be explained?

The query brings us back to the subject of communicative abundance, but not immediately. For the forces that resulted in the various power-

---

[13] Frank Vogl, *Waging War on Corruption: Inside the Movement Fighting the Abuse of Power* (Lanham, MD: Rowman & Littlefield, 2012).
[14] Arthur Koestler, *The Ghost in the Machine* (London: Hutchinson, 1967), p. 48.

scrutinising inventions described above are complicated; as in earlier phases of the history of democracy, generalisations concerning origins are as difficult as they are perilous. Yet two things can safely be said. More obviously, the new type of democracy has had both its causes and causers. Monitory democracy is not a monogenic matter – a living thing hatched from a single cell. It is rather the result of multiple pressures that have conspired over time to reshape the spirit, language and institutions of democracy as we know it today. The other thing about which we can be certain is that one word above all describes the most powerful early trigger of the new era of monitory democracy: war.

In the history of democracy, war and the pity and suffering of war have often been the midwife of new democratic institutions.[15] That rule certainly applied to the first half of the twentieth century, the most murderous recorded in human history. Two global wars plus terrible cruelties shattered old structures of security, sparked pushes and shoves and elbowing for power, as well as unleashed angry popular energies that fed major revolutionary upheavals, usually in the name of 'the people', against representative democracy. Bolshevism and Stalinism in Russia, Fascism in Italy, Nazism in Germany and military imperialism in Japan were effectively twisted and perverted mutations of democracy, which was typically misunderstood within these regimes as a mere synonym for popular sovereignty. These were regimes whose leaders acknowledged that 'the people' were entitled to mount the stage of history – regimes whose hirelings then set about muzzling and maiming and murdering both opponents and supporters among flesh-and-blood people. Western democracy was denounced as parliamentary dithering and muddling, as liberal perplexity, bourgeois hypocrisy and military cowardice. A third of the way into the twentieth century, parliamentary democracy was on its knees. It seemed rudderless, spiritless, paralysed, doomed. By 1941, when President Roosevelt called for 'bravely shielding the great flame of democracy from the blackout of barbarism',[16] when untold numbers of villains had drawn the contrary conclusion that dictatorship and

---

[15] Keane, *The Life and Death of Democracy*; and 'Does Democracy Have a Violent Heart?', talk delivered at the conference War, Culture and Democracy in Classical Athens, 4–6 July 2006, University of Sydney.
[16] President Roosevelt, Address to the White House Correspondents' Association Washington, 15 March 1941. The surviving electoral democracies included Australia, Canada, Chile, Costa Rica, New Zealand, Sweden, Switzerland, the United Kingdom, the United States and Uruguay. Despite its use of an electoral college to choose a president under high-security, wartime conditions, Finland might also be included, as might Eire.

totalitarianism were the future, only eleven electoral democracies remained on the face of the earth.

The possibility of annihilation galvanised minds and gritted determinations to do something, both about the awful destruction produced by war, and the dictatorships and totalitarian regimes spawned by those wars. The great cataclysms that culminated in the Second World War demonstrated to many people the naïveté of the old formula that people should obey their governments because their rulers protected their lives and possessions. The devastating upheavals of the period proved that this protection–obedience formula was unworkable, that in various countries long-standing pacts between rulers and ruled had been so violated that rulers could no longer be trusted to rule. The problem, in other words, was no longer the mobocracy of 'the people', as critics of democracy had insisted from the time of Plato and Thucydides until well into the nineteenth century. The terrible events of the first half of the twentieth century proved that mobocracy had its true source in thuggish leaders (Theodor Adorno dubbed them 'glorified barkers') skilled at denouncing 'democracy' as decadence and calling on 'the people' to make history, only then to terrorise them into submission, so destroying the plural freedoms and political equality (one person, one vote) for which electoral democracy had avowedly stood.[17] The problem, thus, was no longer the mob, and mob rule. Ruling – the arbitrary exercise of power by some over others – was in fact the problem.

The problem of ruling people from above stood at the centre of an important, though unfortunately little studied, batch of political reflections on democracy in the years just before and immediately after 1945.[18]

---

[17] A sustained fascist attack on 'democracy' was developed by Alfred Rosenberg, *Der Mythus des 20. Jahrhunderts, Eine Wertung der seelisch-geistigen Gestaltenkämpfe unserer Zeit* (Munich: Hoheneichen, 1934). Democracy is said to be based on 'abstract popular sovereignty'. It treats 'the people' as 'that part of the state which does not know what it wants'. It stifles 'folkish consciousness'; peddles 'faceless ideas of the state'; spawns 'parliamentary decomposition' and 'mass stagnation'. So-called democracy perpetuates 'mass swindling and exploitation' because in reality it is nothing more than 'a tool of capitalism and the moneyed classes'.

[18] John Keane, 'The Origins of Monitory Democracy', http://theconversation.edu.au/the-origins-of-monitory-democracy-9752 (accessed 13 October 2012). The early years after the Second World War witnessed many new lines of thinking about the future of democracy, within a global context. See, for instance, Thomas Mann, *Goethe and Democracy* (Washington, DC: Library of Congress, 1949); Carl J. Friedrich, *Constitutional Government and Democracy* (Boston, MA: Little, Brown, 1941); Jacques Maritain, 'Christianity and Democracy', a typewritten manuscript prepared as an address at the annual meeting of the American Political Science Association, New York,

The intellectual roots of monitory democracy are traceable to this period, when the possible self-extinction of electoral democracy triggered a moment of 'dark energy': the universe of meaning of democracy underwent a dramatic expansion in defiance of the cosmic gravity of contemporary events. The new energy is for instance evident in the contributions of literary, theological and intellectual figures otherwise as different as Albert Camus, John Dewey, Sidney Hook, Thomas Mann, Jacques Maritain, J.B. Priestley and, strikingly, in a work that soon became a classic, Reinhold Niebuhr's *The Children of Light and the Children of Darkness* (1945). Each of these authors voiced fears that the narrow escape of parliamentary democracy from the clutches of war and totalitarianism might just be a temporary reprieve. Several writers even asked whether the near-destruction of parliamentary democracy served as confirmation that global events were now pushing towards 'the end of the world' (Camus). Thomas Mann gave voice to the trend when noting the need for 'democracy's deep and forceful recollection of itself, the renewal of its spiritual and moral self-consciousness'. Voicing puzzlement and shock at the way the electoral democracies of the 1920s and 1930s had spawned the growth of demagogues, most authors agreed that among the vital lessons provided by recent historical experience was the way the language and practise of majority-rule democracy could be utterly corrupted, to the point where the word democracy was not only wielded in 'a consciously dishonest way' (Orwell), but its mechanisms were used and abused by the enemies of democracy, in the name of the 'sovereign people'. In quest of a new understanding of democracy, more than a few authors openly attacked metaphysical talk of the People and their supposed Sovereignty. 'Everything comes out of the people', said J. B. Priestley in a large-audience, night-time BBC broadcast, then asking exactly who 'the people' are. 'The people are real human beings', he answered. 'If you prick them, they bleed ... They swing between fear

29 December 1949; Oscar Jászi et al., *The City of Man: A Declaration of World Democracy* (New York: Viking Press, 1940); Albert Camus, *Neither Victims nor Executioners* (Chicago, IL: World Without War Publications, 1972 [first published in the autumn 1946 issues of *Combat*]); Reinhold Niebuhr, *The Children of Light and the Children of Darkness: A Vindication of Democracy and a Critique of Its Traditional Defenders* (London: Nisbet, 1945); Pope Pius XII, *Democracy and Peace* (London: Catholic Truth Society, 1945); Sidney Hook, 'What Exactly Do We Mean By "Democracy"?', *The New York Times*, 16 March 1947, pp. 10ff; and Alexander D. Lindsay, *Democracy in the World Today* (London: Command School of Education, 1945).

and hope. They have strange dreams. They hunger for happiness. They all have names and faces. They are not some cross-section of abstract stuff.'[19]

Deeply troubled, more than a few authors called for fresh, untried remedies for the maladies of representative democracy. The abandonment of sentimental optimism was high on their list. Some jurists and political thinkers (Carl J. Friedrich, B.R. Ambedkar) emphasised the need for constitutional restraints upon elected governments. Others called for the injection of religious principles into the ethos and institutions of democracy. Opinions were often divided, but all these writers of the 1940s restated their support for a new form of democracy, one whose spirit and institutions were infused with a robust commitment to rooting out the devils of arbitrary, publicly unaccountable power. The American theologian Niebuhr (1892–1971), who later won prominent admirers, including Martin Luther King, Jr., provided one of the weightiest cases for renewing and transforming democracy along these lines. 'The perils of uncontrolled power are perennial reminders of the virtues of a democratic society', he wrote. 'But modern democracy requires a more realistic philosophical and religious basis, not only in order to anticipate and understand the perils to which it is exposed, but also to give it a more persuasive justification.' He concluded with words that became famous: 'Man's capacity for justice makes democracy possible; but man's inclination to injustice makes democracy necessary.'[20]

In perhaps the boldest move, still other thinkers argued for abandoning the presumption that the 'natural home' of democracy in representative form is the sovereign territorial state. So they pleaded for extending democratic principles across territorial borders. 'The history of the past twenty years', Friedrich wrote, 'has shown beyond a shadow of a doubt that constitutional democracy cannot function effectively on a national plane.' Thomas Mann rubbished attempts to 'reduce the democratic idea to the idea of peace, and to assert that the right of a free people to determine its own destiny includes respect for the rights of foreign people and thus constitutes the best guarantee for the creation of a community of nations and for peace'. He added: 'We must reach higher and envisage the whole. We must define democracy as that form of government and of society which is inspired above every other with the feeling and consciousness of the dignity of man.'[21]

---

[19] J.B. Priestley, *Out of the People* (London: Collins, 1941), pp. 16–17, 111.
[20] Niebuhr, *The Children of Light and the Children of Darkness*, p. vi.
[21] Friedrich, *Constitutional Government and Democracy*, p. 34; Thomas Mann, *The Coming Victory of Democracy* (London: Secker & Warburg, 1943), p. 22.

3 *Monitory Democracy* 125

This way of thinking about the political dangers of arbitrary power undoubtedly helped inspire one of the most remarkable features of monitory democracy: the marriage of democracy and human rights, and the subsequent worldwide growth of organisations, networks and campaigns committed to the defence of human rights. The intermarriage had roots extending back to the French Revolution, certainly, but its immediate inspiration was two major political declarations inspired by the horrors of the Second World War: the United Nations Charter (1945) and the Universal Declaration of Human Rights (1948). The second was arguably the more remarkable candle in the gloom bred by the death of forty-five million people, terrible physical destruction and spiritual misery, and the escalating violence and mounting post-war tensions bound up with such political troubles as ethno-national cleansing in Europe, the bloody partition of Pakistan and India, the Berlin blockade and the unresolved future of Palestine. Drafted in 1947 and 1948, the Universal Declaration of Human Rights seemed to many at the time a mere sideshow of questionable importance. Its preamble spoke of 'the inherent dignity' and 'the equal and inalienable rights of all members of the human family'. It was in effect a call for civil societies and governments everywhere to speak and act as if human rights mattered; its practical effect was to help redefine democracy as monitory democracy. Today, networked organisations like Human Rights Watch, the Aga Khan Development Network, Amnesty International and tens of thousands of other non-governmental human rights organisations routinely deal with a wide range of rights matters including torture, child soldiers, the abuse of women, and freedom of religious conviction. Their job is the advocacy of human rights through well-researched, skilfully publicised campaigns. They see themselves as goads to the conscience of governments and citizens, and they solve a basic problem that had dogged representative democracy: who decides who 'the people' are? Most human rights organisations and networks answer: every human being is entitled to exercise their right to have rights, including the right to take advantage of communicative abundance by communicating freely with others as equals.

COMMUNICATIVE ABUNDANCE

The intermarriage of human rights and democracy and the many monitory institutions that have sprung into life since 1945 proved that democracy is not always cursed by war, and that there are times when terrible violence functions as a trigger for citizens and institution builders to take things into their own hands. But if the horrors of total war were the prime initial catalyst of the birth of monitory democracy, then more recently, without doubt, upheavals in the mode of communication media are proving to be a vital driver of its subsequent growth.

In the era of monitory democracy, all institutions in the business of scrutinising power rely heavily on these media innovations; if the new galaxy of communicative abundance suddenly imploded, monitory democracy would be finished. Monitory democracy and computerised media networks behave as if they are conjoined twins. To say this is not to fall into the trap of supposing that computer-linked communications networks prefigure a brand new utopian world, a carnival of 'virtual communities' homesteading on the electronic frontier, a 'cyber-revolution' that yields equal access of all citizens to all media, anywhere and at any time. The new age of communicative abundance is in fact marked by contradictions, decadent trends and disappointments, for instance the spread of 'post-truth' styles of politics and the widening power gaps between media rich and media poor, who themselves seem almost unneeded as communicators, or as consumers of media products, simply because they have no market buying power.[22] The dark arts of post-truth and communication poverty both contradict the basic principle of monitory democracy that all citizens equally are entitled to communicate their opinions, and periodically to give elected and unelected representatives a rough ride. Yet the fundamental point remains: when viewed from the standpoint of monitory democracy and its future, the advent of communicative abundance ought to be regarded as a most promising development.

The pages that follow show how and why the unfinished communications revolution enables the formation of new information banks, the politicisation of private life and the empowerment of unelected representatives who defend citizens against arbitrary power. Communicative abundance strengthens public muckraking and fuels the growth of new cross-border publics. The combined effect of these criss-crossing trends is to encourage people's suspicions of unaccountable power. Within message-saturated democracies citizens come to learn that they must keep an eye on power and its supposed representatives. They see that prevailing power relationships are not 'natural', but contingent – the resultant of

---

[22] See John Keane, *Democracy and Media Decadence* (Cambridge and New York: Cambridge University Press, 2013).

political processes. One could go further. In the age of communicative abundance, or so it seems, bossy power can no longer hide comfortably behind private masks. Power relations everywhere are subjected to organised efforts by some, with the help of media, to tell others – publics of various sizes – about matters that previously had been hidden away, 'in private'. We live in times when private text messages, Facebook pages, tweets and video footage rebound publicly, to reveal monkey business that forces the resignation of leading government officials. It is an age in which hand-held cameras are used by citizen reporters to upload materials featuring election candidates live, unplugged and unscripted; and this is the age in which mobile telephone images and leaked videos and cablegrams serve as evidence that soldiers in war zones commit war crimes. These and other acts of denaturing power are usually messy business, and they often come wrapped in rumours and hype, certainly. But the unmasking of power resonates strongly with the power-scrutinising spirit of monitory democracy.

Helped along by red-blooded journalism that relies on styles of reporting concerned less with veracity than with 'breaking news' and blockbusting scoops, communicative abundance sometimes hacks into the power relations of government and civil society. It is easy to complain about the methods of muckraking journalism. It hunts in packs, its eyes on bad news, egged on by the newsroom saying that facts must never be allowed to get in the way of stories. It loves titillation, draws upon unattributed sources, fills news holes – in the era of monitory democracy news never sleeps – spins sensations, and concentrates too much on personalities, rather than time-bound contexts. The new journalism is formulaic and gets bored too quickly; and there are times (as we shall see) when it bows down to corporate power and government press briefings, sometimes even serving as a vehicle for the public circulation of organised lies. Such objections to muckraking journalism should be taken seriously; but they are only half the story. Simply put, red-blooded journalism, exemplified by the controversial efforts of Wikileaks to release and circulate secret cablegrams and documents, keeps alive the old utopias of 'government in the sunshine', shedding light on power, 'freedom of information' and greater 'truth' and 'transparency' in the making and implementation of decisions. Given that unchecked power still weighs down hard on the heads of citizens, it is not surprising, thanks to a host of monitory mechanisms, muckraking journalism and easy access to cheap tools of communication, such as multi-purpose mobile phones, that public objections to wrongdoing and corruption are commonplace in the era of monitory democracy. Scandals seem to be a daily occurrence, sometimes to the point where, like earthquakes, breathtaking revelations rumble the foundations of even the most powerful or publicly respected institutions.

In the age of monitory democracy, some scandals have become legendary, like the public uproar in the United States caused by the inadvertent discovery of evidence of secret burglaries of the Democratic Party National Committee headquarters in the Watergate Hotel in Washington DC, and by the subsequent snowballing of events that became the Watergate affair that resulted in threats of impeachment and the eventual resignation (in August 1974) of President Nixon. On the other side of the Atlantic, 'classic' scandals have included the Filesa affair, the rumpus in the early 1990s within Spanish politics triggered by a government auditors' report that confirmed that senior Socialist Party officials had operated front companies, for which they were paid gigantic sums for consultancy services that were never rendered. Then there was the nation-wide investigation by Italian police and judges of the extensive system of political corruption dubbed 'bribesville' (*Tangentopoli*), the so-called *mani pulite* ('clean hands') campaign that led to the disappearance of many political parties and the suicide of some politicians and industry leaders after their crimes were exposed. There was also the resignation of the French foreign minister and the admission by the French president on television that agents of the French secret service (DGSE) were responsible for the murder (in July 1985) of a Greenpeace activist and the bombing of their support vessel, the Rainbow Warrior, a boat that had been due to lead a flotilla of yachts to protest against French nuclear testing at Mururoa Atoll in the Pacific Ocean. And not to be forgotten is the bitter global controversy triggered by the whopping lies about 'weapons of mass destruction' spun by the defenders of the American-led military invasion of Iraq in the early years of the twenty-first century – an invasion, according to the most reliable estimates, that has resulted in many hundreds of thousands of deaths, produced several million refugees and left behind many more traumatised children and orphans.

There is something utterly novel about the intensity and scale of these sagas. From its origins in the ancient assemblies of Syria-Mesopotamia, democracy has always cut through and 'de-natured' habit and prejudice and hierarchies of power. Democracy has always been a friend of contingency. It has stirred up the sense that people can shape and reshape their lives as equals, and not surprisingly it has often brought commotion into the world. In the era of monitory democracy, the constant public scrutiny of power by many differently sized monitory bodies with footprints large and small makes it the most energetic, most dynamic form of democracy ever. The dynamics of monitory democracy are not describable using the simple spatial metaphors inherited from the age of representative democracy. Talk of the 'sovereignty' of parliament, or of 'local' versus 'central' government, or of tussles between 'pressure groups', political parties and governments, is just too simple. In terms of political geometry, the system of monitory democracy is something other and different: a complex web of differently sized monitory bodies that have the effect, thanks to communicative abundance, of continuously stirring up questions about who gets what, when and how, as well as holding publicly responsible those who exercise power, wherever they are situated. Monitory democracy even contains bodies (the Democratic Audit network, the Democracy Barometer and Transparency International) that specialise in providing public assessments of the quality of existing power-scrutinising mechanisms and the degree to which they fairly represent citizens' interests. Other bodies specialise in directing questions at governments on a wide range of matters, extending from their human rights records, their energy production plans to the quality of the drinking water of their cities. Private companies are grilled about their services and products, their investment plans, how they treat their employees, and the size of their impact upon the biosphere. Various watchdogs and guide dogs and barking dogs are constantly on the job, pressing for greater public accountability of those who exercise power. The powerful consequently come to feel their constant pinch.

In the age of monitory democracy, bossy power flourishes, but it can no longer hide comfortably behind private masks; in principle, and often in practice, power relations are subjected to organised efforts by some, with the help of media, to tell others publicly about matters that previously had been hidden away, 'in private', behind closed doors and curtains of secrecy. In the age of communicative abundance, some people complain about its negative effects like 'information overload' and the tendency of media scrutiny to drag down the reputations of politicians and 'politics'. But, from the point of view of monitory democracy, it is at least arguable that communicative abundance on balance has positive consequences, or so it seems.

In spite of all its sensationalist hype and post-truth spin, the new media galaxy makes possible the broadening of people's horizons.

It produces *wise citizens*: experienced citizens who know they don't know everything, and who suspect those who think they do, especially when they try to camouflage their arrogant will to have power over others. Communicative abundance does this by multiplying the genres of programming, information and storytelling that are available to audiences and publics. News, chat shows, political oratory, bitter legal spats, comedy, infotainment, drama, music, advertising, Facebook and Twitter sensations, blogs – all of this, and much more, constantly clamour and jostle for public attention. Communicative abundance has the effect, among others, of tutoring people's sense of pluralism. It reminds them that 'truth' has many faces. Public awareness that 'truth' depends on context and perspective even prods (some) people into taking greater responsibility for how, when and why they communicate. Message-saturated democracies generate plenty of political dissimulation and lying, as I show later in this book; but partly for that reason as well, communicative abundance nurtures people's suspicions of media manipulation and arbitrary power. It tends to heighten awareness that democracy is an unending experiment in taming hazardous concentrations of power. All of the king's horses and all the king's men are unlikely to reverse the trend – or so there are good reasons for thinking. The days of representative democracy and spectrum-scarcity broadcasting and mass entertainment are over. So, too, are the days when millions of people, huddled together as masses in the shadows of totalitarian power, found the skilfully orchestrated radio and film performances of demagogues fascinating, and existentially reassuring.

In the age of communicative abundance, people are learning that they must keep an eye on power and its representatives, that they must make judgements and choose their own courses of action. These wise citizens understand that power monitoring can be ineffective, or counterproductive, and that it has no guaranteed outcomes. These citizens know that public scrutiny campaigns misfire or are poorly targeted. They note with frustration that public outcries sometimes leave everything as it is. They see that power wielders often cleverly find loopholes and ways of rebutting or simply ignoring their opponents. Sometimes wise citizens find the monitory strategies of organisations too timid, or confused, or simply irrelevant to their lives as consumers, workers, parents, community residents and voters. Despite such weaknesses, which need to be addressed both in theory and practice, the political dynamics and overall 'feel' of monitory democracies are very different from the era of representative democracy. Politics in the age of monitory democracy has a definite 'viral' quality about it. Think for a moment about any current public controversy that attracts widespread attention: news about its contours and commentaries and disputes about its significance are typically relayed by many power-monitoring organisations, large, medium and small. In the world of monitory democracy, that kind of latticed pattern – viral, networked – is typical, not exceptional. It helps explain why citizens are being tempted to think for themselves; to see the same world in different ways, from different angles; and to sharpen their overall sense that prevailing power relationships are not 'natural', but contingent. Communicative abundance promotes something of a long-term mood swing in the perception of power. The metaphysical idea of an objective, out-there-at-a-distance 'reality' is weakened; so too is the presumption that stubborn 'factual truth' is superior to power.[23] The fabled distinction between what people can see with their eyes and what they are told about the emperor's new clothes breaks down.

Under media-saturated conditions marked by dynamism, pluralism and competing stories told about how the world works, 'information' ceases to be a fixed category with definite content. What counts as information is less and less understood by wise citizens as 'hard facts' or as chunks of 'reality' to be mined from television and radio programmes, or from newspapers or Internet blogs, and certainly not from the mouths of people who think of themselves as authorities. The famous landscape photographer Ansel Adams (1902–1984) reportedly once remarked that while not everybody trusts the representational qualities of paintings, 'people believe photographs'.[24] Those who repeat the remark (usually out of context) seem so mid-twentieth century, for thanks to photoshop techniques and the paparazzi many people have in fact come to understand that cameras do lie, that photographs should be looked at and looked into, and that every photograph minimally contains two people: the photographer and the viewer. In the age of communicative

---

[23] See Gianni Vattimo, *A Farewell to Truth* (New York: Columbia University Press, 2011).
[24] Ansel Adams, in Nathan Lyons (ed.), *Photographers on Photography: A Critical Anthology* (Englewood Cliffs, NJ: Prentice-Hall, 1966), p. 32: 'To photograph truthfully and effectively is to see beneath the surfaces and record the qualities of nature and humanity which live or are latent in all things. Impression is not enough. Design, style, technique – these, too, are not enough. Art must reach further than impression or self-revelation. Art, said Alfred Stieglitz, is the affirmation of life. And life, or its eternal evidence is everywhere. Some photographers take reality as the sculptors take wood and stone and upon it impose the dominations of their own thought and spirit. Others come before reality more tenderly and a photograph to them is an instrument of love and elevation. A true photograph need not be explained, nor can be contained in words.'

abundance, to put the point more sharply, 'reality', including the 'reality' promoted by the powerful, comes to be understood as always 'reported reality', as 'reality' produced by some for others; in other words, as messages that are shaped and reshaped and reshaped again in the process of transmission. Reality is multiple and mutable, a matter of redescription and interpretation – and of the power marshalled by wise citizens and their representatives to prevent particular interpretations of the world from being forced down others' throats.

4

Wild Thinking

As in every previous communications revolution – think of the upheavals triggered by the introduction of the printing press, or radio, film and television – the age of communicative abundance breeds exaggerations, false hopes, illusions. Thomas Carlyle expected the printing press to topple all traditional hierarchies, including monarchies and churches. 'He who first shortened the labor of copyists by device of movable types', he wrote, 'was disbanding hired armies, and cashiering most kings and senates, and creating a whole new democratic world.' Or to take a second example: D.W. Griffith predicted that the invention of film would ensure that school children would be 'taught practically everything by moving pictures' and 'never be obliged to read history again'.[1] Revolutions always produce fickle fantasies – and dashed expectations. This one is no different, or so it seems to wise minds. Yet when judged in terms of speed, scope and complexity, the new galaxy of communicative abundance has no historical precedent. The digital integration of text, sound and image is a first, historically speaking. So also are the compactness, portability and affordability of a wide range of communication devices capable of processing, sending and receiving information in easily reproducible form, in vast quantities, across great geographic distances, in quick time, sometimes instantly.

Technical factors play a pivotal role in the seismic upheavals that are taking place. Right from the beginning of the revolution, computing

---

[1] Thomas Carlyle, Sartor Resartus, *Fraser's Magazine*, Vol. VIII (London: J. Fraser, 1833–1834); the D.W. Griffith quotation is from Richard Dyer MacCann, *The First Film Makers* (Metuchen, NJ: Scarecrow Press, 1989), p. 5.

hardware has been undergoing constant change, with dramatic world-changing effects on the everyday lives of users. The number of transistors that can be placed inexpensively on an integrated circuit is doubling approximately every two years (according to what is known as 'Moore's law'[2]). The memory capacity, processing speed, sensors and even the number and size of pixels in smart phones and digital cameras have all been expanding at exponential rates as well. The constant revolutionising has dramatically increased the usefulness and take-up of digital electronics in nearly every segment of daily life, and within markets and government institutions as a whole, to the point where timespace compression on a global scale is becoming a reality, sometimes a functional necessity, as in the transformation of stock exchanges into spaces where computer algorithms (known as 'algobots') are programmed automatically to buy and sell equities, currencies and commodities in less than two hundred milliseconds. Cheap and reliable cross-border communication is the norm for growing numbers of people and organisations. The tyranny of distance and slow-time connections is abolished, especially in such geographically isolated countries as Greenland and Iceland, where the rates of Internet penetration (over 90 per cent of the population) are the highest in the world. The overthrow of that tyranny provides a clue as to why, in the most media-saturated societies, people typically take instant communications for granted. Their habits of heart are exposed by the curse uttered when they lose or misplace their mobile phones, or when their Internet connections are down. They feel lost; they wallow in frustration; they curse.

The historical novelty of quick-time, space-shrinking media saturation is easy to overlook, or to ignore, but it should in fact be striking. When four decades ago Diane Keaton told her workaholic husband in Woody Allen's *Play it Again, Sam* (1973) that he should give his office the number of the pay phone they were passing in case they needed to contact him, it was a good frisky gag. But jest soon turned into today's reality. Growing numbers of people are now familiar with real-time communication; as if born to check their messages, they expect instant replies to instant missives. Their waking lives resemble non-stop acts of mediated quick-time

---

[2] The law takes its name from the co-founder of Intel, Gordon E. Moore, whose classic paper on the subject noted that the number of components in integrated circuits had doubled every year from the invention of the integrated circuit in 1958 until 1965. Moore predicted (in 1965) that the trend would continue for at least another decade. See Gordon E. Moore, 'Cramming More Components onto Integrated Circuits', *Electronics*, 38 (1965), 4–7.

communication with others. In the space of one hour, for instance, an individual might send several emails, text or twitter a few times, watch some television on- or off-line, channel hop on digital radio, make an old-fashioned landline telephone call, browse a newspaper, open the day's post, and even find time for a few minutes of face-to-face conversation.

In practice, for reasons of wealth and income, habit and shortages of time, only a minority of people perform so many communication acts in quick time. For most individuals, 'ponder time' has not disappeared. Their mediated acts of communication are sporadic, unevenly distributed and snared in processes of constant change. The available data covering the trends, understandably, tend to be unreliable; it suffers from blunt-edged indicators, lack of historical nuance and built-in obsolescence. Yet when examined carefully, and especially through the lens of broader trends, the aggregate figures suggest a long-term cumulative growth of personal involvement in the multi-media process of communicative abundance. Except for the invention of human language, described by Jean-Jacques Rousseau as the 'first social institution',[3] no previous mode of communication has penetrated so deeply, so comprehensively, so dynamically, into daily human experience. Newspapers circulated through parlours and coffee shops and kitchens, but still they could be ignored, or set aside, or used to line drawers and wrap meat and fish, or to light fires. The telephone had its fixed place, in the office, kitchen or living room; while it had definite halo effects, in that it altered the daily habits and expectations of its users, they were always free to avoid its ring, often for reasons of cost.

The digital media tools that service the architecture of communicative abundance are different. They lie beyond the famous distinction drawn by Marshall McLuhan between 'hot' and 'cool' media.[4] McLuhan rightly saw that different media engage their users in different ways, and to different degrees. Some media (he gave printed works as an example) are 'hot', by which he referred not to their temperature or topicality ('hot off the press') but to the way they involve users, yet keep them detached, as if at arm's length. They favour such qualities as logicality, linearity, analytical precision. Other media, television for example, are 'cool' (McLuhan took the term from the jazz world) in the sense that they

---

[3] Jean-Jacques Rousseau, 'Essai sur l'origine des langues', in *Collection complète des œuvres de J. J. Rousseau, Citoyen de Geneve*, Vol. VIII (Geneva, 1782), Chapter 1, p. 357.
[4] Marshall McLuhan, *Understanding Media: The Extensions of Man* (New York: McGraw-Hill, 1964).

substantially depend upon user participation. The distinction between 'hot' and 'cool' media dovetailed with his thesis that all media invest our lives with artificial perceptions and arbitrary values, and that to a varying degree communication media extend our bodily and sensory capacities, some at the expense of others, so that in a visceral sense they deliver 'amputations and extensions' to our sensory apparatus.

The thesis remains important, but striking is the way communicative abundance sweeps aside the distinction between 'hot' and 'cool' media. Communicative abundance in fact involves a double combination. By fusing, for the first time in human history, the means of communication centred on text, touch, sound and image, the era of communicative abundance draws together and stimulates *most* human senses (fortune and fame awaits the person or group who masters the art of communicating taste and smell). And it involves a second combination: in some circumstances (reading a novel or newspaper on a tablet) the new mode of communication fosters reflective detachment, whereas in other settings (using Skype or messaging a friend on the other side of the planet, or wearing smart glasses) it requires the deep participation of its users and stimulates their various senses, in different combinations.

In the age of communicative abundance, vision is no longer (as many claimed it was in the age of film and television) the principal medium of power and politics. Scholars who insist that democracy based on public debate, and therefore on 'voice', is now obsolete, superseded by a type of 'spectator democracy' in which citizens are mostly passive and 'relate to politics with their eyes',[5] are exaggerating. Talk and text are not fading from political life. The eyes do not always have it. In the unfinished revolution of communicative abundance, democratic politics is a multi-sensual business. Various multi-media techniques and tools of communication draw on text, touch, sound and image. They enter every nook and cranny of daily existence. They touch and transform people's inner selves. Unsurprisingly, communicative abundance triggers constant disputes about the blurry line between 'free communication' and personal insult and criminal blasphemy. For instance, the difference between what can legitimately be said about a person, particularly someone with a public reputation, and what can be said to a person, becomes publicly controversial. The wall separating (say) speaking from an old-fashioned soapbox and making threatening telephone calls is swept away. Twitter posts fuel charges of defamation, hacking of

---

[5] Jeffrey Edward Green, *The Eyes of the People: Democracy in an Age of Spectatorship* (Oxford: Oxford University Press, 2010), p. 4.

Facebook accounts stirs up cries of felony identity theft while students who bombard teachers with e-mails are accused of disturbing the peace, or cyberstalking. Such disputes are due partly to the compactness, user-friendliness, cheapness and portability of the new communication tools; they are equally an effect of their multi-sensual and multi-interactive qualities (their enabling of one-to-many and many-to-one communication) and the decision of users to deploy the new means of communication deep within the territories of their personal lives, and within the lives of others.

The historic novelty of these deep transformations is strongly evident in many global settings, including the United States, perhaps the most media-saturated of the old democracies. There communication with others forms the second largest category of action after paid work, and it is certainly the predominant household activity, whose patterns are distributed quite unevenly. Daily communication preferences are structured by income and wealth; they are also age- and gender-dependent, as suggested by figures (from January 2005 to September 2010) for SMS usage, which show (for instance) that women talk and text more than men do, and that thirteen- to seventeen-year olds do so more than any other age group.[6] The high density of daily communication is reinforced by the tendency of each formerly separate medium to merge with others, to become 'hybrid' media. Contrary to earlier predictions, the new digital media in the United States show no signs of cannibalising old media, such as television and radio and books. Two decades ago, according to one report, the average American household had the television set on for about seven hours a day, with actual viewing time estimated to be 4.5 hours daily per adult; radio listening averaged two hours per day, most of it in the car; newspaper reading occurred between eighteen and forty-nine minutes daily; magazine browsing consumed between six and thirty minutes; and book reading, including schoolwork-related texts, took up around eighteen minutes per day. The implication was that American society was firmly in the grip of its television sets, and would remain so. More recent evidence suggests a more complex trend, in which overall mediated communication grows, along with ever more complex and 'hybrid' patterns of usage. America's love affair with televisions continues

---

[6] Roger Entner, 'Under-aged Texting: Usage and Actual Cost', 27 January 2010, http://blog.nielsen.com/nielsenwire/online_mobile/under-aged-texting-usage-and-actual-cost/ (accessed 10 February 2010); and 'Factsheet: The US Media Universe', 5 January 2011, www.nielsen.com/us/en/insights/news/2011/factsheet-the-u-s-media-universe.html (accessed 5 August 2014).

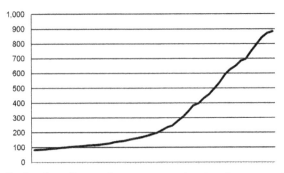

FIGURE 4.1 Ratio of media supply to consumption in minutes per day per household in the United States, 1960–2005
(after W. Russell Neuman et al.)

unabashed, but in altered, multi-media form. The average number of televisions per US household is 2.5; nearly a third of households have four or more televisions. Each week, Americans watch roughly thirty-five hours of television and two hours of time-shifted television via DVR. In the last quarter of 2009, however, simultaneous use of the Internet while watching television reached 3.5 hours a month, up 35 per cent from the previous year; nearly 60 per cent now use the Internet while watching TV. Internet video watching is rising fast; so is the preference for watching videos on smart phones. The overall effect of these various trends is to transform households into media-saturated spaces. In 1960, there were typically 3.4 television stations per household, 8.2 radio stations, 1.1 newspapers, 1.5 recently purchased books and 3.6 magazines; the ratio of media supply to actual household media consumption was 82:1 (see Figure 4.1). By 2005, that figure had risen to 884:1; that is, nearly one thousand minutes of mediated content available for each minute available for users to access content of various kinds.[7]

The shift towards high-intensity, multi-media usage within the daily lives of people, or communicative abundance as it is called throughout this book, is by no means restricted to the United States. The Asia and Pacific region is arguably the laboratory of future patterns. Quite aside from its robust oral cultures,[8] the region currently accounts for the

---

[7] W. Russell Neuman, Yong Jin Park and Elliot Panek, 'Tracking the Flow of Information into the Home', *International Journal of Communication*, 6 (2012), 1022–1041.

[8] The BBC's chief reporter for two decades in India, Mark Tully, notes the continuing importance of word-of-mouth communication within a society increasingly structured by various other means of communication: 'Anyone who has joined a group of villagers

highest global share of Internet users (more than 40 per cent of the total). Its telecommunications markets are rapidly expanding; and with cheaper, more reliable and faster connectivity rapidly becoming a reality throughout the region, the penetration of daily and institutional life by new tools of communication and user-generated information seems bound to grow, especially in democratic countries such as India and Indonesia, whose young people show a remarkable capacity for experimentation. Japan, whose citizens on average watch television four hours a day, is the country with the most avid bloggers globally, posting more than one million blogs per month. Each of its well-entrenched social networking sites and game portals – Mixi, Gree and Mobage-town – has over 20 million registered users. Everywhere in the region, the take-up rate of new media is striking. Micro-blogging (Twitter use in India, for instance) and social networking is all the rage. Australians spend more time on social media sites (nearly seven hours per month) than any other country in the world. Every month in South Korea, the leading social networking site, Naver, attracts 95 per cent of Internet users. The trend is not confined to single territorial states; throughout the region, despite barriers of language, there are signs of rapidly thickening cross-border connections, with many global cross-links. The patterns of regional and global interconnectivity are helped along by many interesting and important trends, including the fact that three-quarters of the world's Internet population has now visited Facebook, Twitter, Wikipedia, YouTube or some other social network/blogging site; that Internet users spend on average almost six hours per month on these sites in a variety of languages; and that some of these sites are now fully multi-lingual, as in the case of Wikipedia, which (by late 2012) contained more than twenty-three million entries, less than a fifth [4.1million] of which were in the English language.

WILD THINKING

Pushed here and there by such trends, it is unsurprising that the developing culture of communicative abundance stokes political visions. With more than a million new devices – desktop computers, mobile phones,

huddled over a transistor set in the dim light of a lantern listening to news from a foreign radio station knows that the spread of information is not limited to the number of sets in a village. Go to that village in the morning, and you will learn that the information heard on that radio has reached far beyond the listenership too', see 'Broadcasting in India: An Under-Exploited Resource', in Asharani Mathur (ed.), *The Indian Media: Illusion, Delusion and Reality. Essays in Honour of Prem Bhatia* (Delhi: Rupa, 2006), pp. 285–286.

televisions and other gadgets – hooked up each day to the Internet, the current revolution is said to have upset standard business models, generated unexpected wealth and changed the lives of millions of people. Sometimes seen as a bulldozer or likened to a great flattener of the world, the new mode of communicative abundance is rated a challenger of all settled hierarchies of power and authority.[9] It fuels hopeful talk of digital democracy, online publics, cyber-citizens and wiki-government. Some speak of a third stage of democratic evolution, in which the spirit and substance of ancient assembly democracy are reincarnated in wired form. 'Telecommunications', or so runs the argument, 'can give every citizen the opportunity to place questions of their own on the public agenda and participate in discussions with experts, policymakers and fellow citizens'.[10] Others promote visions of a 'connected' digital world where 'citizens hold their own governments accountable' and 'all of humanity has equal access to knowledge and power' (the words used by former US Secretary of State Hillary Clinton during an address at Washington's Newseum[11]). In the spirit of the revolution, some pundits venture further. They draw the conclusion that the 'advent and power of connection technologies', with their ever faster computing power, their accelerating shift from the one-to-many geometry of radio and television broadcasting towards many-to-many communication patterns, implies there is something like a 'natural' affinity between communicative abundance and democracy, understood (roughly) as a type of government and a way of life in which power is subject to permanent public scrutiny, chastening and control by citizens and their representatives.[12] Communicative abundance and democracy are thought of as conjoined twins. The stunning revolutionary process and product innovations happening in the field of communications fuel the dispersal and public accountability of power, or so it is supposed.

There is much to be said (it seems) in support of the claim. There are indeed positive, important, exciting, even intoxicating things happening

---

[9] Thomas L. Friedman, *The World Is Flat: A Brief History of the Twenty-first Century* (New York: Farrar, Straus & Giroux, 2005).

[10] Lawrence K. Grossman, *Electronic Republic: Reshaping Democracy in the Information Age* (New York: Penguin, 1996).

[11] US Secretary of State Hillary Clinton, 'Remarks on Internet Freedom', an address delivered at the Newseum, Washington DC, 21 January 2010, www.state.gov/secretary/rm/2010/01/135519.htm (accessed 20 March 2010).

[12] See Eric Schmidt and Jared Cohen, 'The Digital Disruption: Connectivity and the Diffusion of Power', *Foreign Affairs*, 89 (2010), 75–85.

inside the swirling galaxy of communicative abundance. So let more carefully at the details. In examining the affinities between communicative abundance and democracy, a term which so far has been used loosely, several strictures need to be borne in mind, beginning with McLuhan's prudent warning: since every new communication medium tends to cast a 'spell' on its users, in effect imposing 'its own assumptions, bias, and values' on the unwary, seducing them into a 'subliminal state of Narcissus trance', a measure of analytic detachment and diffidence is necessary when analysing and evaluating its social and political impact.[13] The need for detachment implies something positive: the cool-headed analysis of a new historical mode of communication can alert us to its novelties, make (more) visible what previously was less than obvious, so alerting us, in matters of democracy, to its many positive and negative dynamics. That is not to say that interpretations of communicative abundance can 'master' its elusive qualities. Mastery is reserved for the deities; just as any speaker of a language can never comprehensively follow and practise its rules and anticipate and control its past and present and future effects, so the dynamic contours of communicative abundance will retain a measure of elusiveness. Hence this book attempts nothing like what Germans call a *Gesamtdarstellung*, a complete picture of communicative abundance and its dynamics. Nor does it suppose that in future, in some other shape or form, a comprehensive account might be possible. There is much too much dynamic reality for that to happen. The complexity of communicative abundance is too complex, too elusive to be captured in smooth or slick formulae, in propositions based on statistics extracted by using blunt-edged criteria, in hard-and-fast rules, in confident predictions based on the truth of things. We could say that communicative abundance is a modest mistress. She prefers to keep close to her chest more than a few of her secrets.

When it comes to mediated communication with others, we live in a strange new world of confusing unknowns, a thoroughly media-saturated universe cluttered with means and methods of communication whose dynamic social and political effects have the capacity to hypnotise us, even to overwhelm our senses. These puzzling novelties and unknowns are not easily decoded, partly for epistemological and methodological reasons. Put simply, the facts of communicative abundance do not speak for themselves; they do not reveal their riddles spontaneously, of their

---

[13] McLuhan, *Understanding Media*, p. 7.

own volition, without our help. Contrary to those who think of the study of political communications as an empirical 'science', the confusing novelties of communicative abundance cannot be deciphered purely through 'objective' empirical investigation; that is, by cross-referring to so-called brute facts and the corresponding data sets that function as ultimate arbiters of what we know and don't know about the world of communicative abundance. The so-called 'facts' cannot rescue us by guiding and putting right our heads from a distance. This is not just because there are just too many available 'facts' to be grasped as such, so that selective biases (the setting aside of certain 'facts') are inevitable in each and every effort to produce 'objective' knowledge of our media-saturated world (this was the conclusion famously drawn by Max Weber[14]). The problem runs deeper, for 'facts' are always artefacts. How the 'facts' of communicative abundance appear to us, and what strategic and normative significance they have for us, very much depends upon a combination of forces, including the language frameworks through which people who communicate see themselves and express their own situations, and through which the analysts of communicative abundance and its complex dynamics also structure their own research goals and methods. In the age of communicative abundance, 'thick' descriptions, with as many details of the context and the motives and moves of actors, are mandatory. Yet thick descriptions are themselves artefacts. They are always and inescapably structured by frameworks of theoretical interpretation. The key point is this: in efforts to grasp and make sense of complex realities, perspectives are not 'detachable' from empirical methods. Interpretative frameworks do not have a secondary or subsidiary status. They are not barriers to 'adequate' descriptions of 'objective realities', or dispensable luxuries. They are rather vitally important conditions of making sense of the webs of communicative abundance within which people interact, more or less purposefully and meaningfully, for multiple ends using multiple means. In matters of communication, the principle sketched by Einstein is about right: not everything that can be counted counts, and not everything that counts can be counted.

Since the age of communicative abundance brims with puzzling novelties, many old ways of thinking and interpreting media, power and politics are now rendered suspect. Sentimental longings for imaginary better times, when life supposedly was shaped by high-quality national

---

[14] Max Weber, '"Objectivity" in Social Science and Social Policy', in *The Methodology of the Social Sciences* (New York: The Free Press, 1949), p. 110.

newspapers and BBC-style public service broadcasting, are not an option – not even when accompanied by understandable complaints about how the age of communicative abundance fails to overcome language barriers, racist and nationalist hatreds, untamed corporate power and other ills of our time.[15] Awareness of the novelties of our age should not be drowned in outpourings of nostalgia, or pessimism. We need as well to be aware that extrapolations from current trends and predictions about the ultimate uses of new communications technologies are fraught, especially when sustained by analogies to the past. When faced with unfamiliar situations, it is always tempting to suppose that new media will carry on doing familiar things (enabling us freely to communicate with others, for instance) but in more efficient and effective, faster and cheaper ways. Just as the railway was called the 'iron horse' and the automobile the 'horseless carriage', or telephones were viewed in terms of the telegraph, as tools for communicating emergencies or important news, rather than tools for other, more casual purposes, so it is tempting to interpret the new dynamics of communicative abundance through terms inherited from our predecessors. The enticement should be resisted. Presumptions that have outlived their uselessness must be abandoned. What is needed are bold new probes, fresh-minded perspectives, 'wild' concepts that enable different and meaningful ways of seeing things, more discriminating methods of recognising the novelties of our times, the democratic opportunities they offer and the counter-trends that have the potential to snuff out democratic politics.

But what does the call for 'wild' new perspectives actually imply? Minimally, it means abandoning dogmas, clichés and bland formulae, including (to take a short string of examples) the commonplace choice between naïve, simple-minded 'cyber-utopian' beliefs in the liberating nature of on-line communication and the trite mirror-image verdict that communicative abundance is equally a tool of repression, that all techniques and tools of communication, including the Internet, can be used equally for good or bad purposes, and that everything depends upon the context in which they are used.[16] In matters of method, 'wild' new perspectives certainly imply the need for suspicion of neologisms which have a false-start quality about them.

---

[15] James Curran, 'The Internet: Prophecy and Reality', public lecture at the Justice and Police Museum, Sydney, 21 September 2011.
[16] Evgeny Morozov, *The Net Delusion: The Dark Side of Internet Freedom* (New York: PublicAffairs, 2011).

A case in point is the word 'cyberspace'. An artefact of times when computerised digital networks had still not substantially penetrated everyday life and formal institutional settings, the term is not seriously used in this book simply because it misleadingly conveys the sense that things that happen in and through the Internet are not quite 'real', or 'real' in some different way, in a world governed by different principles than those of the corporeal world. Talk of cyberspace radically underestimates the growth of cutting-edge media technologies (the so-called 'Internet of things') that are now structuring people's lives. Examples include robot sensors and microcomputers embedded in objects as varied as kitchen appliances, surveillance cameras, cars and mobile phone apps; and smart glasses that enable wearers, with a touch of the frame or shake of the head or verbal command, to take pictures, record and send videos, search the Web, or receive breaking news or walking directions, without so much as lifting a finger. Other examples include wearable wireless gadgets known as 'sociometers', gadgets attached to the human body or seamlessly integrated into human clothing for the purpose of measuring and analysing people's communication patterns (an example is the name tag device called 'HyGenius', used in hospital and restaurant bathrooms to check that employees are properly washing their hands). And there are wired-up 'smart' cities, such as Korea's Songdu and Portugal's PlanIT Valley, where 'smart' appliances pump constant data streams into 'smart grids' that measure and regulate flows of people, traffic and energy use.[17] In the face of such trends, old-fashioned talk of cyberspace is just that: old-fashioned. It goes hand-in-hand with mistaken questions – such as 'What effect is the Internet having on democratic politics?' – when the priority is rather to understand the origins and development of digital communication networks and tools and the new power dynamics and effects of their revolutionary techniques and tools.

Wild perspectives imply the need for something more: questioning and abandoning outdated clichés, including all descriptions of communication media as the 'fourth estate', a misleading metaphor that originated with Edmund Burke and the pamphlet and newspaper battles of the French Revolution. Contemporary accounts of communication media that

---

[17] These various trends are discussed in Stefano Marzano, Josephine Green, C. van Heerden and J. Mama (eds.), *New Nomads: An Exploration of Wearable Electronics by Philips* (Rotterdam: Uitgeverij, 2001) and Alex Pentland, *Honest Signals: How They Shape Our World* (Cambridge, MA: MIT Press, 2008). For a striking experimental view, using machine vision footage, of how electronic sensors and robots view the world, see http://vimeo.com/36239715 (accessed 22 October 2012).

suppose the continuing validity of that metaphor, for instance analyses of the ideal functions of 'media systems' as 'gatekeepers', independent 'agenda setters', or as 'the fourth branch of government', or even the 'Fifth Estate',[18] are less than persuasive. Their sense of the political geography of media is downright misleading. Communicative abundance dissolves divisions between 'the media' and other institutions. All spheres of life, from the most intimate everyday milieux through to large-scale global organisations, operate *within* heavily mediated settings in which the meaning of messages is constantly changing and often at odds with the intentions of their creators.[19] To say this is not to indulge contemporary talk of 'the media', which is much too abstract and all too loose; in matters of media everything matters, certainly, but not everything connects simply, or is distributed in complex ways that can easily be figured out.

The complex dynamics of contemporary forms of connectivity is a strong reason why disciplinary divisions between political science and communications and other scholarly fields need to be bridged. It is also why democracy and media must be analysed simultaneously, and in new ways – in part, by leaving behind worn-out concepts and perspectives that we have inherited from the era of print culture, radio, television and Hollywood cinema. The following pages show for instance why talk of 'the informed citizen' has become an unhelpful cliché. Engaged citizens whose heads are stuffed with unlimited quantities of 'information' about a 'reality' that they're on top of: that is an utterly implausible and – yes – anti-democratic ideal which dates from the late nineteenth century. Favoured originally by the champions of a restricted educated franchise, and by interests who rejected partisan politics grounded in the vagaries and injustices of everyday social life, the ideal of the 'informed citizen' was elitist. It remains an intellectualist ideal, unsuited to the age of communicative abundance, which needs 'wise citizens' who know that they do not know everything, or so this book argues. It proposes as well the need to set aside once-fashionable presumptions, popular among intellectuals, for instance that the decline of print culture and the advent of electronic media has been an unmitigated disaster; or the prejudices

---

[18] Hannah Arendt, 'Lying in Politics: Reflections on the Pentagon Papers', in *Crises of the Republic* (New York: Harcourt Brace, 1972), p. 45; W.H. Dutton, 'The Fifth Estate Emerging through the Network of Networks', *Prometheus*, 27 (2009), 1–15.

[19] John B. Thompson, *The Media and Modernity: A Social Theory of the Media* (Cambridge: Polity Press, 1995), pp. 34–41.

that all television is children's television; or that the only likeable thing about television is its fleetingness; or that televisions are dream machines that remove citizens, tragically, far from the reality of what is actually happening in the world;[20] or that television-led mass media transform 'the public' into an apathetic blob, 'a black hole into which the political efforts of politicians, advocates of causes, the media, and the schools disappear with hardly a trace'.[21] This book casts doubt on such presumptions, which draw silently upon the older, wider prejudice that 'modern' broadcasting systems breed listless people who live off daily doses of unreality. It is no longer (if it ever was) accurate to say, as the famous American philosopher John Dewey once said, that we 'live exposed to the greatest flood of mass suggestion that any people has ever experienced'. The arts of creating, manipulating and controlling public opinion through media still pose serious problems for democracy. But the warnings issued during the early years of mass broadcasting, during the 1920s and 1930s, need fundamentally to be rethought. It is no longer straightforwardly the case, as Edward Bernays, the godfather of propaganda, put it, that 'propaganda is the executive arm of the invisible government'; or that 'propaganda is to a democracy what violence is to a dictatorship'; or that if 'the people' want to be 'free of chains of iron' and in the name of democracy refuse blindly to 'love, honor, and obey' leaders, then the people must accept the 'chains of silver' produced by organised seduction and propaganda, what Adorno and Horkheimer later called the 'culture industry'.[22]

---

[20] Pierre Bourdieu, *On Television* (New York: The New Press, 1996).
[21] Murray Edelman, *Constructing the Political Spectacle* (Chicago, IL: University of Chicago Press, 1988), p. 8.
[22] John Dewey, 'The United States, Incorporated', in *The Later Works, 1925–1953*, Vol. V (Carbondale, IL: Southern Illinois University Press, 2008), p. 61; Edward L. Bernays, *Propaganda* (New York: Horace Liveright, 1928), p. 48; Harold D. Lasswell, *Propaganda Technique in the World War* (London: K. Paul, Trench, Trubner, 1927), p. 227; Jacques Ellul, *Propaganda: The Formation of Men's Attitudes* (New York: Knopf, 1965), p. 132: 'Governmental propaganda suggests that public opinion demand this or that decision; it provokes the will of a people, who spontaneously would say nothing. But, once evoked, formed, and crystallized on a point, that will becomes the people's will; and whereas the government really acts on its own, it gives the impression of obeying public opinion – after first having built that public opinion. The point is to make the masses demand of the government what the government has already decided to do'; Theodor Adorno and Max Horkheimer, 'The Culture Industry: Enlightenment as Mass Deception', in *Dialectic of Enlightenment* (New York: Herder & Herder, 1972). Bertrand Russell ('China's Entanglements [1922]', in *Uncertain Paths to Freedom: Russia and China, 1919–22* [London and New York, 2000], p. 360) summed up the old view of propaganda thus: 'It is much easier than it used to be to spread misinformation, and,

So here is the rub: just as in the sixteenth century, when the production of printed books and the efforts to read codex type required a fundamental shift of perspective, so today, in the emergent world of communicative abundance, a whole new mental effort is required to make sense of how democracies in various regions of the world are being shaped and reshaped by new tools and rhetoric of communication – and why our very thinking about democracy must also change.

DEMOCRATISATION OF INFORMATION

But what is the most fruitful way to proceed? Which are the key media trends that we need to note, to interpret, to internalise in our thinking about democracy in the age of communicative abundance? A handful of trends seem pivotal. They cry out for careful analysis infused with a strong sense of its own historicity.

Let's begin with the most obvious political effect of communicative abundance: the democratisation of information. Thanks to cheap and easy methods of digital reproduction, we live in times of new information banks and what has been called information spreading, a sudden marked widening of access to published materials previously unavailable to publics, or formerly available only to restricted circles of users. The democratisation process involves the dismantling of information privileges formerly available only on a restricted basis to elites. It operates simultaneously on three intersecting planes.

One flank involves users gaining access from a distance to materials that were once available only within a restricted geographical radius, or only to users prepared to travel great distances and to foot the costs of living locally for a time, in order to make use of the otherwise inaccessible materials. Symbolised by the online editions of *The New York Times*, *The Hindu*, *El País* and *Der Spiegel*, democratisation in this sense refers to a dramatic reduction of the tyranny of distance, the radical widening of spatial horizons, a dramatic expansion of the catchment area of possible users of published materials. It is practically reinforced by a second sense of information democratisation: a great expansion in the numbers of potential users of materials, so that anyone with a computer and Web access, perhaps using tools such as Kindles, Nooks, iPads, or whatever tools succeed them, can now gain access to materials, simply at the click

> owing to democracy, the spread of misinformation is more important than in former times to the holders of power. Hence the increase in circulation of newspapers.'

of a mouse. The online music search engines Grooveshark and Spotify and Piratebay.org, a Swedish website that hosts torrent files, are representative of this sense of democratisation, which means the enhanced availability of materials to people, often at zero cost, on a common access basis instead of a privileged private right basis. Then there is a third and perhaps most consequential sense of the democratisation of information: the process of assembling scattered and disparate materials that were never previously available, formatting them as new data sets that are then made publicly available to users through entirely new pathways. Well-known examples include the multi-million entry encyclopaedia Wikipedia; the Computer History Museum (located in Mountain View California); YouTube, whose 1.3 billion users (in 2017) uploaded at least 300 hours of video footage per minute; the most popular Farsi-language website balatarin.com (a crowd-sourced platform that enables registered users to post and rank their favourite articles); and TheEuropeanLibrary.org, which is a consortium of libraries of the nearly fifty Member States in the Council of Europe, accessed through a single search engine, in three dozen languages.

Do these instances of democratised information have a wider historical significance? They do, but not because they signal the replacement of old-fashioned modern 'narrative' by new computer-age 'databases', as some scholars have proposed.[23] True, the new databases are not normally arranged as intelligible narratives. They do not tell stories structured by a beginning and an end. They are indeed disparate collections of 'information', multi-media materials arranged so that within the collection each item tends to have the same significance as all the others. Yet it does not follow that 'database and narrative are natural enemies'. Just the opposite: exactly because the new information sources are not presented as moral sermons, they are more amenable to being used as the 'raw material' of chosen narratives by publics that enjoy access to them. It is therefore unsurprising that the contemporary use of digital networks to spread all kinds of informative material to ever wider publics has politically enlivening effects. The democratisation of information serves as power steering for hungry minds previously handicapped by inefficient communication. Some observers even hail the advent of times in which citizens regularly 'stand on the shoulders of a lot more giants at the same

---

[23] Lev Manovich, *The Language of New Media* (Cambridge, MA: MIT Press, 2001), p. 225: '[D]atabase and narrative are natural enemies. Competing for the same territory of human culture, each claims an exclusive right.'

time'.²⁴ Such claims invite comparisons with the Reformation in Europe, which was triggered in part by the conviction of dissident Christian believers that access to printed copies of the Bible could be widened, that there were no spiritual or earthly reasons why reading its pages should be restricted to a select few who were proficient in Latin, and that those who could read or had ears to hear were entitled to join reading groups and to savour the pleasures of pondering and disputing printed sermons, spiritual autobiographies and ethical guides to life in all its stages and forms.²⁵ Such comparisons are probably overdrawn, but there can be little doubt that when measured in terms of equal and easy accessibility to materials whose availability was formerly restricted, communicative abundance opens gates and tears down fences separating producers and users of information, some of which is highly specialised, so that new and vitally important information banks become accessible to many more users, often at great distances, more or less at the same time, at zero or low cost.

The trend is for the moment especially powerful in digitally reproduced collections of rare or hard-to-obtain materials. Some developments affect quite particular users groups. Each year, for instance, the electronic collection known as Romantic Circles distributes around 3.5 million pages of material to users living in more than 160 countries. Art historians now have ready access to the Digital Michelangelo Project, which aims to make available to researchers high-quality laser copies of the artist's three-dimensional works. Scholars and members of the general public from around the world have access to such collections as the East London Theatre Archive of many thousands of theatre programmes; the Catalogue of Digitised Medieval Manuscripts; and the Prehistoric Stones of Greece Project. Then there are data banks that (potentially) have wide public appeal because they affect collective memories. Examples include an initiative called American Memory, sponsored by the Library of Congress, which aims digitally to preserve sound recordings, maps, prints and images that form part of the history of the United States. Harvard University Library is planning to digitise its vast collection of Ukrainian-language material, the world's largest, much of it otherwise destroyed or lost in that country during a twentieth century of horrific violence.

---

[24] William Calvin, 'The Shoulders of Giants', in John Brockman (ed.), *Is the Internet Changing the Way You Think? The Net's Impact on our Minds and Future* (New York: HarperCollins, 2011), pp. 66–69.

[25] See Andrew Cambers, *Godly Reading: Print, Manuscript and Puritanism in England, 1580–1720* (Cambridge: Cambridge University Press, 2011).

Other examples include the Holocaust Collection of audio clips, maps, texts, photographs and images of artefacts; and the databases built by citizen networks such as the Association for the Recovery of Historical memory in Spain. These various experiments exemplify the importance of democratised information in combating the twin political dangers of amnesia and confabulation. By preserving details of past traumas, publicly accessible information banks keep alive the politics of memory, in effect extending votes to a constituency that is normally neglected: the dead.

Equally impressive are the 'born digital' collections that are being formed to combat the possible permanent loss of certain materials circulated through the Web itself. Its birth and growth has been synonymous with the higgledy piggledy proliferation of websites, many of which are ephemeral, structured by different and incompatible metadata and often resistant to search engines – hence prone to easy disappearance into the thin air of what some still call cyberspace. In the United States, where government agencies were using e-mail from the mid-1980s, available evidence suggests that for the following two decades most White House correspondence has been lost (on average six million e-mail messages were generated annually by the two Clinton administrations alone). The disappearance of electronic data from lower levels of government, from non-governmental organisations such as universities and in general from private users of various parts of the Web, has been even more extreme. Alarm bells have rung about the dangers of obliterating memories from civil society and government; and, despite shortages of money and technical and legal difficulties, plans for storing and saving digital material are flourishing, along with initiatives such as the Arthur and Elizabeth Schlesinger Library's 'Capturing Women's Voices', a collection of postings by women from a wide range of blogs.[26]

THE NEW PUBLICITY

When considering the political effects of the unfinished communications revolution, there is a second salient trend, one so far mentioned only in passing: communicative abundance stirs up disputes among citizens and their representatives about the definition and ethical and political significance of the public–private division. Publicity is now directed at all things

---

[26] The background is summarised in Robert Darnton, 'The Future of Libraries', in *The Case for Books: Past, Present, and Future* (New York: Public Affairs, 2009), pp. 50–53.

personal; the realm that used to be called 'private' becomes publicly contested; and backlashes in defence of the 'private' develop. Under conditions of communicative abundance, privacy battles are constantly fought, lost or won. Awash in vast oceans of circulating information that is portable and easily reproduced, individuals daily practise the art of selectively disclosing and concealing details of their private selves; anxiety about privacy is commonplace; decisions about whether and to whom they give out their 'co-ordinates' remain unresolved.[27]

Whatever is thought of the disadvantages of the whole process, the rough riding or 'outing' of private life ensures not only that the public–private boundary is the source of constant legal, political and ethical disputes: controversies about the private have a long-term positive effect. They teach citizens that the personal is political, that the realm of the private, once hidden away from the eyes and ears of others but still said by many to be necessary for getting risky and dodgy things done in life, is embedded in fields of power in which rogues take refuge and injustices result. Gone are the days when privacy could be regarded as 'natural', as a given bedrock or sub-stratum of taken-for-granted experiences and meanings. More than a generation ago, the Moravian philosopher Edmund Husserl thought in that way about the 'world of everyday life' (*Lebenswelt*). He proposed that daily interactions among people are typically habitual. Everyday life has a definite 'a priori' quality. It is social interaction guided by acts of *empathy* among people who believe and expect others to behave more or less like themselves. This inter-subjectivity is structured by unquestioned presumptions of mutual familiarity. Actors suppose a 'natural attitude' to themselves and to the world about them; they interact on a bedrock of taken-for-granted beliefs that their own ways of seeing and doing things are 'naturally' shared by others.[28]

Whatever its level of former plausibility, this way of thinking about the everyday world is now obsolete. Those who still think in terms of everyday life as a barrier against the outside world, perhaps even as a safe and secluded haven of freedom in a world dominated by large-scale, powerful

---

[27] Christena Nippert-Eng, *Islands of Privacy: Selective Concealment and Disclosure in Everyday Life* (Chicago, IL: University of Chicago Press, 2010); John B. Thompson, 'Shifting Boundaries of Public and Private Life', *Theory, Culture & Society*, 28, 4 (July 2011), 49–70.

[28] Edmund Husserl, *The Crisis of European Sciences and Transcendental Phenomenology*, trans. D. Carr (Evanston, IL: Northwestern University Press, 1970 [1936]). Compare the line of analysis of contemporary trends by Phil Agre and Marc Rotenberg (eds.), *Technology and Privacy: The New Landscape* (Cambridge, MA: MIT Press, 1997).

institutions, are out of touch. The reality is that everyday life is no longer a substratum of taken for granted things and people. In the age of communicative abundance, for instance, users of the Internet find their personal data are the engine fuel of a booming web-based market economy; traditional methods of matching advertising to the content of people's interests are rapidly giving way to a world structured by digital 'cookies', small pieces of software installed on personal computers that function as unique identifiers of what users are looking at, and can store the tracked information, so building up a picture of the demographics and interests of users that are of high market value to companies such as Facebook and Google, and to their advertising clients. The 'de-siloing' (as they say) of personal data allows advertisers to track users with precision; a class-action lawsuit settled out of court by Facebook revealed that even the 'likes' posted by its users can be deployed as 'sponsored stories' (advertisements) for marketing purposes.[29] Such tactics are part of a deepening trend in which no private matter or intimate topic is left unmediated; that is, cordoned off from media coverage. The more 'private' experiences are, the more 'publicity' they seem to get – especially when what is at stake are matters of taste and consumption, sex and violence, birth and death, personal hopes, fears, skulduggery and tragedy. It is as if we have entered a twenty-first century version of the court of Louis XVI, a world where the waking (*le lever*) as well as the going to bed (*le coucher*) and other intimate details of His Majesty were regarded as 'public' events that induced a sense of wondrous astonishment among all who witnessed them (Asian court societies, such as that of imperial Japan, whose monarchy is a modern European import, also defined the public realm as the courtly household of the ruler, whose 'private' world, as we would see it, was deemed worthy of display to intrigued and sometimes admiring others[30]).

The comparison of our times with the age of Louis XVI is far-fetched, of course; but there is little doubt that in today's media-saturated societies, private life is becoming ever less private. Government agencies install 'black box' surveillance devices within Internet traffic. Digital identities of individuals are mined and tracked by companies. Personal

---

[29] See Somini Sengupta, 'On Facebook, "Likes" Become Ads', www.nytimes.com/2012/06/01/technology/so-much-for-sharing-his-like.html?_r=0; and Dan Levine, 'Facebook "Sponsored Stories" Class Action Settled', www.huffingtonpost.com/2012/05/22/facebook-sponsored-stories-class-action-settlement_n_1537182.html.

[30] Takashi Fujitani, *Splendid Monarchy: Power and Pageantry in Modern Japan* (Berkeley, CA: University of California Press, 1996).

data are big business. Techniques of 'data capture' develop traction. We live in a surveillance economy, in which companies known as data brokers, also called information re-sellers, gather and then market to other companies, including advertisers, hundreds or thousands of details about the consumption patterns, racial or ethnic identity, health concerns, social networks and financial arrangements of most individuals who go online. Cheap and user-friendly methods of reproduction and access to portable networked tools of communication meanwhile ensure that we live in the age of hyper-coverage. Everything that happens in the fields of power stretching from the bedroom and bathroom to the boardroom to the battlefield seems to be up for media grabs. With the flick of a switch or the click of a camera button, the world of the private is suddenly public. Unmediated privacy has become a thing of the past.

These are times in which the private lives of celebrities – their romances, parties, health, quarrels and divorces – are the interest and fantasy objects of millions of people. There is, thanks to genres such as Twitter, television talk shows and talkback radio, an endless procession of 'ordinary people' talking publicly about what privately turns them on, or off. We live in times when millions of people feel free to talk publicly about their private fears, fantasies, hopes and expectations, and to act as if they are celebrities by displaying details of their intimate selves on Facebook. We live in an age when things done in 'private' are big public stories. It is the era (say) in which so-called reality TV cuts from a scheduled afternoon programme to an armed and angry man – holding a hostage, he turns his shotgun on himself, or fires at the police, live, courtesy of a news helicopter, or outside broadcasting unit. There are moments when citizens themselves take things into their own hands, as when a woman spits racist comments to other passengers on a packed London bus, the incident is filmed and posted online, then after sparking a Twitter trend goes viral, attracting ten million viewers within a week. These are times in which things that were once kept quiet, for instance the abuse of children by priests of the Roman Catholic Church, are publicly exposed by newspapers and other media, with the help of the abused, who manage to unearth details of their molesters, sometimes quite by accident thanks to the new tools of communication. And we live in an age when privately shot video footage proves that soldiers in war zones fired on their own side, tortured prisoners, robbed innocent civilians of their lives, raped women and terrorised children.

The culture and practices of communicative abundance cut deeply into everyday life in other ways. Nurtured by aggressive and prying styles of journalism, and by easy-to-use portable media tools, communicative abundance destroys the early modern, originally European supposition that property ownership, market conditions, household life, emotions, and biological events like birth and death are givens, or God-given. All these dimensions of life lose their 'naturalness'. Their contingency comes to the fore; they become potentially the subjects of public questioning and political action. For the same reason, communicative abundance cuts to shreds the older, originally Greek presumption that democratic public life requires pre-political foundations, the tight-lipped privacy (literally, as the Greeks thought of it, the idiocy) that marks the *oikos*, the realm of household and market life in which life's basic needs are produced and distributed and consumed. In the age of media saturation, the privacy of the realm of the so-called private market economy disappears. The injustices and inequalities it harbours are no longer seen as necessary or inevitable, as nobody else's business.

Just as the democratisation of information stirs up public controversies, so the de-privatisation and democratisation of the private power within daily life is both a complicated and heavily contested process. It disturbs lived certainties and presumptions that once seemed to be 'natural'. Yet while the supposed 'a priori' qualities of everyday life are questioned and challenged, backlashes against the whole process develop. Political objections to the destruction of privacy flourish. Some observers argue, extending and upending an eighteenth-century simile, that communicative abundance robs citizens of their identities, that it resembles not a goddess of liberty, but a succubus, a female demon supposed to rape sleeping men and collect and pass on their sperm to other women. Switching similes, some denounce the mounting pressures to expose the secrets of the private as 'totalitarian'.[31] Other critics express things differently by denouncing the killer instincts of high-pressure media coverage of the private; famously spelled out by Janet Malcolm in *The Journalist and the Murderer* (1990), the accusation of media murder is sometimes literally the leitmotif of media events, as when intense publicity tracked the death of Princess Diana following a high-speed car chase by journalists

---

[31] See the comment of Jacques Derrida in Jacques Derrida and Maurizio Ferraris, *A Taste for the Secret* (Malden, MA: Blackwell, 2001), p. 59: 'I have a taste for the secret, it clearly has to do with not-belonging; I have an impulse of fear or terror in the face of a political space, for example, a public space that makes no room for the secret. For me, the demand that everything be paraded in the public square and that there be no internal forum is a glaring sign of the totalitarianization of democracy.'

dubbed *paparazzi*.[32] Still other critics, sensing that a private life is vital for cultivating a sound sense of self, deliberately choose *not* to send tweets, *not* to purchase a smart phone, or *not* to use e-mail. Running in the same direction are calls for journalists to respect others' privacy, to raise their ethical standards and to exercise moral self-restraint as defined by established codes of conduct; challenges to spam and other types of invasive messages; data vault schemes (offered by companies such as Reputation. com) that allow individuals, for a price, to store and manage their private data; and legal cases that aim to prevent journalists from unlimited digging and fishing expeditions, as in the controversies surrounding the 2011–2012 Murdoch press 'hacking' scandal and the major (unsuccessful) appeal brought before the European Court of Human Rights by Max Mosley against the British newspaper *News of the World* for its headline story that he had engaged in a 'sick Nazi orgy with five hookers'.[33]

Some critics of de-privatisation meanwhile call publicly for the legal right of citizens to delete all present-day traces of their past 'private' communications with others. Digital communications technologies are seen as double-edged sharp swords: while individuals find themselves taking full advantage of communicative abundance, their lives are potentially harmed by digitisation, cheap storage, easy retrieval, global access,

---

[32] See for example Tina Brown, *The Diana Chronicles* (New York: Doubleday, 2007). The ethical dangers of media prying into the intimate lives of others are articulated by Janet Malcolm, *The Journalist and the Murderer* (New York: Vintage Books, 1990), p. 1, where the professional journalist is seen as 'a kind of confidence man, preying on people's vanity, ignorance or loneliness, gaining their trust and betraying them without remorse. Like the credulous widow who wakes up one day to find the charming young man and all her savings gone, so the consenting subject of a piece of non-fiction learns – when the article or book appears – *his* hard lesson. Journalists justify their treachery in various ways according to their temperaments. The more pompous talk about freedom of speech and "the public's right to know"; the least talented talk about Art; the seemliest murmur about earning a living.'

[33] See the judgement of the European Court of Human Rights (Fourth Section), *Mosley v. the United Kingdom* (Application 48009/08; Strasbourg, 10 May 2011), paragraphs 131–132. Referring to Articles 8 and 10 of the European Convention on Human Rights, the court recognised the fundamental importance of situations where 'information at stake is of a private and intimate nature and there is no public interest in its dissemination'. It noted as well that 'the private lives of those in the public eye have become a highly lucrative commodity for certain sectors of the media'. The court nevertheless warned of the 'chilling effect' of pre-notification requirements and reaffirmed the principle, which it applied to this particular case, that the 'publication of news' about persons holding public office 'contributes to the variety of information available to the public'. It concluded with a reminder of the 'limited scope' for applying 'restrictions on the freedom of the press to publish material which contributes to debate on matters of general public interest'.

and increasingly powerful software, which together conspire to increase the dangers of the everlasting digital memory of our private lives, for instance outdated information taken out of context, or compromising photos or messages accessed by employers, or political foes. According to these champions of privacy, whereas the invention of writing enabled humans to remember across generations and vast swathes of time, communicative abundance does something altogether different: it potentially threatens our individual and collective capacity to forget things that need to be forgotten. The past becomes ever present, ready to be recalled at the flick of a switch, or the click of a mouse. The trouble with digital systems, runs this line of criticism, is not only that they remember things that are sometimes better forgotten, it is that they hinder our ability to make sound decisions unencumbered by the past.[34] Meanwhile, acting on that point, a new generation of technically savvy privacy activists associated with networked bodies like Privacy International and the Open Rights Group has launched various public campaigns, for instance in favour of stricter application of expiration dates and the development of privacy-enhancing technologies (so-called PETs), and against publicly available geospatial information about private dwellings, government initiatives to regulate access to strong cryptography, the corporate abuse of consumer databases and unregulated wiretapping and hacking powers of media organisations.[35]

All these developments centred on the 'right to privacy' confirm the point that communicative abundance exposes the contingency and deep ambiguity of the private–public distinction famously defended, philosophically speaking, as a sacrosanct First Principle by nineteenth-century liberal thinkers such as the English political writer and parliamentarian John Stuart Mill and Germany's greatest philosopher of liberty, Wilhelm von Humboldt.[36] Their insistence that there are clear distinctions to be drawn between 'the private' (conceived as the sphere of self-regarding actions) and 'the public' (the sphere of other-affecting actions) no longer rings true. In the age of communicative abundance, privacy, defined as the ability of individuals to control how much of themselves they reveal to

---

[34] Viktor Mayer-Schönberger, *Delete: The Virtue of Forgetting in the Digital Age* (Princeton, NJ: Princeton University Press, 2011).

[35] Agre and Rotenberg (eds.), *Technology and Privacy*.

[36] John Stuart Mill, 'On Liberty' [1859] in John M. Robson (ed.), *Essays on Politics and Society* (Toronto, ON: University of Toronto Press, 1977), pp. 213–310; and Wilhelm von Humboldt, 'Of the Individual Man and the Highest Ends of His Existence', in *The Limits of State Action* (Cambridge: Cambridge University Press, 1969), pp. 16–21.

others, their 'right to be let alone',[37] is seen as a complicated and publicly contestable right. Disputes about privacy and its 'invasion' have a long-term political significance. They underscore not only growing public awareness of the contingent and reversible character of the public–private distinction – which is to say that the distinction is no longer readily seen, as it was seen by many nineteenth- and twentieth-century European liberals, as either a binary opposite set in stone or as having a divine, mysterious validity – but thanks to the communications revolution of our time, the private–public distinction is regarded instead as a precious but ambivalent inheritance from former times.

The sphere of 'the private' is seen as a fragile 'temporary resting place'[38] that usefully serves as a refuge from interference by others, but which can function just as well as a refuge for scoundrels. Put differently, communicative abundance exposes deep ambiguities within the private–public distinction. It encourages individuals and groups within civil society to think more flexibly and contextually about the public and the private. Citizens are forced to become aware that their 'private' judgements about matters of public importance can be distinguished from both actually existing and desirable norms that are shared publicly. They learn as well to accept that there are times when embarrassing publicity given to 'private' actions – 'outing' – is entirely justified, for instance when confronted with mendacious politicians, or with men who are duplicitous about their sexual preference, or even leaders (as in Berlusconi's Italy or Donald Trump's America) desperate to confirm that they are men.[39] Finally, citizens come to see that some things are definitely worth keeping private. They learn there are times when privacy – ensuring that certain matters are nobody else's business, that individuals and groups should not freely witness or comment upon their actions – is a precious inheritance.

---

[37] See the oft-cited Samuel D. Warren and Louis D. Brandeis, 'The Right to Privacy', *Harvard Law Review*, 4 (1890), 193–220.

[38] Richard Rorty, 'Introduction: Pragmatism and Philosophy', in *Consequences of Pragmatism* (Minneapolis, MN: The University of Minnesota Press, 1982), pp. xiii–xlvii.

[39] Confronted by magistrates with evidence of his involvement in an alleged prostitution ring, including wiretap evidence in which he boasted that he was only 'prime minister in my spare time', as well as complained that he needed to reduce the flow of women in the face of a 'terrible week' ahead (he was due to see leaders such as Pope Benedict, Nicolas Sarkozy, Angela Merkel and Gordon Brown), Prime Minister Silvio Berlusconi defended himself in a letter published in the Milan-based newspaper *Il Foglio*, whose editor served as minister in one of his former governments: 'I did nothing for which I must be ashamed … My private life is not a crime, my lifestyle may or may not please, it is personal, reserved and irreproachable' (17 September 2011).

That is why they favour keeping certain areas of social and political life 'private' – for instance through efforts by journalists to protect the identity of their sources – and why campaigns against governments' use of closed-circuit TV cameras and other forms of surveillance are therefore of vital public importance.

THE NEW MUCKRAKING

Aside from the democratisation of access to information and the politicisation of definitions of the private–public distinction, a third democratic trend is noteworthy: high-intensity efforts by citizens, journalists and monitory institutions to bombard power holders with 'publicity' and 'public exposure'. This third trend might be described as muckraking, a charming Americanism, an earthy neologism from the late nineteenth century, when it referred to a new style of journalism committed to the cause of publicly exposing corruption.[40] Writers like Lincoln Steffens, Ida Tarbell and Jacob Riis pictured themselves as public journalists writing for a public hungry for the facts of life in contemporary America. True to their name, they saw nothing sacrosanct about privacy. Publicity must be given to the private lives of the rich and powerful wherever and whenever 'the public interest' was at stake, they thought. To this end, they used new investigative techniques, such as the interview; under hails of protest (they were often condemned as busybodies and meddlers) they took advantage of the widening circulation of newspapers, magazines and books made possible by advertising, and by cheaper, mass methods of production and distribution, to write long and detailed articles, even entire books, to provide often sensational exposés of grimy governmental corruption and waste, business fraud and social deprivation.

Along these lines, the Pennsylvania-born journalist Nellie Bly (1864–1922) did something daring but dangerous: for Joseph Pulitzer's newspaper the *New York World* she faked insanity to publish an undercover exposé of a woman's lunatic asylum. Other muckrakers openly challenged political bosses and corporate fat cats. They questioned industrial progress at any price. The muckrakers took on profiteering, deception, low standards of public health and safety. They complained about child labour, prostitution and alcohol. They called for the renewal of urban life – for an end to slums in cities. By around 1905, the muckrakers

---

[40] Keane, *The Life and Death of Democracy*, pp. 341–347.

were a force to be reckoned with, as William Randolph Hearst demonstrated with his acquisition of *Cosmopolitan* magazine; its veteran reporter, David Graham Phillips, quickly launched a much-publicised series, called 'The Treason of the Senate', which poured scorn on senators, portraying them as pawns of industrialists and financiers, as corruptors of the principle that representatives should serve all of their constituents.

In the age of communicative abundance, the new muckrakers keep these themes alive and they do so by putting their finger on a perennial problem for which democracy is a solution: the power of elites always thrives on secrecy, silence and invisibility. Gathering behind closed doors and deciding things in peace and private quiet is their specialty. Little wonder then that in media-saturated societies, to put things paradoxically, unexpected 'leaks' and revelations become predictably commonplace. Everyday life is constantly ruptured by mediated 'events'.[41] These dramatised ruptures pose challenges to both the licit and the illicit. It is not just that stuff happens; media users ensure that shit happens. Muckraking becomes rife. There are moments when it even feels as if the whole world is run by rogues.

Muckraking has definite political effects on the standard institutions of representative democracy. It arguably deepens the already wide divisions that have opened up between parties, parliaments, politicians and the available means of communication. In recent decades, an accumulation of survey evidence suggests that citizens in many established democracies, although they strongly identify with democratic ideals, have grown more distrustful of politicians, doubtful about governing institutions and disillusioned and plain angry with leaders in the public sector.[42] The patterns of public disaffection with official 'politics' have much to do with the practise of muckraking under conditions of communicative abundance. Politicians are sitting ducks. The limited media presence and media vulnerability of parliaments is striking. Despite efforts at harnessing new digital media, parties have often been left flat-footed; they neither own nor control their media outlets and they have lost much of the astonishing energy displayed at the end of the nineteenth century by political parties,

---

[41] Alain Badiou, *Being and Event* (New York: Continuum, 2005).
[42] Ramón Feenstra, Andreu Casales-Riperro, Simon Tormey and John Keane, *Refiguring Democracy: The Spanish Political Laboratory* (London and New York: Routledge, 2017); compare Pippa Norris, *Democratic Deficit: Critical Citizens Revisited* (Cambridge: Cambridge University Press, 2011).

such as Germany's SPD, which at the time was the greatest political party machine on the face of the earth, in no small measure because it was a powerful champion of literacy and a leading publisher of books, pamphlets and newspapers in its own right.

The overall consequence is that under conditions of communicative abundance the core institutions of representative democracy become easy targets of rough riding. Think for a moment about any current public controversy that attracts widespread attention: the news and commentaries it generates typically begin *outside* the formal machinery of representative democracy. The messages become memes quickly relayed by many power-scrutinising organisations, large, medium and small. In the world of communicative abundance, that kind of latticed or networked pattern of circulating controversial messages is typical, not exceptional. It produces constant feedback effects: unpredictably non-linear links between inputs and outputs. The trend renders obsolete once-influential propositions in the field of political communications, especially the claim that democracies are principally defined by 'bandwagon effects', 'running with the pack' and 'spirals of silence' fuelled by fears of isolation among citizens.[43] The viral effects of public scrutiny have profound implications as well for the state-framed institutions of the old representative democracy, which find themselves outflanked by webs of mediated criticisms that often hit their target, sometimes from long distances, often by means of boomerang effects.

Consider a few samples of muckraking, many of them since forgotten, randomly drawn from a twelve-month media cycle (2008–2009) within the world's democracies: a male legislator in the Florida state assembly is spotted watching on-line porn while fellow legislators are debating the subject of abortion. During a fiercely fought presidential election campaign in the United States one of the candidates (Barack Obama) switches to damage control mode after calling a female journalist 'sweety'; he leaves her a voice mail apology: 'I am duly chastened.' In Japan, a seasoned Japanese politician (Masatoshi Wakabayashi) is forced to resign from the Diet after being caught on camera during a budget debate pressing the voting button of a parliamentary colleague who had earlier left the chamber; the disgraced legislator, who had evidently supposed that he was sitting in the blind spot of cameras, later confessed to

---

[43] The influential thesis that public opinion is loneliness turned inside out was developed at length in the classic work by Elisabeth Noelle-Neumann, *The Spiral of Silence. Public Opinion – Our Social Skin* (Chicago, IL: University of Chicago Press, 1984).

breaking the parliamentary rules: 'I wasn't thinking straight. It was an unforgivable act, and I'd like to apologise.'[44] While on a state visit to Chile, the President of the Czech Republic was caught on camera at a signing ceremony pocketing a golden ballpoint pen. In Finland, a senior politician was brought down with the help of a mobile telephone. His private text messages rebounded publicly, to reveal his duplicity and force the resignation of a government minister (as happened in Finland in April 2008 after *Hymy* magazine revealed that Minister of Foreign Affairs Ilkka Kanerva had sent several hundred text messages, some of them raunchy, to an erotic dancer, who sold the messages to the magazine, but then failed to win a court injunction to stop their publication. He tried unsuccessfully to defend himself by saying: 'I would not present them in Sunday school, but they are not totally out of line either'). In the age of communicative abundance, Sony hand-held cameras and iPhones are meanwhile used by off-air reporters and amateur users to file ongoing videos and blogs featuring politicians live, unplugged and unscripted. This is exactly what happened in France; according to video footage quickly uploaded onto LeMonde.fr, the Interior Minister (Brice Hortefeux) agreed to be photographed with a young Arab supporter and responded to an onlooker's joke about 'our little Arab' as a symbol of integration with the heartfelt words: 'There always has to be one. When there's one, it's ok. It's when there are a lot of them that there are problems.'

It is not only elected politicians and formal political institutions that come in for stick. Oiled by communicative abundance, it seems as if no organisation or leader within the fields of government or business or social life is immune from political trouble. Our great grandparents would find the whole process astonishing in its democratic intensity. It certainly spells trouble for 'bad news' accounts of contemporary media, those which are convinced that democracy is going to the dogs because 'the media' is 'dumbing down' or 'entertaining to death' its citizens, for instance by churning out materials of a poisonously low quality. Such pessimism contains a fundamental flaw: it misses the brawling, rowdy, rough 'n tumble qualities of communicative abundance, its propensity to stir up public troubles by exposing hidden discriminations and injustices.

But who or what drives all this gate watching and muckraking? Certainly, they are not the effect of the medium alone, as believers in the magical powers of technology suppose. Individuals, groups, networks and whole

---

[44] Alex Martin, 'Wakabayashi exits Diet due to Illicit Votes', *The Japan Times*, 3 April 2010.

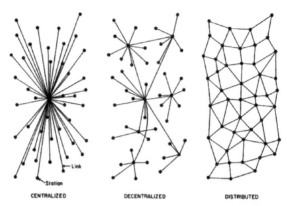

FIGURE 4.2 Centralised, decentralised and distributed networks

organisations make muckraking happen. Yet buried within the infrastructures of communicative abundance are technical features that enable muckrakers to do their work of publicly scrutinising power. From the end of the 1960s, as we have seen, product and process innovations have happened in virtually every field of an increasingly commercialised media, thanks to technical factors, such as electronic memory, tighter channel spacing, new frequency allocation, direct satellite broadcasting, digital tuning and advanced compression techniques.[45] These technical factors have made a huge difference, but within the infrastructure of communicative abundance, there is something special about its distributed networks. In contrast, say, to centralised state-run broadcasting systems of the past, the spider's web linkages among many different nodes within a distributed network make them intrinsically more resistant to centralised control (Figure 4.2). The network functions according to the logic of packet switching: flows of information pass through many latticed points en route to their destination. Initially broken into bytes of information that are then reassembled at the point of delivery, these flows readily find their way through censorship barriers. If messages are blocked at any point within the latticed system, then the information is diverted automatically, re-routed in the direction of their intended destination.

---

[45] For treatments of the background see Manuel Castells, *The Rise of the Network Society* (Oxford: Blackwell, 1998), especially chapter 5; *The Internet Galaxy: Reflections on the Internet, Business, and Society* (Oxford: Oxford University Press, 2003); and *Networks of Outrage and Hope: Social Movements in the Internet Age* (Cambridge: Polity Press, 2012).

This packet-switched and networked character of media-saturated societies ensures that messages go viral, even when they come up against organised resistance. Media-saturated societies are thus prone to contestability and dissonance. Some observers claim that a new understanding of power as 'mutually shared weakness' is required in order to make sense of the impact of networks on the distribution of power within any given social order. The claim is that those who are in positions of power over others are subject constantly to unforeseen setbacks, reversals and revolts. Manipulation and bossing and bullying of the powerless become difficult; the powerless readily find the networked communicative means through which to take their revenge on the powerful. Unchecked power becomes harder to win, much easier to lose. The trend is exemplified by online political initiatives such as the South Korean citizens' journalism site OhmyNews, UK Uncut, the Indian online tool I Paid A Bribe, the American campaigning network MoveOn.org Political Action, and SMS activism of the kind that contributed to the fall of Philippines President Joseph Estrada. It is summarised by the American scholar and activist Clay Shirky: when compared to the eras dominated by newspapers, the telegraph, radio and television, the age of communicative abundance, he says, is an era when 'group action just got easier'. Thanks to networked communications and easy-to-use tools, the 'expressive capability' of citizens is raised to unprecedented levels. 'As the communications landscape gets denser, more complex, and more participatory', he writes, 'the networked population is gaining greater access to information, more opportunities to engage in public speech, and an enhanced ability to undertake collective action.' Others speak of the rising predilection for 'self-organising' and 'connective action' spurred on by the belief that 'life can be more participatory, more decentralized, less dependent on the traditional models of organization, either in the state or the big company'.[46] Still others experiment with the principle in the field of party politics, for

---

[46] Giovanni Navarria, 'Citizens Go Online – Probing the Political Potential of the Internet Galaxy' (PhD dissertation, University of Westminster, 2010); Clay Shirky, 'The Political Power of Social Media', *Foreign Affairs* (January–February 2011), *Here Comes Everybody: The Power of Organizing without Organizations* (London: Penguin, 2008) and *Cognitive Surplus: Creativity and Generosity in a Connected Age* (London: Penguin, 2010); Yochai Benkler, as quoted in Nicholas Kulish, 'As Scorn for Vote Grows, Protests Surge Around Globe', *New York Times*, 27 September 2011; and W. Lance Bennett and Alexandra Segerberg, 'The Logic of Connective Action: Digital Media and the Personalization of Contentious Politics', *Information, Communication & Society* 15 (2012), 1–30.

instance by trying to outflank mainstream political parties using the techniques of 'liquid democracy'. Beppe Grillo's 5 Star Movement in Italy and the Pirate Party in Germany are examples. So is Iceland's Best Party, which won enough votes (in 2012) to co-run the Reykjavik City Council, partly on the promise that it would not honour any of its promises – since all other political parties are secretly corrupt, it would be openly corrupt.

Caution is required at this point because (to repeat) the changes catalysed by networked innovations are not the product of technical design and networked communicative abundance alone. It should go without saying, but it is often forgotten, that the changes that are going on have been driven by a variety of technical causes *and* human causers, including radical alterations of the ecology of public affairs reporting and commentary. As the revolution in favour of communicative abundance has taken root, the whole media infrastructure through which news of worldly events is produced and publicly circulated has become ever more complicated and cluttered. It is much more rough-and-tumble, to the point where professional news journalism is now just one of many different types of power-scrutinising institutions. Within all democracies, many hundreds and thousands of monitory institutions now skilfully trade in the business of stirring up questions of power, often with political effect. Human rights reports, blogs, courts, networks of professional organisations and civic initiatives are just a few examples of the watch-dog, guide-dog and barking-dog mechanisms that are fundamentally altering the spirit and dynamics of democracy.

These public monitors thrive within the new galaxy of communicative abundance. They do not simply give voice to the voiceless; they produce echo effects. An important case in point is the Spanish *indignados* (15-M) movement, which used a wide range of new media tools to monitor and resist police brutality, welfare budget cuts, house evictions, corruption within the credit and banking system, unfair electoral laws, antiquated parliamentary procedures and the suppression of 'inconvenient' news by mainstream media.[47] The political work of such movements is strengthened by the growth of aggressive new forms of professional and citizens' journalism.

The days of journalism proud of its commitment to the principles that 'comment is free, but facts are sacred' (that was the phrase coined in

---

[47] The best accounts are Ramón A. Feenstra, *Democracia monitorizada en la era de la nueva galaxia mediática: La propuesta de John Keane* (Barcelona: Icaria, 2012) and Feenstra et al., *Refiguring Democracy*.

1921 by the *Manchester Guardian*'s long-time editor C.P. Scott) and of fact-based 'objectivity' – ideals that were born of the age of representative democracy, ideals that were always the exception in practice – are fading. In place of the 'rituals of objectivity',[48] we see the rise of adversarial and 'gotcha' styles of commercial journalism, forms of writing that are driven by ratings, political affiliation, sales and hits. There is biting political satire, of the deadly kind popularised in India by STAR's weekly show *Poll Khol* using a comedian anchorman, an animated monkey, news clips and Bollywood soundtracks (the programme title is translated as 'open election' but is actually drawn from a popular Hindi metaphor which means 'revealing the hidden story'). All these criteria sit poorly with talk of 'fairness' (a criterion of good journalism famously championed by Hubert Beuve-Méry, the founder and first editor of *Le Monde*). We witness as well open challenges to professional 'embedded' journalism bound up with the spread of so-called citizen journalism and enclaves of self-redaction.[49] The forces of professional and citizen journalism often intersect, and when that happens (as at Amsterdam's *De Correspondent* and London's *The Guardian*) they are understandably proud of their contribution to the muckraking trend. They like to emphasise that they refuse to take no for an answer, that their job is to uncover things that were previously hidden, to report things as they are, to slam the foolish, to give liars and thieves a hard time. They are sure that the function of journalism is to produce neither pleasure nor harm nor 'objectivity' nor 'balance'. Its purpose rather is to break the habit of breaking news, to point cameras at wounds, to find words to confront justice, to let victims of power speak in their own voices. Sometimes they say journalism should be guided by killer instincts – even if that means there must be victims. Such talk is sometimes simple self-justification, and (as we shall soon see) we need to be more sceptical of the way many professional and citizen journalists like to see themselves as the midwives of 'truth'. But given this gutsy style of independent journalism, there is little wonder that public objection to corruption and wrongdoing nowadays becomes commonplace.

---

[48] C.P. Scott, 'A Hundred Years' [1921], reprinted in *The Guardian* (London), 29 November 2002; Gaye Tuchman, 'Objectivity as Strategic Ritual: An Examination of Newsmen's Notions of Objectivity', *American Journal of Sociology*, 77 (1972), 660–679.
[49] John Hartley, 'Communicative Democracy in a Redactional Society: The Future of Journalism Studies', *Journalism: Theory, Practice & Criticism*, 1 (2000), 39–47.

The new age of communicative abundance is no doubt blighted by trends that contradict the basic democratic principle that all citizens are equally entitled to communicate their opinions, and periodically to give representatives a rough ride.[50] Yet rough riding happens – on a scale and with an intensity never before witnessed. Speaking figuratively, one could say that communicative abundance cuts like a knife into the power relations of government, business and the rest of civil society. Little wonder that public objections to wrongdoing and corruption become commonplace. In the era of media saturation there seems to be no end of scandals; and there are even times when so-called '-gate' scandals, like earthquakes, rumble beneath the feet of whole governments. The frequency and intensity of media-shaped '-gate' scandals are greatly feared by power wielders; and although scandals can have damaging effects on the spirit and institutions of democracy they provide a sober reminder of a perennial problem facing any political system, that there are never shortages of organised efforts by the powerful to manipulate people beneath and around them.

That is why the political dirty business of dragging power from behind curtains of secrecy remains fundamentally important. Nobody should be seduced into thinking that media-saturated societies, with their latticed networks, multiple channels, tough-minded journalism and power-scrutinising institutions, are level playing fields in the democratic sense. Yet even though societies shaped by communicative abundance are not paradises of open communication, historical comparisons show just how distinctive is their permanent flux, their unending restlessness driven by complex media combinations of different interacting players and institutions, permanently heaving and straining, sometimes working together, at other times in contrarian ways. The powerful routinely strive to define and to determine who gets what, when and how; but the less powerful, taking advantage of communicative abundance, keep tabs on the powerful – sometimes with great drama and surprising success.

The consequence is that media-saturated societies are richly conflicted, political orders in which, contrary to some pessimists and purists, politics does not wither away. Nothing is ever settled, or straightforward. In striking contrast to galaxies of communication that were structured by the printing press, the telegraph, radio and television, media-saturated societies enable actors much more easily to cut through habit and

---

[50] John Keane, *Democracy and Media Decadence* (Cambridge and New York: Cambridge University Press, 2013), especially part 2.

prejudice and hierarchies of power. They stir up the sense that people can shape and reshape their lives as equals; not surprisingly, they often bring commotion into the world. Media-saturated societies have a definite 'viral' quality about them. Power disputes are often bolts out of the blue; they follow unexpected pathways and reach surprising destinations that have unexpected outcomes.

The phone-hacking scandal that hit News Corporation in mid-2011 is a striking case in point: it began with investigative reporting by London's *The Guardian* newspaper, which revealed that the company publication *News of the World* had hacked into the voice mail messages of a thirteen-year-old murder victim, Milly Dowler. Public indignation suddenly flared. The global company suffered reputational damage. In quick succession, there followed several arrests of News Corporation executives; the closure of *The News of the World*, which had been in business for 168 years; parliamentary hearings; and a public apology by Rupert Murdoch, the company's chairman and chief executive. He was forced to watch the public embarrassment of his political friends and to witness the collapse of his plans to buy control of a multi-billion pound major satellite television provider, British Sky Broadcasting. Soon afterwards came recommendations to shake up the management of the firm by a major investor advisory organisation that criticised News Corporation's senior executives for their 'striking lack of stewardship and failure of independence' by a board unable to set a strong tone at the top about unethical business practices; and the public inquiry led by Lord Justice Leveson into the culture, practices and ethics of British media.[51]

Other examples of unexpected power disputes spring readily to mind. Groups using mobile phones, bulletin boards, news groups, wikis and blogs sometimes manage, against considerable odds, to heap embarrassing publicity on their opponents. Corporations are given stick (by well-organised, media-savvy groups such as Adbusters) about their services and products, their investment plans, how they treat their employees, and the size of their impact upon the biosphere. Power-monitoring bodies like Human Rights Watch, Avaaz.org, Global Witness and Amnesty International regularly do the same, usually with help from networks of supporters spread around the globe. There are initiatives such as the World Wide Web Consortium (known as W3C) that promote universal

---

[51] The materials gathered by the Leveson Inquiry are at: www.levesoninquiry.org.uk (accessed 5 July 2014); see also Tom Watson and Martin Hickman, *Dial M for Murdoch: News Corporation and the Corruption of Britain* (London: Allen Lane, 2012).

open access to digital networks. There are even bodies (like the Democratic Audit network, the Global Accountability Project and Transparency International) that specialise in providing public assessments of the quality of existing power-scrutinising mechanisms and the degree to which they fairly represent citizens' interests. Politicians, parties and parliaments get much stick from dot.org muckrakers like California Watch and Mediapart (a Paris-based watchdog staffed by a number of veteran French newspaper and news agency journalists). And, at all levels, governments are grilled on a wide range of matters, from their human rights records, their energy production plans to the quality of the drinking water of their cities. Even their arms procurement policies – notoriously shrouded in secrecy – run into trouble, thanks to media-savvy citizens' initiatives guided by the spirit, and sometimes the letter, of the principle that in 'the absence of governmental checks and balances ... the only effective restraint upon executive policy and power in the area of national defence and international affairs may lie in ... an informed and critical public opinion which alone can ... protect the values of democratic government'.[52]

WIKILEAKS

These are times in which terrifying state violence directed at citizens is witnessed and, against tremendous odds, publicly confronted by citizen-uploaded videos, digital sit-ins, online 'hacktivist' collectives and media-savvy monitory organisations, such as the Syrian Observatory for Human Rights, Anonymous and Burma Watch International. There are small citizen groups, such as the Space Hijackers, which manage to win big publicity by acts of daring, for instance driving a second-hand UN tank to Europe's largest arms fair in London's Docklands, ostensibly to test its 'roadworthiness', then to auction it to the highest market bidder, in the process offering prosthetic limbs for sale to arms dealers. Then there are

---

[52] These are the words used by Justice Potter Stewart in the United States Supreme Court's famous opinion in *New York Times Co.* v. *United States* (1971), the so-called Pentagon Papers case: 'In the absence of governmental checks and balances present in other areas of our national life, the only effective restraint upon executive policy and power in the area of national defense and international affairs may lie in an enlightened citizenry – in an informed and critical public opinion which alone can here protect the values of democratic government... Without an informed and free press, there cannot be an enlightened people.'

global headline-making initiatives that lunge non-violently at the heart of highly secretive, sovereign power.

WikiLeaks is still the most talked-about experiment in the arts of publicly probing secretive military power. Pundits initially described it as the novel defining story of our times, but the point is that its spirit and methods belong firmly and squarely to the age of communicative abundance. Engaged in a radical form of muckraking motivated by conscience and supported by a shadowy band of technically sophisticated activists led by a controversial public figure, Julian Assange, WikiLeaks took full advantage of the defining qualities of communicative abundance: the easy access multi-media integration and low-cost copying of information that is then whizzed around the world through digital networks. Posing as a *lumpen* outsider in the world of information, aiming to become a watchdog with a global brief, WikiLeaks sprang to fame by releasing video footage of an American helicopter gunship crew cursing and firing on unarmed civilians and journalists. It then sent shock waves throughout the civil societies and governments of many countries by releasing sprawls, hundreds of thousands of top-secret documents appertaining to the diplomatic and military strategies of the United States and its allies and enemies. Later, it helped secure the safe passage of the most-talked about and politically influential leaker, Edward Snowden.[53]

With the help of mainstream media, WikiLeaks produced pungent effects, in no small measure because of its mastery of the clever arts of 'cryptographic anonymity', military-grade encryption designed to protect both its sources and itself as a global publisher. For the first time on a global scale, WikiLeaks created a viable custom-made mailbox that enabled disgruntled muckrakers within any organisation to release classified data on a confidential basis, initially for storage in a camouflaged cloud of servers. WikiLeaks then pushed that bullet-proofed information into public circulation, as an act of radical transparency and commitment to 'truth'.

WikiLeaks was guided by a theory of hypocrisy and democracy. Its attempt to construct an 'intelligence agency of the people' supposed that individual employees within any organisation are motivated to act as whistle-blowers, not just because their identities are protected by encryption but especially because their organisation suffers intolerable gaps between its publicly professed aims and its private modus operandi.

---

[53] John Keane, 'Why Google is a Political Matter: A Conversation with Julian Assange', *The Monthly* (June 2015).

Hypocrisy is the night soil of muckrakers, whose rakes in the Augean stables of government and business have a double effect: they multiply the amount of muck circulated under the noses of interested or astonished publics, whose own sense of living in muck is consequently sharpened. Muckraking in the style of the WikiLeaks platform has yet another source, which helps explain why its attempted criminalisation and forcible closure is already spawning many similar offspring, such as BalkanLeaks, a Bulgarian-based initiative to publicise organised crime and political corruption in the region. Put simply, WikiLeaks feeds upon a contradiction deeply structured within the digital information systems of all large-scale complex organisations. States and business corporations and other organisations take advantage of the communications revolution of our time by going digital and staying digital. They do so to enhance their internal efficiency and external effectiveness, to improve their capacity for handling complex, difficult or unexpected situations, swiftly and flexibly. Contrary to Max Weber, the data banks and data processing systems of these organisations are antithetical to red tape, stringent security rules and compartmentalised data sets, all of which have the effect of making these organisations slow and clumsy. So they opt for dynamic and time-sensitive data sharing across the boundaries of departments and whole organisations. Vast streams of classified material flow freely – which serves to boost the chances that leaks into the courts of public opinion will happen. If organisations then respond by tightening internal controls on their own information flows, a move that Julian Assange described as the imposition of a 'secrecy tax', the chances are that these same organisations will both trigger their own 'cognitive decline', their reduced capacity to handle complex situations swiftly and effectively, as well as increase the likelihood of resistance to the secrecy tax by motivated employees who are convinced of the hypocrisy and injustice of the organisations which are unrepresentative of their views.[54]

UNELECTED REPRESENTATIVES

The subject of representation brings us to one other trend with significant implications for monitory democracy in representative form: in the age of

---

[54] Julian Assange, 'The Non Linear Effects of Leaks on Unjust Systems of Governance' (31 December 2006), http://web.archive.org/web/20071020051936/http://iq.org/; and 'State and Terrorist Conspiracies' (10 November 2006), http://cryptome.org/0002/ja-conspiracies.pdf.

4 Wild Thinking

communicative abundance, unelected representatives multiply, sometimes to the point where their level of public support casts shadows over the legitimacy and viability of elected representation (politicians and parliaments) as the central organising principle of democracy. The phrase 'unelected representatives' refers to champions of public causes and values, 'democratic public servants',[55] whose authority and power base is located outside the boundaries of electoral politics. It is of course an unfamiliar phrase. Taking us back in time (it seems) to the age of Thomas Carlyle and Ralph Waldo Emerson, and to contentions about the importance of great men and heroes,[56] it grates on democratic ears. Hence, it is important to understand carefully its meaning, and the ill-understood trend it describes.

Our ignorance of the past inevitably breeds misunderstandings of our present, so let us go back to the age when the grafting of the principle and practice of representation onto democracy irreversibly changed the original meaning of both.[57] Representation, once conceived by Hobbes and other political thinkers as simply equivalent to the actual or virtual authorisation of government, had to make room for equality, accountability and free elections. For its part, at least in theory, democracy had to find space for the process of delegation of decisions to others and, hence, open itself up to matters of public responsiveness and the public accountability of leaders. From roughly the last quarter of the eighteenth century, democratic representation came to mean a process of re-presenting the interests and views of electors who are absent from the chambers and forums where decisions are made. Representatives decide things on behalf – and in the physical absence – of those who are affected.

But that was only one side of the complex, dynamic equation. For under conditions of democracy, as so many observers pointed out, those who are rendered absent from the making of decisions must periodically step forward and make their presence felt by raising their hands in public, or (in our times) by touching a screen or placing a cross on a ballot paper in private. Under democratic conditions, representation is a process of

---

[55] Sheldon S. Wolin, *Democracy Incorporated: Managed Democracy and the Specter of Inverted Totalitarianism* (Princeton, NJ and Oxford: Princeton University Press, 2008), p. 291.
[56] Thomas Carlyle, *On Heroes, Hero-Worship and the Heroic in History* [1840] (London: Chapman & Hall, 1870); and Ralph W. Emerson, 'Representative Men', in Joel Porte (ed.), *Essays and Lectures [1850]* (New York: Library of America, 1983).
[57] An extended account of the complex historical origins of representative democracy is found in the mid-section of Keane, *The Life and Death of Democracy*.

periodically rendering or making present what is absent; it is not simply (as Burke supposed) an act of delegation of judgements to the few trustees who make decisions on behalf of those whom they represent. Representation (ideally) is the avoidance of *misrepresentation*. By that is not meant that representation is mimesis, the harmonious, one-for-one mirroring by the representative of the demands and interests of the represented. It is a potentially conflicted relationship structured by the rules of accountability, an ongoing tussle between representatives who make political judgements and the represented, the citizens, who also make political judgements.

The upshot of this dialectic was that representative democracy became a distinctive form of government that simultaneously distinguished and linked together the source of political power – the people or *dēmos* – and the use made of political power by representatives who are periodically chastened by the people whose interests they are supposed to serve. The downside was that the election of representatives became a dynamic process subject to what can be called the disappointment principle.[58] Elections are today still seen as a method of apportioning blame for poor political performance: a way of ensuring the rotation of leadership, guided by merit and humility, in the presence of electors equipped with the power to trip leaders up and throw them out of office if and when they fail, as often they do. Every election is as much a beginning as it is an ending. The whole point of elections is that they are a means of disciplining representatives who have disappointed their electors, who are then entitled to throw harsh words, and paper or electronic rocks, at them. If representatives were always virtuous, impartial, competent and responsive, then elections would lose their purpose.

The disappointment principle coded into the principles and practice of representative democracy not only helps to explain why elected political representatives periodically come in for tough public criticism, or become scapegoats or targets of satire and sarcasm. The factor of disappointment helps explain why, under conditions of communicative abundance, alternative forms of representation become attractive, so that *unelected representatives* attract great media attention and public support. Thomas Carlyle spotted that the fame of 'heroes' such as Shakespeare, Luther, Goethe and Napoleon was made possible by the modern printing press; he would be dumbfounded by the amplifying effects of communicative

---

[58] John Keane, 'Hypocrisy and Democracy', *WZB-Mitteilungen*, 120 (June 2008), 30–32.

abundance. Media-saturated societies multiply the variety and scope and sophistication of publicity outlets hungry for 'stars'. An unsurprising consequence is the rapid growth and diffusion, well beyond the reaches of elected government, of famous individuals, groups and organisations who stand up for causes and carve out public constituencies that are often at odds with the words and deeds of established political parties, elected officials, parliaments and whole governments. Whatever may be thought of their particular brand of politics, or the merits of the particular issues for which they stand, unelected representatives alter the political geography and political dynamics of democracies. These respected public personalities with a difference add to the commotion of democratic politics – while often causing established representative mechanisms serious political headaches.

But who exactly are unelected representatives? What does the unfamiliar phrase mean? In the most elementary sense, unelected representatives are authoritative public figures who win public attention and respect through various forms of media coverage. Documentaries are made about their lives; interviews with them go viral; they have websites and they blog and tweet. Often extroverted characters, they sometimes seem to be everywhere, even though they usually have a strong sense of contract with the citizens who admire them, who see in themselves what they would like to become. These representatives have to be media savvy. They enjoy notoriety and they are good at its arts. They are famous but they are not simply 'celebrities', a term which is too wide and too loose and too normatively burdened to capture their core quality of being unelected representatives of others' views. Unelected representatives are not mindless fame seekers who have climbed the ladders of renown. They are not 'million-horsepowered entities' (McLuhan), individuals well-known for their 'well-knownness'.[59] And they are not in it for the money. They are not exaltations of superficiality; they do not thrive on smutty probes into

---

[59] Marshall McLuhan, in *Explorations 3*, republished in *Marshall McLuhan Unbound 1* (Toronto, ON: University of Toronto Press, 2005); and Daniel J. Boorstin, *The Image, Or, What Happened to the American Dream* (New York: Atheneum, 1962), p. 57. Treatments of the phenomenon of the celebrity include Nick Couldry, *The Place of Media Power: Pilgrims and Witnesses of the Media Age* (London: Routledge, 2000); Chris Hedge, *Empire of Illusion: The End of Literacy and the Triumph of the Spectacle* (New York: Nation Books, 2009); Joshua Gamson, *Claims to Fame: Celebrity in Contemporary America* (Berkeley, CA: University of California Press, 1994); Chris Rojek, *Celebrity* (London: Reaktion Books, 2001); Graeme Turner, *Understanding Celebrity* (London: Sage, 2004); and Daniel J. Boorstin, *The Image: A Guide to Pseudo-Events in America* (London: Methuen, 1961, 1971).

their private lives; and they do not pander to celebrity bloggers, gossip columnists and tabloid *paparazzi*. The figure of the unelected representative is not what Germans call a *Hochstapler* (a 'high piler'), an imposter who brags and boasts a lot. Unelected representatives instead bear the marks of humility. Their feet are on the ground. They stand for something outside and beyond their particular niche. More exactly: as public representatives they simultaneously 'mirror' the tastes and views of their public admirers as well as fire their imaginations and sympathies by displaying leadership in matters of the wider public good, seen from their and others' point of view.

Unelected representatives have the effect of widening the horizons of the political, even though they are not chosen in the same way as parliamentary representatives, who are subject to formal periodic elections. It is true that there are times and places where unelected representatives decide (for a time) to reinvest their fame, to make a lateral move into formal parliamentary politics and a ministerial position. An example is Wangari Maathai (1940–2011), the first African woman to win the Nobel Peace Prize and the founder of the pan-African grass-roots Green Belt Movement. Other figures do exactly the reverse, by pursuing public leadership roles after elected office. Many examples spring to mind. Among them are the efforts of former German Chancellor Helmut Schmidt, who helped found (in 1983) the InterAction Council, a group of over thirty former high office holders; Mikhail Gorbachev's and Nelson Mandela's running commentaries on world affairs; Al Gore's *An Inconvenient Truth* campaign; the Africa Progress Panel and peace negotiation efforts of former UN Secretary General Kofi Annan, for instance during the violently disputed elections of 2007/2008 in Kenya; and the multiple public activities of Jimmy Carter, whose self-reinvention as an advocate of human rights makes him the first ex-president of the United States to insist that the world is so shrinking that it needs new ways of doing politics in more negotiated and principled ways, nurtured by bodies like The Elders, which he helped to found in 2007.

Elsewhere I have attempted to assess the long-term viability and significance of these unelected representatives who once occupied high office.[60] Their public prominence demonstrates positively that the age is over when former elected leaders lapsed into mediocrity, or spent their

---

[60] John Keane, 'Life after Political Death: The Fate of Leaders after Leaving High Office', in John Kane, Haig Patapan and Paul 't Hart (eds.), *Dispersed Leadership in Democracy: Foundations, Opportunities, Realities* (Oxford: Oxford University Press, 2009).

time 'taking pills and dedicating libraries' (as Herbert Hoover put it), sometimes bathed in self-pity ('after the White House what is there to do but drink?', Franklin Pierce reportedly quipped). Equally clear is the way that elections or governmental politics are not the normal destiny or career path of unelected representatives. Fascinating is the way they most often shun political parties, parliaments and government. They do not like to be seen as politicians. Paradoxically, that does not make them any less 'chosen' or legitimate in the eyes, hearts and minds of their followers. It often has the opposite effect.

Untainted by office, unelected representatives walk in the footsteps of Mahatma Gandhi: beyond the confines of government, they carve out constituencies and win over supporters who as a consequence are inspired to act differently, to strive to be better than they currently are. The upshot is that in their role as public representatives they often cross swords with elected authorities. They put the represented on trial as well: they challenge them to hold fast to their convictions and/or urge them to take a stand on an issue. And despite the fact that they are not mandated by periodic votes, unelected representatives most definitely have a strong sense of being on trial, above all by acknowledging their 'contractual' dependence upon those whom they represent. Their supporters and admirers are in effect their creators. That is why they have to handle their self-importance carefully: their fame requires them to be both different from their admirers and yet similar enough so that they are not aloof, or threatening. Unelected representatives are in this sense not to be confused with 'oligarchs' or 'demagogues' or scheming demiurges such as Vladislav Surkov, the style architect of 'sovereign democracy' in contemporary Russia.[61] The grip of unelected representatives on popular opinion is much more tentative. Their fame can be thought of as the democratic descendant of aristocratic honour. It does not come cheaply. It has its price: since their reputation for integrity depends upon a strong media profile, unelected representatives can find, sometimes with surprising speed, that their private lives and public reputation are quickly ruined by the active withdrawal of support of the represented. The old maxim, a favourite of Harry Truman when he was out of office, that money, craving for power and sex are three things that can ruin political leaders, applies with real force to unelected leaders. Unlike celebrities, who can thrive on bad press, they find scandals fatal, ruinous of their whole public

---

[61] Peter Pomerantsev, 'Putin's Rasputin', *London Review of Books*, 33 (2011), 3–6.

identity. They know the meaning of the old maxim: reputations are hard won and easily lost.

Unelected representatives draw breath from communicative abundance but by no means does this imply that they are 'second best' or 'inferior' or 'pseudo-representatives' when compared with their formally elected counterparts. Emerson noted how the printing press made it seem that some great men had been elected. 'As Sir Robert Peel and Mr. Webster vote, so Locke and Rousseau think for thousands', he wrote.[62] In the age of multi-media culture, unelected representatives similarly enjoy robust public reputations and they exercise a form of 'soft' or 'persuasive' power over others, including their opponents. They are listened to, admired, sometimes adored, often mimicked or followed; and to the extent that they are influential in these ways they may, and often do, present challenges to formally elected representatives, for instance by confronting their claims or questioning their actions. So what is the basis of their unelected fame? How do they manage to produce political effects? To put things simply: what's the source of their popularity and how are they able to use it to stand apart from elected representatives, either to praise their work or to call their actions into question?

There are many different types of unelected representatives. Some draw their legitimacy from the fact that they are widely regarded as models of *public virtue*. Figures such as Martin Luther King Jr., Princess Diana and Aamir Khan (a Bollywood film star and television presenter known for spotlighting festering issues such as domestic violence and caste injustice) are seen to be 'good' or 'decent' or 'wise' or 'daring' people who bring honesty, fairness and other valuable things to the world. Their reputations are untarnished by allegations of corruption; although they are not presumed to be angels they are widely supposed to be living illustrations of alternative pathways, a challenge for people to aspire to greater moral heights, to inspire them to live differently. Other unelected representatives – Mother Teresa or Desmond Tutu – win legitimacy because of their *spiritual or religious commitments*. There are unelected representatives whose status is based instead on *merit*; they are former nobodies who become somebody because they are reckoned to have achieved great things. Amitabh Bhachan (India's screen star whose early reputation was built on playing the role of fighter against injustice), Colombian-born Shakira Mebarak and the Berliner Philharmoniker (the latter two

---

[62] Emerson, *Representative Men*, p. 715.

are Goodwill Ambassadors of UNICEF) belong in this category of achievers. Still other figures are deemed representatives of *suffering, courage and survival* in this world (His Holiness the 14th Dalai Lama of Tibet is an example). There are other unelected representatives – in marked contrast to political party leaders and governments who 'fudge' issues – who draw their legitimacy from the fact that they have taken a principled stand on a particular issue, on which they campaign vigorously, in the process appealing for public support in the form of donations and subscriptions. Bodies like Amnesty International or initiatives such as the Live 8 benefit concerts are of this type: their legitimacy is mediated not by votes, but by means of *moral monetary contracts* that can be cancelled at any time by admiring supporters and subscribers who are equipped with the power to draw the conclusion that these ad hoc representatives are no longer representative or worthy of their financial support.

Whatever is thought of their stardom, unelected representatives play a vital democratic role in the age of communicative abundance. They certainly refute the old presumption, championed by Thomas Carlyle and Ralph Waldo Emerson, that unelected leaders serve to reinvent monarchical and aristocratic standards of proper behaviour and greatness, that in effect 'representative men' stand outside of time and can be its master, re-binding the fractured polities of the modern world. This way of thinking about unelected leaders no longer makes sense; their dynamic effects are different. Unelected representatives can do good works for democracy, especially when politicians as representatives suffer a mounting credibility gap. They stretch the boundaries and meaning of political representation, especially by putting on-message parties, parliaments and government executives on their toes. Sometimes posthumously (Gandhi is a prime example), their figure draws public attention to the violation of public standards by governments, their policy failures, or their general lack of political imagination in handling so-called 'wicked' or 'devilish' problems that have no readily agreed upon definition, let alone straightforward solutions. Unelected representatives also force existing democracies to think twice, and more deeply, about what counts as good leadership. They serve as an important reminder that during the course of the past century the word leadership was excessively politicised, to the point where we have forgotten that the words *leader* and *leaderess*, from the time of their first usage in English, were routinely applied to those who coordinated such bodies as singing choirs, bands of dancers and musicians and religious congregations.

Unelected leaders can have profoundly transformative effects on the meaning of leadership itself. They serve not only as an important corrective to the undue dominance of state-centred definitions of leadership, and not only do they multiply and disperse different and conflicting criteria of representation that confront democracies with problems (such as whether unelected leaders can be held publicly accountable for their actions using means other than elections) that were unknown to the earliest champions and architects of representative democracy, but thanks to their efforts, leadership no longer means (as it meant in Max Weber's classic state-centred analysis) bossing and strength backed ultimately by cunning and the fist and other means of state power, a *Realpolitik* understanding of leadership that slides towards political authoritarianism (and until today has given the words *Führer* and *Führerschaft* a bad name in countries such as Germany).[63] Leadership also no longer means manipulation through the bully pulpit (a peculiarly American term coined by Theodore Roosevelt to describe the use by leaders of a 'superb' or 'wonderful' platform to advocate causes and agendas). Leadership instead comes to be understood as the capacity to mobilise 'persuasive power' (as Archbishop Desmond Tutu likes to say). It is the ability to motivate citizens to do things for themselves.

---

[63] Max Weber's famous account of the qualities of competent political leadership (*Führerschaft*) in parliamentary democracies is sketched in '*Politik als Beruf*' (originally delivered as a speech at Munich University in the revolutionary winter of 1918/1919), in *Gesammelte Politische Schriften* (Tübingen: Mohr Siebeck, 1958), pp. 493–548. During the speech, Weber said that democracies require leaders to display at least three decisive qualities. Genuine leadership first of all necessitates a passionate devotion to a cause, the will to make history, to set new values for others, nourished from feeling. Such passion must not succumb to what he called (Weber here drew upon Georg Simmel) 'sterile excitation'. Authentic leaders – this is the second imperative – must avoid 'self-intoxication' all the while cultivating a sense of personal responsibility for their achievements, and their failures. While (finally) this implies that leaders are not merely the mandated mouthpieces of their masters, the electors, leaders' actions must embody a 'cool sense of proportion': the ability to grant due weight to realities, to take them soberly and calmly into account. Passionate, responsible and experienced leaders, Weber urged, must be relentless in 'viewing the realities of life' and must have 'the ability to face such realities and ... measure up to them inwardly'. Effective leadership is synonymous with neither demagoguery nor the worship of power for its own sake. Passionate and responsible leaders shun the blind pursuit of ultimate goals; such blindness, Weber noted sarcastically, 'does rightly and leaves the results with the Lord'. Mature leaders must be guided instead by the 'ethic of responsibility'. Recognising the average deficiencies of people, they must continually strive, using state power, to take account of the foreseeable effects of particular actions that aim to realise particular goals through the reliance upon particular means. Responsible leaders must therefore incorporate into their actions the prickly fact, in many contexts, that the attainment of good ends is dependent upon (and therefore jeopardized by) the use of ethically doubtful or (in the case of violence) even dangerous means.

4 Wild Thinking

The arts of unelected leadership are certainly demanding. 'A determination to be courageous; an ability to anticipate situations; the inclination to dramatise political effects, so as to warn citizens of actual or potential problems; above all, the willingness to admit that mistakes have been made, to urge that they must be corrected, without ever being afraid of making yet more mistakes', is how one unelected leader explains it.[64] Unelected leadership is many things. It involves flat rejection of the devils of blind ambition, what Carlyle called 'Lionism'. It is the learned capacity to communicate with publics about matters of public concern, to win public respect by cultivating 'narrative intelligence' that includes (when unelected representatives are at their best) a mix of formal qualities, such as level-headed focus, inner calm, courteousness, the refusal to be biddable, the ability to listen to others, poking fun at oneself, and a certain radiance of style (one of the confidants of Nelson Mandela once explained to me his remarkable ability to create 'many Nelson Mandelas around him' – the same thing is still commonly said of Jawaharlal Nehru). The qualities of unelected leadership also include the power to use media to combine contradictory qualities (such as strength and vulnerability, singularity and typicality) simultaneously, and apparently without effort, as if leadership is the art of *Gestalt* switching. Above all, unelected leadership demands awareness that true leaders are not to be regarded as privileged Elect. Under conditions of communicative abundance, in the age of monitory democracy, true leaders are public figures who know that they are deeply dependent upon the people known as the led, that their ability to lead stems from their knack of getting people to look up to them, rather than to be hauled by the nose through flattery, greed, bigotry or fear.

---

[64] From an interview with Emílio Rui Vilar, former senior minister of the first democratic governments after the defeat of the Salazar dictatorship, former Deputy Governor of the Bank of Portugal and Director-General of the Commission of the European Union, and director of the Calouste Gulbenkian Foundation, a non-governmental foundation known for its active support for public accountability and pluralism in matters ranging from political power to aesthetic taste (Lisbon, 27 October 2006).

5

Lying, Truth and Power

Monitory democracy has undoubtedly doubled public sensitivity towards the phenomenon of lying. Commentaries on the subject are flourishing. Pseudology is suddenly fashionable. It has become conventional to quote the work of Plato on noble lies; or to make mention of Kant's discussion of whether it is justified to save the life of a friend by telling a lie (he didn't approve of that because being truthful was for him 'a sacred and absolutely commanding decree of reason'); or to draw upon the writings of Hannah Arendt about the significance of the Pentagon Papers.[1] Less well known is the fact that it was the Russian-born historian and philosopher of science Alexandre Koyré who first posed afresh questions about the changing historical significance of lying and emphasised its potentially catastrophic consequences in the age of media-saturated democracy. His treatment was not only careful, sophisticated and unsettling; its strengths and its weaknesses ensure that it remains of great relevance today – or so the following pages will try to show.

Many scholars remain unaware of his work, which is a pity, given the distinctiveness of Koyré's approach to the subject of lying. His thoughts were first sketched in a 1943 essay conceived when working in Cairo, 'Reflexions sur la mensonge' (translated into English and published in

---

[1] Plato 'The Republic', in B. Jowett (ed.), *The Dialogues of Plato*, Book III (New York: Charles Scribner's Sons); Immanuel Kant, 'On a Supposed Right to Lie from Altruistic Motives', in *Critique of Practical Reason and Other Writings in Moral Philosophy* (Chicago, IL: University of Chicago Press), pp. 346–350; Hannah Arendt, 'Lying in Politics: Reflections on the Pentagon Papers', in *Crises of the Republic* (New York: Harcourt Brace Jovanovich, 1972), pp. 3–43.

New York in the summer of 1945).[2] His starting point was a provocation: since human beings are equipped with the capacity for embodied speech, they have a remarkable in-built capacity to 'say what is not so'. Lying is an intentional act of obfuscation, he argued. It takes many varied forms, scattered through a range of settings, extending from the intimacies of everyday life through to powerful institutions of government and business. Sometimes the buncombe humans utter is motivated by playfulness, said just for the fun of it. At other moments, humans handle the truth carelessly, without much thought, or because, as the old saying has it, a little inaccuracy saves a world of explanation. Lying without saying a word, the gesture of refusing to open one's mouth, or faking an orgasm, is another possibility. And saying what is not so is sometimes done in self-defence, as when telling untruths can be a weapon of the underdog, a tool for empowering the powerless slave against the omnipotent master. Koyré further observed that societies often tolerate or recommend lying under certain circumstances, for instance when taradiddles told are judged to be 'harmless' or even helpful, as when a child is told by its parent that they're so good at something when clearly they are not; or when good outcomes depend upon not telling the whole truth and nothing but the truth to everyone; or when bitter truths that otherwise would cause pain are masked by courtesy and civility. Koyré surely had Plato in mind when he added that early political philosophy was tied to the same principle: since most people (the *dēmos*) must live in lies because they are incapable of grasping the truth, whose mishandling and bowdlerisation can be dangerous to political order, veracity 'must be spooned out, diluted and specially prepared for them'.

For Koyré, war serves as the troubling big exception to these conventional views that lying is sometimes permissible. During moments of military conflict, as he knew from active service on the Russian front during the First World War, lying is typically treated by commanders as a just weapon designed to overwhelm the enemy. Lying to friends is impermissible; lying to foes is mandatory, and desirable. The point was of course made by Machiavelli, von Clausewitz and others. 'But what if war, an abnormal, episodic, transient condition, should come to be permanent and taken for granted?', Koyré asked, as if to taunt previous

---

[2] Alexandre Koyré, 'Les réflexions sur le mensonge', *Renaissance*, 1 (January–February 1943), translated as 'The Political Function of the Modern Lie', *Contemporary Jewish Record*, 8 (1945), 290–300; and 'The Liar', *Philosophy and Phenomenological Research*, 6 (1946), 344–362. All quotations are drawn from these texts.

analysts of war. In such circumstances, when whole political orders feel themselves to be under siege, with an all-powerful enemy wielding a knife at their throat, lying 'would become obligatory and be transformed into a virtue'. Truth telling would no longer be regarded as chivalrous, as pious or plain honest. It would rather be seen as a sign of decadent weakness, a willingness to capitulate to enemies whose defeat requires lying to become more than simply necessary. It must be considered 'a condition of sheer existence', remarked Koyré, an inviolable rule of human survival.

In an age of asymmetric warfare, unending combat against 'terrorism' and chronic military interventions by the United States (more during the past three decades than at any other moment in its history) and by other states (Russia in Syria, Saudi Arabia in Yemen), Koyré's reasoning surely still has a sting in its tail. It was intended to discompose his readers. Writing during the most terrible war in human history, with totalitarian power ascendant in both Europe and East Asia, the thesis he spelled out was chilling in its novelty: 'there has never been so much lying as in our time', he wrote. The point can easily be misunderstood, for Koyré did not mean to emphasise quantitative trends. The really novel quality of contemporary lying was its omnipotent and all-embracing or *total* character. According to Koyré, we live in an age when the scope of political lying dramatically expands. Lying becomes coterminous with life. It becomes not just the canopy but the infrastructure of existence. 'The written and spoken word, the press, the radio, all technical progress is put to the service of the lie. Modern man – *genus totalitarian* – bathes in the lie, breathes the lie, is in thrall to the lie every moment of his existence.' Koyré described modern-day lying as 'mass output for mass consumption'. Despite its utter corruption of democratic values and institutions, the total lie – the kind peddled by totalitarian regimes and (Koyré ventured further) by profit-seeking advertisers who peddle 'patent falsifications' – most definitely belongs to the age of the universal franchise. The Age of the People is the Age of Big Lies. In the 'democratic era of mass civilization', the body known as the People had now to be granted recognition as a sociological fact. They could no longer be ignored, or treated as clueless matter, as ignorant swine to be herded with the stick. Their presence on the stage of history was now undeniable. From the point of view of power elites, they had thus to be acted upon, using state-of-the-art instruments of deception, including second-degree lies, which cleverly weave truths into the fabric of total lies. Like hapless animals stranded in fields of power, the People must be sucked upwards into a gigantic tornado of lies, which transforms them into an organised force for permanent lying.

According to Koyré, leaders like Hitler, who trade in systematic lying, bring to perfection its frightening arts. Political liars of his kind are new. They are power-loving creatures of the new age of mass broadcasting media and democracy. Pseudo-aristocrats who are contemptuous of flesh-and-blood people, they suppose 'the common run of mortals' is credulous, that most human beings are thoroughly gullible creatures, just as Machiavelli had observed in *The Prince*. 'Men are so simple and yield so readily to the desires of the moment', the Florentine adviser of princes had observed, 'that he who will trick will always find another who will suffer to be tricked'.[3] But twentieth-century totalitarians go further, Koyré argued. In effect, they democratise the Machiavellian principle. They suppose that trickery can be a tool of total popular mobilisation. The people are a fickle force, but they can be reckoned with and guided from above, tingling in awe, tears in their eyes, inspired by newspapers, radio broadcasts, films and television programs. Led by their noses, ears and eyes, people can be harnessed as an engine of power, as an instrument of triumphant totalitarian rule legitimated by large-scale lying that is popularly believed and popularly circulated. The really frightening thing about totalitarian liars is their treatment of untruths as a weapon, as a means of deceiving people systematically, for the sake of building and securing total power. Totalitarian liars have little or no respect for the complex realities of the world. Conventional religious objections to lying are also overthrown; the precept that lying, saying what is not, deliberately obfuscating reality, is a grievous sin of pride against the spirit, is rejected as just so much worthless old rubbish from timid and unenlightened times. The principle that 'there exists a single objective truth valid for everybody' is considered claptrap, for political reasons. In totalitarian circles, it is replaced by the primacy of the lie: the Big Lie peddled over and over again by political forces whose leader is worshipped for his ability to manipulate and practise lies with such skill, especially when trapped in tight corners. The numbers of victims and the scale of destruction are unimportant. What counts is victory – over all opposition, across the whole earth.

LYING AND DEMOCRACY

Why bother with such thoughts on political lying and democracy, especially given that they belong to circumstances very different to our own – to

---

[3] Niccolò Machiavelli, *The Prince* (New York: The Modern Library, 1950), pp. 64–65.

dark and baneful times when it was quite probable that totalitarianism would triumph globally in a hellish cauldron of barbarism and total war? Sceptics might point out that with the possible exception of the North Korean regime ruled by bizarre figures such as Kim Jong-il, the Great Leader daily worshipped by the state-controlled DPRK mass media for his efforts to build 'socialism' and 'stop the rain and make the sun come out' (a phrase used during his state visit to Russia in August 2001), totalitarian regimes are no more. Born of the twentieth century, the totalitarian regimes of Germany, Cambodia, China, Albania and Romania have since been reshaped by the forces of internal reform, or political collapse, or military defeat. And (these sceptics might add) democracy has come up smelling of roses in many different places on our planet. So, all things considered, these sceptics might conclude, Koyré's analysis has been superannuated by events, to the point where it is now mostly of antiquarian interest.

There are several possible responses to this line of reasoning. The most obvious has to do with the fact that Koyré spotted the way big lies indeed have a close, if contradictory and heavily contested affinity with democracy. Koyré did not fully grasp the logic of the stormy relationship but his intuition that the positive revaluation of the People and the coming of democracy is certainly of striking relevance in our twenty-first century age of monitory democracy and communicative abundance. Once upon a time, for instance in the early modern Europe described in the classic treatise of Johannes Althusius, *Politica Methodice Digesta, Atque Exemplis Sacris et Profanis Illustrata* (*Politics Methodically Digested, Illustrated with Sacred and Profane Examples* [1603]), organised lying was restricted in geographic scope and social depth. Lies have short legs, ran a sixteenth-century English proverb. When spun by the powerful, their webs did not penetrate easily into a political landscape comprising a mosaic of emerging territorial state monarchies co-existing with many differently sized consociations intersecting from a distance, a world of royal courts, free cities, religious emperors, provincial lords and the Holy Roman Empire, a kaleidoscope of different, sometimes overlapping jurisdictions whose inhabitants were mainly illiterate and normally had little or no contact, except for messages conveyed by means of rumour, or by foot, horse or donkey.

Our times are different. Political lying can easily flourish in the age of media saturation, especially under conditions of fear and war, when rising or ascendant groups can satisfy their hunger for power over others by persuading them to feed on vast untruths, peddled through communication media that penetrate deeply into people's everyday lives. Mobile telephones, radio, film and television and the Internet lengthen lies' legs, their propensity to spread rapidly through vast populations, persuading fearful or confused people that the powerful are correct in their descriptions of reality, even though they deliberately say things that they themselves know are not so. Think of just two epochal moments in our lifetime: the 1964 Gulf of Tonkin incidents during the Vietnam War, the first televised war; or the Weapons of Mass Destruction saga in the so-called war against terrorism of our times. War does indeed nurture the doctrine that the powerful must be allowed to operate in secrecy, according to reasons of state, using hidden counsels wrapped in cultic mystery (*arcana imperii*). More than that, lying is 'a useful instrument of statecraft in a dangerous world', as when President Franklin Roosevelt manoeuvred the United States into the Second World War against Nazi Germany by lying to American citizens about the German attack on the USS Greer in August 1941.[4] That is why, in an era of global mass communications, war is not just destructive of human life. It also poses grave dangers for democratic institutions and their spirit of openness and plurality.

But how does it happen that mass media-saturated societies are unusually prone to the production, reproduction and public circulation of lies? It has been said by Martin Jay, drawing on the work of Hannah Arendt, that since politics is the realm of public action, and since by definition it always involves the capacity to be inventive and to bring novelty into the world, it typically draws on our capacity for imagination, which is a mark of our capacity for freedom.[5] On this view, lying, which is nurtured by our capacity for imagination, is ontological. It is unworthy of knee-jerk moral outrage. It should not be condoned by way of the amoral 'realist' argument that lying is ineluctably bound up with politics, that lying is its necessary ingredient. Lying, says Jay, is a clear alternative to violence. It is generative, a creative act that is coterminous with the art of engaging others in public, as political beings.

The thesis is both too abstract and insensitive to the time–space variations of meaning and function of lying. It comes close to praising the virtue of mendacity, which is why we need to drill more deeply than he did into the symbiotic relationship among democracy, communications

---

[4] John J. Mearsheimer, *Why Leaders Lie: The Truth about Lying in International Politics* (Oxford: Oxford University Press, 2011), pp. 24–25.
[5] Martin Jay, *The Virtues of Mendacity: On Lying in Politics* (Charlottesville, VA: The University of Virginia Press, 2010).

media and lying. The most obvious connection is seen in the fact, confirmed by opinion poll samples taken in every democracy on our planet, that politicians tell lies. Why do they lie? It is not because of their inherent mendacity (though some of them seem hell-bent on proving exactly that) but everything to do with the dynamics of democracy itself. Democracy in representative form is structured by the principle that citizens periodically elect representatives who in effect are put on trial as leaders for a given period of time. Representative democracy is thus guided by the disappointment principle. The presumption is against the performance and credibility of those who have been elected, or those vying to succeed them. The whole point of periodic elections is that electors grant the winners a temporary licence to succeed, or to fail. The threat of failure, the strong possibility that the winners will disappoint the represented, is backed by severe sanctions: public disgrace, in the form of public denunciations and subsequent removal from office, with all the personal and material uncertainties that follow.

If incumbent representatives are to avoid being flung from office, then they have to do everything in their powers to cheer up citizens. Representatives must try to erase or pre-empt their disappointment, to persuade citizens that they are worthy of another term in office or (if and when fixed-term rules kick in) to prepare for life after office by persuading the represented that theirs was a job well done. Especially when things are not going well, and they are under pressure from rivals and citizen voters, persuasion needs a helping hand from old friends, especially the perfumed figure of mendacity. And so representatives are tempted to cast themselves in the role of the Cretan figure of Epimenides of Knossos in the sixth century BCE, to behave like a latter-day Cretan who insisted, hand on heart, that all other Cretans are utter liars. Saying what is not so is risky business, of course; but for the representative who wants to succeed, lying becomes an attractive or seductive option, a vital strategy of re-election, the price of staving off defeat, or salvaging reputation from possible public disgrace. Lying becomes a means of self-protection, a sop to vanity and certain cure for possible humiliation (a point well made by Dorothy Rowe[6]). That is the moment that the Richard Nixon 'I am not a crook'

---

[6] Dorothy Rowe, *Why We Lie* (London: Fourth Estate, 2010), p. x: 'sometimes we lie in response to feeling that we are in great danger, even though there is no threat to our life. We are frightened, and so we lie. What we see as being in danger is something we value even more than our life. It is our sense of being a person ... We move very quickly to protect it.'

political liar is born. It is also the 'Mission Accomplished' moment when George W. Bush announced (1 May 2003) American military victory in Iraq; and it is the saga of the string of deceptions that marked the Tony Blair strategy of clever, hands-on, state-of-the-art media manipulation.

All democratically elected governments are today pro-actively involved in mendacity: clever, cunning struggles to kidnap their citizens mentally through the exercise of what Machiavelli called *astuzia*. Their deepening involvement in the business of manipulation of appearances, the tendency that leads us into 'the age of contrivance' (a phrase coined by the American historian Daniel Boorstin in *The Image* [1962]) or into what some Americans are calling, following Stephen Colbert of Comedy Central, the age of 'truthiness' and 'post-truth', is made plain by the Blair governments' media management tactics. They took the art to new heights. They fed 'leaks' as exclusives ('you can have this, but only if you put it on page 1'). When embarrassing stories broke, they put out decoys. They tried to master the art of releasing bad news on busy days (they called it 'throwing out the bodies'). They denied. They said what was not so. Alastair Campbell, Blair's chief tactician, regularly practised the art of deception, and did so with great cunning and finesse. His deputy (Lance Price) recalls that Campbell, testing the waters, to prove his skill in the game of mendacity, deliberately told a *News of the World* journalist that Blair had stayed on the eighth floor of a hotel that in fact was only six storeys tall (the journalist never bothered to check); and that Campbell went to a Britney Spears concert and managed to get her autograph, then bet somebody £200 he could get the *Evening Standard* to splash a story that she supported New Labour. He won the bet that very day. The dissembling mentality shaping such stunts is revealed graphically, quite by accident, in Blair's recently published autobiography *A Journey*. On the last evening of the second millennium, when the government's extravaganza spectacles (the Millennium Wheel and 'River of Fire' fireworks) had not gone to plan, Blair recalls with horror his discovery that the country's newspaper editors, who had been invited to attend the midnight Millennium Dome celebrations in the presence of the royals and the Prime Minister, had been left queuing for hours at Stratford Station, which had become clogged with New Year's eve revellers. Blair describes how he grabbed by the lapels the minister in charge, his old friend and flatmate Lord 'Charlie' Falconer. 'Please, please, dear God', writes Blair, 'please tell me you didn't have the media coming here by tube from Stratford just like ordinary members of the public.' Lord Falconer replies: 'Well, we thought it would be more democratic that way.' Blair responds:

'Democratic? What fool thought that? They're the media, for Christ's sake. They write about the people, they don't want to be treated like them.' Falconer: 'Well, what did you want us to do, get them all a stretch limo?' Thundered Blair: 'Yes, Charlie, with the boy or girl of their choice and as much champagne as they can drink.'[7]

Efforts by politicians to trick and charm the pants off journalists are of course neither the monopoly of British politics nor the personal penchant of a mendacious politician who was later nicknamed Tony B Liar. Stories of political dissembling by governments and candidates are commonplace in all existing state-bounded democracies. Indian democracy regularly passes through lying about corruption scandals. American democracy has had its recent fair share of political lying. In just one week, during the 2008 US presidential race, the campaign strategy of John McCain fabricated crowd estimates for a rally in Virginia and cunningly circulated several handfuls of untruths, including claims that Barack Obama supported 'comprehensive sex education' for children in kindergarten ('dishonest' and 'deceptive' said *The Washington Post*); that Mr. Obama used the colloquial expression 'lipstick on a pig' to describe Sarah Palin; that Mr Obama would raise taxes on middle-class families and force families into a government-run health care plan; and that Ms. Palin visited Ireland and Iraq (her airplane refuelled in the former and never crossed the border into the latter).[8]

According to most theorists of democracy, journalists and public commentators, such monkey business explains why a free and open communication system is a vital weapon for preventing the spread of lying. From the early modern period, speaking truth to power (the reliance on 'facts' and the pursuit of 'objectivity' are the ritual words used by many journalists) has become the conventional way of putting the point.[9] In recent decades, the principle of speaking truth to power has been reinvigorated by the hope that the new communicative abundance sustained by multimedia digital networks will enable citizens to put a stop to lying by promoting universal 'access', citizen 'participation' and public 'accountability and transparency'. The troubling paradox is that in contemporary monitory democracies, hope is too often scuppered by a decadent trend

---

[7] Tony Blair, *A Journey* (London: Random House, 2010), p. 260. His governments' early obsession with image, style and novelty is described from the inside by Stephen Bayley, *Labour Camp: The Failure of Style Over Substance* (London: B. T. Batsford, 1998).
[8] Michael A. Cohen, 'The Politics of Lying', *The New York Times*, 16 September 2008.
[9] See my account of the early modern claims in defence of 'liberty of the press', in *The Media and Democracy* (Cambridge: Polity Press, 1990).

that favours the rapid circulation of lies. There are more than lies peddled by the politicians and the political class; there are also media lies that have serious political consequences.

Lies take root and flourish everywhere in the soil of communicative abundance. Why does this happen? Common-sense explanations often point the finger at journalists, who are accused of being compulsive liars. That at least was the charge levelled famously by Peregrine Worsthorne, former editor of *The Sunday Telegraph* in Britain. He once asked which part of a newspaper was more truthful: the news stories or the adverts. His answer: the ads. In advertisements for airlines, planes fly and land safely; in news stories, they crash. The ads show households sitting around cosy fires in the depths of winter; in news reports, their houses burn down. Planes rarely crash and houses rarely burn down. Ergo, adverts are more accurate than news.[10] This standard line of attack on news journalism is usually backed up by a litany of complaints voiced by citizens and politicians about 'media', and journalists in particular. They are said to hunt in packs, their eyes on bad news, egged on by the newsroom saying that facts must never be allowed to get in the way of stories. Journalism is organised lying. It obliterates the vital distinction between 'opinion' and 'fact'. It sensationalises everything. Journalism loves titillation, draws upon un-attributed sources, fills news holes – in the age of communicative abundance, news never sleeps – spins sensations, and concentrates too much on personalities rather than time-bound contexts. It is said, especially by bookish types, that journalism is formulaic, that it gets bored too quickly and that it likes to bow down to corporate power and government press briefings.

Such generalisations are undoubtedly exaggerated. Journalists are literally under the gun in many global settings; they bravely risk their lives when they report, and if they find themselves in the wrong place at the wrong time, then they pay the ultimate sacrifice, with their lives. In contemporary democracies, moreover, there are many hardworking, honest and ethically open-minded journalists; and, as Michael Schudson has pointed out, bellyaching against journalists is on balance not such a bad thing for monitory democracy, especially if it sharpens the wits of citizens and encourages their healthy sense of scepticism about power, including the power of journalists to represent and narrate the world in

---

[10] Malcolm Dean, *Democracy Under Attack: How the Media Distort Policy and Politics* (Bristol: Policy Press, 2012), p. 376.

which we live.[11] The bellyaching nevertheless has had damaging effects on the reputations of journalists. Judging by their low popularity ratings, journalists in many democracies are struggling to hold their own against politicians, real estate agents, car salesmen and bankers.

Yet the problem actually runs much deeper than matters of flawed reputation and the reciprocal tit-for-tat dislike that some journalists have for their audiences. Complaints about reputation are in fact symptomatic of a more worrying dynamic, a problem that Koyré, writing in radically different historical circumstances, never quite managed to grasp. For reasons having to do with market pressures and top-down managerial control, most journalists no longer work 'off diary'. In democracies otherwise as different as Japan, Canada, the United States, Australia and Britain, they have little or no time in which to go out into the field and find their own stories and carefully check the material they are handling. Swept along by ever-rising floods of digital information and pulled by working conditions, they become highly vulnerable to ingesting and reproducing the packages of information that are supplied to them by the public relations industry and governments. Like a human body lacking a properly functioning immune system, many media platforms sprinkle lies all over the place. Journalists produce lots of distorted or pseudo-news or pseudo-coverage about pseudo-events – lots of flat earth news.[12] Often the stories journalists spin amount to 'small' or 'casual' lies; in a rush, one eye on advancement, the other on the looming deadline, they handle truth carelessly. They produce what President Donald Trump and his supporters dubbed 'fake news'.

The flat earth news trend within the ranks of professional journalism is often reinforced by the growth of blogging, twitter and other forms of so-called citizen journalism. There are undeniably good things coming out of this rough-and-tumble, kaleidoscopic world of competing and conflicting opinions about matters of public interest; in contexts such as Iran and China, for instance, citizen journalism poses a genuine threat to secretive, heavy handed abuses of power. Picking up on this trend, John Hartley and others have praised the recent rapid expansion of a culture of redaction. He speaks of a 'redactional society' in which citizens are engaged as producers in sifting through the chaos of their information worlds by 'learning how to share, deploy, trust, evaluate, contest and act upon

---

[11] Michael Schudson, *Why Democracies Need an Unlovable Press* (Cambridge: Polity Press, 2009).
[12] Nick Davies, *Flat Earth News* (London: Chatto & Windus, 2009).

collective knowledge'.[13] In much the same vein, Umberto Eco and others have spoken of the contemporary importance of 'overstanding', a form of interpretation of the world that does more than ask questions and produce answers posed by the myriad of symbolic artefacts surrounding us. Over-standing, which should not be confused with over-interpretation, is the thoughtful activity of posing questions that these power-ridden symbolic materials otherwise take for granted, frustrate, silence or deny outright.[14] These and other interpretations of the contributions to public life by citizens are important. They highlight the possibility of expanding and democratising the role of public commentary in the age of monitory democracy. But their chief limitation, in my view, is the way they ignore the threats to veracity posed by the displacement and destruction of what might be called edification.

Edification: the family of terms linked to the words editing and education, and to their Latin root (*aedificare*: to build, from *aedis* 'dwelling' and *facere* 'make'), remind us not only of the vital and inescapable importance for democracy of intelligent editorial judgements about how publicly to represent the world in which we dwell; these terms point to a darker trend, the downside effects that happen when conventional editorial practices are wrong-footed by working conditions, and by 'amateur' journalists and their defenders, who are prone to talk loosely of the importance of replacing authoritative truth with what is sometimes called 'horizontal truth', collectively produced opinions that are said to be more or less of equal worth. It is all very well to place emphasis on self-chosen citizen representatives actively hashing through competing interpretations, instead of deferring to authoritative sources of information. But the inconvenient point is that sloppy journalism and online mis-reportage, false rumours and nonsense evidently flourish in the age of communicative abundance. Take just one randomly selected early example, the moment (November 2010) of panic and confusion surrounding news of the mid-air explosion of a jet engine on a Qantas A380 bound for Sydney from Singapore. The event triggered a chaotic bluster of random tweets and other messages, unchecked and un-sourced, many of them wildly inaccurate. Speed dictated that even sources such as ABC News

---

[13] John Hartley, 'Communicative Democracy in a Redactional Society: The Future of Journalism Studies', *Journalism*. 1 (2000), 39–47.

[14] See Umberto Eco, *Interpretation and Overinterpretation: Umberto Eco with Richard Rorty, Jonathan Culler and Christine Brooke-Rose*, edited by Stefan Collini (Cambridge: Cambridge University Press, 1992); see also Wayne C. Booth, *Critical Understanding: The Powers and Limits of Pluralism* (Chicago, IL: University of Chicago Press, 1979).

(@abcnews) compounded the bedlam with posts such as: 'Kyodo news wire is reporting a passenger plane thought bound for Singapore has crashed in Indonesia.' The ill-chosen words prompted a Qantas spokesperson to confess that reports on the Internet and Twitter were 'wildly inaccurate'. By then the failed engine itself had chipped in with a tweet via @QF32_Engine_2: 'I've been a very, very bad engine.' The absurdity was well summarised by a tweet from Sydney journalist (@Jen_Bennett): 'I have an unconfirmed report that says your unconfirmed report is unconfirmed. More speculation as it breaks.'

Such episodes underscore how crumbs of news of events can and do generate nonsense rumours that go viral, sometimes to the point where they morph from mere pitter-patter, water-cooler chatter into re-blogged and re-tweeted inaccuracies and outright falsehoods. Recycled information without edification produces falsification, as when reputable newspapers like the *Washington Post* published no fewer than eighteen editorials in favour of the view that weapons of mass destruction (WMD) existed; or when (according to the *Pew Research Center* [19 August 2010]) nearly half of American Republicans believed that President Barack Obama was a Muslim, over a quarter doubted that he is a citizen, and fully half, again falsely, believed that the massive bailout of banks and insurance companies was enacted by Obama, not by President Bush. The cut-and-paste carelessness of mainstream media, their lack of questioning and absence of editing is compounded by the impatient fame seeking fuelled by bloggers' and tweeters' desire to prove they are the source of breaking news; that they are capable of attracting substantial numbers of clicks and readers' eyeballs; some of them (oft-cited examples include Gawker and Guido Fawkes) are interested in maximising clicks because they believe it will attract advertisers, build brand value and generate income and wealth.

The famous lithograph by A. Paul Weber, 'Das Gerücht (The Rumour)' serves as a reminder that the trouble with unchecked messages of questionable veracity is their propensity to grow long legs, and long tails (Figure 5.1). In the age of communicative abundance, the task of keeping lids on wilful and half-intended distortions often proves challenging, especially because the means are freely available for spreading apparently credible information rapidly to large numbers of people. Since in everyday settings most citizens are preoccupied with a range of personal matters, and therefore do not have the time or inclination to double-check the information passing through their lives, a 'tipping point' can be reached, a 'cybercascade' moment when confusion, anxiety and fear drive

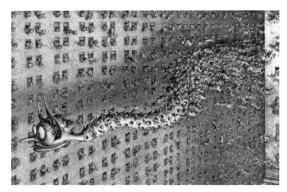

FIGURE 5.1 A. Paul Weber, *Das Gerücht* (The Rumour) 1943

a dramatic shift of collective opinion. Large groups of people end up believing something – regardless of whether or not that something is true – simply because other people, in the relevant community, seem to believe that it is true.[15] Whether, or to what extent, there is substance in the claim, sometimes implied by media critics, that the production and spread of lies is proof negative that many 'digital native' citizens are vulnerable to 'gaslighting' and are gradually losing their ability to make intelligent judgements about matters of public importance, is examined elsewhere.[16] In fact, there is little but anecdotal evidence for the view that the unfinished communications revolution is nurturing self-absorbed and degraded characters gripped by incomprehension, the self-deluded, groping, death-sentenced 'I of whom I know nothing' types found in Samuel Beckett's *The Unnamable* (1953). More plausible is the worry, taken up in the following pages, that there is another form of lying for which 'churnalism', in both its professional and citizen forms, is responsible. Let's call it no earth news. It could be called the narration of public silence, or perhaps malevolent silence, since it takes the form of important events and processes, which journalists around the world deliberately fail to take an interest in, or to tell. They choose a sub-form of lying, wilful ignorance. They choose not to take an interest in reporting the way things are. They lie from a distance, so to speak; and they do so, in no small

---

[15] Cass R. Sunstein, *Republic.com* (Princeton, NJ and Oxford: Princeton University Press, 2002), p. 44.
[16] John Keane, *Democracy and Media Decadence* (Cambridge and New York: Cambridge University Press, 2013).

measure, because such subjects as the global redistribution of poverty, efforts to build cross-border institutions, species destruction, the arms trade and leveraging in the banking and credit sectors are highly complicated and perforce require intensive concentration, language skills and in-depth research to cover thoroughly, or to cover well. Journalists simply don't bother with such matters. They conspire in taciturnity tinged with ignorance. The result: deliberately crafted hush about the wider world upon whose push–pull dynamics the lives of millions of citizens dangle.

TRUTH?

The affinities between democracy and lying are clear, and they ought to be unsettling for democrats everywhere. But what can be said about the business of truth, said often to be the binary opposite of lying? Truth and lying are relational terms. Yet what is the difference between them? Is the distinction still plausible? If so, how are we to speak of truth in an age when naïve conceptions of veracity and 'objectivity' have been picked and pulled apart by such disparate developments as the disconnection of religious authority and science, the linguistic turn in philosophy and the multiplication of representatives under conditions of monitory democracy?[17] To put things in a more precise, if abstract way: if truth (as I shall suggest) has a history, and if today it is the name we give to statements governed by rules that define what we mean when we speak of truth, even when we wilfully go against it – that is, tell lies – surely this implies that truth and lying, its binary opposite, have no ultimate foundations unburdened by the contingencies of time and space? And, if that is so, if in other words truth is neither a fixed nor reliable marker by which to measure lying, doesn't that imply that the act of telling lies, wilfully saying what is not so, in effect is licensed to go on the rampage, unconstrained by its other half, the objectivity of truth?

It is not easy to answer these vexing questions. Parents who demand of their children to tell the plain truth, or those who swear in a court of law to 'tell the truth, the whole truth and nothing but the truth', do so for reasons they think to be compelling. They suppose that truth is the opposite of lying, that whenever a lie is told, the liar by definition knows that s/he is going against the truth. Unfortunately, things are not so straightforward. The distinction between truth and lying has a heavily

---

[17] Gianni Vattimo, *A Farewell to Truth* (New York: Columbia University Press, 2011).

contested history, as Perez Zagorin has highlighted in his powerful account of such forms of dissimulation in early modern Europe as the Catholic doctrine of mental reservation, crypto-Judaism and the dissimulation of religious unbelief among philosophers and men of letters.[18] There is considerable evidence as well that in Europe the birth of subjects who thought of themselves as capable of distinguishing truth from falsity, and who considered the practice of avowal and truth-telling (*le dire vrai*) as a form of self-purification, was the contingent outcome of religious forces and post-religious institutions in such fields as law, medicine and psychiatry.[19] These and other enquiries suggest that what counts as truth is a matter of opinion; and that truth, supposedly the touchstone of what counts as lying, is a persuasive set of metaphors, points of view (Nietzsche's words) that through time come to 'seem firm, canonical, and obligatory to a people', attitudes that draw their sustenance from 'a sum of human relations, which have been enhanced, transposed, and embellished poetically and rhetorically'.[20]

But let us pause for a moment, to examine a puzzling trend. Sceptics say that talk of truth is implausible, or a downright fraud, but remarkable – and strange – is the tenacity of the whole idea of truth. It's widely said we live in the age of 'truthiness'; that truth is a trope; and that everything's relative to everything else. Yet despite the scepticism and prevarication, public references to the 'truth' of things are flourishing. The post-modernist sensibility seems correspondingly to be making no headway, or weakening. There's much talk of the value of 'objectivity', references to indisputable 'facts' and resorts to Truth Commissions. Fed by websites such as www.factcheck.org, and by Truth-O-Meters provided by organisations like Politifact, there is a new enfranchisement of Certainties and Facts, an embrace of the view that the clear and vocal verdicts of Truth must be respected. People from all walks of life meanwhile regularly say things like 'true!', or 'that's not true'. And we live in times

---

[18] Perez Zagorin, *Ways of Lying: Dissimulation, Persecution and Conformity in Early Modern Europe* (Cambridge, MA and London: Harvard University Press, 1990).
[19] Michel Foucault, *Wrong-Doing, Truth-Telling: The Function of Avowal in Justice*, edited by Fabienne Brion and Bernard E. Harcourt (Chicago, IL and London: University of Chicago Press, 2014).
[20] Friedrich Nietzsche, 'On Truth and Lie in an Extra-Moral Sense [Über Wahrheit und Lüge im außermoralischen Sinn]', in *The Viking Portable Nietzsche*, translated by Walter Kaufmann (New York: Viking Press, 1976), pp. 46–47.

when sorting out the truth in politics hatches great political scandals that double as media events, episodes when 'telling the truth' becomes of paramount value to the parties caught up in a public conflict.

Backed by these trends, the practice of truth-telling is stubbornly resistant to doubt, so marking monitory democracies with a strange paradox: while this new form of democracy encourages great outpourings of public truth-telling, its dynamics of public scrutiny of arbitrary power encourage serious doubts to be cast on the whole idea of unquestionable truth. For complicated historical reasons that run deep, and stretch back at least to Luther's famous, explosive, influential attack on popery as the sole interpreter of scripture in *An Open Letter to the Christian Nobility of the German Nation Concerning the Reform of the Christian Estate* (1520), talk of 'Truth' or 'truth' has become philosophically and politically questionable under conditions of monitory democracy. Gone are the ages marked by keywords such as grace, salvation, evolution, progress, natural law, reason and perfectibility.[21] Tropes like 'We hold these truths to be self-evident' nowadays arouse suspicions. The whole tendency is fed by a growing abundance of platforms where power is interrogated and chastened, so that monitory democracies nurture uncertainty, doubt, scepticism and irony. They help spread the conviction that truth has many faces, the recognition that truth understood as the firm grasp of the 'real world' and its dynamics is never fully attainable.

Philosophers in the European tradition have complicated matters further by pointing to the disputed plural meanings of the 'truth' word. For instance, truth can refer to 'factuality',[22] propositions that correspond to 'reality', to the accurate 'mirroring' of reality by ideas in our heads, or in bar graphs or statistical charts that purport to represent 'objectively' some or other state of affairs. Alternatively, truth can refer to watertight, logical reasoning, to the learned art of developing a chain of premises which lead to a valid conclusion, such as 'snow is white is true if and only if snow is

---

[21] Compare the famous and forward-looking remark by Carl L. Becker, *The Heavenly City of the Eighteenth-Century Philosophers* (New Haven, CT: Yale University Press, 1932), p. 47: 'In the thirteenth century the key words would no doubt be God, sin, grace, salvation, heaven and the like; in the nineteenth century, matter, fact, matter-of-fact, evolution, progress; in the twentieth century, relativity, process, adjustment, function, complex. In the eighteenth century the words without which no enlightened person could reach a restful conclusion were nature, natural law, first cause, reason, sentiment, humanity, perfectibility.'

[22] Harry G. Frankfurt, *On Truth* (New York: Alfred A. Knopf, 2009), p. 54.

white'. Other philosophers, by contrast, have thought that truth can only mean 'the disclosure of what keeps itself concealed'.[23] Wittgenstein and other language game philosophers have meanwhile said that truth or knowledge is in the end always based on acknowledgement, the more or less shared 'world picture' and language framework (Thomas Kuhn would later say the paradigm) in which we live our lives, a framework that 'imagines' and 'interprets' the world and pre-structures what meaningfully is communicated to others.

Koyré had sympathy for the view that what counts as truth in any time–space context has a deeply 'imaginative' dimension. He grasped that lying and truth-telling belong to the same linguistic universe, if only because both are nurtured by leaps of imagination concerning what 'reality' is; both suppose the human ability to imagine in mental pictures the world around us, 'as it really is'. That's why fools can neither lie nor spot the truth. This was of course a vital point inscribed within Oscar Wilde's scurrilous defence of art as the struggle to tell lies, as the active pursuit of 'beautiful untrue things'.[24] Koyré himself proposed that acts of imagination have played a vital role throughout the history of science. He did not regard the pursuit of truth in scientific matters as the quest progressively to strip away simulations, veils or appearances from things 'as they really are'. Truth is not the quest to find the happy correspondence between the statements we make and objects of fact. Truth has many faces. It is marked by a definite elusiveness, which is why, he understood, the act of telling lies is much easier than revealing the truth. ''Tis as easy as lying', Shakespeare says in *Hamlet* (Act 3). The remark underscored the way liars have in their heads definite pictures of what they are denying. Tell a lie, and find the truth, runs an old English proverb. By definition, a lie is a wilful act of fabulation, of saying what is not so. What is so is taken for granted – unlike truth, which even in the hands of the most hard-nosed believers in unvarnished Truth (think of Thomas Gradgrind, in Dickens' *Hard Times*, a 'man of realities ... of facts and calculations') is always said to involve pains-taking and time-consuming efforts to release reality from the distorting dross of fabrications.

---

[23] Martin Heidegger, 'The Origin of the Work of Art', in *Poetry, Language, Thought* (New York: Harper & Row, 1975), p. 56.
[24] Oscar Wilde, 'The Decay of Lying: An Observation', in *Intentions* (London: Methuen, 1913), pp. 1–56.

THE POLITICAL DANGERS OF LYING

Koyré's proposition that what counts as truth is always marked by 'imagination' put him at odds with Hannah Arendt's later defence of 'factual reality' and 'meticulous loyalty to factual, given reality'.[25] Koyré acknowledged that for many observers truth and human reality are twins. For them, truth is the aspiration to tear down curtains and to demolish falsehoods through the re-description of living realities, with some measure of accuracy. But Koyré rejected the view, fashionable among contemporary philosophers of science, that truth is gleaned empirically through hypothesis formation and testing by means of practical experimentation. In perhaps his best-known work, *From the Closed World to the Infinite Universe*, Koyré pointed out that the rise of early modern science crucially entailed a conceptual revolution, a fundamental *Gestalt* switch among scientists during the period stretching from Nicholas of Cusa and Giordano Bruno through to Isaac Newton.[26] It was not just that Copernicus and the newly invented telescope dramatically widened human horizons by calling into question notions of an ordered universe of 'fixed stars'. The key point for Koyré is that the scientific quest for truth, the aspiration to know the secrets of the universe, is always and inescapably embedded in specific historical circumstances; that is, in the time–space world of language, institutions and characters in which perforce human beings dwell on earth.

Koyré's sensitivity to the contingencies of knowledge, his scepticism about naïvely empiricist accounts of truth, his sympathy for the view that in matters of truth (as President Bill Clinton later famously put it) everything 'depends on what the meaning of "is" is': all of this arguably retains its bite in the age of monitory democracy. It is not just that Koyré's approach cuts against the grain of simple-minded or un-ironic beliefs in Truth, or that it nudges our democratic sensibilities towards a more plural understanding of truth. More surprising is the way Koyré's thinking implies the need to guard against organised efforts to destroy outright the idea of truth and its antagonist, lying. To illustrate this paradox

---

[25] Hannah Arendt, 'Lying in Politics: Reflections on the Pentagon Papers', in *Crises of the Republic* (New York: Harcourt Brace Jovanovich, 1972), p. 11; and 'Truth and Politics', in *Between Past and Future: Eight Exercises in Political Thought* (New York: Viking Press, 1968), pp. 227–264.

[26] Alexandre Koyré, *From the Closed World to the Infinite Universe* (Baltimore, MD: The Johns Hopkins University Press, 1957).

imagine for a moment ('counter-factually') a world where talk of truth and Truth had been abolished. What would be the consequences?

There would most likely be several tangible effects. The whole phenomenon of lying would by definition disappear. We don't usually think of things this way, but since truth and lies are twins, lying, the opposite of truth, keeps the whole idea of truth alive. Lying is the deliberate saying of what is not so. It is wilful deception – covering up things that the liar supposes to be 'true'. Harry Truman said: 'Richard Nixon is a no good, lying bastard. He can lie out of both sides of his mouth at the same time, and if he ever caught himself telling the truth, he'd lie just to keep his hand in.'[27] Truman meant: when Richard Nixon lies, he supposes he knows what is true. When inventing effective lies, he designs falsehoods under the guidance of truth. When all's said and done, Richard Nixon, the no good lying bastard, knows the meaning of, and pays homage to, truth.

So if in a world without truth, lying would by definition disappear; we could no longer say 'all politicians are bloody liars'. Citizens, journalists and politicians could not accuse bogus think tanks, corporations and lobbyists of 'handling the truth carelessly'. Emancipated from the scourge of lying, people might feel welcome relief, and propose three cheers, but that would be premature, for the disappearing of truth would entail several probable downsides for democracy. The most obvious setback would be that the powerful, those who decide on behalf of others who gets what when and how, would find it much easier to get their way. Speaking truth to power, the originally eighteenth-century mantra of philosophers, journalists and citizens, always forced the powerful to do battle with public accusations of their illegitimacy. Talk of truth (she was often represented as a woman) was one of arbitrary power's limits, as I tried to show in two studies of power: the late eighteenth-century life and writings of Tom Paine, who triggered the Silas Deane affair, the first public scandal of the young American republic; and a history of power in twentieth-century Europe centred on Václav Havel, a citizen playwright who courageously defied arbitrary power for several decades before 1989 in the name of the principle of 'living in the truth'.[28] One broad

---

[27] Harry S. Truman, in Merle Miller, *Plain Speaking: An Oral Biography of Harry S. Truman* (New York: Berkley Books, 1974), p. 179.

[28] John Keane, *Tom Paine: A Political Life* (New York and London: Little Brown, 1995); Václav Havel, *The Power of the Powerless*, edited by John Keane (London: Hutchinson, 1984) and John Keane, *Vaclav Hável: A Political Tragedy in Six Acts* (London: Bloomsbury, 2000).

implication of these particular studies is that the abolition of truth would abolish more than lying. Truth is a trope, but when cleverly used its champions can and do have unsettling effects on arrogant and powerful governors. In a world where references to God have lost their absolute grip and no longer serve as checks upon hubris, ditching truth would require citizens and their elected and unelected representatives to lay down a powerful weapon when confronted by arbitrary power. The powerless would become more vulnerable to the powerful.

The disappearing of the language of truth from public life would likely have another consequence: a world that disregarded veracity would become vulnerable to the spread of a special kind of language popularly known as bullshit.[29] The growth of advertising, combined with press releases from public relations agencies and constantly issued government 'announcables',[30] are among its key present-day drivers. From the perspective of truth and lying, bullshit is a dangerous phenomenon with democratic qualities: since every politician, every organisation and every citizen is supposed to have views on things, no matter how ill-conceived or carelessly put, the whole matter of veracity can easily be set aside, or sent packing. Consider a randomly chosen example: a sentimental war veteran speaking before a crowd, in the presence of television, radio and newspaper journalists, emphasising how great his country is, and how he and his fellow soldiers who gave their hearts, their guts and their blood, on foreign shores made their homeland ('us') the greatest country in the world. In this context, the speaker isn't trying to deceive or truthfully enlighten the audience; the speaker simply doesn't care what the audience thinks. Matters of what's true and what's false are irrelevant. The speaker as 'bullshit artist' wants simply to be seen as a patriot, sincere all the way down to his socks, or underwear. His sincerity is a form of bullshit. It's a performance, certainly; but like excrement, from which all nutrients have been removed, his bullshit is empty speech. Bullshit is excrement without nutrient. It's 'hot air', improvised speech from which informative content and truth claims have been extracted, hence potentially the fertiliser of the soil in which publicly unaccountable, arbitrary power flourishes.

---

[29] Harry G. Frankfurt, *On Bullshit* (Princeton, NJ and London: Princeton University Press, 2005).

[30] Lindsey Tanner, *Sideshow: Dumbing Down Democracy* (Melbourne: Penguin Books, 2012).

MULTIPLE TRUTHS

Wherever power is exercised over others in publicly unaccountable ways, it can and often does have crippling effects. Things go wrong and the mishaps maim people's lives, especially in circumstances in which the powerful fall narcissistically in love with their own particular sense of judgement. When that happens, the radius of their circle of advisors shrinks. They denigrate and push aside their critics. Hubris sets in. The powerful fall prey to the bad human habit of believing what is convenient and telling themselves what they want to hear. So they tell lies and generally become dismissive of all opinions and evidence that run counter to their own views. They hallucinate while talking hot air. What they are doing and why they are doing this or that comes clothed in mendacious phantasms, to the point where problems, policy failures and enforced retreats either go unrecognised or are interpreted, falsely, as irrelevancies, or triumphs.

The hubris problem brings us back face-to-face to the truth paradox, raised earlier. Koyré taught that lying poses grave dangers to democracy. The pages above have set out to complicate his thesis, by suggesting that even though truth claims are always questionable, the eviction of lying as a lived category from public life would serve the interests of arbitrary power. Speaking truth to power would become a meaningless phrase. Bullshit would flourish. So would wilful ignorance. Four decades ago, the American psychologist Irving Janis labelled hubristic behaviour as 'groupthink', the tendency of decision makers operating in group settings to lie to others and to ignore counter-evidence in the interests of towing the line, getting things done and protecting their flanks.[31] He showed how groupthink played a fundamental shaping role in the fiasco of the American invasion of Cuba at the Bay of Pigs. More recent examples of political decisions, or political non-decisions, protected by groupthink spring to mind, among them the invasion and occupation of Iraq and Afghanistan, the mishandling of the 2003 SARS epidemic by the Hong Kong Chief Executive and the pseudo-regulation of BP that led to the Deepwater

---

[31] Irving Janis, *Victims of Groupthink: A Psychological Study of Foreign-Policy Decisions and Fiascoes* (New York: Houghton Mifflin Company, 1972); see also Paul 't Hart, *Groupthink in Government: A Study of Small Groups and Policy Failure* (Baltimore, MD: The Johns Hopkins University Press, 1994) and Paul 't Hart *et al.* (eds.), *Beyond Groupthink: Political Group Dynamics and Foreign Policy-making* (Ann Arbor, MI: University of Michigan Press, 1997).

Horizon oil spill. Groupthink was also at work in the negligence of many democratic governments in allowing banking and credit institutions to regulate their own affairs, unhindered by objections and fears that the large-scale 'leveraging' of risk in money markets would result eventually in giant market bubbles, whose bursting would bring the world nearly to the point of a global great depression.

Such groupthink-fuelled policy disasters are no laughing matter. In Iceland, for example, the 2,300-page Truth Report released by a Special Investigation Commission shows how that tiny country was led into misery and global disgrace by an unchecked, shadowy and dissembling government and a banking sector that grew within seven years to become ten times the size of the whole economy.[32] Key decisions were confined to a few government ministers; lines of communication throughout the political economy were deliberately kept unclear; no reports on the banks were written. Everything was off the record. Such organised mendacity always and everywhere has far-reaching effects. In the twenty-first century world of long-distance interdependence, institutional lying shapes and damages the lives of millions of people; for a variety of reasons to do with communicative abundance, technological scale and the geographic mobility of capital and governmental power, the global footprint of lying is widening. It gives a new meaning to the old proverb that fools never differ: wilfully ignorant power is unchecked power, and unchecked power is dangerous power, ultimately because it turns a blind eye to the universe of great complexity, great unknowns and great unintended consequences in which it operates.

If hubris nurtured by groupthink and its lies is a disease produced by publicly unaccountable power, then the only known human cure for its deadly effects is the free circulation of courageous conjectures, corrective judgements, the institutional humbling of power by means of public checks and balances on liars. The cure requires the preservation of the truth/falsity dualism; but differing viewpoints about what is true and false must also logically be part of the remedy. Truth must be kept alive, in more humble form. Truth is a necessary democratic trope. Yet upper-case Truth is the enemy of democracy. Truths in the plural are by contrast its mainstay. Truth seeking is against Truth. Truth seeking involves doubt, scepticism, stubborn incredulity, a willingness to stand back temporarily

---

[32] See 'Causes of the Collapse of the Icelandic Banks – Responsibility, Mistakes and Negligence', in *Report of the Special Investigation Commission* (Reykjavik, April 2010), www.rna.is/media/skjol/RNAvefurKafli21Enska.pdf.

from the world for the purpose of questioning and rejecting non-sensical claims made on its behalf. Truth seeking is suspicious of bullshit, forms of speech in which concern for veracity is extinguished. Truth seeking requires independent reflection on the world. It is aware of its own elusiveness. Truth seeking welcomes semi-colons, the awareness of nuances, plural propositions and complex realities. Truth seeking requires courage – what Greek democrats called *parrhesia* – and it implies breaking the rules that govern definitions of what we mean by truth. For that reason, truth seeking refuses convictions, Truth-fuelled commitments to ideologies such as the Market, the Nation, dogmatic Christianity, self-righteous Judaism or purist Islam. Truth seeking is equally tough on liars, and not just because they tell lies. Despite their knavery, liars belong to the category of the gullible because they make a double mistake. Not only do they suppose that truth is an unproblematic given, so ignoring its many faces. Liars presume, again mistakenly, that others are incapable of seeing through lies because they cannot think for themselves, in complex ways. The quest for truth demands awareness of inconsistencies and contradictions; it requires a sensibility to difficulties and complexities, the capacity for thought and judgement. It therefore has no truck with what Hannah Arendt sometimes praised as the 'despotic character' of truth when it seeks entry into the world of politics.[33]

WISE CITIZENS

Can monitory democracies shield themselves from organised lying at the same time as living without the presumption of singular Truth? Can they cope in practice with the existential ambiguities and political complications posed by plural truths? It's not an easy act. 'If a lie had no more faces but one, as truth hath', remarked Montaigne, 'we should be in farre better termes than we are: For whatsoever a lier should say, we would take it in a contrarie sense. But the opposite of truth hath many-many shapes, and an undefinite field.'[34] For better or worse, the 'undefinite field' with which monitory democracies now have to live is more 'undefinite' than

---

[33] Hannah Arendt, 'Truth and Politics', in *Between Past and Future* (New York: Viking Press, 1968), p. 241: 'The modes of thought and communication that deal with truth ... are necessarily domineering; they don't take into account other people's opinions, and taking these into account is the hallmark of all strictly political thinking.'
[34] 'Of Lyers', in *The Essayes of Michael Lord of Montaigne*, Book 1 (London: Grant Richards, 1908), chapter 9, p. 39.

Montaigne could have imagined. In its most vibrant moments, monitory democracy thrives on *parrhesia*: differing viewpoints about what is true and false, bold challenges to lies and bullshit and groupthink, free-spirited talk, conjectures and counter-conjectures, the institutional humbling of power by means of checks and balances placed on the merchants of Truth, all of this done with a strong sense that 'truth' has many faces. Monitory democracy is shaped by what Daniel Kahneman has called 'slow thinking', structured by institutions that pick apart 'illusions of certainty' by nurturing 'a culture in which people watch out for one another as they approach minefields'.[35] Monitory democracy casts public doubt on the cliché that every society is dominated by a 'regime of truth', the line of formulaic thinking later often repeated by supporters of Michel Foucault, for whom the valorisation of contingent belief as truth uttered by some who are charged with saying what is true is an effect of power/knowledge games.[36] Instead, monitory democracy generates public diffidence towards power wrapped in truth claims, and lies. It thrives on unceasing battles 'for truth' and 'around truth'. It is equally alive to the way small lies have a nasty habit of metamorphosing into big lies, and that that is why the robust public scrutiny of power, for instance by means of such monitory mechanisms as judicial review, muckraking and other forms of investigative journalism,[37] truth commissions and social audits, is the wisest and most effective early warning system, the most powerful means of coping with uncertainty and anticipating, recognising and preventing big mistakes, and big evils.

---

[35] Daniel Kahneman, *Thinking, Fast and Slow* (London and New York: Allen Lane, 2011), p. 418.

[36] Meaghan Morris and Paul Patton (eds.), *Michel Foucault: Power, Truth, Strategy* (Sydney: Feral Publications, 1979), p. 46.

[37] An example is the Dutch crowd-funded news site *de Correspondent*. Launched in 2013, it is committed to a new and more pluralist understanding of 'truth' and 'news'. Its editor, Rob Wijnberg, explains that 'news' claiming to be 'true' and 'objective' is the great unrecognised addiction of our time. He insists that those who only see the world via 'the news' are unlikely to know how the world works, and that what is therefore needed is a digital experiment that presents news differently, from a variety of perspectives, more slowly, more contextually. 'I don't believe in "the news" in the objective sense of the word', says Wijnberg. 'You can describe the world in infinite ways, and "the news" happens to be one of them ... I want the correspondents to make their choices explicit – what do they think is important, and why should readers care about it? You do that by making clear that you're not following an objective news agenda, but a subjective journey through the world'; see www.niemanlab.org/2013/04/a-dutch-crowdfunded-news-site-has-raised-1-3-million-and-hopes-for-a-digital-native-journalism/?relatedstory.

So if the free circulation of small truths is a weapon against the potentially deadly effects of singular Truth, and if as well they are a potent palliative against bullshit, groupthink and the Big Lies feared by Koyré, monitory democracy has a close affinity with the outlook recommended by Wittgenstein. 'Suppose it were forbidden to say "I know" and only allowed to say "I believe I know"', he reflected.[38] Writing in the age of mass circulation newspapers, radio and television, Wittgenstein could not have foreseen the many ways in which the unfinished communications revolution of our time has fortified his understanding that nothing in this world can be certain – not even this statement – and that truth has more than a few faces. All things considered, every dark moment included, this unfinished revolution is on balance a friend of pluralism. Gone are the days when millions of people, huddled together as masses in the shadows of totalitarian power, found the skilfully orchestrated radio and film performances and big lies of demagogues fascinating, and existentially reassuring. Message-saturated democracies generate plenty of political lying, certainly; but liars find themselves subject to intense public scrutiny and restraint. People's suspicions of manipulation by media performances grow; liars consequently find that while they need to lie more convincingly they are more easily 'outed' publicly.

Under conditions of monitory democracy, the new galaxy of digitally networked media tends to nourish people's sensitivity to power, in its manifold forms. Communicative abundance tends to widen people's horizons. It helps spread different perspectives on the world. It does so by multiplying the genres of storytelling that are readily available to inquisitive publics. Breaking news, investigative journalism, chat shows, blogs, political oratory, comedy, infotainment, advertising, drama, music – all this, and more, jostle for public attention. The whole trend is unfinished, and fragile, but it suggests the need to abandon the cherished old ideal of 'the informed citizen'. Fully engaged citizens whose heads are stuffed with unlimited quantities of 'information' about a 'reality' they have mastered: the image of the model citizen is both utterly implausible and anti-democratic, a worn-out ideal dating from the late nineteenth century.[39] Favoured originally by the champions of a restricted, educated franchise, and by interests who rejected partisan politics grounded in the vagaries

---

[38] Ludwig Wittgenstein, *Über Gewissheit/On Certainty* (New York: Harper Torchbooks, 1972), aphorism 366, p. 47e.
[39] Michael Schudson, *The Good Citizen: A History of American Civic Life* (New York and London: The Free Press, 1998), pp. 69–77, 182–185.

and injustices of everyday social life, the ideal of the 'informed citizen' was elitist in effect. It has since become an intellectualist ideal. It's unsuited to the age of plural truths, lying, bullshit and groupthink. It has no place in times that badly need not 'informed citizens', but wise citizens: people who know they don't know everything, citizens who are suspicious of those who think they do, especially when they try to camouflage their arrogant will to power over others.

6

Silence, Early Warnings and Catastrophes

When wise citizens look around and think about the world they easily see that we are living in an age marked by 'megaprojects': large-scale corporate and state adventures of power that touch and transform the lives of millions of people and their bio-habitats in dramatic ways. These big-footprint power adventures include not just superhighway schemes, carbon filtration plants (the world's first has just opened in Norway), under-sea tunnels and mining operations centred on gold, or coal, uranium, tar sands and rare earth metals, they also include shadow banking projects, inter-city high-speed railway networks, new airports and airport extensions, the research and development of new weapons systems, liquid natural gas plants, new communications systems and nuclear power stations. These megaprojects are distinguished by their astronomical design and construction costs (at least US$1 billion) and by their substantial complexity, scale and deep impact upon communities of people and their environment. In power terms, they are typically hybrid arrangements that involve consortia of variously sized businesses as well as funding and logistical support from governments.

Megaprojects defy the conventional distinction between 'capitalist' markets and 'bureaucratic' states. It is safe to say that their power dynamics typically violate democratic ideals and institutions. Sometimes born of elections and signed off by parliaments, megaprojects resemble sizeable tumours of arbitrary power within the body politic of democracy. They violate the familiar rhythm of politics associated with elections; details of their design, financing, construction and operation are typically decided from above; and especially when it comes to military and commercial megaprojects, things are decided in strictest secrecy, with virtually no monitoring by parliaments, outside watchdog groups or voting citizens.

Such projects are a mixed blessing for democratic politics. Yes, they create jobs and measurable wealth, exchangeable commodities, scientific-technical know-how and improved services. Many make our lives easier – the invention of the Internet is proof positive of that. Often a source of local and national pride, they can generate large profits, but even when no golden harvest results they add hugely to the private fortunes of their owners, managers and shareholders. Megaprojects make some people mega-rich. But this is just half the story.

Given their high sunk costs, their complexity and scale, and measured in terms of the numbers of people whose lives are affected, megaprojects can have damaging effects. It is not just that they resemble predators with large appetites in a democratic environment or, to switch similes, that megaprojects suspend democratic politics through the enactment of permanent forms of emergency rule. When megaprojects malfunction, as they are prone to do, they destructively impact upon human beings and our biosphere on a scale unimaginable to our ancestors.

Scale provides a clue as to why this is the case. Megaprojects are systems of highly concentrated power whose footprints, or radius of effects, are without precedent in human history. Once upon a time, even under imperial conditions, most people on our planet lived and loved, worked and played within geographically limited communities. They never had to reckon with all of humanity as a factor in their daily lives. Whenever they acted recklessly within their environment, for instance, they had the option of moving on, safe in the knowledge that there was plenty of Earth and not many other people. Whenever bad things happened, they happened within limits. Their effects were local. When things went wrong elsewhere, at a distance, over their horizons, it was none of their concern or business. They could say (as the old Scots proverb has it) that 'what's nane o' my profit will be nane o' my peril'. Distance and time protected them from the trials and misfortunes of others.

The new adventures of mega-power radically alter this equation. Their size and connectedness with regional and global processes ensure that growing numbers of people and swathes of their environment are affected by things that happen in far-distant places. These projects pose potentially a double misfortune for our world. Their unparalleled ability to put in place systems of arbitrary power that enable some members of our species to lord over many others, and over our biosphere – what the Czech philosopher Jan Patočka called 'titanism'[1] – is matched by the growing possibility that whenever their risky ventures go wrong, the disasters that result always have incalculable and potentially irreversible damaging effects, on a gigantic scale.

POWERED BY SILENCE

Megaprojects do go wrong. During their design and execution phases, they suffer construction problems, budget blow-outs and delayed completion schedules. The cost-inflation effects of Hong Kong's airport at Chek Lap Kok – the most expensive airport project ever – were so great that for a time the whole of the local economy suffered. London's Olympic Games bid was originally costed at £2.37 billion; the probable final cost was an estimated £24 billion. The Sydney Opera House project (dubbed by its architect Jørn Utzon 'Malice in Blunderland') suffered a cost overrun of 1,400 per cent and opened ten years late. In today's Australia, a land (it seems) of megaprojects, only 1 out of 15 megaprojects approved during the past decade (Conoco Phillips' US$3.3 billion liquid natural gas project) has been completed on schedule, and within budget.

When up and running, megaprojects are plagued by chronic operation problems and 'normal accidents' triggered by unforeseen and irreversible chains of tightly coupled disruptions.[2] Sometimes the mishaps do irreparable damage. Hence the household names: event sequences that include the Bhopal gas and chemical leak, the nuclear meltdown at Chernobyl and gigantic oil spills courtesy of the Exxon Valdez and Deepwater Horizon. Disasters of their type are growing in number and frequency. They point to a grim future – one in which whole peoples and many parts of our planet are the potential victims of risky power experiments whose dysfunctions generate cross-border, potentially life-or-death effects.

Why do they happen? Why do megaprojects so often fail to measure up to the lavish claims made in their defence? Is it because (as popular folklore and serious analysts sometimes propose) these projects are typically in the hands of alpha-males whose 'serial' thinking is inferior to women's capacity for 'parallel' thinking? Or due to the fact (alleged by the evolutionary biologist Robert Trivers) that natural selection favours

---

[1] Jan Patočka, 'Titanism', in Erazim V. Kohák (ed.), *Philosophy and Selected Writings* (Chicago, IL: University of Chicago Press, 1989), pp. 139–144.
[2] Charles Perrow, *Normal Accidents: Living with High Risk Technologies* (Princeton, NJ: Princeton University Press, 1999).

self-deception, or perhaps because humans have been turned loose on the world in the industrial age equipped with prehistoric brains that recognise only simple Newtonian causes and effects, and can think only in primitively visual terms?[3]

Reductionist one-track explanations are unconvincing. There are multiple causes and causers of megaproject failures and each case is shaped by different combinations. Such forces as simple human miscalculation; the blind arrogance and impatience of leaders; inadequate 'hedging' for surprise events; bad decisions caused by poor coordination and diffused responsibility chains; systematic lying (what policy analysts call 'strategic misinformation'); and unintended chain reactions – all play their part in ensuring things go wrong, when they go wrong, as they sometimes do.

The gargantuan size and hyper-complexity of megaprojects make matters worse, but more than their 'cognitive failure' (Francis Fukuyama's bland term) is at stake.[4] Substantial evidence is mounting that their dysfunctions stem ultimately from their refusal of robust internal and external public scrutiny. Not all disasters are human and megaprojects don't always fail, it is true. Yet when they do fail, in 90 per cent of cases, the proximate cause is the privatisation of power. Those in charge of operations suppose, mistakenly, that their mega-organisations can be governed in silence – silence within and outside the organisation. There's a paradoxical dynamic at work in this anti-political trend because the silence is *produced*, usually through intensive public relations campaigns that have the effect of cocooning the power adventure, shielding it from rigorous public scrutiny by fabricating positive stories of its performance within media-saturated settings. The strange dynamic closely resembles what anthropologists call the 'Rashomon Effect' (named after the 1950 Akira Kurosawa film *Rashomon*).[5] The whole point is that the power relations embedded within the megaproject come wrapped in a canopy of multiple realities; hidden agendas are protected by various efforts at producing silence that functionally depends upon volumes of public rhetoric, things being said and displayed to the outside world.

---

[3] These explanations are proposed by Robert Trivers, *Deceit and Self-deception: Fooling Yourself the Better to Fool Others* (London: Allen Lane, 2011); and Gerhard Vollmer, 'Wissenschaft mit Steinzeitgehirnen?', *Mannheimer Forum*, 86 (1986), 9–61.

[4] Francis Fukuyama, 'Afterword', in *Blindside: How to Anticipate Forcing Events and Wild Cards in Global Politics* (Washington, DC: Brookings Institution Press, 2007), p. 170; compare Bent Flyvbjerg, Nils Bruzelius and Werner Rothengatter, *Megaprojects and Risk: An Anatomy of Ambition* (Cambridge: Cambridge University Press, 2003).

[5] James W. Fernandez, 'Silences of the Field', in Maria-Luisa Achino-Loeb (ed.), *Silence: The Currency of Power* (New York: Berghahn Books, 2006), pp. 161–163.

6 Silence, Early Warnings and Catastrophes 211

When that happens, silent complacency about the complex operations wins the upper hand, both within and outside the megaproject. Institutional dysphasia sets in; group-think, wilful blindness, unchecked praise and anti-learning mechanisms (Daniel Ellsberg's famous phrase) flourish. Thinking the unthinkable, public questioning of the goals and *modus operandi* of the megaproject, seems unnecessary, a taboo topic. Those in charge of operations discourage bad news from moving up the inner hierarchy. Cults of loyalty reinforced by aloofness and cold fear are their thing. There is no management by walking around, or by talk back. Troublemakers are ousted from the organisation. Contrarians are blanked, or rebuked as 'Chicken Littles'. Discussing the un-discussable requires guts, which are usually in short supply. Silence traps employees into distancing themselves from matters of ethics; they draw the conclusion that it is someone else's job to solve the problems, or that problems will resolve themselves. Journalists play along; a standard combination of promises of access, sinecures and over-dependence on official hand-outs renders them obedient. They become what could be called 'plane spotters', captive cheerleaders of the power adventure, silent cogs in its machinery of compliance.

SILENCE

The public silences produced by large-scale adventures of power are surely among the strangest, most paradoxical features of media-saturated societies, which otherwise thrive on high levels of open clamour and public hubbub that fuel complaints about excessive media scrutiny and sensationalism, and demands for a new politics of noise reduction.[6] So it's worth probing these mega-silences in depth. Given their fundamental importance as a power resource in the design, implementation and operation of megaprojects, it is unfortunate that a political treatise on silence and its various effects remains unwritten. It is as if a great political silence has descended on the subject of silence, that its study is reckoned properly to belong elsewhere – for instance, in the fields of semiotics, anthropology and socio-linguistics, where the analysis of human language has underscored the many ways in which 'the stupendous reality that is language cannot be understood unless we begin by observing that speech consists

---

[6] Matthew Flinders, 'A Defence of Politics against the Media', in *Defending Politics: Why Democracy Matters in the Twenty-first Century* (Oxford: Oxford University Press, 2012), pp. 142–169.

above all in silences'.[7] Just as the spaces, punctuation marks and patterns of aeration within any written text establish strategic silences that serve as signals that direct readers in their encounter with the text, so (it is pointed out) all communication with others rests inevitably on invisible beds and blocks of silence. Silence is not just the aftermath of communication; every moment of communication using words backed by signs and text is actively shaped by what is unsaid, or what is not say-able. Communication is the marginalia of silence – the foam and waves on its deep waters.

Proverbs and aphorisms pick up this theme. They foreground the significance of the unsaid as a maker of meaning, the ways in which silence talks, the advantages of well-timed silence, even (as the old Swiss saying goes) the superiority of golden silence compared with silver speech. Theologians reinforce the point by emphasising the vitally important role played by sacred silence in all of the world's religions. Think of the Kaddish prayers in synagogue for recently departed loved ones; or the Quaker assembly practising the principle that human silence enables Divine Presence: silence is a technique of self-discipline, a powerful solvent of worldly cares, a sign of respect for a deity, an acknowledgement of the inadequacy of words to capture the experience of sacredness.[8]

Historians chip in with reminders of the many early modern efforts to codify the etiquettes of everyday silence.[9] There are library shelves stuffed full with manuals on the delicate arts of cultivating silence as a desirable way of communicating with others. Idle talk was condemned. Respectful silence was praised. There were warnings that what is said cannot be taken back. Lurking behind the moralising were fears of rebellion founded on what August Comte first called a 'conspiracy of silence'. He that is silent gathers stones, ran an old English proverb. It hit the mark: silence could be impolite, speaking volumes, such that yawns could be silent shouts and underdogs could speak back to their masters by means

---

[7] José Ortega y Gasset, 'What People Say: Language. Towards a New Linguistics', in *Man and People* (New York: Norton, 1957); see also Stephen A. Tyler, *The Said and the Unsaid: Mind, Meaning, and Culture* (New York: Academic Press, 1978); George Steiner, *Language and Silence: Essays on Language, Literature and the Inhuman* (New Haven, CT: Yale University Press, 2008); Keith H. Basso, 'To Give up on Words: Silence in Western Apache Culture', in *Language and Social Context* (New York: Penguin, 1970), pp. 67–86; Edward T. Hall, *The Silent Language* (New York: Doubleday, 1959).

[8] The classic work is Gustav Mensching, *Das heilige Schweigen: Eine religionsgeschichtliche Untersuchung* (Giessen: Töpelmann, 1926).

[9] Peter Burke, 'Notes for a Social History of Silence in Early Modern Europe', in *The Art of Conversation* (Cambridge: Polity Press, 1993), pp. 123–141.

of mocking silence – a practice later dubbed 'dumb insolence' by British army officers. If toothy silence could express scorn, then it followed that there were more than a few circumstances in which subjects had to learn when and when not to be silent. Children were expected to understand that silence was a form of polite behaviour appropriate to beings of little status. Silence was certainly gendered: women were widely expected to wear the fine jewels of calculated quietude. Their faithful reserve and obedient hush, without appearing to be speechless, was deemed imperative. The same went for subjects of government. 'Silence is sometimes an argument of Consent', remarked Hobbes.[10] The caveat 'sometimes' was important. It underscored the importance of *respectful* silence among underlings. 'Tell not all you hear, nor speak all you know', servants were told. Others warned that fools are wise as long as they are silent. The optimists added: silence seldom hurts.

CATASTROPHES

How wrong that maxim proved. It's true that in matters of politics, hush can be a productive tool; an example is the well-known tactic used by British Prime Minister Theresa May, to trip up her rivals during meetings, by letting silence fill a room, so tempting her opponents or fence-sitters to bumble, or to put their feet in their own mouths. In politics, silence can also have civil effects, as when a call for silence precedes the entry of a judge into a court of law; or when crowds are requested by the authorities to observe a minute's respectful silence; or when jurors are obliged to remain publicly silent about their deliberations (as in the grand jury system in the United States). People politely rise, respectfully stand, or they hold their tongues. The political effects are benign, and limited, certainly compared to the dilapidating effects that flow from dysfunctional megaprojects. When things go wrong within large-scale adventures of power, many ancillary organisations and services grind to a halt. People are made homeless; some are robbed of their lives. Habitats are pushed beyond the limits of sustainability. They seize up, or breakdown.

'Catastrophe' is another term for such devilish outcomes. It is a potent word (originally from ancient Greek, *katastrophe*, 'sudden turn, overturning') that cries out for definition and begs to be used carefully,

---

[10] Thomas Hobbes, *Leviathan*, Book 2 (Harmondsworth: Penguin Books, 1968 [1651]), Chapter 36, p. 138.

especially because (it seems) the numbers of large-scale misadventures are rising. I emphasise that to speak of catastrophes – unexpected sensational events that inflict long-term ruinous damage on humans, or our biosphere, or both – is not to indulge apocalyptic thinking or to be nostalgic for halcyon times when life was calm and peaceful. The new catastrophes of our age are not the climax of inevitable historical trends; they should not be understood (say) as markers of the final triumph and breakdown of Western metaphysics, as Heidegger proposed.[11] The new catastrophes are not inevitable. More than a few are triggered by bizarre projects that should never have been attempted; with hindsight, had the megaproject been conceived and run differently, plenty of other catastrophes could have been avoided. That is a reason why these catastrophes are not taking us backwards. We are not returning in any simple sense to the pattern of vile events that paralysed the world from just before the outbreak of the First World War to 1950, a forty-year 'age of catastrophe' when whole societies stumbled from one calamity to another through the wreckage of economic collapse, inter-state rivalries, total war, totalitarianism, murder and genocide.[12]

The catastrophes of our times are different. Their *slow-motion quality* is striking. There is no Big Bang, but there are plenty of loud explosions whose numbers are growing in frequency. Our catastrophes are *cumulative*; and their *sources are different*. They are not products of fascism, capitalism or socialism. They are the effect of big adventures of power operating in many different settings, and at *many different points on our planet*. Our catastrophes cut deeper and more aggressively into our *biosphere* and distinctive as well (thanks to communicative abundance) is that they stand centre stage in *real-time media events* that trigger fascination, fear and foreboding on a global scale. Catastrophes shatter the public silence that bred them in the first place. They attract millions of witnesses. They are also the raw material of risk-hedging business investment deals ('catastrophe bonds', they are called at the Chicago Board of Trade and on Wall Street) and (to name an early 'classic') *The Last Man on Earth*-style blockbuster movies and other forms of popular entertainment.

---

[11] Martin Heidegger, 'Letter on Humanism', in David F. Krell (ed.), *Basic Writings* (New York: Harper & Row, 1976), pp. 193–244.
[12] Eric Hobsbawm, *The Age of Extremes: A History of the World, 1914–1991* (New York: Pantheon, 1994).

FUKUSHIMA

Catastrophes are difficult to capture in words; as the French writer Maurice Blanchot reminded us, those who experience them first hand are often unable to communicate their horror.[13] Samuel Beckett's *Catastrophe* (a short play written thirty years ago in honour of Václav Havel) comes close to capturing the point that silence is the currency of catastrophes both before and after they strike. Some part of their ugliness stems from their destruction of the ability to communicate with others. Ugly as their details are, as we now know from the catastrophe that occurred at the Fukushima Daiichi nuclear power plant during the months of March–April 2011.

Fukushima quickly became the greatest industrial catastrophe in the history of the world. Triggered by the largest-ever recorded earthquake in the country's history (so large it made our planet spin faster on its axis), the disaster was not simply the effect of 'natural' causes, as many observers initially claimed. The catastrophe came covered in the fingerprints of organised silence. Fukushima records show that warnings by experts and citizens about safety hazards were swept aside, right from the mid-1950s, when, against the strong advice of the Japan Scientists Council, the United States backed the policy of developing nuclear power in Japan using American-designed, enriched-uranium plants unsuited to earthquake zones and voices of dissent were ignored, or silenced. The silencing or 'blackout' policy was defended by successive governments, and by the Tokyo Electric Power Company (Tepco), which became skilled at forging and doctoring safety data; issuing blanket Rashomon Effect assurances through the media that their plants were invulnerable; and harnessing the *kisha* club system of embedded journalism to the point where the company's organised dissimulation made it difficult to improve safety arrangements in the face of unreported dangers. The old habits of hush guaranteed, during the earliest phases of the unfolding disaster, that company directors and government officials were determined to speak with one voice, regardless of what was actually happening on the ground. Silence embraced one disaster after another. The president of the company crumbled under the strain; knowing (as the Japanese say) that the dog had fallen into the river, he stopped attending meetings and quarantined himself in silence in his office for five days and nights. Millions of

---

[13] Maurice Blanchot, *The Writing of the Disaster* (Lincoln, NE: University of Nebraska Press, 1995).

television viewers soon witnessed fires and minor explosions, even a whole nuclear reactor flying apart in a cloud of dust and debris. More than 10,000 tonnes of highly contaminated water was dumped into the nearby ocean; despite protests from the wider region, the company carried on spraying seawater on several reactors and fuel cores, in the process generating many hundreds of thousands of tonnes of highly radioactive waste, for which it had no disposal plans.

With evacuation plans in disarray, and several reactors melting down, over 100,000 people, many children among them, were forced to flee the Fukushima area, many into temporary shelters, uncompensated and jobless, anxious about their exposure to contaminated food, water and soil, their futures tattered and torn. There was confirmation that a geographic area of nearly a thousand square kilometres – an area roughly one-eighth the size of metropolitan London – would remain uninhabitable for the foreseeable future. Quantities of strontium, caesium and plutonium isotopes, so-called 'hot particles', had meanwhile been detected in local water tables and in car engine air filters as far away as Seattle. It was confirmed as well that something worse than a meltdown had happened at the plant: a hot fuel 'melt through' of layers of the reactor plant's cracked and compromised bottom casing. Tepco, facing massive clean-up and compensation costs, tried to regain its media footing by outlining a roadmap for the future safe 'cold shutdown' of the plant. Canny journalists who first visited the site replied that full decommissioning and robotic clean-up of the wrecked and radioactive plant would minimally take a decade; the more prudent in their midst pointed out that nuclear disasters never end.

POLITICAL EFFECTS

Those who coined the old proverb that silent people are dangerous people could never have foreseen just how dangerous are those anti-political people who organise and manage public silence in the early years of the twenty-first century. Covered-up disasters on the scale of Fukushima are stomach-turning; and with the exponential growth of megaprojects, the probability of catastrophes triggered by organised silence is rising. Tagged with names like 'Three Mile Island', 'Chernobyl', 'Lehman Brothers', 'The Royal Bank of Scotland' and 'Deepwater Horizon', catastrophes are becoming unexceptional. They are a new normal.

So what are their probable political implications? The question is pertinent because historians such as Jean Delumeau and Norman Cohn remind us that past catastrophes typically triggered public mood swings and reactions. Think of the world of medieval Europe, where events such as the Black Death (which wiped out a quarter, perhaps a third of the population of Europe in the space of three or four years) and periodic outpourings of belief in the end of the world served several times as the spark that ignited the gunpowder of millenarian movements.[14] The gigantic earthquake that devastated Lisbon in 1755 ignited violent political tensions in the Kingdom of Portugal, damaged the monarchy's colonial ambitions, inspired various innovations, ranging from the birth of modern seismology and earthquake engineering to Enlightenment criticisms of theodicy and fresh philosophical thinking about the sublime. Closer to our era, the battlefield slaughter of the First World War trampled on beliefs in one-way progress (think of Walter Benjamin's angel of history, turning its back on the future, gazing backwards on 'one single catastrophe that keeps piling wreckage upon wreckage'[15]). The first global military catastrophe triggered fears of the end of the world mixed with hopes of universal redemption through apocalyptic violence, the refusal of 'bourgeois' parliamentary 'chatter' and magnetic attraction to loud-talking Mussolini, Hitler and other Men of the People. The catastrophes associated with the Second World War nearly destroyed parliamentary democracy. Few prophecies of perfection surfaced. For many, the world instead felt emptied of meaning and transcendent purpose, a nightmare reality (as Hannah Arendt noted) haunted hereon by the problem of how to understand and restrain human evil, for instance through human rights, rule of law and other monitory democracy mechanisms in cross-border form.

FREEDOM OF COMMUNICATION: NEW HORIZONS

So what about our times? It is too early to forecast the full political impacts of the catastrophes of our age, but they are already triggering observable effects. Catastrophes are symptoms of *democracy failure*. They are warnings that big power adventures are exercises in the destruction of politics. By establishing spaces of arbitrary power that defy

---

[14] Jean Delumeau, *Le péché et la peur: La culpabilisation en Occident, XIIIe–XVIIIe siècles* (Paris: Fayard, 1983); Norman Cohn, *The Pursuit of the Millennium: Revolutionary Millenarians and Mystical Anarchists of the Middle Ages* (Oxford: Oxford University Press, 1970).
[15] Walter Benjamin, 'Theses on the Philosophy of History', in Hannah Arendt (ed.), *Illuminations* (New York: Schocken, 1969), p. 257.

election cycles and bear some resemblance to medieval fiefdoms where barons rule over commoners, these adventures carry us towards a future where mechanisms of freely chosen representation by citizens and keeping tabs on those who exercise power play a minor role in most people's daily lives. Big power adventures gone wrong do damage, or permanently deform, citizens' lives; and they have potentially hurtful effects upon the whole of humanity, and the rest of our biosphere. Not only do catastrophes turn patches of our planet into permanently uninhabitable zones, they also pose worrying questions about irreversible tipping points. As we will see later in this book, they prompt 'greening effects', public anxieties about the possibility that the human species is passing through a door of no return, that we are falling victim to our own titanism and (a point forcefully made by Haruki Murakami when reflecting on the long-term significance of the Fukushima catastrophe) that we may be incapable hereon of living self-reflexively as 'uninvited guests on planet Earth'.[16]

Catastrophes fuelled by silence are politically significant for another reason. They show not only that politics based on open communication systems greatly matter to the future of our world, they force us as well to rethink the reasons why (let's call it) the First Amendment principle of 'free and open communication' is desirable – far more precious than our ancestors could possibly have imagined.

In these early years of the twenty-first century, under conditions of monitory democracy, is it possible to inject new energy and life into the old political principle of freedom of communication, to effect its re-description so that it assumes a new and expanded political relevance? Can we leave behind the old arguments for 'liberty of the press' inherited from the age of the printing press and print culture? Can we move beyond the conventional consequentialist views that freedom of communication is a good thing because it is a means of informing and mobilising voters, investigating governmental power, providing intelligible frameworks of interpretation, lending different styles of life a stamp of public acceptability, binding disparate groups into common publics and educating them in the virtues of democracy? In other words, is there a way of regarding freedom of public communication as a political principle uniquely suited to our new age of catastrophes?

---

[16] Jared Diamond, *Collapse: How Societies Choose to Fail or Succeed* (New York: Viking Press, 2005); Haruki Murakami, 'As an Unrealistic Dreamer', speech delivered upon receiving the Catalunya International Prize, Barcelona, 2011, www.senrinomichi.com/?p=2728.

6 Silence, Early Warnings and Catastrophes

There is. Simply put, the principle of freedom of public communication is a means of damage prevention. It is an indispensable early warning mechanism, a way of enabling citizens and whole organisations and networks to sound the alarm whenever they suspect that others are causing them harm, or that calamities are bearing down on their heads in silence. 'See something, say something' is a widely used motto invented by the New York Metropolitan Transit Authority and today used elsewhere in many different settings. The motto captures the deepest political significance of freedom of public communication. In principle, it rejects silent nonchalance in human affairs. 'Whereof one cannot speak, thereof one must be silent', wrote Ludwig Wittgenstein in his *Tractatus*,[17] but the elegant last-sentence formula of his key early work must be revised. There are moments when silence is not an option. Refusal to hold one's tongue in the face of organised silence is necessary because it brings things back to earth. It serves as a 'reality check' on unrestrained power; it is a potent means of ensuring that those in charge of organisations do not stray into cloud cuckoo land, wander into territory where misadventures of power are concealed by silence wrapped in fine words of trust, loyalty, growth and progress.

When rethought in this way, the early warning principle of communication has global implications. It is not just that it no longer indulges blandly rationalist, Habermas-style fantasies of conjoining citizens into harmonious agreement, or that it is no longer wedded (as earlier justifications of freedom of communication were) to a First Principle, be it Truth or Happiness or Human Rights or God, Public Service or the Common Good. Suspicious of organised silences and arbitrary power, a champion of the weak against the strong, especially when the weak find themselves silenced by the strong, the early warning principle of communication is politically meaningful in a wide range of contexts. It is on the lookout against all forms of arbitrary power, wherever they take root. It is just as applicable to transport projects in China and multi-billion dollar tar sand extraction schemes in Canada as it is to the 'modernisation' of military forces and credit and banking sector institutions elsewhere on the planet. Gripped by a strong sense of the contingency of things, the principle is a fair-minded defender of openness, a friend of perplexity when in the company of cock-sure certainty.

---

[17] Ludwig Wittgenstein, *Tractatus Logico-Philosophicus* (London: Routledge, 1922), p. 7.

That explains its candour. Nothing about the behaviour of human beings comes as a surprise to the early warning principle of public communication. It doubts that human beings are straightforwardly 'gaffe-avoiding animals'.[18] It sees that humans are capable of the best, and the worst. For that reason, the political principle stands against hubris and the privatisation of risk. It considers that concentrated power is dangerous; it supposes that human beings are not to be entrusted with unchecked power over their fellows, or their circumstances. It stands against stupidity and dissembling; it is opposed to silent arrogance and has no truck with bossing, bullying and violence. The early warning axiom is attuned to conundrums and alive to difficulties. It is serious about the calamities of our times; it tracks the calamities to come. The axiom stands opposed to those post-modernists who, with a sigh, treat catastrophes as proof of the rottenness of our 'modernity', or as marvellous challenges to the reigning banalities of mass culture. The early warning principle of communication offers a powerful reply to their political wistfulness. The reply, simply put, is that societies plagued by pockets of public silence are asking for trouble. For when big-footprint adventures of power succumb to the unsaid, sweep things under the carpet, become victims of what some writers have called the *'non-dit'*, they flirt and dance with disaster.

A POLITICS OF CATASTROPHE PREVENTION

But what exactly does the early warning communication principle imply in practice? What is to be done about the organised silence that breeds catastrophes? Can anything help prevent them?

A politics of catastrophe prevention is possible, and quite literally it can begin at home and in the workplace, driven by the recognition that our lives begin to end the moment we become silent about things that matter. The story is told that one evening in 1974, during the period the American chemist F. Sherwood (Sherry) Rowland realised that chlorinated fluorocarbons, or CFCs, might well destroy our planet's ozone layer, his partner Joan asked him, a man of unusual calm, how things were going at work. 'It's going very well', he replied. 'It just means, I think, the end of the world.' The couple stopped purchasing spray can devices, and vowed never to use them again. This was a political act. It reinforced

---

[18] Ernest Gellner, 'The Gaffe-Avoiding Animal, or a Bundle of Hypotheses', in *Relativism and the Social Sciences* (Cambridge: Cambridge University Press, 1985), pp. 68–82.

6 Silence, Early Warnings and Catastrophes 221

Rowland's conviction that CFCs were not innocent or inert gases. Commonly used as aerosol compounds in such products as deodorants, refrigerators and hair sprays, Rowland and a laboratory colleague suggested that CFCs were by no means inert.[19] Their persistence yielded results: the landmark Montreal Protocol (1987) that effectively banned the production and stockpiling of CFCs and other ozone-depleting chemicals.

Numerous other examples of the politics of catastrophe prevention spring to mind. Following the Deepwater Horizon catastrophe, for which it encountered deep trouble in the courts, British Petroleum launched a rudimentary programme of 'town hall' meetings for its employees and managers. Électricité de France S.A., among the world's largest energy producers, operates a full media disclosure policy. The family-run global clothing retailer C&A has long embraced watchdog 'performance channels', close links with radical non-governmental organisations, annual citizenship seminars and sworn dependence upon a legally freestanding unit (SOCAM) responsible for monitoring questionable practices within the company. These companies take their cue from risk-management bodies such as the Oxford-based Major Projects Association (MPA), which urges large-scale projects to adopt 'stand back reviews', periodic 'pulse checks', 'honest reporting' and an internal 'challenging' culture that draws upon 'intelligence' from multiple 'stakeholders'. As the Leveson Inquiry in the United Kingdom demonstrated, parliamentary committees and public inquiries can also bare sharp teeth. Longstanding laws against 'wilful blindness' can be activated by courts. Investigative journalism – the clever patience and good quality writing at newspapers such as the *New York Times* and *De Correspondent* – serve to counter plane-spotting 'churnalism'. Citizens themselves can invent and operate silence-breaking mechanisms designed to prevent or minimise the impact of catastrophes, as in Saskatchewan, where (Elaine Scarry reminds us[20]) dispersed rural

---

[19] Rowland and his colleague Mario Molina estimated that a single chlorine atom could absorb more than 100,000 ozone molecules. They predicted that CFCs might well linger for more than a century in the stratosphere, damaging parts of its ozone layer. 'Chlorofluoromethanes are being added to the environment in steadily increasing amounts', they noted. 'These compounds are chemically inert and may remain in the atmosphere for 40–150 years, and concentrations can be expected to reach ten to 30 times present levels. Photodissociation of the chlorofluoromethanes in the stratosphere produces significant amounts of chlorine atoms, and leads to the destruction of atmospheric ozone' (Mario J. Molina and F. S. Rowland, 'Stratospheric Sink for Chlorofluoromethanes: Chlorine Atom-catalysed Destruction of Ozone', *Nature*, 249 [28 June 1974], 810–812).

[20] Elaine Scarry, *Thinking in an Emergency* (New York: Norton, 2011).

communities have signed legally binding mutual aid contracts, or as in Japan since the Fukushima catastrophe where radiation detection counter-systems operated by citizens have been built, helped by the launch of the world's first mobile phone (Softbank's Pantone) that doubles as a Geiger counter.

The common thread running through these manifold efforts to monitor and resist arbitrary power is as simple as it is demanding. They doubt the claimed virtues of golden silence. They understand that pockets of silent power are both bad for democracy and politically dangerous in that they have twisting and buckling effects on people's lives. These political experiments in the art of breaking the grip of arbitrary power are early warning signals. They call upon citizens to do more than engage in reasoned deliberation, or to vote. They invite us to recover what Bernard Crick once beautifully called the 'pearl beyond price in the history of the human condition':[21] politics, which includes the art of making public noise, smart public noise, well-targeted din and disquiet loud enough to shatter the eerie silences that so easily can cause things to go so terribly wrong for so many people.

---

[21] Bernard Crick, *In Defence of Politics* (London: Bloomsbury Continuum Impacts, 1962), p. 3.

PART III

RE-IMAGINING EQUALITY

7

Capitalism and Civil Society

So far in this book, despite its fundamental importance for the theory and practice of monitory democracy, the subject of civil society has been left largely unmentioned. So now is the moment to explore its significance, especially for the way the old subject of civil society forces us to think in fresh ways about such matters as labour and capital, big business and market competition, inequality and the future of democracy.

The focus on civil society in what follows seems at first sight unpromising. Easily the most striking feature of the remarkable body of literature and public discussion of civil society during the past half century is its utopian quality. Something of a prim and purist view of civil society has come to be dominant. Civil society is treated as a market-free zone. In documents produced by bodies such as the Global Agenda Council on the Role of Civil Society and Civicus, a global alliance for citizen participation, civil society is said to comprise a non-governmental space of associations in which a complex plurality of individuals, groups, organisations, civic initiatives and social movements cultivate virtues such as communication, solidarity, openness, toleration of differences, non-violence, the yearning for freedom with justice. Civil societies – in contrast to money-driven, risk-taking, power-protected markets – are said to be structured by 'mutual recognition' or by 'autonomy', 'public space', 'pluralism', even by the rules of 'a certain kind of universalising community' marked by 'interactional practices like civility, equality, criticism, and respect'.[1]

---

[1] Jeffrey C. Alexander, 'Introduction', in *Real Civil Societies. Dilemmas of Institutionalization* (Newbury Park, CA: Sage, 1998); compare Lester M. Salamon and Helmut K. Anheier, *Defining the Nonprofit Sector: A Cross-National Analysis* (Manchester:

In some quarters, civil society is even assigned the historic role of heir to the proletariat, as a universal subject-object. Civil society is seen as the protector of citizens against the ravages of money-driven markets and governmental power. This 'third sector' or 'third force' is a space of resistance to 'colonisation', the domain where citizens discover the power of the powerless, an enclave in which the republican ideals of the French Revolution (*liberté, egalité, fraternité*) are nurtured.[2] An extreme version of this understanding of civil society as a liberated base from which the despotic powers of markets and governments can be challenged and politically defeated is developed in a famous tract by Michael Hardt and Antonio Negri: it envisages a world civil society that is capable of sparking off a revolutionary struggle for a new form of communism conceived dialectically as the child of bio-capitalism's quest for global mastery.[3]

PREDATORY MARKETS

When examining the history of civil society, an important counter-fact becomes striking. It is this: during the modernisation of the concept of civil society that took place in the Atlantic region, roughly between the years 1750 and 1848, every commentator on commodity production and exchange thought of markets as an organising principle of civil society. Some praised, some criticised and some remained ambivalent about the rise of commodity production and exchange; more than a few observers emphasised their predatory practices, and their potentially corrosive ethic of possessive individualism. The misery produced by markets (commerce and exchange) was a constant theme of the literature. Adam Smith's *Lectures on Justice, Police* (1763) noted how the workmen in the commercial parts of England were trapped in a 'despicable condition ... through want of education they have no amusement ... but riot and debauchery. So it may very justly be said that the people who clothe the whole world are in rags themselves.' His *Wealth of Nations* (1776) generally admired the civilising thrust of markets, but (in Book V) it lamented the decline of

---

Manchester University Press, 1997); and David Green, *Reinventing Civil Society: The Rediscovery of Welfare without Politics* (London: Institute of Economic Affairs, 1993).

[2] Jürgen Habermas, *Theorie des kommunikativen Handelns*, Vol. II (Frankfurt am Main: Suhrkamp, 1982); compare Václav Havel, *Power of the Powerless*, edited by John Keane (London: Hutchinson, 1985).

[3] Michael Hardt and Antonio Negri, *Empire* (Cambridge, MA: Harvard University Press, 2000).

martial spirit and the 'drowsy stupidity' and pauperisation produced by the great wheels of commerce and exchange.[4] During the same period, Thomas Paine's *Common Sense* (1776) referred positively to the enterprise and wealth of the 'civilised society' and the *doux commerce* of the Americans who struggled against the British Empire. Later (in *Agrarian Justice* [1797]) he proposed a far-reaching system of market-correcting grants, funded by government inheritance taxation, to assist the newly married, the sick and the old. Without saying so in so few words, Paine gave poverty its name and in the same breath envisioned its abolition. His words were to become famous. 'It is not charity but a right, not bounty but justice, that I am pleading for', he wrote. 'The present state of civilisation is as odious as it is unjust. It is absolutely the opposite of what it should be, and it is necessary that a revolution should be made in it. The contrast of affluence and wretchedness continually meeting and offending the eye, is like dead and living bodies chained together. Though I care as little about riches as any man, I am a friend to riches because they are capable of good.'[5]

Hegel later noted the hectic dynamism of markets and their predatory potential. Civil societies were seen as modern inventions in which the *Bürgerstand* permanently unsettle and revolutionise social needs and produce a 'rabble of paupers'. That way of thinking about civil society and social inequality prepared the ground for the most savage early modern critique of *bürgerliche Gesellschaft*: Marx's attack on civil society as a self-paralysing bourgeois society dominated by the ruthless logic of commodity production and exchange.[6]

During the first phase of modern interest in civil society, these different Atlantic-region accounts of civil society had important political consequences. There were tensions and radical disagreements, ranging from the preoccupation of Malthus with overpopulation to Marx's call for the

---

[4] Adam Smith, *An Inquiry into the Nature and Causes of the Wealth of Nations*, edited by Edwin Cannan (Chicago, IL: University of Chicago Press, 1776); compare *Lectures on Justice, Police* (1767).

[5] Thomas Paine, *Common Sense: On the Origin and Design of Government in General, with Concise Remarks on the English Constitution* (Philadelphia: R. Bell, 1776); and *Agrarian Justice, Opposed to Agrarian Law, and to Agrarian Monopoly: Being a Plan for Meliorating the Condition of Man, by Creating in Every Nation a National Fund* (London: T.G. Ballard, 1797); first published as Thomas Payne, *À la Législature et au Directoire, ou la justice agraire opposé à la loi et aux privileges agraires* (Paris: W. Adlard).

[6] G.W.F. Hegel, *Grundlinien der Philosophie des Rechts* (Frankfurt am Main, 1976 [1820]); Karl Marx, 'On the Jewish Question', and Karl Marx and Friedrich Engels, 'The German Ideology', in Lloyd D. Easton and Kurt H. Guddat (eds.), *Writings of the Young Marx on Philosophy and Society* (New York: Doubleday & Company).

revolutionary abolition of civil society. But note the agreement within the disagreement: without exception, all commentators saw waged labour and capital, investment, production, exchange and the consumption of commodities – the forces and relations of production, mediated by nature – as both a constitutive feature, a dynamic motor of civil society, and a fundamental (some insisted: the fundamental) source of social inequality.

SOCIAL INEQUALITY

Thomas Piketty's much-discussed *Capital in the Twenty-First Century* agrees.[7] It resurrects old themes that were central in the early modern analysis of markets and civil society. Acknowledging that the nature of capital has changed radically (from land and other real estate in the eighteenth century to industrial and financial capital in the twenty-first century), he reminds us that a market economy based on private property, if left to itself, contains 'powerful forces of divergence' that are potentially destructive of democracy and its ethic of equality. The principal 'destabilising force', says Piketty, is the historical fact that for long periods of time the private rate of return on capital (r) has often been significantly higher than the rate of income and output (g). The inequality $r>g$ implies that there is a built-in tendency for wealth to accumulate more rapidly than output and wages. 'The entrepreneur inevitably tends to become a rentier, more and more dominant over those who own nothing but their labor.' It took the catastrophes of the twentieth century to reverse this trend, and significantly to reduce the return on capital. For a time, notes Piketty, the Keynesian welfare state and other redistributive mechanisms created the illusion that the structural inequality problem had been resolved. It manifestly hasn't. Enhanced GDP growth is no solution, because countries at the technological frontier typically cannot grow faster than 1–1.5 per cent in the long run, no matter what economic policies are adopted (history shows that only countries engaged in catch-up can temporarily grow at Chinese-style rates). Even when the rate of growth is modest, says Piketty, the $r>g$ inequality gap is never automatically reduced. Greater equality in the ratio between the return on capital (r) and income and output (g) requires the political correction of market forces.

---

[7] Thomas Piketty, *Capital in the Twenty-First Century* (Cambridge, MA and London: Harvard University Press, 2014).

CIVILISING EFFECTS

More than a few observers and practitioners baulk at such talk. They say in reply that the inequality dynamic within contemporary civil societies is attenuated, its sharp edges softened, by the fact that civil societies have *socialising effects*. And indeed certain social rules and habits of the heart are common to 'the market experience'[8] and other civil society institutions. The market process of producing, buying and selling commodities not only needs to be embedded in a social *habitus* anchored in the unpaid work of households, markets also have certain socialising or 'civilising' effects (as Marx himself noted when analysing the 'socialisation of production' under capitalist conditions). Civil societies structured by market processes functionally require non-violence; money and the capacity for monetary calculation; the self-restraint of actors and their carefully defined self-love (otherwise known as sympathy); and a sense of level-headed responsibility for one's actions, even the expectation that failures have penalties, that there is a price to be paid for mistakes.[9] As well, neither civil society nor markets can function without the cultivated ability of actors to negotiate with strangers (as in business deals), to trust others, and to make sense together (as in the social identity formation that takes place through advertising-driven consumption of commodities). Civil societies are marked by a definite impersonality: the stranger is a figure common to markets and all other civil society institutions. Civil societies effect a separation between things and persons.[10] Money permits possession and exchange at a distance, which is why (think of Francisco Goya's *Alegoría del Comercio*) markets stretch spatial horizons, so making possible the transition from *Gemeinschaft* to *Gesellschaft*. Markets and other civil society institutions are basic preconditions of transforming the space–time coordinates of individual personality and social co-operation.[11] There is one other important consideration, say the

---

[8] Robert E. Lane, *The Market Experience* (Cambridge: Cambridge University Press, 1991); and Robert E. Lane, *The Loss of Happiness in Market Democracies* (New Haven, CT: Yale University Press, 2000).
[9] Víctor Pérez-Díaz, 'Markets as Conversations: Markets' Contributions to Civility, the Public Sphere and Civil Society at Large', in Victor Pérez-Díaz (ed.), *Markets and Civil Society: The European Experience in Comparative Perspective* (New York: Berghahn Publishers, 2014), pp. 27–76.
[10] Marcel Mauss, *The Gift: Forms and Functions of Exchange in Archaic Societies* (London: Cohen & West, 1966).
[11] Georg Simmel, 'Die Großstadt und das Geistesleben', in *Die Großstadt: Jahrbuch der Gehe-Stiftung*, 9 (1903).

defenders of markets: when they are embedded in civil society arrangements, markets offer the resources, including freedom of association, with which to repel and tame the uncivil effects of commodity production and exchange. Co-operative associations, friendly societies, scientific and literary circles, publishing houses, newspapers, chapels, guilds, craft and trades unions, political parties: historically speaking, these and other inventions served as levers of empowerment, sites where the powerless, through small works, could achieve grand things.

MARKET FAILURES

The socialising effects of markets are well-established axioms in the social sciences, but when they are treated in isolation they seriously underestimate the ways in which market dynamics and market inequality are destructive of the norms and practices of any actually existing civil society. Market power and market dynamics are aggressive. They have domineering qualities that destroy such civil society virtues and practices as civility, mutual recognition and social solidarity.

Why do they do this? To begin with, markets are not 'naturally' zones of social co-operation and friendship. The civil society idealists are right about this. For all their socialising effects – von Hayek even speaks of the 'catallaxy' of markets (from the Greek verb *katallatein*, 'to exchange', but also 'to admit into the community' and 'to change from enemy into friend')[12] – markets regularly disrupt and spoil social interaction. They stir up social competition and (because someone has to lose) reduce social pluralism; as political economists from Adam Smith to Thomas Piketty have pointed out, they have ruinous effects on shared perceptions and feelings of sociability. The historical record is clear on this point: the much-vaunted civilising effects of markets are everywhere counterbalanced and undone by *uncivil* effects, such as the nurturing of a culture of narcissistic greed and the damage inflicted on people's lives by low wages and unemployment.

But why do markets have these endogenously damaging effects on civil societies? Contemporary theories of civil society need to revisit – and to revise – the classical theories of market failures that once upon a time were part and parcel of virtually all modern accounts of civil society. There are many examples, including the theory of alienation, with its

[12] Friedrich von Hayek, *Law, Legislation and Liberty*, Vol. II (London: Routledge, 1976), pp. 108–109.

critique of the character-deforming effects of the modern division of labour and the counterfactual, positive vision of a world where humans could hunt in the morning, fish during the afternoon and enjoy polite criticism after dinner.[13] More recent critiques of markets have concentrated upon the problem of 'externalities': the activities of firms are seen to produce unintended effects, 'public bads' like air and water pollution, jammed roads and urban over-crowding, that do not figure in the costs and benefits associated with the firm. There has also been much theorising of the crisis tendencies of markets: for instance, the 'anarchy' and periodic convulsions caused by falling rates of profit and class antagonisms; their tendency to promote under-consumption or consumer dissatisfaction; the propensity of firms to cause unemployment by hanging on to their capital, by *not* placing investment 'bets'; and the tendency of markets to whip up socially destructive storms of technical innovation.[14]

These and other theories of market failures deserve reconsideration. Some critiques of markets, like the Romantic theory of alienation and its vision of individuals living authentically in social harmony with others, are implausible and should be rejected by a civil society perspective.[15] Other analyses, such as C.B. Macpherson's emphasis on the 'extractive power' of markets and the inequalities produced by the fact that in market competition there are always losers, continue to be important.[16] The earliest complaints about markets as sources of inequality and class domination date from the early nineteenth century. They remain plausible.[17] Consider the United States: its otherwise vibrant civil society is scarred by the fact that a mere 1 per cent of households owns at least 38 per cent of the national wealth, while the bottom 80 per cent of households owns only 17 per cent of national wealth. Or France, where the average disposable income, after transfers and taxes, of the wealthiest 0.01 per cent of the population now stands at seventy-five times that of the bottom 90 per cent.[18] Such figures suggest that markets are not

---

[13] Karl Marx and Friedrich Engels, 'The German Ideology' (1845–1846).
[14] Joseph Schumpeter, *Capitalism, Socialism, and Democracy* (New York: HarperCollins, 1942).
[15] See John Keane, *Democracy and Civil Society* (London and New York: Verso, 1988).
[16] C.B. Macpherson, 'Problems of a Non-market Theory of Democracy', in *Democratic Theory: Essays in Retrieval* (Oxford: Clarendon Press, 1973).
[17] Charles Hall, *The Effects of Civilization on the People in European States* (London: Gilpin, 1805).
[18] Pierre Rosanvallon, *Society of Equals* (Cambridge, MA and London: Harvard University Press, 2013).

describable in the happy terms of Pareto efficiency; they can be, and often are, 'prisons' of powerlessness and protectors of 'dead capital' that stifles the operation of so-called trickle down effects.[19]

NEW MARKET DYSFUNCTIONS

In recent times, additional arguments have surfaced to explain why markets produce dysfunctions and self-paralysing trends with socially unequal effects. The conceptual shift marks off our times from the age of classical political economy. Two examples spring to mind. The first, already analysed in the previous section, has become axiomatic in fields such as architecture and planning: giant market actors frequently manipulate local information for their own interests, to the point where corporate 'mega-projects' so distort information that they result in massive cost miscalculations and projects that are never ready on time, as well as suffer other types of dysfunctions.[20] In such cases, the self-adjustments triggered by market failures do not apply to corporate actors. It turns out that the Hayekian claim that markets offer an effective set of interrelated co-ordination functions under conditions of complexity – in other words, that the beauty of markets is that they are decentralised mechanisms for incorporating and processing local information into large-scale productive and distributive outcomes – is untrue, or greatly exaggerated.[21] In the worst-case scenarios, as this book's analysis of the politics of silence has already noted, un-monitored corporate mega-projects can produce catastrophes that badly damage or thoroughly wreck civil society institutions, exacerbating their patterns of unequal wealth and income.

A second example of innovative, critical thinking about market dysfunctions and inequalities focuses on the environmental recklessness of markets. The argument is that 'free markets' typically lack normative and institutional restraints on the profit-driven exploitation of 'natural resources'. The consequence is that contemporary civil societies are for the first time being forced to come to terms self-reflexively with their co-dependence upon, and dwelling within, the biosphere. Civil societies are

---

[19] Hernando De Soto, *The Mystery of Capital: Why Capitalism Triumphs in the West and Fails Everywhere* (New York: Basic Books, 2000).
[20] Bent Flyvbjerg, *Megaprojects and Risk: An Anatomy of Ambition* (Cambridge and New York: Cambridge University Press, 2003).
[21] F.A. Hayek (1944), *The Road to Serfdom* (London: Routledge & Kegan Paul, 1966) and F.A. Hayek, *Dr. Bernard Mandeville (Master-Mind Lecture)* (London: British Academy, 1966).

'de-naturing' the modern project of dominating nature. By that I mean these societies are demonstrating in practice that nature is a fictitious commodity; in so doing, they are slowly but surely exposing the market fundamentalism inherent in talk of the 'efficiency' of markets that began in the late nineteenth-century work of Leon Walras and others. The implication is that markets should not be trusted to ensure (these used to be standard terms) the best possible use of resources in the context of alternative possible uses by means of what was called *tâtonnement* (groping), the process through which prices are clumsily adjusted in response to excess demand or supply.[22] In the name of 'efficiency', 'wealth generation' and profit, so-called 'free markets' foul the nests of our biosphere – permanently and, possibly, irreversibly. Around the globe, for instance, species of every kind are dying out, invisibly, silently; according to conservative estimates, the rate of species extinction is a thousand times faster than the rate of extinction before humans arose.[23] In this sense, the market-driven domination of the biosphere is exceeding its limits. The point is that no civil society can indefinitely withstand the destruction of its ecological foundations. No civil society can live indefinitely with a glaringly unequal power gap between humans and non-humans. Hence the emerging political battles over corporations' responsibility for climate change, bio-diversity loss and chemical proliferation; and the emergent politics of consumption, its environmental shadows and their unequal social and political effects.[24]

WHY EQUALITY?

Let us pause, to ask why citizens in the early years of the twenty-first century should lament, or grow upset about, the patterns of rising social and political inequality that are the effects of the multiple dysfunctions of markets. The question is by no means innocent. Once upon a time, inequality, for which in many language domains there was not even a word, was understood as the hand of the deities, or of a God, or a product of fate or 'nature', as simply a given and unalterable fact. So why should citizens and their representatives now strive for the reduction of

---

[22] Leon Walras, *Elements of Pure Economics* (London: George Allen & Unwin, 1954).
[23] Elizabeth Kolbert, *The Sixth Extinction: An Unnatural History* (London: Bloomsbury, 2014).
[24] Peter Dauvergne, *The Shadows of Consumption: Consequences for the Global Environment* (Cambridge, MA: MIT Press, 2008).

inequalities of wealth and income, push towards a civil society marked by less unequal outcomes? After all, cynics might say that human beings everywhere quickly grow used to the realities of inequality. The rich and powerful certainly do. When it comes to the problem of inequality, they have a habit of falling back on the conclusion drawn by a character in Dostoevsky's *Notes from Underground*: 'Yes, I'd sell the whole world for a farthing, straight off, so long as I was left in peace. Is the world to go to pot, or am I to go without my tea? I say that the world may go to pot for me so long as I always get my tea.'

A range of (secular) possible replies can be given to this sardonic, jaundiced, world-weary way of thinking. Most obviously, as the early modern champions of civil society themselves first pointed out, nothing is inevitable or 'natural' or automatically desirable about social inequality. The pursuit of more socially equal outcomes, for instance through government policies that lift the income floor for the poor (say, through guaranteed basic income schemes) or publicly restrict the private accumulation of wealth (through taxation bracket changes), does not necessarily stifle initiative and the economic activity on which people's lives depend. The argument that civil societies need inequalities, and the corresponding incentives they create, in order efficiently to grow economically, is implausible.[25] The evidence in fact favours the reverse equation. As political economists from Smith to Piketty have pointed out, sustained economic growth is typically linked to inequitable distributions of economic rewards. Higher levels of inequality lead to underinvestment in education (as those left behind are priced out of higher education) and in public goods and infrastructure (as skewed income distribution erodes tax revenues). Low rates of social inequality nurture demand, and sustainable economic growth, across any given economy. Stark and sustained inequality, by contrast, perverts incentives, discourages those at the bottom of the income distribution (whose hard work goes unrewarded) and encourages those at the top to engage in short-sighted speculation, much of which (think of predatory lending and usurious credit card rates) exploits the poor, and widens the gap in their living conditions compared with those of the rich.

---

[25] Compare the remark of the former New Zealand Prime Minister David Lange, who presided over the country's path-breaking radical experiment with pro-market policies: 'social democrats must accept the existence of economic inequality because it is the engine which drives the economy' (cited in Seymour Martin Lipset, 'The Americanization of the European Left', *Journal of Democracy*, 12, 1 (2001), 80.

The objection to market-produced inequality can be put differently: from the point of view of market economies, pervasive inequality of wealth and income tends to undermine economic dynamism and growth, if only because, at a certain point, stark income gaps begin to hollow out consumption. 'A millionaire cannot wear 10,000 pairs of $10 shoes', an advertiser famously warned on the eve of the 1929 Great Depression, 'but a hundred thousand others can if they've got the $10 to pay for them, and the leisure to show them off'.[26] During our times, rising inequality has created the same tension, eased only temporarily and highly unevenly by the availability of consumer credit, or market-inflated home equity. In the age of the 'attention economy',[27] efforts to patch together substitutes for aggregate demand, in turn, have created their own market risks, including a bloated, shadowy and parasitic financial services sector, fed by the desperate demand for credit from those falling behind, and by the frantic search for speculative returns by those who are galloping well ahead of everybody else.

There is another, equally serious objection to social inequality, this time to do with the many ways in which its effects cannot easily be 'quarantined'. Inequality matters, most obviously and directly, to those left behind by ever greater concentrations of income and wealth. The point is obvious to the poor, the so-called underclass, who have long been cordoned off from social rewards and opportunities. But the corrosiveness of social inequality in more than a few actually existing civil societies also touches the lives of the rest of the population, including the broad middle class, who begin to taste what it means to live precariously, within a society where growing inequality has generally begun to erode wealth and income, reduce living standards, and generally restrict life chances and choices.[28]

There's a further *democratic* objection to inequality, which is that it shapes the quality of life of *all* social strata, of society at large, simply because it directly affects the health and sense of well-being of rich and

---

[26] Cited in Maury Klein, *Rainbow's End: The Crash of 1929* (Oxford and New York: Oxford University Press, 2001), p. 108.
[27] Thomas H. Davenport and John C. Beck, *The Attention Economy* (Boston, MA: Harvard Business School Press, 2001).
[28] See my exchanges with Francis Fukuyama, 'Do the Middle Class Want Democracy?' (ABC Radio National, 27 August 2013), www.abc.net.au/radionational/programs/latenightlive/22no-bourgeois2c-no-democracy22/4912324; and 'Can Democracy Survive a Disappearing Middle Class?' (Centre for Independent Studies, Sydney 2013), www.youtube.com/watch?v=-oJiUUOlieM.

poor alike. Inequality results in what Rousseau (in *Discourse on the Origins of Inequality*) called *égale gueuserie* (equality in misery). Citizens in unequal societies, researchers have shown, more likely end up sick, obese, unhappy, unsafe, or in jail. These social outcomes, in turn, undercut the productivity and efficiency of the economy as a whole, as the high costs of poor public health, heavy policing and mass incarceration siphon off resources and leave human capital underprepared, and underutilised. They have ruinous effects on *all* structures of civil society.

There is another vital objection to market-generated inequalities: unequal distributions of dignity and life chances tend to endanger democracy, both in terms of the open violation of the core democratic principle of equality and the institutional bias these inequalities consolidate. Institutionally speaking, market power always pre-conditions political outcomes. The rich are blessed with both the material resources and the stocks of motivated know-how that count for much more than the individual votes they might cast during an election. Bank accounts and bonds always trump ballots. Inequality has broad political consequences. The powerful rich have the ability to veto dissenting voices and to outflank and crush public watchdog bodies. The rich tilt public government policy towards short-sighted rewards or special treatment (deregulation, tax breaks), and away from the provision of public or collective goods (education, infrastructure) essential to future economic growth. Inequality of wealth and income breeds political inequality, which stands clearly at odds with the core ethical principles of democracy. Democratic institutions, when they operate well, provide a basic (physical, legal, fiscal) infrastructure in which markets can thrive. These institutions also ameliorate or regulate the excesses of market competition, and provide the public goods and services that markets are unable or unwilling to generate on their own. Under conditions of stark economic and political inequality, by contrast, all of these positive functions begin to unravel. *Democracy failure* happens. Short-sighted and recklessly speculative market activities are rewarded, rather than restrained. Collective investment in the economy's infrastructure, everything from good schools to good roads, withers. Deepening economic inequality robs the whole political process of the public commitments and resources needed to deal with its poisonous effects.

RETHINKING SIMPLE OR ARITHMETIC EQUALITY

Among the difficult challenges facing democrats in these years of the twenty-first century is to re-imagine what is meant by the word 'equality'.

7 Capitalism and Civil Society 237

In broad-brush terms, it is clear that market-generated inequality contradicts the democratic spirit of equality, whose roots run deep. Historically speaking, voices from within democracy in every form have consistently questioned and rejected the presumption that the wealthy are 'naturally' entitled to rule, that (as Sieyès put it in *Qu'est-ce que le tiers état?*) the rich have a right to wallow in their riches, so that they 'scarcely even think of themselves as belonging to the same humanity'.[29] Considered as both a political form and a whole way of life, democracy committed itself to the equalisation of wealth and power. That was, and remains, its exceptional quality. From the outset, democracy

> demanded that people see that nothing which is human is carved in stone, that everything is built on the shifting sands of time and place, and that therefore they would be wise to build and maintain ways of living together as equals, openly and flexibly. Democracy required that people see through talk of gods and nature and claims to privilege based on superiority of brain or blood. Democracy meant the denaturing of power. It implied that the most important political problem is how to prevent rule by the few, or by the rich or powerful who claim to be supermen. Democracy solved this old problem by standing up for a political order that ensured that the matter of who gets what, when and how should be permanently an open question. Democracy recognised that although people were not angels or gods or goddesses, they were at least good enough to prevent some humans from thinking they were. Democracy was to be government of the humble, by the humble, for the humble. It meant self-government among equals, the lawful rule of an assembly of people whose sovereign power to decide things was no longer to be given over to imaginary gods, the stentorian voices of tradition, to despots, to those in the know, or simply handed over to the everyday habit of laziness, unthinkingly allowing others to decide matters of importance.[30]

The old democratic principle that democracy means self-government among equals seems straightforward, but striking is the way this principle is challenged under conditions of monitory democracy. In matters of equality, democracy undergoes a double transformation. It comes to mean institutionalised pluralism, a shared sense among citizens and their representatives of the complexity of their worlds, and their opposition to arbitrary power in every form. This transformation in turn implies the theoretical and political need to re-imagine and practically reconfigure the principle of equality, to understand it in more complex terms. Pierre Rosanvallon's *The Society of Equals* pushes in this direction. Strangely,

---

[29] Abbé Sieyès, 'Essai sur les privileges (1788)', in *Qu'est-ce que le tiers état?* (Paris: PUF, 1982), p. 9.
[30] John Keane, *The Life and Death of Democracy* (London and New York: Simon & Schuster, 2009), p. xii.

given his long-standing interest in the subject, his analysis of the future of equality dispenses with the category of civil society; and, arguably, his proposal for re-imagining equality depends much too heavily on the thinking of Tocqueville, whose exaggerated emphasis on equality as sameness during the age of representative democracy has often been noted. Rosanvallon is nevertheless right to appeal for a new political vision of equality based on 'singularity, reciprocity, and communality'.[31] The question for democrats is what exactly does this mean in the age of monitory democracy?

What is required is a fresh re-description of the relationship between equality and democracy, a way of speaking differently, more democratically, about the principle of equality. The fresh approach would recognise that *simple notions of equality*, understood as equal treatment and equal prospects of advancement for each individual citizen, can become unworkable, even undesirable when they are treated as the sole measure of the meaning and practice of equality. Within democratic settings, it is true, some notions of simple equality remain politically important; one person, one vote and universal entitlements to health care and education and decent pensions are obvious cases in point. But notions of simple equality cannot be the sole measure of equality under conditions of monitory democracy. What is required is a more *complex notion of equality* that recognises that there are circumstances in which, for the sake of reducing inequality, democracies sometimes must privilege some citizens at the expense of others.

The paradox can be explained by imagining for a moment a totally different world: a socially undivided and homogeneous political community in which, in the name of equality, all individuals are continuously treated the same. In this paradise of pure and simple equality, summarised in George Orwell's glowing account of daily life in revolutionary Barcelona in December 1936,[32] resources would be divisible into equal

---

[31] Rosanvallon, *Society of Equals*, p. 260.

[32] 'It was the first time', George Orwell wrote, 'I had ever been in a town where the working class was in the saddle. Practically every building of any size had been seized by the workers and was draped with red flags or with the red and black flag of the Anarchists; every wall was scrawled with the hammer and sickle and with the initials of the revolutionary parties ... Every shop and café had an inscription saying that it had been collectivized ... Waiters and shop-walkers looked you in the face and treated you as an equal.' He added: 'The thing that attracts ordinary men to Socialism and makes them willing to risk their skins for it, the "mystique" of Socialism, is the idea of equality; to the vast majority of people Socialism means a classless society, or it means nothing at all'; *Homage to Catalonia* (London, 1938), Chapter 1.

amounts. Each citizen would benefit in exactly the same way and, since people are presumed to be so much alike in their wants and needs, no disputes would break out over the significance and effects of the equal portions given to all as equals. Differences of taste and conflicts among differing goals would be unknown, or treated as irrelevant. In this society of arithmetic equals, the fully centralised allocation of resources and the absence of politics would render obsolete the need for any institutions of representative government. Why would there need to be mechanisms for monitoring the exercise of power if, at the end of each day, every citizen dutifully accepted that she or he was the simple equal of each and every other citizen?

Scenarios of simple equality have often greatly bothered past analysts of democracy. 'The gradual progress of equality is something fated', wrote Tocqueville in a famous lament about the crushing consequences of the drive towards equalisation during the age of representative democracy. This 'irresistible revolution advancing century by century' in favour of simple equality, so Tocqueville thought, might dangerously steamroll the world into a flat and simple form of equality, what he called levelling into sameness (*semblablement*). The movement for equality would stop at nothing, he warned. It would have the unintended consequence of building a new form of state servitude brought on by the democratic quest to make and treat everybody equal. 'Does anyone imagine that democracy, which has destroyed the feudal system and vanquished kings, will fall back before the middle classes and the rich? Will it stop now, when it has grown so strong and its adversaries so weak?'[33]

Aside from his habit of understating the factual inequalities in nineteenth-century societies, Tocqueville's prediction failed to spot the ways in which the irremediably concrete and complex ways of democracy would remould the ideals and practices of equality into something far more complicated than anybody had envisaged in the era of representative democracy. In our age of monitory democracy, awareness is growing that there are many different kinds of equalities that are, in turn, capable of having many different kinds of relationships with one another. The simple word equality is transformed into a much more *complex grammar of equality*. It becomes apparent to many people that the fractured quality of social and political life demands not only that recognition be granted to more than one practical meaning of equality. Many people realise as well

---

[33] Alexis de Tocqueville, *Democracy in America*, Vol. I, edited by J.P. Mayer (New York: Doubleday, 1969), p. 12.

that the principle of equality cannot itself serve as a basis for choosing among them. In a curious and surprising way, this growing awareness of the complex grammar of equality confirms Aristotle's critique of 'numerical equality'.[34] Writing in the era of assembly democracy, he contrasted 'numerical equality' with 'proportional equality', which he defined as a form of equal treatment of others who are considered as equals in some or other important respect, but not others. 'In the many forms of government which have sprung up there has always been an acknowledgement of justice and proportionate equality.' He contrasted democracy with oligarchy. Democracy 'arises out of the notion that those who are equal in any respect are equal in all respects; because men are equally free, they claim to be absolutely equal'. Under conditions of oligarchy, by contrast, inequality is valued. Oligarchy 'is based on the notion that those who are unequal in one respect are in all respects unequal; being unequal, that is, in property, they suppose themselves to be unequal absolutely'. For Aristotle, the contrast was striking. 'The democrats think that as they are equal they ought to be equal in all things; while the oligarchs, under the idea that they are unequal, claim too much, which is one form of inequality.' Aristotle considered that both approaches were faulty, and were prone to 'stir up revolution'. And so, in opposition to all simple understandings of equality and inequality, he opted for a middle course. Aristotle proposed that the best polity is one in which a mixture of both numerical and proportionate forms of equality are cultivated. 'That a state should be ordered, simply and wholly, according to either kind of equality [numerical or proportional], is not a good thing', he wrote. 'Both kinds of equality should be employed; numerical in some cases, and proportionate in others.'

It is of more than passing interest that in the United States the landmark legal case of *Fullilove* v. *Klutznick*, 448 U.S. (1980) pointed in this direction. The famous case split the nine-judge United States Supreme Court into five separate opinions about whether the federal government was entitled to give preferential treatment in some part of its public works programs to minority-owned companies. In the end, the Court held such set-aside treatment was justified, but the case highlighted a watershed clash: between equality understood in terms of equality of results or outcomes, and the quite different understanding of equality as equality of opportunity, a form of equality that typically results in unequal outcomes, in 'winners' and 'losers'.

---

[34] Aristotle, *Nichomachean Ethics*, 1130b–1132b; and *Politics*, 1301a26–39, 1302a03–15.

Things become still more complicated when these different understandings of equality are applied either to individuals, or to groups, or to specific policy areas, or to large territorial areas, or to cross-border relations of power. In each case, the quest for 'equality' has different – and often unequal – effects. The scope of equality can be local or territorial or global, and these different domains often conflict with one another, so that, for instance, the act of placing singular emphasis on the equality of citizens living within a state ('all are equals in this country') easily works against citizens equipped with different needs and concerns within the same state, as well as works against citizens of other states, or those without any state at all. The implication is clear: like salt to the sea, the principle of equality lies at the heart of democracy, but it is not a straightforward Universal Principle that can be applied like a sharp saw to rough wood, or a bulldozer to uneven ground. Aristotle's contrast of 'numerical equality' and 'proportional equality' remains pertinent. Or, to switch similes by borrowing from Walt Whitman's well-known likening of democracy to fruits and flowers: contrary to the complaints and platitudes of its opponents, the thrust of democratic ideals and a democratic politics committed to the complex equalisation of power is not to cut down tall poppies, to level everything to the ground. It is rather to ensure that a wide variety of species everywhere on the planet can flourish, in fields of plants and animals that are otherwise at risk from harm and extinction at the hands of parasites and predators.

WHAT CAN BE DONE?

We live in times still very much in the grip of market thinking, deep dysfunctions and pathologies of market power and (paradoxically) the seeming political inability to do much about them. So can the actors and institutions of any given civil society today help to alleviate, or outright reverse, the drift towards highly unequal capitalist societies?

In some quarters, it used to be fashionable to say that the whole idea of a civil society offers 'a new kind of capitalism critique', simply because markets are principally defined by the logic of 'competition, exchange and the maximisation of individual benefits'.[35] The argument is too easy, and

---

[35] Víctor Pérez-Díaz, 'Markets as Conversations: Markets' Contributions to Civility, the Public Sphere and Civil Society at Large', in Victor Pérez-Díaz (ed.), *Markets and Civil Society: The European Experience in Comparative Perspective* (New York: Berghahn, 2014), p. xii.

actually misleading. It is worth repeating the fundamental point: the civil society/markets dualism ignores the deep functional interdependence of inequality-producing markets and other civil society institutions. The intellectual and political point here is to retrieve and elaborate the insight of classical political economy that all known markets, past and present, are non-governmental, money- and nature-mediated, power-ridden relations of investment, production, exchange and consumption in which buyers and sellers of commodities are constituted and constrained by linguistically mediated social rules that amount to obligations that govern the behaviour of all market actors. Karl Polanyi's definition of a market economy as 'an economic system that is controlled, regulated and directed by market prices; order in the production and distribution of goods is entrusted to this self-regulating mechanism'[36] is misleading. Regardless of how dependent civil society actors are upon money or budgets, financial reports, buying, selling and advertising, linguistically mediated social rules are *within* and not somehow *outside* market relations.

The infusion of markets with webs of social relations is quite in accordance with the early modern observation that civil societies are differentiated in complex ways by a multiplicity of non-governmental rules: intimacy and friendship, public debate and social conversation, forms of play and rites of passage to do with birth, marriage, procreation and death, but also by the rules of money, property, commodity production, exchange and consumption. Commentators from Smith and Paine to de Tocqueville understood well that the propensity to 'truck, barter and exchange one thing for another' is co-structured, co-determined by other rules of social interaction. Markets require these social rules in order to function. No civil society, no markets (this is one lesson to be drawn from the Soviet model of socialism). The inverse is also true: no markets, no civil society (the lesson of cases as different as Solidarność, Mao's China and Pol Pot's Cambodia). The marriage between markets and other civil society institutions may be (and often is) unhappy, but for the sake of their mutual survival their divorce is forbidden.

FICTITIOUS COMMODITIES

A strategic political insight follows from this abstract formulation: for the sake of monitory democracy, and the radical reduction of market-generated

---

[36] Karl Polanyi, *Origins of Our Time: The Great Transformation* (London: Victor Gollancz, 1945), p. 74.

inequality, what is needed is a new quest to embed markets within other civil society institutions that are protected by legal and governing arrangements. This was the key point made by Karl Polanyi: the unbreakable dependence of capitalist markets upon *other* civil society institutions highlights the fact that labour is a 'fictitious commodity'. Despite his constricted definition of a market economy, Polanyi's point was that labour power cannot live with the dualism of market and civil society. While labour is organised as a commodity in the markets of contemporary capitalist economies, it is not produced for sale and cannot in real life behave as a pure commodity. Put differently, labour is just another name for a type of social activity that is ultimately not detachable from *six* other entangled, variously combined types of civil society institutions that are always and everywhere in need of political protection by citizens and their representatives:

- *non-market forms of production* within households, voluntary and charitable groups and other 'parallel economy' activities;
- forms of *recreation*, in which people spend at least some of their disposable time in such activities as sport, travel, tourism and hobbies;
- the (often overlapping) organisations of the *arts and entertainment*, including galleries, cinemas, music and dance clubs, theatres, pubs, restaurants and cafés;
- the *cultivation of intimacy* through friendships and household spaces of co-operation, sexual experimentation, procreation and the social nurturing of infants and adults;
- non-governmental *communication media*, such as user-friendly web platforms, newspapers and magazines, bookshops, television studios and community radio stations; and, finally,
- public spaces that define and nurture the *sacred*, including cemeteries, institutions of religious worship, monuments and sites of historical importance.

These various types of non-market social organisation are indispensable preconditions of labour power. Sometimes they are described through terms like 'social capital' and 'cultural capital' and 'human capital', but that is misleadingly to suppose that employees are mere adjuncts of market forces. Whatever may be thought of (let's call it) the Hitachi model of corporate life – an arrangement in which workers are required to socialise with other company staff through corporate clubs and organisations – it drives home the general point that labour power depends for its existence upon the social ecosystems of civil society. Employees cannot be reduced to the process of rationally calculated, commodity production, exchange and consumption. It is true that their lives can be more or less media-saturated, more or less religious and – certainly – more or less market-dominated. But short of sociocide, the nervous breakdown of the social, civil societies can never fully be transformed into capitalist markets, into something like a greed-driven factory or stock exchange or shopping mall. Robbed of the protective clothing afforded by civil society and reduced to the status of a mere factor of production, social actors would die of social exposure. 'To allow the market mechanism to be the sole director of the fate of human beings and their natural environment ... would result in the demolition of society', wrote Polanyi. 'For the alleged commodity "labour power" cannot be shoved about, used indiscriminately, or even left unused, without affecting also the human individual who happens to be the bearer of this particular commodity.'[37]

THE RE-SOCIALISATION OF MARKETS

In contexts otherwise as different as Ireland, Taiwan, India and South Africa, there are signs of a developing sense that social inequality is a poisonous fruit of capitalist accumulation. There is rising public awareness that for the sake of our biosphere and our democratic ways of life a new politics of social equality is urgently needed. There are new citizens' initiatives, the founding of new political parties, and demands for new government policies that can put a stop to the ruinous anti-democratic effects of rising inequalities of wealth and income.[38]

So what exactly is to be done? How can the vicious 'Bossuet paradox' ('God laughs at men who complain of the consequences while cherishing the causes') be practically overcome, so that many more people feel that what they deplore in general (rising social inequality) they can deal with in their own particular contexts? Might new and more complex forms of the old ideal of simple equality come once again to inspire public passions, as they did from the end of the eighteenth century? The nineteenth-century communist, socialist and anarcho-syndicalist vision of abolishing

---

[37] Karl Polanyi, *Origins of Our Time: The Great Transformation*, pp. 78–79.
[38] Ramón Feenstra, Andreu Casales-Riperro, Simon Tormey and John Keane, *Refiguring Democracy: The Spanish Political Laboratory* (London and New York: Routledge, 2017).

markets is admittedly dead. It failed. More honestly: it ruined itself in an orgy of hubris, violence and political despotism. The utopia of abolishing markets proved disastrous (as *Democracy and Civil Society* tried to show[39]) either because it trusted in the full state take-over of the exchange with nature (as Hayek in *The Road to Serfdom* predicted it would[40]) or because it thought in anarchist and anarcho-syndicalist terms, weighed down by imaginings that law and government could be abolished by forging social harmony based on the solidarity of the collective producers.

Either way, civil society was supposed to become a mere memory, an unpleasant experience from the past. Given the follies and cruelties associated with the past century's efforts by states to exterminate civil society, and given also that today's blind trust in the arrogance of market-centred policies must be rejected, how can normative theories of civil society find a new way in the politics of reducing inequality? Who or what is the heir of the socialist and anarcho-communist project of reducing the grip of markets on people's lives? How can markets be re-embedded in the mosaic of legally guaranteed social relations we call civil society, so as to bring into our world greater freedom and equality, understood in new and more complex ways, on a global scale?

Specifically, what does the eighteenth-century vision of moral economy mean today?[41] Which demands shall in future succeed the nineteenth-century call for Eight Hours Work, Eight Hours Recreation, Eight Hours Rest? It's too easy to observe that market-driven capitalism has a history and is unlikely to last indefinitely, for in the face of rising inequality the pressing question centres on the urgency and viability of a new settlement between governments, civil societies, citizens and their chosen representatives. Does this settlement require a major shift towards a carbon-neutral, circular, open-data economy? Is there scope for the development of social innovation and investment funds, and crowd-sourced funding for social initiatives? Does the 'de-commodification' of civil societies require their stronger embrace of a 'relational economy' that creates value out of social relationships, as in digital 'second skin' initiatives, such as peer-to-peer collaboration carpooling

---

[39] John Keane, *Democracy and Civil Society* (London and New York: Verso, 1988); see also John Keane (ed.), *Civil Society and the State: New European Perspectives* (London and New York: Verso, 1988); and *Global Civil Society?* (London and New York: Cambridge University Press, 2003).
[40] von Hayek, *The Road to Serfdom* [1944].
[41] E.P. Thompson, 'The Moral Economy of the English Crowd in the Eighteenth Century', *Past and Present*, 50 (1971), 76–136.

and AirB&B-type schemes, social innovation cities (such as Seoul and Copenhagen) and the growth of caring industries in such fields as ageing and refugee settlement? Rephrased, the question is whether a vision of 'civic capitalism'[42] is a politically legitimate and plausible norm. Is it feasible in democratic countries to pursue a politics of *noblesse oblige*: a politics that aims at seducing, threatening, legally forcing businesses to acknowledge and to honour their social responsibilities? Can whole areas of civil society effectively be de-commodified through bans on bill-board advertising in cities (as in Sao Paolo), anti-corruption initiatives (such as India's Ipaidabribe.com), public–private partnerships (PPPs), support for public service media and new types of consumer citizenship? Can efforts to strengthen shareholders' and stakeholders' rights play their part in the whole process? What about strengthened works councils, the extension of trade union rights, the reduction of working time and the more systematic inclusion of households within labour market policies? Does the survival of local civil societies require the global cancellation of debts of poor countries, their fair representation in global institutions, an end to tax-avoidance havens and new global taxes on corporate profits? Does the humbling of corporate power require the defence of new forms of citizenship, such as the legal right to decent maternity/paternity leave, schemes geared to the social needs of women, adequate care for the old, a basic citizens' income and the legal recognition of ecosystems? How important are policies that foster inter-generational justice, for instance the empowerment of children, civil society's most market-vulnerable participants?

Arguably, none of these innovations can be attempted, or implemented and managed, unless civil societies are protected and nurtured by government and para-governmental institutions. The historical evidence suggests that civil societies cannot overcome the forces of market fundamentalism simply by means of their own resources and efforts. For most avowed democrats of the past century, this strategic point was self-evident. For these democrats, the democratisation of markets typically meant greater state intervention and control of markets. More recently, confronted with the collapse of the Soviet model of socialism, many democrats recognise that since parliamentary democracy is constantly vulnerable to corporate 'kidnapping', updated versions of the social democratic vision of

---

[42] John O'Neill, *Civic Capitalism: The State of Childhood* (Toronto, ON: University of Toronto Press, 2004).

liberating ('de-commodifying') areas of life currently in the grip of unregulated markets are now needed. What is required, they say, are new government policies that 'socialise' the unjust effects of markets by 're-embedding' them within civil society institutions guaranteed by election victories, welfare mechanisms and legal protection. Their broad vision is clear: in defence of the democratic principle of equality, government instruments are needed to limit 'predatory' forms of capitalism and to protect and extend social citizenship rights through such 'pre-distribution' strategies as raising the minimum wage and enforcing new contract law arrangements that empower workers and consumers.[43]

Whether such regulation can succeed without crossing borders and through state efforts alone remains an open question. Both the reflections and tactical considerations presented here suggest that in political struggles against market-produced inequality, governments need the support of active civil societies, which raises a further question, as to whether a wider vision of 'post-capitalist' or 'socialist' civil society is politically viable and capable of winning public legitimacy. In the era of financial capitalism, neo-liberal economics and big money, public talk of socialism seems mainly to be forbidden, out of fashion, or unwise. These are times in which the old sarcasm of Rousseau has a strange, new relevance: 'Societies have assumed their final form: no longer is anything changed except by arms and cash.'[44] That being so, how shall the old political project of 'socialising' markets and making civil societies more equal and more open and more 'civil' be kept alive and nurtured in the coming years? From the new perspective of monitory democracy, the point is not only to change the world, but also to interpret it in new ways. Stale answers need to be questioned. Fresh questions need to be put. And new emphasis must be given to the wise words of William Morris about the history of struggles for the reduction of inequality. People 'fight and

---

[43] Thomas H. Marshall, *Citizenship and Social Class and Other Essays* (Cambridge: Cambridge University Press, 1950); Peter A. Hall and David Soskice (eds.), *Varieties of Capitalism: The Institutional Foundations of Comparative Advantage* (Oxford: Oxford University Press, 2001); Geoff Mulgan, *The Locust and the Bee: Predators and Creators in Capitalism's Future* (Princeton, NJ and London: Princeton University Press, 2013); Robert B. Reich, *Saving Capitalism: For the Many, Not the Few* (New York: Knopf, 2015); Philippe van Parijs and Yannick Vanderborght, *Basic Income: A Radical Proposal for a Free Society and a Sane Economy* (Cambridge, MA: Harvard University Press); and the classic work by Claus Offe, *Contradictions of the Welfare State*, edited by John Keane (London: MIT Press, 1984).

[44] Jean-Jacques Rousseau, *Essai sur l'origine des langues* (Paris: A. Belin, 1817).

lose the battle', he wrote, and yet it sometimes happens that 'the thing that they fought for comes about in spite of their defeat'. When there is this kind of success, he continued, it sometimes 'turns out not to be what they meant', so that other people 'have to fight for what they meant under another name'.[45]

---

[45] William Morris, *A Dream of John Ball and a King's Lesson* (London and New York: Longmans, Green & Company, 1896).

8

The Greening of Democracy

As human despoliation of our planet gathers pace, the subject of green politics presses ever harder on corporations, governments and mainstream public opinion. The challenges and changes are not confined to the democratic world, but they are striking, and without precedent. The greening of democracy runs far beyond spreading public talk of sustainability and climate justice and is more consequential than disputes about the price of carbon and emissions trading schemes. In less than a generation, green-minded intellectuals, civic initiatives, movements and political parties have managed to reshape public agendas; in consequence, matters such as nuclear power, chemical pollutants, carbon emissions, climate change and species destruction are now firmly on the policy agenda of democratic politics. Public awareness that humans are the only biological species ever to have occupied the entire planet, with potentially catastrophic consequences, is growing (as the controversies surrounding a new geological era called the Anthropocene suggest[1]). Green politics has helped popularise new philosophical perspectives (such as critical animal studies, feminist care ethics, neo-Marxism, capability approaches and talk of environmental justice). It has championed precautionary attitudes towards 'progress' and its blind embrace; green politics might even be described as a contribution to a new type of 'slow democracy' aimed at arresting the pace of decision making that has wrecking effects. Green politics has also tabled important tactical questions. Important strategic matters now absorb considerable amounts of political energy: for

---

[1] Christophe Bonneuil and Jean-Baptiste Fressoz, *The Shock of the Anthropocene: The Earth, History and Us* (London and New York: Verso, 2016).

instance, whether priority should be given to civic initiatives, civil disobedience and networked social movements or the formation of alliances with mainstream parties, how green political parties can best be kept open to their members and supporters, and whether their political success requires broadening their agendas to include topics such as immigration, sexual orientation, health care and pensions.

Much less effort has been devoted to clarifying the long-term democratic significance of these achievements of green politics. The profoundly radical implications of green politics for the way people imagine and live democracy are still poorly understood. It is true there are activists, probably a dwindling minority, for whom the priority is to give up on democratic politics and to live simply, in 'harmony with nature', as if wilderness is medicinal for lives 'bound by clocks, almanacs ... and dust and din' (John Muir, co-founder of the Sierra Club). Much more striking is the way levels of support for democratic principles run high within green circles, as confirmed by the discomfort triggered by James Lovelock's widely reported suggestion that it 'may be necessary to put democracy on hold for a while'.[2] Greens' commitment to such democratic principles as equality, openness and respect for diversity and one-person-one-vote equality seems unwavering. Yet why people with green sympathies should embrace democracy for more than tactical reasons, whether democratic principles themselves can be 'greened' and what that might imply for the way people imagine to be the 'essence' or 'spirit' of democracy are matters that remain rather obscure within green circles and beyond – or so the following pages suggest.

ENERGY REGIMES

Finding our bearings requires seeing that green politics has triggered what physicists call a moment of dark energy: the universe of meaning of

---

[2] See his interview with Leo Hickman in *The Guardian* (www.guardian.co.uk/environment/blog/2010/mar/29/james-lovelock [accessed 6 January 2013]): 'We need a more authoritative world. We've become a sort of cheeky, egalitarian world where everyone can have their say. It's all very well, but there are certain circumstances – a war is a typical example – where you can't do that. You've got to have a few people with authority who you trust who are running it. And they should be very accountable too, of course. But it can't happen in a modern democracy. This is one of the problems. What's the alternative to democracy? There isn't one. But even the best democracies agree that when a major war approaches, democracy must be put on hold for the time being. I have a feeling that climate change may be an issue as severe as a war. It may be necessary to put democracy on hold for a while.'

8 The Greening of Democracy

democracy is undergoing a dramatic expansion, in defiance of the cosmic gravity of worldly events. The changes are not cosmetic, but transformative, at least as radical as the semantic and institutional shift toward 'representative democracy' that took place at the end of the eighteenth century. Green politics and 'green democracy' are not simply neologisms that enrich the language of democracy, say, in the way novel phrases like 'social democracy', 'Christian democracy' and 'liberal democracy' altered the vocabulary of representative democracy during the era of representative democracy. Green politics is not just a new lexicon. It cuts deeper and runs wider, and it therefore demands fresh political thinking guided by a strong sense of its own historicity and future strategic and normative potential.

There are few directional signposts, let alone meaningful precedents, but one way of grasping the novel greening of democracy and its long-term significance is to draw upon the spirit of Montesquieu's path-breaking exploration of the link between political institutions and their geographic environment[3] by asking questions about the relationship between different historical forms of democracy and the environmental milieux in which they are embedded. Think of things this way: every human society is defined by its particular *energy regime*, the sum total of arrangements whereby energy is extracted from human or animal muscle power or harvested (say) from running water, sun, tides, wind, coal or uranium atoms, then applied, stored, bought and sold, used to fuel machines, or wasted, and eventually dissipated.[4] Environmental historians reminds us that human energy regimes are variable, that their form and content undergo changes in space and through time, yet in each case energy regimes are defined by clusters of techniques, institutions and methods of producing and distributing energy for defined purposes. Energy regimes are more than just technical arrangements or tools that can be picked up and put down at will, for any particular purpose. Energy regimes produce path dependencies and have power effects; embedded within social and political institutions, they co-determine who gets what, when and how. Energy regimes, that is to say, typically operate from

---

[3] Montesquieu's theory of the influence of geographic environment on political forms is presented in *The Spirit of the Laws*, where the temperate climate of middle Europe is seen to be optimal for the cultivation of political liberty, in contrast to warm countries, where peoples are rendered 'too hot-tempered', and more northern climes, whose peoples are 'icy' and 'stiff'; Charles Montesquieu, *The Spirit of the Laws [1748]*, edited by Victor Goldschmidt (Paris: Garnier-Flammarion, 1979).

[4] J.R. McNeill, *Something New Under the Sun: An Environmental History of the Twentieth-Century World* (London: Allen Lane, 2000).

within and through the various institutions of any given political order, and it is in this sense that their impact is pervasive. They do much more than enable certain people to get things done. Energy regimes sink into their skins, structure the way they think and interact. Even the metaphors through which they speak are affected, for instance when they use words and phrases like 'electrifying', 'switched on', 'bright spark' and 'carbon footprint'. Energy regimes also have wider environmental consequences: the habitats within which humans dwell are transformed by the energy modes they employ. In extreme cases, energy regimes so interfere with local biomes that they trigger dynamics that can have catastrophic consequences for human inhabitants.[5]

All known forms of democracy have been embedded within and materially shaped by energy regimes. Consider the case of the assembly democracies of the ancient Greek world. They were a labour-intensive form of democracy. While cleverly harnessing sail power for long-distance shipping and animal energy (oxen, donkeys, mules and horses), early Greek democracies were founded primarily on muscle power: human labour for such activities as rowing triremes, farming, construction, mining and manufacturing. As the best-known case of Athens shows, much of this labour was supplied by chattel slaves. Citizens themselves pitched in. While rich citizens enjoyed lives of *skhole* ('leisure'), most non-elite Athenians either laboured alone or alongside their own slaves. The heavy dependence upon labour power was expressed through the vernacular language of democracy. Male citizens often called themselves 'the labouring men'; and members of the lowest class were named *hoi thetes*, literally 'the hired labourers' (the common word for the lower-class as 'the poor', *hoi penētes* [plural] comes from the verb *penomai*, meaning 'to labour').[6]

The environmental impact of the assembly democracies of the ancient Greek world remains much-disputed. Nineteenth-century European Romantics tended to portray classical Greece as an Arcadian land of noble forests and crystal fountains, but more recent archaeological evidence suggests that the Greek democracies did impact upon their local environments, sometimes negatively. Aristotle's *Meteorologica* (Book 1, chapter 14) notes the transformation of Mycenae into a 'dry and barren' landscape; and there

---

[5] Jared Diamond, *Collapse: How Societies Choose to Fail or Succeed* (New York: Viking Press, 2005).
[6] Further details are provided in David Pritchard, *Sport, Democracy and War in Classical Athens* (Cambridge and New York: Cambridge University Press, 2012).

are plenty of other recorded cases where soil erosion followed reckless over-cultivation of fields, or the over-exploitation of forests. Yet the commitment to self-sufficiency (*autárkeia*), limited scale and popular belief in deities combined to limit environmental destruction. Hunting of animals took place for prestige (rather than pecuniary) reasons; livestock husbandry involved small flocks associated with arable agriculture, which was geared to satisfying needs by cultivating small fields using crop rotation and multiple cultures. Widespread belief in deities served as an additional brake upon misuse of the environment. The assembly democracy of the ancient Greeks flourished in an enchanted garden governed by deities, in whom citizens invested great hopes. They feared them as well. The public trial and execution of the philosopher Socrates in 399 BCE for importing fake gods into the city of Athens, and for impiously corrupting its youth, confirmed that those who snubbed the deities would suffer harsh punishment. Within the Greek democracies, priests and old men were in the habit of reminding citizens (the story was taken originally from Homer) that at the entrance of the home of Zeus, the god of freedom, stood two large barrels, from which he dispensed ill to some newcomers, good to others, and to the rest a few ladles of good from one barrel and, from the other, a bit of ill. Tales like that put early democracies on edge. Many citizens thought of themselves as members of a community of worshippers who believed that deities like Zeus would punish them collectively if they or their leaders behaved unjustly; he and other deities were thought to enjoy the power to ruin democracy, for instance by bringing bad weather or failed harvests, or the death of oak trees, or the disappearance of fish from the seas.

GETTING RID OF THE SUN

When we turn to the energy regime that prevailed during the era of modern representative democracy, we see the continuing importance of human labour power as a key energy source. Yet there is a striking difference with the assembly democracies of the ancient world: modern forms of representative democracy were born and grew to maturity in exactly the same time period as the transition to carbon-fuelled energy regimes. The historic tipping point happened towards the end of the eighteenth century, and it is surely among the strangest coincidences in the history of democracy: an energy revolution of epochal importance was unleashed on peoples struggling politically to re-define and build forms of self-government based on the periodic election of representatives.

The coincidence has barely been noted by environmental historians or political thinkers.[7] What we find instead within the literature on democracy and its material environment are compelling but separate accounts: environmental historians note the switch to carbon-based energy regimes while political thinkers focus on the invention of representative democracy.[8] The effect of keeping apart the two entangled histories is unfortunate, if only because of the undeniable importance of the profoundly transformative effects of the industrial revolutions that gripped various societies in the Atlantic region during the last decades of the eighteenth century. These revolutions were initially propelled by animal and human muscle power and water-driven textile mills. Beginning around 1820, however, the dominant energy regime gradually became carbonised, in two overlapping stages.

Put simply, we could say that the first phase of the energy regime upheaval led to the coronation of King Coal. For nearly a century, supported and protected by a coal-consuming, coal-exporting British empire,[9] the coal-fired monarch reigned over urban concentrations of heavy industry in smokestack cities connected by railways, steamships, newspapers, letters and the telegraph. These 'coketowns' (Charles Dickens called them in *Hard Times*) profoundly transformed many people's lives and their habitats. They are remembered as unhealthy and ugly places. 'Look up and around this place you will see the huge palaces of industry. You will hear the noise of furnaces, the whistle of steam', wrote de Tocqueville during a visit to Manchester, at the time the global epicentre of laissez-faire, steam-powered capitalism. 'A sort of black smoke covers the city. The sun seen through it is a disc without rays. Under this half daylight 300,000 human beings are ceaselessly at work.'

---

[7] An example is Mark Fiege's *The Republic of Nature: An Environmental History of the United States* (Seattle, WA: University of Washington Press, 2012), an interesting example of environmental history that attempts to narrate the rise of the American republic in terms of its interdependence with material nature, unfortunately by concentrating mainly on the many ways the republic fed upon broad (Jeffersonian) conceptions of an orderly universe and a strong public sense of entitlement to riches wrested from the earth by human ingenuity.

[8] See for example Sonia Alonso, Wolfgang Merkel and John Keane (eds.), *The Future of Representative Democracy* (Cambridge and New York: Cambridge University Press, 2011) and Nadia Urbinati, *Representative Democracy: Principles and Genealogy* (Chicago, IL: University of Chicago Press, 2006).

[9] Kenneth Pomeranz, *The Great Divergence: China, Europe, and the Making of the Modern World Economy* (Princeton, NJ: Princeton University Press, 2001); Andreas Malm, *Fossil Capital: The Rise of Steam Power and the Roots of Global Warming* (London: Verso, 2015).

He added: 'From this foul drain the greatest stream of human industry flows out to fertilise the whole world. From this filthy sewer pure gold flows. Here humanity attains its most complete development and its most brutish.'[10] King Coal's reign was marked by multiple paradoxes. To mention just a few: the worship of coal-fired electrification did more than anything else to banish the fear of ghosts from people's night-time lives. Soot-stained skies blocked the rays of the sun, but coal hastened the abolition of darkness by gas lamp-lit streets, electrified signs and even human attempts to simulate sunrises and sunsets. Coal-fired railways comprising wooden boxcars, cross-ties and sleepers gobbled up forests and triggered the growth of conservation movements and national parks initiatives (an example was Theodore Roosevelt's support for a national forest service to rationalise the use of America's remaining forests). Carbon-based energy generated employment, soiled natural landscapes but enabled struggles for representative democracy, including fiercely fought political efforts to widen the franchise and to reshape governments into welfare states. It is easy to see in retrospect that fossil fuels were the underwriter of representative democracy. Consider the way electrified capitalist economies, connected by coal-fired trains, printing presses and postal and telegraph systems, were instrumental in enabling the growth of civil societies, independent public spheres, co-operatives, friendly societies, trades unions, social democratic working class parties and votes for women. There was resistance from bodies like the Association for the Prevention of Smoke, and from anarchists and socialists who imagined 'a politics of beauty and conviviality in harmony with nature'.[11] But the general trend among democrats during this period was to regard 'nature' as an unlimited resource, to be fully exploited by the new energy regime, for the use and enjoyment of 'the people'. Alexis de Tocqueville's letters from America, written in the year 1831, are chocked full of such sentiments. 'All is hustle and bustle. And money is the universal divinity', he wrote. The young American 'democracy devoid of limits or measures' was marked by a feverish will to conquer forests, land and water. 'Here the earth itself wears a new face every day', he continued. Citizens 'wage war against the forest in a thousand different ways.' They are 'unhappy if they

---

[10] Alexis de Tocqueville, *Journeys to England and Ireland*, edited by J.P. Mayer (London: Transaction Publishers, 1963), pp. 107–108; compare Stephen Mosley, *The Chimney of the World: A History of Smoke Pollution in Victorian and Edwardian Manchester* (Cambridge: White Horse Press, 2001).
[11] Christophe Bonneuil and Jean-Baptiste Fressoz, *The Shock of the Anthropocene*, p. 272.

aren't plowing new soil, tearing up roots, cutting down trees, fighting wild beasts and Indians: therein lies their pleasure for other men in making money hand over fist and living within four walls'.[12]

Now consider phase two of the carbon revolution, which began in earnest during the 1920s, when leading national economies began to supplement their dependence upon coal with a growing allegiance to the Sultan of Oil. The United States, soon to become the richest and most powerful democracy, took the lead.[13] Its domestic oil and gas industry – spurred on by the first big gusher (in 1901, at Spindletop well, east Texas) and feeding hungrily upon liquids exhumed from ancient forests – soon became a powerful driver of assembly line manufacturing of aircraft and automobiles, fertilisers, petrochemicals and plastics. The new black gold loyalty spawned spectacular inventions, such as gasoline-powered chainsaws, which resembled giant forest-eating invaders from another planet, capable of snipping trees at their base, up to a thousand times quicker than men wielding sharp axes. There were tools like lawnmowers, tractors and trucks, bulldozers, motorcycles and automobiles, whose irresistible popularity stemmed from the convenience of mobility, social status, affordability and the jobs they created. Oil and gas came to shape 'where we live, how we live, how we commute to work, how we travel – even where we conduct our courtships'.[14]

Amidst wild scenes of jubilation, huge fortunes were often made overnight by the discovery and marketing of oil and gas, which seeped into the structures and dynamics of every representative democracy. Think counter-factually for a moment: for instance, without fossil fuelled electricity, such things as political parties, campaign advertising, election rallies, newspaper, radio and television coverage of elections would be impossible. Television debates and radio interviews and party-political announcements would be unthinkable; ballot papers could not be printed or delivered in sufficient quantities. Voter turnout levels, especially among frail and older citizens with limited mobility, would be low due to lack of transport or fear of the dark. Electronic voting and the counting of ballot papers would be impossible; and the razzamatazz of announced results would be no more.

---

[12] Alexis de Tocqueville, *Letters from America* (New Haven and London: Yale University Press, 2010), pp. 33, 68, 103, 243–244.
[13] Daniel Yergin, *The Prize: The Epic Quest for Oil, Money and Power* (London: Simon & Schuster, 1991), pp. 82–86.
[14] Ibid., p. 14.

MONITORY DEMOCRACY

We are living in times of unprecedented restiveness about carbon-fuelled growth and its destructive impact upon the biosphere in which we humans dwell. The opportunities and the troubles they pose are intimately connected to the rise of monitory democracy.

The public questioning and refusal of carbon-based energy arrangements admittedly have deep taproots. They are traceable to the historic switch from sun-powered energy that took place at the end of the eighteenth century. Think of early modern poetry and literature, the protests of Romanticism, the birth of the co-operative and labour movements, rural anarchism and variants of nature-tinged nationalism: all these initiatives and more played a part in stimulating and keeping alive the common sense that something was not quite right in the shift towards carbon-intensive energy regimes. The late nineteenth-century conservation movement, which gave birth to public zoos (Taronga was opened in 1884, on a site known as Billy Goat Swamp) and to the first conservation groups (Birds Australia was founded in 1901) was part of the same pattern of resistance to blind dependence on carbon-based energy systems. So too were loud protests against the recklessness of the oil industry, for instance the American novelist Upton Sinclair's best-selling *Oil!* (1927), which features a character named Vernon Roscoe, a greedy business man who helps bribe the government to acquire land to drill oil in a place called Teapot Dome, along the way doing all in his might to crush the trade unions that opposed him, and doing so by bribing the government authorities to throw union members into jail.

By the last quarter of the twentieth century, growing numbers of citizens, environmental organisations and scholars had concluded that democracy does not mix well with coal, gas and oil, that an energy regime fuelled by these substances damages monitory institutions and undermines their ecological foundations.[15] The critics noted, for instance, that the carbon dependence of the United States, Europe and Japan, places not self-sufficient in fossil fuels, required a massive oil transport industry. Tankers grew rapidly in size, around 30-fold between 1945 and 1977. The volume of oil moved around the globe jumped to staggering levels: by 1970, about five gallons of oil were in transit at any moment on the high seas for every woman, man and child on planet Earth. Big tankers developed the bad habit of dumping excess oil and flushing out their tanks when at sea; and

---

[15] The seminal work is Timothy Mitchell, *Carbon Democracy: Political Power in the Age of Oil* (London and New York: Verso, 2011).

accidents became routine. These 'normal accidents' became infamous media events: the break-up (in 1967) of the *Torrey Canyon* off the Cornwall coast; the offshore blowout (1979) at Tabasco in Mexico, which released an oil slick nearly the size of Connecticut in the direction of Texas; and the 34,000 tons of crude oil splashed along the Alaskan coast in 1989 by the grounded Exxon *Valdez*. By 1990, there were estimates that during the course of the twentieth century ten times more oil had been dumped into our oceans than was released by natural seeps.

Meanwhile, from the 1950s, fossil fuels proved to be the single largest contributor to atmospheric increases of temperature (due to the addition of carbon dioxide to our planet's atmosphere – a 30-fold increase between 1900 and 2000) and a major cause of the poisoning of the biosphere by toxic petrochemicals and the fuelling of machines that ripped like knives into its delicate fabrics. Especially in urban settings, carbon-fuelled vehicles, for all the mobility they offered human beings, took their toll. By the end of the twentieth century, around 400,000 people were killed annually in so-called road accidents, many more than in war. Car use and production produced staggering waste: in the automobile manufacturing process in Germany, for instance, by the 1990s every one ton of finished car produced 29 tons of waste, with the production of each car emitting as much air pollution as driving a car for ten years.

ON COUNTRY PATHS

In the age of monitory democracy, such negative environmental impacts of the carbon energy regime, and the not unrelated attempted shift to nuclear power, are becoming plain for all to see, if they want. It should be unsurprising that environmental despoliation is triggering intellectual backlashes. Among the earliest and most challenging in the age of monitory democracy was Heidegger's critique of the human quest to invade and dominate the biosphere using techniques based on the rationale of measurement, mechanisation and total control, or *Machenschaft* as he called it. Comprehensive technical control of things and people is the fundamental feature of the modern world, Heidegger argued. 'The world now appears as an object open to the attacks of calculative thought, attacks that nothing is believed able any longer to resist. Nature becomes a gigantic gasoline station, an energy source for modern technology and industry.'[16] Our encounter with

---

[16] Martin Heidegger, 'Memorial Address' (1955), in *Discourse on Thinking* (New York and London: Harper & Row, 1966), p. 50.

'nature' is no longer conceivable in terms of letting it be, or enabling it to become what it might become, of 'bringing forth' its own potential. Modern technology is an all-encompassing apparatus, a whole way of life (*Ge-stell*) geared to the 'challenging' and 'ordering' and 'power-seizing' conquest of our habitats, for specified human purposes. Modern humans imagine themselves to be 'lords of the earth'. They suffer the illusion that everything is man-made. People lose contact with their earthly habitats. They become homeless, uprooted; the biosphere is 'set upon'. The 'old wooden bridge that joined bank with bank for hundreds of years' and the 'old windmill' whose sails were 'left entirely to the wind's blowing' are replaced by the human will for power over nature: 'The earth now reveals itself as a coal mining district, the soil as a mineral deposit', Heidegger noted. 'Agriculture is now the mechanized food industry. Air is now set upon to yield nitrogen, the earth to yield ore, ore to yield uranium … uranium is set upon to yield atomic energy, which can be released either for destruction or for peaceful use.'[17]

Heidegger feared the modern will to universal calculation and domination. Synonymous with the self-absorbed hubris of humans hell-bent on mastering nature, a recipe for 'homelessness', 'monstrousness' and 'world darkening', modern technology has become the destiny of the world. So is resistance to technology possible? Might 'meditative reflection' and a new 'openness to mystery' combine to whet the appetite of humans for what he called the 'releasement toward beings [*Gelassenheit*]'? In other words, could humans cultivate their sense of fruitfully being rooted within a biosphere that must be respected and protected, not dominated? Through a new 'rootedness' or 'autochthony', or what he termed *Bodenstandigkeit*, could humans come to dwell 'poetically on the earth' by acting as shepherds who refuse to lord over other beings and instead (as Heidegger puts it) seek to preserve them 'in their nearness to the truth of being'?[18]

Efforts at greening democracy can learn much from the fraught answers given by Heidegger to these questions. It is important to note that his rightful emphasis on the need for a new human mode of 'thinking' and earth-friendly 'dwelling' and 'building' confined the alternative to *one* mode of 'unconcealment of being': the revealing of beings that occurs through *poēsis*, which for him included both creatively 'bringing forth' (*Vollbringen*) something (say, solar power) to its full potential *and* the

---

[17] Martin Heidegger, 'The Question Concerning Technology', *Basic Writings* (New York: Harper & Row, 1977), p. 296.
[18] Ibid.

lived experience of the aesthetic beauty of the world. Guided by the vision of *poēsis*, Heidegger sometimes sounded melancholy, as when he concluded that the spell of 'technology' and its menacing consequences cannot be broken, so that the destiny of humans and their non-human environment is the tragic story of failed efforts to defy the will to complete mastery. More cheerful moments can be found in his writings, for instance when he suggests that the 'saving power' of *poēsis* is inscribed *within technē*, understood in the classical Greek sense of creative potency, ways of doing things that eschew manipulation and control. Humans might after all be rescued by embracing technology, which teaches us to think of another, closely related but more enriching form of *poēsis*, our willingness to open ourselves to the beauty of the world, 'brought forth and made present', as Heidegger says. 'The irresistibility of ordering and the restraint of the saving power draw past each other like the paths of two stars in the course of the heavens', he wrote, citing a poem of Hölderlin. 'But precisely this, their passing by, is the hidden side of their nearness.'[19] This was a vision of people 'being-in' or dwelling in the world, caring for others (*Fürsorge*), feeling at home within its meaningful arrangements through self-transcending acts of disclosure (*Entbergung*). Then there are those moments when Heidegger's thoughts on *poēsis* come wrapped in mystery, talk of God laced with touches of hope tied with a bow of anti-political resignation: 'the frenziedness of technology may entrench itself everywhere to such an extent that someday, throughout everything technological, the essence of technology may come to presence in the coming-to-pass of truth'.[20]

Guided by these tensely related formulations, Heidegger's fixation on manipulation and beautification as two overlapping modes of revealing arguably led him astray, initially by understating the importance of *alternative* ways of living in the world. His dismissal of democracy was symptomatic, and it resulted from his failure to grasp the way in which the experience of democracy fundamentally challenges the arbitrary power of technical reason. Heidegger thought just the opposite. Once upon a time, during the early 1930s, he had spoken in fascist terms of states as 'the way of Being of a people' and 'the people' (*das Volk*) their

---

[19] Heidegger, 'The Question Concerning Technology', pp. 314–315. Heidegger cites two lines from Hölderlin's 'Patmos' ('But where danger is, grows/The saving power also'), in *Friedrich Hölderlin: Poems and Fragments* (Ann Arbor, MI: University of Michigan Press, 1966), pp. 462–463.

[20] Ibid., pp. 316–317.

'supporting ground'.[21] Following the military defeat of Nazism, he showed no fondness for monitory democracy. 'How can a political system accommodate itself to the technological age, and which political system would this be?', he asked in his posthumously published *Der Spiegel* interview. 'I have no answer to this question. I am not convinced that it is democracy', came the reply.[22] The key reason offered throughout his works of the post-1945 period is that the norms and institutions of 'democracy' are functionally integrated with the prevailing order of power. Representative democracy is a tool of technical domination. It is just another form of machination, or *Machenschaft*. Democracy is an obsession with manipulative power. It is deeply implicated in the human struggle to manipulate and control the Earth, and beyond. 'Seizures of power are no longer "total" in the sense of confinement to a single state or people', he wrote. 'They now extend their reach to the limits of the inhabited Earth, and even into the atmosphere and stratosphere.'[23] Democracy equally nurtures the blind preoccupation with quotidian affairs, an indulgence Heidegger dubbed 'ensnarement' (*Verfallensein*). He offered the example of the newspaper industry and its cultivation of unthinking public opinion. Once upon a time, foresters wielding axes walked the forest paths used by their grandfathers. Forestry soon became an 'industry that produces commercial woods' and foresters 'made subordinate to the orderability of cellulose, which for its part is challenged forth by the need for paper, which is then delivered to newspapers and illustrated magazines'. Those products consolidate a 'dictatorship of the public realm [*die Öffentlichkeit*]' in which the manufactured public opinion 'swallows what is printed, so that a set configuration of opinion becomes available on demand'.[24]

QUESTIONS OF REPRESENTATION

Heidegger's conflation of democracy and technological manipulation was neither original nor convincing. It belongs squarely to a period peppered

---

[21] Martin Heidegger, *Nature, History, State 1933-1934* (London, New Delhi, New York, Sydney: Bloomsbury, 2013), p. 43.
[22] 'Nur noch ein Gott kann uns retten', *Der Spiegel*, 30 (May 1976), 193-219.
[23] Martin Heidegger, *Besinnung*, in *Gesamtausgabe*, vol. 66 (Frankfurt am Main: Klostermann, 1997), p. 18.
[24] Martin Heidegger, 'The Question Concerning Technology', p. 299; Martin Heidegger, 'Letter on Humanism', in David F. Krell (ed.), *Basic Writings* (New York: Harper & Row, 1976), p. 197.

with anxious outbursts among intellectuals about the potentially threatening effects of 'technology'.[25] What Heidegger and his bomb-struck contemporaries failed to recognise is that democracy is a form of politics that sharpens people's understanding of the contingency of the power relations through which they live their lives. It nurtures a shared sense of the time-bounded quality or contingency of power; it enables and encourages them as equals to question and to reject manipulative arbitrary power, to struggle against what Heidegger generally called technology.

The insurgent, disruptive dynamics of democracy are amplified by its embrace of practices of representation. Democracy in representative form was unknown to the ancient world; the ancient Greeks never even had a word for it. The early modern effort to combine democracy and representation, to develop new institutions such as political parties, periodic elections and parliaments, fundamentally changed the spirit and language and practical dynamics of democracy. The invention of 'government democratical, but representative' (Thomas Jefferson) changed the meaning of both democracy and representation. It also nurtured public tensions rooted in the division between the represented and the representative. Representation was not understood as mimesis, mere delegation of powers to another who is supposed to reproduce the opinions and actions of the represented. Political representation was not seen as a process of issuing political mandates. In the new understanding of democracy, representatives do not receive direct, minute-by-minute instructions from the many they represent. The job of representatives was necessarily to define and interpret the interests of those whom they represent. Representation is substitution; functionally differentiated from the represented, the representative decides things potentially in opposition to the represented.

This means that representation is a dynamic process marked by conflict and highly contingent outcomes. Representation is subject to the disappointment principle.[26] The choice of representatives, for instance through periodic elections, is a method of apportioning blame for poor political performance, a way of ensuring the rotation of leadership, guided by merit and humility, in the presence of electors equipped with the power to trip leaders up and throw them out of office, if and when they underperform, as often they do. Every act of choosing a representative is as

---

[25] Examples from this period include Max Bense, *Technische Existenz* (Stuttgart, 1950); Friedrich Georg Jünger, *Die Perfektion der Technik* (Frankfurt, 1953); and Günther Anders, *Die Antiquiertheit des Menschen* (Munich: C.H. Beck, 1956).

[26] John Keane, 'Hypocrisy and Democracy', *WZB-Mitteilungen*, 120 (June 2008), 30–32.

much a beginning as it is an ending. The whole point of elections is that they are a means of disciplining representatives who disappoint their electors, who are then entitled to throw harsh words, and paper or electronic rocks, at them. If representatives were always virtuous, impartial, competent and responsive, then elections would lose their purpose. In other words, the ability of representatives to define and interpret the interests of those whom they represent depends upon a process of permanent contact and deliberation and potential conflict between representatives and the represented. Representation always has a vicarious dimension: it implies a relationship between the representative and the represented that goes well beyond a pure and simple face-to-face contract. Ideally conceived, representation is an act of delegation through which the represented grant to representatives the task of defending their interests, all the while insisting that they remain directly accountable to the represented for their actions.

GREENING REPRESENTATION

The dynamics of representation seem to be of marginal theoretical importance to green-minded scholars who fashionably champion some or other vision of 'deliberative democracy'.[27] Theories of deliberative democracy suffer multiple weaknesses. Their self-understanding of their own historicity, and the age of monitory democracy to which they belong, is weak. Their penchant for small-scale, face-to-face deliberative forums begs difficult tactical questions about scalability, including whether micro-level schemes can be replicated at the national regional and global levels. Deliberative democrats are prone to understate such strategic challenges as the 'artificiality' of pilot scheme experiments (where indefatigable citizen deliberators are expected to behave as if they are rational communicators in a scholarly seminar) and the veto power of power-hungry vested interests. Inspired originally by the work of Jürgen

---

[27] See John S. Dryzek, *The Politics of the Earth: Environmental Discourses* (New York: Oxford University Press, 2013); and the introduction to *Deliberative Democracy and Beyond: Liberals, Critics, Contestations* (New York: Oxford University Press, 2002), where the 'essence of democracy' is said to be 'deliberation, as opposed to voting, interest aggregation, constitutional rights, or even self-government'. What is called 'authentic deliberation' is 'the requirement that communication induce reflection upon preferences in non-coercive fashion'. It is claimed that the emphasis on deliberation in this sense renews concern with 'the authenticity of democracy: the degree to which democratic control is substantive rather than symbolic, and engaged by competent citizens' (pp. 1–2 ff).

Habermas, deliberative democrats are secretly Greek: convinced that democracy is quintessentially assembly democracy, or 'participatory democracy',[28] they downplay the strategic and normative importance of courts, media platforms and other power-monitoring institutions and generally seem blind to the ubiquity of representation within political life.[29]

The maltreatment of representation by theorists of deliberative democracy is regrettable, especially because the 'stretching' of democratic forms of political representation to include the biosphere is among the remarkable novelties of our age of monitory democracy. Non-human nature of course cannot speak and act for itself, in any human sense. It cannot enjoy 'rights'; to do so (by definition) would require it to observe sets of duties. But non-human nature can be represented in human affairs. In Heidegger's language, it can be convoked, coaxed into appearance (*apophainesthai*). Non-human nature can be brought forth from 'concealment' into 'unconcealment'. Its political representation enables it to 'come forward' and to 'arrive' in human affairs. Political representation in this sense might be considered a form of *poiēsis*, a bringing forth (*Hervor-bringen*). But representation is neither a form of attempted mastery of nature nor submission to its aesthetic beauty. Political representation defies this Heideggerian distinction: it is a special dynamic relationship through which humans *limit* and *restrain* their own will to master the biosphere by offering to protect and nurture the non-human nature to which they belong.

---

[28] Some observers are certain that green politics heralds the re-birth of 'participatory democracy', a twenty-first-century version of the originally Greek ideal of assembly democracy. An example is Tim Flannery's *Here on Earth: An Argument for Hope* (Melbourne: Victoria Text Publishing, 2010), which speaks of a 'globally participative democracy' (p. 252) and gives as an example the Vote Earth campaign during the 2011 Copenhagen negotiations, a partnership between Google Earth and WWF's Earth Hour which managed to distribute electronic ballot boxes across thousands of web portals, then to urge people to 'vote Earth' in support of a robust outcome of the negotiations, guided by the visionary principle (as Flannery puts it) of 'online elections, organised by the people, of the people and for the people' (ibid.). This line of political thinking is misleading in several ways. Aside from its underestimation of the dangers of populism, the blind worship of 'the people', green calls for 'direct democracy' misread the ways in which many monitory bodies underscore the fact and positive effects of representation in political affairs.

[29] The weaknesses within the theory of undistorted communication of Jürgen Habermas are examined at length in my *Public Life and Late Capitalism* (Cambridge and New York: Cambridge University Press, 1984).

Representation is a fiduciary relationship in which humble people aware of their own bio-limits are entrusted to act on behalf of biomes incapable of representing themselves. Non-human nature is voiceless; it cannot speak and act for itself, though it withers and dies if maltreated by humans. As fiduciaries (from Latin *fiduciarius*, meaning '[holding] in trust'; from *fides*, meaning 'faith', and *fiducia*, meaning 'trust'), humans are charged with taking care prudently of the needs and interests of non-human nature, to protect and nurture it as a partner, to act as its loyal shepherd, not its saviour. To represent non-human nature is to acknowledge that humans (as agents) have a duty to provide its biomes (as principals) with the highest standards of care. It does not suppose that 'nature' is a fixed or given-for-all-time or uncontroversial sub-stratum of human existence. Political representation is not mimicry or communion with Nature conceived as an unalterable foundation linking the Earth with the dead and the living and the unborn, as was supposed by Maistre, Burke, Taine and other early modern European conservatives. Human efforts to represent non-human nature politically invite public controversies, both about the nature of 'nature' and the ways in which it has changed through time, not just according to its own endogenous dynamics but also (and now increasingly) under the impact of changing forms of human interaction with the bio-environments in which humans dwell.[30] Heidegger failed to see that political representation is not another, more subtle and insidious tool for mastering non-human nature. It is rather guided by human awareness that human judgements about what non-human nature 'is' or is 'becoming' are fallible, contestable, publicly revisable. The political representation of non-human nature is synonymous with the public monitoring and restraint of currently unequal and destructive power relationships – not a formula for imagining a new perpetual peace, an earthly paradise in which humans and non-human nature are united, freed at last from problems caused by ignorance, misunderstanding, doubt and arbitrary power.

It may be objected that the whole notion of extending powers of representation to non-human nature is not a recent invention. It is indeed true that (a) all human societies have created ways of registering or re-presenting their interdependence with the biosphere and its (sometimes invisible) elements by means of verbal, oral and pictorial expressions;[31]

---

[30] Philippe Descola, *The Ecology of Others* (Chicago, IL: University of Chicago Press, 2013).

[31] Alessandro Nova, *The Book of the Wind: The Representation of the Invisible* (Montréal: McGill-Queen's University Press, 2011).

and (b) within the representative tradition there are older customs and traditions of politically defending 'nature'.[32] Medieval and early modern Europe saw many durable practices of this kind, including rural assemblies ('tings') and the common peasant custom of bringing animals, plants and vegetables into local courts for the purpose of settling ownership disputes. Other examples included the powerful water boards (known as *waterschappen*) that sprang up in the low-lying parts of the North Sea coast; and the water tribunals of the Iberian peninsula, representative assemblies invented and operated by farmers in drought-prone regions to manage their crop irrigation systems through periodic public meetings of elected representatives.

These ancient schemes supposed that the world of 'nature' had political rights, blessed with a voice that prompted local people to take it into their care through human schemes of representation. Shepherds and farmers were deeply mindful that their labours would be in vain without heeding nature's powers – and without getting others to do the same. Exactly this sentiment in multi-mediated democratic form is making its presence felt in our times, helped greatly by the invention and diffusion, for the first time in the long history of democracy, of power-scrutinising and power-chastening monitory mechanisms that openly contest the human domination of the biosphere by representing its fate in human affairs. This book has emphasised throughout that the age of monitory democracy complicates and enriches the prevailing common-sense understandings of democracy; the old belief that democracy is 'one person, one vote, one representative' has gradually been replaced by practices guided by the rule of 'one person, many interests, many voices, multiple votes, multiple representatives'. Green politics enriches and redefines the meaning of representation. It helps rid the whole idea of democracy of its anthropocentrism (what could be more anthropocentric than a political ideal that originally supposed humans are masters and possessors of 'nature'?). Green politics makes way for the entrance of the biosphere into the political life of human beings, who reconnect the political and natural worlds in hybrid public spaces that Bruno Latour has called 'parliaments of things'.[33] The new politics does more than urge humans to re-imagine themselves as humble beings deeply

---

[32] Keane, *The Life and Death of Democracy*, pp. 188–193.
[33] Bruno Latour, 'From Realpolitik to Dingpolitik or How to Make Things Public', in Bruno Latour and Peter Weibel (eds.), *Making Things Public: Atmospheres of Democracy* (Cambridge, MA and London: MIT Press, 2005), pp. 14–41; and *We Have Never Been Modern* (Cambridge, MA and London: MIT Press, 1993).

entangled in the ecosystems upon which they depend. It redefines democracy to mean, descriptively speaking, a way of life that renders power publicly accountable by means of institutions in which humans and their biosphere are treated symmetrically, as interdependent equals, in opposition to the reigning view that humans are the pinnacle of creation, lords and ladies of the universe, 'the people' who are the ultimate source of sovereign power and authority on Earth.

The age of monitory democracy coincides with manifold efforts to wean the world off its dependence upon coal mines, fracking, oil refineries, filling stations and fuel-oil engines, to replace them with a new post-carbon energy regime founded on solar- and wind-power and revolutionary electricity-storage techniques.[34] The energy regime transformation overlaps with many new power-restraining platforms that function as early warning detectors, public broadcasting stations and sites of active resistance and power reversals. Most obviously, there are green political parties (the first in the world were the United Tasmania Group [1972] and the Values Party in New Zealand[35]). Green themes have surfaced in 'liquid democracy' parties such as the Pirates in Sweden and Germany, the *grillini* in Italy and the Best Party in Iceland. There are meanwhile local government covenants, 'rewilding' projects, environmental impact hearings and citizen science projects (the Open Air Laboratories [Opal] project in the UK is an example). There are global agreements, such as the Convention on Biological Diversity, and the Aarhus Convention, which calls upon states to guarantee their citizens' rights of information, justice and participation in environmental decision making. Daring multi-media civic occupations multiply. There are green think tanks and green academies (such as Berlin's Grüne Akademie funded by the Heinrich Böll Foundation). A new genre of 'gonzo' nature writing – literary works emphasising humans' interdependence with the non-human 'natural' world – has been born: among the earliest examples is Erich Kästner's classic children's tale of an assembly of the world's animals that calls on humans to behave more decently in the world.[36] There are regional

---

[34] Popular accounts of the transition include Christiane Grefe, *Global Gardening: Bioökonomie – Neuer Raubbau oder Wirtschaftsform der Zukunft?* (Munich: von Verlag Antje Kunstmann, 2016) and Chris Goodall, *The Switch: How Solar, Storage and New Tech Means Cheap Power for All* (London: Profile Books, 2017).
[35] Stephen L. Rainbow, 'Why Did New Zealand and Tasmania Spawn the World's First Green Parties?', *Environmental Politics*, 1, 3 (1992), 321–346.
[36] Erich Kästner, *The Animals' Conference* (Zurich: Europa Verlag, 1947). More recently, see the vivid personal account of the 'exhilarating inaccessibility' that greets human

initiatives such as the Mediterranean Action Plan (MAP) and regional fisheries management organisations (RFMOs), some of them specialising in monitoring highly migratory species of fish (an example is the Commission for the Conservation of Southern Bluefin Tuna) or others concerned with the living marine resources within a region (an example is the Commission for the Conservation of Antarctic Marine Living Resources). There are earth watch summits and, for the first time, court judgments supportive of indigenous peoples; legal redefinitions of lands (the Te Urewera Act 2014 in Aotearoa New Zealand is an example) as enjoying 'all the rights, powers, duties and liabilities of a legal person'; and clauses within written constitutions designed to protect the biosphere. Mongolia's constitution expressly states that citizens must enjoy rights to a 'healthy and safe environment, and to be protected against environmental pollution and ecological imbalance' (Chapter 2, Article 16). Slovenia's constitution stipulates that 'everyone has the right to drinkable water', while the democratic Constitution of the Kingdom of Bhutan specifies that every citizen 'is a trustee of the Kingdom's natural resources and environment for the benefit of the present and future generations and it is the fundamental duty of every citizen to contribute to the protection of the natural environment, conservation of the rich biodiversity of Bhutan and prevention of all forms of ecological degradation including noise, visual and physical pollution through the adoption and support of environment friendly practices and policies' (Article 5).

The innovation known as bio-regional assemblies is exemplary of the trend.[37] Born in the early 1980s, bodies such as the Beaver Hills Initiative in Alberta are watchdog and action networks that work to renew critical awareness and public respect for whole ecological communities, to take their side against the painful 'solastalgia' produced by blindly destructive 'growth'.[38] These networks craft new ways of shaming and chastening human predation. Their representatives favour the transition to a post-carbon energy regime. They imagine territory in fresh ways. They suppose

efforts to live as badgers and otters in Charles Foster, *Being a Beast: Adventures Across the Species Divide* (New York and London: Metropolitan Books, 2016).

[37] Kirkpatrick Sale, *Dwellers in the Land: The Bioregional Vision* (Athens, GA: University of Georgia Press, 1985); G. Robert Thayer, *LifePlace: Bioregional Thought and Practice* (Los Angeles: University of California Press, 2003); and Mike Carr, *Bioregionalism and Civil Society: Democratic Challenges to Corporate Globalism* (Vancouver, BC: UBC Press 2004).

[38] Glenn A. Albrecht, 'Solastalgie: Heimweh in der Heimat', in N. Jung *et al.* (eds.), *Natur im Blick der Kulturen* (Opladen, 2013), pp. 47–60.

that in order to secure the clean air, water and food humans need to survive healthfully, people must become guardians of the places where they live. Bio-regional assemblies encourage people to see the wondrous in the common. They probe the reasons why people do not act in order to get people to act. They highlight the costs generated by public ignorance of bio-surroundings. They insist that the best way for families, friends, neighbours, indigenous peoples and other human beings to take care of themselves and their successors is to protect and restore regions, to pay attention to what is happening to land, plants and animals, springs, rivers, deserts, lakes, groundwater, reefs and oceans, and the quality of air. These assemblies insist that some things are just not for sale. They call upon human beings to swap their innocent attachments to 'historical progress' and 'modernisation' with a more prudent sense of deep time that highlights the fragile complexity of our biosphere and its multiple rhythms.[39] These initiatives sometimes demand a halt to consumer-driven 'growth'; at other times, they call for green investments to trigger a new phase of expansion based on a post-carbon energy regime. They reason that if history is a train journey between stops, then progress requires reaching for the emergency brake, to put an end to acts of wanton vandalism now rebounding on our planet. These assemblies accuse middle-of-the-road political parties, including social democratic parties, of being trapped in a dead end. They typically reject the old fossil-fuel imagery of the old Left – think of warrior male bodies gathered at the gates of pits, docks and factories, singing hymns to industrial progress, under smoke-stained skies.[40] Bio-regional assemblies rightly find such images worse than antiquated. They interpret them as bad moons, as warnings that unless we human beings have the courage to change our ways with the world, things may turn out badly – very badly indeed.

---

[39] John Keane, 'A New Politics of Time', *The Conversation* (3 December 2016), https://theconversation.com/a-new-politics-of-time-69137.
[40] See my essay 'The End of Social Democracy', *Australian Literary Review*, 1 (2011), 1–5.

9

Child Citizens

Can children, civil society's most market-vulnerable participants, become full members of a democratic political order? Do they have the capacity as citizens to enjoy its rights of association and property, legal protection and powers to vote, as equals of older citizens, for representatives of their choice, in free and fair elections?

In France, the United States, Japan and elsewhere most people think they do not, for reasons that are woven firmly into the fabric of contemporary common-sense definitions of civil society and citizenship. Citizens of a democracy are said to belong to a civil society and political community of common laws, and to share its entitlements and duties equally with other grown-ups. When Aristotle famously defined a citizen as any adult who can 'hold office', he invoked a powerful thought that still lives on: to be a citizen is to be the opposite of a powerless subject. To enjoy the status of a citizen is to engage freely and equally with others who are mature enough to act politically by exercising the power to define how to live together peacefully, to decide who should get what, when and how. Seen in this way, citizenship is not just about fair and open legal decisions or democratic government or living as equals with other adult members of civil society. According to some old and venerable traditions of political thinking, citizenship is their condition of possibility.

Children – according to the same common-sense definition – are minors. Their ontogenesis is incomplete and so by definition they cannot be citizens who enjoy the entitlements that enable them to live as the equals of others. To speak of citizens is minimally to speak of beings equipped with the capacity to choose self-reflexively when navigating their daily courses of action through the institutions of civil society and government. Children do not choose to be born and at the beginning of their lives, by definition, they have no say in who is to parent them and which institutions, beginning with their household and its psychodynamics, are to guard over and mark their lives indelibly, forever. Consistent with this ascribed powerlessness, there is also the brute fact – it is said – that children are nowhere acknowledged as entitled to govern their own lives until well into their teenage years. Hence the conclusion: children are children and only time and proper upbringing can bring them into the adult world of civil society, government and citizenship.

Viewed in this way, orthodox thinking about children may be persuasive, but it nevertheless begs important descriptive and normative questions about their status and power. Are children fated to be the temporary possession of adult-dominated institutions and policies? Since children are by definition beings that have not yet passed through the gates of adulthood, surely their childhood, and thus their unequal relationship with adults must be recognised and protected under democratic conditions? Or might it be that this unequal relationship between child subjects and adult citizens is unnecessary? Might young people deserve to be considered as worthy of greater equality of treatment, perhaps even as the formal equals of grown-ups, so that their dignity is protected? Could it be that actually existing monitory democracies are confronted with a new challenge – how to create spaces for children considered as citizens.

Among the interesting things about the subject of childhood is that such questions have arisen only in contexts that have been touched by modern hands. Put simply, contingent categories like 'childhood' and 'children' belong to the universe of thinking and acting structured by institutional complexes that we have come to call civil society, representative government and democracy. Once upon a time, the idea of childhood as a special and alterable phase of life simply didn't exist. Every culture of course has had its views about living beings in their early years of life. The temptation was always strong to think of them as natural creatures – as naturally innocent, or as naturally depraved, or as naturally expendable, as for instance was the custom in classical Greece, where sickly youth were commonly left in the countryside to die of exposure, or their healthy counterparts were sold into slavery, especially if a family needed money. This belief in the absolute primacy of nature had the effect of suppressing awareness of either the continuities or discontinuities in the transition between infancy and adulthood. In medieval Europe, for example, around the age of five or six or seven, the young were commonly deemed no longer in need of constant attention from their mothers and were jettisoned into the workaday world of adults. Young people were viewed simply as miniature adults – a picture reinforced by the male-centred 'ages of man' imagery inherited from classical antiquity, and by beliefs in the four humours, and by the parallels that were often drawn between the stages of life and the behaviour of the seven planets.

All this changed with the reinvention and geographic spread of the language and institutions of civil society and representative government. The sixteenth century was a particularly decisive watershed in this respect. The causal links between the fate of young people and the push for constitutional government underpinned by vibrant civil societies oiled by commerce and exchange and Christian norms of conjugal duty were certainly complicated, but the clear consequence was that modern civil societies became associated with the nurturing of a new category of beings called 'children'. This 'discovery' of childhood, according to a classic study by Philippe Ariès,[1] was in fact no 'discovery' of a pre-existing social terrain. The simile is wrong: childhood was rather an invention of certain social groups – middle class moralists, lawyers, priests, men of property and philanthropists – who felt the ground of certainty shaking under their feet, who sensed that the abandonment of old patterns of authority and the push for self-government required the definition and special treatment of young people, to shape their earliest emotional experiences, so that they could be prepared for the shock of adult citizenship.

THE GREAT QUARANTINE

The task of pinning down the history of children and childhood is not easy, initially because there is an obvious problem of sources. In their diaries, letters and autobiographies, members of the literate and educated elites and upwardly mobile social groups have left behind traces of their thoughts and feelings about children; by contrast, the ways in which the vast majority of people regarded their children, peasants and rural and urban labourers for instance, have passed into oblivion.

The surviving evidence suggests that bourgeois Protestant circles clustered around figures like Luther and the English Puritans were among the first to express sustained interest in the young and their proper place in an

---

[1] Philippe Ariès, *L'Enfant et la vie familiale sous l'ancien régime* [1960], translated as *Centuries of Childhood: A Social History of Family Life* (New York: Knopf, 1962).

emergent civil society.[2] The contributions of these rising lower middle class believers to the invention of childhood sometime during the sixteenth century were initially justified using many different and conflicting labels – Christian duty, civility, civilisation, civil society, the commonwealth, the order of liberty, the republic, education – but the quarantining effects linked to these epithets were pronounced, and historically speaking without precedent. Young people were made to pay a high price. Defined by powerful groups within civil society, children were positioned outside and underneath civil society. The resulting dualism of children and civil society placed children of all classes in the position of being powerless objects of attention by political actors and institutions. Reminded constantly of mental and bodily and height differences by adults who called them 'kids' – the same slang word first used in the seventeenth century to describe young goats, an animal thought to be naturally stupid and renowned for its insatiable appetite – children were subjected for the first time to highly invasive forms of arbitrary power. Fine talk of civility and civilisation aside, children in fact resembled slaves fit for incarceration within the walls of families, or foundling homes. William Blackstone's lectures on the common law, given at Oxford in 1758, spoke revealingly of the family as 'the empire of the father'. He reported that women were 'entitled to no power, but only reverence and respect'; and that the absolute legal power of fathers over their (male) children ended only when they reached the age of twenty-one years, at which point the young male adult entered 'the empire of reason'. Until that moment arrived, 'the empire of the father continues even after his death; for he may by his will appoint a guardian to his children', Blackstone added. 'He may also delegate part of his parental authority, during his life, to the tutor or schoolmaster of his child; who is then in loco parentis, and has such a portion of the power of the parent committed to his charge, viz. that of restraint and correction.'[3]

Under the impact of such thinking, the historical change in the lives of young people was dramatic. Children were no longer principally seen as incorrigible slaves of their wicked nature, brutish and devilish creatures tainted by the sin that began at the time of creation, and that was subsequently passed down from generation to generation (a view that

---

[2] See John C. Sommerville, *The Discovery of Childhood in Puritan England* (Athens, GA: University of Georgia Press, 1992).

[3] William Blackstone, 'Of Parent and Child', in *Commentaries on the Laws of England in Four Books*, 12th edn, Book 1 (London: T. Cadell, 1793), Chapter 16, pp. 451–453.

lingered well into this period, and that was often associated with the theology of St Augustine). Young people were also no longer principally regarded as miniature adults whose simplicity, sweetness and drollery provided relaxation and (sexual) amusement for adults in their vicinity (a view represented in some seventeenth-century paintings that featured children dressed in their own distinctive clothes, with their own distinctive mannerisms). Young people instead became objects of adult definition, adult psychological interest and adult moral solicitude. They were viewed as creatures that stood half way between animals and adults – creatures that were capable of correction and instruction, and thus in need of confinement in families through special practices that gave them the special treatment sufficient to enable them to pass from the half-animal world of minors to the world of adults, replicating in a few short years the stages of civilisation that human beings themselves had taken several millennia to achieve.[4] The exceptions, such as ill-bred peasant scoundrels, the urban beggar children wearing ragged trousers, the pickpockets and scoundrels with snotty noses who somehow managed to slip through the nets of paternal supervision, were living proof of this new preoccupation with children. So too was the fascination with the figure of the *puer senex*, the rare male child prodigy who behaved from the beginning like an old man. Such freaks defined the rules of an age in which the young were deemed non-adults. Thomas Williams Malkin was a much-talked about example: born in 1795, he started his career at the age of three, proved himself to be an expert linguist at four, an outstanding philosopher at five, and then began reading the fathers of the Church at six, only to die of old age and excess at seven.[5]

So the invention of children and childhood went hand in hand with new strategies of control that on the surface of things had little to do with the norms and institutions of civil society or citizenship or representative democracy, as they would later be understood. Measured in power terms, the new strategies of control were their antithesis, as evidenced by the rapid spread throughout eighteenth-century Europe of homes of correction for abandoned children. London's Foundling Hospital, established by Royal Charter in 1739, is today still often considered a shining example of a golden age of philanthropy, but for the children who found

---

[4] See the illuminating observations of Norbert Elias on children and 'civility', in *The Civilizing Process. The History of Manners* (New York: Urizen Books, 1978), especially pp. 53–54, 73–74, 140–141, 168–177, 188–189, 203.
[5] Benjamin Heath Malkin, *A Father's Memoirs of his Child* (London: Longman, 1806).

themselves confined within its solid brick walls life rather resembled a military camp. On entering the Hospital, children had their hair cut in the same style; they were issued with a standard uniform and given the same meagre diet, repeated weekly. Hunger and bullying and violent punishment were endemic; hard work and God-fearing obedience to adult superiors was expected; and the young inmates quickly discovered that every aspect of their existence was geared to their future role of dutiful and productive servants, artisans and soldiers.

Children considered 'legitimate' found that life within their own families bore a striking resemblance to that of 'bastard' foundlings. Respectable children were regarded as fresh clay in the hands of adult potters and dressed accordingly in civilising metaphors that suggested the primacy of nurture over nature. The Dutch humanist Desiderius Erasmus (1466–1536) spoke of the possibility of overcoming the 'monstrous bestiality' of the human condition by cultivating the 'quality of rawness and freshness' of children's minds. The famous English philosopher John Locke noted that he regarded the child for whose father he had written the 1693 treatise *Some Thoughts Concerning Education* 'only as white Paper, or Wax, to be moulded and fashioned as one pleases'. Standing behind these metaphors of bestiality, rawness and pliability were eager thoughts of power over the future: the presumption that the hands that rocked cradles would one day rule the world. Locke was quite clear about this. 'Of all the Men we meet with', he wrote, 'Nine Parts of Ten are what they are, Good or Evil, useful or not, by their Education.'[6]

The popular methods backing this presumption varied through time and space, but they consistently supposed not only a deep consciousness of childhood – a strong will to brand young people with the name of 'child' – but also a deep desire to isolate children in order better to bend them to the will of their adult rulers. Printed advice came thick and fast. 'Sleep neither too little nor too much. Begin each day by blessing it in God's name and saying the Lord's Prayer. Thank God for keeping you through the night and ask his help for the new day. Greet your parents. Comb your hair and wash your face and hands', advised an early sixteenth-century German manual on discipline (two centuries later, the English poet Lord Byron was among those still complaining that children disliked washing and hence always smelled of bread and butter, or worse[7]). Encouraging children to

---

[6] John Locke, *Some Thoughts Concerning Education*, edited by John W. Yolton and Jean S. Yolton (Oxford: Oxford University Press, 1989 [1693]), pp. 265, 83.
[7] Lord Byron, *Beppo* (1818), Stanza 39.

internalise social norms and to cultivate their sense of individual conscience was given top priority among the Dutch Protestants of the seventeenth century. From a republican perspective, Rousseau's *Émile, ou de l'education* (1762) developed similar thoughts. Though indebted to the quarantining imperative and its universe of presumptions, his manual of advice gave a radical twist to images of children. It was a forerunner of the view that childhood was a realm of purity and dynamic innocence subsequently lost to adults. *Émile* begins with the famous line: 'Everything is good as it leaves the hands of the Author of things, everything degenerates in the hands of man.' Then followed the advice: 'Respect childhood, leave nature to act for a long time before you get involved with acting in its place.'[8]

The advice supposed that children were (potentially) creatures blessed with a depth of moral wisdom about the world that adults find hard to comprehend. From there it was just a short step towards the conclusion that children should be given more space outside civil society in which to develop their capacities, for instance through play with objects made available to them by adults. In the closing decades of the eighteenth century, the first hints of the child as player of games and consumer of commodities appeared. Parents were encouraged to tap into the emerging toy industry to occupy their children's attention by supplying them with marbles, dolls, tops, board games, jigsaw puzzles and model soldiers; by the middle of the nineteenth century, manufacturing centres such as the Black Country in England and Nürnberg in Germany turned out huge quantities of cheap metal and wooden toys that even working-class households could afford to buy.

But during the age of the great quarantine, childhood was not all play. Hegel's image of the family, which belongs to the very end of this period, pictured the domestic as the 'first ethical root of the state', as a sphere of sensuous reciprocity, of harmony nourished by unadulterated love. The image was greatly idealised, as revealed by the systematic spread of rougher methods of crushing the wills and training up children to the standards of adulthood, backed by threats of force. The age of quarantined children was marked by great violence against them – in the name of their civilisation. The lingering belief in the innate depravity of children encouraged parents and guardians to pick up the rod so as not to spoil the child. Raw leather could be made to stretch; soft wax would take any impression; as the twig was bent, so would the tree be inclined, ran the

---

[8] Jean-Jacques Rousseau, *Émile, ou de l'education* (1762).

common sayings of the new 'poisonous pedagogy'.[9] Children were hanged for committing minor offences, such as rebelling against their parents. Whipping, beating, scolding and generally abusing children, so as to fling them into a state of fear, was widespread through all social ranks. Not even toddlers were spared: the future seventeenth-century king, Louis XIII, was reportedly whipped by his nurse from the age of two (a fitting tribute to an age that believed in the aphorism, 'Woe to the kingdom whose king is a child'); and Susanna Wesley, the mother of Methodism and herself the twenty-fifth of as many children, noted that from the age of one, at the latest, her own children were taught to fear the rod and to cry softly.

THE AGE OF WELFARE REGULATION

There is no space here to detail the complex variety of challenges to the enslavement of children – for that is what it was – but striking is the fact that well into the nineteenth century the majority of children living in the Atlantic region managed in various ways to escape the worst effects of the quarantine process. There was tremendous resistance, most of it unorganised and 'private', to the efforts of the middle class friends of citizenship to define young people as children, then forcibly to isolate and civilise them. Material necessity, fear of starvation and infant mortality, and the simple imperative of survival, gripped the offspring of the peasantry and craftspeople and urban workers and vagrants. Young people were thus expected to grow up fast, to earn or thieve a crust by working for money or kind, as well as to help their elders with tasks around the farm, or the workbench, or the home, if indeed there was a home.

Among the civilisers of the emergent civil societies and political orders of the Atlantic region, the ruffians and vagabonds who absconded were regarded as less than children, as in need of new forms of government and philanthropic regulation that more effectively 'policed' children, using more benevolent methods. 'Every person that frequents the out-streets of this city', declared a group of New York city reformers in 1824, 'must be forcibly struck with the ragged and uncleanly appearance, the vile language, and the idle and miserable habits of great numbers of children, most of whom are of an age suitable for schools, or for some useful employment'. The reformers added: 'The parents of these children, are,

---

[9] Alice Miller, *For Your Own Good. Hidden Cruelty in Child-Rearing and the Roots of Violence* (New York: Farrar, Straus, Giroux, 1983), especially pp. 3–91.

in all probability, too poor, or too degenerate, to provide them with clothing fit for them to be seen in at school; and to know not where to place them in order that they may find employment, or be better cared for.'[10] By the middle of the nineteenth century, within the Atlantic region, this new way of thinking flourished. The upshot was that legislators, Christian philanthropists, newspapermen, writers and public moralists imagined a better future for children. They questioned the use of violence and quarantine as means of reproducing childhood – and rejected the principle of dealing with recalcitrant children by humiliating them, sometimes by taking their lives.

We know from the reception afforded Charles Dickens' *Oliver Twist* (1838) that literature played a vital role in persuading publics of the urgent need to view children and childhood differently. Among the most powerful appeals to stop the wanton cruelty against children was the fictionalised autobiography by Jules Vallès, *L'Enfant* (1879). An open attack on the double standards of bourgeois culture, a plea for greater civility directed at young and old alike, the novel was dedicated to 'all those who were bored stiff at school or reduced to tears at home, who in childhood were bullied by their teachers or thrashed by their parents'. It featured a young boy, Jacques Vingtras, who suffered persistent scapegoating and violent abuse at the hands of a schoolteacher father and peasant mother who seem mainly interested in climbing social ladders. The boy's mother is especially pleased to find divine authority for her sadistic impulses in the biblical injunction that sparing the rod spoils the child. So at home she gets on with the daily act of worship, all the while subjecting her young son to ingenious humiliations. He appears to internalise his mother's zeal, and indeed he seems most at home and free of emotional suffering when he is receiving his regular sacrament of beatings and humiliations. He seems to enjoy being forced to eat onions that make him vomit. He apparently likes being battered black and blue. He obeys orders to wear trousers that are so rough and ill-fitting that they draw blood. He willingly swallows his mother's regular doses of pennypinching public humiliation and his father's attempts to have him incarcerated. So brutalised is the boy that he seems to pity those among his mates who are the victims of non-violent parental affection. He even feels unwell when his mother refrains from chastising him. 'I'd give a great deal

---

[10] *Documents Relative to the House of Refuge, instituted by the Society for the Reformation of Juvenile Delinquents in the City of New York, in 1824* (New York: Hart, 1832), p. 13.

to get a clout – it makes my mother happy, it cheers her up; it's like the flip of a wagtail or the dive of a duck.' Or so things seem. Much of the action in *L'Enfant* is hideously farcical, so charged with emotional coldness and cruelty that the reader is encouraged to identify with the angry introspection of a misunderstood child, who eventually learns in subtle ways to escape his prison of punishment and to stand up to his parents, even to love them in time. Despite everything, the morally and physically abused child is in fact a model for others, an example of how to endure injustice, and how to use early moral intuitions to overcome it in the name of dignity and simple decency – against its self-appointed adult guardians. The young child's conclusion even had political implications: 'I'll defend the Rights of Children in the same way others defend the Rights of Man.'[11]

Language like that sent reformers scurrying in all directions, to find new ways of rescuing children from violence, material deprivation and ill breeding – and from their unduly short childhoods. The horrible conditions suffered by the lower class young were no longer seen simply as a fact of life; and young people in general were now considered capable of escaping their immaturity. For that to happen, they needed to be trained into obedient maturity, to see that one day they would become adults, and that until that day arrived, like young animals not yet ready to cope in the wide world, they had to be trained up into literacy, and socially useful practices. 'The feebleness of infancy demands a continual protection', noted Jeremy Bentham, who was among the first to express the new wisdom in the language of child welfare. 'Everything must be done for an imperfect being, which as yet does nothing for itself. The complete development of its physical powers takes many years; that of its intellectual faculties is still slower.' He added: 'At a certain age, it has already strength and passions, without experience enough to regulate them. Too sensitive to present impulses, too negligent of the future, such a being must be kept under an authority more immediate than that of the laws.'[12]

The process of producing happier, literate, socially useful children through families, hospitals and foundling homes was presumed to take time. The period of childhood was consequently extended, and the new pedagogies and laws and government policies combined to usher in a second phase of childhood: an age of welfare regulation that demonstrated

---

[11] Jules Vallès, *The Child* (New York: New York Review Books, 2005), p. 327.
[12] Jeremy Bentham, *Theory of Legislation*, Vol. I (Boston, MA: Weeks, Jordan, 1840), p. 248.

not only that there was no such fixed condition called childhood, but also that childhood could be a prelude to membership of a civil society and full citizenship exercised within a political community. The old spatial metaphors that had defined childhood as subservience were shattered. New spatial metaphors appeared. Children were still reckoned to live outside of civil society and government, beyond their margins; but from hereon they were supposed no longer to stand beneath their structures, as in the age of the great quarantine. Children were regarded instead as positioned alongside and just outside the boundaries of civil society and government – as proto-adults who were capable of entering into their dynamics, as labourers, servants, mothers, owners of property, civil administrators and military and naval men, and as citizens.

How did the change come about? The age of welfare regulation was inaugurated and subsequently driven by many forces, including the advent of public inoculation against smallpox and other fatal diseases; public outcries against cruel employers and the trans-Atlantic opposition to slavery; new claims about the benefits of public education, including teaching children to read and write; and the dramatic reduction of fertility rates, of the kind that first happened in the United States and France. The shrinking numbers of young people in these countries were triggered by a change of expectations unleashed by their revolutions against absolutism. Dreams of material improvement, equality and liberty spread rapidly through the Atlantic region. It soon became something of a laboratory where young people were rescued from violence, over-working and ill breeding by philanthropic and state intervention in households, especially the homes of the poor scum that comprised the majority of the population. Among the vital champions of such intervention were children's home improvement societies, of the kind that flourished in nineteenth-century America. Rooted in civil society and fostered originally by the Protestant churches, middle-class bodies like the New York Children's Aid Society (founded in 1853 by Charles Loring) and the Boston Children's Aid Society (founded in 1860) specialised in the placement of poor, neglected and orphaned children in farms and small towns – and did much to popularise new methods of care for children that were said to be firmly embedded in the best interests of the children, not merely those of the adults.

The resultant of these various trends had considerable social effects. Young people were gradually removed from the official labour market, sub-categorised, compulsorily educated, required by law and social pressure to spend a growing proportion of their lives in the publicly regulated spaces of childhood, alongside the institutions of civil society and government. Many striking paradoxes marked the era of welfare regulation. In an age when children were still poor people's riches, children, in the name of civil society, were forcibly removed from its labour markets. Formally excluded from involvement in its market structures, children were increasingly housed in schools. Regarded as beings that were not yet capable of responsibly shifting for themselves, children who violated social standards, for example by committing a crime, suddenly found themselves treated – and punished – as if they were adults. Public muddle about the status and powers of children was commonplace during this period. It was certainly stained by the juices of paternalism: while there was much talk of 'care' and 'improvement' in connection with civil society, representative government and democracy, children were regarded as objects of welfare administration. They were seen as the aim and effect of top-down policies designed to minimise violence and humiliation, to prepare them for their discharge into adult life. A case in point, at the end of the nineteenth century, was the rise of the 'child savers' in the United States: reform-minded intellectuals, professionals and organisations who were rhetorically committed to 'protecting' children from their own selves, and from the 'delinquency' that was said to be produced by the physical and moral dangers of an increasingly industrialised and urban society.[13]

Especially in the field of government, the building of pioneering systems of welfare protection was often slow, in no small measure because they triggered bitter conflict and resistance. In Britain, for example, the 1802 Health and Morals of Apprentices Act limited the hours worked by children in textile mills to 12 per day; and the 1833 Factory Act prohibited the employment of children under the age of 9. But it was not until the passing of the 1880 Education Act that schooling became compulsory for children aged between five and ten – and not until 1900 that the school leaving age was raised to 14 years, so effectively removing younger people from the vagaries of labour markets. The American case equally highlights the drawn-out difficulties that frustrated welfare reformers. In 1916, for the first time in the country's history, a Democratic Congress passed a child labour law (known as the Keating-Owen Child Labor Act) by substantial majorities. Its proponents considered the legislative victory a triumph, and with good reason. Signed into law by President Woodrow Wilson, it condemned the perceived evils of child labour by prohibiting

---

[13] Anthony M. Platt, *The Child Savers: The Invention of Delinquency* (Chicago, IL: University of Chicago Press, 1969).

the sale in interstate commerce of goods manufactured by children. But two years later, in a cliffhanging judgement, the Supreme Court held the law to be unconstitutional. Within eight months of that judgement, a newly elected, Republican-dominated Congress passed another child labour law, again by a sizeable margin. The Supreme Court dug in its heels, and three years later, it rejected the law as unconstitutional by a margin of 8–1. Congress took its revenge; it ensured that judicial obstruction was to produce a much bigger, unintended effect. In 1924, Congress introduced a constitutional amendment. It passed through the House and Senate by big margins. The issue of protecting children against exploitative employers then spread to the state legislatures. By 1938, twenty-eight states with a clear majority of the country's population had passed the amendment. In that same year, Congress agreed the Fair Labor Standards Act, which contained provisions outlawing child labour. By 1942 – half a lifetime after the pioneering legislation – the cause in favour of children was finally upheld by the Supreme Court.[14]

Efforts to abolish child labour formed part of a bigger shift, a great historical transformation of the definition and treatment of children. Government and philanthropic intervention into the world of childhood had not merely the effect of lengthening the time young people spent as minors; it triggered a paradigm change in how they were regarded by others. Mental and physical violence directed at young people was increasingly viewed as illegitimate. Child poverty was seen to be unnecessary. All children were said to be capable of literacy and in need of a certain level of material and spiritual wellbeing; as fragile beings, they were thought to be deserving of adult feelings of compassion and mercy. The history of legislation covering compulsory schooling exemplifies the mood change. Consider again the case of Britain, where governments became involved for the first time with the schooling of children, in 1833, with an education grant of £20,000. The first Education Act (which conceived education as neither compulsory nor free) did not reach the Statute Books until 1870; only in 1876, with Sandon's Education Act, did government stand behind efforts to encourage as many children as possible to attend schools, and to make their parents responsible for ensuring that they received basic instruction. In 1891, the Fee Grant Act finally made elementary education free of charge – at which point, government effectively acknowledged that all adult members of the society had a

---

[14] Robert A. Dahl, *A Preface to Democratic Theory* (Chicago, IL: University of Chicago Press, 1965), pp. 106–107.

responsibility for the youngest generation, who were hereon presumed to be capable of leaving the world of childhood to become adult citizens capable of satisfying their duties, but also blessed with entitlements, including the rights to live and work and organise as citizens within a civil society protected by the casting of votes in elections.

THE COMING ENFRANCHISEMENT

The most recent phase of childhood – let us call it the age of the child citizen – is one in which the principle that children are capable of living under democratic conditions *within* civil societies, and that they are honorary citizens, serves as both a rallying point for many organisations, networks and groups, and as the focus of conduct and policymaking in the fields of government, law and civil society. Although the emancipation of children as full citizens is bitterly contested – there is plenty of resistance from government administrators, paediatricians, social workers, nurses, day care centre employees, school teachers, church organisations and child therapists – there are also many indications that the release of children from bondage, into full citizenship and its political and legal entitlements, is now under way. The old dogmas of quarantine and welfare regulation are crumbling; it is as if civil societies and governments have decided that they cannot live with the incivility that they formerly inflicted on children. The consequence is not only that the dualism between children and citizenship becomes blurred in many people's minds; as the global outcry against wanton cruelty against children by the Catholic Church shows, the power-ridden division between child and adult becomes questionable, and is publicly questioned, with politically unsettling effects.[15]

Although unstable, self-contradictory and by no means fully consolidated, the age of the child citizen, roughly speaking, had its beginnings in the years immediately following the end of the Second World War. It coincided with the moment of the birth of monitory democracy. It is true

---

[15] Some accounts of this trend include John O'Neill, *Civic Capitalism: The State of Childhood* (Toronto, ON: University of Toronto Press, 2004), especially pp. 101–109; Xiaobei Chen, 'The Birth of the Child Citizen', in Janine Brodie and Linda Trimble (eds.), *Reinventing Canada: Politics of the 21st Century* (Toronto, ON: Prentice-Hall 2003), pp. 189–202; and Urie Bronfenbrenner and Peter R. Neville, 'America's Children and Families: An International Perspective', in Sharon L. Kagan and Bernice Weissbourd (eds.), *Putting Families First: America's Family Support Movement and the Challenge of Change* (San Francisco, CA: Jossey-Bass, 1994), pp. 3–27.

that the changes affecting the definition and treatment of children since that time have older roots. Not to be underestimated are the long-term boomerang effects, the unintended consequences, of the two earlier phases of childhood. The quarantine of children, for instance, presupposed that there was no such thing as the innocence of childhood. Much later, it also stimulated awareness that the cruel treatment of children was incompatible with the values and rules of citizenship, civil society and constitutional government. The age of welfare regulation, with its talk of 'care' and 'the best interest of the child', similarly produced allergic reactions to the condescension of children. Both epochs subsequently prompted distinctions to be drawn between biological 'time' and 'social' time, so that, for example, the biological immaturity of children is today routinely distinguished from the many different ways in which that immaturity can be symbolically understood, and made publicly meaningful and institutionally effective.[16]

If the age of the child citizen is partly the unintended consequence of two earlier historical epochs, then it also has more immediate roots in the efforts of citizen campaigners, professional experts, governments and businesses to do something about the powerlessness of minors induced by the earlier history of childhood. Thanks to their efforts, which are not always altruistic, the conditions in which children live their lives are coming to be seen as contingent, as therefore capable of improvement. The democratisation of childhood gathers pace. The subjection of children to arbitrary power comes to seem strange. The task of vindicating their rights to live well finds its way onto political agendas. Once presumed to be the section of society best suited to the rod, creatures that were little and prone to misbehaviour, children nowadays find themselves at the centre of policy disputes and political fights. Some of them also find a voice of their own; through youth parliaments, children's forums and other bodies, they are heard and come to expect to be listened to by others.

In the Atlantic region, the contemporary politicisation of childhood is driven by a wide variety of forces. Summarised in the briefest way, the most important trends include:

- *The twentieth-century assault on the patriarchal family.* The contemporary (if geographically uneven) retreat of the patriarchal family is

---

[16] John Keane, 'A New Politics of Time', *The Conversation* (3 December 2016), https://theconversation.com/a-new-politics-of-time-69137.

not the result of what some structural-functional sociologists blandly call 'modernisation'. The restructuring of household life has been driven by such concrete forces as two global wars, the Russian and Chinese Revolutions, the construction of welfare states, feminism and new labour market obligations and opportunities for women. These forces have had the combined effect of weakening patriarchy on a scale never before witnessed in such a short time.[17] In the Atlantic region, the changes have been a mixed blessing for children. The early death of infants has radically declined in tandem with a comparative decline of the numbers of children. That has meant better conditions of life for many children, including their cherishing as children (the matter-of-factness with which earlier generations handled high infant mortality rates is almost unimaginable to most people today). But for some children, life has come to be plagued by such factors as fatherly neglect, pauperisation and (increasingly reported) domestic violence. The continuing wide gap between women's legal equality with men and the fact that on average in OECD countries women enjoy not much more than half (55–60 per cent) the wealth and income of men is not to the general advantage of children. The point is that while the breakdown and decline of patriarchal families has not led automatically to the improvement of the lives of children, their actual living conditions are nevertheless changing fast.

- *The development of government and civil society schemes in support of the principle that children, considered as young citizens, have the right to certain universal entitlements.* Free dental and health care and schooling schemes have become commonplace, but there are signs on the political horizon of more radical schemes, such as the provision of basic income to children as citizens. The former US Treasury Secretary, Paul O'Neill, championed federal government proposals for opening an investment saving account in the name of every child at her or his birth, to place a specified sum of several thousand dollars into the account at every birthday until the age of 18, with the accumulated funds then allowed to grow at a compounded rate until the individual reached retirement age. The proposal has since been stalled. Yet legislation to establish more modest Kids Accounts – in a society in which up to 20 per cent of households have no bank account – has once reached Congress; at state level, experiments are under way to create

---

[17] Goran Therborn, *Between Sex and Power. Family in the World 1900–2000* (London: Routledge, 2004).

children's accounts through Cradle to College Commissions, supported by banks, colleges, businesses and foundations; and the SEED Initiative, sponsored by the Ford Foundation and other civil society bodies, is so far the most intensive effort to invest in children of different ages and family incomes by providing an initial deposit matched by family contributions, over a four-year period. In Britain there was (until 2011) a more ambitious scheme in operation: the Child Trust Fund, under whose rules each child born on or after September 2002 received a voucher of at least £250, rising to £500 for poorer families, then an additional payment of the same order when they reached seven years, the amount paid into a special cash or stock-market based account, which could not be touched by the young person until she or he reached 18.

- *Changes in the field of civil and family law.* The jurisprudential status of children is undergoing dramatic transformation. There is growing agreement that law must make the child's needs paramount; that there is an unquestioned right of parents (including care- or step-parents) to raise their children as they see fit, free of government intrusion; but that in cases of neglect, maltreatment and abandonment, or in circumstances where adults themselves are unable to reach agreement and are forced to resort to legal processes, the role of the courts is to take the side of the child, in support of their needs, in order that they can become a person living in dignity, and capable of becoming an adequate parent for children of the future.[18] Consider just three statutes in Britain during the past several decades: (a) the 1984 Appeal Court decision in favour of Gillick, a ruling that established the principle that in the absence of an express statutory rule, all parental authority 'yields to the child's right to make his [sic] own decisions when he reaches a sufficient understanding and intelligence to be capable of making up his own mind on the matter requiring decision'; (b) the 1991 Age of Legal Capacity (Scotland) Act, which established that young people have full (or 'active') legal capacity at sixteen years, and that although the courts can set aside certain transactions as 'prejudicial' (like buying a computer or a bike), a child aged twelve or over can make a will, be entitled to consent or not to an adoption order; the same Act also declared that a child of any age has 'passive

---

[18] Among the classic and most highly influential defence of these principles is Joseph Goldstein, Anna Freud and Albert J. Solnit, *Beyond the Best Interests of the Child* (New York: The Free Press, 1973).

capacity', for example, the right to own heritable and moveable property; and the Act had the effect of replacing the term 'minor' with 'age 16' in certain statutes; (c) the 1995 Children (Scotland) Act which established that any child under sixteen years, if s/he has sufficient understanding of the nature and consequences of the proceedings, now has legal capacity to instruct a solicitor in connection with any civil matter.

- *The rapid growth of power-scrutinising organisations and networks dedicated to the improvement of young people's lives.* Many monitory bodies concerned with children are rooted in civil society, within state borders. Well-known examples include Action on Rights for Children, ChilOut (Children Out of Detention) and the Child Welfare League of Canada. Some child-monitoring initiatives operate across borders, often inspired by the 1989 UN Convention on the Rights of the Child, whose clauses specify the entitlements of all young people under eighteen years of age, or at least until the age of majority, if that comes earlier. Examples of cross-border social initiatives include Plan International; End Child Prostitution, Pornography and Trafficking; and the Campaign for Universal Birth Registration, which takes its cue from Article 7 of the UN Convention on the Rights of a Child, in support of the entitlement of each and every child to enjoy a legal identity (each year an estimated 48 million children are born without such an identity). What is striking about most or all of these power-monitoring initiatives is their rejection of the political language associated with the age of welfare regulation. Instead of condescending descriptions of children as frail and vulnerable creatures in need of protection and compassion, they speak firmly of the rights of children to enjoy their rights. Acts of preying upon children – including paedophilia – are deemed unjustified abuse.
- *Histories of childhood.* Guided by the work of Philippe Ariès and others, scholars from several disciplines have tried to show, for the first time and often with surprising effect, the varying spatial and temporal ways in which people and institutions have defined childhood, and how children themselves experience childhood as a particular phase of their lives. Such research has stimulated awareness that our childhood is not simply a bundle of formative experiences that we forget or remember; it forces recognition that the way we think about childhood itself has a history. The new histories have definite democratising effects on the understanding of children – effects that have been compounded by the growing public impact of various species of

psychoanalysis and child therapy. In spite of many in-house disagreements, the science and art of child development has emphasised that the experiences of adulthood are permanently linked to the formative episodes of childhood. Freud's famous observation, that a child suckling at his or her mother's breast is the prototype of every relation of love, serves as a clue to the bigger point – one that becomes obvious to those who think about it – that childhood and adulthood operate within the same spectrum; that at any moment an individual's life is propelled into the future by the repetition of past (sexual and emotional) experiences that are more or less recognised, evaded or unwittingly consummated. Seen in this way, it is a brute fact that all adults were once children, but how exactly childhood works within adults, and what significance it has for them, is a 'contingent fact', a matter for adults themselves to recognise and to act upon. Put differently: children are equipped with the strong wish to grow up, to become like adults, but adults are forever (like) children. 'A life', Adam Phillips explains, is 'an idiosyncratic repertoire of repetitions.'[19]

- *Children's literature.* In the burgeoning literature by or about children, young people are now considered, like adults, as readers with tastes and powers to set trends.[20] The age of the child citizen witnesses the advent of a huge global children's book industry; well-publicised listed ratings of children's books, featuring many different sub-genres; and the popularity of Roald Dahl, Jacqueline Wilson and J.K. Rowling (the most borrowed author in Britain's libraries) and other authors who write explicitly in defence of the democratic principle that children are at least the equals of adults. There are as well huge-selling works that are now widely considered 'children's classics', like Astrid Lindgren's *Pippi Longstocking* series, Antoine de Saint Exupéry's *The Little Prince*, E.B. White's *Charlotte's Web*, as well as 'blockbuster' works, like thirteen-year-old Anne Frank's diaries, which contain the following kinds of entries: 'Monday 28th September 1942 ... I think it's odd that grown-ups quarrel so easily and so often and about such petty matters. Up till now I always thought bickering was just something children did and that they outgrew it. Of course, there's sometimes a reason to have a "real" quarrel, but the verbal exchanges that

---

[19] Adam Phillips, 'Childhood Again', in *Equals* (New York: Basic Books, 2002), p. 150.
[20] Karin Lesnik-Oberstein, 'Defining Children's Literature and Childhood', in Peter Hunt (ed.), *International Companion Encyclopedia of Children's Literature* (London: Routledge, 1996), pp. 17–31.

take place here are just plain bickering. I should be used to the fact that these squabbles are daily occurrences, but I'm not and never will be as long as I'm the subject of nearly every discussion. [They refer to these as "discussions" instead of "quarrels", but Germans don't know the difference!] They criticise everything, and I mean everything, about me: my behaviour, my personality, my manners; every inch of me, from head to toe and back again, is the subject of gossip and debate. Harsh words and shouts are constantly being flung at my head, though I'm absolutely not used to it. According to the powers that be, I'm supposed to grin and bear it. But I can't! I have no intention of taking their insults lying down. I'll show them that Anne Frank wasn't born yesterday. They'll sit up and take notice and keep their big mouths shut when I make them see that they ought to attend to their own manners instead of mine. How dare they behave like that! It's simply barbaric.'[21]

- *Youth subculture.* Beginning during the 1950s, for the first time ever, there appeared new life styles for young people that quickly came to be called 'youth culture'. Defined by distinctive symbolic styles and tangible choices in matters such as clothing, slang, politics and music genres, the youth-based subculture offered participants membership and identities outside of those ascribed by family, work, school and other civil society and governing institutions. The long-term effects of youth subculture remain controversial. Some observers interpret it as a ritualised resistance from below to dominant (bourgeois) culture; others claim that the subculture has made young people, whose hormones change earlier and faster than ever before, more worldly wise; still others insist that youth subculture has become so dominant that the worship of adolescence ensures many people now retain immature attitudes well into adulthood.[22] Less controversial is the way youth subculture, in defiance of the old adage that old heads cannot be put on young shoulders, has powerfully encouraged children to think of themselves as members of a younger generation. Consider just one example from the early youth generation: *'Rock 'n Roll'*, a famous song written and performed in the early 1970s by Lou Reed, a louche, musically talented New Yorker with a drug habit, good connections

[21] Anne Frank, *The Diary of a Young Girl* (London: Penguin, 2002), pp. 43–44.
[22] Compare Stuart Hall and Tony Jefferson, *Resistance Through Rituals: Youth Subcultures in Post-war Britain* (London: Routledge, 1993); Steven Mintz, *Huck's Raft: A History of American Childhood* (Cambridge, MA: Harvard University Press, 2004); and Marcel Danesi, *Forever Young: The 'Teen-Aging' of Modern Culture* (Toronto, ON: University of Toronto Press, 2003).

and a large chip on his shoulder.[23] Those who heard it performed live usually agreed that it was among the most sublime contributions to music of that generation. Quite at odds both with Reed's cultivated talent for making himself permanently misunderstood through dark and brooding performances, the simple lyrics summarised one (imaginary) view of the history of the outbreak of youth culture: 'Jenny said, when she was just five years old/You know there's nothin' happening at all/You know my parents will be the death of us all/Two TV sets, two Cadillac cars ... ain't help me nothin' at all ... One fine morning, she heard on a New York station/She couldn't believe what she heard at all. Despite all the amputation/ You could dance to a rock 'n' roll station/ It was all right.'

- *The rise of the child consumer and a politics of children's consumption.* Business corporations, especially in the field of communication media, show unprecedented interest in youthful outlets for their products. While the figure of the child as a participant in the world of commodities made its first appearance towards the end of the quarantine phase of childhood, and while children as buyers and consumers of toys, books, clothing and other commodities expanded considerably during the welfare phase of childhood, it was usually the spectre of childhood pauperisation that gripped the imaginations of contemporaries. Under more recent conditions of enforced austerity, when in Britain (for instance) an estimated 3.9 million children are living officially in poverty, images of children suffering malnutrition, gout, rickets and obesity have again returned to headlines.[24] During the age of the child citizen, however, even children suffering the effects of inequality have become the target of concerted advertising and marketing strategies that have proved to be as controversial as they have been profitable to manufacturers and retailers. On an unprecedented scale, children have been drawn fully into markets, where they are targeted by businesses keen to exploit whatever buying power they or their parents or guardians have. The whole process is not quite the one-way street that some observers have supposed it to be. Those observers who worry about children being drowned in an endless flood of choosing, buying and expending commodities have a point. But for all the claims that

---

[23] See my obituary, 'Rock 'n Roll Democracy', *The Drum* (Australian Broadcasting Commission), www.abc.net.au/news/2013-11-15/keane-lou-reed-democracy/5094594.

[24] 'Inquiry: Child Poverty and Health – the Impact of the Welfare Reform and Work Bill 2015–2016', All Party Parliamentary Group on Health in All Policies, London, 2016.

children are the victims of organised efforts to manufacture a future generation of dead-head consumers who will serve as the obedient slaves of a totalitarian consumer society of 'comfortable, smooth, reasonable, democratic unfreedom' (Herbert Marcuse), the terrain of children's consumption is now heavily contested. Many efforts to de-commodify young people's lives have begun: Jamie Oliver's media-led assault on the British school lunch culture of turkey twizzlers, including his *Democracy Cookbook* (2006) initiative 'for youth workers to help them engage young people in politics, show them what it means, how it works, and demonstrate the difference they can make with their vote'; campaigns against the use of Scooby-Doo, Bob the Builder, Shrek and other film and cartoon and celebrity characters to sell food stuffed with salt, fat and sugar to minors whose obesity rates are rising; and the enforcement of legal limits on advertising targeted at children. The unsustainability of present and predicted future patterns of high-intensity consumption is also prompting campaigns to highlight to children their long-term responsibilities as earthly bio-citizens.

- *Initiatives to reduce the voting age for young people.* The early history of representative democracy was marked by the presumption that young people were entitled to become citizens with full voting rights only when they reached the age of twenty-one years; voting and office holding was sometimes confined to elected representatives who were even older (a practice that remains in countries such as Italy, where in Senate elections voters must be aged twenty-five years). Many adults today think such rules are set at about the right level. They are against reform, and say so openly. Their language bears striking parallels, in the history of representative democracy, to the rhetoric used by those who opposed the emancipation of slaves, or who resisted granting the vote to male workers, or women, or colonial subjects. Conservatives say that 'kids' lack 'maturity'; their ability to think logically through an argument, to understand cause and effect and to take responsibility for their own actions, is sub-standard, or so it is said. The claim is of course circular and true by definition: kids are naturally kids; maturity is thought to have no history, so that youth and politics will never mix. So it follows that teenagers, in their imprudence, will misuse the vote. At sixteen (say opponents) teenagers are negative and rebellious; they are more keen on making a statement than acting responsibly. Like hysterical suffragettes bent on dragging passions into politics, or ill-mannered nineteenth-century workers, young people are a danger unto themselves. The champions of voting reform contradict this way of thinking, with some success. The era of the child citizen unleashes pressures for reducing the voting age below eighteen. The earliest successful moves to set the voting age at sixteen began during the 1990s, at the municipal and state levels in Germany. In 2007, Austria became the first of the world's leading monitory democracies to adopt a voting age of sixteen for all purposes. Elsewhere, civil society campaigns pursue the same goal. Examples include groups like Article 12 in Scotland; Americans for a Society Free from Age Restrictions and Rock the Vote in the United States; and Germany's K.R.A.T.Z.A., a youth support network that stands for the abolition of all age limits for voting. Proposals are also in circulation to adopt some or other version of a Demeny voting system that enables parents to cast proxy votes on behalf of their children, until they reach the minimum voting age.[25]

CHILD CITIZENS?

The changes unleashed by a combination of these and other forces are arguably of major significance in the history of citizenship and democracy. The overall transition that is now under way, in many richer countries of the Atlantic region, and despite setbacks and continuing injustice, including rising levels of child poverty, is one that leads from a condition of childhood that treated children as mere subjects of adults' power, towards a world in which children are gradually coming to be seen as citizens who are the equals of adults. Something like a de-colonisation and democratisation of children and childhood is going on. No longer are young people regarded, for instance, as little animals in need of a good thrashing, or as delicate creatures that should be seen but not heard. Overweening adult presumptions are breaking down. In various fields of law and government and civil society, children are coming to be seen as thoughtful and sentient beings, as citizens who are entitled as of right to lives unblemished by fear and violence, happy and fulfilling lives unscarred by enforced labour, or the pressures of poverty mixed with market consumption, or the prejudiced bossing of those who have already reached the age of so-called majority. The old presumption that the physical immaturity of children consigns them of necessity to generalised immaturity is crumbling. Just as the physical 'disabilities' of groups once

---

[25] Paul Demeny, 'Pronatalist Policies in Low-Fertility Countries: Patterns, Performance and Prospects', *Population and Development Review*, 12 (supplement, 1986), 335–358.

referred to in derogatory ways as 'the crippled' and 'the old' are now seen as needing compensation, so that the 'differently abled' and 'elderly citizens' can live their lives in dignity, in the sunshine of respect from others, so the biological facts of physical immaturity of children are seen increasingly to be detachable from questions about how, in social and political ways, this so-called immaturity is to be compensated in ways that are meaningful and satisfying to children themselves. Reminders are served that immaturity means something positive: far from connoting inertness or mere lack or the inability to shift for oneself in the world, it signifies the positive power of children to act meaningfully and in dignity – to live, play, work, shed tears, love and ponder things in peace and quiet, just as grown-ups do.

Enfranchisement by stealth is one way of describing the long-term trajectory that makes children living in the Atlantic region, and in various other parts of the globe, the beneficiaries of policies and support that win them greater dignity and respect and freedom. Symptomatic of the long-term enfranchisement is the way that the so-called minority status period is pressured increasingly by anomalous patterns of definition, duty and entitlement. In today's Britain, for instance, young people can vote in general elections at eighteen; but at sixteen, they can pilot a glider, sleep together, marry (without parental consent in Scotland) and have children. In Scotland, sixteen year olds can do more than vote. They can bring an action for aliment – or even when they are under sixteen – so long as they display the capacity to instruct a solicitor. All sixteen year olds in the United Kingdom can be independently domiciled and give their consent to surgical, medical and dental treatment; they can be company directors, or be tried by jury in Crown Court and locked up, or change their name by deed poll, or leave school. Under the 1991 Child Support Act, whose central legal concept is the 'qualifying child', a person ceases to be a child at sixteen. Young men (women have to wait another year) can even join the armed forces.

Anomalous definitions of childhood are symptomatic of the democratisation of childhood. In Canada, at the federal level, young people become full adult citizens at the age of eighteen; in some provinces, Newfoundland and British Columbia for instance, nineteen is the age of majority. In Quebec – but not in Ontario – younger people can assume the legal status of an 'emancipated minor', which means they become legally separated from their parents or guardians and no longer subject to their decision making powers, and so on. We have entered times in which the fields of early age come to be ploughed by deep political controversies; on a scale never before seen, the experience of childhood comes widely to be seen as contingent. That results in a widening repertoire of images and interpretations of childhood; monistic presumptions about children's necessary servitude, or their bestiality, or their utility as young beasts of burden, or as angels, give way to a kaleidoscope of views about childhood and children. It might even be said that childhood is so pluralised that childhood is no more. The spaces opened up for different definitions of the experience of minority even enable some children, for the first time, to win political and legal protection for their claims, and even to find a public voice, for instance through school councils, youth parliaments and children's forums.

There are admittedly mountains of prejudices and double standards that still burden and spoil children's lives, but symptomatic of the trend towards their inclusion as citizens under conditions of monitory democracy is the accelerating breakdown of philosophical confidence in the old practices of treating children as feral or fragile creatures. Suppositions that the fundamental power division between adult and child is rooted in factual differences are admittedly still alive today. In subtle form, we could say, they live on in recent proposals for extending a second vote to parents, who are understood as 'interested guardians' of the interests of their children. Starker versions of such thinking have old roots. The nineteenth-century English journalist James Fitzjames Stephen gave voice to the supposed differences when discussing the legal status of being a child. Although admitting that 'minority and majority are questions of degree, and the line that separates them is arbitrary', he blasted as meta-barbaric those who dared to raise questions about children's legal status. 'If children were regarded by law as the equals of adults, the result would be something infinitely worse than barbarism. It would involve a degree of cruelty to the young which can hardly be realised even in imagination. The proceeding, in short, would be so utterly monstrous and irrational that I suppose it never entered into the head of the wildest zealot for equality to propose it.'[26]

The old confidence exuded by Fitzjames Stephen and others of this period has been withering for some time. It shows every sign of withering away completely. In the age of the child citizen, there is growing awareness of the need for distinctions and discriminations that are much more subtle than thresholds – the twenty-first or eighteenth or sixteenth

---

[26] James F. Stephen, *Liberty, Equality, Fraternity* (Cambridge: Cambridge University Press, 1967), pp. 142, 193.

birthday – that seem utterly arbitrary, and misleadingly so, if only because they suppose that mature, sane, responsible adults appear magically, at an instant, like butterflies from the cocoon of childhood. The opening sequences in the passage from birth to adulthood to old age (with which childhood shares more than a few passing resemblances) to death are not like that. Just like adults of any age, children enjoy well-developed capacities to feel and abhor pain. It is not true that the young feel no pain, or less pain, or that there is something like a rule that stipulates that the younger a child the less pain s/he 'naturally' feels, or remembers. Hence the campaigns, waged by groups such as War Child and Amnesty International, to highlight the hellish suffering experienced by child soldiers, whose numbers have reportedly swelled to more than 300,000 worldwide.

While children are certainly not adults in miniature, there are other deep continuities between the worlds of minority and majority. Those who are lucky to have and/or know children also understand that whatever their degree of self-centredness, their actions are always tempered by some measure of self-less concern for others, as well as a strongly imagined sense of self-respect. These are of course qualities shared with adults, some of whom, in moments of honesty, will admit that their own sense of self-respect is not only bound up with the concern for others, but that contact with children often has the effect of reminding adults that they can unlearn qualities that are sometimes better developed in children. 'Few grown-up persons', remarked John Dewey, 'retain all of the flexible and sensitive ability of children to vibrate sympathetically with the attitudes and doings of those about them. Inattention to physical things (going with incapacity to control them) is accompanied by a corresponding intensification of interest and attention as to the doings of people.'[27]

Dewey's insightful point prompts the vexed question of whether or not children know how to live – as citizens – in the big, wide world. It is often said, and common sense seems to dictate, that they know little or nothing, that lacking conceptions of how they should live, parents, guardians, teachers and other adults have no alternative but to teach the young by imposing their own standards upon minors. According to this conventional view, 'young people do not have the ability to properly evaluate their options and make sound decisions' and 'may not have enough

---

[27] John Dewey, *Democracy and Education* (New York: Macmillan, 1925), pp. 51–52.

knowledge and experience to participate in an activity'.[28] Adult guardians of 'reason' think along the same lines. 'The child literally does not know how to live, and must be taught to do so', wrote the political philosopher John Plamenatz six decades ago. He drew from this the conclusion that since s/he has neither knowledge nor experience of the world, the child is incapable of making choices worthy of the name, and therefore deserves arbitrary rule. 'If it is not taught in one way, it will be taught in another; it feels the need to be influenced, to be guided, to be put on its feet morally and spiritually. We impose our standards on our children, not because our standards are better than theirs, but because they have none of their own.'[29]

From the point of view of the norm of the child citizen, there are several troubles with this view. Ignorance is not a monopoly of childhood; nor is inexperience or uncertainty about how to live in the world. The acknowledgement by adults that people do not know enough to navigate their way through the world – that they are humble creatures in need of humility and help from wise others – is in any case a fundamental democratic virtue, as this book is arguing at length.[30] Moreover, the view that children are ignorant of the world, and are therefore incapable of dwelling responsibly on the (distant) consequences of their own actions, is again not a defect of so-called minors; the history of adult struggles for and against self-government is splattered with ignorant fools, headstrong knaves and (as Winston Churchill famously noted) characters who learned that the worst thing about political suicide is living with the regret of it all. Finally, the view that children are ignorant and irresponsible, and that it is therefore 'in their own best interests' to be subjected to external controls, begs large questions. These doubts centre not only on who defines the 'interests' of children, but also which forms of control are most appropriate and legitimate – exactly the same questions that have proven to be the stuff of every known previous attempt to extend democratic citizenship, for instance to workers, women, slaves, the colonised, racial and ethnic minorities. Rash ignorance and efforts to minimise its harmful effects are not specialities of the young. Governmental intervention into the affairs of adults for the stated purpose of minimising

---

[28] Cited from a handbook distributed by the Centre for Public Legal Education (Edmonton, Alberta, 2015), www.law-faqs.org/alberta-faqs/youth-and-the-law-in-alberta/how-old-do-i-have-to-be/youth-faqs-general-questions/.
[29] John Plamenatz, *On Alien Rule and Self-Government* (London: Longmans, 1960), pp. 23–24.
[30] The theme of humility is analysed earlier in John Keane, *The Life and Death of Democracy* (London and New York: Simon & Schuster, 2009).

or preventing misguided acts that have harmful effects – think of John Stuart Mill's reasoned call for the regulation of soldiers who drink alcohol on the job, or of someone unwittingly about to swallow cyanide – are of course a feature of all known forms of government. What is distinctive and special about democracy, beginning with its assembly-based forms in the classical period and today featuring various forms of monitory democracy, is that it is an always unfinished, practical experiment in exactly the same art of naming and regulating the precipitant behaviour of citizens and their representatives, but doing so by means that are subject to processes of public accountability and the public giving of consent.

THE FUTURE?

What are the probable long-term effects of the quiet revolution in favour of children's rights as citizens? How will things turn out in the end? It is far too early to guess, let alone to tell. All that can be said safely is that for two centuries, European theories of citizenship and democracy have prided themselves on thinking of politics as the business of grown-ups, as an adults' affair, as a sphere of life well beyond and higher in status than what goes on in households. Written in the age of representative democracy, think of Hegel's classic treatment of domestic life in *Philosophie des Rechts:* the family is parochial, body-bound, oiled by sentiments of closeness, the proximity of adults concerned with the animal-like concerns of lust and procreation, the nurturing of uncivilised children, who are 'outside' of civil society and state or, more accurately, duty bound to behave as objects of transcendence, as preludes to the higher worlds of civil society, law and the state.

The hour has long past when this kind of thinking was credible. In conceptual and practical terms, it has been rendered obsolete; from the perspective of political strategies and democratic norms, it is now better described as an anti-democratic remnant of the age of representative democracy that has now come to an end. In the early phase of that era, the eighteenth-century aphorist and wit Sébastien-Roch-Nicolas Chamfort (1741–1794) remarked that the best measure of the quality of any society is the way its institutions and citizens treat women.[31] That rule remains pertinent, but it needs to be supplemented with another: a fundamental measure of equality among citizens and the overall quality of any

---

[31] Sébastien-Roch-Nicolas Chamfort, *Products of the Perfected Civilization: Selected Writings of Chamfort* (London: Macmillan, 1969).

democracy is the way it treats its young people, who are after all a master key to the doors of the future of all government and society. It follows from this maxim that for the sake of the future of citizenship and democracy, there is today, in the Atlantic region and elsewhere, an urgent political need to do something about the condescension and disempowerment of children. Necessary reforms include campaigns for universal registration; the strengthening of the Gillick criteria in courts of law; the prohibition of child trafficking and solitary confinement and forcible strip searching of young offenders; and the reduction of the age at which young people can vote for representatives. The current spike in the levels of child poverty – documented by growing numbers of reports on children's living conditions in rich countries[32] – must be reversed. Evidence that the radical reduction of child poverty can be achieved is suggested by the striking fact that given levels of child well-being are policy-susceptible, and that there is no obvious relationship between child poverty and GDP per capita. The cluttering of children's lives with unnecessarily different and confusing thresholds of adulthood should be seen as a public problem; for the sake of their own dignity and their learned ability to juggle and make sense of different situations, their domestic and wider societal lives should be better synchronised, not broken into fragments. All forms of cruelty and violence against children must be outlawed. So, too, should the outright victimisation of children by contingent and removable prejudices, many of them masquerading as generosity and benevolence. Energies can be invested in the creation of new monitory mechanisms for enabling children publicly to represent their own interests. But the basic requirement for any or all this to happen is a switch of perception, a change of heart and mind, a willingness to see things differently: commencing with the recognition (as Tocqueville said of slavery in nineteenth-century America) that democracies that try to harbour the ships of servitude and injustice will find their shores battered by the gales of contempt for their hypocrisy. That rule certainly applies to children, who are no longer to be regarded simply as the citizens of the future. A new truth is out: children are now the measure of how all other citizens should be treated.

---

[32] Examples include the United Nations Children's Fund, *Child Poverty in Perspective: An Overview of Child Wellbeing in Rich Countries* (Florence: UNICEF Innocenti Research Centre, 2007); Peter Adamson, *Measuring Child Poverty: New League Tables of Child Poverty in the World's Rich Countries* (Florence: UNICEF, 2012); and C.J. de Neubourg et al., 'Child Deprivation, Multidimensional Poverty and Monetary Poverty in Europe', *Innocenti Working Paper* (Florence: UNICEF Innocenti Research Centre, 2012).

PART IV

DEMOCRACY ACROSS BORDERS?

10

Quantum Metaphors

Political crises are normally described as sudden turning points, moments of gripping drama, flashpoints when everything is up for grabs, when bold judgements and decisions become necessary. But archaeologists, palaeontologists, historians and others teach us that the radical transformation and/or ruination of old orders and their replacement by new power arrangements often happen slowly. The rhythms of disruption and dis-integration are not always sudden. Crises can smoulder. They may well take time to materialise because they obey the laws of the *longue durée*, not the mayhem of convulsive fits and starts.[1]

Slow-motion ruptures are naturally much harder to spot, and to analyse, but arguably they must be central to the analysis of monitory democracy and its uncertain future, or so the following reflections on territory, borders and cross-border democracy propose. The trigger thought within the next few pages is that the old ideals and institutions of representative democracy, especially political parties, parliaments and general elections, are today snared in a deepening crisis. The roots of this protracted crisis are traceable to the plain fact that every nation-state democracy is today living in *post-sovereign* conditions, caught up in a salmagundi of power-wielding institutions designed to solve problems and produce and administer decisions that are not tied in any simple sense to territory. Entangled in worldwide webs of interdependence backed by space- and time-shrinking flows of mediated communication, politics within actually existing democracies no longer stands in splendid

---

[1] Jacques Le Goff, *Must We Divide History into Periods?* (New York and London: Columbia University Press, 2014).

isolation from the rest of the world. Boundary disputes, 'spooky action at a distance' (Einstein), spillover effects, arbitrage pressures and butterfly effects are common. Here–there dialectics are chronic. Things that happen politically in one place have effects elsewhere, in far-away locations. The reverse dynamic is equally commonplace: events, information flows, declarations and deals that happen in far-off places can and do touch off immediate local consequences.

These cross-border trends pose the key question of whether democracy can be re-imagined in kaleidoscopic terms; that is, understood as a political form, a type of politics and a whole way of life structured by multiple interacting spatial frameworks in which peoples, with the help of their representatives, govern themselves and their ecosystems in differently sized settings marked by different spacetime rhythms that are not exclusively framed and contained by state borders. The task of re-imagining democracy in this way supposes that democratic theory now requires something like a quantum leap, a major breakthrough equivalent to a sudden jump of a particle from one energy level to another. Such a quantum turn has far-reaching implications. It radically questions the dominant place-based, territorial imaginary of contemporary democratic politics. It sets its sights on explaining in fresh ways why questions of territory, place and space matter to democracy; why they need to be moved to the heart of democratic theory; and why the concern of quantum approaches in physics and astronomy with such matters as 'extra dimensions', 'entanglement' and 'spacetime' are highly relevant for democratic politics. The whole approach weighs against the place-based mentality of contemporary democratic thinking and politics. It also probes the conceptual and empirical weaknesses of 'cosmopolitan democracy' perspectives, 'democracy' theories and other present-day efforts to find a post-territorial language of democracy. It explores why, against considerable odds, the spirit, language and institutions of monitory democracy today survive and thrive in cross-border settings; and why the twenty-first century future of democracy now vitally depends on challenging the scholarly flatlands by developing quantum styles of thinking and a new practical politics of democratic space.

NON-LINEARITY

In this proposed quantum turn, let's call it, the trigger hypothesis is that democratic ideals and institutions are snared in a smouldering crisis traceable to their implication in processes of *non-linearity*.[2] Just as scientists have realised that systems cannot be studied in isolation because everything has an effect on everything else in our universe, and that since every single particle of matter has some gravitational effect on every other particle of matter, non-linear systems structured by feedback loops, interactions that can grow exponentially, are the norm. The principle of non-linearity equally applies to the realm of human affairs, for instance in the multiple ways in which democratic mechanisms 'at home' are increasingly shaped and twisted by forces 'abroad'. It is not just that nation-state democracies are confronted with ever-heavier bundles of problems that can be solved only through outside help; or that these democracies are now so entangled with other democracies that they regularly comment on their home affairs, copy policies and institutions, negotiate disagreements and learn from each other's mistakes. Less positive things are happening. The deepening worldwide integration of states and peoples means that, within any given democracy, things that are decided 'at home' by citizens and their governing representatives shape and often damage peoples 'abroad', with limited chances of redress or compensation. In these circumstances, the old axiom that 'every actual democracy rests on the principle that not only are equals equal but unequals will not be treated equally'[3] assumes a fickle new meaning. For when democratic politics in (say) German or American form delivers injustices to distant others, leaving them to suffer injurious decisions, or non-decisions, over which they have no control, it becomes a hypocritical exercise in dispensing arbitrary power. Finally, insofar as democracies find themselves entrapped in cross-border force-fields, political choices are constrained and policy decisions are frustrated, or blocked outright. Such matters as immigration, banking, exchange rates, tourism, education, policing and military are now regularly co-decided by others at a distance, regardless of what legislatures, voters and leaders at home may want, or choose to do. The upshot is that life within territorial democracies feels ever less 'sovereign'. In extreme circumstances, dysfunctions within the multilateral sprawl of cross-border arrangements have threatening consequences for democracies, as when bad banks, economic austerity, rotten

---

[2] John Keane, *Democracy and Media Decadence* (Cambridge and New York: Cambridge University Press, 2013); Parag Khanna, 'Remapping the World', *Time*, 11 March 2011; and Charles S. Maier, *Once within Borders: Territories of Power, Wealth, and Belonging since 1500* (Cambridge, MA and London: Belknap Press, 2016).
[3] Carl Schmitt, *The Crisis of Parliamentary Democracy* (Cambridge, MA: MIT Press, 1988), p. 9.

air, violence or nuclear spills in one country damage democracy among its neighbours. There are cases of small island states (such as the democracies of Kiribati and Tuvalu) where environmental damage threatens forcibly to displace citizens to new territories, from where they seek to exercise jurisdictional control over their former homelands, from a distance. And there are democracies, such as Estonia, which store terabytes of government and citizen data (covering such matters as banking details, electoral rolls, birth records, property deeds and other government data) in secure offshore locations and joint data management projects with other states.

Within the field of democratic theory, these empirical anomalies and real-world complications are typically ignored, or treated as random exceptions. Most researchers remain convinced that democracy only ever happens within fixed and bounded territorial settings.[4] For some scholars, territorial place not only remains central in matters of power and politics, it is said to be of rising importance.[5] Reinforced by taken-for-granted methodologies and sizeable investments in Freedom House-style 'national' databases, democracy researchers chronically think in terms of fixed-place settings, such as rural communities, urban neighbourhoods and territorial states. Their *territorial mentality* is strongly evident in contemporary scholarly accounts of the functional prerequisites of democracy, which are said to include (a) a territorially defined 'sovereign' territorial state that guarantees through its various sub-units the physical security of a resident population of citizens who are subject to the rule of law; (b) a political culture compatible with electoral mechanisms, including competition among political parties, periodic elections and parliamentary government; (c) a more or less homogeneous social infrastructure or 'national identity' bound together by a common language, common historical customs and a common sense of shared territory; and (d) a territorially bound market economy capable of generating wealth that lifts citizens out of poverty and guarantees them a basic standard of living sufficient to enable them to take an interest in public affairs, and to vote in periodic elections.

The whole idea of monitory democracy spotlights the growing strangeness of this originally eighteenth-century understanding of democracy in territorial

---

[4] Examples include Adam Przeworski, *Democracy and the Limits of Self-Government* (Cambridge: Cambridge University Press, 2010); Michael Coppedge and John Gerring, 'Conceptualizing and Measuring Democracy: A New Approach', *Perspectives on Politics*, 9, 2 (2011), 247–267.

[5] Göran Therborn, 'Why and How Place Matters', in Robert E. Goodin and Charles Tilly (eds.), *The Oxford Handbook of Contextual Political Analysis* (Oxford: Oxford University Press, 2006), pp. 509–533.

state form. Representative democracy 'rendered practicable ... over a great extent of territory',[6] was undoubtedly a uniquely modern achievement. By any measure, it was a breathtakingly novel form of self-government, a polity defined by written constitutions, independent judiciaries and laws that guaranteed such procedures as periodic election of candidates to legislatures, limited-term holding of political offices, voting by secret ballot, competitive political parties, the right to assemble in public and liberty of the press. Representative democracy in this sense greatly extended the geographic scale of political life. As time passed, and despite its localised origins in towns, rural districts and large-scale imperial settings, democracy came to be 'housed' mainly within territorially defined states, backed up by administrative, law making and taxation powers, and by standing police forces and armies.[7] These states were qualitatively bigger and more populous than the political units of assembly democracy. The democracies of the classical Greek world were small-scale affairs. Most of them, Mantinea and Argos for instance, were no bigger than a few score square kilometres. Hence the standard observation that the leap from 'the vision of democracy in the city-state that prevailed ... from the Greeks to Rousseau' to the 'approved school-solution ... the nation-state' was nothing less than a paradigm revolution. 'Representative government in the nation-state is in many respects so radically – and inescapably – different from democracy in the city-state', runs the standard conclusion, 'that it is rather an intellectual handicap to apply the same term, democracy, to both systems, or to believe that in essence they are really the same'.[8]

NEW QUESTIONS

The monitory democracy perspective developed in this book critically engages this orthodox view in *three* different but intersecting ways.

First, the whole idea of monitory democracy points to the *hidden connections* between the models of ancient assembly democracy and modern 'territorial democracy'.[9] These models unquestionably stood at

---

[6] Antoine L. C. Destutt de Tracy, *A Commentary and Review of Montesquieu's Spirit of Laws* (Philadelphia, PA: William Duane, 1811), p. 19.
[7] Michael Mann, *The Sources of Social Power: The Rise of Classes and Nation States, 1760–1914* (Cambridge: Cambridge University Press, 1993).
[8] Robert A. Dahl, 'The City in the Future of Democracy', *The American Political Science Review*, 61 (1967), 953–970.
[9] Daniel J. Elazar, 'Territorial Democracy and the Metropolitan Frontier', *The American Mosaic: The Impact of Space, Time, and Culture on American Politics* (Boulder, CO: Westview Press, 1993), chapter 9.

opposite ends of a size spectrum: the former were small-scale and the latter were large-scale versions of democracy. The monitory democracy perspective nevertheless notes that the two contrasting models of democracy share a common presumption that popular self-government is always 'naturally' and irrevocably anchored in defined physical place. Both supposed that democracy, ancient and modern, required demarcated territorial ground that served as the fixed framework of citizens and their encounters, deliberations and decisions. Democracy has telluric qualities. Place is its condition. Democracy is infused with location; it is self-government through the medium of meaningful belonging to a defined place.

The monitory democracy perspective is keenly interested in this entrapment of ancient and modern democratic vistas within a *fixed place-based mentality*. It explores the contours of this mentality, and why the trouble democrats have in thinking beyond *place* merits critical reflection. The perspective investigates how past democracies in home-grown form were typically attached to territory (from *terra*: land, earth, nourishment, sustenance). It asks why they often served as both the guardian of *territorium* (a place from which people are warned) and the springboard of war and terror (*terrere*). It notes the extent to which democracy today still operates in demarcated physical places, such as capital cities and local city assemblies (the modern-day version of the *pnyx* in Athens), or in the *Stadtstaaten* (Berlin and Hamburg), capital city territories, districts and provinces of federal states, or in whole territorial states. These places, the new understanding of democracy observes, are the privileged sites of election; in some cases, as in the upper chambers of bicameral systems, they enjoy rights of representation. Despite all the variations, geographic place is 'where' democracy happens. Place supposes a 'locational' view of things. The *topos* and anchor of meaningful belonging and affective attachment, place is definable by criteria such as measurable distance; latitude and longitude; and elevation. Place is a three-dimensional patch of the earth or sea that is not equivalent to any other. Place is bounded, a 'natural' unit, a fixed location where democratic things 'happen' – where power is exercised through institutions, subject to the consent of voting citizens, by means of representatives. Place is the address of democracy; it is the address where democracy lives, or so the orthodoxy supposes.

In a *second* move, the monitory democracy perspective poses pointed questions that expose a fundamental contradiction: if democracy minimally means a 'sovereign' political form that enables people to govern themselves, to win control over their lives by voting for political parties in 'free and fair' elections, within any given patch of the earth, then isn't democracy fast losing ground to the multiple dynamics of publicly unaccountable cross-border chains of corporate, legal and governmental power? Don't these publicly unaccountable cross-border dynamics strike deeply at the heart of both the meaning (semantics) and efficacy (pragmatics) of democracy in place-based form? Isn't place-based democracy within 'sovereign' territorial states losing its grip? Might its crippling entanglement within cross-border dynamics signal its growing obsolescence as a grand political ideal?

What is interesting about this set of questions is the wide range of conflicting replies they elicit. The abreactions range from glum cynicism and populist backlashes to scholarly efforts to revisit the meaning of democracy in cross-border settings. Five types of response to the contradiction are worth noting:

Fatalism: Fatalists suppose that little or nothing can be done to unpick or soften the contradiction between 'sovereign' territorial democracy and cross-border power dynamics. Citizen initiatives and democratic innovations and talk of cross-border democracy are rendered helpless by these cross-border dynamics, it is said. Democracy is a shrinking violet, a victim of the advance of 'abstract space'[10] imposed by globalising corporate and governmental agencies. Prospects for democracy are said to be further weakened by the hyper-complexity of cross-border decision-making, which renders impossible the 'public enlightenment' and 'civil discourse and compromise' so necessary for democracy.[11]

Rebuilding Territorial Democracy Often associated with populist parties and leaders, this understanding of democracy supposes that politicians, political parties, voters and governments can combine forces to turn back the clock, to shore up the fortress walls of parliamentary democracy through the 'claw back' of cross-border powers to the territorial state. These democrats want to take back their country. Territorial barriers need to be strengthened. Citizens must feel proud of their country. Strengthened state institutions must again become the principal guardian of the democratic principle of sovereign territoriality backed by 'the people'.

---

[10] Henri Lefebvre, *The Production of Space* (Oxford: Blackwell, 1991).
[11] Robert A. Dahl, 'The Past and Future of Democracy', revised manuscript version of a lecture at the symposium Politics from the 20th to the 21st Century at the University of Siena, 14–16 October 1999; and Robert A. Dahl, *On Democracy* (New Haven, CT: Yale University Press, 1998), pp. 114–117.

Local Empowerment: There are other democrats who set themselves the task of breathing life back into local self-government, in effect by recapturing what they imagine to be the spirit and substance of Greek-style assemblies of the people. Some scholars envisage a new geography of 'open cities' and 'refuge cities'.[12] Others revive talk of 'power to the people!', the slogan used by groups like Students for a Democratic Society during the 1960s rebellions, in order to show that self-government requires decentralised decision making. This alternative envisages citizens' self-determination through innovative 'grass roots' forms of 'deep' democracy that serve to enhance 'the commitment and capacities of ordinary people to make sensible decisions through reasoned deliberation and empowered because they attempt to tie action to discussion'.[13]

Global Federalism: Still other democrats embrace a neo-Kantian vision of a 'system of geo-governance unlike any other proposed to date', a two-tiered system of 'cosmopolitan democracy' in which all peoples enjoy certain basic human rights and are treated as ends in themselves. These cosmopolitans advocate 'a model of political organisation in which citizens, wherever they are located in the world, have a voice, input and political representation in international affairs, in parallel with, and independently of, their own governments'.[14]

Demoicracy: This approach thinks in terms of a peaceful assemblage of intersecting and self-governing states.[15] Used mainly to describe and legitimate the European Union, this perspective recommends a composite polity of polities answerable to multiple distinct peoples

---

[12] Jacques Derrida, *On Cosmopolitanism and Forgiveness* (London: Routledge, 2001).

[13] Benjamin Barber, *If Mayors Ruled the World: Dysfunctional Nations, Rising Cities* (New Haven, CT: Yale University Press, 2013); Archon Fung and Erik O. Wright (eds.), 'Thinking about Empowered Participatory Governance', in *Deepening Democracy: Institutional Innovations in Empowered Participatory Governance* (London: Verso, 2003), p. 5.

[14] Daniele Archibugi and David Held, *Cosmopolitan Democracy: An Agenda for a New World Order* (Cambridge: Polity Press, 1995), pp. 1–16; Jürgen Habermas, 'The Constitutionalization of International Law and the Legitimation Problems of a Constitution for World Society', *Constellations*, 15 (2008), 444–455.

[15] Jan-Werner Müller, 'The Promise of Demoi-cracy: Diversity and Domination in the European Public Order', in Jürgen Neyer and Antje Wiener (eds.), *The Political Theory of the European Union* (Oxford: Oxford University Press, 2010); Kalypso Nicolaïdis, 'The Idea of European Demoicracy', in Julie Dickson and Pavlos Eleftheriadis (eds.), *Philosophical Foundations of European Union Law* (Oxford: Oxford University Press, 2012), pp. 247–274; Francis Cheneval and Frank Schimmelfennig, 'The Case for Demoicracy in the European Union', *Journal of Common Market Studies*, 51 (2013), 334–350.

(*demoi*). This perspective supposes that cross-border government in democratic form has no need of a single 'sovereign' people whose common identity serves as its foundation. Demoicracy is a new type of 'confederation'. It is a political form that values pluralism, urges the mutual public recognition of differences and recognises both the growing interdependence of states and peoples and the possibility that multiple separate peoples can together effectively restrain and legitimate the power of cross-border governing institutions.

A *third* concern of the monitory democracy perspective is to pay close attention to these different approaches by asking whether their combined effect, paradoxically, is to disable the democratic imagination, essentially because all are wedded to some or other version of a place-based, territorial understanding of democracy. It should be noted that each regards democracy as popular self-government; but noteworthy is the way each is tacitly committed to a flat-earth view of democracy as grounded in a fixed physical location. Seen in this way, these attempts to breathe life back into the democratic project are better described as efforts at resistance and substantial repair, patched on to the crumbling edifice of territorial democracy. Their disagreements are in-house, in that they concern questions of feasibility and *size*. They ask: What is the optimum geographic size of a democracy? What are the comparative advantages and disadvantages enjoyed by democratic systems of different magnitude? Can a system of representative democracy become too large to be controlled by its citizens?[16]

A QUANTUM TURN

The principal difficulty with such common sense, 'Chinese box' questions concerning place and size, is their failure to grasp the multiple *spacetime dynamics* that are today simultaneously shaping, enervating and energising all real-world democracies. Here the monitory democracy standpoint attempts a quantum turn, initially by setting out to learn from the outlooks, concepts and methods developed within the exciting research fields of contemporary cosmology and particle physics. Their quantum perspectives serve as catalysts that prompt questions about the many ways in which the mentality of territorial democracy is insufficiently complex and

---

[16] Robert A. Dahl and Edward R. Tufte, *Size and Democracy* (Oxford: Oxford University Press, 1974).

(wilfully) ignorant of the '*quantum weirdness*'[17] of phenomena that require a fundamental rethinking of democracy as we have known it.

In matters of democracy, this quantum perspective aims to show how things are happening that are not merely stranger than theorists and practitioners once thought; many developments are far stranger than they can presently think. Trapped on scholarly flatlands, territorial democracy, with its common sense, three-dimensional fixation on latitude, longitude and altitude, ignores the need for more democracy within the expanding *multiverse* of differently sized, spatially entangled institutions and networks of power that straddle our Earth. As we will shortly see, territorial democracy also ignores new forms of democracy marked by a multidimensional dynamism: unusual forms of monitory democracy that operate within interconnected fields of power that stretch in all directions, from the local to the global, and beyond, and back. To speak metaphorically, in quantum language, the monitory democracy approach asks whether theories of territorial democracy ignore phenomena ranging from quarks, neutrinos and other elementary particles through to the planets, stars, dark energy zones, red dwarfs and Earth-size exo-planets within our rapidly expanding (and disappearing) galaxy, as we know it. The theory of monitory democracy goes further: models of territorial democracy, it suggests, fail to understand that these high-energy quanta operate in more than three dimensions, and that they are constantly in motion, vibrating and oscillating within quantum fields, pushing and pulling in multiple directions, often defying gravity, expanding the universe of democracy, nudging it towards unknown destinations.[18]

The monitory democracy perspective is deeply interested in the complex uncertainties generated by these quantum processes. Although such *indeterminacies* appear to render exact formulations and calculations impossible, theories and observations are necessary and feasible, just as they are in the research fields of contemporary cosmology and particle physics. Contemporary democratic theory is confronted by more than its share of undiscovered 'dark matter' but, so this new approach implies, puzzling unknowns must not prevent it from mapping the contours of present-day democracy with quantum characteristics. In a strange way, these unknowns harbour solutions: they are the bearers of puzzlement,

---

[17] David Z. Albert, *Quantum Mechanics and Experience* (Cambridge, MA: Harvard University Press, 1992).
[18] Steven Weinberg, *The Quantum Theory of Fields*, Vol. I (Cambridge: Cambridge University Press, 1995).

but they also prompt new questions, new ways of thinking and new solutions to strange anomalies and unsolved problems.

CASE STUDIES

In tandem with its mapping and dissection and critique of the territorial mentality, the theory of monitory democracy is deeply interested in several *new types of present-day democratic institutions* that are anomalous when measured by the old textbook standards of territorial democracy. Let us consider briefly three basic types of innovations that are indicative of a much broader trend. Historically speaking, these 'quantum' phenomena are without precedent: they squarely belong to the era of monitory democracy, and their theoretical and practical importance lies in their open defiance of the territorial mentality that continues to grip the democratic mentality.

Consider the birth of new forms of *bio*-democracy. These are modes of self-government that consider people, animals, trees, rocks and rivers as woven together in a common fabric and therefore reject the presumption that the land on which people dwell is simply definable 'territory', understood as a resource exploitable by states, corporations, citizens and representatives. Just as particle physics research successfully challenged the presumption that the atom is the ultimate building block of the universe, so the bio-democracy experiments think of themselves as embedded in living dynamic networks of human interactions that run 'deep' into the world of the non-human, and vice versa. Trend-setting experiments with indigenous self-government, for instance in the north-east Pacific archipelago Haida Gwaii (Islands of the People) and Uluru-Kata Tjuta National Park in central Australia, push in this direction. Striking is the way these democratic experiments are infused with a strong sense of (a) the dynamic and fragile complexity of our world; (b) the inter-connectivity and self-organising potential of all living and non-living elements within the political environment; and (c) the deep respect for the non-human and its legitimate 'right of representation' in human affairs. Equally striking is the way these experiments with indigenous self-government display (d) recognition of the non-linear effects and, hence, the chronic indeterminacy and potential instability within human efforts to govern themselves within ecological settings; (e) awareness of the fundamental importance of councils, cultural heritage forums and other methods of political decision making in refusing arbitrary power and promoting public awareness of all these qualities and boosting capacities for effectively handling non-linear and potentially unstable outcomes; and (f) deep acknowledgement of the difficulty of drawing strict boundaries between 'local' and 'far-away' peoples and political institutions and, hence, the imperative hereon to think of democracy in quantum terms of multiple spaces whose horizons stretch well beyond 'homeland' settings.

A second set of innovations can be described as *cross-border self-government*. These new democratic mechanisms operate in cross-border settings using artful methods of linking together far-flung geographical places across many different time zones. Think of the Bonn-based Forest Stewardship Council (FSC), a multi-stakeholder, global civil society organisation founded in the early 1990s to promote responsible management of the world's forests.[19] Comprising a decentralised set of global network partners, the FSC is an open membership, self-governing body committed to 'participation, democracy, equity and transparency'. Its members belong to one of three 'chambers' (social, economic, environmental). Their southern- and northern-hemisphere participants enjoy equal representation and voting rights in the highest decision-making body, the General Assembly. The FSC might be thought of as an exemplar of long-distance methods of handling power responsibly across borders, a type of political organisation that decides who gets what, when and how within multi-dimensional spaces not tied to territory in any straightforward, three-dimensional sense. Mindful of the dangers of arbitrary power, committed to self-government, the FSC does more than embrace a quantum 'multiple worlds' perspective, it supposes these spaces are dynamically interlinked. Motion is presumed to be inherent in these interconnected multiple worlds; what happens in one space is constantly shaped by things that happen in other spaces. *Quantum entanglement* is chronic. The universe of democracy is never local; despite doubts and protests expressed by democrats and democratic theorists still convinced that democracy must be grounded in a defined place, *superposition* and 'spooky action at a distance' among territorial democracies and democratic politics in defined places is becoming the norm.

When analysing these new forms of cross-border self-government, the monitory democracy perspective asks whether old dualisms such as time–place and time–space simply no longer make sense.[20] Might it be that not

---

[19] David Humphreys, *Forest Politics: The Evolution of International Cooperation* (London: Earthscan, 2008).

[20] The subject of time and monitory democracy is treated elsewhere in John Keane, 'A New Politics of Time', *The Conversation* (3 December 2016), https://theconversation.com/a-new-politics-of-time-69137.

territory, but multiple fields of spacetime are now the guiding quantum framework of these new democratic experiments, some of which have no fixed headquarters, or permanent address? In attempting to address this question, the polity known as the Central Tibetan Administration (CTA) has high relevance for the theory of monitory democracy. Some scholars might be tempted dismissively to liken it to an airport or motorway, a 'non-place',[21] and thus a non-phenomenon. Things are otherwise. The spacetime architecture of the CTA oozes quantum weirdness. It is in fact a novel form of parliamentary self-government beyond territory: now operating in northern India, its 'homeland' lies elsewhere, across borders, in other geographic places ('historic Tibet'). The polity operates in the space of another time: an imaginary homeland positioned in a distant future. Legislative authority is vested in the CTA parliament, which is popularly elected every five years by exiled citizens living in many different foreign countries. Its members are constantly on the move. Rights of representation in the legislature are shared by geographic constituencies (deputies from Europe and North America) and functional groupings (different schools of Buddhism, and the pre-Buddhist Bon faith). In accordance with a written constitution, citizenship is granted to any person (or their offspring) born in the imaginary future homeland; in practice, since proof of place of birth is often difficult, citizenship is established by interview, conducted at one of many government offices worldwide. Striking is the way many citizens value democracy because they regard their lives as inconstant, as permanently impermanent. Mandated by the 14th Dalai Lama, democracy is seen as more than the champion of equality of individuals and compassion and concern for all human and non-human beings.[22] Democracy is considered the guardian of impermanence – a warning of the dangers of attachment (to worldly power), a positive guarantor of flux and fluidity, a living reminder to citizens that they belong to a future world prefigured by a present-day world in which nothing is essentially itself.

A third set of democratic innovations centres on *mobile elections*. A possible objection to monitory democracy is that bio-democracy and cross-border self-government with quantum characteristics are of marginal scholarly importance, at least when compared with the presumed

---

[21] Marc Augé, *Non-Places: An Introduction to Supermodernity* (London: Verso, 1995).
[22] His Holiness the Dalai Lama, 'Buddhism, Asian Values, and Democracy', *Journal of Democracy*, 10 (1999), 3–7; and Stephanie Roemer, *The Tibetan Government-in-Exile* (Abingdon: Routledge, 2008).

wellspring of democracy: periodic elections. The fulcrum point of contemporary democracy (so the orthodox argument runs) remains elections in fixed territorial settings. The theory of monitory democracy explores a counter-hypothesis: elections are marked increasingly by quantum characteristics. Consider, for instance, the ways in which campaigns, voters and political parties regularly feel the pinch of what quantum physicists call the *principle of non-locality*: just as experimental fiddling with one particle instantly alters the behaviour of its sister particles elsewhere, so non-local effects are woven through the universe of elections.[23] The theory of monitory democracy accepts that the principle of 'free and fair elections' remains important for democracy.[24] But it questions the territorial mentality of existing scholarly research on 'international opinion swings' and the 'neighbourhood effect' of 'free and fair' elections.[25] It notes the quantum dynamics of cross-border elections in multi-state polities (an obvious prototype is European Parliament elections), and of voting processes within international civil society organisations, such as the International Olympic Committee, whose executive bodies are subject to election by secret ballot, by a majority of votes cast, for limited terms of office. The monitory democracy approach is especially interested in the shaping effects of digital media and communicative abundance,[26] above all the opportunities they offer to campaigners, journalists and election monitors to intervene from a distance in local elections, which thereby become non-local affairs. The theory of monitory democracy draws attention to the virtually undocumented history of the multiple processes through which United States presidential elections, since the 1960s, have become deeply enfolded (implicate, as quantum experts say) in the affairs of other polities. Of central interest are cases of territorial state elections whose local dynamics are shaped in real time by non-local campaigning at a distance. The fiercely fought 2013 general election in Malaysia is a remarkable case in point. The first-time use of postal voting for all

---

[23] David Bohm, *Wholeness and the Implicate Order* (London: Routledge & Kegan Paul, 1980).
[24] John Keane, *A Short History of the Future of Democracy* (Amsterdam: Hans van Mierlo Stichting, 2016).
[25] Hee Min Kim and Richard C. Fording, 'Voter Ideology, the Economy, and the International Environment in Western Democracies, 1952–1989', *Political Behavior*, 23 (2001), 53–73.
[26] Manuel Castells, *Networks of Outrage and Hope: Social Movements in the Internet Age* (Cambridge: Polity Press, 2012); John Keane, *Democracy and Media Decadence* (Cambridge and New York: Cambridge University Press, 2013).

overseas Malaysians triggered what physicists call *'quantum tunneling'*: Malaysian citizens, candidates, campaigners, Election Commission staff, flashmobs and election monitors scrambling in all directions, travelling and messaging across borders, behaving in non-local ways, in far-flung contexts from Singapore and southern Thailand to Kalimantan in Indonesia.

POLITICAL IMPLICATIONS

The use of quantum perspectives to rethink the territorial mentality of representative democracy arguably offers descriptive, strategic and normative advantages. By harnessing the mentality and metaphors drawn from such fields as particle physics and cosmology, monitory democracy is an exercise in reshaping the democratic imaginary. It is an effort to show how monitory democracy can survive, and thrive, in the difficult conditions of the twenty-first century. Most obviously, the quantum turn helps free democratic politics from the grip of 'psephocracy', the floundering presumption that democracy, all things considered, ultimately is free and fair elections, periodic voting by citizens of a nation in territorially defined settings. With the help of quantum metaphors, monitory democracy implies a strategic and normative re-definition of democracy as much more, though nothing less, than free and fair elections. The re-definition recognises that elections are of declining importance in battles to restrain arbitrary power. The vision of monitory democracy is thus driven by a strong sense of urgency. It highlights the ways in which the spirit, language and institutions of democracy in territorial state form are being undermined and swamped by a variety of cross-border causes and causers. The theory of monitory democracy calls for bio-democracy and other emerging democratic alternatives to be taken seriously by scholars and democrats alike, not treated as marginal anomalies. It proposes that a quantum perspective, with its emphasis on the need to think in terms of differently sized and dynamically interconnected spaces, is better equipped to offer democracy a good chance of survival, especially in a world very different from the age of representative democracy: a twenty-first-century world shaped by powerful global corporations and dangerous heavily armed states, a planet bound together by instant cross-border communications and determined as well by global bodies such as the WHO, the IMF and the AIIB, webs of entangled cities and regional organisations, 'mini-lateral' arrangements, cross-border codes of conduct and networks of non-governmental citizen actors determined to humble those who presently abuse their power, with damaging consequences for millions of people and the environments in which they dwell.

The monitory democracy perspective is radical. It aims to have disruptive effects. It questions mainstream scholarly presumptions that theories of cross-border democracy are fated to fail because they run up against such intractable problems as public ignorance about global matters, the impossibility of assembling citizens as equal stakeholders, without majority tyranny, across territorial borders.[27] The theory of monitory democracy attempts to show, to the contrary, why the confinement of democracy to state barracks is having disabling effects on the democratic imagination and how it can be remedied positively. The quantum approach it embraces poses large and substantial questions as to whether it is possible, in these early decades of the twenty-first century, to re-define democracy, to effect its 'de-territorialisation'. Rephrased, the questions are thus: Can it be set loose on the world? Can democracy hereon be thought of as a never-ending political project through which flesh-and-blood people, and their representatives, together seek public controls over the exercise of power, wherever it is exercised, in non-local ways, in a multiverse of interconnected spacetime settings?

A theory of democracy with quantum characteristics offers new and exciting ways of ensuring, in an age of post-sovereignty, that the spirit and substance of democracy can survive and thrive under pressure from its growing entanglement within webs of arbitrary power backed by space- and time-shrinking flows of mediated communication. It should be emphasised that the quantum theory of democracy is not to be confused with place-based 'mixed constitution' (Polybius) solutions. Armed with quantum metaphors, monitory democracy is more dynamic, more radically plural, more recursive and more alert to contradiction and self-contradiction. Within (say) the Asia and Pacific region, and within the wider global order, the vision of monitory democracy is quite at home within entangled fields of decision making, demarcation disputes and power struggles. It is comfortable with the strange and unfamiliar principle that power can legitimately be exercised, monitored and restrained in multiple spacetime settings by citizens and representatives who will never meet each other in their lives. The preoccupation of monitory democracy with spacetime dynamics means that it is keenly sensitive to the worrying absence of democratic mechanisms in such key

---

[27] Thomas Christiano, 'A Democratic Theory of Territory and Some Puzzles about Global Democracy', *Journal of Social Philosophy*, 37 (2006), 81–107.

policy areas as the banking/credit sector, the global arms industry, regional trade deals and territorial states' handling of stateless refugees. Within these and other fields of power, it sets its sights on greater public accountability of those who rule over others, and the biomes in which they live. Monitory democracy with quantum characteristics urges that growing numbers of political problems can be resolved openly and justly only within and among sub-state, regional and global spaces that are in perpetual motion. That is why it champions a 'polycentric' understanding of democracy. It joins Elinor Ostrom and others in the conviction that the future of democracy requires not only a fundamental break with territorial 'sovereignty' thinking, but also new efforts to cultivate a rich mixture of democratic innovations, within multiple spacetime settings, linked together through free information flows, nurtured by the confidence that multi-scalar public monitoring and restraint of arbitrary power have definite problem-solving advantages over more centralised and state-centred political methods.[28]

---

[28] Elinor Ostrom, *A Polycentric Approach for Coping with Climate Change* (Washington, DC: The World Bank, 2009).

11

The European Citizen, 1970–2005

> Since new citizens cannot be created all at once, you must begin by making use of those who exist, and to offer a new path for their hopes is the way to make them want to follow it...
>
> Jean-Jacques Rousseau, Considérations sur le gouvernement de Pologne (1772)

Nearly half a century ago, the French scholar and publicist Raymond Aron poured ice-cold water on a brand new idea at its moment of birth. 'There are no such animals as "European citizens"', wrote Aron. 'There are only French, German, or Italian citizens.'[1] If he were still with us today, Raymond Aron would be forced to concede that a new political animal has since been born. The European citizen speaks in a very faint voice and in many different languages, but her talk of European citizenship can nevertheless be heard in various quarters. Its presence is felt in university teaching and research initiatives; within school curricula like the Council of Europe's *Speak Out on European Citizenship* programme; in multi-media messaging and street demonstrations; and in the manifestos of some political parties and in parliamentary debates. European citizenship functions as a 'trigger norm' in various fields of law covering such matters as consumer protection, asylum and immigration;[2] and, of course, the principle of European citizenship has an important place in the

---

[1] Raymond Aron, 'Is Multinational Citizenship Possible?', *Social Research*, 41 (1974), 638–656, at 652–653.
[2] Stephan Wernicke, 'Au nom de qui? The European Court of Justice between Member States, Civil Societies and Union Citizens', *European Law Journal*, 13 (2007), 380–407.

Treaty of Amsterdam (signed in October 1997); in the reiteration of 'citizenship of the Union' in the Nice Treaty (signed in February 2001); and (most comprehensively) in the draft Constitution that encountered ratification difficulties during the first half of 2005, and in the subsequently approved Treaty of Lisbon. Whatever long-term effects the latter Treaty may have on the project of European integration, it is safe to say that Raymond Aron was mistaken: despite all the misfortunes that befell Europe during the past decade,[3] there is today talk and some institutional backing and action in support of 'European citizenship'. The theory and practice of European citizenship deals a blow to the presumption that citizenship is the property of bordered 'sovereign' states. Its novelty, in the history of European integration, is also indisputable. There have so far been few Big Ideas invented by the engineers of integration, but this one – alongside such slogans as 'The Community of Europe' and the vision of a 'Single Market' – arguably came to rank as among the most important during the past few decades, despite the fact, emphasised throughout the pages to come, that the project of European citizenship is poorly defined, challenged by processes of dis-integration and certainly in need of intellectual and political friends.[4]

RETHINKING CITIZENSHIP, ACROSS BORDERS

Let us begin with its friends: who were the champions of European citizenship during the period under review? Which people, groups and organisations tried to disprove Raymond Aron's judgement? Put most simply, the answer is: those who foresaw that the stresses and strains of European integration would foster the need for a new collective sense of purpose that would bind the disparate populations of Europe together into some higher European unity; in other words, those who spotted that the Monnet model of European integration would burn out – that regulatory effectiveness and economic achievements would not be enough because integration would stimulate public demands for having a say in decision making, as came to happen, sometimes with dramatic effects. The foresight of the supporters of European citizenship was rewarded

---

[3] A summary of these difficulties is presented in John Keane, 'Europe is Suffering a Multi-Morbidity Crisis: A Conversation with Claus Offe in Berlin' (February 1, 2017), www.huffingtonpost.com/the-conversation-global/europe-is-suffering-multi_b_14521262.html

[4] Jan Zielonka, *Is the EU Doomed?* (Cambridge: Polity Press, 2014) and *Counter-Revolution: Liberal Europe in Retreat* (Oxford: Oxford University Press, 2018).

which is why, before it is too late, and details dissolve in the mists of time, democrats, historians, political thinkers and others need to record the 35-year-long history of how the project of European citizenship happened.

Such a history would include the path-breaking recommendations to the 1974 Paris meeting of the European Council, where for the first time there was talk of the importance of increasing mobility as a source of 'European consciousness and the development of European citizenship'; and the Tindemans Report,[5] where the aim of creating a political community of citizens was first clearly articulated. Appeals to 'European citizenship' later appeared in a wide variety of contexts: for instance, in Helmut Kohl's campaign in favour of 'Unionsbürgerschaft' in 1990, which is perhaps the first recorded case where the language of European citizenship became part of an active dialogue between citizens and their government; and in a string of judgements issued by the European Court of Justice, where perhaps most progress was made in defining and extending new citizenship entitlements and duties to the peoples of the European Union. The whole effort to define 'the European citizen' became prominent in Article 9 of the Treaty of Amsterdam, which declared: 'Citizenship of the Union is hereby established. Every person holding the nationality of a Member State shall be a citizen of the Union.' That provision specified that the citizens of the new Union would enjoy freedoms that included the qualified right to move and reside freely within the territory of the Member States; the right of European citizens to have access to an ombudsman in any of the official languages and to petition the European Parliament, to vote and stand for municipal elections – and to vote in European elections – while resident in Member States of which they are not nationals. It also included their right, at home and abroad, to consular representation and diplomatic protection by any Member State. The appended Charter of Fundamental Rights in the draft Constitution added other, more forward-looking entitlements, for instance, the 'right to good administration'. The same line of citizen-based reasoning was evident in the Treaty of Lisbon, signed in mid-December 2007. Introduced to equip 'the Union with the legal framework and tools necessary to meet future challenges and to respond to citizens' demands', the Treaty provided for a strengthened European Parliament, placing it on an equal footing with the Council for the bulk of Union legislation, the EU budget

---

[5] Leo Tindemans, 'European Union. Report by Mr Leo Tindemans, Prime Minister of Belgium, to the European Council', *Bulletin of the European Communities*, Supplement 1/76, (1975), Brussels.

and international agreements; extended qualified majority voting; introduced a Charter of Fundamental Rights into European primary law; and provided for the use of a Citizens' Initiative, for the purpose of calling on the Commission to bring forward new policy proposals.

Note that these citizens' entitlements were in each and every case *political* in the richest meanings of the word. This is consistent with the fact, in the European region, that the etymological roots of the word citizenship refer back to the citizen (*civis*) who dwells and co-operates with others within a city (*civitas*).[6] Citizenship is an abstract or 'imagined' identity – a self-reflexive form of civic allegiance – that replaces or transcends the 'natural', more or less taken-for-granted bonds of household or tribe or local community. Rephrased: from Aristotle to the Treaty of Lisbon via Roman law, the twelfth-century revival of neo-Roman jurisprudence, the Italian city-states, the self-governing towns of Zeeland and Holland, the Polish *Sejm*, to the slogans of the English and French revolutionaries – in all of these contexts to be a citizen meant being an individual who belongs to a *political community of common laws* and thereby shares its *entitlements and duties equally with others*. When Aristotle defined a citizen as anyone who can 'hold office', he invoked a thought that still lives on: to be a citizen is not to be a powerless subject. It rather entails equal opportunities of access to the politically defined rights and duties of the polity. To enjoy the status of a citizen is to de-nature power, to engage freely and equally with others by exercising the power to define how to live together peacefully, to decide who should get what when and how. Citizenship is not just about legal decisions or governmental policymaking and implementation. According to some old and venerable traditions of European thinking, it is their condition of possibility.

CHALLENGES

If politics lies at the heart of the meaning of the term citizenship, then it is obvious that in the years after 1970 the project of European citizenship resembled the wonderful fable told by José Saramago's *Tale of an*

---

[6] Max Weber, *Economy and Society: An Outline of Interpretive Sociology*, Vol. II (Berkeley, CA: University of California Press, 1978), pp. 1212–1372; Quentin Skinner and Bo Strath (eds.), *States and Citizens* (Cambridge: Cambridge University Press, 2003); and John Keane (ed.), *Civil Society: Berlin Perspectives* (New York and Oxford: Berghahn Press, 2006).

Unknown Island: it was a political odyssey, an exercise in making up rules along the way, an encounter with new problems for which there were no names, let alone automatic or easy solutions. During this period, the vision of European citizenship was confronted by a bundle of challenges, for which there were no straightforward resolutions on the horizon. It may be that these challenges – four of them are outlined below – will help to define something like a new political vision, even a political programme that could lead, if it were successful, to the reshaping and positive revaluation of 'Europe'. Time will tell.

So during the years 1970–2005 what were the most pressing challenges faced by the novel vision of European citizenship?

The first had to do with the fact that European citizenship was (and remains) a *derived* and not an independent legal status. The Treaty of Amsterdam and the Lisbon Treaty granted 'citizenship of the European Union' to any person having the nationality of a Member State, but it excluded the harmonisation of powers to grant nationality. It followed that if third-country nationals (at the time, there were more than 15 million legally resident in the Union) wished to become European citizens then they first had to acquire the citizenship of a Member State. The first point, rephrased, is this: because of its political dependence upon Member States, the vision of European citizenship was perforce in the hands of the living-dead past. Each Member State contained not only different and contested historical understandings of actually existing citizenship rights and duties. There was also great variation of the historical 'depth' and contemporary 'feeling' for citizenship, especially when it was considered as a meaningful normative vision. It was upon this uneven and jagged foundation – for the first time anywhere in the world – that an overarching vision of *European* citizenship was to be built.

It remains to be seen whether these diverse meanings and feelings for 'citizenship of the Union' will prove durable, but what became clear during this period is the urgent need for a new history of citizenship in the European region. The task of satisfying that need is neither easy nor straightforward. While we have various studies of the history of citizenship of particular countries or regions,[7] no serious attempt has yet been

---

[7] Charles Tilly and Michael Hanagan (eds.), *Extending Citizenship, Reconfiguring States* (Lanham, MD: Rowman & Littlefield, 1999); Simon Schama, *Citizens: A Chronicle of the French Revolution* (New York: Knopf, 1989); Milan Podunavac, 'The Principles of Citizenship and Pluralism in Identity', in Zagorka Golubović and George F. McLean (eds.), *Models of Identities in Postcommunist Societies* (Washington, DC: Council for Research in Values and Philosophy, 2003).

made to write a comparative European history of the notion of citizenship in the different languages of the region. Such a forward-looking history of citizenship – a present-day history of the future – would need to overcome the clichéd distinctions between 'eastern' and 'western' Europe and conventional divisions among its Member States (as if there were only 'French, German or Italian citizens', to repeat the words of Raymond Aron). It would initially do so by developing a typology of the different languages and institutions of citizenship in various regions of Europe. The research would crosscut and so challenge conventional geographical units of comparison by concentrating on regions of Europe (such as the Mediterranean basin) or combinations of regions (south-eastern and northern Europe) that have never before been systematically compared.

This new history of citizenship would of course need to note the earlier concerns of Max Weber and others by asking whether, or to what extent, the appearance of citizenship traditions within the European region was unique in world-historical or global terms. The conventional wisdom is that only in Europe did the constellation of preconditions for (modern) citizenship emerge: territorially bounded, law-governed states; the institutional separation of the sacred and the profane followed by secularisation; the emergence of civil societies; and the invention of representative government, power-sharing assemblies, political parties and periodic elections.

A reconsideration of citizenship in Europe would need to test this wisdom, in part by pursuing a comparative investigation of analogous or parallel traditions of citizenship in other regions of the world. Some consideration could be given – two randomly chosen examples can be mentioned briefly – to competing Chinese legal and political traditions of citizenship (*shimin shehui* ['city-people's society'] and *gongmin shehui* ['citizen's society']), for instance as they have been shaped by the Daoist celebration of natural, virtually anarchistic spontaneity, legalist defences of centralised political order, and the 'middle way' of Confucianism, with its focus upon moral cultivation and legitimate power in constitutional form. Special emphasis would need to be given to the reworking of these traditions during the early twentieth-century nationalist revolution – the so-called 'Chinese awakening' – in favour of the unity and sovereignty of a Chinese territorial state, and the continuing ripple effects of this revolution into the twenty-first century.[8]

---

[8] John Fitzgerald, *Awakening China: Politics, Culture and Class in the Nationalist Revolution* (Stanford, CA: Stanford University Press, 1996); Richard Madsen, 'Confucian

A global re-examination of citizenship in Europe might give consideration as well to the old politico-legal traditions of the Islamic world, especially (given its geographic proximity and socio-cultural influence upon Europe) the Ottoman Empire. The research would revisit the conventional claim that the world of Islam, until its colonisation by European powers, contained no strongly developed endogenous politico-legal traditions of citizenship. A careful eye would need to be trained upon the mounting counter-evidence, provided by recent scholarship, of well-developed practices of open-ended political communities structured by clusters of religiously sanctioned urban institutions: the *umma* (the community of believers); an autonomous civic system of *sharia* laws; the cultivation of social solidarity and social pluralism through the *waqf* foundations and Sufi brotherhoods (*turuq*); and the cultivation of public spheres for the purpose of monitoring and checking the exercise of political power.[9]

It is probable that such global comparisons would show that Europe is *not* exceptional in developing shared traditions of belief in the equality of citizens living within legally defined political communities. But – to take a different tack – among the striking and unique features of the European region is the way in which Europeans at various times and in different places have *self-reflexively* meant different and conflicting things when they referred to 'citizens' and 'citizenship'. In Europe, that is to say, the languages of citizenship have been – and continue to be – semantically antagonistic, politically contested and unequally distributed in a geographic sense. So we come to a working hypothesis: during modern times, five different, partly overlapping languages of citizenship have played a

---

Conceptions of Civil Society', in Simone Chambers and Will Kymlicka (eds.), *Alternative Conceptions of Civil Society* (Princeton, NJ: Princeton University Press, 2002), pp. 190–206; Thomas A. Metzger, 'Modern Chinese Utopianism and the Western Concept of Civil Society', in San-ching Chen (ed.), *Kuo T'ing-i hsien-sheng chiu-chih tan-ch'en chi-nien lun-wen-chi, Papers Commemorating the Ninetieth Birthday of Prof. Kuo Ting-yee*, Vol. II (Taipei: Institute of Modern History, Academia Sinica, 1995), pp. 273–312.

[9] Amir Arjomand, 'Philanthropy, the Law, and Public Policy in the Islamic World before the Modern Era', in Warren F. Ilchman, Stanley N. Katz and Edward L. Queen (eds.), *Philanthropy in the World's Traditions* (Bloomington, IN: Indiana University Press, 1998); Aziz Al-Azmeh, *Muslim Kingship: Power and the Sacred in Muslim, Christian and Pagan Politics* (London: Tauris, 1997); Marshall G.S. Hodgson, *The Venture of Islam* (Chicago, IL: University of Chicago Press, 1974); Miriam Hoexter et al. (eds.), *The Public Sphere in Muslim Societies* (Albany, NY: State University of New York Press, 2002); Ira M. Lapidus, *A History of Islamic Societies* (Cambridge: Cambridge University Press, 1988). See also John Keane, *The Life and Death of Democracy* (London and New York: Simon & Schuster, 2009), part 1.

key role in shaping the institutions of government and civil society of Europe as we know it today.

Listed as 'ideal-types', these citizenship languages first of all include the understanding of *citizenship as obedience to authoritarian state structures*. According to this first view, articulated for instance in Jean Bodin's *Six livres de la république* (1576; occasioned by the Huguenot rebellions) and Thomas Hobbes' *De Cive* (1642; inspired by the outbreak of civil war in Britain), political stability requires subjects' obedience to the institutions of the territorially defined state and its sovereign powers backed up by the sword. Citizenship implies the passive subordination of subjects who consider themselves duty-bound to an absolutist regime, within which law is the expression of the sovereign's will, and subject only to certain God-given natural laws.[10] The citizen as subject enjoys no rights of public criticism or disobedience or rebellion; faction and civil strife are to be avoided, since they are causes of disorder, cruelty and injustice. The (male) citizen is subject unconditionally to the powers and laws of the state, which in turn enables him to enjoy the institutions of private life, especially through the family, private property and certain religious freedoms. Citizenship as a compulsory form of political-legal identity is paramount; plural identities are restricted and tightly monitored. Civil society understood as a complex ensemble of non-governmental identities is absent.

Traces of this statist understanding of citizenship are still today evident in certain linguistic usages, for instance in the German expressions *Staatsangehörigkeit* (citizenship; nationality) and *Staatsbürger einer Monarchie* (subject of a monarchy); in Article 3 of the Slovenian constitution, which speaks of 'a state of all its [male and female] citizens' (*država vseh državljank in državljanov*); and in the Croatian word for citizen, *državljanin* (from *država*, meaning 'state'). In each case, the connotations differ from a second understanding of citizenship: *citizenship as membership of a well-governed polity that avoids despotism by defining and protecting the freedoms and virtues of its leading social groups*. In this second understanding of citizenship, tensions between citizenship and social identities are evident. Citizenship is seen to be

---

[10] Peter Riesenberg, *Citizenship in the Western Tradition* (Chapel Hill, NC: University of North Carolina Press, 1992); Michael Stolleis, *Geschichte des öffentlichen Rechts in Deutschland, Volume II, 1800–1914* (Munich: Beck, 1992); Manfred Riedel, *Zwischen Tradition und Revolution: Studien zu Hegels Rechtsphilosophie* (Stuttgart: Klett-Cotta, 1982).

nurtured through polities, but only on the basis of organised power sharing with *non-governmental* organisations and ways of life. Such polities first appeared in the Iberian peninsula during the twelfth century, where in the adjoining kingdoms of Leon and Castile public recognition was given to the customary right of representatives (*procuradores*) to gather and to present petitions, and to insist that their acceptance by a parliament (*cortes*) implied that they had binding legal effect upon all members of the polity.[11] Citizenship – the entitlements and duties of all to live within a political community of laws – was negotiated through parliaments, which were the site of intense bargaining about the overall welfare of the realm. Parliaments ratified treaties and debated questions of war and peace. They appointed ambassadors and exercised control over the naturalisation of strangers entering the kingdom. New or extraordinary taxes could not be levied without their prior approval, and their consent was required as well for proposed changes in either their rate or their mode of collection. Some early parliaments even enjoyed the power to investigate allegations of breaches of the law by officials or the monarch, and to call for justice in cases of wrongdoing. In all these customs – the Croatian thinker Iurii Krizhanich's *Politika* (1670) and Montesquieu's *De l'esprit des lois* (1748) later spotted – citizenship implied freedom from political despotism through the cultivation 'from below' of political representation and *social limitations upon power*.

A third approach, the republican, defines *citizenship as full and equal membership of a free and indivisible republic*. The ideal polity is not a monarchy, but a commonwealth of laws, one that is made and continually re-made by citizens and their representatives. Citizenship is the equal enjoyment of rights and duties defined by public consent, not dutiful obedience. Note that citizenship is an all-encompassing identity: the 'faction' and division of social life, especially the rifts that stem from property, are to be kept out of and beneath political life. Citizens certainly enjoy such freedoms as those of *habeas corpus*, liberty of the press, private property, periodic elections, even the right to resist arbitrary government, if need be through revolutionary force that aims to eliminate *'incivisme'*. But these same citizens are entitled to resist only insofar as they are loyally bound to the higher order of the polity, which knows no division between government and civil society. Examples of this demanding normative ideal of citizenship include George Buchanan's

---

[11] Keane, *The Life and Death of Democracy*, part 2.

De Iure Regni apud Scotos (1579); Jean-Jacques Rousseau, *Du contrat social* (1762); and Aleksandr Radischev, *A Voyage from St. Petersburg to Moscow* (1790). Traces of this republican version of citizenship as 'active citizenship' are evident, for instance, in Dutch references to *burger* (citizen) and *burgerschap* (citizenship), which terms carry no negative connotations of 'bourgeois'. Note that especially during the eighteenth century, this republican vision of citizenship became cosmopolitan: the freedoms and corresponding duties of citizenship were seen to criss-cross borders. Interesting and important cases include the transformation during the 1790s of the Swedish language of *medborgare* (citizen) and *medborgarskap* (citizenship). From the early sixteenth century, they denote the common relationship enjoyed by burghers of the same town; during the eighteenth-century these terms are transformed – and mixed with the term for 'subject' (*undersåte*) – to mean persons that by virtue of certain rights and duties belong to a particular state; while during the 1790s, this old language of citizenship is radicalised through proliferating references to *werldsborgare* (citizen of the world).[12] A similar transformation is evident in the final draft of the Girondin constitution of 1791, which stipulated that any foreigner wishing to reside in France and willing to take the civic oath could be granted naturalisation by the Legislative Assembly (hence the famous remark of Jean Lambert Tallien: 'The only foreigners in France are those who are bad citizens'). This cosmopolitan turn was evident as well in the first outlines of a philosophical vision of citizenship across borders sketched in Johannes Althusius, *Politica Methodice Digesta* (1603) and later developed in the writings of Immanuel Kant (e.g., *Idee zu einer allgemeinen Geschichte in weltbürgerlicher Absicht* [1784]) in defence of a 'law of world citizenship' (*ius cosmopoliticum*) which binds citizens and states together into a higher republican commonwealth of states.

The fourth – and perhaps most influential – understanding of citizenship is nation-centred. It formed as an abreaction to talk of world citizenship. It defines *citizenship as the cultivation of the sovereign powers of the nation by means of state power legitimated through national symbols*. So understood, citizenship reveals the strong influence of the late eighteenth-century doctrine of national self-determination.[13] Each nation is said to

---

[12] Peter Hallberg, *Age of Liberty: Social Upheaval, History Writing and the New Public Sphere in Sweden, 1740–1792* (Stockholm Universitet, 2003).
[13] See John Keane, 'Nations, Nationalism and European Citizens', in Sukumar Periwal (ed.), *Notions of Nationalism* (Budapest: Central European Press, 1995), pp. 182–207.

be entitled to govern itself through territorially defined institutions of government and law. Citizens enjoy their freedoms and shoulder their burdens as equal members of *nation-states*. In practice, struggles for national self-determination created their own symbolic universe, often by assimilating sacred liturgies and organisational models from the Christian tradition, then adapting and transforming them into secular forms. National identity – considered as the most basic identity – functioned as a 'civil religion' that rendered the politics of citizenship into a component of the educational mission of the state. Citizenship was seen to require the cultivation of a political community of believers, an idealised *people* united in the cult of the 'patriotic religion' (Mazzini) that could embrace the whole of Europe. This understanding of *nation-state-centred citizenship* has had a marked effect on contemporary languages of citizenship. An example is the 'nationalisation' and partial replacement of such terms (in the language of Serbian, for instance) as *stanovnik* (citizen, from the verb *stanovati*, meaning 'to inhabit'), *stanovnik grada* ('one who lives in a city'), and *gradjanin* (citizen), with *državljanin* (from *država*, meaning state, hence 'citizen of a state'). Sometimes the meaning of citizenship has been so 'nationalised' that many contemporary Europeans either use the terms 'citizenship' and 'nationality' interchangeably, as when they carry or produce their passports, or (as in Hungarian) see citizens (*állampolgár*) and citizenship (*állampolgárság*) as creatures of the territorial state (*állam*).

Finally – and most familiar to Europeans today – is the understanding of citizenship as the cultivation of civil, political and social rights and duties within a territorial state shaped by national customs and governed by democratic procedures. This understanding of citizenship belongs to the era of representative democracy. It is the only understanding that openly recognises and sanctions multiple social identities. It had its immediate roots within battles to extend the franchise and to strengthen municipal self-government. It came relatively late to the European region, being confined mainly to the past one-and-a-half centuries. Its contours appear strongly within contemporary appeals to 'informed citizens' and to 'citizenship' (*cittadinanza*; *citoyenneté*; *Staatsbürgerschaft*), understood as the right and duty to vote, to engage in jury service and to respect civil liberties. The ideal of democratic citizenship was most famously expressed in T.H. Marshall's classic reflections on citizenship. They analyse, for the case of Britain, the historical evolution of bundles of citizenship entitlements, from legally guaranteed civil rights that ensure freedom from arbitrary government and the enjoyment of civil society (habeas corpus, private property, the right of association) to political rights that enable citizens to exercise, directly and indirectly, control over their state institutions by means of votes, independent political parties and jury service; and to the enjoyment of social rights to family life (the principal domain of women), employment in the labour market, the freedom to join trade unions, and state-guaranteed education and health care for all citizens, regardless of their income or wealth.[14]

MONNET

The first intellectual and practical challenge that faced the vision of European citizenship during its first several decades might be summarised thus: how to develop a viable and publicly attractive vision of citizenship within a cluttered European heritage; that is, within a kaleidoscope of sometimes overlapping, sometimes conflicting traditions of citizenship that have deep roots, that therefore grant a voice to the past to ensure that it lives on beyond the territorial state level.

Of course, during the period 1970–2005 these different traditions of citizenship began to overlap and criss-cross state borders. They unfolded within the framework of an emergent polity, loosely called 'Europe'. This polity was born nearly seven decades ago in the circumstances of total war, concentration camps, and devastated economies. Underground visions of a 'united Europe', the early failures (during the 1940s) to institutionalise these grand visions, and American efforts (e.g. the Marshall Plan) to 'rescue' Europe from Soviet domination all combined to encourage the first modest efforts to develop European-wide initiatives in strictly limited policy areas, such as coal, iron and steel production, and agriculture and transportation.[15] These *petits pas* (Monnet) were to have much bigger effects. They would eventually lead to the voluntary creation of a new form of multi-layered and multi-jurisdictional polity that was both rooted within and stood 'above' the structures of its Member States. Throughout the period under review here, there was no convincing political science term for this polity. The main crucible of European citizenship, the European Union, was neither a federation nor a confederation

---

[14] T.H. Marshall, *Citizenship and Social Class and Other Essays* (Cambridge: Cambridge University Press, 1951).
[15] Derek W. Urwin, *The Community of Europe: A History of European Integration Since 1945*, 2nd edn (London: Longman, 1995).

nor an empire nor a territorial macro-state. It resembled a *condominio*[16] marked by multi-tiered structures of governance whose competence cut through and across the powers of its Member States. The polity was defined by legal rules and processes, and by compulsory acceptance of the *acquis communautaires*. It became a polity that lacked a clearly defined supreme authority or a stable, contiguous territory; a polity that had no effective monopoly over the legitimate means of coercion and had no standing army and only a limited defence strategy and an uncertain identity in world affairs (despite the Lisbon Treaty provision for a new High Representative of the Union in foreign affairs and security policy). Finally – here we come to a second challenge confronting the project of European citizenship – Europe was a political form that was heavily, and increasingly, dependent upon the *sub-governmental dynamics* of an emergent European civil society.

From its inception, the process of European political integration was guided by the presumption that institution building from above could dispense with the bottom-up process of public legitimation of governmental power. This Monnet model, as it has been called, certainly took for granted the existence of vibrant democratic mechanisms operating at the Member State level. But this model supposed not only that an ever stronger net of European-level institutions could be cast over its Member States, the whole process was also supposed to be separable from the time-wasting and controversy-producing mechanisms of public accountability that would otherwise slow down and unnecessarily complicate the complex processes of bargaining and agreement formation so necessary if Europe was to shake off the legacy of war and totalitarianism, as well as create a single, integrated European market. The political legitimacy of Europe was to be supplied by shame and wealth. Painful memories and the strong sense of shame generated by the background experience of total war, cruelty and several types of totalitarian rule would suffice – like a negative counterfactual – to bind the peoples and governments of Europe together. Similar conglomerating effects upon the peoples and institutions of the region would flow from the positive investment, production, trade and consumption benefits of supra-national integration – or so it was supposed.

---

[16] Philippe Schmitter, *How to Democratize the European Union ... and Why Bother?* (Lanham, MD: Rowman & Littlefield, 2000); Philippe Schmitter and Alexander H. Trechsel, *The Future of Democracy in Europe: Trends, Analyses and Reforms* (Strasbourg: Council of Europe Publications, 2004).

11 The European Citizen, 1970–2005

The Monnet model of European integration was in reality always subject to the push-pull forces of domestic politics within the Member States, but from roughly the end of the 1970s it began visibly to disintegrate. Perceptions grew, both among policymakers and policytakers, that the European project had not won the trust and loyalty of its subjects. There was mounting awareness that the character of the European process of political integration and its modes of legitimation were closely intertwined. Although differently envisaged at the beginning, the project had initially concentrated upon economic integration, understood in terms of the regional enlargement of political power in order to deregulate markets. An immediate consequence of this preoccupation with the creation of a single market was the perceived neglect of government. A further, intensive round of political integration thus became an urgent priority. But with further steps toward political integration, important and difficult questions about the democratic accountability of the new political structures came to the table. European integration was confronted by diffuse social grumblings, active political refusals to consent – as in the French and Dutch referendum votes against the draft Constitution during the first half of 2005 – and the generalised sense that the institutions of government do not rest upon the articulated will of a European *dēmos* or *dēmoi*.

This process of de-legitimation arguably deepened with the creation of a European Parliament and (in 1979) the holding of the first European elections. For the first time, the structures and ethos of the European integration process became subject to cross-border democratic mechanisms of free and fair elections, open public debate and parliamentary supervision – all of which enabled the articulation of public grumblings and reticence about Europe. The time between the 1987 Single European Act and the Amsterdam Treaty of Union most definitely saw an upsurge of public withdrawal, public controversy and public involvement through the use of referenda, parliamentary debate and the formation of many thousands of civil society organisations concerned to lobby the European institutions. The policy failures of the European Community during the violent break-up of Yugoslavia deepened the feelings in some quarters that the supra-national structures were distant and not wholly legitimate, and therefore ineffective. The end stage of this growing legitimacy problem was the politically embattled, double-barrelled effort to win acceptance of a written constitution and to create and expand a common currency designed both to underpin a single, integrated market and to create a common bond of loyalty among the populations of the region.

More than any previous policy initiatives, the quest for a written constitution and currency union touched raw nerves, tapped deep feelings of national sentiment – and compounded the sense that the whole European integration process was in need of a new ethos, a new guiding vision, a collective sense of purpose that binds the disparate populations of Europe into some higher European unity. The traditional legitimation model of European integration – legitimation by historical shame, regulatory effectiveness and economic achievements – was in decline. With increasing political integration, public demand for having a say in decision-making increased. There was a growing consensus that the European polity now needed support – through the cultivation of new collective identities, a sense of political community and – according to some – new forms of European citizenship.

But the question was whether or not the norm of European citizenship could successfully function as both a new legal status and a meaningfully lived mode of legitimation? To what extent was European citizenship likely to operate as a guarantee of the primacy of European law, or of property rights or of strategies for democratisation? Would European citizenship have important implications for social policy, or immigration rights and procedures? Or was European citizenship (as Ralf Dahrendorf and others claimed) fated to be a 'soft' form of citizenship – 'soft' in the sense that it would remain dependent empirically and normatively upon the primary determining power of citizenship dynamics within the Member States?

EUROPEAN CIVIL SOCIETY

Looking back on this period, satisfactory answers to such questions could only be given by first situating European citizenship within the wider context of its sub-governmental dynamics. It is still often held that European citizenship was largely due to political, legal and administrative instruments (*'Königsmechanismus'*) that had an impact 'from above', *against* a multitude of social and cultural interests and identities, divisions and fragmentations. According to this view, a common European sense of social and cultural citizenship was largely lacking – with little or no thrust towards a European citizenship developing 'from below'. There was some evidence in support of this view. European citizenship has indeed been strongly defined and promoted 'from above' through institutions such as intergovernmental conferences, the European Council and the European Court of Justice. For that reason, it seemed likely that for the foreseeable future European citizenship would have to accommodate a much greater diversity of political and legal forces than any national citizenship of previous centuries ever did. In contrast, both to its older state-centred or 'cosmopolitan' forms, efforts to render citizenship compatible with governmental diversity would be among the characteristics – and major challenges – of European citizenship. At the very least, as the Amsterdam Treaty of Union made clear, European citizenship would remain a *derivative* form of citizenship, one that was dependent upon the behaviour of Member States that retain the power to define the form and content of citizens' rights and duties.

Yet there was another side to the whole story of 'top-down' European integration: during the years after 1970, there were strong forces 'from below' that required and supported the emergence of European citizenship. These forces were bigger and wider than those generated by the Single European Act, which was largely a child of Mrs Thatcher's political imagination and no doubt (a grand irony here) for a time among the most radical contributions yet to the integration of Europe. There were, in addition to single market pressures, strong social and cultural trends towards the formation of a *European civil society*: a vast, dynamically interconnected and multi-layered European social space consisting of many thousands of non-governmental initiatives, networks, personalities, movements and organisations. This cross-border civil society was not completely congruent with the present-day European Union but its density was highest there, especially in the old Member States and several of the new accession states. This civil society comprised individuals, households, businesses, non-profit and non-governmental organisations, coalitions, conferences, social movements and cultural-religious groups. Their situated actions comprised the stuff out of which civil society is made and in turn feeds the work of charities, lobby groups, citizens' movements, independent media, trade unions and sporting bodies. During the period 1970 to 2005, the symbols of this civil society were breathtakingly diverse: Airbus, Nokia, UEFA, Wim Wenders, Médecins sans frontières, Benetton, IKEA, El Pais, Jürgen Schrempp, the Pope, Rem Koolhaas, a Berlin Philharmonic in the hands of Sir Simon Rattle, and a London Symphony Orchestra featuring a Russian double-bass player, a Maltese violinist of mixed Sicilian and Scottish origin, and a Serbian-born leader of the orchestra who was the bearer of a French passport.

This European civil society of course has a history. It is in fact an old and deep-rooted process, evident for instance in the anti-slavery initiatives, labour movement activities and demonstrations for peace on an international scale that date well back into the nineteenth century. There was however evidence that the 'socialisation of Europe' accelerated during the period under review. Thanks to such factors as market pressures, tourism fuelled by low-cost transportation, sporting events, travelling ideas, migrations and transnational networks of education, the density and complexity of border-transcending social relations grew rapidly. Whatever may be said about its 'harmonising' effects – think for a moment of the European flag, with its circle of twelve gold stars symbolising solidarity, harmony, perfection – this emergent European civil society was by no means a space of tranquillity. Civil society meant a tendency towards conflict, protest, contestation, and this conflict potential posed new theoretical and political challenges to the project of European citizenship. Due to the fact that it was embedded in civil society activities, European citizenship was citizenship with a difference. It was a form of citizenship that did not produce the harmony and homogeneity of a *Gemeinschaftsglaube* (Weber). European citizenship instead displayed *plural* qualities. It was expressive of *multiple, potentially conflicting identities*, something of a guarantee of the right of citizens to be *socially different* within the European Union.

The point can be put differently: the development of rules of European citizenship was a vital precondition of the nurturing of a European civil society because cross-border civil society activities, whether in business or sport or media or religion or education and research, required cross-border rules and regulations which, when taken together and handled politically, added to the momentum of European citizenship. It was clear from the outset that the future European citizen would never become an 'omnicompetent citizen' (Lippmann), a political animal who had a full-time, undivided loyalty to a sovereign political community. The European citizen bid *auf Wiedersehen* to republican and state-centred definitions of citizenship. She was, and would remain, a restrained and divided political animal: a part-time citizen caught up in a patchwork quilt of socio-economic milieux, a *habitus* of multiple identities anchored but tossed about within a vast sea of social preoccupations.

This is to say that the trigger norm of European citizenship broke with the traditional understanding of citizenship as a *common identity*: a universal attachment of individuals to a common framework of legally specified entitlements and duties. Traditional definitions of citizenship were perforce often hostile to differentiation and 'faction', as can be seen in early modern republican discourses on citizenship.[17] Such reticence

---

[17] Michael Schudson, *The Good Citizen: A History of American Civic Life* (New York: Martin Kessler Books, 1998), p. 309.

meant that prior models of citizenship were marked by a low regard for minority rights and a rather miserly vision of what social differences could be appreciated, tolerated and even cherished. Such miserliness appeared to have no place in the understanding of European citizenship born of the 1970s. Not only did policies based on the norm of cultivating citizenship in Europe unfold within the context of a mosaic of robust and dynamic, actually existing civil societies that tended to intermingle as an emergent European civil society, this patchwork quilt of civil societies, comprised a multiplicity of identities – linked to regional loyalties, gender, market position, sport, music and respect for the sacred, to name just a few – that had the effect, for a time, of challenging and de-centring *national identity*.

European citizenship implied a unique form of *post-national citizenship*. Within the European region, definitions and visions of citizenship had hitherto been locked within national identities. Since the late eighteenth century, the doctrine of national self-determination functioned to 'modernise' the much older theme of citizenship. From that time onwards, the individual considered as a citizen was supposed to share with others a common sense of 'national identity', understood as a form of belonging defined by certain rules of grammar, including a shared language or dialect; shared memories of the past; shared positive feelings about the local ecosystem; and shared understandings of such 'cultural' matters as food, jokes, clothing styles, religion, such that the identities 'I' and 'Thou' could co-mingle and serve as something like a 'home-in-the-world' for individuals and groups.[18] National identity so defined always implied territorial state protection, or the quest for such protection. Citizenship was presumed to be possible only when nations could articulate their needs and determine their fates through territorially structured government. From the time of the French Revolution, this equation courted the well-known dangers of *nationalism* and territorial state violence. To be a citizen implied a duty of loyalty to a polity conceived as a political community rooted in national identity.

The new language of European citizenship represented a direct challenge to such thinking. It underscored one of the big issues faced by the emergent European polity: how institutionally to protect and nurture a

---

[18] Fredrik Barth, 'Ethnic Groups and Boundaries', in *Process and Form in Social Life: Selected Essays of Fredrik Barth* (London: Routledge & Kegan Paul, 1981), pp. 198–227; John Keane, *Civil Society: Old Images, New Visions* (Cambridge: Polity Press, 1998), 79ff.

multiplicity of (complex, overlapping, hybrid) national identities, which for obvious reasons would not wither away into some common 'European' identity based upon a common language, ecological sensibility, sense of history and shared culture. Seen in this way, the project of European citizenship attempted something never before attempted on a continental scale: to detach nationality and citizenship; to guarantee and protect citizens' entitlements to their own national identities; and (hardest of all) to protect the whole political order from politically dogmatic or violence-prone ideological renditions of national identity, expressed either as extra-parliamentary *nationalism* or as confused or mindlessly revengeful 'Euroscepticism'.

EQUALITY?

If European citizenship was to be understood as a fluid identity that internalised ongoing negotiations of particular differences ('multiple identities') mixed with common loyalties, as a new type of *complex citizenship* that guaranteed citizens their 'right to be different', then naturally questions arose concerning citizens' access to the social and economic resources that would enable them to secure their sometimes common, sometimes different loyalties – as social and political equals.

The whole idea of citizenship is a precious democratic inheritance, if only because it reminds us of the possibility of *equality*. Here, in one tiny word, was the third challenge posed by European citizenship, a challenge that can be clarified by referring back to T.H. Marshall's seminal work on class and citizenship.[19] Marshall emphasised that the project of citizenship required institutions and policies that could reduce and eliminate market-created socio-economic inequalities. The entitlements to civil rights (*habeas corpus*, freedom of association, the ownership of property) and political rights (to vote, to run for office, to join or support political parties) were not enough, he argued. According to Marshall, citizenship required 'a general enrichment of the concrete substance of civilised life, a general reduction of risk and insecurity, an equalisation between the more and the less fortunate at all levels – between the healthy and the sick, the

---

[19] T.H. Marshall, *Citizenship and Social Class and Other Essays* (Cambridge: Cambridge University Press, 1951); Martin Bulmer and Anthony M. Rees (eds.), *Citizenship Today: The Contemporary Relevance of T.H. Marshall* (London: UCL Press, 1997).

employed and the unemployed, the old and the active, the bachelor and the father of a large family'.[20]

What were the prospects for a new form of cross-border citizenship that recognised that the citizenship specified in the Treaty of Amsterdam and the Nice Treaty would be just a word unless it was linked to the equalisation of life chances and the reduction of social risks? Put briefly, the prospects during the period 1970 and 2005 appeared to be dim, and not only because the fair-weather friends of European integration were dead opposed to talk of a 'social Europe' that provided some measure of social security for all European citizens. European citizenship also suffered a sequencing problem. Since national welfare states (like those of Sweden and France) came decades before European integration, and since most national governments remained convinced that the Keynesian welfare state ensured public identification with the nation-state (rather than, say, being a major cause of public budget deficits), their leaders were more or less suspicious of competing welfare systems at the European level, as well as strongly resistant to proposals for a pan-European public welfare system. That is partly why only 1 per cent of Europe's GDP was re-distributed through the institutions of the European Union (in contrast to the 40–50 per cent of GDP that circulated through its Member States). The entry of neo-liberal thinking and policies into mainstream policy thinking arguably made matters worse. Plans for new European social legislation centred on social citizenship and regulatory intervention were scuppered by controversies about public finances, pension problems, rising budget deficits and diffuse scepticism towards traditional welfare state policies. The single-minded commitment of the European Central Bank to the task of preventing inflation ruled out new forms of Keynesian intervention.[21] Neo-liberalism meanwhile found its adherents in the European Commission, such that, at the European level, large-scale redistribution became hard to legitimise, especially given the relative lack of social cohesion and solidarity at the level of European civil society. The absence of European social legislation not only served as a *limiting factor*, as a brake upon the process of nurturing European citizenship; the limiting factor was also a *consequence* of the underdeveloped state of European citizenship.

---

[20] Ibid., p. 56.
[21] Howard James, *Making the European Monetary Union* (Cambridge and London: Belknap Press, 2014).

The weakening or setting aside – for the time being – of the vision of a social Europe is now part of the history of European integration and it has had serious implications for the whole ideal of European citizenship. While the construction of a 'single European market' happened, and while a new form of European polity defined by multi-level governance, mechanisms of representation, and the supremacy of EU law over the laws of its Member States crystallised, a common social identity defined by socio-economic rights and duties, aspirations and obligations hardly emerged. It is true that mechanisms of redistribution between economic sectors were at the core of what the EU meant to its Member States. The EU did indeed contribute to reducing socio-economic inequalities between its wealthy and its less wealthy regions, for instance through regional transfer funding schemes. Both initiatives functioned as elements of an 'EU social policy'. It is equally true that progress was made in such areas as passengers' rights and mobile phone charges, and that official European-level documents sometimes indicated the need for bold new social provisions, for instance in the form of promises to recognise that 'all people who are disabled or are in danger of becoming so, regardless of their age and race, and of the nature, origin, degree or severity of their disablement, should have a right to the individual assistance required in order to lead a life as far as possible commensurate with their ability and potential'.[22]

All these bold statements and modest innovations seemed to confirm the slow development of a cross-border culture of legally enforceable rights (e.g., to equal pay for equal work, or in the field of ecological protection) within a 'social Europe' – by stealth.[23] But during this period, the basic reality of European citizenship proved more intractable. The existing and new Member States made little substantial commitment to harmonise or co-ordinate their social policies; some were downright hostile to all talk of social equality in Europe. The Member States of an expanded EU thus found themselves riddled with zones of poverty and positioned at highly different levels of economic and social wellbeing.

---

[22] Council of Europe, Committee of Ministers Recommendation No. R (92) 6, 9 April 1992.
[23] Herbert Obinger, Stephan Leibfried and Francis G. Castles, 'Bypasses to a Social Europe: Lessons from Federal Experience', *Journal of European Public Policy*, 12 (2005), 1–27; Andrew Dobson and Derek Bell (eds.), *Environmental Citizenship: Getting from Here to There* (Cambridge, MA: MIT Press, 2005); Klaus Schubert, Simon Hegelich and Ursula Bazant, 'Europäische Wohlfahrtssysteme: Stand der Forschung – theoretisch-methodische Überlegungen', in Klaus Schubert, Simon Hegelich and Ursula Bazant (eds.), *Europäische Wohlfahrtssysteme* (Wiesbaden: VS Verlag, 2008), pp. 13–43.

Their taxation regimes and social policy provisions and expectations varied widely, as did the coalitions of social associations (e.g., trades unions and business interests) that were instrumental in defining and redefining social citizenship entitlements. The powerful policy influence of the neo-liberal market ethos, with its generalised hostility to government intervention and preference for private, market-driven solutions, arguably reflected and reinforced the skewed patterns of social representation and social inequality within the European polity. Frequently, policy definitions of European citizenship unfolded within a political community whose policymaking structures provided privileged access and accountability to business interests – to the comparative disadvantage of policy-takers, such as consumers, workers, pensioners, patients, students, migrants, denizens and the impoverished.[24] In the absence of equalised social access to political representation, the EU tended to function as a guarantor of social inequalities. Its dependence upon Member States and powerful coalitions of socio-economic interests rendered improbable a shift towards a 'Social Europe'. From the perspective of European citizenship, that had a profoundly worrying implication: in the absence of major policy initiatives guided by the aim of positive integration based upon common systems of social compensation and social redistribution, European citizens were marked by a split identity. Caught between a *Marktwirtschaft* and their *Staatsbürgerschaft*, Europeans were prohibited from becoming citizens in a socio-economic sense. Despite whatever gains they made in matters of legal and political citizenship status, they were *market* citizens – owners of capital, workers and consumers caught up in forms of competition that necessarily produced *victims and losers*.

ARMS-BEARING CITIZENS?

Finally: during the period 1970 to 2005, the project of European citizenship faced one other highly unusual, historically unprecedented challenge. It proved to be a project that took place under conditions of *de-militarisation* and a 'civilian Europe'. It is important to recall the historical fact that the vision of citizenship within the European region was deeply entangled within experiences of violence and war. Ever since preparations for war against infidels in the name of Europa were made nearly a millennium

---

[24] Philippe Schmitter and Wolfgang Streeck, 'From State Weakness as Strength to State Weakness as Weakness: Welfare Corporatism and the Private Use of the Public Interest', Max-Planck-Institut für Gesellschaftsforschung Working Paper 03/2 (March 2003).

ago, the continent of Europe and its adjoining islands enjoyed a reputation as the heartland of new – modern and terrible – forms of violence and war that left a deep scar on the face of citizenship.

Citizens were *men* entitled to enjoy the benefits of equal legal status because they had already borne arms, or would in future be expected to bear arms in support of their polity. The rhetoric of citizenship was usually marked with presumptions about the importance of cultivating military virtues. In extreme circumstances, citizens were expected to show their loyalty to their polity and to demonstrate their courage, tenacity and capacity for self-government by proving themselves upon the battlefield. The replacement of mercenaries by professional standing armies in small city-states; the insistence (driven by the opposite suspicion of standing armies) upon the right of citizens to bear arms; the expressed concerns about the 'decline of the martial spirit' (Adam Smith); the insistence that men who had fought for their country should be entitled to full civil, political and social rights – all this was part of an historical period in which the citizen was a man on horseback armed with a sword or crossbow or musket or rifle.

Research on European citizenship needs to reconsider the ways in which the various languages of citizenship crystallised under conditions of warfare and within violent revolutionary confrontations. These languages were evidently the by-products of – critical reactions against – the religious and plebeian violence of early modern Europe.[25] The troublesome fact is that every citizenship language positively regarded military service, not just as a means of defending one's own territorial state, but as a vital and necessary condition of attaining such masculine civic virtues as courage, bravery and brotherhood. Until quite recently, the history of citizenship in the European region was for this reason (among others) a history of the exclusion and subordination of women – in favour of men who were deemed capable and willing to bear arms against actual or potential enemies.

The prejudice that fighting men were the citizens' fortress rested upon exclusionary gendering mechanisms, ranging from the rigorous equation of arms-bearing with civic capacity in the recommendations of Machiavelli, who had a strong preference for a citizen (male) militia over

---

[25] Dominique Colas, *Le glaive et le fléau: Généalogie du fanatisme et de la société civile* (Paris: B. Grasset, 1992); Julius R. Ruff, *Violence in Early Modern Europe 1500–1800* (Cambridge: Cambridge University Press, 2001); John Keane, *Violence and Democracy* (Cambridge: Cambridge University Press, 2004).

other types of military force, through various appeals to citizens' right to bear arms against tyrants to contemporary policies (in countries such as Greece, Finland and Romania) of compulsorily drafting young men for military service. Any account of the origins and development of European citizenship must note the catalogue of arms-related reasons given for excluding women from citizenship (women as feeble and feeble-minded; as unreliable because periodically incapacitated; duplicitous; as 'by nature' too tender for war, and so on). Such a history needs as well to examine how the obligation to undergo military training and to fight wars was a key element in 'sacralising' and 'masculinising' citizenship; and how the political process of connecting citizenship rights with matters of life and death, sacrifice and honour, imbued military conscription with high symbolic value – at the expense of women.

Seen in retrospect, the policy vision of European Union citizenship signalled a break with old European ideals and practices of citizenship and their bellicose masculine prejudices. The reduction of conscription duties that took place in Europe in the decades after 1970 proved to be a political breakthrough, a gateway to a 'de-militarised' and less gendered and more genuinely universal vision of citizenship whose norms and forms were shaped by 'civilian service' within a 'civilian Europe'. The de-masculinisation of citizenship evidently had older roots. It can be said that European citizenship developed as an allergic reaction to the violence and cruelty of the Second World War. It was encouraged by the so-called revolution in military affairs: the shift towards smaller armies backed by technology-intensive weapons systems linked to air power. European citizenship was nurtured as well by such disparate processes as de-Nazification, the civilian overthrow of military dictatorship in Spain and Portugal and Greece, the rise of anti-nuclear peace movements, and the so-called 'velvet revolutions' of 1989–91. The combined effect of these forces was to revise fundamentally the image of Europe as war-mongering and murderous. In many parts of Europe, it became difficult for millions of citizens to understand why, a generation earlier, many observers applauded Jean-Paul Sartre's angry dismissal of Europe as a fat, pale, murderous region, whose fingers on every corner of the globe had to be slashed, until she fully let go. In place of guilt-ridden rhetoric of that kind, talk of 'civilian Europe' flourished. This implied the peaceful resolution of conflicts and disputes through processes of law and open (inter-governmental) negotiation. It also implied a commitment to the non-violent reunification of the two halves of Europe and the weakening of policed and militarily guarded borders. The ideal of a civilian Europe further implied the nurturing of civil society institutions and key virtues such as civility and non-violent openness; and the public recognition that toleration of differences implies diversity, and that diversity requires toleration. Through the coordination of diplomatic services and standing armies, a citizens' Europe pointed to the need for a common security and defence policy that could be implemented, with peaceful effects, not only in the borderlands of Europe, but in the world beyond.

During this period, we could say, the political animal called the European citizen dismounted from his horse, and laid down his arms. Residual patterns of military conscription notwithstanding, the legal status of being a citizen unfolded within the context of a post-heroic civilisation and a demilitarised 'security community' (Karl Deutsch) in which the experience of war tended to become more distant, less tangible, principally accessible through the visual imagery of communications media.[26] But how sustainable was this model of post-military citizenship, we might ask? Could the benefits of citizenship within a socio-political environment freed from the scourge of violence generated by armies locked in power battles over territorial borders be durably enjoyed by many millions of European people?

During the heyday of European citizenship, these tricky questions became both pertinent and difficult, not least because the vision of a 'civilian Europe' began to suffer visible stresses and strains. There were various threatening developments: tragic wars and ethnic cleansing within the former Yugoslavia; growing pressures for 'humanitarian intervention' in various global conflicts; sadistic forms of urban violence associated with the new terrorism;[27] and the outbreak of an American-led 'war on terror' that had direct security implications for the European polity and its peoples. These challenges evidently forced new questions onto the political agenda of the European Union. For instance: granted that European citizens could enjoy a political life of non-violence, how could the ethos and substance of European citizenship be extended to those regions, especially south-eastern Europe, with a recent history of cruel violence and forcible displacement of hundreds of thousands of people? Supposing that there would be a continuing need for (military) policing of Europe's (potential) trouble spots, would a 'European army' or 'European Peace

---

[26] Robert Cooper, *The Breaking of Nations: Order and Chaos in the Twenty-first Century* (London: Atlantic Books, 2003).
[27] John Keane, *Global Civil Society?* (Cambridge: Cambridge University Press, 2003), pp. 92–128.

Corps' be necessary? If so, how should it be organised, and funded? And given that the model of post-military citizenship functioned as something of a global norm, as the draft Constitution made clear, could European citizens avoid taking up arms in opposition to cruelty and violence elsewhere in the world? Was greater priority to be given by the European Union to nurturing a global civil society and global governing institutions, like the International Criminal Court and a drastically reformed United Nations? Or was 'military muscle' still a necessary external condition of European citizenship? Just how viable would be the new European-level armed forces (a 7,500 person-strong crisis and peacekeeping group and a 60,000-strong rapid reaction force) that began to be assembled following an Anglo-French initiative at Saint-Malo in December 1998? Would the further development of these forces be a necessary condition of the creation and nurturing of citizenship at home and abroad? And what would be the proper relationship of these forces with the military apparatuses of NATO, the United States and the United Nations? In other words: Could there be European citizenship without Europe taking steps to defend itself militarily?

These difficulties confronting the trigger norm of European citizenship were symptomatic of the wider entrapment of the emerging European polity within the vice grip of a devilish dialectic. The deep-seated pressures that for some time worked in favour of a common European citizenship now began to mark it with 'fractured' and resisted qualities. The extended troubles spawned by the draft European constitutional treaty tempted some observers to predict that the political animal called the European citizen was dying. 'We who lead Europe have lost the power to make Europeans proud of themselves', said Jean-Claude Juncker, Luxembourg's prime minister and holder of the European presidency at the time of the French and Dutch referendum votes against the European constitutional treaty.[28] Unlike Juncker, who subsequently led a successful pro-Constitution referendum campaign in his home state, some witnesses saw in these rejections a reaffirmation of the First Principle that the basic obligation of any Member State is to itself, its own territorial integrity, its own security, and the effective functioning of its own 'sovereign' institutions. Others claimed to have spotted the resurgent forces of populist nationalism ('We want to stay Dutch' was among the slogans used to mobilise votes against the Constitution); and still others drew the

---

[28] See the contemporary assessment of William Pfaff, 'What's Left of the Union?', *The New York Review of Books* (14 July 2005), pp. 26–29.

conclusion that the French and Dutch rejections, like the Irish and Danish rejections before them, signalled the end of economic reform and of the Eurocurrency, a repudiation of the arrogance of meddlesome European political elites – perhaps even the beginning of the end of European integration.

LOOKING BACK

The sea is deep, the Greeks say. So it was with the fledgling European project of nurturing cross-border citizenship, just as it was with the extended struggles, over eight centuries, to cultivate modern forms of territorial citizenship at the sub-national and nation-state levels. In the years after 2005, further progress on constitutional integration seemed doomed, crushed by a long list of intersecting forces, ranging from dysfunctions in the banking system, economic stagnation, compulsory austerity, terrorism and war inside and on the margins of Europe to rising social inequality, popular disaffection with political elites, the breakdown of cartel party systems and the spread of racism and xenophobic populism. Pressured by these and other ugly forces, disheartened conclusions about the future of European citizenship flourished. They were perhaps premature. The naysayers frequently failed to take into account the paradoxical fact that after 2005 levels of mediated interest in European affairs grew to an all-time high in every Member State. Despite the proclivity of more than a few citizens to project onto 'Brussels' domestic dissatisfactions with the sterility, injustices and stagnation of their own states, diffuse feelings of belonging and active citizen identification with 'Europe' were by no means dead. Meanwhile, on the plane of institutions, the European Union continued to be governed by established treaty arrangements. Pressures for deeper spacetime integration meanwhile continued to grow in areas like policing, immigration, environment and foreign policy. The bigoted secessionism of a short-sighted British government aside, common problems of renewable energy systems, sustainable economic reform, political re-adjustment and social equity were not scheduled to disappear. A 'new Yalta' agreement that effectively severed the ties between 'Europe' and the peoples of Romania, Bulgaria, Georgia, Ukraine and the post-Yugoslav states of Croatia, Serbia, Montenegro and Kosovo seemed most improbable. The problem of how to deal with Russia and war in Syria and Libya, and the need to forge imaginative new arrangements with Ukraine, Turkey, Israel, the whole Middle East region, China and beyond, were challenges unlikely to recuse themselves.

Whatever happens in the coming years and decades, it seems safe to say that the ideals and practices of European citizenship are most unlikely to 'mature' into an overarching political identity, into a civil religion that serves as the common European identity of a common European polity. That is not necessarily a cause for lament, if only because the trends that pushed towards European citizenship, however weak and incoherent, served to enlarge our understanding and acceptance of cross-border citizenship. The fact and the vision of European citizenship de-territorialised citizenship. It helped to rescue Europeans from their blighted past, to foster the quest for reconciliation, now and in the future. In the field of law, the project of European citizenship highlighted the discriminations of alienage and the need to overcome them. Talk of European citizenship also served as a warning against the political dangers of recidivist nationalism. It functioned as a reminder to neo-liberals (and others for whom Euro-citizenship is a *Schimpfwort*) that market processes typically have socially corrosive and unjust effects. And talk of European citizenship resembled a trumpet blast in favour of constitutionalising and publicly monitoring – democratising – the growing volume and density of so-far unaccountable cross-border institutions and processes within the European region.

All things soberly considered, what are the chances of survival of the European citizen? The question is by definition unanswerable, but it does drive home the elementary point that the project of European citizenship never enjoyed historical guarantees. It was just the opposite. For a generation, the gates of heaven have been closed to Europeans. The trigger norm of European citizenship serves as a reminder to them, and to the wider world, that European integration was a different process than most other political experiments of modern times. In contrast, say, to the founding of territorial states like France and the United States in the name of the *summum bonum* based on norms like liberty, equality and public happiness, European integration was born of the desire to avoid the *summum malum* of terror, war, genocide and totalitarianism. During the decades after 1970, we could say, the norm of European citizenship was the David to the Goliath of war, injustice and servitude. It was perhaps even a tiny contributor to the giant task of blocking the whims and desires of the Grand Ideologies that several times ravaged Europe and brought misery to its peoples, and the whole world. There the analogy with the tiny armed warrior who courageously did battle with a slingshot ends. That is because European citizens have another, more powerful weapon through which to defend themselves, their ideals and their European institutions: a precious inheritance called democratic politics.

Careful reconsideration of the micro- and macro-processes through which claims were tabled and deals struck concerning European citizenship makes quite clear that neither 'History' nor 'modernisation' nor 'spillover effects' nor any other abstract force or single subject was responsible for the practical advances made during the four decades after 1970. The decisive factor in every case was the manoeuvres, negotiations, threats, compromises and agreements of organised forces within the domains of civil society and government. The inclusion of paragraphs related to citizenship within the Rome meeting of the European Council, the Treaty of Maastricht and the Amsterdam Treaty of Union, for instance, were the resultant of a Spanish text on European citizenship, two favourable resolutions adopted by the European Parliament, resistance by the Danish government in the name of nation-state citizenship and last-minute complaints by the Spanish Prime Minister, Felipe González, about the political dangers of forging a Treaty that only sanctioned market integration. All of this can be called log-rolling and horse-trading amateurishness, but the plain fact is that such political processes of deciding non-violently who gets what, when and how are, and ought to be, unavoidable within a polity infused with the spirit of democracy. It is for this reason alone that democratic politics will undoubtedly remain at the heart of what's left of the citizenship project in Europe – and why politics will ensure its eventual demise and destruction, or instead serve as a vital condition of its future renewal and flourishing, so confirming in practice that a new form of citizenship that calls into question the territorial mentality is possible, and desirable.

12

Antarctica: Democracy at the End of the World

Democracy is a small word that harbours the big idea that people can restrain arbitrary power and govern themselves through their chosen representatives. These days, as this section of the book has pointed out at length, democracy and the territorial state are treated as twins. Democracy is said to be national: it is German or French or Chilean, South African, Brazilian or Canadian. International democracy (a term that first appeared out of the ruins of the First World War) and 'cosmopolitan democracy' (a more recent neologism) are condemned as either simpleminded oxymorons, or as impracticable ideals. And so, in an age when key decisions from afar increasingly push and pull the local lives of citizens, this way and that, it should come as no surprise that more than a few believers in democracy today experience a sinking feeling, or conclude that democracy has no chance of survival in the face of regional and global forces that powerfully undermine the whole ideal of citizens governing themselves as equals, for instance through national parliaments, periodic national elections and national governments subject to written constitutions. The trend produces discomfort and panic. It leads pundits and practitioners towards one of two conclusions: either democracies must strive to claw back as much 'foreign' power as they can, or the whole ideal of democracy must be abandoned, replaced by what is variously called 'governance', or one-party rule, or 'smart power' exercised by technocrats and other unelected officials.

What is genuinely interesting about Antarctica, the vast sixth geological continent at the bottom of our world, is the way its governing arrangements defy all these real-world trends, and ways of thinking. Although competitive political parties, parliaments, elected governments and other familiar paraphernalia of representative democracy are largely absent from the continent, Antarctica resembles a laboratory in which, for more than half a century, political experiments have been going on that are of great relevance to the future of democracy. The pages that follow suggest that these experiments can teach us important things about the present and future contours of democracy – and whether it can take advantage of the opportunities and survive the worrying challenges of the twenty-first century.

STEWARDSHIP

To grasp the great significance of Antarctica for understanding the present and future of democracy requires going back in time, to the moment of its first sighting by European eyes. Most men who encountered the continent for the first time thought of it as a foreign world. It resembled the strangest of places, another planet on Earth. The vast expanse of ice and snow, along with its exotic wildlife, was experienced as an untamed wilderness deeply threatening of human existence. Antarctica was *terra nullius* in the extreme. It was not only the highest and driest continent, but also the coldest and stormiest. Antarctica was judged a beastly place, a terrain of 'wild' and untamed qualities.

It is unsurprising that the continent's first visitors were gripped by anxieties and fears. Feelings of threat invariably morphed into their polar opposite: presumptions of human superiority, the unrestrained will to unlock the continent's secrets, perhaps even to exploit its untapped rich resources for all that they were worth in market terms. So the diaries and notebooks of the early adventurers are filled with a sense of buccaneer adventure, tales of bravery in the face of extreme danger, strong sentiments of romance, the pathos of disappointment, a *machismo* manifested as triumph over the wild and untamed. Gendered images were plentiful. 'At the bottom of this planet', wrote the first man to fly over the South Pole, Admiral Richard Byrd, 'is an enchanted continent in the sky, pale like a sleeping princess. Sinister and beautiful, she lies in frozen slumber.'[1] Fears of sinister sleeping mistresses readily bred the will to conquer. That sentiment reached its apogee in the famous neck-and-neck race between the British explorer Captain Scott and the Norwegian Roald Amundsen to reach the South Pole in the southern summer of 1911–1912. 'The country lay before us in the brilliant light', wrote the winner of the race

---

[1] Richard E. Byrd, *Discovery* (New York: Putnam, 1935); and *Alone* (New York: Putnam, 1938).

in his diary on 13 November 1911. 'Shining white, bright blue, utterly black illuminated by sunlight, the country looks like a fairy tale. Precipices, peaks on peaks, so cragged and so wild, it lies unseen and virgin-like.'[2]

The controversies among historians unleashed by that struggle are still today charged with talk of heroism in the face of adversity and the 'frigid mistress';[3] but what is remarkable just a century on is the 180-degree revamping of Antarctica's image. Nothing short of a fundamental quantum switch of perspective is taking place. The change has global relevance and positions Antarctica in the vanguard of a global trend. No longer considered an object of conquest and domination, the continent is seen as fragile and vulnerable, an endangered space in which humans must tread lightly and be mindful of their obligations as stewards of its complex and delicate living landscape. An important aspect of this new way of imagining the continent is a gathering sense of danger, growing awareness that the actions of humans could reduce the continent to a *terra nullius*.

The intuition that the continent might become what it was once imagined to be is more than ironic. It has a political significance. It nourishes a revolution of perceptions, so that the old human quest to dominate nature is replaced by human awareness of our own dependence upon a fragile biome entitled to human respect and protection. Examples abound. The banning of the myopic practice of disposing waste materials by floating them out to sea on ice, the prohibition of the use of dogs (an alien species of super-predator) to pull researchers and sledges, and the opening (in 2007) of the world's first zero-emissions polar science station at Princess Elisabeth, are just three of many symbols of how the urge to conquer Antarctica through absolute power has been humbled, brought

---

[2] *The Roald Amundsen Diaries: The South Pole Expedition 1910–12* (Oslo: Fram Museum, 2010).
[3] Tom Griffiths, *Slicing the Silence: Voyaging to Antarctica* (Cambridge, MA: Harvard University Press, 2008); Ranulph Fiennes, *Race to the Pole: Tragedy, Heroism, and Scott's Antarctic Quest* (New York: Hyperion, 2004); and George A. Doumani, *The Frigid Mistress: Life and Exploration in Antarctica* (Baltimore, MD: Noble House, 1999), whose dust jacket blurb draws upon more than a few prejudices: 'Details the trials and tribulations, the laughter and sorrow experienced as part of the efforts during and after the International Geophysical Year (IGY) to unlock the secrets of this harsh and uncompromising environment unwilling to give up its secrets. While most books on polar exploration focus on the heroics and adventure, The Frigid Mistress focuses on the human side of the story depicting the interaction among the scientists, civilians, and military personnel and the humour and friction that develops whenever humans are tossed together in close quarters under trying circumstances and inhuman conditions.'

down to earth. It is replaced by a strong sense of the need for humans to act as stewards of a fragile environment requiring protection and deserving of political representation in human affairs.

Many forces drive the quantum shift of perspective. The discovery that the continent of Antarctica sits atop more than 400 sub-glacial lakes that (possibly) flow like rivers into one another has undermined the imagery of the 'frozen continent'. Awareness is rising that Antarctica is experiencing warming and its effects; fears are growing that it may go the way of the Arctic region, where the years 2005–2010 were the warmest on record, so that during summer months the Arctic Ocean will probably be completely ice-free within the next three or four decades.[4] Some scientists meanwhile insist that Antarctica is a vital benchmark that provides practical clues concerning how future generations can reverse the damage to the Earth caused by human activity. It is important not to forget another key driver and symptom of the shift of perspective: the successful campaign by Greenpeace to declare the continent a World Park. That global commons principle had to be fought for politically, as Greenpeace activists showed for the first time during the 1980s with the establishment of an independent base camp at Ross Island and the subsequent occupation (in the 1987/1988 season) of the French airstrip construction site at Dumont, a controversial project that involved plans to dynamite the habitats of nesting penguins. The Greenpeace actions succeeded. In 1991, the global commons principle was formally adopted in the Protocol on Environmental Protection to the Antarctic Treaty, the so-called Madrid Protocol. It commits the contracting parties to 'the comprehensive protection of the Antarctic environment and dependent and associated ecosystems' and designates 'Antarctica as a natural reserve, devoted to peace and science'. The Protocol prohibits all activities relating to Antarctic mineral resources, except for scientific research, and it led immediately to measures that banned all incineration and dumping of refuse on the continent.

ENFRANCHISEMENT

It could be said that Antarctica is a cutting-edge case of the self-democratisation of humans, the rejection of our own long-standing arrogant presumption that we are masters and possessors of nature. But its

---

[4] Antarctic Climate and Ecosystems CRC, *Position Analysis: Climate Change and the Southern Ocean* (2011); Arctic Monitoring and Assessment Programme, *Snow, Water, Ice, Permafrost in the Arctic* (2011).

significance is greater than this. Antarctica is a continent engaged in world-leading experiments in the art of enfranchising nature, ensuring its tangible presence as an equal in human politics. The experiments pose a fundamental challenge to those scholars who fix on fair and free elections as the core mechanism and ethical principle of democracy, and who suppose that the question of who is entitled to vote and be represented in human affairs has long been a settled issue. The challenge of Antarctica has several dimensions, each to do with the widening and deepening of the meaning of political representation.

The continent is host to elections in the conventional democratic, representative sense. There are no permanent residents, but throughout the year between 1,000 and 5,000 denizens reside at research stations scattered across the continent. Voting (as in democracies such as Mongolia) is among nomads. Countries such as New Zealand proudly organise general elections at a distance, in testing circumstances; in that country's 2008 general election, under the watchful eye of a newly appointed Overseas Returning Officer to Antarctica, voting papers were flown to and from Scott Base, where 100 New Zealand citizens from several stations cast their votes on a turnout of nearly 100 per cent. Technically speaking, voting under these conditions is impressive. It also raises interesting questions about the appropriate boundaries of democratic politics. At a minimum, the case of Antarctica demonstrates that in the matter of elections quantum tunnelling happens, that thanks to digital communications voting by citizens in spaces located at vast distances from territorial states is feasible, and desirable.

More fascinating still is the manner in which, throughout the continent of Antarctica, the franchise is being stretched in ways that would astonish our great-grandparents. Invisibly, slowly but surely, the interests of a whole new constituency have come to be registered in the affairs of Antarctica. The continent is host and contributor to the monitory democratic revolution of our times, a transition marked by the 'empowerment' through representation of the biosphere in human affairs. Antarctica is another case of the bio-democracy discussed in previous pages. Its political significance goes well beyond talk of simian sovereignty, animal rights and respect for other sentient creatures. Antarctica surmounts familiar arguments about whether open democratic societies are capable of cultivating public awareness of future generations (they can) or whether democracies can act quickly enough to handle the coming mega-disasters (they can). Developments in Antarctica confront us with fundamental questions about the meaning of democracy, and whether it has a future. It forces us to think about how we think about democracy.

The case of Antarctica prompts the fundamental question of whether we human beings are capable of democratising ourselves, in a triple sense: in other words, not only whether we can humble ourselves by collectively recognising our ineluctably deep dependence upon the ecosystems in which we dwell, or whether, simultaneously, we can find new ways of practically extending voices and votes in human affairs to our ecosystems, but also (and consequently) whether it is possible in theory and practice to rid the whole idea of democracy of its anthropocentrism. The fundamental question is: Can democracy come to mean, descriptively speaking, a way of life and a potent method of rendering power publicly accountable by means of institutions in which humans and their biosphere are treated symmetrically, as equals, as interdependent *actants* (Bruno Latour), as subjects and objects who simultaneously act and are acted upon within geographical contexts that mediate and bind humans and their biomes together, in opposition to the still-dominant view that humans are the pinnacle of creation, lords and ladies of the universe, 'the people' who are the ultimate source of sovereign power and authority on Earth?

This way of playing with words may seem strange, or opaque, but it shouldn't be. For it must be remembered that all human societies have created ways of registering or re-presenting their interdependence with the natural world and its elements by means of verbal, written and pictorial expressions, even when these elements (wind, for instance) are intangible and invisible.[5] It should also not be forgotten that the democratic tradition is salted and peppered with many old customs, ways of politically representing 'nature', some of them, such as water tribunals, tings and dyke committees, stretching back well into medieval times.[6] Memories of their importance have mostly been extinguished, although from time to time their spirit has been kept alive, especially in the world of literature, for instance in Erich Kästner's classic children's tale of an assembly of the world's animals that votes to call on humans to behave more decently in the world.[7]

The continent of Antarctica brings to life and puts into practice new ways of imagining the political inclusion and representation of the biosphere within human affairs. These innovations have profound implications for the way we think about democracy in the twenty-first century. Antarctica is a

---

[5] Alessandro Nova, *The Book of the Wind: The Representation of the Invisible* (Montréal: McGill-Queen's University Press, 2011).

[6] John Keane, *The Life and Death of Democracy* (London and New York: Simon & Schuster, 2009).

[7] Erich Kästner, *The Animals' Conference* (Zurich: Europa Verlag, 1949).

continent where the nature/politics dualism no longer makes sense. It is a place where the omnipresence of non-human nature constantly registers and makes its presence felt among the humans who dwell there. But it is also, conversely, a place where awareness runs high among humans that there are different ways of seeing and acting upon the biosphere, that it is not just raw, non-human, 'out there' nature but a complex set of interacting living elements whose dynamics and meaning are shaped by human perceptions and actions, which are themselves bound up with the deep structures of the biosphere. The point can be sharpened: Antarctica forces us to realise that we humans move among miracles, that in the words of the American naturalist and philosopher Edward L. McCord, we've a common primordial bond with every other living species, that we're part of the earth's 'unfathomable flow of impacts over billions of years of evolution'.[8]

The point that human and non-human nature are two co-dependent and entangled parts of a common but vulnerable dynamic is confirmed in virtually every first-hand account of the challenge of living and working in constant sub-zero temperatures. Visitors typically make much of how their senses are affected by the dense fogs on the sea ice and by the massive 'white-outs' caused by unforgiving winds. They grasp at words to describe the surreal feeling of being surrounded by absolutely nothing but white, with no visible horizon or visible features of any kind. They are struck by a wide variety of other encounters: the slow-motion sunsets that last for hours because the sun never really sets; the 'sun dogs', white rainbows formed from tiny snow crystals in the air; the seals that want to play and interrupt scientists as they go about their fieldwork; and the emperor penguins that seem as naturally skilled at the arts of posing and performing before cameras as they are in organising altruistic wave-motion huddles to ensure that each individual penguin member stays warm.

There is as well much made of the reverse effects, the impact that humans automatically have on the local biomes. Here's one example: scientists currently working in the McMurdo Dry Valleys are acutely aware that their presence transforms the environment they are trying to study. These freeze-dried polar deserts, which are thought most closely to resemble the terrestrial environment of Mars, are of particular interest because they are home to tiny roundworms known as nematodes. Within the pared-down ecosystem, these millimetre-long creatures occupy the top rung of the food chain and their population size is deemed a vital

---

[8] Edward L. McCord, *The Value of Species* (New Haven, CT: Yale University Press, 2012), p. 125.

indicator of possible alterations of the patterns of carbon turnover, the storage and recycling of carbon from one useful form to another. Nematode numbers appear to be in decline although investigators, known affectionately as 'worm herders', cannot be entirely sure. This is partly because these herd book keepers (let's call them) are highly mindful that their fieldwork is beset by a peculiar methodological dilemma: their access to the McMurdo Dry Valleys would be impossible unless they were ferried to and from their field camps by helicopters, yet the engine emissions of those flying machines tend to upset the delicate carbon dioxide measurements that are so vital for the accuracy of their overall research findings.

MONITORS

Many other similar examples could be cited, but here it is enough to point out that what is politically most interesting about Antarctica is the way the sensed 'closeness' and fragility of its biosphere has triggered efforts to find innovative ways of handling, publicising and controlling the power relationships inherent in the patterns of human interaction with the biomes of the continent. These innovations could be called (following Bruno Latour) 'parliaments of things'.[9] They function as monitory bodies that operate outside and beyond the reach of conventional electoral and parliamentary institutions. A large number of these monitors operate in and around the continent. They vary in footprint size and effectiveness. Their entanglement is striking, although at first glance they seem to bear no generic relationship to one another. These monitors range from public declarations, conciliation and arbitration mechanisms, International Polar Year programmes, youth ambassador schemes, law panels and councils of scientific experts through to NGO information networks such as the Antarctic and Southern Ocean Coalition (ASOC) and radical direct-action, media-intensive initiatives like the Sea Shepherd Conservation Society (SSCS), an international non-profit, marine wildlife conservation organisation whose stated mission is to safeguard the bio-diversity and end the destruction of habitat and slaughter of wildlife species in the waters surrounding Antarctica.

---

[9] Bruno Latour, 'From Realpolitik to Dingpolitik', in Bruno Latour and Peter Weibel (eds.), *Making Things Public: Atmospheres of Democracy* (Cambridge, MA and London: MIT Press, 2005).

CITIZEN SCIENTISTS

Antarctica is a strange political space for democrats. Although it is home to neither political parties, parliaments nor periodic elections it hosts many power-scrutinising and power-chastening mechanisms and processes which have the combined effect of preventing concentrations of power common to traditional monarchies, authoritarian dictatorships, totalitarian regimes and other forms of modern despotism. Antarctica defies description in these orthodox terms. It is also not a case of 'governance without government', a popular phrase in some scholarly circles that is rather too fuzzy and insufficiently sensitive to the problem of arbitrary power to be of use in grasping the contours of the politics of the continent. Considered as a polity, Antarctica is something other, something new on the face of the planet. It is best described as a species of *monitory democracy* in which arbitrary power is subject to institutional restraint, intense public scrutiny and key decisions made by unelected representatives.

Unfamiliar talk of unelected representatives grates on democratic ears; but evidence is growing that representatives whose power base is located beyond the fringes of parliamentary elections can and do play important roles in the age of monitory democracy, especially in times when the authority and effectiveness of formally elected representatives wanes, or is absent. Even though they are not chosen directly by citizens, these representatives can do good works for democracy. They serve as correctives to the undue dominance of state-centred definitions of leadership, while their personal or group authority enables them to draw attention to the policy failures and violation of public standards by governments and businesses.[10] They frequently make valuable contributions to the public chastening and humbling of power, especially during periods between formal elections. Unelected representatives change the definition of democracy, which in the age of monitory democracy comes to mean something well beyond free and fair elections, a new form of democracy centred on ongoing and unending processes of publicly scrutinising and chastening power, wherever and by whomever it is exercised in governmental and non-governmental settings.

---

[10] John Keane, 'A Productive Challenge: Unelected Representatives Can Enrich Democracy', *WZB-Mitteilungen*, 131 (2011), 14–16; see also Sonia Alonso, John Keane and Wolfgang Merkel (eds.), *The Future of Representative Democracy* (Cambridge: Cambridge University Press, 2011).

The exemplars of unelected extra-parliamentary representation in Antarctica are scientists and scientific associations and networks. Their role in the politics of Antarctica cannot be understated. Sometimes outlandish claims are made on their behalf; one study of the global importance of the continent even concludes that the role of scientists there proves that 'science is the keystone for the "progress of mankind"'.[11] Things are not so straightforward, yet most observers rightly agree that from the 1950s scientists and scientific organisations have played a vital role in driving the transformation of perceptions of nature and the growth of monitory institutions.

With a touch of exaggeration designed to clarify things, it can be said that Antarctica is a strange new form of monitory democracy in which citizen scientists have replaced voters as the source of political legitimacy. By this conjecture, I emphasise several trends. The most obvious development dates from the 1950s, to the decade when scientists played a vital role in the first efforts to establish a governing architecture for the continent.[12] The founding moment was the decision by various groups of scientists from a dozen countries to participate in the International Geophysical Year (IGY). On 1 July 1957, they launched systematic, simultaneous scientific research programmes covering the ice and atmospheric conditions of the continent. Their collaborative successes over eighteen months inspired the Antarctic Treaty of 1959, which formalised their peaceful pursuit of scientific knowledge. The Treaty is a remarkably bold document. The prominence it gives to freedom of scientific research is striking. 'Antarctica shall be used for peaceful purposes only', it begins (Article I). It goes on to specify that representatives of the contracting governments shall do all in their powers to further the objectives of the Treaty, which include the 'facilitation of scientific research' and 'international scientific co-operation'; the 'preservation and conservation of living resources' (Article IX); a guarantee to designated observers of 'freedom of access at any time to any or all areas of Antarctica' (Article VII); and the banning of all measures of a military nature, including 'nuclear explosions and the disposal of radioactive waste material' (Article V).

---

[11] Paul Arthur Berkman, *Science into Policy: Global Lessons from Antarctica* (San Diego, CA: Academic Press, 2002), p. 222; compare the different approach and conclusions of Gordon Fogg, *A History of Antarctic Science* (Cambridge and New York: Cambridge University Press, 1992).

[12] Dian Olson Belanger, *Deep Freeze: The United States, the International Geophysical Year, and the Origins of Antarctica's Age of Science* (Boulder, CO: University of Colorado Press, 2010).

EXPERTISE AND THE EARTH SYSTEM SCIENCES

The Antarctic Treaty System is the first-ever binding international treaty to acknowledge the central role of scientists in matters of government. No less important is the fact that it legitimised their role as citizen 'watchdogs' and 'guardian' representatives of human power over the biosphere, so contributing in a major way to the redefinition and 'democratisation' of expertise. Put differently, the scientists of Antarctica cut a path towards what is now called citizen science or 'community science'. When they warn, as they are now doing, that the volume of methane hydrate ('fire ice') stored under Antarctic ice sheets is on a par with that trapped in the northern hemisphere's frozen permafrost soils,[13] their expertise is publicly distributable. They breathe life into the ideal of what is called 'participatory action research'; that is, forms of data collection and enquiry guided by the principle that scientific research is a collaborative process for the benefit of publics and the species, processes and habitats in which they dwell.[14]

The leading role played by scientists in Antarctica is a reminder that the subject of expertise is highly relevant for democracy, yet the key points are unfamiliar and need explanation. Historically speaking, the relationship between expertise and democracy has typically been tense. Talk of experts and expertise is a product of the same nineteenth-century Europe that wrestled with fundamental issues prompted by the rapid spread of democratic impulses. During the nineteenth century, the older English-language meaning of 'expert' as someone who is adept because of their experience in any given field (from the Latin *experiri*: to try) gave way (in 1825) to a new understanding of an 'expert' as someone whose authority derives from special knowledge or skill and (in 1869) to the new-fangled word 'expertise', meaning expert knowledge or the quality of being expert in a particular field of knowledge or technical skill. Hostility towards experts stems from that period, when thinking about democracy came to be intoxicated with belief in the possibility of levelling and remoulding society into harmonious political communities of self-governing equals. From this period dates the orthodox conviction that expertise and democracy don't mix – that democracy is a recipe for self-government of the ignorant, or that the very idea of expertise is an insult to democracy,

---

[13] Jemma L. Wadham *et al.*, 'Potential Methane Reservoirs beneath Antarctica', *Nature*, 488 (2012), 633–637.
[14] See the special issue devoted to citizen science in *Frontiers in Ecology and the Environment*, 10 (2012).

either because everybody is an expert, or because nobody is an expert. The conviction feeds questions that are still heard today. How possibly can democrats approve of claims to superior knowledge and technical know-how? Surely, the cold and aloof arrogance of experts clashes openly with the democratic principle of equality of all people and their opinions? Isn't the so-called scientific-technical or professional knowledge on which experts stake their know-all claims bound up with a bid for power over others?

The scepticism buried deep within such questions is understandable. In matters of power, self-described experts have a tainted past. Think for a moment of the many well-documented cases during the past century in which so-called experts sided with powerful authorities against the principles and practice of democratic power sharing. The active fascination of intellectuals with the God of totalitarian power, the willingness of medical doctors to turn a blind eye to the Hippocratic oath by performing hideous experiments on their victim patients, the organised harnessing of scientific knowledge to produce deadly chemical, biological and nuclear weapons: these are just the tip of the iceberg of the propensity of experts to side with abusive arbitrary power, or so many critics and observers have noted.[15] So a note of caution is most definitely needed. In practice, experts can and do abuse their authority. They are indeed prone to believe unquestioningly in their own esoteric insights, especially when 'groupthink' pressures set in. Like others caught up in webs of power relations, experts can also easily violate their own standards of non-partisanship, by being on somebody's side, and not the side of others.[16]

---

[15] Richard Crossman (ed.), *The God that Failed: A Confession* (London: Harper, 1949); Robert Jay Lifton, *The Nazi Doctors: Medical Killing and the Psychology of Genocide* (New York: Basic Books, 1988); and Richard Rhodes, *The Making of the Atomic Bomb* (New York: Simon & Schuster, 1986).

[16] The point that experts are neither angels nor wizards is made clear when re-examining the kind of claims made after the First World War by the most famous American journalist, Walter Lippmann, who called for the creation of think tanks filled with experts, 'political observatories' he called them, whose job was to save democracy from the ignorance of its own citizens. See Walter Lippmann, *Public Opinion* (New York: Harcourt, Brace & Co., 1922). Lippmann's proposal admittedly harboured ambivalence, if only because he was well aware of the need to keep government by experts on a leash. Just as citizens regularly reject the advice or seek second opinions when dealing with architects, accountants, dentists and doctors, so they need to do the same with experts who advise governments or civil society organisations, Lippmann reasoned. Yet he also emphasised that experts, by dint of their professional training and peer- or publicly-monitored codes of conduct and competence, tend to bring different standards of judgement and views of the world

12 Antarctica: Democracy at the End of the World 359

It is unclear from the limited available research whether, and to what extent, the citizen scientists of Antarctica are in this sense nowadays in breach of the rules of expertise, for instance because of 'groupthink' pressures, publishing pressures and the distorting effects of government sponsorship and funding. Many Antarctic scientists acknowledge the need for a measure of democratic openness within their own ranks, in that they strictly observe clearly defined codes of professional conduct and subject themselves to ongoing peer group reviews designed to prevent their expertise from degenerating into 'pal-ship'.[17] These experts display humility. They recognise that institutionally distorted science is the *violation of expertise*, if by that word is meant what Niels Bohr, the Nobel prize-winning physicist famous for his contributions to quantum mechanics, had in mind when pondering the subject. 'An expert', he liked to say, 'is someone who knows some of the worst mistakes that can be made in their subject, and who manages to avoid them'.[18] When expertise is understood in this revised and more modest way, as the capacity to puncture inflated expectations with the needle of specialised wisdom, then the relationship between democracy and experts looks rather different. The case of Antarctica most definitely reinforces this shift of perspective. It suggests that independently minded expertise can play a vital role in the public control and democratisation of arbitrary power.

Consider for a moment the example of efforts in Antarctica to develop Earth system science. Widely considered to be among the most promising efforts to expand our understanding of complex global environmental processes, earth system science is a challenge to scientific and political business as usual. It is a bold research programme that sees our planet Earth as a complex ensemble of interactive components that include biotic and a-biotic forces as well as bio-geophysical components and anthropogenic drivers. The programme aims to provide integrated and comprehensive interpretations of the dynamic interactions between humans and the Earth. An example is current research on the East Antarctic and West Antarctic ice sheets of the continent. Superlatives are required to grasp their scale and motion. Nearly 90 per cent of ice (and 70 per cent of fresh

---

into the alleyways and corridors of power, which is good for democracy, or so he concluded.

[17] Michael Schudson, 'The Trouble with Experts – and Why Democracies Need Them', in *Why Democracies Need an Unlovable Press* (Cambridge: Polity Press, 2008), pp. 108–125.

[18] Cited by Edward Teller, in Robert Coughlan, 'Dr. Edward Teller's Magnificent Obsession', *LIFE* magazine (6 September 1954), p. 62.

water) on our planet is locked into these sheets. Together they are one-and-a-half times the size of the United States, twice the size of Australia and much larger than Europe. They comprise one-tenth of the land surface of the Earth. Positioned well above sea level on a continent that is on average three times higher than any other, these ice sheets are at their deepest over five kilometres thick and break off into the ocean at the rate of many thousands of cubic kilometres each year. With mean temperatures now rising, Earth system scientists warn that any alteration of these patterns would have serious consequences for the rest of our planet. If the East Antarctic Ice Sheet was to suffer meltdown, then sea levels worldwide would rise more than 50 metres. The melting of the West Antarctic Ice sheet – thought by scientists to be a more likely prospect during the foreseeable future – would increase sea levels by at least five metres.

What do these estimates tell us more generally about the role of scientific expertise? It is routinely observed by visitors to Antarctica that although scientists there are outnumbered ten to one by their support staff, they like to think of themselves as the top dogs of their respective field stations. Yet far more significant is the way these same elite scientists understand their work as beginning from scratch. For instance, members of SCAR, the Scientific Committee on Antarctic Research, a body charged with providing international, independent scientific advice to the Antarctic Treaty System institutions, typically do not think of themselves as know-alls. They refrain from acting as though they are philosopher queens and kings who have mastered the arts of certainty, objectivity and universal knowledge that can be implemented with technical precision and effectiveness. They instead regard themselves as caught up in the open-ended uncertainties of research. Like geologists sifting through endless piles of rocks in search of fossils (a scene captured in Annie Aghion's documentary, *Ice People* [2008]), scientists think of themselves as 'actants' confronted not just with the vagaries of grant applications, budgets, equipment and working conditions but, above all, with chronic muddles and fuddles to do with such elementary matters as the design of research frameworks, methods of collecting data and human disturbances of the biomes under investigation. Their most daunting challenge is how to decide the significance and meaning of the things they research. What relevance has the discovery of mystery species of bacterial life that have been living in isolation within Antarctica's sub-glacial lakes, under intense pressure, and with no sunlight, for millions of years? How adaptable to ocean acidification and reduced salinity (both caused by rising carbon emissions) are the marine species of the Southern Ocean? Why exactly do scientists who over-winter on the continent (French scientists call themselves 'hivernauts') run high risks of 'free run' disturbances of their circadian rhythms, random re-settings of their internal body clocks that trigger their sense of 'being dead', or 'not real'?

These are just a few of the many questions that show that under conditions of tantalising uncertainty, expertise in Antarctica tends to have sobering effects on scientists and all parties concerned, just as Bohr predicted. Scientists there raise many more questions than they can answer. They are bearers of doubt, specialists in contrapuntal reasoning. As the example of the possible break-up of the Antarctic ice sheets suggests, experts are quite capable of flinging counter-points and counter-perspectives at the powers that be. Pundits often describe this as speaking 'truth' to power, but (as we have seen earlier) given the many well-known difficulties with that weasel word, wisdom counsels against its use. Much better to see that what Antarctica experts do when they act properly as experts is to feed into political processes alternative perspectives that can and do put pressure on both governments and businesses and citizens, encouraging them all to think twice, to refine their thinking, even to change their ways.

THE END OF SOVEREIGNTY

Thanks to the foundational role played by citizen scientists in events that led to the signing of the Antarctic Treaty, Antarctica became the first continent to abandon and push beyond the modern doctrine of sovereign territorial states. That doctrine supposed that states can rightfully lay claim and possess territory if they demonstrate in practice that their grip on that territory is effective and durable. As a muscular motivating force in world affairs, the doctrine proved virile in the history of attempted conquests of the lands and seas of Antarctica by various European powers. A version of the doctrine certainly played a key role in the Antarctic Treaty negotiations. Its force is registered in Article IV, which emphasises that the existing sovereignty claims of the contracting states remain intact. Within the Treaty system, the sovereignty mentality remains alive. It was famously articulated by General Augusto Pinochet, during his visit to Antarctica in 1977, when he told French journalists: 'I have been all over Chile, only this part was missing.' The same territorial mentality is encoded in the 2010 Argentine legislation that makes compulsory the use of a bi-continental map in every government agency, and at all levels of that country's education system. These examples serve as reminders that in matters concerning Antarctica and its future, sovereignty remains a keyword. But has the settlement of Antarctica altered, or at least compounded, its range of meanings? Has Antarctica begun to loosen the grip of sovereignty on our political imaginations?

To answer these questions, the category of sovereignty needs briefly to be reconsidered. Its theological origins are worth noting. So, too, are its 'meme' qualities, its propensity for replication and mutation and time–space variation (an example is the early modern doctrine of popular sovereignty, which is an earthly form of the originally Christian theological doctrine of God as the singular source of political authority). It's worth remembering as well that the sovereignty principle has triggered bitter controversies about both its meaning and legitimacy.[19] What is nevertheless striking is the resilience of the early modern European doctrine of sovereignty, whose earliest definitions are traceable to such political writers as Jean Bodin: 'All the characteristics of sovereignty are contained in this, to have power to give laws to each and everyone of his subjects, and to receive none.'[20] This way of political reasoning, repeated by Thomas Hobbes and a thousand subsequent writers, was bound up with the expansion of European empires through webs of corridors and enclaves, such as sea lanes, rivers and roads connecting island bases, missions, trading posts, towns and garrisons.[21] The establishment of sovereignty over foreign lands, we can say, took place not merely by force of arms. It also happened through imperial acts of legal possession against the claims of rivals. In addition to legal talk of sovereignty, various other techniques were used to establish sovereign claims: the planting of flags and crosses; the establishment of settlements; the drafting of maps and travel itineraries that eased officials' navigation within distant realms; and the creation of new governing structures that served as carriers of the sovereignty imaginary.

It was within this historical context that William Blackstone's well-known and influential *Commentaries on the Laws of England* (1765–1770) forcefully presented a version of the sovereignty principle. 'How the several forms of government we now see in the world at first actually began, is a matter of great uncertainty, and has occasioned infinite

---

[19] An example is the early work of Harold J. Laski, *Studies in the Problem of Sovereignty* (New Haven: Yale University Press, 1917).

[20] Jean Bodin, *Les Six Livres de la République* (Paris: Jacques du Puy, 1576), Book 1, chapter 9.

[21] Lauren Benton, *A Search for Sovereignty: Law and Geography in European Empires, 1400–1900* (New York: Cambridge University Press).

disputes', he wrote. 'However they began, or by what right soever they subsist, there is and must be in all of them a supreme, irresistible, absolute, uncontrolled authority, in which the *jura summi imperii* or the rights of sovereignty, reside.'[22]

Such thinking, the belief that 'sovereign is he who decides on the exception', owed at least some of its force to its theological bent, or so argued the Weimar jurist and political thinker Carl Schmitt. 'All significant concepts of the modern theory of the state are secularised theological concepts', he wrote, so that 'the omnipotent God became the omnipotent lawgiver ... The exception in jurisprudence is analogous to the miracle in theology.'[23] In other words, sovereignty is a word bound up with disagreement, mounting tensions, political outbursts, power struggles that may well end in the surprise declaration of a state of emergency (what Schmitt called the *Ausnahmezustand*). The principle of sovereignty is bellicose. It supposes the possibility and desirability of unlimited power, omnipotence. Sovereignty can't be shared. It is indivisible. It comes alive at the moment when those who control state institutions decide arbitrarily for others what is to be done, and see that it is done, if necessary by robbing their opponents of their liberties, properties, livelihoods and lives.

SLOW DEMOCRACY

Antarctica, we could say, took revenge on this particular understanding of the doctrine of sovereignty. For reasons of space, the detailed circumstances that led to the signing of the 1959 Antarctic Treaty cannot be probed here. What is important to note is the way the treaty enabled Antarctica to become the first continent to abandon, and to push beyond, the modern doctrine of sovereign territoriality. It was as if the architects of the Antarctic Treaty anticipated the recommendation 'to deconstruct the concept of sovereignty, never to forget its theological filiation and to be ready to call this filiation into question wherever we discern its effects'.[24] A version of the old doctrine of sovereignty certainly played a key role in the Antarctic Treaty negotiations. Its force is registered in Article IV, which emphasises that the existing sovereignty claims of the

---

[22] William Blackstone, *Commentaries on the Laws of England* (Oxford: Clarendon Press, 1766–1769), book 1, introduction, section 2.
[23] Carl Schmitt, *Political Theology: Four Chapters on the Concept of Sovereignty* (Cambridge, MA: MIT Press, 1985), p. 36.
[24] Jacques Derrida, *The Beast and the Sovereign*, Vol. I (Chicago, IL: University of Chicago Press, 2009).

contracting states remain intact. Yet what is really interesting about the Treaty, which was signed by twelve states, seven of which lodged territorial claims, is that its drafters proceeded to specify that no new sovereignty claims, or enlargements of existing sovereignty claims, are permitted so long as the Treaty is in force. In effect, the agreement among sovereign states, most of which were democracies (the clear exceptions were the Soviet Union and South Africa), was an agreement to disagree about their respective sovereignty claims. 'No acts or activities taking place while the present Treaty is in force', states Article IV, 'shall constitute a basis for asserting, supporting or denying a claim to territorial sovereignty in Antarctica or create any rights of sovereignty in Antarctica.'

Here was the equivalent of a theological miracle: the fiery doctrine of sovereignty was placed on ice. Its deep freezing preserved a contradiction, certainly. But it also made possible the construction of a complex new architecture of government that bears no relationship to any known textbook account of government. But what kind of polity is Antarctica? Some observers commend it as a workable hotchpotch arrangement of entangled states, or as a model of 'sovereign neutrality'.[25] Most observers pass over the question in silence. That is a pity, for considered in descriptive terms, as a functioning set of governing institutions, Antarctica is a trend-setter, a new type of cosmopolitan law-bound polity defined by a mixture of overlapping power-sharing jurisdictions that are connected with the rest of the world, and (arguably) have important implications for how it might in future be governed.

The novelty of its polity, its practical dismantlement of territorial state sovereignty, is evident on a variety of fronts. Talk of sovereignty always implied, in circumstances when push comes to shove, that states can rightfully lay claim, possess and defend territory if they demonstrate in practice that their grip on that territory is effective and durable. As a macho-muscular and frequently bellicose force in world affairs, the originally European doctrine, as is well known, proved virile in the history of attempted conquests of the lands and seas of Antarctica by various European powers. Yet today Antarctica has no standing armies or police forces or (as far as we know) surveillance agencies operating on its territory. Argentina's Operación 90 (1965) is one of the few documented

---

[25] Gillian Triggs, 'The Antarctic Treaty System: A Model of Legal Creativity and Cooperation', in Paul A. Berkman, Michael A. Lang, David W. H. Walton and Oran R. Young (eds.), *Science Diplomacy: Antarctica, Science, and the Governance of International Spaces* (Washington, DC: Smithsonian Institution Scholarly Press, 2011), pp. 39–49.

cases of a military land manoeuvre on the continent. Conducted in secret, so as not to upset the two superpowers of the time, the manoeuvre in support of Argentina's land claims ended happily. Thanks to a chance encounter with an American radar operator, and confirmation they were not Soviet troops, the Argentine soldiers were invited to his base, where the food, according to their commander, General Jorge Leal, was the best his troops had eaten in some weeks.

In Antarctica, there is no executive power in the form of a presidency or prime ministerial system. The continent has no centralised taxation agency, no national judiciary, no bureaucracy (the Antarctic Treaty Secretariat, established in 2004, isn't comparable to a civil service) and no welfare state institutions. The new polity of Antarctica doesn't even have a proper textbook name. It's a mode of self-government comprising a dynamic and highly complex mosaic of different types of overlapping legal and governmental institutions guided by the principle that unconstrained ('sovereign') power is power that is arbitrary, dangerous and illegitimate.

The governing architecture of Antarctica has decidedly unusual qualities. Amidst the jungle of acronyms – the European Union has no monopoly on upper case stage names – there are many paradoxes. Things aren't what they often seem to be. Its polity has kaleidoscopic qualities. For instance, the instruments through which the continent is governed simultaneously pay homage to the principle of state sovereignty while in practice transcending its limits by means of a tangle of supra-national structures. The Antarctic Treaty, agreed by a dozen states reluctant to cede powers to their competitors, has resulted in a rather sizeable and elaborate web of government and legal institutions whose regulatory powers far exceed what was originally envisaged. The creation of a permanent Secretariat to administer the Antarctic Treaty and its offshoot bodies feeds the trend towards post-sovereignty, or what I have elsewhere called cosmocracy.[26] The same trend is evident in the expansion of the number of so-called Consultative Parties (there are now twenty-nine member states in this category) and also the central role played by the supra-national Antarctic Treaty Consultative Meeting (ATCM). Since 1994, it has become something of a parliament. It is an annual meeting of various representatives, observers and invited experts hosted for two weeks by one of the Consultative Parties, in the

---

[26] John Keane, *Global Civil Society?* (Cambridge: Cambridge University Press, 2003), pp. 92–128.

alphabetical order of their English-language name; like the European Parliament, which convenes in Strasbourg and Brussels, the ATCM is a geographically mobile legislature of voting representatives.

From the standpoint of modern textbooks and classic authors, the compound, polycentric architecture of government in Antarctica is an incomprehensible mutant, yet its durability and functionality are striking. Compared with rigidly geometric hyper-centralised institutions, the architecture of government in Antarctica comprises a flexible, dynamic system of positively clumsy institutions marked by what might be dubbed 'useful inefficiencies'. These inefficiencies are useful in the sense that they facilitate access to power by outsiders and the sharing of power among the various represented parties. Such clumsiness – awkwardness of rhythm or performance – is not normally considered a political virtue. In the case of Antarctica, the word well describes a definite virtue of its governing system, which through time has become ever more differentiated, subtle and sophisticated. The polity of Antarctica is a type of 'mixed constitution' (Polybius) in a higher, more plural, more democratic form. Governing processes are openly 'messy', recursive and sometimes self-contradictory. Thanks to the tangled, rhizomatous (or rootstalk-like) structures of decision making, demarcation disputes abound. Matters are discussed, batted about, sometimes vetoed; details are probed, second and third opinions are solicited, compromises are struck, often after infuriating bouts of brinkmanship and slow-motion negotiations.

Antarctica could be said to be a strange new form of slow democracy. By that I am not referring to the familiar point (once attributed to Thomas Carlyle, the lover of noble talent, no great friend of democracy, and recently repeated by David Runciman[27]) that democracy is cumbersome, slow and inefficient, and that in due time the voice of the people will be heard, and their latent wisdom will prevail through good leadership. I rather have in mind something more complicated, more enigmatic and more pragmatic: under Antarctic conditions, when questions arise concerning who gets what, when and how, and who represents whom, matters are typically subject to open deliberation and decided through what are called decisions, measures and resolutions – each following their own practical rule-bound logic, and each subject to a unanimity rule. *Decisions* bear upon internal organisational matters of the ATCM. *Resolutions* are not legally binding on the contracting parties; they are

---

[27] David Runciman, *The Confidence Trap: A History of Democracy in Crisis from World War I to the Present* (Princeton, NJ: Princeton University Press, 2013).

hortatory texts, directed beyond their ranks to include various interested parties. Then there are *measures*, which are legally binding once they have been approved by all the Consultative Parties.

Decisions, resolutions and measures are all encased within multilateral legal networks that highlight the passing away of the fiction of the legal sovereignty of territorial states. Yes, talk of sovereignty survives. Perhaps it is on the increase, fuelled by anxieties about the return of China to the global stage and often sustained by bizarre definitions (the claim by Argentina, for instance, is based on such ragbag criteria as 'historical heritage coming from Spain', former 'seal-hunting activities', 'installation and management of lighthouses', scientific and military operations and the 'rescue' of two Englishmen from misfortune[28]). The propensity of member states to fast-track decisions, and so to challenge the multilateral legal framework designed to serve the common good, is also alive and well, as shown by the Japanese Whaling case, brought by the Humane Society International in the Australian Federal Court.[29] Despite these anomalies, the new Antarctic reality has moved beyond the old world of sovereignty. The polycentric governing institutions of the continent are proving durable, in no small measure because they come clothed in law. Subject to legalisation through forms of 'soft' and 'hard' (*erga omnes*) legal arrangements, these institutions regularly function as brakes on

---

[28] Anne-Marie Brady, *China as a Great Global Power* (Cambridge and New York: Cambridge University Press, 2017). See also the eclectic extended list of sovereignty claim criteria provided in Dirección Nacional del Antártico – Instituto Antártico Argentino, 'Argentina in Antarctica', at www.dna.gov.ar/INGLES/DIVULGAC/ARGANT.HTM (accessed 9 September 2012): 'Main claims are as follows: 1. Geographical and geological continuity, 2. Historical heritage coming from Spain, 3. Seal-hunting activities since their starting in the area; 4. Standing occupation of a scientific station running since the beginning of the century until the present: the Meteorological and Magnetic Observatory of South Orkney Islands, inaugurated in 1904; 5. The installation and maintenance of other temporary stations in the Antarctic peninsula and nearby islands, as well as in the Filchner ice shelf, as well as a number of shelters in different spots of the sector; 6. Exploration works, scientific and cartographical surveys on a regular basis; 7. Installation and management of lighthouses and aid to navigation; 8. Rescue, help or support tasks, such as the saving at the beginning of the XIX century of the eminent Swedish explorer and scientist Otto Nordenskjöld and his crew, the rescue of a sick man and an victim of an accident, both Englishmen from the distant Fossil Bluff Station; 9. Argentine presence on land, sea and air in the whole Sector, including the South Pole, reached for three times alternatively by Navy and Air Force aircrafts and by the terrestrial Army expedition so-called Operation 90.'

[29] Details of the case brought by the conservation group, Humane Society International (HSI), under section 475 of the Environment Protection and Biodiversity Conservation Act 1999, are found at www.envlaw.com.au/whale.html.

attempts by states to exercise power arbitrarily, without public scrutiny, in the old sovereignty ways.

If Antarctica is a law-abiding post-sovereign polity comprising a salmagundi of clumsy power-sharing institutions, themselves designed to produce and administer decisions subject to the exercise of voting rights, then matters are made even more complicated, conceptually speaking, by the fact that its governing instruments are not tied in any simple sense to territory. The Antarctica polity has quantum qualities. Entangled in worldwide webs of interdependence that are oiled by space- and time-shrinking flows of communication, Antarctic politics does not stand in splendid isolation from the rest of the world. Spillover effects, arbitrage pressures and butterfly effects are common. The upshot is that things that happen politically within and around the continent sometimes have effects elsewhere, in far-away locations. The reverse also commonly happens: events, information flows, declarations and deals that happen in far-off places can and do have immediate consequences in Antarctica. The decision (in 2006) by a South Korean court to allow action against a Togo-registered ship engaged in illegal, unreported and unregulated fishing in the Southern Ocean; the whale-protection campaigns waged by the Sea Shepherd Conservation Society (banned in mid-December 2012 by the US Ninth Circuit Court of Appeals); and the Whaling in the Antarctic case led by Australia against Japan – these are just three of a burgeoning number of examples of the hybrid push–pull ways power is checked, and the continent governed according to the principle of non-locality, through monitory mechanisms, sometimes at vast distances from its shores.

SOVEREIGNTY AND THE DOMINATION OF NATURE

It is not often noted that Antarctica has dispensed with the formal imagery of sovereignty. It's true there is an emblem of the Antarctic Treaty, featuring a white continent marked by lines of latitude and longitude; as well, there's a richly contested variety of both serious and satirical cartographic representations, ranging from the continent wrapped in national flags, including the ensign of the short-lived Nazi protectorate of Neuschwabenland, to the multi-coloured LGBTI flag map of Antarctica. Yet the fact is that Antarctica has no official flag, no national anthem or currency or coat of arms.

Something much more historically unusual and of deeper long-term significance is also at work. Put simply, Antarctica is the first continent to rid itself of the bestial metaphors in which the doctrine of sovereignty

12 Antarctica: Democracy at the End of the World 369

always came wrapped. The point is typically ignored by journalists, diplomats and scholars alike. Expressed in terse terms, sovereignty always had a feral snarl.[30] The big and pompous modern European idea of sovereignty typically supposed that a people living within a territory would otherwise quarrel and be violent, and tear one another to bits, unless governed, above all in moments of exception, by a sharp-edged form of armed power that is unified, unconditional and indivisible. The whole idea of state sovereignty supped with the devilish image of the sovereign ruler pitted against the wild animal. Think for a moment of Mustapha Kemal, who named himself Atatürk (Father of the Nation) and was nicknamed the 'grey wolf': sovereign are those rulers who manage to separate themselves from, and rise above, the world of nature, which was typically thought of as a fear-ridden domain ruled by beasts locked permanently in deathly power struggles. Sovereign rulers are different, or so it was argued. They bring orderly rule. Yet in laying down the laws, within a demarcated territory, using force if necessary, they reserve for themselves the prerogative of acting outside the laws, just like wild animals.

Take a well-known early example of this seductive but self-contradictory vision of sovereign rule: Machiavelli's recommendation (chapter 18 of *The Prince*) that the good and powerful ruler must act as both a lion and a fox. Sovereign are those rulers who know that they must of necessity roar like a lion and be as crafty as a fox, so as to scare and cajole the resident population into conformity, for the sake of its own self-preservation, within a demarcated territorial setting, protected from its external enemies. In this well-known formulation, the condition of possibility of sovereignty is also its undoing. For it turns out that the ruling sovereign and the wild animal beast are an oddly matched pair. In order to act in sovereign ways, the sovereign by definition must overcome the beast within itself. But by acting in an unbounded fashion, the sovereign behaves just like a beast, ruling ultimately through fear and violence, unconstrained by customs, laws and procedures, which, for the sake of order and good government, it nevertheless creates and then imposes on to others from the outside.

Since the 1950s, developments in Antarctica have strongly challenged, and in some cases rejected outright, the deeply anti-democratic, bestial imagery coded into the old sovereignty principle. As scholars have

---

[30] Jacques Derrida, *The Beast & the Sovereign* (Chicago, IL and London: University of Chicago Press, 2009), especially pp. 1–31.

warned, the paralysing uncertainty surrounding the polity of Antarctica should not be underestimated. Antarctica is feeling the pinch of climate warming and ocean acidification. Tourism is expanding, along with safety and environmental risks. There are signs of growing rivalry among some claimant states interested in extracting Antarctic resources and disrupting the consensus of the 'Antarctic club'.[31] Even so, long-term changes should not be overlooked. In fact, the rejection of bestial imagery may be the most important, and irreversible, achievement of the governing arrangements of Antarctica, where metaphors of fixed territory, rule and wild animals are conspicuous by their absence.

The symptoms of this metamorphosis are plain to see. Most obviously, governing arrangements in Antarctica reject the fixed territorial mentality and the will to dominate nature built into the doctrine of sovereignty. Just like the continent's birds, sea cucumbers and free-swimming snails, which know no fixed abode and (remarkably) find the energy and bearings to migrate annually from pole to pole, the legal and governmental institutions targeted at the continent are co-defined by, and connected to, parallel and sometimes overlapping mechanisms located elsewhere. Antarctica is the embodiment of the quantum principle of non-locality: those who seek to govern the continent are daily reminded that the continent is not 'dead' or lifeless territory. It is a vibrant biosphere, comprising living systems permanently in motion, interconnected with the rest of the planet. Symbols of this dynamism include the seals that want to play and interrupt scientists as they go about their fieldwork; and the emperor penguins that seem as naturally skilled at the arts of posing and performing before cameras as they are in organising altruistic wave-motion huddles to ensure that each individual penguin member stays warm. The UN Highly Migratory Fish Stocks Agreement and the High Seas Fisheries Compliance Agreement are two revealing institutional cases of the same point: both agreements involve efforts to protect endangered species of fish, which of course recognise no fixed territorial boundaries, and whose protection and nurturing require alternative arrangements guided by precautionary principles.

Humble stewardship of the dynamically contingent, the fragile and the vulnerable: especially since the adoption (from the end of the 1980s) of the Environmental Protocol and its numerous Annexes, these metaphors, and general sympathy for the biosphere, have come to replace the old bestial

---

[31] Ben Saul and Tim Stephens (eds.), *Antarctica in International Law* (Oxford: Hart Publishing, 2015).

12 Antarctica: Democracy at the End of the World

images of sovereignty. The flipside of this semantic switch is a new politics of representation of the non-human world. When analysing the 'spirit' and practices of such bodies as the Convention on Biological Diversity (CBD), the International Maritime Organization (IMO) and the Agreement on Conservation of Albatrosses and Petrels (ACAP), all of which politically shape Antarctica as we know it today, what is striking is how they widen and deepen inherited meanings of political representation.

What's meant by this? We have already noted that all human societies create ways of registering or re-presenting their interdependence with the natural world and its elements by means of verbal, oral and pictorial signifiers. Antarctica obeys this rule, but gives it a twist. It's perhaps an exaggeration to put things this way, but the continent is a world-leading laboratory in the arts of enfranchising nature. It brings to life, and puts into practice, new ways of imagining the political inclusion of the biosphere as a legitimate, potentially equal partner, within human affairs. In Antarctica, the nature/politics dualism of the doctrine of sovereignty no longer makes sense. It's not just a continent where non-human nature constantly makes its presence felt among the humans who dwell or visit there. It's also (conversely) a place where awareness runs high among humans that there are different ways of representing and acting upon the biosphere. In other words, the biosphere is not seen as raw, non-human, 'out there' nature, ripe for human exploitation, but as a complex set of interacting living elements whose significance is shaped by human perceptions and actions, which are themselves bound up with the deep dynamics of the biosphere.

By experimenting with new ways of practically extending voices and votes to our fragile biomes, Antarctica does more than revive and stretch the principle of the political representation of non-human domains. Arguably, the most far-reaching political significance of Antarctica is the way both positive and threatening developments there prompt fundamental twenty-first-century questions about whether human beings are capable of humbling ourselves by collectively recognising our ineluctably deep dependence upon the biomes in which we dwell. Are human beings capable, in theory and practice, of ridding ourselves of our own anthropocentrism? Can we live beyond the still-dominant view that we humans are the pinnacle of creation, lords and ladies of the universe, 'the people' and their states who are the ultimate source of sovereign power and authority on Earth? Is Antarctica perhaps even an important harbinger of the global commons principle, a reminder that the Earth's surface should not be carved up by national jurisdictions?

THE FUTURE?

These are fundamental political questions that await twenty-first century answers, and actions to reinforce them. Growing numbers of observers are acutely aware of their importance. They wax eloquent about Antarctica as an unusual scientific laboratory, a global commons of immeasurable value to the world, the last unspoiled wilderness, a bellwether of global trends. But the point emphasised in this chapter is that Antarctica is also a remarkable political experiment of great global relevance. It is a site of the self-democratisation of humans. Human pride is suffering a fall; old arrogance towards the biosphere has given way to a new humility; human awareness of our dependence upon fragile biomes entitled to human respect and protection has gained much ground. Antarctica is a continent where new ways of politically enfranchising and representing nature have been invented. It is also the first continent to abandon and go beyond the modern doctrine of sovereign territorial states. Antarctica is a law-abiding, post-sovereign polity comprising many 'clumsy' power-sharing institutions designed to produce and administer decisions subject to public scrutiny and the exercise of voting rights. Its governing instruments are not tied to territory in any simple sense. Entangled in worldwide webs of interdependence, Antarctica can be seen as an unusual species of monitory democracy defined by its reliance upon many public scrutiny mechanisms, a parliament in the making (the ATCM) and by unelected and extra-parliamentary representatives, including scientists, whose role as 'watchdogs' of human power and 'guardian' representatives of the biosphere are contributing to the redefinition and 'democratisation' of expertise.

Can this novel species of dispersed democracy in monitory form survive the mounting pressures of our century? The question is unavoidable, if only because Antarctica faces a veritable mountain of unresolved difficulties. Their symbol is Erebus, the volcano that spits fire and fumes over the frozen continent, in memory of the son of the primordial god Chaos, the personification in Greek mythology of deep darkness, an underworld where the dead spend time after dying. Antarctica promises a bright new future for monitory democracy, but it is not heaven on earth. It has its own Erebus of mounting troubles, dark trends that now bear down on both its delicate biomes and its fragile architecture of self-government.

The contours of these new threats are not difficult to detect. Original signatories to the Treaty are beginning to make noise about the need to occupy their share of claimed Antarctica territory.[32] Fears are rising that the continent will be subjected to commercial exploitation. The Protocol on Environmental Protection to the Antarctic Treaty (the Madrid Protocol) bans all forms of mining until 2048, when (according to Article 25) any party can summon a conference to propose modifications, or outright abandonment, of the protocol. In practice, such changes will prove difficult: 75 per cent of the original parties to the protocol would have to agree. In the interim, the continent nevertheless remains vulnerable to corporate market rumblings. Evidence of mineral deposits stored beneath the continental rocks and ice is plentiful. Large deposits of iron ore have been discovered in the Prince Charles Mountains region. The continent, once rich in flora and fauna millions of years ago, when Eastern Antarctica was located at the equator, also contains large deposits of coal. The dirty spectre of an Arctic oil and gas rush haunts the continent, especially given that the confirmed oil and natural gas deposits in the Ross Sea could be accessed using new extraction technologies designed to withstand extreme cold.

Scientists meanwhile remain alert to the meaning and significance of odd anomalies. The ozone hole, which in the month of September covers much of its land mass, is still growing in size. In 2005, an area of ice the size of California briefly melted, and research suggests that Antarctica is warming due to human carbon dioxide emissions. The citizen scientists are noting warmer ocean temperatures, changes in the seasonality and coverage of sea ice and the disappearance and below-surface melting of floating ice shelves. Glacier outflow rates in West Antarctica are on the rise; and in the Antarctic Peninsula, where during the past 50 years temperatures have risen four times faster than the global average, there have been several ice shelf collapses, including at Larsen-B, whose 3,000-square kilometre ice shelf, stable for 12,000 years, suddenly collapsed during a three-week period (in 2002).

---

[32] An example is the recommendation of Ellie Fogarty, *Antarctica: Assessing and Protecting Australia's National Interests* (Sydney: Lowy Institute, 2011), pp. 10–11: 'With claimant states now representing only one quarter of ATS consultative States Parties, it is important for Australia to determine which other states might share common positions on divisive questions such as sovereignty claims and resource exploitation.' Fogarty adds: 'Although any state activity undertaken while the Treaty is in force cannot be seen as asserting or supporting a claim to sovereignty, Australia nonetheless needs to increase its occupation and presence. Greater occupation, and the ability to access all of its claimed territory, will make it less difficult for Australia to argue its case for sovereignty in future.'

Numbers of tourists have meanwhile grown from small-scale 'expedition tourism' in the 1960s into a big business, rising steadily from around 27,000 tourists visiting the continent during the 2011–2012 season to more than 38,000 during the 2015–2016 season. Their movements are currently self-regulated by the International Association of Antarctica Tour Operators (IAATO), a body which has a direct interest in expanded numbers, unfortunately within biomes so delicate (to take one example: a single human footprint in moss lingers decades before it disappears) that calls are growing louder for legally binding action against mass tourism, ever larger and accident-prone vessels and land-based hotels. The role of tourism in the introduction of alien species and diseases to wildlife is unknown. There are meanwhile calls for the tighter synchronisation or 'harmonisation' of currently conflicting laws and jurisdictions, so as to deal more effectively with such issues as biological prospecting, the growing volume of plastic bags and bottles and other pollutants, and the political conflicts in the Southern Ocean over whaling and unregulated fishing of species such as Antarctic and Patagonian tooth fish (marketed as Chilean sea bass). Especially controversial is the 'suction' harvesting of krill, paper-clip sized crustaceans with translucent reddish bodies and black eyes. Used as food for fish farms and as a source of Omega 3 oil in health supplements, krill populations have already declined (Antarctica scientists estimate) by around 80 per cent since the 1970s. The most probable cause is thought to be global warming, which is melting the ice that is home to the plankton and algae eaten by krill. Further decline in their numbers would likely threaten their predators (such as whales, albatrosses, petrels and penguins). By consuming very large quantities of carbon-rich food, krill additionally play a vital role in the large-scale 'sequestering' of carbon dioxide from the atmosphere of our planet.

Like monitory democracies elsewhere, the polity of Antarctica is subject as well to demands for *democratisation*. There seem to be rising concerns that the governing institutions of Antarctica are insufficiently representative of different social and political interests, that states themselves exercise too much influence, and that civil society organisations and networks should play a stronger role in the continent's 'clumsy' institutions, which remain vulnerable to penetration by the best-organised, richest and most powerful non-governmental bodies, especially commercial interests. As things stand, the whole polity could do with toothier public scrutiny mechanisms and more plural and inclusive patterns of representation, especially when it is considered (to take a few examples) that the US-based Antarctic and Southern Ocean Coalition (ASOC) is the only civil society organisation with expert observer status to the Antarctic Treaty System; that around 50 per cent of the states involved in the Antarctic Treaty System do not abide promptly by its rules of information exchange; and that, except for ritual opening photography sessions, the annual sessions of the parliament (the ATCM) typically happen behind closed doors, while even its working documents are embargoed until after its business is concluded.

So when all things are considered can this highly original political experiment called Antarctica rise to the occasion and handle these challenges? Future historians will be able to provide answers, but if the lines of questioning and analysis provided here have substance, then much depends on whether and how fast the world's political understanding of Antarctica can be enriched, great power rivalries and corporate interference refused, and public support among citizens and their representatives for its governing structures, and their democratic reform, strengthened.

PART V

VIOLENCE, FEAR, WAR

13

Does Democracy Have a Violent Heart?

The difficult subject of war and the traumas of war has so far been left unmentioned in these pages; now is the moment that their troubling connection with democracy must be analysed. Their topicality has recently been brought to life by the fact that virtually all democracies are today caught in the sticky threads of a permanent war against 'terror'. In the name of 'democracy protection' and 'democracy promotion', armies have been gathered and sent to foreign countries; forms of 'blowback' violence have come to plague the heartlands of monitory democracy; with the consequence that more than a few democratic institutions have been militarised, as if the permanent war for democracy has necessitated the trimming of their power-sharing, representative mechanisms. Civilians are subjected to dummy exercises, new forms of surveillance and routine 'security' checks; police powers have been expanded; the dark arts of surveillance are flourishing; and enemy torture has been justified publicly. All citizens have meanwhile been warned to be on guard, at all times, to conduct themselves as if their daily lives are a permanent battlefield. Electorates have even heard loud calls by politicians and intellectuals to protect governments, at home and abroad, by taking 'pre-emptive military actions against grave threats to their survival or to their civilian population'.[1]

Pressured by these trends – nothing yet needs to be said of the counter-trends – it is unsurprising that more than a few observers have recently drawn the conclusion that democracies have violent proclivities. Democracy is said to have a 'dark side' that sups with the devils of political

---

[1] Alan Dershowitz, *Preemption: A Knife That Cuts Both Ways* (New York and London: W. W. Norton & Company, 2006), p. 239.

violence; or it is claimed that democracy 'kills'.[2] One scholar has drawn the colourful conclusion that 'the origin and heart of democracy is essentially violent'. Violence, defined (loosely) as 'action forceful enough to produce an effect', is not just the result of contingent policies of particular democratically elected governments. It is inherent in every effort to establish or maintain democracy, if by that is meant 'any political system grounded in the idea that sovereignty lies with the people'. The principle of the sovereignty of the people can never be established democratically, or so it is argued. Democracy (it is said) is a strange impossibility. It always and everywhere rests upon foundational acts of violence: 'the massacre of indigenous populations, or the crushing of those who oppose a new foundation of the people's sovereignty' as well as 'the ongoing history of forgetting this original violence, not out of spite or indifference, but because the violence at the origin of democracy threatens democracy itself'.[3]

THE DEMOCRATISATION OF VIOLENCE

The conjecture that democracy and bellicosity are terrible twins is a healthy corrective to evolutionist views of democracy (like those of Francis Fukuyama[4]) that see only its benign freedom-loving qualities, or prefer to emphasise its 'world-historical' tendency to spread secular, science-induced economic growth across the whole earth. To insist that democracy has a violent heart is correctly to draw attention to the entanglement of democratic institutions and ideals in the facts and fantasies of war, but the protest it launches against democracy as an engine of war – paradoxically – feeds upon a deep-seated historical tendency for democracies to 'denature' war and other forms of violence. Like the rebellious teenager whose hot-tempered behaviour owes much to careful parental nurturing in the arts of resisting deference, so the thesis that democracy has a violent heart is symptomatic of the unusual sensitivity of actually existing democracies to war, and to other forms of violence. Monitory democracy enables the 'democratisation of violence'. By this unfamiliar phrase, I do

---

[2] Paul Collier, *Wars, Guns, and Votes* (London and New York: Vintage, 2009); Michael Mann, *The Dark Side of Democracy* (Cambridge and New York: Cambridge University Press, 2005); and Humphrey Hawksley, *Democracy Kills: What's So Good About the Vote?* (London: Macmillan, 2009).

[3] Daniel Ross, *Violent Democracy* (Melbourne: Cambridge University Press, 2005), especially the introduction, from which the citations are drawn.

[4] See the new afterword of Francis Fukuyama, *The End of History and the Last Man* (New York: The Free Press, 2006).

not mean that they encourage the arming of all citizens and their engagement in acts of violence of their choice – something like a macabre reversal of the historic 'ballots, not bullets' principle. To speak of the democratisation of violence is rather to say that democracies as we have come to know them unleash a process of the denaturing of violence in policy fields as different as the treatment of children and women in household settings through to efforts to rein in political leaders and military personnel who show no respect for others' dignity and instead practise cruelty as a way of life. The neologism (from the late 1950s) of 'domestic violence', the invention of satyagraha ('velvet') protest tactics, the spread of human rights culture and the public trial of bellicose heads of state all bear witness to this trend. The historical roots of this denaturing of violence run deep and are complicated. Their causes and causers – all unknown to the world of Athenian *dēmokratia* – include the invention of political mechanisms of peaceful compromise (parliaments, for instance[5]), the birth of civil societies, the growth of constitutional government, changing modes of warfare and bad experiences with the cruelty of both anti-democratic and democratic regimes doing things in the name of 'the people'. There is no space here to examine these trends in all their complexity, but the myriad symptoms are clear.[6] Institutions and acts of violence are no longer seen exclusively as willed by gods or a God, or determined by historical fate or by dastardly 'human nature'. Non-violent methods of publicly checking and regulating institutions of violence take root; they seek to ensure that these institutions – police forces, armies, secret intelligence bodies, private security companies – neither perpetrate surplus violence nor become permanently 'owned' by any particular power group, including the government of the day. The democratisation of war and other types of violence is a process that has the effect of rendering institutions and acts of violence publicly accountable and therefore as contingent: as acts of destructive power that are alterable and preventable through human will and effort. This process of 'democratisation' even affects the terms war and violence. The scope of application of these descriptors broadens; their meaning comes to be seen as heavily context-dependent and, hence, as variable in time and space; in consequence of

---

[5] John Keane, 'Dictatorship and the Decline of Parliament: Carl Schmitt's Theory of Political Sovereignty', in John Keane, *Democracy and Civil Society* (London and New York: Verso, 1988), pp. 153–189.

[6] More detailed analysis can be found in John Keane, *Violence and Democracy* (London and New York: Cambridge University Press, 2004) and *The Life and Death of Democracy* (London and New York: Simon & Schuster, 2009).

which the terms 'war' and 'violence' and their legitimacy come to be contested in such fields as criminal law, journalism, government policy – and (as is evident in recent controversies about torture) even within the ranks of armies whose ultimate job brief is to kill other human beings.

Why and how do democracies 'democratise' or de-nature war and other forms of violence? For a start, they enable public criticism of its necessity by means of clusters of monitory institutions that facilitate citizens' efforts to organise themselves and to speak about power and its abuse. (The force of open public criticism is usually felt during transitions to democracy, when public suspicion of men and institutions of violence is expressed with a sudden vengeance, like a geological upheaval: the *ancien regime* is accused of rape and murder; searches begin for those who have been disappeared; clandestine mass graves are exhumed; citizens are urged to tell their stories of cruelty and suffering.) The literature and art produced and/or circulated under democratic conditions, or with democratic aspirations, have been leaders in the critical representation of war and violence, and its pity. Various forms of democratic art aim to sensitise their audiences to the contingency or non-necessity of violence: think of *De Profundis* by Shostakovich, music set to the words of lament written by Lorca for loved ones murdered by Franco's troops; or the satires of war and warmongers that flowed from the typewriters of Robert Graves and other English war poets; or the novels and short stories of writers otherwise as different as Nabokov, Céline and Kafka. Democracies also suffer a normative problem with the cruelty and death that war brings. If monitory democracy, to put it simply, is a set of institutions and a whole way of life structured by non-violent means of equally apportioning and publicly monitoring power within and among overlapping communities of people who live according to a wide variety of morals, then war and violence – the unwanted interference with the bodies and personality of subjects – are anathema to its substance and spirit. But there is something about democracy that runs deeper than ethics: a distinctive feature of democracy, one that is usually given insufficient attention by observers but captured powerfully in one of the greatest odes to the democratisation of 'spirit' that democracies encourage and require, Ludwig Wittgenstein's *Über Gewissheit* (1959). It is this: the institutional dynamics and everyday culture of democratic institutions require for their operation shared perceptions of the complexity and contingency of things, of the non-necessity of what is given, an understanding that reality is not 'real', that claims to veracity can be doubted because they inevitably depend upon the acknowledgement of others, that in principle the extant power relations in any context can be named, re-described, challenged and altered.

EMPIRE AND DEMOCRACY

The contemporary democratisation of war and violence is merely a trend, with no historical guarantees of success, yet it implies and demands greater sensitivity to time–space variations of the vexed relationship between war and democracy. Essentialist propositions such as 'democracy is inherently bellicose' or 'violence is at the heart of democracy' should be doubted. They must be set aside in favour of efforts to think more deeply about their historically contingent relationship, beginning but not ending with the case of the *dēmokratia* of Athens.

The evidence assembled by archaeologists and classicists convincingly shows that the Athenian experiment with power-sharing and power-constraining democratic institutions was thoroughly entangled in contingent circumstances of city state rivalry, empire-building, war and rumours of war.[7] Especially from the time of the first efforts to assume leadership of a confederacy of Greek states, called the Delian League, whose several hundred members vowed 'to have the same friends and enemies' and whose military aim was the liberation from Persian control of the Greek island states and cities of Asia Minor (modern Turkey), Athens, step by step, state by state, turned herself into an imperial power – what the Athenians called an *arkhē*. Athenian democracy became good at launching and winning wars; despite the profusion of opportunities for citizens to become involved in politics, there were few signs of the democratisation of violence. If anything, the opposite was the case: imperial democracy in Athenian form developed a reputation at home and abroad for its *prophasis*, its growing power to strike fear into the hearts of others and, thus, to precipitate violent reactions. Among the most shocking things about Athens, it must be said, is that belligerence ran so deeply through its veins that the most famous oration in its defence (as Nicole Loraux has pointed out[8]) was a strangely aristocratic discourse that revealed much about the fascination of Pericles with imperial power and the 'normality'

---

[7] See David M. Pritchard, *Public Spending and Democracy in Classical Athens* (Austin, TX: University of Texas Press, 2015), and *Sport, Democracy, and War in Classical Athens* (Cambridge and New York: Cambridge University Press, 2013).
[8] Nicole Loraux, *The Invention of Athens: The Funeral Oration in the Classical City* (Cambridge, MA: MIT Press, 1993).

of democratic violence. Even more shocking – this point has hardly been explored in scholarship on Athens – is that the very word *dēmokratia* was infected by the spirit of war.[9]

Judged in terms of the democratisation of violence principle, the Athenian experiment with democracy started badly. To see why requires a closer examination of the connection between empire and democracy – a connection insufficiently researched in the literature on war and democracy. The Athenian democracy quickly grew to be an imperial polity: a dominant power whose rulers were prone to measure their strength against all their rivals combined. Pericles put the point succinctly: the power of democratic Athens at the beginning of the Peloponnesian War lay in her possession of naval forces more numerous and efficient than those of the rest of Hellas. So did Alcibiades, who doubted the possibility that Athens could exercise a 'careful stewardship' of its empire, exactly because those powers who do not 'hold empire over other peoples' themselves risk succumbing to 'the empire of others'.[10] It was from this

---

[9] See my *The Life and Death of Democracy*, especially pp. 55–62. The word *dēmokratia* (from *dēmos* and *kratos*, rule) became common currency in Athens during the early decades of transition sparked by the reforms of Cleisthenes and popular resistance to military intervention by the Spartans under Cleomenes. Historians like to say that the word carried several connotations, including for instance descriptive references to the deme and more positive links with the assembly of citizens, the *dēmos*. That is a fair but limited observation, for it fails to spot how the deeply negative connotations of the word *dēmokratia* – a form of polity defined by the exercise by some of self-interested or sectional power over others – are buried within the very word itself. The verb *kratein* (κρατεῖν) is usually translated as 'to rule' or 'to govern', but in fact its original connotations are harsher, tougher, even brutal. To use the verb *kratein* is to speak the language of military manoeuvring and military conquest: *kratein* means to be master of, to conquer, to lord over, to possess (in modern Greek the same verb means to keep, or to hold), to be the stronger, to prevail or get the upper hand over somebody or something. The story of the origins of the world and the birth of the deities told by the Greek poet Hesiod in his Theogony uses *kratein* in this way: the personified figure of Kratos is seen as the no-nonsense, loyal agent of the much-feared Zeus. Homer's Odyssey and Sappho's Supplements use *kratein* in the same sense. The noun *kratos* (κράτος), from which the compound *dēmokratia* was formed, similarly refers to might, strength, imperial majesty, toughness, triumphant power and victory over others, especially through the application of force. The now obsolete verb *dēmokrateo* (δημοκρατέω) brims with all of these connotations: it means to grasp power, or to exercise control over others. Seen from a twenty-first century vantage point, these are strange connotations, exactly because the word *dēmokratia* had the opposite meaning of what most democrats today mean when they speak of democracy, in much more positive and complex ways, as non-violent inclusiveness, as power-sharing based on compromise and fairness, as equality based upon the legally guaranteed respect for others' dignity.

[10] Thucydides, *History of the Peloponnesian War*, Book 1, 143, 1 and Book 6, 18, 3; among the long-neglected works on democracy and empire are John A. Hobson, *Imperialism:*

standpoint that democracy in Athens became synonymous with the armed struggle for freedom and power over others. Fighting against enemies not only made men feel that they were worthwhile citizens (the Athenians spoke of *khrēstos politēs*), it also brought wealth to their pockets. The consolidation of imperial power tempted the Athenians to centralise their control over key legal cases, in effect to bring capital cases from the periphery to Athens' revenues. That move created more opportunities for the citizens of Athens to earn income and to participate in its legal machinery, which consequently grew in size and importance within the overall structures of the polity.[11] Empire also brought wealth to the democracy, partly to pay for its machinery of government and to employ vast numbers of ordinary Athenian males as soldiers. Save for a small number of states that chose to keep their nominal independence by providing ships that sailed in the Athenian fleets, all cities of the empire were required (by the early 440s BCE) to pay an annual tribute; they were required as well to fork out duties on exports and imports that passed through the hub port of Piraeus.

The extent to which the wealth generated by empire was vital for the survival of democracy remains disputed, but without doubt among the most potent effects of empire was to expand the power and influence of the military in the day-to-day functioning of the polity.[12] More money from the public budget was spent on war and preparations for war than on any other activity. The revenues generated by empire were used to revolutionise the standard methods of war. The Athenians experimented with siege warfare and tactical retreat. They trained their hoplites and naval crews for weeks and sometimes months, and developed the art of using their ships as high-speed, offensive weapons. Huge numbers of ships and fighters were moved around the whole of the eastern Mediterranean for campaigns that sometimes lasted months or, when sieges were used,

---

A Study (London: 1902); Franklin H. Giddings, *Democracy and Empire, with Studies of Their Psychological, Economic, and Moral Foundations* (New York: Macmillan, 1900); and George Veitch, *Empire and Democracy: 1837-1913* (London, 1913).

[11] See the remarks of John M. Camp, *The Athenian Agora: Excavations in the Heart of Classical Athens* (London: Thames & Hudson, 1986), pp. 46-47.

[12] G.E.M. de Sainte Croix, 'The Character of the Athenian Empire', *Historia* 3 (1954), 1-41 and *Athenian Democratic Origins and Other Essays*, edited by D. Harvey and R. Parker (Oxford: Oxford University Press, 2004); K.A. Raaflaub, 'Democracy, Power and Imperialism in Fifth-Century Athens', in J.P. Euben *et al.* (eds.), *Athenian Political Thought and the Reconstruction of American Democracy* (Ithaca, NY and London: Cornell University Press, 1994), pp. 103-146; and the comments by Russell Meiggs, *The Athenian Empire* (Oxford and New York: Oxford University Press, 1999), chapter 23.

up to a year; even during peace time, up to a hundred ships on practice and guard missions spent several months a year cruising the seas.

The democracy, already enjoying among its friends and enemies a reputation for being a busybody, for its eternal restlessness (*polypragmon*), hatched and executed new plans for fighting simultaneously on several fronts. During the fifth century, as David Pritchard notes, Athens found itself at war on average two out of every three years; never once did it enjoy more than a decade of peace.[13] Especially with the introduction of pay for military service in the 450s BCE, war came to dominate the everyday lives of Athenians, their visual arts, the proceedings of their assembly. Citizenship and military service grew to be indistinguishable: the spirit and institutions of democracy felt deeply 'martial'.

The dalliance of democracy and armed force had wider, geopolitical implications. The democracy obviously carried within it the seeds of expansion by bellicose, anti-democratic means. At first, it is true, the impulse of Athens to expand was restrained; and the spread of Athenian power usually went hand in hand with 'democracy promotion', the creation and nurturing of democratic ways of life: new architectural forms; public space; a form of government run by citizens for citizens; a legal system that followed the rule that nobody was to be above the laws, and that laws must apply equally to everybody. These inventions undoubtedly proved attractive to others; in various parts of the burgeoning empire, there were times when citizens downtrodden by their local nobility or suffering from *stasis* openly welcomed Athenian intervention and influence in their local affairs. A model example was the rebuilding in 444/443 BCE of the ancient city of Sybaris, which received an influx of settlers, a new layout and a brand new democratic constitution. The trouble was that democracy did not spring naturally from the depths of the Aegean, or the region's soil, or from the deities or souls of its peoples. The democratic lawgivers sometimes found their subjects to be less than law-abiding. Democratic laws therefore had to be imposed, perhaps by

---

[13] See the additional evidence provided in Y. Garlan, 'War and Peace', in J.-P. Vernant (ed.), *The Greeks* (Chicago and London: University of Chicago Press, 1995), pp. 53–85; and K.A. Raaflaub, 'Archaic and Classical Greece' in K. Raaflaub and N. Rosenstein (eds.), *War and Society in the Ancient and Medieval Worlds: Asia, The Mediterranean, Europe, and Mesoamerica* (Cambridge, MA, and London: Harvard University Press, 1999), pp. 129–162 and 'Father of All, Destroyer of All: War in Late Fifth-Century Athenian Discourse and Ideology', in D.R. McCann and B.S. Strauss (eds.), *War and Democracy: A Comparative Study of the Korean War and the Peloponnesian War* (Armonk and London: Routledge, 2001), pp. 307–356.

cunning or, if necessary, by means of violence, or so they concluded. But when that happened, Athenian democracy found it increasingly hard to 'place things in the middle', as their citizens liked to put it. Athens then came face to face with an ugly possibility: in the name of democracy, and for the sake of holding or expanding its own position, it was sometimes forced (as in 416/415 BCE, during the expedition launched by Athens against the Aegean island of Melos) to set up garrison colonies, to plunder whole cities, even to heap cruelty on those who tried to stand in its way.

OTHER DEMOCRACIES

The countless military adventures of Athens showed not only that a domestically peaceful democracy could inflict violence upon its neighbours, it also implied that violence was a double-edged sword for the Athenian democracy. It could become subject to the charge of double standards – and to acts of military reprisal. The heroic survival of the Athenian democracy against its Spartan and Persian enemies had a flip side: by arming to protect itself, by acting as if it had been born into the world to give no rest to either itself or to others, it encouraged its rivals – Philip II of Macedon, for instance – to seek and to win the ultimate prize of drowning Athens in the blood of its citizens. The bellicose dynamic within the ancient Greek world has understandably fed recent worries among scholars of democracy who wrestle with the possible conclusion that democracy is a violent form of polity.[14] But before handing down this verdict, and any strategic or normative conclusions that might flow from it, we need to pause, to ask whether the variable forms of ancient, assembly-based democracy in the wider Greek world might make a difference to our understanding of the subject of violence and war.

The traces of evidence of scores of democracies in the Hellenic world, some of them much older than that of Athens, should make us think twice about drawing easy conclusions, simply because we do not know a great deal about what the democrats of these other democracies actually thought about war, and how they practised or resisted it. The usual caveats about sources apply with a vengeance to these old political

---

[14] See the tentative remarks on 'the failure to observe much democratic peace in the different conditions of ancient Greece', in Bruce M. Russett, 'Democracy, War and Expansion through Historical Lenses', *European Journal of International Relations*, 15, 9 (2009), 22; compare Wolfgang Schuller, 'Zur Entstehung der griechischen Demokratie ausserhalb Athens', in Horst Sund and Manfred Timmermann (eds.), *Auf den Weg gebracht: Festschrift Kurt Georg Kiesinger* (Konstanz, 1979), pp. 433–447.

communities: time has ravaged the evidence and few of the jumbled fragments that remain have been blessed with the kind of intensive efforts at archaeological resuscitation that their Athenian equivalents have enjoyed.[15] We can nevertheless be sure that the art of self-government by assemblies of people was not an invention of the Athenians. The ancient Greek world knew no single type of assembly-based democracy; outside of Athens there flourished a whole range of different democracies. Often standing in tension with Athens, these democracies showed that the formula (famously defined by Aristotle) that democracy is a unique type of polity in which the *dēmos* is *kyrios* could be applied differently, and in different contexts, with different sets of institutions and – most probably – different understandings of what democracy was all about. In the Greek world, assembly-based democracy was not a single or fixed form: it was more like an odyssey in which different theoretical imaginings and various practical experiments were the norm.

There were altogether some two hundred Greek city states scattered throughout the Mediterranean; up to a half of these had a taste of democracy at one time or another, some of them well before Athens claimed to be democratic. The details of these early *dēmokratai* may initially seem tedious, but their cumulative effect on our understanding of the subject of war and democracy is potentially strong, and important to absorb. The fragmentary evidence from democracies like Ambracia, Chios, Cyrene and Heraclea Pontica is not always good news for democrats. Sometimes it describes in painful detail the destruction of democratic institutions, either by military conquest, or by violent conspiracies of the rich, or by demagogues or single-minded tyrants, or by all four in some sequence. In each case, there is an important reminder of the utter contingency of democracy – of the ease with which it can be blown away by violence, like a leaf in the autumn winds.

The Greek democracies that operated at a distance from Athens also raise questions about their political compatibility with democracy in imperial form. These other democracies are of special interest, and not just because they highlight the sobering point that ancient democracies were rarely established democratically, and that even when they were born of *resistance* to military interventions and violent power grabbing

---

[15] See Eric W. Robinson, *The First Democracies. Early Popular Government Outside Athens* (Stuttgart: Franz Steiner Verlag, 1997) and the sceptical but cryptic review by Mogens Herman Hansen in *Bryn Mawr Classical Review*, 17 (September 1999); and John Keane, *The Life and Death of Democracy*, especially pp. 78–107.

they often came into being through the exercise of arbitrary power, backed by threatened or actual violence. These other democracies underscore another point: that in matters of democracy war is a wild horse. It is true, paradoxically, that the whole trend towards democratisation in the Greek world was deepened by such events as the outbreak of war in the Peloponnesus between Athens and Sparta (431–404 BCE). On the coasts and islands of the Aegean, many members of the vast military coalition under the command of Athens were already, or soon became governed, by democratic rules. That was the deliberate policy of the Athenians, who for the sake of empire building lent a hand to democratic factions wherever they could, in contrast to the Spartan taste for well-ordered oligarchies. The military victory of Sparta nevertheless resulted in a brief period of autocracy in Athens. Early in 411 BCE, there was an oligarchic coup after the assembly – its composition distorted by the absence of many poor citizens absent on naval duty, and by organised conspirators wielding the swords of fear and propaganda – voted to abolish itself. The military victory of Sparta meanwhile led to the overthrow of democracy among many of its allies. The return of tyranny in Syracuse around the same time threatened an end to the experiment in self-government throughout the whole region.

War was generally bad for democracy. But thanks to the growing unpopularity of the ruling Council of 400 and a brief flurry of street fighting, Athenian citizens managed to shake off oligarchy and renew their democratic institutions. The Athenian resistance proved not to be exceptional. Threatened with *stasis*, many states in the Aegean also clung on to their democracies. On the mainland, the Argives followed the pattern; so did Sicyon, Phleious and Thebes. The Arcadian confederation did so as well, at least for some years. During the 360s, it even tried something never before attempted: to form a confederacy structured by the rules of democratic negotiation and compromise. Among the key institutions that the Arcadians invented was a confederal assembly called the *myrioi*.[16] Open to all citizens of the region, it was the first-ever recorded experiment in cross-border or regional democracy. The experiment rested on a working principle that remains as rock-solid today as it did then: in order to survive and flourish, democracies must tame the

---

[16] Hans Schaefer, 'ΠΟΛΙΣ ΜΥΡΙΑΝΔΡΟΣ', *Historia* (1961), 292–317; James Roy, 'Problems of Democracy in the Arcadian Confederacy 370–362 BC', in Roger Brock and Stephen Hodkinson (eds.), *Alternatives to Athens: Varieties of Political Organization and Community in Ancient Greece* (Oxford: Oxford University Press, 2000), pp. 308–326.

military and political pressures on their borders. We might even speak of an Arcadian Law: the viability of any democracy is inversely proportional to the quantity of outside ('geopolitical') threats to its existence. That Arcadian Law contained a gloomy corollary: a warning that democracy could be misused to kill off democracy. The Arcadian initiative in cross-border democracy showed not merely that things took place in the Greek world of city states that were not covered by, or were directly at odds with, the Athenian model of democracy. The case of Arcadia suggests that the Athenian model had worrying implications for the plurality of democracies of the region – that the Athenian empire was capable of gobbling up democracies in the name of democracy, and that therefore democracies had a strong self-interest in banding together, peacefully, to ensure their political survival, so as to avoid their massacre through rivalry, expansion and armed conflict. Put differently: many citizens within these democracies seem to have grasped just how easily their polities could succumb to events triggered by plots, violent disturbances and military catastrophes. They knew that democracies were constantly vulnerable to what contemporaries called *stasis*, a very broad term used to describe the factional squabbling, outright sedition, open civil war, bloodshed and mass exile that was endemic in a geopolitical system of independent city states that lacked any co-ordinating centre and, hence, constantly violated their geographical isolation and political autonomy by sucking them into a vortex of permanent rivalries.[17]

REPRESENTATIVE DEMOCRACY

There are vital lessons to be learned from the other Greek experiments with democracy, including the lesson, in matters of war, that the tight grip of Athens on our democratic imagination needs to loosened, simply because the logic of induction alone forbids any simple-minded conclusions about democracy and bellicosity. The appeal here for greater open-mindedness and sensitivity to context when analysing the relationship between democracy and war is strengthened by turning our attention to

---

[17] The meaning of stasis is discussed in J.C. Octen, 'Stasis in the Greek World ... from the End of the Peloponnesian War to the Death of Alexander the Great', unpublished dissertation (Cambridge University, 1967); Kathryn A. Morgan (ed.), *Sovereignty and its Discontents in Ancient Greece* (Austin, TX: University of Texas Press, 2003); and Hans-Joachim Gehrke, *Stasis: Untersuchungen zu den inneren Kriegen in den griechischen Staaten des 5. und 4. Jahrhunderts v. Chr.* (Munich: Beck, 1985), especially part 1.

more modern times, to the invention of a new historical form of democracy no longer centred on the open-air assembly of sovereign male citizens.

From around the tenth century CE, democracy entered a second historical phase whose centre of gravity was Europe. Shaped by forces as varied as the rebirth of towns, the rise (in northern Spain) of the first parliaments, and the conflicts unleashed by self-governing councils and religious dissent within the Christian Church, democracy came to be understood as *representative democracy*. This at least was the term that began to be used in the Low Countries, France, England and the new American republic during the eighteenth century, for instance by constitution makers and influential political writers when referring to a new type of government with its roots in popular consent. Representative democracy was a novel way of thinking about democracy; it was unintelligible by the standards of Athenian citizens, who even lacked an equivalent word for 'representative' or 'representation'. Other observers (Jean-Jacques Rousseau, for instance) were to denounce the whole idea as oxymoronic, but in practice representative democracy grew in popularity and influence to become a new form of government in which people, understood as voters faced with a genuine choice between at least two alternatives, are free to elect others who then act in defence of their interests; that is, *represent* them by deciding matters on their behalf.

Much ink and blood was to be spilled in defining what exactly representation meant, who was entitled to represent whom and what had to be done when representatives disregarded those whom they were supposed to represent.[18] But common to the second historical phase of democracy was the belief that good government was government by representatives. Often contrasted with monarchy, representative democracy was praised as a way of governing better by openly and *non-violently* airing differences of opinion – not only among the represented themselves, but also between representatives and those whom they are supposed to represent. Representative government was also hailed for encouraging the rotation of leadership guided by merit. It was said to introduce competition for power that in turn enabled elected representatives to test out their political competence before others. It was in effect an effort at internalising the

---

[18] See the various contributions to Sonia Alonso, Wolfgang Merkel and John Keane (eds.), *The Future of Representative Democracy* (Cambridge: Cambridge University Press, 2010) and John Keane, 'The Least Worst Form of Government: The Rise and Fall of Representative Democracy', unpublished manuscript.

ancient Athenian practice of *ostrakismos*. Some observers were to say that representative democracy would rid politics of fools and knaves, even that it would promote peace among nations. The earliest champions of representative democracy also offered a more pragmatic justification of representation. It was seen as the practical expression of a simple reality: that it wasn't feasible for all of the people to be involved all of the time, even if they were so inclined, in the business of government. Given that reality, the people must delegate the task of government to representatives who are chosen at regular elections. The job of these representatives is to monitor the spending of public money. Representatives make representations on behalf of their constituents to the government and its bureaucracy. Representatives debate issues and make laws. They decide who will govern and how – on behalf and in the name of the people.

As a way of imagining and handling power, representative democracy was an unusual type of political system. Compared with the previous, assembly-based form of the Greek world, it greatly extended the geographic scale of institutions of self-government. As time passed, and despite its localised origins in towns, rural districts and large-scale imperial settings, representative democracy came to be housed mainly within territorial states protected by standing armies and equipped with powers to make and enforce laws and to extract taxes from their subject populations. The new historical form of democracy altered the architecture of politics. Territorially defined governments fed by their control of resources like taxation, law, administration and the means of violence began to wield enormous power over their subjects. These Mortall Gods, as Thomas Hobbes called them, began to shape and reshape the lives of their subjects. It turned them into taxpayers; objects of law and civil administration; and soldiers and victims of war among states. In modern Europe, representative democracy resembled a plant that grew in the hot house of these territorial states, which were typically much bigger and more populous than the political units of ancient democracy (most states of the Greek world of assembly democracy, Mantinea and Argos for instance, were no bigger than a few score square kilometres). Representative democracy was equally unusual in that it rested upon written constitutions, independent judiciaries and laws that guaranteed procedures that still play vital roles in the democracies of today: inventions like *habeas corpus* (prohibitions upon imprisonment and torture), periodic election of candidates to legislatures, limited-term holding of political offices, voting by secret ballot, referendum and recall, electoral colleges, competitive political parties, ombudsmen, civil society and civil liberties such as the right to assemble in public, and liberty of the press. All these inventions were designed to ensure that in matters of politics, the subjects of government would have their heads counted – instead of being chopped off by those who governed.

A RIGHT OF NATIONAL SELF-DETERMINATION?

The novel system of representative democracy in territorial state form was widely praised as an improvement upon ancient Greek democracy, but the truth is that representative democracy was permanently vulnerable to violent conflict and war fuelled by struggles for national self-determination. Their long-term, self-destructive effects were missed in the famous account of democracy and war presented by the French writer and politician Alexis de Tocqueville (1805–1859). Looking at the case of the young American republic, and peering into the future, Tocqueville imagined – with one qualification – that peace would come to be a general principle of modern democratic life. 'Fortune, which has conferred so many peculiar benefits upon the inhabitants of the United States, has placed them in the midst of a wilderness, where they have', he wrote, 'no neighbours; a few thousand soldiers are sufficient for their wants.'[19] Tocqueville warned that democracies should be permanently watchful of armies, whose officers and other ranks (unlike the armies once led by aristocrats) are gripped by material ambition and therefore tend to be dissatisfied with their lot. They come to see that war is in their self-interest, even though wars and rumours of war eat like an acid at the structures and habits of democratic life. Fortunately, Tocqueville observed, most American citizens understood that war whips up animosity towards others, concentrates the means of administration in a few hands and destroys material infrastructure and wealth. Privileged by geography and committed to the principle of equality, the American democracy thus tended to pacifism. 'The ever increasing numbers of men of property who are lovers of peace, the growth of personal wealth which war so rapidly consumes, the mildness of manners, the gentleness of heart, those tendencies to pity which are produced by the equality of conditions, all these causes concur to quench the military spirit.'[20]

---

[19] Alexis de Tocqueville, *Democracy in America*, vol. 2, edited by J. P. Mayer (New York: Doubleday, 1969), chapter XXII, p. 279.
[20] Ibid.

The assessment proved to be wildly inaccurate. Leaving aside the shameful near-annihilation of native Americans, a vicious civil war driven by two conflicting understandings of American democracy and the subsequent rise of a global American empire, Tocqueville failed to see that the invention and deployment, during the eighteenth century, of the doctrine of the sovereignty of nations proved to be a curse for democracy. The formula was unknown to Greek democrats. It seemed to be simple enough and thoroughly consonant with the ideal of representative democracy: each nation living within a given territory was to be entitled to govern itself through its own governmental institutions. There were manifold troubles with this doctrine. Not all people defined themselves primarily or exclusively as members of a 'nation'; the doctrine implied that they should be encouraged or forced to do so. Nations in any case did not release their passions or procreate or live separately from others, in discrete territorial frameworks; lust, pregnancy and childbirth were great scramblers of national identities and state boundaries. The call for 'national self-determination' thus implied the compulsory demarcation and 'cleansing' of nations from lands where they were said not to belong. This further implied, as a last resort, murder and violence. And since self-determining nations living in territorial states resembled atoms without a gravitational force to hold them together, jostling and elbowing and outright fisticuffs were by implication permanent probabilities. The 'democratic' doctrine of national self-determination implied not just bickering, diplomacy and negotiation. Something worse was implied: sabre-rattling, demagoguery and brinkmanship leading to declarations of war. On the eve of the First World War, Prince von Bulow, who had directed German policy as Imperial Chancellor from 1900 to 1909, put the point chillingly: 'If it were possible for members of different nationalities, with different language and customs, and an intellectual life of a different kind, to live side by side in one and the same state, without succumbing to the temptation of each trying to force his own nationality on the other, things on earth would look a good deal more peaceful', he said. He added: 'But it is a law of life and development in history that where two national civilisations meet they fight for ascendancy. In the struggle between nationalities one nation is the hammer and the other the anvil; one is the victor and the other the vanquished.'[21]

---

[21] Prince Bernhard von Bülow, *Imperial Germany* (London: Dodd, Mead & Co., 1914), pp. 245–246.

FRENCH EVENTS

The new democratic formula of national self-determination was undoubtedly revolutionary. It had incendiary effects, in the form of major disturbances in the Low Countries, as well as in other hot spots of Europe, for instance in Switzerland and Ireland. But the formula had its greatest triumph in the French Revolution. An earthquake that sent shock waves throughout Europe, and far beyond, for instance throughout Spanish America, the spectacular events of 1789 introduced Europeans and the rest of the world to the representative-democratic idea that government could be 'for the people' and 'by the nation'. Four years into the Revolution, Robespierre's five-minute speech on Virtue and Terror in the Convention on 5 February 1794 registered the pulse of events, and the link between representative democracy and nation states. 'Democracy', he thundered, 'is a state in which the people, as sovereign guided by laws of its own making, does for itself all that it can do well, and by its delegates what it cannot ... Democracy is the only form of state which all the individuals composing it can truly call their country.' Robespierre went on to make a prediction – one that proved as inaccurate as it was supercilious. 'The French are the first people in the world to establish a true democracy, by calling all men to enjoy equality and the fullness of civil rights; and that, in my opinion is the real reason why all the tyrants allied against the Republic will be defeated.'[22]

Robespierre's boast played to the high drama of the moment, but it was to be spoiled and in some circles discredited by its association with the practice of terror and war. With one leg in the Convention and the other firmly planted in the revolutionary clubs and cells of Paris, Robespierre clambered to the summit of power by presenting himself as the great reconciler of direct and representative democracy. He was 'the people'.[23] Robespierre turned out to be the first democratic dictator of modern times. Partly through luck, but partly through his own calculations and tactical prowess, he positioned himself to play the role of master within a political void. The symbol and stage director of the Jacobin rule that culminated (from 2 June 1793) in the expulsion of the Girondins from the Convention, a purge soon magnified into the Terror, Robespierre saw himself as the

---

[22] Maximilien Robespierre, *Discours et rapports à la Convention* (Paris: Union Générale d'Éditions, 1965), pp. 213ff.
[23] François Furet, *Marx et la Révolution française* (Paris: Editions Flammarion, 1986), p. 86.

great champion of modern democratic progress. He sealed an alliance between the popular *sans culotte* movement and the most radical segments of the middle class, and moved quickly to root out all dissent. He was obsessed with unanimity, which he considered a prime revolutionary virtue. He thought and acted like a fanatic, an obsessive who believed that the leading role of 'the people' and the 'general will' necessitated not only the provision of radically new policies like public education, poor relief and the universal suffrage, but also the rooting out of 'faction' and 'particular interest' – through force of arms, whenever necessary.

It was partly because of the bellicosity of the Revolution that great excitement in favour of democracy quickly spread through parts of Europe. The extent of foreign support for its ideals has often been exaggerated; great care needs to be taken when trying to assess the impact of the Revolution on democratic ideals and institutions. Contemporaries who were sympathetic to the Revolution, especially intellectuals, typically thought of the upheaval as an epochal moment, as a clean break with the corrupted past, as a giant leap upwards, onto a higher historical plane. That reaction was especially strong within the German lands, where philosophers like Immanuel Kant thought, in rather cosmopolitan but ethereal terms, of the Revolution as something like a metaphysical fact of relevance for the whole world. The revolutionaries' own denunciations of despotism added to the headiness. People living under oppressive regimes, anywhere in Europe or in the rest of the world, were in effect invited to take matters into their own hands. Kings and clerics were warned. Insurrection for the sake of democratic liberty was no longer a crime: the right of all peoples to self-regeneration was a universal right.

In retrospect, it is unclear exactly who were supposed to be, or in fact were, the addressees of such heady principles. In 1789, illiterate peasants still comprised the big majority of Europe's population. In the central-eastern half of the continent, there were few cities, limited trade and commerce and a weakly developed, educated middle class. Besides, those who ruled Europe's populations through states and empires – including so-called 'enlightened despots' – had little interest in allowing the spirit of democratic liberty to flourish, as it had done in France and Britain and the Low Countries through the subterranean development of printing presses, reading circles, clubs and *salles de lecture*. Crackdowns flourished, as in Russia, where Catherine the Great (1729–1796) revealed her true reactionary instincts by spying on, arresting and imprisoning her democratic opponents.

The combined effect of these barriers to the spread of revolutionary ideals was to increase the temptations of the French authorities to resort to military force, in the name of representative democracy. So history repeated itself – the imperial democracy of Athens versus neighbouring Melos – this time on a continental scale.[24] Democratic liberty was not negotiable. Its lofty ideals quickly gave way to talk of *pays ennemis* and *pays conquis*. Democracy went on the march, in uniform, caught up in the practical imperatives of conquest and occupation. Annexation in the name of democratic ideals was either carried out through the signing of a treaty (as happened in the Rhineland) or territory was simply annexed and sub-divided into arbitrarily defined, French-style departments, without consultation, as took place in Belgium in 1795 and Piedmont in 1802. It is true that there were places, like the Batavian Republic and the Helvetic Republic, where the Napoleonic armies claimed that the birth of a sister republic was the work of its most 'advanced' patriots. But in every case, French control over territory, resources and people was the primary imperative. National self-determination by citizens was arranged on French terms. Democratic constitutions designed to bring order and guarantee certain basic freedoms – subject to strong executive authority and a limited property franchise, *a la française* – were imposed. Administrative systems based on departments and districts, cantons and communes were put in place. A local press sympathetic to French orthodoxy was cultivated. Property systems based on seigneurialism were broken up; every effort was made to dissolve the power of the Catholic faith.

Whatever locals thought of these reforms was largely irrelevant, for the fundamental point was that all the democratic reforms were imposed by conquest, not formulated or accepted through consent. Especially after 1793, when the French expanded its military campaign and found itself at war with most of monarchical Europe, the logic of brute conquest prevailed. In practice, the revolutionary slogan '*Guerre aux châteaux, paix aux chaumières*' ('War on castles, peace to cottages') meant what the Committee of Public Safety meant when (on 18 September 1793) it

---

[24] The following section draws upon Suzanne Tassier, *Histoire de la Belgique sous l'occupation française en 1792 et 1793* (Brussels, 1934); Simon Schama, *Patriots and Liberators: Revolution in the Netherlands, 1780–1813* (New York, 1977); Alfred Rufer, *La Suisse et la Révolution française* (Paris, 1974); T.C.W. Blanning, *The French Revolution in Germany: Occupation and Resistance in the Rhineland, 1792–1802* (Oxford: Oxford University Press, 1983); Stuart Woolf, *A History of Italy, 1700–1860: The Social Constraints of Political Change* (London: Methuen, 1979); and *Occupants-occupés, 1792–1815: Colloque de Bruxelles, 29 et 30 Janvier 1968* (Brussels, 1968); and Jacques Droz, *L'Allemagne et la Révolution française* (Paris, 1949). The thoughts on the long-term impact of the rise and fall of the French democratic empire are elaborated in John Keane, *The Life and Death of Democracy*, pp. 455–581.

instructed the commanders of French armies to live off the land and its people, to 'procure, as far as possible from enemy territory, the supplies necessary to provision the army, as well as arms, clothing, equipment, and transport'. *Commissaires militaires* were charged with extracting taxes and supplies on the spot. Huge sums were expected, and without delay. It was not long before the search for military resources became the prime goal of occupation, as when the revolutionaries marched into northern Italy for the purpose of providing a new granary for the French armies and new funding to help pay off the costs of war. Civilians were seen as fair game and officers, knowing the unreliability of food convoys, turned a blind eye to the bad behaviour of their troops, despite the grave risks of military indiscipline. The people's army bit into the flesh of the peoples they occupied. In the name of ballots, they billeted themselves using bullets. Horses and cattle were rounded up and fields were stripped to feed starving battalions. Troops smashed their way into homes, where they helped themselves to money, bedding, clothing, wine, food and kitchen utensils. There was drunken abuse, wanton vandalism and beating and rape of the women who stood in their way.

Few troops were ever brought to justice and little gratitude ever flowed from the conquered. Countless Italians, Belgians, Spanish and Rhinelanders understandably saw the conquest with the eyes of conquered people: they saw equality bathed in misery, fear and poverty, but no liberty or fraternity. The sheer size of the French armies, plus their youth and hunger and military inexperience, spread fear and stirred up national resentments among the local communities through which they passed. The French effort to sow the seeds of democratic revolution by military force and influence faltered. It certainly altered boundaries and changed institutions. But it largely failed to win minds, let alone hearts. It bred resentment and resistance and the consequence, not surprisingly, was that the whole trend towards democratisation (a neologism of this period) stalled. It was as if history had taken a strong dislike to representative democracy. War in its name promoted petty tyranny or authoritarianism, as well as clampdowns on press freedom, public assembly and other civil freedoms. War gave democracy a bad name, as can be seen in almost all satirical cartoons of the period. At the end of the Napoleonic Wars in 1815, not one government in the whole of Europe could be described as democratic – if by that we mean, as was meant at the time, a civilian government of representatives subject to openly contested elections and voting by adult males.

OVERKILL

The French events revealed how representative democracy could degenerate into violently 'democratic' despotisms that proved menacing to more than just their subjects at home. As with democracy in the ancient Greek world, modern representative government had both 'inside' and 'outside' dimensions, which implied that political manipulation at home could be enhanced by dalliances and skulduggery abroad. So the neighbouring citizens of states were potential victims of outside manipulation, fear and outbreaks of war. This was not simply a French problem. From the time of the French Revolution, all representative governments found themselves in the devil's company of geopolitics. The question confronting these democracies was whether elected government that paid lip service to 'the people' could be combined with a system of armed territorial states that acted as if they were 'sovereign' powers, and whose leaders knew well that just as nature abhors a vacuum so state politics moves to fill gaps and to take advantage of opportunities. During the course of the nineteenth century, the combination produced unhappy results that resulted eventually in the first-ever global war. In the absence of the European Union and other viable cross-border peace-making mechanisms that were later to be built on the ruins of representative democracy, European experience during the age of representative government confirmed that a system of squabbling, nominally sovereign states bristling with arms was prone constantly to war, and to rumours of war. It proved as well that war was the crucible within which unaccountable rulers muster intrigue and machination to embark upon military adventures by mobilising 'the people' – in order better to pulverise them.

It is important to note that the geopolitical instability in which representative democracies were born coincided with major transformations of the mode and means of warfare. Those transformations, like the military innovations of Athenian democracy, suggest a more general rule: each major historical phase of democracy has been linked with a radical transformation of the mode and means of fighting war. The imperial democracy of Athens coincided with the hoplite revolution on land and the massive expansion of trireme power at sea. The struggle for representative democracy – symbolised by Cromwell's Ironsides and the people's armies of the Napoleonic era – coincided with the organisation of machine-like mass armies equipped with swords and muskets and great killing power, together with canon-firing warships capable of all-devouring confrontations on the high seas, in which the aim was skilfully to destroy one's opponents and their equipment completely. The widespread implosion of representative democracies in the first decades of the twentieth century coincided with the 'perfection' of these military trends, their mutation into something that had never before happened: the invention of 'overkill' weapons systems capable of exterminating the entire human species.

All weapons of violence tend towards overkill, of course. From the beginning, the weapons invented by humans – the rock, spear, javelin, dart, arrow – bestowed a form of power to produce effects out of all proportion to the means employed. That power transformed hominids into humans by enabling them to become the first sizeable creatures on earth to effect change by committing acts of violence at a distance – and so surviving and exploiting even the largest land animals. Humans became what they threw. The arts of manipulating fire and the later means of killing at a distance – the crossbow, the trebuchet, Greek fire – greatly added to the stock of human powers of violence. The invention of gunpowder, by the Chinese, at the end of the first millennium BCE, facilitated the rise of the so-called gunpowder empires, such as those of the Ottomans, Russians and Mughals.[25] The subsequent harnessing of gunpowder for far more destructive ends – the development of weapons with a potentially global reach – brought human beings into contact, for the first time, with the possibility of *total war* that turned any point on the planet into a battle front, resulting in large-scale death. Mechanised total war was a European invention of the late eighteenth century, but it only reached perfection – and the height of self-contradiction – during the long twentieth century of violence, in exactly the same period that the species of representative democracy tottered on the edge of extinction, at all four corners of the earth.

The frightening development of techniques of *overkill* – the military capacity to overwhelm *all* institutions of government and civil society and to reduce to zero their power of securing their subjects' lives against the ravages of violence – was compounded by the invention and use of means of war such as chemical weapons, motorised tanks, land mines and concentration camps. These are now well-known ugly facts of contemporary life, but less well understood are four key military developments

---

[25] An excellent short survey of the history of weaponry is to be found in Alfred W. Crosby, *Throwing Fire: Projectile Technology Through History* (Cambridge and New York: Cambridge University Press, 2002).

unique to the last half-century that arguably changed everything in matters of war and democracy: American B-29s in 1945 unloading comprehensive destruction from the unprecedented height of 20,000 feet; the counter-detonation by the Russians of their first atomic bomb in 1949; the Americans' deployment in 1956 of B-52 intercontinental bombers capable of flying round trips to Moscow; and the development, by the early 1960s, of intercontinental ballistic missiles capable of reaching their far-flung targets within half-an-hour. The net effect of these and other potentially barbarous military inventions has been to draw the populations of actually existing democracies into a global 'triangle of violence' – a point explained at length in my *Violence and Democracy*[26] – in which the military security of democracies has come to depend in part upon a 'bad conscience' about past wars of total destruction by weapons that continue to have an overkill capacity.

DEMOCRATIC PEACE?

The fact that overkill is today an *ultimate* problem, not just for democracies grappling with the task of democratising violence, but for the whole of the planet, stems from the widespread realisation that the new technologies of warfare have the potential to annihilate many millions of people, perhaps even to exterminate the whole of *homo sapiens*. We have been catapulted, say, from the early nineteenth-century world of representative democracy and Colonel Shrapnel testing his deadly new fragmenting shell on the wildlife of Foulness Island, into a world in which weapons of war potentially render (certain forms of) war obsolete, simply because human beings could no longer survive their devastating effects.

It is against the backdrop of this contradictory development that democracy, as understood by our grandparents, is undergoing profound changes. Reshaped from all sides by new institutions, civic initiatives and political pressures, democracy has entered a third historical era. The emerging era of monitory democracy, which dates roughly from the mid-twentieth century, was born of the experience of overkill and total war, including the crushing military defeat of German and Japanese fascism, the beginnings of de-colonisation and the post-war reconstruction of Europe and Japan. The global experience of total war, and of military victory and military defeat, helped push the language and institutions and 'spirit' of

---

[26] See Keane, *Violence and Democracy*, p. 182.

democracy into a new epoch, in which democracy continues to mean (as in Athens) nothing less than a form of self-government based (as in the era of representative democracy) on free and fair elections, but something much more: the continuous public scrutiny or monitoring of power by extra-parliamentary mechanisms that target both governmental and non-governmental organisations, at home and abroad. Once seen as given by the grace of a deity, or as grounded in First Principles such as the Nation or God, democracy comes to be viewed much more pragmatically, as a vital weapon for use against dangerous concentrations of unaccountable power, wherever they exist. In the era of monitory democracy, the word democracy means: the non-violent public accountability and public control of decision makers, whether they operate in the field of state or interstate institutions or within so-called non-governmental or civil society organisations, such as businesses, trade unions, sports associations, environmental and human rights networks and charities.

The age of monitory democracy is uniquely sensitive to outbreaks of war and violence. It may be that the so-called 'war on terror' led by the United States will change everything, but it is safe to say that most of today's democracies have a declining appetite for bellicosity. Their citizens often feel horror and disgust at the psychic traumas, damaged tissues of sociability and ecological and infrastructural damage inflicted by the senseless sanctification of cruelty and violence. Decisions by governments to go to war are for that reason typically done behind veils of secrecy, as in the growing reliance on drone warfare. It is also why decisions to go to war are typically met with doubt, anguish and public disturbance, as can be seen whenever democratically elected governments are confronted with the dilemma of whether or not to intervene to put a stop to cruelty and killing in uncivil war zones. If democratic governments stand back and do nothing (as happened initially in Timor Leste), then they are accused of contradicting their own standards of self-government without violence; but if they intervene militarily to put a stop to wanton violence (as when Indian troops entered Bangladesh), then they are accused of exactly the same contradiction. Efforts to resolve the dilemma typically fuel public controversy, as do all other types of military intervention and operation.

Why is there a hypersensitivity to war and other forms of violence? When compared with the Greek model of assembly democracy and the modern European age of representative democracy, why does violence become a sizeable fishbone in the throat of many democrats? One answer is that life within monitory democracies is shaped by the advent of many new violence-scrutinising mechanisms. Examples include the growth of peace movements rooted in civil society, disarmament initiatives, global summits and war crimes tribunals; the list also includes truth and reconciliation commissions, campaigns against torture, outcries against violence targeted at women and children, human rights networks and experiments (the European Union and its Copenhagen criteria are the leading case) in crafting power-sharing institutions that criss-cross and complicate the borders of states and their 'sovereign' military powers. All these monitory inventions – symbolised in many people's minds by such bodies as Amnesty International, Médecins Sans Frontières and Reporters without Borders – remind citizens and representatives of the frightful things happening around them and, in so doing, they underscore the dilemmas and threats posed by 'overkill' weapons, war and violence for the ideals and institutions of publicly accountable, power-sharing ways of life.

The sensed discomfort with war and its toxic effects is amplified by stories and images and sounds circulated by a globally interdependent system of communication media. But the discomfort is equally reinforced by the return of an old problem that has twice before haunted democracy: the temporary ascendancy of a democratic empire, this time in the form of the United States, the world's first-ever democracy to operate as a (potentially) bellicose dominant power in global form. Its post-1945 commitment to securing 'global order' in the name of 'democracy' as a way of life suited to all peoples of the earth is arguably proving a mixed blessing for monitory democracy, as can be seen by carefully scrutinising a favourite recent conjecture of American presidents, government officials, journalists and academics: the credo that democracies like the United States are reliable lovers of peace. 'During the Cold War', stated President Bill Clinton, shortly after the final collapse of the Soviet Union, 'we fought to contain a threat to the survival of free institutions. Now we seek to enlarge the circle of nations that live under those free institutions, for our dream is that of a day when the opinions and energies of every person in the world will be given full expression in a world of thriving democracies that co-operate with each other and live in peace.'[27] The conjecture was

---

[27] President Bill Clinton, 27 September 1993, cited in Tony Smith, *America's Mission. The United States and the Worldwide Struggle for Democracy in the Twentieth Century* (Princeton, NJ: Princeton University Press, 1994), p. 311. The same point was repeated in President Clinton's 1994 State of the Union address: 'Ultimately, the best strategy to ensure our security and to build a durable peace is to support the advance of democracy elsewhere. Democracies don't attack each other, they make better trading partners and partners in diplomacy', www.pub.whitehouse.gov/urires/I2R?urn:pdi://oma.eop.gov.us/1994/1/26/1.text.1.

soon turned by academics into what could be dubbed a Law of Democratic Peace. 'Democracies never go to war' was the boldest version. 'Democracies almost never go to war with each other' was the more modest rendition.[28]

The conjecture has proven faulty, for a string of reasons. The destructive assaults on Lebanon by Israel in the so-called July War of 2006 showed that under circumstances of regional or global tension, highly armed democracies can readily work themselves into a fearful frenzy, then project their anxieties onto their neighbours, by force of arms, with hugely destructive effects on the lives of citizens, infrastructure and the surrounding ecosystem.[29] There is also the sobering point – documented rather poorly, often using questionable definitions and methods – that representative and monitory democracies, despite the more general trend towards the democratisation of violence, have left more than a few victims in their wake because they regularly pick fights and start wars, often in disputed circumstances, using trumped up charges and claims that many voters may swallow, at least for a time.[30]

The champions of the Law of Democratic Peace have overstated the case for the democratisation of violence thesis; in effect, they have turned it into an awkward dogma. They have meanwhile found to their embarrassment that their overstated 'scientific' propositions were easily used against them, as in the build-up to the 2003 American invasion of Iraq. If it is true that democracies love peace, some elected political leaders reasoned, then that is more than enough justification for launching war on designated enemies, so as to transform them into democracies that

---

[28] The quantity of literature produced by such claims is vast, but notably includes Michael Doyle, 'Kant, Liberal Legacies and Foreign Affairs', *Philosophy and Public Affairs*, 12, 3–4 (1983), 205–235, 323–353; Bruce Russett, 'Bushwhacking the Democratic Peace', *International Studies Perspectives*, 6 (2005), 395; and F. Chernoff, 'The Study of Democratic Peace and Progress in International Relations', *International Studies Review*, 6 (2004), 49–78.

[29] Samir Khalaf, 'The July War on Lebanon', *Conflict in Focus*, 14–15 (December 2006), 7–9.

[30] Compare Melvin Small and J. David Singer, 'The War-proneness of Democratic Regimes', *Jerusalem Journal of International Studies*, 1, 4 (1976), 50–69, where it is claimed that between 1816 and 1965, 58 per cent of inter-state wars were provoked by democracies – wars being defined as violent conflicts claiming at least 1,000 lives. The claim is unconvincing, if only because democracies are defined (poorly) as regimes in which just 10 per cent of the population are enfranchised. Compare Harald Mueller, 'The Antinomy of Democratic Peace', *International Politics*, 41 (2004), 494–520, where 'pacifist democracies' willing to co-operate with dictatorships are contrasted with 'militant democracies' that are fundamentally hostile to such regimes.

would in turn shore up democratic peace with their neighbours.[31] The Law of Democratic Peace has found itself in a topsy-turvy world where the blind worship of electoral democracy – demolatry, let us call it – passed for democracy, and democracy itself is tarred with the brush of war. In these circumstances, even the much-discussed parallel claim that 'democracies win wars' has found itself struggling to stay afloat. 'Since 1815', write the two best-known champions of this view, 'democracies have won more than three quarters of the wars in which they have participated'. They added: 'This is cause for cheer among democrats. It would appear that democratic nations not only might enjoy the good life of peace, prosperity, and freedom; they can also defend themselves against outside threats from tyrants and despots.'[32]

Even by this reckoning, democracies lose up to a quarter of the wars they fight, which proves to be cold comfort, especially in those bungled military conflicts – Vietnam and Iraq and Afghanistan are examples – where not only the global reputation of the United States has been put on trial, but democracy itself has been forced to suffer a measure of disgrace. The probability of democratic disgrace has been bolstered by the vulnerability of American-style methods of fighting to so-called 'asymmetric' wars.[33] In plain speech: destructive precision-guided weapons dropped from the skies are usually no match for the methods practised by rag-tag guerrillas and tightly disciplined, carefully decentralised armies enjoying strong local support nurtured by local feelings that American-style military interventions are shameful. The disproportion between the limited casualties suffered by the military invaders and the terrifying violence heaped upon civilian victims is staggering; so high are the levels of self-protection of the invading armies that their violence is felt by observers and victims alike to have a 'terrorist' quality about it. With their unusually high sensitivity to casualties, monitory democracies have found

---

[31] See the confession of Bruce Russett, 'Bushwhacking the Democratic Peace', *International Studies Perspectives*, 6 (2005), 395–408: 'Many advocates of the democratic peace may now feel rather like many atomic scientists did in 1945. They had created something intended to prevent conquest by Nazi Germany, but only after Germany was defeated was the bomb tested and then used – against Japanese civilians whose government was already near defeat. Our creation too has been perverted.'

[32] Dan Reiter and Allan C. Stam, *Democracies at War* (Princeton, NJ and Oxford: Princeton University Press, 2002), p. 2.

[33] The discussion of forms of warfare in which the weaker combatant uses unconventional strategies and weapons to offset the advantages of the stronger combatant owes much to the seminal essay by Andrew J.R. Mack, 'Why Big Nations Lose Small Wars: The Politics of Asymmetric Conflict', *World Politics*, 27, 2 (1975), 175–200.

it increasingly hard to 'win' asymmetric conflicts. True, there are plenty of occasions when democracies make better choices of military strategy; and it is often true (this was not what Tocqueville thought) that 'democratic soldiers fight with better leadership and greater initiative'.[34] But it is equally the case that monitory democracies are under constant domestic pressure to make wars short. Publics are understandably intolerant of their own casualties; monitory democracies show signs of 'democratising' violence, minimally by meting out electoral punishment to governments who become embroiled in foolhardy or risky or prolonged wars.[35] Doubting the necessity or wisdom of taking and destroying lives, many citizens do not suffer fools gladly and are therefore prone to express impatience with their representatives when results are not forthcoming. That is another reason why the imperial American democracy is more and more forced to settle for draws, or to suffer humiliating losses dressed up as victories.

The reputation of both the American empire and its democratic ideals has not been helped by wars carried out in the name of promoting democracy. Most such 'fight them, beat them, teach them to be less autocratic, perhaps even democratic' wars have proven to be fraught, or outright failures – in about 85 per cent of cases, according to one report that examined ninety American military interventions from 1898 to 1992. Another study, covering 228 United States military operations stretching from forcible interventions to peacekeeping, border control and military training, showed that just 28 per cent became more democratic.[36] The earliest military interventions in the former Spanish empire set the trend towards self-contradiction, which in our times shows no signs of abating.[37] The poor record of success of

---

[34] Dan Reiter and Allan C. Stam, *Democracies at War* (Princeton, NJ and Oxford: Princeton University Press, 2002), p. 198; cf. Alexis de Tocqueville's remark that 'in the control of society's foreign affairs democratic governments do appear decidedly inferior to others' (*Democracy in America*, edited by J.P. Mayer [New York: Doubleday, 1969], p. 228).

[35] This is a basic point developed in Keane, *Violence and Democracy*.

[36] Mark Peceny, *Democracy at the Point of Bayonets* (Pennsylvania: Penn State University Press, 1999); John A. Tures, 'Operation Exporting Freedom: The Quest for Democratization via United States Military Operations', *Whitehead Journal of Diplomacy and International Relations*, 6 (2005), 97–111.

[37] See the pathbreaking studies by Tony Smith, *America's Mission: The United States and the Worldwide Struggle for Democracy in the Twentieth Century* (Princeton, NJ: Princeton University Press, 1994) and Christopher Hobson, *The Rise of Democracy. Revolution, War and Transformations in International Politics Since 1776* (Edinburgh: Edinburgh University Press, 2015).

democracy at the point of bayonets, and under the flight paths of drone bombers, does not at all prove that democracy is suited only to a few lucky peoples, so that the building of democracy remains an impossibly daunting 'leap in the dark', as Lord Derby famously claimed to Prime Minister Benjamin Disraeli in the 1860s. The mixed record of success rather highlights the point that in the age of monitory democracy successful 'democracy promotion' is always and everywhere subject to the most stringent conditions. Self-government requires the creation or preservation of a functioning government – not necessarily a territorial state but, minimally, a set of political institutions capable of exercising authority over a territory, making and executing policies, extracting and distributing revenue, producing public goods, and of course protecting its citizens by wielding an effective monopoly over the means of violence. The contradiction between the promise of self-government and the reality of forcible occupation by an invading democratic power such as the United States has to be handled sensitively; the military power to force others into submission does not translate spontaneously into the power of the conquered survivors to form stable democratic governments and law-enforced civil societies. Self-government minimally requires, for instance, a form of 'trusteeship' or 'shared sovereignty' managed by multilateral institutions that help produce a viable, wider regional settlement. The contradiction can be resolved, or dampened, by following a clear timetable for withdrawal, cultivated wherever possible by building the institutions of a civil society, including functioning markets. Equally necessary are determined efforts to cultivate local trust, not only through respect for local traditions and political aspirations, but especially by enabling the occupied population to organise and speak out against the occupiers, to subject them to the mechanisms of monitory democracy.[38]

---

[38] Among the more important research in this area is Karl Deutsch, *Political Community and the North Atlantic Area: International Organization in the Light of Historical Experience* (Princeton, NJ: Princeton University Press, 1957); John Ikenberry, *After Victory: Institutions, Strategic Restraint, and the Rebuilding of Order after Major Wars* (Princeton, NJ: Princeton University Press, 2001); Simon Chesterman, *You, the People: The United Nations, Transitional Administration, and State-Building* (Oxford: Oxford University Press, 2004); and the revealing summary of the early débacles that resulted from the American invasion of Iraq in March 2003, an account written by a former advisor to the administration of George W. Bush, Larry Diamond, 'Promoting Democracy in Post-Conflict and Failed States: Lessons and Challenges', *Taiwan Journal of Democracy*, 2, 2 (2006), 93–116.

FUTURE RESEARCH

Whether or not monitory democracies, including the United States, can sustain the process of democratising violence in the face of such complexities, or more generally survive territorial state rivalries and the unprecedented forms of 'overkill' and 'asymmetric' violence of our time, remains an open question. Things will very much depend upon the ability of citizens and their representatives to handle wisely problems of war and violence for which there are no precedents, and no easy solutions – new problems that include the destabilising effects of the American empire and the new 'triangle of violence' that includes planetary outbreaks of uncivil wars, nuclear anarchy and 'asymmetric' terrorist attacks. In attempting to defuse and wind down such threats, using the institutions of monitory democracy, can anything be learned about the subject of war and democracy by revisiting such cases as the Athenian democracy? Most certainly there is much to be absorbed, but with several important qualifications.

As Josiah Ober and others have pointed out, for instance, the case of Athens shows that from the beginning democracy, considered as a form of self-government founded upon the equality of its citizens, contained within it uniquely important mechanisms for calling into question the blind worship of war and other forms of violence.[39] In the absence of civil society, political parties, periodic elections and monitory bodies in the contemporary sense, the Athenians nevertheless experimented with many different ways of publicly checking and balancing exercises of power. Public officials were subject to scrutiny (*dokimasia*) before taking up office, for instance. They had to lodge regular reports on their activities; under pain of prosecution, their conduct was subject to review; and, in sessions of the assembly, citizens were entitled to lodge complaints (*probole*) against public officials for their wilful manipulation of people, their failure to deliver their promises, or their misbehaviour at public festivals. The Athenians bequeathed to the democratic tradition the principle that open scrutiny or public accountability mechanisms enable actors, citizens and elected leaders alike, to handle intelligently and prudently apply the means of violence, for instance in self-defence or in opposition to rampant cruelty directed against others. But in matters of war, the case of Athens implies, democracy is potentially much more than the art of knowledge gathering, 'good counsel' (*euboulia*), tactical agility and prudence – in a

---

[39] Josiah Ober, *Democracy and Knowledge: Innovation and Learning in Classical Athens* (Princeton, NJ: Princeton University Press, 2008).

word, pragmatism. Its self-questioning dynamics nurture what no other type of polity can achieve: a process that I have called the 'denaturing' or 'democratisation' of war and other forms of organised violence, which become publicly questionable and potentially eradicable means of resolving disputes and making gains.

So, at a minimum, what can be learned from the case of Athens is that democracy is not 'naturally' bellicose. Its heart is not necessarily violent. Yet less positive things are to be learned from the case of Athens. For a start, careful examination of the Athenian democracy casts serious doubt on the recently fashionable proposition that democracies are 'naturally' peaceful. The case of Athens shows in particular that transitions to democracy can feed and be fed by war and rumours of war, and that in extreme cases democratic polities can morph into empires; that is, dominant and dominating powers that prove dangerous for the ideals and institutional legitimacy and effectiveness of democracy. When democracies – Athens, revolutionary France, the United States of America are the three known historical cases – transform themselves into big powers bent on expansion, they risk more than just the hubris that comes with the militarisation of their domestic politics. When they become mixed up with inter-state rivalries and cavort with the devils of war, as they are prone to do, imperial democracies encourage enemies, who are typically forced to protect themselves against the double standards of a democracy that by its actions contradicts the language of equality and peaceful self-determination of citizens.

In the age of overkill, asymmetric violence and a permanent 'war on terror', surely the double realisation that democracies are uniquely capable of calling into question so-called military and security imperatives just as much as they can stir up geopolitical trouble and stoke the fearful fires of war is an invaluable Greek gift to all thinking students of democracy?

14

The Triangle of Fear

> It is not power that corrupts but fear. Fear of losing power corrupts those who wield it and fear of the scourge of power corrupts those who are subject to it.
>
> Aung San Suu Kyi (1991)

Many things shall be said for a long time about the 2001 death squad attacks on two key American symbols of globalisation, but among the most certain of their effects is the fear they reportedly struck into the hearts of many citizens around the world, above all in the United States itself.[1] A month after the attacks, fighter jets in that country scrambled daily over key cities on 'homeland defence' missions. Security was tight at sporting events, and in and around all government buildings. The airport at the country's capital city had scarcely reopened. Reports whizzed through the media of two men infected with Anthrax, a deadly agent widely said to be the most likely weapon in a biological attack. Stories circulated as well of the shut-down for eight hours of the national Greyhound bus network – following a crash caused by a razor-wielding man who attacked the driver – and an incident in the capital city, one of whose underground stations was closed and passengers quarantined after a fare-dodger turned on transit police with a spray bottle filled with carpet cleaner. CNN researchers confirmed these jitters in a feature called 'The New Normal': in response to questions about the meaning of normality, a

---

[1] Edward Alden and Sheila McNulty, 'Fear and Rumour Leave America in Grip of Anxiety', *Financial Times Europe*, 11 October 2001, p. 18; Paul Krugman, 'Fear Itself', *The New York Times*, 30 September 2001.

sample of middle Americans responded mainly with stories about their fears about the loss of normality. Sales of ammunition, guns, bullet-proof jackets, and gas marks meanwhile remained brisk. So too were sales of antibiotics, bottled water, and canned goods. Talk of the 'fear economy' began to spread, helped along by new statistics on the cancellation of vacations, the widespread refusal to fly, the big reductions in consumer spending on luxuries and the scaling back of business investment plans. Despite the largest investigation and intelligence-gathering operation in the republic's history, most citizens acknowledged being caught in the vice-grip of fear. They spoke of their profound uncertainty about when, how, or even if, other attacks might occur. Many of those old enough to remember said their sense of dread was comparable to that caused by the nuclear scares of the early years of the Cold War.

DESPOTISM

The spread of fear outwards from the United States, helped by the rapid circulation across borders of images, sounds and reported speech, arguably represented a new phase of the globalisation of fear that began after the First World War and was reinforced by the events of the following world war and the invention and deployment of nuclear weapons. For the fourth time in a century, fear cast a long shadow over the whole world. The odd thing is that political thinking has been caught naked by this new phase of the globalisation of fear, essentially because in recent decades questions about fear have rarely featured in discussions within the fields of political philosophy and political science. Franz Neumann's masterful Berlin lecture on the subject a half-century ago[2] was among the last sustained treatments of a theme that has since fallen into abeyance. Whenever it has arisen, it usually appears as a matter of antiquarian interest, most often in connection with the classic work of Montesquieu, *De l'esprit des lois* (1748).[3] Montesquieu there captured the imaginations of several generations of political thinkers and writers who found themselves caught up in one of the crucial political developments of the eighteenth century: the rising fear of state despotism and the hope, spawned by the military

---

[2] Franz Neumann, 'Anxiety and Politics', in *The Democratic and Authoritarian State. Essays in Political and Legal Theory* (London: Collier-Macmillan, 1964), pp. 270–300.
[3] Charles Montesquieu, *The Spirit of the Laws [1748]*, edited by Victor Goldschmidt (Paris: Garnier-Flammarion, 1979).

defeat of the British monarchy in the American colonies, and by the first moments of the French Revolution, of escaping its clutches.[4]

Montesquieu was freely read and liberally quoted during this period, especially because his work contained an entirely new understanding of the concept of despotism. Montesquieu transformed the classical Greek understanding of despotism (*despótēs*) as a form of kingship exercised legitimately by a master over slaves. Rejecting as well Bodin's and Hobbes' subsequent positive rendering of despotism as a form of political rule justified by victory in war or civil war, Montesquieu entered the eighteenth-century controversies prompted by the Physiocrats' defence of 'despotisme légal'. In a highly original move against all previous reflections on the subject, he viewed despotism, with trepidation, as a type of political regime that was founded originally among Orientals, but that now threatened Europe from within. Despotism, he thought, is a type of arbitrary rule structured by fear. It ruthlessly crushes intermediate groups and classes within the state and forces its subjects to lead lives that are divided, ignorant and timorous. Within despotic regimes, Montesquieu remarked, fear and mutual suspicion are rampant. The lives, liberties and properties of individual subjects are scattered to the winds of arbitrary power. Everyone is forced to live at the mercy of the frightening maxim 'that a single person directs everything by his own will and caprice'.[5]

Montesquieu's analysis of despotism no doubt contained strongly imaginative or 'fictional' elements, especially in its reliance upon a prejudiced or Orientalist view of Muslim societies.[6] Yet by linking together the subjects of fear and despotism, Montesquieu powerfully gave wings to the intellectual flight from the status quo of absolute monarchy within the Atlantic region. He helped to convince many of his readers that despotism was a new and dangerous form of unlimited – concentrated and unaccountable – secular power. Guided by no ideals other than the blind pursuit of power for power's sake, and feeding upon the blind obedience

---

[4] See my 'Despotism and Democracy: The Origins and Development of the Distinction between Civil Society and the State, 1750–1850', in John Keane (ed.), *Civil Society and the State: New European Perspectives* (London and New York: Verso, 1988), pp. 35–71.

[5] Montesquieu, *The Spirit of the Laws* (New York: Hafner Press, 1949 [1748]), Book 2, Chapter 1, p. 8.

[6] See Alain Grosrichard, *Structure du sérail: la fiction du despotisme asiatique dans l'Occident classique* (Paris: Seuil, 1979); and Christopher Sparks, *Montesquieu's Vision of Uncertainty and Modernity in Political Philosophy* (Lewiston, NY: E. Mellen Press, 1999).

of its subjects, Montesquieu implied that despotism is a half-crazed, violent and self-contradictory form of governance. It crashes blindly through the world, leaving behind a trail of confusion, waste and lawlessness, to the point where it tends to destroy its own omnipotence. It consequently undoes the fear upon which it otherwise thrives. Despotism becomes the scourge of decency. It shocks and repels those who are afraid; and it encourages those who yearn to live without fear. It inspires its opponents to seek alternatives, for instance republican government, representative parliamentary power-sharing arrangements, the cultivation of free public opinion within the rule of law, and the education of citizens into the ways of civic virtue.

DEMOCRACY

Through this line of reasoning, the critics of despotism after Montesquieu helped prepare the way for the view that representative democracy, a peculiarly modern form of government in which the exercise of power is shared through general elections and is subject to permanent public scrutiny, reduces fear to the point where it becomes of minor importance in politics. The presumption that democracies are fear-less, or fear-discharging, systems is sometimes stated explicitly, as in the thoughtful study of contemporary politics and fear by Juan Corradi and his colleagues.[7] There it is argued that while democracies do not altogether do away with fear – a political order without fear is an unattainable utopia – they are historically unique in their capacity to sublimate, reduce and control human fears creatively. Established democracies tend to 'privatise' fear, which becomes at most a personal matter to be handled by individuals in their daily lives – as an intimate problem to be analysed and treated in the company of either the spouse or the friend or the psychoanalyst or the priest. Little wonder that political philosophy and political science lose interest in the subject, which is handed over to the sub-field of political psychology, leaving a few isolated thinkers to ask: How do democracies actually manage to marginalise fear, to push it into the domains of intimate and transcendent experience? Corradi and his colleagues were understandably concerned with state despotism in Latin America, so the thesis that electoral democracies solve the age-old problem of fear functioned in their work mainly as a counterfactual presumption.

[7] Juan E. Corradi, Patricia Weiss Fagen and Manuel A. Garretón (eds.), *Fear at the Edge: State Terror and Resistance in Latin America* (Berkeley, CA: University of California Press, 1992).

They simply presented a list of the various means used by American-style democracies to discharge fear, including the decentralisation of power, citizen participation in local associations, the encouragement of state-protected religious freedoms, the possibility of rapid geographic and social mobility and, above all, representative government.[8]

The thesis that democracies privatise fear is stimulating. But it is unconvincing, in no small measure because it only hints at the dynamic processes through which actually existing monitory democracies do indeed tend – but never fully successfully – to reduce the role played by fear in the overall structures of power. What then are these processes, peculiar to monitory democracy, that perform the positive role of reducing and 'privatising' fear? And could it be that there are counter-processes that ensure fear is a problem that this type of democracy never entirely resolves? The possible answers to these questions are not immediately obvious, but common-sense reflection – let us call it the orthodox view of democracy and fear – typically identifies three overlapping processes that seem to guarantee that democracies trivialise fear. In preparation for a more nuanced – less politically naïve – account of democracy and fear, these processes are sketched below.

Non-violent power-sharing According to the orthodox view, representative democracies tend to reduce the fears of governors and governed alike because they institute the practice of non-violent power-sharing at the level of governmental institutions. Just how unique that innovation is can be seen by considering that all previous modern territorial states and military empires typically sought to exercise monopoly control of the means of violence, and to rule by making others afraid of the threatened use of that violence. The armed power of these states and empires, often wielded in the name of reducing their subjects' fears, had the effect of *inspiring* fear among their subjects and rivals at home and their enemies abroad. As Guglielmo Ferrero emphasised, state and imperial rulers, equipped with the awesome capacity to take life away – the sword of the ruler should always be reddened with blood, noted Luther – developed a taste and a reputation

---

[8] Ibid., pp. 1–10, 267–292. The thesis is well-summarised by Norberto Lechner, 'Some People Die of Fear: Fear as a Political Problem', in E. Corradi, Weiss Fagen and M.A. Garretón, *Fear at the Edge: State Terror and Resistance in Latin America* (Berkeley, CA and Oxford: University of California Press, 1992), pp. 33–34: 'Democracy involves more than just tolerance; it involves recognizing the other as a coparticipant in the creation of a common future. A democratic process, in contrast to an authoritarian regime, allows us to learn that the future is an intersubjective undertaking. The otherness of the other is then that of the alter ego. Seen thus, the freedom of the other, its unpredictability, ceases to be a threat to self-identity; it is the condition for self-development.'

for harsh action. All rulers armed with the sword were capable of inspiring fear, even of the extreme kind that Montesquieu called despotic.[9] The violent persecution and attempted destruction of religious minorities, such as the Huguenots, was only an extreme instance of this rule: the use of spies and informants, the militarisation of the civilian population, brutal punishments, forced conversions, and the torture and massacre of men, women, and children helped produce fear on a scale far exceeding anything described or recommended in the early modern textbooks on government written by figures like Bodin and Hobbes. Rulers' capacity for making others afraid applied as well to their (potential) rivals. Those who plotted the seizure or paralysis of armed power, for instance through a coup d'état or regicide, usually risked their lives, and lived in fear of doing so. That was a good and necessary thing, recommended Machiavelli. Musing on the reputation for cruelty of Cesare Borgia, he openly criticised Cicero's advice that love compared with fear is a much more effective resource in government: 'it is much safer to be feared than loved'.[10]

According to the orthodox view, representative democracies minimise such fear, initially by establishing a pact of non-violence among rulers and their potential rivals and opponents. What might be called the Law of Damocles helps to explain the basis of this pact. In the court of Dionysius, the much-feared tyrant of Syracuse, there was a sycophantic courtier named Damocles. He yearned to wield power like his master, so Dionysius decided to teach him a lesson by inviting Damocles to preside over a splendid royal banquet. Wrapped in frippery, Damocles was flattered and acted the part remarkably well – until the moment he discovered, dangling above his lavish golden throne, a huge sword on the end of a single strand of hair. The foolish courtier-turned-ruler cried out in horror. He had begun to learn the lesson that those who rule by fear can potentially die by fear, and that they are therefore best advised to seek means other than fear through which to govern. Modern representative democracies claim to recast this rule in constitutional form: they respect the Law of Damocles by developing a consensus, among governors and governed alike, that threats of violence and government by fear are not easily containable, that nobody is safe, and that therefore such threats should not be used as techniques of government, or of opposition.

---

[9] Guglielmo Ferrero, *The Principles of Power: The Great Political Crises of History* (New York: G.P. Putnam's Sons, 1942).
[10] Niccolò Machiavelli, *The Prince*, in Max Lerner (ed.), *The Prince and The Discourses* (New York: Carlton House, 1950), Chapter 17, p. 61.

Civil Society The orthodox view supposes that democracies also diminish the use of fear as a weapon wielded by those who govern by institutionalising arms-length limits upon the scope of political power, in the form of civil society. The historical invention in early modern Europe of spaces of non-violence called civil societies has proved to be a self-contradictory and therefore highly unstable – but nonetheless precious – process.[11] The birth of these societies was made possible by the extrusion or 'clearing' of the principal means of violence from daily life and their concentration in depersonalised form in the hands of the repressive apparatuses of imperial or territorial-based governing institutions. As ownership of the means of violence shifted from the non-state to the state realm – it was always, and still remains, a heavily contested process[12] – these civil societies became permanently vulnerable to standing armies and police forces, which could harass them from within, or periodically call on the citizens of these societies to kill external enemies in wars between heavily armed states.

According to the orthodoxy, the civil societies that survived, and today flourish, nevertheless served to protect an important liberty: the freedom of individuals and groups to live without the everyday fear of violent death at the hands of others. Modern civil societies tend to transform potential enemies into 'strangers' whose strangeness, Simmel pointed out, derives from their simultaneous remoteness and closeness to others around them.[13] Especially in contemporary civil societies, when things go well, strangers abound, and savage pleasure and unfettered hatred in destroying anything considered hostile becomes rare. The members of civil society become capable of suppressing or sublimating their aggressive impulses, whether they are directed at governments or at fellow-civilians themselves. They display remarkable self-restraint, even in the face of hostility. It is as if they are guided by an inner voice warning them not to inflict violence upon others who annoy or threaten them. The social

---

[11] The classic work in this field is that of Norbert Elias, *Über den Prozess der Zivilisation* (Basel: Haus zum Falken, 1939) and 'Violence and Civilization: The State Monopoly of Physical Violence and Its Infringement', in John Keane (ed.), *Civil Society and the State: New European Perspectives* (London and New York: Verso, 1988), pp. 177–198; compare my *Violence and Democracy* (London and New York: Cambridge University Press, 2004).

[12] Janice E. Thomson, *Mercenaries, Pirates, and Sovereigns: State-Building and Extraterritorial Violence in Early Modern Europe* (Princeton, NJ: Princeton University Press, 1994).

[13] Georg Simmel, 'Der Fremde', in *Soziologie: Untersuchungen über die Formen der Vergesellschaftung* (Leipzig: Duncker & Humblot, 1908), pp. 685–691.

spaces connecting individuals tend to become non-violent and 'civility' itself becomes a cherished norm. There are plenty of counter-trends, admit the champions of the orthodox view, but the capacity of civil societies to live non-violently ideally means that 'otherness', the figure of the stranger or foreigner, for instance, can in principle be accepted, even welcomed, without fear. Alterity is not regarded as an inconvenience to be eliminated, either by forcible exclusion or reduction to sameness. Otherness is instead the object of respectful, sometimes indifferent and sometimes rewarding encounters among subjects for whom that otherness sometimes may well lie beyond comprehension, as if it had an irreducible strangeness. To speak for a moment in the language of Emmanuel Levinas: within a civil society, the subject who acts as an individual or within a group is neither 'at home with itself' [*chez soi*] nor 'in itself' [*en soi*]. It is most certainly not (as Jean-Paul Sartre famously argued in *L'Être et le néant*) a 'for itself' [*pour soi*]. It rather understands that it exists in proximity to others, that it is constituted *by* and *as* its exposure to them, and that therefore it can communicate non-violently with them through the 'risky uncovering of oneself, in sincerity, in the breaking up of inwardness and the abandon of all shelter, in exposure to traumas, in vulnerability'.[14] *Homo civilis* understands herself as the hostage of others. Exposure to their powers is the bedrock of her existence. She understands that she is another for others – and that responsibility for them is therefore neither an accident that befalls (or does not befall) her nor a sign of her 'natural' love or 'natural' benevolence towards them. *Homo civilis* instead understands something that is both more basic and more contingent: that civility is an expression of temporal and spatial interdependence, and that it is only thanks to 'the condition of being hostage that there can be in this world pity, compassion, pardon and proximity – even the little there is, even the simple "After you, sir"'.[15]

Publicity Actually existing democracies today operate within a global framework of communications media. These media, the orthodox theory supposes, have the effect of transforming the nature of the fear experienced by the members of civil societies by publicising it – thereby reducing the quantity of genuine fears they experience. Beginning with the early modern printing press, so the argument runs, these communications media helped to publicise the arbitrary power of governmental

---

[14] Emmanuel Lévinas, *Autrement qu'être ou au-delà de l'essence* (The Hague: Nijhoff, 1974), pp. 82–83.
[15] Ibid., p. 186.

institutions, so encouraging the public spheres that sprang up with media help to believe that fear should not rule, indeed that government by fear was illegitimate. The cultivation of public opinion within non-violent public spheres came to be seen as a weapon against the paralysing effects of fear.[16] Much the same process encouraged the formation of civil societies by establishing spaces within which things could be said and done without fear of the consequences, and by helping to publicise their members' diffuse anxieties and their explicit fears – and so to suggest that there might be remedies for fear other than private suffering. The drying up of rumours, which once operated as the great waterway of fear,[17] was one of the long-term consequences of modern communications media, it is argued. Rumours circulate fear by depending upon formulations like 'people are saying', or 'I heard', or 'there's a rumour going around'. Such hearsay has no individual subject and it is therefore hard to refute; it is a hot potato that is quickly juggled and passed on to the next listener. A rumour is a quotation with a loophole; it is never clear who is being quoted or who originally set it in motion.[18] By contrast, the non-violent conjecture and refutation, controversy and disputation that routinely takes place within a public sphere has the effect of checking the veracity and tracing the source – 'de-naturalising' or 'de-sacralising' – everyday fears.

THE TRIANGLE OF FEAR

The proposition that democracies tend to reduce and trivialise the fears of their citizens seems so far to be plausible, but another moment's reflection easily uncovers a basic problem in the analysis of democracy and fear: the problem of how to define fear itself. Few keywords in the field of politics have been as neglected as fear. By comparison with the huge controversies generated by other keywords like the state, democracy and power, fear as a concept tends to be used as a 'face-value' term – as a concept that does

---

[16] See John Keane, 'Liberty of the Press', in *The Media and Democracy* (Cambridge: Polity Press, 1991), pp. 2–50.

[17] Jean Delumeau's study of fear during the early modern era, *La peur en Occident, XIVe–XVIIIe siècles* (Paris: Fayard, 1978), notes that the rumour is 'equally acknowledgement and elucidation of a general fear and, further, the first stage in the process of abreaction, which will temporarily free the mob of its fear. It is the identification of a threat and the clarification of a situation that has become unbearable' (p. 247).

[18] See Hans-Joachim Neubauer, *Fama: Eine Geschichte des Gerüchts* (Berlin: Berlin Verlag, 1998).

14 The Triangle of Fear

not merit even a definition because it is presumed that everyone who has experienced fear in their lives, or has learned about it from others, knows what it is.[19]

The presumption that fear is fear is manifestly misleading, as controversies within neighbouring scholarly fields, like psychology, physiological psychology and philosophy, reveal.[20] Much could be said about these controversies, and their importance for democratic theory, but for the moment it is only necessary to draw upon them selectively for the purpose of sketching a new account of fear, understood here as an 'ideal-typical' concept that can bring greater clarity to our understanding of a political subject that in the age of monitory democracy has suffered much neglect, and is now in urgent need of attention.

Fear is the name that should be given to a particular type of psychic and bodily abreaction of an individual or group within a triangle of interrelated experiences. This triangle of experiences within which fear arises in certain times and places among human beings – and among vertebrate animals as well[21] – is historically variable. Through time, humans and animals evidently develop, in phylogenetic terms, different fear thresholds; so too, through the process of ontogenesis, beginning in the earliest moments of infancy, individuals can and do develop their capacities for conquering fears of various kinds; and, as Montesquieu well understood, different political systems have displayed radically different forms and concentrations of fear. In every case, however, the phenomenon of fear develops within a triangle of socially and politically mediated experience. The corners of this triangle are marked by (a) objective circumstances that are perceived by a subject or group of subjects to be threatening; (b) bodily and mental symptoms that are induced by that object and experienced as such by the individual subject or group; and (c) the individual's or group's abreactions against the object that has induced those symptoms in the first place (see Figure 14.1).

---

[19] An example of this face-value usage of the concept of fear is Barry Buzan, *People, States and Fear: An Agenda for International Security Studies in the Post-Cold War Era* (Boulder, CO: Lynne Rienner, 1991).

[20] Anthony Kenny, *Action, Emotion and Will* (London: Routledge & Kegan Paul, 1963), Chapter 3.

[21] Eric A. Salzen, 'The Ontogeny of Fear in Animals', in Wladyslaw Sluckin (ed.), *Fear in Animals and Man* (New York: Van Nostrand Reinhold, 1979), pp. 125–163. Compare p. 9: 'provided we have evidence of some capacity for receiving and decoding information from the environment concerning dangers or threats, and some capacity for learning what are dangerous circumstances (or being provided with innate capacities for registering these), the concept of fear may be applied to animals other than human beings'.

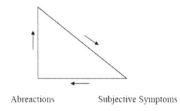

FIGURE 14.1 The Triangle of Fear

When seen in this way, it becomes clear that fear is not a naturally occurring substance; it is rather the product of a dynamic relationship among individuals, their fellows and their socio-political circumstances. When fear is analysed as a particular experience that arises within the dynamic 'boundaries' of these triangular co-ordinates, its relationship to similar but different experiences becomes clear. Outside and beyond the 'boundaries' of the triangle the concept of fear simply doesn't apply. Consider the case of a subject who neither experiences symptoms nor reacts against dangerous circumstances – the soldier who goes numbly into battle under the influence of drugs or duty – or the case of an individual who reacts against dangerous circumstances but experiences no symptoms of fear, as when a person chooses, on the spur of the moment and almost without thinking, to avoid moving towards an army checkpoint which is felt or known to be hostile. In both cases, the concept of fear is inapplicable.

The understanding of the concept of fear as a particular set of experiences co-defined by the interaction of subject and object certainly helps us to see the difference between fear and anxiety. Anxiety is not a species of fear: it is rather a type of agitated reaction to events that have occurred in the past – sexual abuse by a parent, a close brush with death – or to possible future events, such as a forthcoming examination that could result in failure, a nuclear explosion caused by a 'normal accident', or concern about growing old. In each case, the events that trigger anxiety are somewhere in the distance; or they might in future not happen at all. Anxiety can of course be transformed into fear, but the difference remains. Compared with anxiety, fear is immediate. It is a subjective reaction to actually existing objective circumstances.[22]

---

[22] A version of this distinction between fear (the abreaction against a concrete, external danger) and anxiety is outlined in Søren Kierkegaard, *The Concept of Dread* (Princeton, NJ: Princeton University Press, 1944), p. 38.

Guided by this sharpened concept of fear, let us then probe in more detail what actually goes on within the triangle of experience called fear.

Subjective Symptoms Fear normally is experienced as subjectively felt symptoms, in the form of physiological, mental and emotional changes. Groups in the abstract cannot experience these changes; of course, groups become afraid, but they only do so insofar as fear grips each one (or most) of their individual members. Fear is always an intensely personal experience. Its physiological, mental and emotional components come in more or less concentrated form, both in terms of the 'depth' with which they are experienced by the individual, and the speed with which they come and go. Fear can be experienced on the surface – as when it is experienced 'second hand', at a distance, in empathy with others – or it can penetrate deep down, even hiding itself in the nightly dreams of the afraid, whose sleep it disturbs. The experience of fear can be more or less sudden. It can creep up on the individual, take its time, and trap its victim by stealth. Or it can suddenly pounce upon the individual, like a prowler lurking in the dark, in which case its effects are felt immediately and frontally.

Fear is a dictator of time, for in all cases, shallow or deep, slow or fast, time seems to slow down or even stop when the individual is afraid. This is because the body is plunged into a different world. It suddenly shrinks, grows weaker, and feels vulnerable, heavier some say, as if it is filled with cold, viscous liquid. Fear is forcible submersion in a fathomless ocean. The body stiffens. Then it shivers. Outside voices and sounds become muffled, directionless, then jangle in the head. Tics start up in the neck, the temples, the eyelids, jumping, thumping, like an insect under the skin. Shoulders knot. The mouth grows dry. Fear rises in the throat, like bile; then it turns into a tumourous lump that sticks in the throat, like a stone. Speech stammers. The heart races. Fingers become shaky, inept. Hands tremble. Concentration on anything other than fear, and being afraid, becomes impossible. Fear closes the mind and fills it with thoughts that whir like bats suddenly deprived of radar. The pulse by this time seems to be everywhere: in the legs, arms, face, chest. Breathing naturally is difficult. It comes in short, ragged gasps. Or it seems to stop completely, so that there is no more in and out, in and out, only a gaping hole in the chest.

Objective Circumstances The subjective symptoms of fear are always experienced within certain surroundings. Fear is a reaction by a subject to an object or objects that are perceived to be hostile or outright dangerous. It is true that fear-like symptoms can occur despite the fact that there are no signs of circumstances that are fear-producing. When a person acknowledges that there are no (immediate) signs of danger, but says, 'I'm not afraid of anything in particular. I just feel like this most of the time', all the while feeling incapable of doing anything about that feeling, they may be said either to not know the meaning of the word fear or to be suffering from a form of anxiety connected to something experienced at some point in the past. In all other cases, the fear experienced by individuals or groups is typically induced by threatening circumstances within their immediate or more distant milieu.

Fear can be triggered by a very large variety of objective circumstances: a critically ill child, or a sudden explosion, getting the sack, or being cornered by a thief, the cracking roar of jets overhead, or by television images of civilian aircraft transformed into deadly missiles, for instance. In every case, these circumstances are sensed by the individual or the group to be ill-boding, sinister, menacing or perhaps even life-threatening.

Intended reactions Experienced as felt symptoms induced by objective circumstances, fear usually results in some kind of intentional reaction or abreaction against the perceived object of fear. In extreme cases, fear can have destructive effects on the individual or group. It hounds the afraid into self-persecution. They become incapable of warding off their fears and instead regress into morbid symptoms, like panic and muddle. Fear can also be projected outwards, against others, as a form of persecutory behaviour, in which the experience of fear prompts the subject to look with hateful eyes for an enemy; the afraid, sometimes with the help of demagogic leaders, then off-load their fears nastily onto others – as in xenophobia – or violently eliminate or paralyse – kill or injure – what makes them afraid. These and other reactions are typically unpredictable, for fear is a form of radical uncertainty. With the body in such an unfamiliar and agitated state, it is never clear what will happen next. For the individual who is afraid, fear resembles peering coldly down from some shadowy height, without being able to see the ground below and without knowing how to act. The stomach churns. The afraid may suddenly feel wet and warm between their legs. Scared shitless can pass from phrase to fact. The self that is afraid is under siege. It is a desperate self. Transfixed on its object, it may freeze, or shake uncontrollably. Or the self may scream while taking a step back from the shadowy heights on which it is perched, or stand firm, or run away, or jump blindly towards the ground below.

Miraculously, the afraid may also grow wings – *timor addidit alas*, runs the original Latin expression – and fly defiantly over the heads of its object, determined to make it flee. Scores of self-help manuals advise readers how to turn their fears and indecision into confident actions.[23] There it is called 'fearbusting', but those influenced by classical Greek and Roman writings harbour the same point; fear can breed courage, 'grace under pressure' (Aung San Suu Kyi[24]) – and courage, in the circumstances, can nourish creative or daring acts that are quite literally out of the ordinary. Exactly how this happens is strongly context-dependent, although when large numbers of people lose their fear the triangle of fear is typically broken by catalysis. Individuals or groups boldly wade out of the mire of fear, thereby inspiring others to follow. This escape from fear is always an *individual* act, although the act itself can be more or less group-based and more or less dramatic. Commenting on Edgar Allan Poe's story of three fisherman caught in a maelstrom, Norbert Elias points out that two of them died after being paralysed by fear, whereas the survivor managed to conquer his fear after recognising that round objects are sucked less quickly into a watery abyss, and so jumping into a barrel to save himself. The lucky survivor, Elias comments, 'began to think more coolly; and by standing back, by controlling his own fear, by seeing himself as it were from a distance, like a chessman forming a pattern with others on a board, he managed to turn his thoughts away from himself to the situation in which he found himself ... Symbolically representing in his mind the structure and direction of the flow of events, he discovered a way of escape.'[25]

Then there are moments when the escape from fear at the individual level is a group-based process, an event that is as dramatic as it is co-dependent upon the 'saintly' abreactions of others. The October 2000 revolution in Serbia is a case in point.[26] The unexpected overthrow of the *ancien régime* arguably would have been impossible without fearless catalysts like the youth group *Odpor* (Resistance), which in the face of harsh repression struggled to resist the 'sociocide' or implosion of civil society and to stand up to the Milosević regime through non-violent acts

---

[23] See for example Susan J. Jeffers, *Feel the Fear and Do it Anyway* (London: Arrow, 1991) and Gavin de Becker, *The Gift of Fear: Survival Signals That Protect Us from Violence* (London: Bloomsbury, 2000).
[24] Aung San Suu Kyi, 'Freedom from Fear [1991]', in *Freedom from Fear and Other Writings* (London: Penguin Books, 1995), p. 184.
[25] Norbert Elias, 'The Fisherman in the Maelstrom', in *Involvement and Detachment* (Oxford: Blackwell, 1987), p. 46.
[26] Dragica Vujadinović-Milinković, 'Degradation of Everyday Life, Destruction of Society and Civil Society Suppression', unpublished paper presented at the University of Bradford, 25–26 March 2000.

of open defiance, including door-stepping citizens in towns large and small, hosting music concerts and publicly circulating banners and leaflets that contained what seemed at the time to be make-believe slogans, like 'He is finished!' Their actions were saintly in the best and most exact sense.[27] They felt called upon to bear a responsibility that they alone had chosen to bear. Their standards could not be statistically unremarkable, or commonplace. They felt themselves required to exceed ordinary standards, to do things that others – being afraid, or too selfish – were unwilling to do, or could not reasonably be expected to do. Like all previous saints, they were *unique* people in the face of fear. They strived to accomplish the impossible, and that is why they did not expect others to seek the unattainable in the way that they did. That is what made them saints: their ability to assume personal responsibility for doing things that were way above the call of duty.

Fear that gives wings to courage and freedom is only one type of abreaction to fear. The capacity to shake it off by confronting the perceived sources of fear can indeed be enlivening. The personal effort to draw on inner and outer resources to nurture the habit of refusing to let fear dictate one's actions can fortify the individual. And the ability to join with others in dignity and solidarity to resist the enervating miasma is a form of empowerment. The surmounting of fear can certainly add to people's self-confidence, as it does normally in the process of ontogenesis, and at a certain magical moment during the outbreak of every revolution (as Ryszard Kapuściński's fine study of the overthrow of the Pahlavi regime emphasised[28]). Yet fear should not be glorified universally, as if it was something like the necessary condition of courageous action, itself the precondition of democratic freedom with dignity. This is so for two main reasons.

In the first place, the abreactions produced by fear can be destructive of the freedom and dignity – sometimes the lives – of others. Fear can produce anti-democratic sentiments and outcomes. The covenants extorted by fear outlined and justified in Thomas Hobbes' *De Corpore Politico* and other works can be understood as a simile of a type of fearful reaction by individuals and groups that results in their own subjugation.[29]

---

[27] See the remarks of Emmanuel Lévinas, 'Mourir pour ...', in *Entre nous: Essais sur le penser-à-l'autre* (Paris: Bernard Grasset, 1991), pp. 228–229.

[28] Ryszard Kapuściński, *Shah of Shahs* (London: Picador, 1986), pp. 109–111.

[29] Thomas Hobbes, *De Corpore Politico: Or the Elements of Law, Moral and Politic*, in William Molesworth (ed.), *The English Works of Thomas Hobbes of Malmesbury*, Vol. IV (London: J. Bohn, 1840), Part 1, Chapter 2, Section 13, pp. 92–93.

The huddling together of the afraid and their combined efforts to project their fears nastily onto others, for instance in the form of racism, hatred of foreigners or populist pride, is another instance of the possible anti-democratic effects of fear.

There is a second reason why fear should not be glorified as the mother of courageous freedom. During the experience of fear, there are always moments that feel interminably long, when the person who is afraid fails to react, or takes no appropriate action to protect themselves, as when a person turns pale, breaks into a sweat, screams ... and later says that they were 'scared stiff' or 'glued to the ground'. The details of such non-action could of course be counted – plausibly – as a type of reaction, even though it is minimal and involuntary, which serves to highlight the key point that fear is no friend of freedom. All fear is bondage, goes an old Italian and English proverb.[30] Fear is indeed a thief. It robs subjects of their capacity to act with or against others. It leaves them shaken, sometimes permanently traumatised. Fear as bondage and theft can certainly happen under conditions of monitory democracy. When large numbers fall under the dark clouds of fear, no sun shines on civil society. Fear saps its energies and tears and twists at the institutions of political representation. Fear eats the soul of democracy.

FEAR AS A PUBLIC PROBLEM

And so the question returns: do monitory democracies, considered ideally as dynamic systems of publicly accountable and restrained power, contain within them mechanisms for 'privatising' and therefore trivialising, or even eradicating outright, the fears that otherwise threaten the social and political freedoms that are the lifeblood of democracy? Fresh thinking is certainly required when responding to this question, if only because the conventional argument that democracy indeed 'privatises' fear is less than convincing. Much more needs to be said in particular about the several counter-trends within the realms of state institutions, civil societies and communications media. These counter-trends arguably ensure not only that fears are not washed away by monitory forms of democracy – they guarantee that fear is a permanent *public* problem within actually existing democracies.

---

[30] James Sanford, *The Garden of Pleasure: Contayninge Most Pleasante Tales ... Done out of Italian into English* (London: Bynneman, 1573), p. 52.

War Consider the obvious problem of war: contrary to the 'democratic peace' thesis, democracies do not enjoy an excellent record in either avoiding war with one another or reducing citizens' fears generated by war and rumours of war.[31] War is not somehow forgotten. It does not disappears over the horizon of experience. In the age of the permanent 'war on terror', there is undoubtedly public support for minimising the loss of life – the number of body bags – and the casualties that result from full-scale war. The reliance upon robotic, 'risk-free' aerial bombardment as the preferred means of military intervention and the growth of a 'post-heroic' view of war, even an unwillingness among men and women to wave the flag, slip into military uniform and go off to fight wars, are the main consequences. Some scholars have drawn from this the conclusion that the world has sub-divided into two parts: a zone of violent anarchy that is troubled by war, warlords, lawlessness, repression and famine; and a 'security community' of peaceful and prosperous democracies in which fear generated by war disappears.[32]

The conclusion may be comforting, but it is misleading, as current trends show strikingly. The so-called democratic zone of peace cannot shake off the problem of fear generated by war, and not only because the commitment to a permanent 'war on terror' and the violence-ridden drugs trade and globalised arms production binds it to the fate of war-torn zones elsewhere. Public calls for military intervention wherever human rights are violated – into areas suffering plagues of private violence and uncivil war stoked by gunrunners, warlords, gangsters, armed sects, rebel armies – keep fear of war in the headlines. So too does the growth of a global system of communications media, whose editors often feature war and cruelty in accordance with the rule, 'If it bleeds, let it lead.'[33] Then there is the unresolved problem of the role played by nuclear-tipped states in the post-Cold War world system. This system is dominated by the United States, the world's single superpower, which can and does act as a 'swing power' backed by nuclear force. As a swing power, it is engaged in several regions although not tied permanently to any of them, but its manoeuvres are complicated by the fact that it is presently forced to co-exist and interact with several other nuclear great powers, including

---

[31] R.J. Rummel, *Understanding Conflict and War*, Vols. I–V (Beverly Hills, CA: Sage, 1975–1981).

[32] Max Singer and Aaron Wildavsky, *The Real World Order: Zones of Peace/Zones of Turmoil* (Chatham, NJ: Chatham House, 1993).

[33] These points are detailed in my 'The Long Century of Violence', in *Reflections on Violence* (London: Verso, 1996).

China and Russia. The geometry of this arrangement clearly differs from the extended freeze imposed by the Cold War, when (according to Raymond Aron's formula) the democracies lived in accordance with the rule, 'peace impossible, war unlikely'. With the collapse of bipolar confrontation, this rule has changed. There is no evidence of the dawn of a post-nuclear age, and the freedom from the fear of nuclear accident or attack that that would bring. Nowadays, as Pierre Hassner put it so well, peace has become a little less impossible and major wars are a little less unlikely, principally because a form of unpredictable anarchy is settling on the whole world.[34] The probability of a nuclear apocalypse, in which the earth and its peoples are blown sky-high, may have been reduced, but major wars remain a possibility, including even the use of nuclear-tipped weapons in conflicts that originate in local wars.

Nuclear weapons abound – the arsenals of the United States and Russia each contain somewhere around 7,000 nuclear warheads.[35] Depleted uranium shells are now routinely dropped on the victims of war. And despite the 1972 Anti-Ballistic Missile Treaty, nuclear capacity is spreading. The nuclear armament of North Korea, the nuclear arms races between Pakistan and India, and the festering military tensions among Israel, Turkey, Russia, Iran and the Arab states all suggest that the rules of nuclear confrontation are disputed, and that the global issue of nuclear weapons is now deeply implicated in the proliferation of so-called conventional weaponry in local wars, and the widespread fears they generate.

Civil Society Failures Toughly realist accounts of the fear-reducing qualities of contemporary civil societies need to be sensitive to their self-paralysing tendencies, as well as to the measures required to ameliorate or overcome them. Civil societies undoubtedly contain fear-producing dynamics. Their restlessness (an apt word used by Hegel to describe a feature of modern civil societies) frustrates any natural tendency towards social equilibrium; and the social bonds nurtured by the conflicts they produce do not guarantee citizens' freedom from fear. Pressured by such forces as unemployment, large-scale immigration, criminal violence and racism, civil societies are structured by multiple organising principles and institutional forms that can and do disorientate actors, generate risks

---

[34] See the concluding interview in Pierre Hassner, *La violence et la paix: De la bombe atomique au nettoyage ethnique* (Paris: Esprit, 1995).

[35] Arms Control Association, *Nuclear Weapons: Who Has What at a Glance* (Washington DC, January 2017), www.armscontrol.org/factsheets/Nuclearweaponswhohaswhat.

and enforce hard choices. Disorientation can be creative, a source of inspiration for individuals and groups, of course. Yet as Franz Neumann pointed out, the anxieties that result can function as the soil in which fears of various kinds spring up.[36] The disorganising effects of market failures, the dysfunctions endemic within processes of commodity production and exchange associated with market economies are an obvious example. The freedom of capital to invest and dis-invest produces well-known symptoms: periods of creative destruction associated with technical innovations; surges of capital investment and hyper-speculation followed by downturns; and the periodic dis-employment and wholesale redundancy of labour power. The resulting stresses and strains can and do generate genuine fears – of losing one's material livelihood (as a worker) or one's shirt (as an owner or manager of capital). To the extent that market economies intertwine and form themselves into a global economy, these fears come to be felt globally. As we have seen earlier in this book, the fears are compounded by the perpetual ecological disturbances caused by market-driven, fossil fuel-based economies. Led by the United States, whose inhabitants currently devour between fifty and 100 times more energy per capita than those of Bangladesh, these economies have consumed ten times more energy during the past century than did their predecessors during the thousand years before 1900.[37]

Fears also result from the tendency of civil society to generate moral turbulence and collisions among its constituent individuals and groups. So-called communitarian critics of civil society dwell at length upon this point. Mourning the loss of imagined stable communities of the past – and suffering from a condition that might be called *Gesellschaftsangst* – they dream fancifully of stitching together the torn shreds of morality with the blue thread of political community. That could not be done without destroying civil society itself, but their emphasis on its disorganising effects, and the trepidations they generate, although exaggerated, puts a finger on the point that civil societies produce fear in considerable quantities. True, they cultivate resources – the arts of kindness and civility, the ability to

---

[36] Franz Neumann, 'Anxiety and Politics', in *The Democratic and the Authoritarian State: Essays in Political and Legal Theory* (New York: The Free Press, 1957), p. 271: 'Modern society produces a fragmentation not only of social functions but of man himself who, as it were, keeps his different faculties in different pigeonholes – love, labor, leisure, culture – that are somehow held together by an externally operating mechanism that is neither comprehended nor comprehensible.'

[37] John R. McNeill, *Something New under the Sun: An Environmental History of the Twentieth-Century World* (London: Allen Lane, 2000), pp. 14–17.

duck conflicts, to make jokes, to bargain and to make give-and-take compromises – that help them weather storms of controversy and the fears they induce. When they function well, the institutions, networks and informal connections of civil societies provide a 'holding environment' in which individuals experience their bodies as the place wherein they securely dwell.[38] A good case can be made as well for the view that conflict is an essential factor of socialisation, and that civil societies benefit from the cumulative experience of tending and muddling through their own social conflicts, particularly the kind that are non-threatening or 'divisible'.[39] In practice, of course, the distinction between threatening and non-threatening conflicts is itself controversial to their protagonists, and that is the rub: civil societies conjure up fears of what others have done, or are doing, or might be planning to do – sometimes to the point where the participants themselves become mildly or acutely afraid. A disturbing example is the unease that surfaced during recent years within the European Union about national identity and the xenophobic outbursts driven by wild fantasies of 'take-overs' by 'foreigners' and the need to redraw borders and reclaim 'sovereignty' against threatening Others.[40]

COMMUNICATIONS MEDIA AND THE FASCINATION WITH FEAR

No account of the subject of fear and monitory democracy would be plausible without considering the ways in which networked communications media fascinate their audiences with stories that not only report and circulate fears, but also *induce* fears. Why is it, beginning with the Graveyard poets and the first gruesome tabloid newspaper stories, through Dracula, the films of Alfred Hitchcock and Stephen King, millions of people have spent so much time wilfully scaring themselves, to the point where they experience mysterious pleasures associated with sudden intakes of breath and momentary prickles of the skin? Why do the communications media of contemporary democracies enjoy the power to fascinate people with matters that they should run screaming from?

---

[38] D.W. Winnicott, 'The Theory of the Parent-Infant Relationship', *The International Journal of Psycho-analysis*, 41 (1960), 585–595.
[39] See Albert Hirschman, 'Social Conflicts as Pillars of Democratic Market Society', *Political Theory*, 22 (1994), 56. The socialising effects of conflict are analysed in Georg Simmel's path-breaking essay, 'Der Streit', in *Soziologie: Untersuchungen über die Formen der Vergesellschaftung* (Leipzig: Duncker & Humblot, 1908).
[40] John Keane, 'Europe is Suffering Multi-Morbidity: A Conversation with Claus Offe in Berlin', *Huffington Post* (31 January 2017).

Providing plausible answers to these questions is not easy, although one way of doing so is to examine the ways in which fear is rooted in the experience of death. The whole Western history of reflections on the subject of fear and politics, beginning with Thucydides, may be thought of in 'existential' terms, as a sub-set of the more general, deeply visceral reactions to the irremediable fact that each individual on Earth is fated to die. Death always preoccupies and intrigues individuals, whether they know or accept it, or not. The preoccupation begins at an early age, when death is the object of intrigue and curiosity, but death is most often subject to taboos imposed by adults. Death and dying always come culturally coded. In functional terms, adult individuals, and small and large groups, cope with death through a great variety of strategies with often unpredictable reactions. They may lapse into melancholy; with a sigh of resignation and a touch of despair, they turn in seriousness towards the great questions of life, thereby earning themselves the reputation as melancholics and depressives in the company of others, the kind of people who compulsively read obituaries to reassure themselves they aren't listed among them. Others who are preoccupied with the idea and certainty of death seek out a religion, which has the consoling effect of putting death in its place, sometimes (in the case of Christian Science, for instance) by denying it outright or (the teachings of the Buddha) by believing that death is not the end of life, merely the end of the body we inhabit in this life, the beginning of the attachment of our spirit to a new body, in a new life.

There are of course more common methods of forgetting death. Exalting the dead through fond memories and making 'a supreme effort to deny death'[41] by declaring it a taboo subject are just two examples of the many ways in which the living cope temporarily with the necessity of their death. They live content, convinced for the time being of their own immortality. It is well known that putting death on the shelf has its costs. Individuals normally pay for their denials. Sometimes the cost is high, in the form of severe symptoms like bouts of depression and psychosomatic illness. More common are those moments when individuals experience, sometimes intensely, what Freud called the uncanny (*das Unheimliche*), that diffuse feeling of fascination with the spooky, the shadowy, the spine-chillingly strange. During these moments when

---

[41] Hattie Rosenthal, 'The Fear of Death as an Indispensable Factor in Psychotherapy', in Hendrik M. Ruitenbeek (ed.), *Death: Interpretations* (New York: Dell, 1969), pp. 169–170.

they are drawn into the lairs of the uncanny, seemingly against their will, people resemble children who are both afraid of the dark and yet riveted by it. Comfortable in the conscious, if strained recognition that there is no immediate or actual danger to their lives, they indulge their deeper concerns about death.

Whether or not 'the aim of all life is death', and whether individuals chronically suffer the secret wish to die,[42] need not detain us here. The key point is this: since the conscious fear of death would make individuals unable to function normally in everyday life, they repress that fear. In turn, that repression generates tension which, from time to time, is released through a safety valve, in order to avoid accumulating too much of it.[43] The old joke about the individual who was so afraid of death that they killed themselves captures something of this equation. Under democratic conditions, there are times, in other words, when individuals are drawn fearfully towards death in order better to escape its clutches. Under democratic conditions, such fears are no longer projected onto the imagined 'spirits' of nature; and religious institutions lose their monopoly powers of handling the uncanny through sacred imagery that rivets believers to images of the living God, who is represented either as a loving and compassionate God or as a terrible power capable of divine wrath. The modern experience of the uncanny consequently tends to become 'homeless'. Enter modern communications media: their success in attracting and retaining audiences partly stems from their power of creating sites that enable individuals to fixate on symbolic representations of dying and death. Communications media enable individuals to indulge their fears of death, as if they were obsessed with a disturbing painting, like that of Dürer depicting Death as an intruder hell-bent on strangling his victim.

THE DEMOCRATISATION OF FEAR

Within contemporary democracies, the fear industry – the widespread promulgation of images and stories of fear through communications media – is often publicly criticised for exaggerating the scope and intensity

---

[42] Sigmund Freud, 'Beyond the Pleasure Principle', in J. Strachey (ed.), *The Standard Edition of the Complete Psychological Works of Sigmund Freud*, Vol. XVIII (London: Hogarth Press, 1955).
[43] Gregory Zilboorg, 'Fear of Death', *Psychoanalytic Quarterly*, 12 (1943), 465; see also Rosenthal, 'The Fear of Death as an Indispensable Factor in Psychotherapy'.

of violent crime and other personal and group disasters.[44] It is accused of *inciting* fears in others, sometimes to the point of so blurring their judgements about 'reality' that they begin unnecessarily to be panicked into believing that they are living in some late modern version of the lawless state of nature described by Thomas Hobbes. Driven by ratings, newspaper, radio, television and web-platform media turn fear into a commodity. They bombard audiences with stories of homicidal au pairs, mass murderers, paedophile preschool teachers, road ragers, and merciless killer viruses. The corresponding – anti-democratic – belief in Hobbesian solutions logically follows, or so it is claimed. The afraid take refuge in talk of worsening crime and getting tough on the causes of crime; they huddle under the protection of insurance policies, burglar alarms, tougher policing, and gated communities dotted with 'armed response' signs; and they back candidates who promise to be tough on 'terrorism'.

Repressive forms of law and order may well be the offspring of citizens who are afraid, although the politics of fear is a wild horse capable of surprising twists and turns. A good counter-case can be made for paying greater attention to the dialectics of the commercialisation of fear through media such as film, television and music. These media arguably have the long-term effect of relocating fears that are experienced privately into the public domain. They publicly identify those who are afraid, give them a voice, partly by giving their fears a name. The fears once experienced privately by individual victims at the hands of bullies, stalkers, child molesters, or rapists are comparatively recent examples of this trend. By identifying these fears and enabling the afraid to speak out publicly, communications media enable all citizens to understand these fears as a *public* problem for which *public* remedies can and should in principle be found.

This long-term transformation of fear into a public problem is subject to many and various exceptions, no doubt. Yet the vital significance of the metamorphosis can be gauged by placing it within a wider historical context. Until the eighteenth century, until the time of Montesquieu's path-breaking reflections, fear had been regarded by those who studied it as a sad necessity in human affairs. Although there had been a string of laments for the undue power and folly induced by fear, discourses on its nature usually treated it as human fate. Fear was considered to be a sticky web spun by the gods, as natural as thunder and lightning, an inevitable

---

[44] See, for example, Barry Glassner, *The Culture of Fear: Why Americans Are Afraid of the Wrong Things* (New York: Basic Books, 1999).

part of the human condition – as Thucydides himself thought when analysing fear as rooted in the human drive for security, glory and material wealth.[45]

During the eighteenth century, for a variety of intersecting reasons, this presumption of the inevitability of fear began to crumble. A long revolution in the understanding of fear broke out. So fear came to be given various names and was then studied by writers who distinguished between its causes and pretexts. Its roots in the densely textured fabric of psychic, social and political life were investigated, and the possibility emerged, or so these writers thought, that fear and its paralysing effects could be overcome, not just comforted and consoled, for instance through religious faith. Fear came to be regarded as a thoroughly human problem for which there are thoroughly human remedies. Some writers even thought politically about the subject, sometimes in radical ways, for instance by suggesting that a certain type of political system, a democratic republic, would prove to be something of a 'school of courage' (Ferrero) and, hence, the best antidote to fears that destroy citizens' capacities for self-chosen action.

To the extent that fears once suffered in private have come to be perceived and dealt with as public problems, the ground is prepared for the understanding of fear as contingent, as a *political* problem. This long-term transformation may be described as the 'democratisation' of fear, not in the ridiculous sense that everyone comes to exercise their right to be afraid, or is duty-bound to be so, but rather that fear, especially its debilitating and anti-democratic forms, ceases to be seen as 'natural' and comes instead to be understood as a *contingent* human experience, as a *publicly treatable* phenomenon, as a political problem for which tried and tested political remedies may be found.

A fundamental first step in this modern democratisation of fear was its categorisation. Partly in emulation of the methods pioneered by Linnaeus, imaginative word-building by analysts of fear became voguish. By the first quarter of the nineteenth century, the suffix *phobia* – from the Greek *phobeio*, meaning 'I fear' and 'I am put to flight' – began to be used widely by medical and psychological writers, so widely in fact that figures like Benjamin Rush satirically suggested new terms like 'rum phobia' ('a very rare distemper') and 'church phobia' and 'doctor phobia'.[46] Carl

---

[45] William Desmond, 'Lessons of Fear: A Reading of Thucydides', *Classical Philology*, 101, 4 (2006), 359–379.
[46] Benjamin Rush, 'On the Different Species of Phobia [1789]', in Dagobert Runes (ed.), *The Selected Writings of Benjamin Rush* (New York: Philosophical Library, 1947),

Westphal's less jocular invention of the term *agoraphobia* pinpointed cases of morbid fear of open places.[47] Others spoke for the first time of such fears as *photophobia* (fear and avoidance of light), *hydrophobia* (fear of water, earlier called *phobodipsia*, fear of drinking), and *xenophobia*, fear and avoidance of strangers and foreigners. On the eve of the First World War, one authority noted the contemporary usage of 136 different neologisms with the suffix *-phobia*.[48] A century later, the list has come to include such terms as *allodoxaphobia* (fear of opinions), *ataxophobia* (fear of disorder, or untidiness), *neophobia* (fear of anything new) and *phobophobia* (fear of phobias).[49] The new and (it seems) constantly expanding vocabulary for describing and analysing fear no doubt has served to endow its investigators with 'expertise' and clinical 'authority'. But it has also paved the way for the view that fears can be named and classified and their aetiology publicly explained. Freud's early thoughts on the zoophobias of children – the horse phobia of 'little Hans' and the wolf phobia of the young Russian known as 'the wolf-man'[50] – helped bolster this trend. Fear was seen neither as a natural product of birth (as Otto Rank had claimed) nor (as Ernest Jones had surmised) an expression of an inborn faculty,[51] nor as an illness. The fears of disturbed individuals were rather interpreted as clues to the existence of repressed anxieties and wishes that have been displaced by the ego, only to resurface in consciousness in disguised form. Those disguises were said to function as mechanisms of avoidance, alibis whose self-disturbing or self-crippling effects

---

pp. 220–225; see also the pertinent remarks of Leopold Loewenfeld, *Die psychischen Zwangserscheinungen* (Wiesbaden: Bergmann, 1904), pp. 330–355.

[47] Carl F. O. Westphal, 'Die Agoraphobie: Eine neuropatische Erscheinung', *Archiv für Psychiatrie*, 3 (1871), 138–161. Westphal describes a disturbed patient who felt that Tiergarten, where there were no signs of houses, and a certain square in Berlin were both many miles wide. The patient did not mind traffic or the company of other people, but whenever alone in such places he suffered severe symptoms, like head sensations, palpitations and trembling.

[48] G. Stanley Hall, 'A Synthetic Genetic Study of Fear', *American Journal of Psychology*, 25 (1914), 149–200, 321–392.

[49] Ivan Ward, *Phobia* (Duxford, Cambridge: Icon Books, 2001), pp. 26–27.

[50] Sigmund Freud, 'Analysis of a Phobia in a Five-year-old Boy [1909]', in *The Standard Edition of the Complete Psychological Works of Sigmund Freud*, Vol. X (London: Hogarth Press, 1955), pp. 31–49, and 'From the History of an Infantile Neurosis [1918]', in ibid., Vol. XVII, pp. 3–122.

[51] See Freud's critique of Rank in *The Problem of Anxiety* (New York: Norton, 1936), chapter 10; cf. Ernest Jones, 'The Pathology of Morbid Anxiety', in *Papers on Psychoanalysis*, 4th edn (London: Benn, 1911).

could in principle be cured by cultivating the victims' capacity for self-reflection, by talking about their tangled dynamics.

The contemporary concern with traumas – experiences of fear that are so intense that an individual's ordinary coping mechanisms break down – feeds into this older process of democratising fear. Many studies in the burgeoning fields of psychiatry and psychoanalysis emphasise that intense experiences of fear are not confined to those who survived the Shoah, or nuclear attack, or refugee and prison camps, or who as soldiers survived combat at the battlefront. Traumas are found closer to home, sometimes too close to home for comfort. The common symptoms of what was once called 'shell shock' and 'battle fatigue' and is now called Post Traumatic Stress Disorder (PTSD) – symptoms such as emotional numbing, feelings of helplessness, anger, anxiety, disturbed sleep, flashbacks, panic attacks, hyper-alertness, suicidal thoughts, survivor guilt, self-punishment, anxiety about losing others, general confusion – show up in large percentages of other groups that have been scared half to death, for instance those who have experienced rape or incest or violent crime.[52] The individuals and groups who survive concentrated fear do not easily extricate themselves from its clutches. Fear lives on in its victims. It stalks their every step. Despite the fact that they may have no direct memory of what was done to them, the victims of fear remain disturbed. It is as if everything that subsequently happened to them brings them back to their original fears. Their 'normal' lives within civil society cannot become routine affairs, or purified. The afraid are haunted by a normalcy shot through with the bizarre fears from which they thought they had escaped. Hence their felt need to bear witness, to tell stories to others about the horrors that they tasted – and to reconstitute their damaged lives, painfully, not through tranquillisers, but through the catharsis of teaching themselves and others how the truths and dangers of what they have been through might be comprehended.

The political effort to identify fears, to name them, to witness and care for their victims, and to hunt down their perpetrators so that they might

---

[52] Good summaries of these trends can be grasped by comparing *Report of the War Office Committee of Enquiry Into 'Shell-Shock'* (London, 1922); the Veteran Administration publication, Selected Bibliography 2: *Post-Traumatic Stress Disorder with Special Attention to Vietnam Veterans*, Revision 25 (Phoenix, VA: VA Medical Center, 1986); Charles R. Figley (ed.), *Stress Disorders among Vietnam Veterans: Theory, Research and Treatment* (New York: Brunner/Mazel, 1978); Alice Miller, *Am Anfang war Erziehung* (Frankfurt a.M.: Suhrkamp, 1980); and Kali Tal, *Worlds of Hurt: Reading the Literatures of Trauma* (Cambridge: Cambridge University Press, 1996).

be brought before courts of law is something positive, yet incomplete. It is hard to know where today's monitory democracies are positioned on the scale of either understanding the fears that they (or other regimes) generate, or their counter-capacity to cultivate fearlessness, for instance through publicly witnessing the dastardly effects of fear. One thing is however certain: despite the flight of contemporary political science and political philosophy away from the land of fear, its inhabitants do not remain silent. Fear is a topic that cannot be ignored, or made to wither away, simply because democracies themselves stimulate the public awareness that those who ignore fear do so at their own peril.

PART VI

WHY MONITORY DEMOCRACY?

15

Is Democracy a Universal Ideal?

THE DEMOCRACY THING

Is democracy a good thing? That was the question that surfaced in the sun-scorched vineyards of Kandahar province, in October 2004, during a gathering of a thousand Pashtun tribal elders called to discuss Afghanistan's first awkward steps towards electoral democracy. The *shura*, or assembly, was reportedly treated by the organisers with roast lamb and a list of instructions: check that the tents, tables, indelible ink and stationery have been delivered to polling centres, some with addresses like 'beside the Joi Nau stream' or 'near the water station pump'; use tractors and taxis and donkeys to transport voters to those locations; make sure that both wives and husbands can recognise the president's photo on the ballot. 'We show them: here is the ballot, here is Karzai. Don't mark his head or put a line through his symbol – just tick the box', said Ahmed Wali Karzai, a Kandahar businessman and one of several speakers urging the assembly to cast a vote for his brother, Hamid Karzai, the incumbent president and election front runner. 'They don't have a clue what is going on', Ahmed Ali said after the assembly had concluded its business. 'They come to us and say: "Why are we having an election? Everything is going well." Or they say: "We don't need the government. It's done nothing for us. I live in a tent. What do I care about politics?" I tell them – they often frown – it's this democracy thing.'[1]

---

[1] 'Afghans take first awkward steps towards democracy', *Financial Times* (London), 9–10 October 2004.

This democracy thing: Is it a desirable political ideal? No treatment of monitory democracy and its future would be plausible without tackling the question, and its corollaries. Might monitory democracy be a universal norm, as relevant and applicable to the vineyard people of Kandahar and the Douro Valley as it is to bankers in Frankfurt, Lisbon and London and business people in Taipei and Cape Town, as well as to *dalit* women in India who battle for *panchayat* representation, or to the factory workers and peasants of China, the Kurds of Turkey, or even to powerful bodies that operate across borders, like the WTO and the World Bank? Or might it be that under pressure from all of the threats and challenges cited in this book the word democracy has become a soothing lullaby, perhaps even, as Nietzsche thought, a fake universal norm, just one of those pompous little Western values that jostles for our attention, dazzles us with its promises and, for a time, cons us into believing that it is not a mask for power, a tool useful in the struggle by some for mastery over others?

Most political commentators around the world today dodge such questions. A great normative silence envelops democracy at the very historical moment – paradoxically – that it cries out for help. There are multiple reasons for this hush. During the past several decades, the most influential has been the ascendancy of the 'end of history' and 'third wave' liberal democracy school. Journalists, politicians and political thinkers of this persuasion commonly noted that democracy in recent decades became, for the first time ever, a global political language. They pointed out that its dialects are now spoken in many countries on every continent – in India, Taiwan, Egypt, Ukraine, Argentina and Kenya – and they took heart from think tank reports that sang the praises of democracy using back-up evidence to prove its unstoppable advance. One well-known report spoke of the twentieth century as the Democratic Century. It pointed out that in 1900 monarchies and empires predominated. There were no states that could be judged as electoral democracies by the standard of universal suffrage for competitive multi-party elections; there were merely a few 'restricted democracies' – twenty-five of them, accounting for just 12.4 per cent of the world's population. By 1950, with the military defeat of Nazism and the beginnings of de-colonisation and the post-war reconstruction of Europe and Japan, there were twenty-two democracies accounting for 31 per cent of the world's population; a further twenty-one states were 'restricted democracies' and they accounted for 11.9 per cent of the world's population. By the end of the century, the report observed, the so-called Third Wave brought the experience of democracy to Latin America, post-communist Europe and

15 Is Democracy a Universal Ideal?

parts of Africa and Asia. Out of 192 countries, 119 could be described as 'electoral democracies' – 58.2 per cent of the globe's population – with eighty-five of these countries – 38 per cent of the world's inhabitants – enjoying forms of democracy 'respectful of basic human rights and the rule of law'. So the report found that the ideal of liberal democracy is now within reach of the whole world. 'In a very real sense', ran the conclusion, 'the twentieth century has become the "Democratic Century" … A growing global human rights and democratic consciousness is reflected in the expansion of democratic practices and in the extension of the democratic franchise to all parts of the world and to all major civilizations and religions.'[2]

Many quietly drew from reports of this kind the conclusion that liberal democracy had become a *de facto* universal. Brushing aside suggestions that democracy is a particular ideal with particular roots somewhere in the geographic region located between ancient Syria-Mesopotamia and the early Greek city-states, they noted, with satisfaction, that liberal democracy had triumphed over all other political values. Around the world, it has been embraced *as if* it were a way of life that had global validity – as 'a universal value that people anywhere may have reason to see as valuable' (Amartya Sen), as the 'end point of mankind's ideological evolution' and 'the final form of human government' (Francis Fukuyama).[3]

Not everyone agreed with these sentiments. Some commentators, Richard Rorty among them, were quite cynical – more sensitive to the ethical and political problem of why democracy should be considered desirable. Rorty minced no words. He admitted that modern representative democracy is a 'peculiarity' of 'North Atlantic culture'. But he was sure that democracy is 'morally superior' because it is an ingredient of 'a culture of hope – hope of a better world as attainable in the here and now by social and political effort – as opposed to the cultures of resignation characteristic of the East'. So even though democracy is only one norm among others it is self-evidently superior in practice, he claimed. 'There is much still to be achieved', Rorty explained in the *Süddeutsche Zeitung* shortly after President Bush had begun to talk war and freedom, 'but basically the

---

[2] See the Freedom House Report, *Democracy's Century: A Survey of Global Political Change in the 20th Century* (New York: Freedom House, 1999).
[3] Amartya Sen, 'Democracy as a Universal Value', *Journal of Democracy*, 10, 3 (1999), 3–17; Francis Fukuyama, *The End of History and the Last Man* (New York: The Free Press, 1992), p. xi.

West is on the right path. I don't believe it has much to learn from other cultures. We should aim to expand, to westernise the planet.'[4]

Pragmatic reasoning of this kind stood alongside the 'democracy promotion' efforts of the United States and other countries, but such reasoning easily became mixed up in violent power games in devils' playgrounds, as we learned from daily reports about democratisation experiments in Iraq, and in Afghanistan, where (by July 2006) new-minted members of the national parliament, most of them men linked to warlords and drug dealers and human rights violators, moved around in heavy vehicles, with armed guards fore and aft, dodging daily threats and declared bounties on their bodies (US$25,000 dead; $50,000 alive).[5] And there was plenty of evidence that suggests, especially when talk of the ethical superiority of democracy is backed up by military force, that the outcomes are probably bound to give democracy a bad name – resulting in what has been called 'pushback' of the kind that is happening today in various parts of the Middle East and elsewhere.[6] The harsh words against American democracy promotion efforts spoken by Lebanese Druze leader and opposition parliamentarian Walid Jumblatt may be read as the writing on the wall of democracy whenever and wherever it blindly or arrogantly supposes itself to be a universally 'good' North Atlantic norm. Describing President Bush as a 'mad emperor' who thinks of himself as 'God's deputy on earth', Condoleezza Rice as 'oil coloured' and Tony Blair a 'peacock with a sexual complex', Jumblatt sarcastically defined democracy as a type of imperial government in which 'their skies are American airplanes, their seas are American fleets, their bases are American bases, their regimes are US–British regimes, their rivers are American boats, their mountains are American commandos, their plains are American tanks and their security is at the service of American interests'.[7]

Such sweeping attacks on the democratic ideal serve as a reminder that the belief that the West has a patent on the universal ideal of democracy is a politically dangerous and self-crippling dogma. There is mounting evidence, tabled throughout this book, that the liberal democratic dogma is losing its self-confidence, losing its way in the world, and troubled by

---

[4] From an interview with Mathias Greffrath and others, 'Den Planeten verwestlichen!', *Süddeutsche Zeitung* (Munich), 20 November 2001 (translation mine).
[5] Paul McGeough, 'A Nation Built at the Point of a Gun', *Sydney Morning Herald* (15–16 July 2006), pp. 34–35.
[6] Thomas Carothers, 'The Backlash against Democracy Promotion', *Foreign Affairs* (March–April 2006).
[7] Cited in *The Daily Star* (Beirut), 3 February 2003.

inner demons: such phenomena as class inequality, ecological destruction, populism and xenophobia. Pressured by these dark ghosts from the past, the liberal democratic dogma is looking vulnerable. It is certainly philosophically questionable. The dogma begs a straightforward but tricky ethical question that has important strategic value: What is so good about the ideal of democracy as self-government of people through their chosen representatives?

To grasp why this question is important, let us return to the writings of Richard Rorty. When pressed further to explain why the Western 'experiment' with liberal democracy is desirable, Rorty replied that all forms of universal reasoning should be abandoned because democracy needs no philosophical justification at all. In normative terms, democracy should travel light: rejecting mumbo jumbo, it should whistle its way through the world with an air of 'philosophical superficiality and light-mindedness'.[8] The norm of democracy should not be understood as something like an extension of, or a substitute for, the principles once prized by theology. Democratic ideals can stand on their own feet. They are not desirable because they are somehow true to an order that is antecedent to and given to us – a foundational 'reality' that is non-contingent, necessary and prior to its particular forms. Democracy should shun dubious philosophical friends. It has no need of them. Indifference towards them is the beginning of democratic wisdom.

It has been said that this line of reasoning about democracy tacitly, by default, supposes the controversial metaphysical claim that there is no prior and independent ethical order. Rorty rightly brushes off that objection by saying that philosophy is both incapable of adducing such an order and, at the same time, that it has no business in dabbling in speculations about its existence or non-existence. The trouble with this conclusion – that democracy has absolute priority over philosophical norms – is not only that it ignores just how much philosophy as we know it has been changed by the democratic experience, but, more importantly, that it also ignores, conversely, just how much democracy as we experience it today continues to be shaped by grandiloquent philosophical propositions, themes and sentiments. It is not just that the word democracy (as Philip Pettit, John Dunn and others have pointed out) is a thickly evaluative term. Whether we recognise it or not, much thinking about

---

[8] Richard Rorty, 'The Priority of Democracy to Philosophy', *Objectivity, Relativism, and Truth: Philosophical Papers*, Vol. I (Cambridge: Cambridge University Press, 1991), p. 193.

democracy worldwide continues to live under the spell of early modern normative justifications of democracy that have the effect of turning it into a dogma.

FIRST PRINCIPLES

Any effort to free democracy from these inherited justifications needs to examine them in much more detail and with less wistfulness than Rorty supposes. As we are about to see, the single-mindedness of these traditional justifications – their secret or stated commitment to a foundational First Principle – is incompatible with a new understanding of democracy that allows both for a diversity of justifications of why democracy is desirable and explicit recognition of the plurality of conflicting and often incommensurable notions of the good affirmed by people living in actually existing democratic – and non-democratic – societies. The point is that today's silence about why democracy is supposed to be a desirable universal norm harbours much inherited philosophical arrogance that is itself undemocratic – and not likely to wither away unless it is vigorously exposed and opposed. The norm of democracy needs actively to be democratised: brought down to earth, stripped of its philosophical foundations so that it can better serve our planet and its peoples even-handedly, with less fanatical presumption and more humility.

Traces of old-fashioned arrogance are easy to spot within the contemporary belief that democracy is a universal value. Consider to begin with the nineteenth-century Christian view that support for the ideal of democracy is desirable, even necessary because it is based on 'the principles of eternal justice, the unchanging laws of God'. These words, famously spoken by the New England minister and campaigner, Theodore Parker, before a large public rally against slavery in Boston,[9] subsequently surfaced in the speeches of many an American president, most recently in

---

[9] From the speech, 'The American Idea', delivered by Theodore Parker to an anti-slavery rally in May 1850: 'A democracy, that is a government of all the people, by all the people, for all the people; of course, a government after the principles of eternal justice, the unchanging laws of God; for shortness sake, I will call it the idea of freedom'. Parker elsewhere noted that 'the democratic idea has had but a slow and gradual growth even in New England', but that it was nevertheless spreading throughout the American republic, such that 'government becomes more and more of all, by all and for all', a testimony to the fact that democracy is 'the enactment of God's justice into human laws' (quotations respectively from *Additional Speeches, Addresses, and Occasional Sermons*, Vol. I (Boston, 1855), p. 33; and 'The Nebraska Question', in ibid., p. 327).

15 Is Democracy a Universal Ideal?

those of George W. Bush. They also command strong support today among many Christians of different persuasions around the world. Christians were not always so inclined; the case for the marriage of Christian ethics and the norm of democracy was itself an historical achievement and had to be made politically the hard way, including through tough philosophical argument. An example is Jacques Maritain's justification of democracy as a predicate, or sublimated form, of Christian ethics.[10]

Maritain draws on the well-known remark of Henri Bergson that the motive power of democracy is love in order to describe the motivations that must be cultivated by citizens if democracy is to be born, or to survive and to flourish. Sense experience suggests that democracies require a 'common consciousness and common moral experience'. Citizens must be convinced in their hearts that rulers who produce injustices and commit crimes by using 'iniquitous and perverse means' are the sworn enemies of democracy. Citizens need a measure of secular faith in the forward march of humanity; they must be persuaded that human history does not go around in circles, or that it moves inevitably towards decline, or disaster. On that basis, democrats must believe that human beings, whether in their capacities as voters or as workers or as members of social groups, are rights-bearing citizens who are equal before the law, even in the face of inequalities that are regarded by most people as functionally necessary for the survival of democracy. Democrats must also understand that they are members of a state and that their lives and liberties and wellbeing depend upon its structures and policies. Yet the citizens of a democracy must grasp as well that their own dignity transcends the state and its powers. Democracy demands respect for the belief that legitimate government is exercised by virtue of the consent of the governed – not by the trickery and threats of the governors.

Among the unusual twists in Maritain's philosophical defence of democracy is its stress on the point that in any democracy worthy of the name the principle of 'the will of the people' is not its founding principle.

---

[10] From Jacques Maritain, 'Christianity and Democracy', a typewritten manuscript prepared as an address at the annual meeting of the American Political Science Association in New York (29 December 1949). The manuscript is preserved in the University of Notre Dame Archives, Notre Dame, Indiana, Jacques Maritain Papers, 6/04 F. The following quotations are drawn from pp. 2, 5, 4 and 2–3. See also his *Christianity and Democracy* (London: The Century Press, 1945), pp. 10–11, where Maritain speaks of 'a new democracy whose Christian inspiration will call forth not only, in the West, the living traditions of Christ's religion, but, throughout the world, the moral forces of "the naturally Christian soul"'.

Conventional, simple-minded democratic views of the sovereign people are blind to the ways in which democracy can degenerate into mere rule of a majority that considers itself the sole judge of good and evil, so setting democracy on the road to totalitarian rule. The prevention of totalitarianism and other forms of violent injustice requires institutional *limits* on the formula of popular (majority) sovereignty – in favour of a 'common democratic charter' that privileges such aforementioned motivations as faith in the possibility of human progress, the inviolability of human dignity and the conviction that human suffering and injustice can be overcome through 'political work'. These motivations serve as correctives of simple-minded understandings of democracy, which suffer from blindness of a second sort: the blindness that accompanies their old-fashioned commitment to the dogma that the people of any single state are sovereign masters of their own sovereign house. The dogma of sovereignty overlooks the pressing need to cultivate 'brotherly love' across borders, to extend 'civic friendship ... to the entire human race'.

Conventional notions of democracy suffer a third form of blindness: they indulge a misguided belief that 'the people' can do without transcendental standards while living on earth. Here Maritain moves by way of reflexive abstraction from considerations of sense experience to the metaphysical claim that democracy is the 'temporal manifestation of the inspiration of the Gospel'. Democracy is rooted in God-given Being; it is the sublimate of God's creation and guidance of the earth and its peoples. Historically speaking, Christian teachings provided by degrees the evangelical inspiration of the secular democratic consciousness that was born of modern times. Human beings with democratic instincts are not soulless apes for whom the accidents of zoological mutation and adaptation just happened by chance to turn out favourably. 'The democratic sense or feeling', says Maritain, 'is, by its very nature, an evangelical sense or feeling, its motive power is love, the essential thing in it is fraternity, it has its real sources in Gospel Inspiration.' The corollary of this thesis is that the democratic state of mind cannot survive in purely secular form. 'The people are not God, the people do not have infallible reason and virtues without flaw.' Democratic efforts to decide what is just or unjust require the inspiration of the Gospel. Authority ultimately has its source in God. No person or group or people can claim the right to rule others. That is why, Maritain concludes, the voluntary re-Christianisation of the world, the 'internal awakening' of individuals who become spiritually committed to the teachings of Jesus of Nazareth, is a basic condition of reviving and quickening democracy in troubled times.

Traces of Christian thinking are blended into a quite different justification of democracy in the widely read, hotly-debated polemic by Giuseppe Mazzini, 'Thoughts Upon Democracy in Europe' (1847).[11] It begins with a stirring anthem: 'The democratic tendency of our times, the upward movement of the popular classes, who desire to have their share in political life – hitherto a life of privilege – is henceforth no Utopian dream, no doubtful anticipation. It is a fact; a great European fact, which occupies every mind, influences the proceedings of government, defies all opposition.' Mazzini interpreted this 'upward movement' towards democracy as confirmation of the Principle of Man. This guiding foundational principle has a 'religious' quality: faith in its workings is mandatory because everybody and everything in the world is both its expression and potential beneficiary. Democrats 'are believers without a temple'. The Principle of Man – together with its corollary that all living men and women can come to enjoy freedom and equality – is becoming the measure of all things, says Mazzini. The world is subject to what he called 'the law of continual progress'. Nudged along by political will and due effort, it leads everywhere to the self-improvement and equality of human beings.

The Principle of Man stands opposed to competition, selfishness, 'party spirit', and the present-day 'analysing, dividing, and sub-dividing' of Man into unequal fragments. It is opposed to talk of individual rights and to efforts (like that of Thomas Paine's *Rights of Man* [1791–1792] and Mary Wollstonecraft's *A Vindication of the Rights of Woman* [1792]) to ground democracy on a theory of rights. The Principle of Man also abhors the exploitation of Man by men. It seeks to overcome the divisions between 'the Glasgow workman and his master, the Irish labourer and the middleman, the child who works in the mine and he who with a rod prevents him from falling asleep'. Democracy is a 'creed of fusion'. It 'thirsts for unity'. It stands for co-operation, love, association and enthusiasm: the individual living for his or her family, the family for its country, the country living for humanity as an integrated whole.

Mazzini was at pains to point out that democrats know that inequality disfigures people. 'Give the suffrage to a people unfitted for it, governed by hateful reactionary passions, they will sell it, or will make a bad use of it; they

---

[11] Giuseppe Mazzini, 'Thoughts Upon Democracy in Europe', first published in the *People's Journal* (1847) and reprinted in Joseph Mazzini, *A Memoir by E.A.V. with Two Essays by Mazzini* (London, 1875), pp.171–257. The quotations that follow are found on pp. 171, 175, 171, 179, 202–203, 178, 185, 177, 180, 194, 239, 205, 239, 233 and 217.

will introduce instability into every part of the state.' That is why democrats wish human beings to be better than they currently are. 'Democracy says to us – "If you wish to attain it, let man commune as intimately as possible with the greatest possible number of his fellows" . . . It bids us – "Endeavour all to unite. Invite all to the banquet of life. Throw down the barriers which separate you. Suppress all the privileges which render you hostile or envious . . . Make yourselves equal, as far as it can be done."' Democrats champion 'the idea of the mission of humanity'. They work for the nurturing of dutiful love within the Family, where the child's first lesson in the Principle of Man is offered by 'the mother's kiss and the father's caress'. Democrats see the Family as the nucleus of the Nation and in turn they champion the self-determination of all Nations, considered as equals, as entities that nurture the solidarity of citizens, for instance through the ownership of property and the right of suffrage. According to Mazzini, solidarity in the home is linked to the solidarity that comes through membership of a Nation. And just as he objects to the fracturing of Family and Nation by the greedy exploits of 'the well-lodged, well-clothed, and well-fed classes', so he finds abhorrent 'the usurping and monopolising nation, conceiving its own grandeur and force only in the inferiority and in the poverty of others'. Democracy lives for the day when all forms of privilege and inequality within nations shall be turned into dust and ashes. For the same reason it yearns for the peaceful integration of all Nations into a common Humanity based on family and 'fatherland' – a new world order of democracy based on sovereign nations bound together 'by progress, and consequently by liberty'.

A pinch of religion, an ounce of nation-thinking, two spoonfuls of the belief in progress, a large serving of Humanism: Mazzini's eclectic thought patterns had the effect of widening the repertoire of philosophical justifications of modern representative democracy while deepening its embrace of stable foundational principles that afford a comprehensive view of the world. The same effect – and the grip of the philosophical past on the present – is evident in efforts to define democracy as founded on the principle that power sharing arrangements are desirable because concentrated power always has unhappy or dangerous effects.

Among the first formulations of this particular justification of the democratic ideal was an influential tract called *Government* (1820), written for an encyclopaedia by the Scottish preacher and teacher and civil servant, James Mill (1773–1836).[12] It explained that democracy in representative

---

[12] James Mill, 'Government', *Encyclopaedia Britannica* (1820), reprinted as *An Essay on Government* (Cambridge: Cambridge University Press, 1937).

form maximizes the happiness of the governed by providing them with the means of sacking those governors who make them miserable. Democracy conforms to the fundamental Principle of Utility that states that 'if the end of Government be to produce the greatest happiness of the greatest number, that end cannot be attained by making the greatest number slaves'. The 'evils of unbridled power' and the enslavement to rulers is a constant political problem because all men – Mill thought women and children were non-players in the game of politics – strive constantly for power over others. Power is a universal aphrodisiac. Men cannot resist its charms. It sets off insatiable desires for the total conquest of others. Power hunger is 'boundless in the number of persons to whom we would extend it, and boundless in its degree over the actions of each'.

It follows from this 'grand governing law of human nature' that the great problem in matters of government is somehow to turn necessity into virtue by restraining those in whose hands is lodged the powers needed to protect the political community. Absolute monarchy is an objectionable type of government because it potentially takes whatever it pleases from its subjects and, in the extreme, ends in 'terror'. Government by a propertied aristocracy is not much better; for all its talk of virtue and civilisation, in practice it drags people down 'to the condition of negroes in the West Indies'. That leaves 'Democracy'. Mill reasoned that the ancient understanding of democracy by assembly, while admirable in its search for government for and by the whole community, in fact proved to be unworkable, at least for modern times. This is because it thwarted 'calm and effectual deliberation' by stirring up violent passions that encouraged some to shout down or speak over the heads of others, and because the regular assembly of a whole community would cut short the time spent producing wealth so vital for the survival and self-improvement of a community. Democracy therefore requires representatives, who do the job of governing, on behalf of others, but are prevented from becoming their masters because the representatives are themselves subject to voters' power to correct their actions or to get rid of them using the fair trial of periodic elections.[13]

---

[13] Mill, *An Essay on Government*, pp. 4, 49, 18, 17, 22, 25, 9. It is worth noting that in this tract Mill did not favour universal adult suffrage, as might have been expected from his reasoning about the common interest of the people in preventing their suffering at the hands of arbitrary power. Women, children, younger adult males and those without property – ten-twelfths of the population – are struck off the possible list of the enfranchised, on the ground that 'an interest identical with that of the whole community, is to be found in the aggregate males, of an age to be regarded as *sui juris* [Mill set the limit at 40], who may be regarded as the natural Representatives of the whole population' (p. 45).

EMIGRATION

When the language of democracy began to travel across seas and continents during the nineteenth and early twentieth centuries, brand new justifications of its superiority as an ethical ideal appeared. One of the long-lasting effects of the growing worldliness of democracy was to widen the philosophical case for it by adding to its existing menu of justifications. The curious thing is that despite its development of many tails of different colours, the norm of democracy continued to be wedded to universalist claims based on some type of metaphysical First Principle. A case in point, developed in New Zealand during the Second World War, is Karl Popper's knowledge-based theory of democracy as a unique type of polity that produces policies through evolutionary learning by enabling the public refutation of nonsense through public conjectures linked to truth claims. Democracy is an opponent of 'the closed society' and to all forms of 'historicism', by which Popper meant the dogmatic belief that history develops inexorably and necessarily, according to knowable general laws, towards a determinate end. Democracy is also an implacable opponent of unthinking acceptance of whatever seems fated, or necessary. 'One hears too often the suggestion that some form or other of totalitarianism is inevitable', wrote Popper. 'They ask us whether we are really naïve enough to believe that democracy can be permanent; whether we do not see that it is just one of the many forms of government that come and go in the course of history. They argue that democracy, in order to fight totalitarianism, is forced to copy its methods and thus to become totalitarian. Or they assert that our industrial system cannot continue to function without adopting the methods of collectivist planning, and they infer from the inevitability of a collectivist economic system that the adoption of totalitarian forms of social life is also inevitable.' Such ways of explaining and justifying the end or decline of

---

Further discussion of Mill's defence of representative democracy is to be found in the contrasting views of C.B. Macpherson, *The Life and Times of Liberal Democracy* (Oxford: Oxford University Press, 1977), Chapter 2; Joseph Hamburger, 'James Mill on Universal Suffrage and the Middle Class', *Journal of Politics*, 24 (1962), 167–190; and Mill's own claim, recorded later by his son, John Stuart Mill, that in the tract *Government* he presumed that the times were such that the franchise had to be restricted, so that he was asking only what seemed to him an allowable or achievable franchise (see John Stuart Mill, *Autobiography* [London, 1924], pp. 87–88). But as Macpherson points out (ibid., p. 41), the wording of the article *Government* 'suggests not that he regarded the restrictions as unfortunately necessary concessions to political realism, but rather that he regarded them as useful in securing that the electors would make a good choice.'

representative democracy ignore its principal normative advantage: 'only democracy provides an institutional framework that permits reform without violence, and so the use of reason in political matters'.[14]

Popper's central claim is that democracy is a non-violent and permanently self-reforming polity whose governments and citizens are guided by rational public deliberations that are subject to the principle of the rejection of falsehoods and the development of falsifiable claims to Truth. Democracy in this sense is the political complement of what happens in the field of scientific-technical innovation, where the progress of knowledge – the improved human ability to solve human problems by coming to know better the world of nature – is facilitated by the use of scientific methods that Popper calls 'critical rationalism'. Popper is sure that the growth of human knowledge is a causal factor in the evolution of human history; he is equally insistent that the accumulation of knowledge is no straightforward (empiricist) matter of observing 'reality' and verifying theories through inductivist reasoning and the marshalling of the 'facts' of that so-called reality. Scientific theories, and human knowledge generally, are irreducibly conjectural: they are nurtured by acts of creative imagination for the purpose of solving problems that have arisen in specific historical and cultural settings. Positive results from the experimental testing of truth claims cannot confirm their truth status; what is logically decisive in the effort to demonstrate their validity is that such claims can withstand vigorous and rigorous attempts to falsify them. Not verification but falsifiability is the key criterion of the boundary between what is and is not genuinely scientific: a theory should be considered scientific if and only if it is open to, and can withstand, falsification. Just as in science, so as in democracy: fallibilism is their common property. Under democratic conditions, truth claims by citizens, parties and governments are under constant public scrutiny. When democracy works well, actors make conjectures, marshal evidence and use rational argumentation to pour cold water on hot-headed rhetoric, bogus truth claims and dangerous ideologies. In this way, democracy displays its 'fitness' and ultimate justification: that it holds hands with metaphysical and historical indeterminism and so makes possible evolutionary progress towards the elimination of errors, the solving of socio-economic and political problems, and the search for greater equality. Democracy is synonymous with the advance of reason. 'Men are not equal; but we can decide to fight for

---

[14] Karl R. Popper, *The Open Society and Its Enemies* (Princeton, NJ: Princeton University Press, 1950), pp. 4, 6.

equal rights', concludes Popper. 'Human institutions such as the state are not rational, but we can decide to fight to make them more rational. We ourselves and our ordinary language are, on the whole, emotional rather than rational; but we can try to be a little more rational, and we can train ourselves to use our language as an instrument not of self-expression, but of rational communication.'[15]

Popper's re-grounding of democracy as a form of polity guided by the unending quest for truth exemplified the growing muddle within democratic theory. Expressed in a less judgemental way, one could say that as the ideal of democracy travelled to all four corners of the earth, its arsenal of normative weapons grew in size and variety; or, to switch similes, the norm of democracy began to resemble an exotic plant whose seeds were carried to foreign soils, where they took root and flourished as healthy plants in various mutant forms. This syncretism of the democratic ideal no doubt helps to explain how its language could adapt to so many different habitats, for instance to lands where it had previously been absent. An example is Sun Yat-Sen's famous account of the arrival of democracy in China – 'the age of the people's power' – as the teleological culmination of Four Stages of History. Picturing modern Europe as a latecomer to the ideas of democracy that were already sketched by Confucius and Mencius (for whom 'most precious are the people; next come the spirits of land and grain; and, last, the princes'), Sun Yat-Sen summed up a world-historical movement as powerful and unstoppable as the eastwards-flowing Yangtze River: 'the first period was one of struggle between man and beast in which man employed physical strength rather than any kind of power; in the second period man fought with Nature and called divine powers to his aid; in the third period, men came into conflict with men, states with states, races with races, and autocratic power was the chief weapon. We are now in the fourth period', said Sun Yat-Sen, 'of war within states, when the people are battling against their monarchs and kings. The issue now is between good and evil, between right and might, and as the power of the people is steadily increasing we may call this the age of the people's sovereignty [*Min-ch'uan*] – the age of democracy.'[16]

Then – a more recent example – new justifications of democracy have sprung up in the Muslim world, of the kind championed in Iran by Mohsen

---

[15] Popper, *The Open Society and Its Enemies*, p. 461.
[16] Delivered in Canton as weekly lectures that concluded during the first months of 1924 and published as Dr Sun Yat-Sen, *San Min Chu I. The Three Principles of the People* (Shanghai: China Committee, 1927), pp. 165–166.

Kadivar. 'From the point of view of Islam', says Kadivar, 'human beings are endowed with magnanimity *[keramat]*. They are the carriers of the spirit of God ... and are therefore entitled to act as God's viceroy or Caliph on earth.' Human beings are deemed trustworthy, but this implies that each individual is saddled with the God-given duty to decide how to live, and to live well, according to certain norms. Core transcendent precepts certainly play (for believers) an important role in fulfilling this duty, but Kadivar emphasises that religious precepts are of two types: immutable and variable. Some broad religious principles, such as the unity of God, the prophecies of Mohammed and the certainty of the Hereafter, are unquestionable. They are God's gift to humanity, providing us with answers to questions that are otherwise impossible or too difficult or time-consuming to pose, let alone to answer. But God has left for human beings great scope for the exercise of human judgement. It is not only that the interpretation (*ijtihad*) of scriptural texts and traditions is intrinsically temporal, that is subject to freshly decided edicts by human beings themselves, *ijtihad* itself finds its limits in the fact that the texts and traditions are either silent about worldly affairs (the realm of *mubahat*) or inapplicable to a wide variety of matters (*manteghatul fragh*) that include such disparate challenges as operating an air traffic control system or deciding how best to secure the welfare of children within marriages that fall apart. This necessity of human judgement means that in many contexts the religious texts and traditions must be thought of as directives that are only capable of providing non-binding general guidelines (*akham-e irshadi*) for dwelling on earth. Hence the inescapability of *politics*: the collective definition and handling by human beings of their collective affairs.

Kadivar insists that politics in this sense is not a fixed, unchanging activity that is based on immutable principles, such as command and obedience. Democracy is just one of three broad types of politics – along with autocracy and aristocracy – and each has a contingent relationship with the religious precepts of Islam. Government conducted in the name of Islam (or any other religion) has no fixed or universal form; theocracy is not a type of government *sui generis*. Government can be autocratic, or aristocratic, or democratic, but only democracy can satisfy the formal requirements of Islam. Kadivar once called this form of government peculiarly suited to Muslim societies a 'religious democracy'; more recently, he prefers to speak of a 'democracy in Islamic society or democracy for Muslims'.[17] He has in mind democratic institutions and procedures that

---

[17] Correspondence with Mohsen Kadivar, Tehran, 26 June 2006. See also his 'Mardom Salari-ye Dee-ni [Religious Democracy]', *Tabarestan-e Sabz* (Tehran), 31 June 2001,

are infused with the religious conscience of citizens who think of their polity as legitimate because it is authorised by God. Since God has entrusted *all* people with the responsibility of living well on earth, and since living well depends upon the learned capacity to contribute as equals to the common ordering of collective affairs, democracy – not the system of appointive, absolute guardianship known as *velayat-e faqih* – is a requirement of serving God. Democracy breathes new life and new meaning into the old Islamic custom of swearing an oath of allegiance to leaders (*bay'at*). It does not treat humans as if they were orphaned children in need of guardians. Democracy provides the procedures for demonstrating human magnanimity. It has the added advantage of minimising 'the likelihood of making erroneous decisions in the public domain through maximising public participation in the decision making process'.[18] Civil society institutions, free and fair elections, the rotation of office holders, respect for citizens' rights, the public supervision of governmental power, and the civil, political and legal equality of opportunity of Muslims and non-Muslims with respect to race, ethnicity, gender, religion and political beliefs: these and other democratic mechanisms are the condition of possibility of living in dignity as a Muslim in the contemporary world.

---

pp. 5–7; also available online at www.kadivar.com. The vexed relationship between democracy and the system of Shi'ite Islamic government known as *velayat-e faqih* is analysed in 'Wilayat al-faqih and Democracy', in Asma Afsaruddin (ed.), *Islam, the State and Political Authority: Medieval Issues and Modern Concerns* (Basingstoke: Palgrave Macmillan, 2011). In these and other publications, Kadivar spells out his objections to those followers of Islam who base their objections to religious democracy on the following cluster of assertions: human beings are untrustworthy creatures who are easily led astray by satanic temptations or self-created fantasies, and hence are in need of guardians appointed by God; Islam is a comprehensive, totalising religion in that it provides guidance for the solution of all problems and the satisfaction of all needs of human beings, from the cradle to the grave; the guiding deliberations of the *ulama*, especially the grand jurists or *mujtahids*, must be paramount in the process of defining problems and satisfying needs of the people, who are duty-bound to accept and to comply with their teachings and rulings; the secular principles of civil and political equality are not in accordance with Islamic teachings, since believers are not equal with non-believers, men are not equal with women, the learned (*a'alim*) are not equals of the ignorant (*ja-hil*), while the people are most certainly not equals of the Guardian Jurist (*vali faqih*), whose say in all matters is final. On the writings of Kadivar and the history of different interpretations of democracy in Iran, I have drawn upon the insightful commentary of Ali Paya, 'Islam and/or Democracy? Some Views from Iran', Centre for the Study of Democracy Research Report, London, September 2004.

[18] '*Velayat-e Faqih* and Democracy', 17 November 2002, p. 4.

THE ORIGINALITY OF DEMOCRACY

What are we to make of these many and various attempts to find a normative foundation for democracy? Their heterogeneity is striking and it might be said by way of inference that the tendency for democracy to mean so many different things to so many different people is both an expression of its remarkable 'indigenisation' in many different contexts – the language and institutions of democracy have 'gone native' on every continent of the earth – and one of the key reasons why it has been able to spread and to win popularity in so many different socio-cultural contexts. The forces of indigenisation and diversification have combined to enhance its global popularity: *e unus pluribum* might be a short-hand formula to describe this trend towards semantic pluralism. Future historians who look back on our times may well conclude that this chameleonic quality of the democratic ideal proved to be its winning smile, in much the same way as the partly overlapping words 'liberty' and 'rights' have managed to win friends who see many different and conflicting things in the mirror of those terms.

It is painfully true, in contexts such as the townships of South Africa, that the word 'democracy' often means things less esoteric, like clean running water, bread and electricity. And while it is of course impossible to know how things will turn out, the polysemic quality of the democratic ideal is arguably a mixed blessing, if only because it arouses the deep suspicion – among those who think about the subject – that it is a thoroughly incoherent norm. The simple juxtaposition of its different justifications – here I am following the well-known method employed in Abu Hamid Al-Ghazali's *The Incoherence of the Philosophers* (*Tahafut al-falasifah*)[19] – exposes their incommensurability. Plenty can of course be learned positively from their comparison, including the imperative to acknowledge their legitimate place in any revised normative theory of democracy. Yet logical flaws and slips of reasoning are plentiful; the plausibility of each is weakened by blind eyes or dulled senses about important matters; and when assembled and compared, it is obvious that the problem they each set out to solve – to settle once and for all questions about what is so good about democracy – is compounded by their incompatibility. None of this should be surprising, since elsewhere in

---

[19] Abu Hamid Al-Ghazali's *The Incoherence of the Philosophers/Tahafut al-falasifah*, translated, introduced and annotated by M.E. Marmura (Provo, UT: Brigham Young University Press, 2000).

the field of philosophy all efforts to provide a rational foundation for ethical principles seem to have failed. One need not accept the melancholy conclusion of Wittgenstein – that 'the tendency of all men who ever tried to write or talk of Ethics or religion was to run against the boundaries of language. This running against the walls of our cage is perfectly, absolutely hopeless'[20] – to appreciate the gravity of the problem. Since Wittgenstein, techniques of rational argumentation and analytical reasoning have become more sophisticated, but in the world of the philosophy of ethics everything remains the same: disagreement and tower-of-Babel confusion tempered only by temporary trends and fashions led by this or that approach – yesterday existentialism and universal pragmatics and liberal theories of justice, today communitarianism and deconstruction and theories of sovereignty – whose success in the world is mainly determined by rhetorical charm, institutional funding, personal charisma, the art of timing and a dollop of luck.

The multiple attempts to find an ultimate foundation of democracy have similarly failed to put a stop to controversies and to heal disagreements. Like yeast mixed with flour, these efforts may well have leavened the philosophical case for democracy, but they have done so by yielding a strange-tasting bread. Incoherence turns out to be the price of diversity. Can an ideal that is backed up by little platoons of clashing metaphors and colliding justifications be anything other than 'essentially contested', even downright muddled? Can democracy mean so many things to so many different people in so many different contexts that – like a Coke adds Life advertisement – it comes to mean everything and nothing? And, if that is so, then surely it is no longer possible to believe naïvely that democracy has a special philosophical status, that it is based on an incontrovertible First Principle? In an age that offers technical expertise, blind deference, nationalism, theocracy, Chinese-style one-party rule, the fists of brute power and other alternative ways of governing, isn't democracy to be seen as just one – dispensable – norm among many others?

Tough questions of this kind should make us realise that the age of innocent belief in democracy is over; as well, they should serve as a warning that democratic ideals have no meta-historical guarantees, no inbuilt anti-virus protectors that shield democracy from its critics and dedicated foes. Richard Rorty's rather cynical pragmatism is symptomatic of this deflowering of democracy. So too is the audible increase in

---

[20] Ludwig Wittgenstein, 'A Lecture on Ethics', in Peter Singer (ed.), *Ethics* (Oxford: Oxford University Press, 1994), pp. 146–147.

expressions of outright boredom and contempt for democracy, sometimes in disturbingly high places, like Donald Trump's macho rule by tweeted edict and Silvio Berlusconi's mischievous tactics and televised appeals, directed like darts over the heads of parties, government officials and civil society groups, to be granted a simple majority so that he could get on with the job of taking care of business.[21] The loss of innocence of democracy is manifested in the deep unease generated by Napoleonic big talk of 'managed democracy' (Vladislav Surkov) and 'democracy with Chinese characteristics'.[22] And the deflowering of the democratic ideal is suggested as well by the replacement of normative discussions about democracy by various types of consequentialism, including the strangely tautological claim that democracy proves its ethical superiority and distinguishes itself from other polities because it maximises the ability or propensity of citizens to participate effectively in matters of collective decision making.

Those who favour consequentialist arguments for democracy heap praise on its practical ability to achieve specified goals. It is claimed that democracy is good because it stimulates economic growth, or forms of development that are mindful of justice (Rajni Kothari). Others have claimed that democracy tames the beasts of war, or that it can and does reduce 'terrorist' threats to 'national security'. Still others suppose that democracy fosters 'human development more fully than any feasible alternative' (Robert Dahl). Empirically and conceptually speaking, all of these claims are highly doubtful (they beg too many tricky questions about the nature of 'human development' or the desirability of 'economic growth', or what is 'national security', for instance), so doubtful in fact that potentially they do more harm than good for democracy, considered as a theoretical norm. The recent turn towards theories of 'deliberative democracy' arguably provides no convincing solution in this respect. Quite aside from strategic problems, to do with whether and how democratic deliberation is best maximised through reformed representative institutions, mass public spheres, judicial or constitutional guarantees,

---

[21] See 'Un'idea chiara di democrazia', *Unita* (Rome), 14 June 2004, quoting Prime Minister Berlusconi: 'When I take a decision, there begins a process of confrontation ... You then have to go to a [parliamentary] commission and to the House of Representatives [Camera dei Deputati]. All of this takes a long time. Then comes the turn of the Senators to prove [to the public] that they come to Rome not only to have a love affair. Give me 51% and I'll take care of everything.'

[22] See my *When Trees Fall, Monkeys Scatter: Rethinking Democracy in China* (London and Singapore: World Scientific Europe, 2017).

electronic voting or oppositional initiatives, self-styled 'deliberative democrats' praise democracy as a regulative norm because of its insistence that 'people's votes ought to reflect their *considered* and *settled* judgements, not top-of-the-head or knee-jerk reactions'.[23] Exactly why it is a good thing that citizens should act reflectively, responsively and responsibly, whether or to what extent that stipulation can come to mean the same thing, and why the norm of deliberation is to be counted as a universal norm, remains quite unclear. It is as if deliberative democracy is desirable because it maximises deliberation, which in turn has the good effect of keeping citizens busily involved in the business of deliberation.

In an era in which more people than ever before treat democracy as a worldly ideal, but without any sure grasp of why it is a universal good, something more radical is required. The last justificatory word in matters of democracy should not be left to pragmatists or cynics or ephemeral politicians like President George W. Bush, or to their clichés about 'democracy promotion' and the global war in support of 'democracy' against 'terrorism'. The democratic imagination now needs to protect the specificity of democracy from the criticisms of its opponents and doubters and charlatans by venturing into new territory. Consider the following possibility: the effort to democratise the norm of democracy by 'burrowing' underneath all previous efforts to ground democracy in arrogant talk of First Principles.

Attempts to fix the meaning and superiority of democracy using First Principles are not only incoherent, they also harbour an arrogance that undermines its historical originality – an originality that needs to be underscored by building it into the norm of democracy itself. What is this originality of democracy? Like gunpowder and print and other exotic imports from afar, the arrival of popular assemblies and (later) the strange-sounding word *dēmokratia* in the region that today we call the West changed the course of human history. Understood simply as people governing themselves, democracy implied something revolutionary: it supposed that humans could invent and harness special institutions to

---

[23] Robert E. Goodin, *Reflective Democracy* (Oxford: Oxford University Press, 2003), p. 1. Compare p. 228, where democratic deliberation is praised for its requirement that each individual tries to step into the shoes of others: 'It asks each of us to look at the situation from all those various perspectives, and to come to a judgement as to what is best from all those perspectives. But in saying "what is best overall", or "what is best for all", there is no sense of any "community" or "public interest" that is more than a function of the interacting interests of all those representative individuals, their preferences and perspectives.'

decide for themselves how they would live together on Earth. It may seem simple and straightforward to us, but the whole idea that flesh-and-blood mortals could organise themselves as equals into forums or assemblies, where they could pause and consider and then decide for themselves this or that or some other thing – democracy in this sense was an extraordinary invention of breath-taking scope. It was in effect the first-ever *human* form of government. All government is of course 'human' in the sense that it is created and built up and operated by human beings. The exceptional – out-of-the-ordinary – thing about the type of government called democracy is that it demanded that people see that life is never merely given. It called on them to understand that nothing that is human is set in stone, that all human institutions and customs are built on the shifting sands of time and place, and that if people are to acknowledge their equal vulnerability to the evanescence of human existence, then they have no option but to build and to maintain ways of living openly and flexibly. Democracy, the most power-sensitive form of government ever invented, implied the de-naturing of power. It called on human beings to understand that we are not necessarily what we are, so that within any political order questions about who manages to get what, when and how should be regarded as permanently open, as subject to ongoing public scrutiny.

Democracy urged people to see through talk of gods and nature. It called on them to reject claims to privilege based on some or other irrevocable criterion of superiority. Its ethic poured cold water on believers in *karma*: presumptions that individuals wishing to improve their prospects in the next life must properly fulfil the (caste) roles assigned to them in this life. Democracy meant self-government of equals, the lawful rule of an assembly of people whose sovereign power to decide things was no longer to be given over to imaginary gods, the stentorian voices of tradition, to cruel despots, or simply handed over to the everyday habit of unthinking indifference, so allowing others to decide matters of any importance on behalf of their subjects. The point can be put more abstractly: as a contingent mode of being in the world, democracy was born of a this-worldly orientation. It brought government closer to Earth. It supposed not just the willingness of people to spot a disjunction between the trans-mundane and mundane worlds, to think and act in terms of a chasm that separated a higher transcendental moral or metaphysical order and the everyday world of human beings living together within various earthly institutions. Democracy further supposed that there was no straightforward homology between these two otherwise connected worlds, and that therefore the mundane realities of the everyday world were 'up for grabs'; that is, capable of ordering and reordering by human beings whose eyes were fixed for at least some of the time on *this* world and not *that* world extending through, above and beyond human intervention.

Among the paradoxes in the history of democracy is that this originality of democracy was largely concealed in the best-remembered Athenian discourses on the subject – the very discourses that most observers still suppose are the degree zero of thinking about democracy. Positive justifications of democracy – democratic ways of speaking about democracy – were scarce in classical Greece, and not simply (as the English scholar Moses Finley once claimed) because 'the philosophers attacked democracy; the committed democrats responded by ignoring them, by going about the business of government and politics in a democratic way, without writing treatises on the subject'.[24] The reasons why the best-recorded early experiment with democracy left no democratic theory of the value of democracy run deeper. The French scholar Nicole Loraux has put one finger on the problem. She has shown that Finley's pragmatic interpretation begs too many questions and misses the key point: that the Athenian democracy actively mistrusted and never used writing as an instrument of theoretical reflection because that would have required withdrawal from the active life of the city. Exiled figures like Thucydides; Isocrates, who kept his distance from public life because he was shy and had a weak voice; outright opponents such as pseudo-Xenophon; and figures like Plato whose political career had been cut short: it was characters like these who condemned democracy and were in turn condemned as failed citizens because they were deemed both inactive (*apragmones*) and useless (*achreioi*). The touted exceptions – the funeral orations by Pericles (who proposed *arête* as the fundamental principle of democracy) and Lysias (who spoke of 'the ancient valour' of democracy's 'ancestors') – both contradicted the originality of assembly-based democracy by picturing it as a beautiful, harmonious whole, which it most certainly was not. Put simply – the point should be surprising for

---

[24] M.I. Finley, *Democracy Ancient and Modern* (London: Chatto & Windus, 1973), p. 28; cf. A.H.M. Jones, 'The Athenian Democracy and Its Critics', in *Athenian Democracy* (Oxford: Blackwell, 1957), p. 41, where it is noted that 'it is curious that in the abundant literature produced in the greatest democracy of Greece there survives no statement of democratic political theory'. Compare Nicole Loraux, *The Invention of Athens: The Funeral Oration in the Classical City* (Cambridge, MA and London: MIT Press, 2006) and *The Divided City: On Memory and Forgetting in Ancient Athens* (Cambridge MA, and London: MIT Press, 2002).

us today – classical Greece cannot rescue us from our confused ignorance about why democracy is a good thing because Greek commentators offer us only foundational justifications – or silence. Stranger still is the fact, mentioned in passing many pages ago, that the active friends of *dēmokratia* typically justified democracy by linking it to empire. Even the word itself oozed connotations of imperial conquest. Kurt Raaflaub and others have shown that by the middle of the fifth century BCE, 'power' and the striving for its accumulation stood at the centre of the lives, the experiences and the expectations of the Athenians. Power politics and imperialism were seen as typically Athenian and as typically democratic. The reputation of Athens as a busybody (*polypragman*) constantly striving to acquire (*ktasthai*) became synonymous with democracy itself. Hence the well-known remark of Thucydides: 'Remember, too, that the reason why Athens has the greatest name in all the world is because she has never yielded to misfortunes, but has lavished more lives and labours upon warfare than any other city, thus winning the greatest power that has ever existed in history. The memory of this greatness ... will be left to posterity forever.'[25]

HUMBLE DEMOCRACY

In the face of silence combined with the anti-democratic resort to First Principles or imperial advantage, what is needed is a new democratic way of thinking about the advantages of democracy. Here is one possible alternative: a theory of humble democracy. This approach does not regard the ethic of democracy as a universal norm founded upon some or other First Principle. It rather understands democracy as the condition of possibility of values and valued forms of life. It is a desirable norm whose 'universality', its applicability across borders and in different contexts, stems from its commitment to 'pluriversality'; that is, its militant striving to protect people and their biosphere everywhere and always against bogus First Principles and arrogant Grand Ideologies and their associated claims upon power.[26] The norm of humble democracy knows

---

[25] Kurt A. Raaflaub, 'Democracy, Power, Imperialism', in J. Peter Euben, John R. Wallach and Josiah Ober (eds.), *Athenian Political Thought and the Reconstruction of American Democracy* (Ithaca, NY: Cornell University Press, 1994), pp. 103–146; Thucydides, *History of the Peloponnesian War* (Cambridge, MA: Harvard University Press, 1956), Book 2, 64.3.

[26] John Keane, 'Democracy, Ideology, Relativism', in John Keane, *Democracy and Civil Society* (London and New York: Verso, 1988), pp. 213–245.

that in practice such Universals – dogmatic belief in the Nation, the Party, Men, the Market, the People or the State, for instance – have a bad track record because they camouflage and nurture struggles to monopolise and abuse power in the domestic and cross-border fields of both government and civil society.

The ethic of humble democracy therefore favours the invention and preservation of institutions and ways of life that stand guard against abusive Universals. It recognises and fosters the need to understand that multiple and different forms of power-sharing, power-restraining democracy are thinkable, and practicable. It stays calm when asked the unnerving question, likened by the Turkish writer Orhan Pamuk to a pistol shot in the midst of a music concert,[27] whether the West could endure forms of democracy created by its foes. The ethic of humble democracy everywhere aims to be the consistent champion of key virtues like toleration of differences, respect for legality and non-violence. Its strong sense of irony does not lead it astray, into the ranks of naysayers and so-called 'relativists', for whom nothing can be defined or asserted with certainty, and nothing done and nothing resisted. The ethic of humble democracy seeks actively to comfort the afflicted and to afflict the comfortable. It takes the side of the downtrodden. It favours institutional pluralism, differentiated equality and a variety of mechanisms of public accountability designed to ensure that wrong-headed decisions and outright folly can be prevented, or undone.

The ethic of humble democracy is inclined to action. It is courageous and audacious. But it does not embrace revolt for the sake of revolt. It knows that a taste for contingency and revolt can excite the desire for unlimited power over others. That is why humble democracy aims to humble. It favours the equalisation of power and stands opposed to manipulation, bossing and violent rule. It knows that efforts to prevent monopolies of power must never be abandoned, even though they are often in vain. Humble democracy dislikes hubris. This is not because it thinks of democracy as True and Right. It is rather because the ethic of humble democracy sees democracy as the best political weapon so far invented for publicly humbling armies, governments, parties, corporations and other NGOs, especially when their lust for power is aroused by the conviction that True and Right are on their side.

---

[27] Orhan Pamuk, *Snow* (London and New York: Knopf, 2004).

Seen in this way, democracy is a whole way of life whose durability depends upon the cultivation of the thoroughly political virtue of humility. Democrats should not shy away from talk of virtues. Benedetto Croce's well-known warning that those who engage in politics should learn to respect the power of the foundations of the political, applies especially to democracies, which require more than respect for the law, institutions designed to prevent the abuse of power, citizens' desire for participation, freedom of communication and periodic elections in order to function well. Monitory democracies also need democratically virtuous citizens. Virtues are the substructure of a peaceable monitory democracy. There are of course many great democratic virtues. Patience, mercy, courage and equal respect for otherness are among them. So is the propensity to compromise, the art (runs the old German proverb) of dividing a cake in such a way that everyone believes they have the biggest piece (Ein Kompromiß ist die Kunst, einen Kuchen so zu teilen, daß jeder meint, er habe das größte Stück bekommen). But, all things considered, the cardinal democratic virtue is humility. Humility is a friend of democracy because it refuses to put itself and other virtues on a pedestal: to be proud of certain virtues, including one's own or others' humility, is to suffer from its lack. Although sometimes symbolised by the quiet and boring person of modest upbringing, humility should not be confused with docility or submissiveness. Nietzsche insisted that humility is the morality of slaves, and therefore deserves nothing but contempt. 'Humility *[humilitas]* is sadness born of the fact that a man considers his own lack of power, or weakness', wrote Spinoza, but both he and Nietzsche provide misleading accounts of humility.[28] Had they been privileged to witness first hand public figures like Rosa Luxemburg or Martin Luther King or the Dalai Lama, they would have seen that the humble are not necessarily private, insignificant, or inconspicuous individuals – mere subjects who will never become rulers, or who die without leaving any other mark on the world except a few belongings and (if they are lucky) a grave. Humility is neither meekness nor lowliness (what Aristotle called *micropsuchia*) nor servility. Humility is in fact the antithesis of arrogant pride: it is the quality of being aware of one's own and others' limits, and the responsibility of ensuring these limits are always and everywhere observed.

---

[28] Friedrich Nietzsche, *Beyond Good and Evil*, in *Complete Works of Friedrich Nietzsche*, Vol. XII, edited by Oscar Levy (London, 1964), aphorism 260, p. 229; and Benedict de Spinoza, *The Ethics*, in Edwin Curley (ed.), *A Spinoza Reader: The Ethics and Other Works*, Vol. III (Princeton, NJ: Princeton University Press, 1994), definition 26, p. 192.

Humility has an allergic reaction to the self-satisfied Hobbesian rule *homo homini lupus est* (man is a wolf to men). It does not suppose it to be the starting point for understanding contemporary power, politics and international relations. Those who are humble try to be without illusions. They dislike vanity and have an affinity with honesty; the humble have an allergic reaction to calculated silence, nonsense on stilts, lies and bullshit on thrones. Humble human beings feel themselves to be dwellers on earth (*humus*, from which the word humility derives). They are aware of their obligations to the non-human world. They know that they do not know everything, that they are not God, or a god or goddess. Humility is their vital resource. It strengthens the powerless and tames the powerful by questioning their claims to superiority. It is the opposite of haughty hunger for power over others, which is why humility balks at humiliation. In a world of arrogance tinged with violence, humility emboldens. Unyielding, it gives individuals inner strength to act upon the world. It dislikes hubris. It yearns for its dethronement. Humility detests violence and the violent who always suppose, for a time, that they are right. Humility shuns showy arrogance and all forms of aggressiveness. Humility radiates in the presence of others, calmly, and cheerfully – it is a sociable virtue – enabling them to 'be themselves'. It does not arrogantly demand reciprocity. It implies equality. It is generous. Augustine wrote: 'Wherever there is humility there is also charity.' Descartes agreed: 'the most generous people are usually also the most humble'.[29] Aimed at the haughty and the bossy, humility implies tolerance, and since it shuns abusive power, it anticipates a more equal and tolerant – and less violent – world. The humble live off the simple conviction that the world to which they aspire is better than the world in which they are forced to dwell.

POLITICAL IMPLICATIONS

This is all very well, a sceptic may say, but what might this radical revision of our understanding of democracy imply for citizens, activists and institutional decision makers? What are the practical implications of supposing that democracy is a universal norm defined by its opposition to First Principles and to all forms of arrogant rule? Are there any implications at all?

---

[29] See John Keane, *Whatever Happened to Democracy?* (London: Institute of Public Policy Research, 2002).

There are various possibilities. Within any given context, the most obvious implication is the need to preserve as many power-monitoring and power-humbling mechanisms as possible. Actually existing monitory democracies do not need to reinvent wheels like periodic elections supervised by uncorrupted electoral commissions, requirements that politicians must resign when they are involved in conflicts of interest, or laws and independent media that guarantee the right of citizens publicly to question nonsense, to speak bitterness, and to organise against their elected representatives. These tried and tested procedures all tend to have humbling effects upon those who step out of line when they exercise power over others. They are methods more refined and effective and egalitarian than those of previous polities. Hunting and gathering communities excommunicated those who aroused the wrath of the spirits by falling in love with their own arrogance. Sumerian kings had their face slapped once a year by a priest to remind them of the importance of humility. Medieval kings in Europe were forced on occasion to swear to God that they would not abuse their power. Democracy instead prefers more down-to-earth methods with regular effects. It mobilises a much wider variety of non-violent means of subjecting the exercise of power to public scrutiny in order that constituents become free to choose decision makers who will eventually lose the trust of others, get the blame, and get thrown out of office, without triggering violence and uncivil war.

Such methods as periodic elections, competitive parties and parliamentary assemblies are an important inheritance, but they are not enough. There is today an urgent need worldwide to develop innovative methods of safeguarding and enlivening actually existing democracies – by strengthening the hand of humility as citizens tussle with power brokers in the fields of government, civil society and areas in between. The reason for the urgency is that all actually existing monitory democracies, whether in India or Australia or the United States or the older democracies of the European Union, are today suffering definite symptoms of aging and degeneration. There are troubles in the house of democracy.[30] The cluster of institutions that we call representative democracy is a product of the nineteenth and early twentieth centuries. In many countries, for the many reasons cited earlier in this book, this power-humbling system of representative democracy – periodic elections, the secret ballot, competitive party systems, parliamentary and expert supervision of state policy,

---

[30] See John Keane, *Whatever Happened to Democracy?* and the end section of John Keane, *The Life and Death of Democracy* (London and New York: Simon & Schuster, 2009).

cabinet or presidential forms of executive leadership, publicly funded governmental administration – is working poorly, or not as well as it might. The degenerative symptoms include the growing sense among publics that government is distant and too much like show business, or that politicians are pitiful creatures, or that joining a political party is for losers. The pores through which societies humble those who exercise power, through which they breathe and are represented within government, are beginning to feel partly or wholly blocked, which is also why talk of 'post-democracy' or even 'democrazy' is today flourishing. Such talk, despite all its imprecision, is the carrier of the feeling that there are things going on that we do not understand – even that there are bad developments for which we have no good theories, let alone practical remedies.

The list of such developments is perforce long because the scale of the emerging problems is already large, and growing. Their effects run wide and cut deep. Actually existing monitory democracies are subject to demographic trends – a dramatic ageing of the citizenry – that prompt some observers to speak of an emerging age of 'silver democracy'. These democracies are experiencing the corrosive effects of deepening social inequality caused by market and democracy failures. The spread of corporate power and the dismantling of Keynesian welfare state 'safety net' arrangements work to the benefit of the rich. The world of wealthy democracies is joining ranks with the world of the poor, not in the literal sense that wealth disparities and poverty of (say) Indian proportions are now haunting the wealthier democracies of the Atlantic region, but rather that democracy everywhere is coming to be blighted with the problem of how to create greater equality in such matters as life expectancy and health and housing when unrestrained market competition necessarily produces social losers. Actually existing democracies are facing as well the decline of social solidarity – a new round of social fragmentation and social contests caused by such forces as immigration, flourishing diasporas, populism and the developing self-awareness of rights-bearing civil societies. Then there are difficulties that result from the renewed impetus to de-democratise or insulate certain institutions (like corporations, central banks and newly privatised organisations) from electoral pressures, legal challenges and public accountability procedures. The militarisation of policing, the growth of state security apparatuses and secret surveillance operations are especially worrying examples of the growth of despotism in the name of defending democracy.

15 Is Democracy a Universal Ideal?

Contemporary democracies face additional challenges, including new and bitter controversies concerning the role and legitimacy of expertise in democratic politics. When and through which forums should so-called experts be allowed to dictate the terms of policymaking in such fields as stem cell research and nanotechnology? What counts as expertise? These and other questions first surfaced during the nineteenth century. They remain poorly formulated and badly handled in democratic theory and practice, partly because it remains unclear whether or where a line in the sand needs to be drawn against the use of power-humbling democratic procedures. Meanwhile, there are anxieties in the house of democracy about the long-term implications of the embedding of democratic politics in a new galaxy of communication media that could erode the public spheres that nurture and protect democracy, replacing them with some or other form of populist rule featuring 'block-busting' leader-performers like Rodrigo Duterte and Thaksin Shinawatra. The sarcastic complaint of Gore Vidal long ago served as a warning: 'a democracy is a place where numerous elections are held at great cost without issues and with interchangeable candidates'.[31]

All these ailments underscore the kind of internal dysfunctions and external threats now facing the spirit and institutions of monitory democracy. These deficiencies show that the efforts of past generations to humble power are no straightforward recipe for the building of paradise on earth, that the quest to tame the tigers of power is never entirely successful – hence, a quest of eternal importance. Democracy is an elusive norm. It is never a condition achieved. Monitory democracy has always to become democracy. It is a thing of action – not something capable of being piled up or squirreled away, like gold in a vault. That is why actually existing monitory democracies urgently need new thinking and practically effective remedies for the threats and challenges they face. The cultivation of a more just power-sharing democracy is among the imperative trends of our times; a theory of humble democracy helps make sense of its contours and lends it a stronger significance.[32] In practical matters, some of the required democratic innovations have already been placed on

---

[31] Gore Vidal, *A View from the Diners Club: Essays 1987–1991* (London: Andre Deutsch, 1991).

[32] See my 'Democracy Field Notes' series at www.johnkeane.net; Archon Fung and Erik Olin Wright (eds.), *Deepening Democracy: Institutional Innovations in Empowered Participatory Governance* (London: Verso, 2003); and Claus Offe (ed.), *Die Demokratisierung der Demokratie: Diagnosen und Reformvorschläge* (Frankfurt a.M.: Campus Verlag, 2003).

the political table. Neighbourhood forums, such as Chicago-style monthly 'community beat meetings' designed to give interested residents a chance to humble police officers by holding them accountable for their actions, count as an example. So too does the originally Brazilian practice of participatory budgeting, which offers humble city residents the chance of improving public facilities by codetermining public budgets that were previously distorted by elite-driven patronage payments. Many of these innovations are local in spirit and effect. Regional and country-wide initiatives – like new publicly funded 'watchdogs' or 'integrity commissions' for spotting and stamping out corruption, or the use of citizens' assemblies to re-design electoral systems – are less plentiful, though of equal importance. But the biggest challenge to the survival of democratic imagination and democratic ingenuity arguably lies in the field of cross-border corporate and state power relations. Our world currently witnesses a growth spurt in what was earlier described as quantum tunnelling. Power exercised arbitrarily by large-scale organisations is flourishing. But so, too, is the invention of new arguing and bargaining mechanisms like conferences, alternative summits and social forums, a flourishing cross-border journalism and culture of public debate. There is even the expansion of a global civil society – something like a worldwide version of Gandhi's idea of the *lok sevak sangh*, global networks of committed and politically unaffiliated activists who articulate local injustices, educate public opinion, mounting *satyagrahas* when necessary, thereby acting in general as watchdogs and champions of public life on a global scale.[33]

When examining these and other innovations, the friends of monitory democracy should not deceive ourselves. The radical idea of democracy, the most potent human weapon ever invented for humbling power, remains theoretically confused and institutionally impoverished. Actuality seems to be getting the upper hand against the democratic imagination and democratic politics. Who today knows how to put an end to the arrogant behaviour of our species by extending the vote and giving a 'voice' to non-human nature? Should actually existing monitory democracies try to develop new mechanisms for intervening in violent conflicts, using 'soft' and 'hard' means? And what should democrats around the world think about the United States? How can the first-ever global dominant power that is itself a democracy be democratised – subjected

---

[33] John Keane, *Global Civil Society?* (Cambridge: Cambridge University Press, 2003).

to power-humbling democratic mechanisms? The fact is that democrats currently have no solutions to these problems. We barely know how to ask questions about them. And when we do, the questions themselves sometimes seem unintelligible.

Not for the first time in its long and stormy history, democracy is again confronted with the unexpected, the un-named, the unknown and the unsolved. 'Thunder on! Stride on! Democracy, Strike with vengeful strokes', said the poet, Walt Whitman. Indeed. But with the humility that comes from the wisdom that knows that the (fashionable) distinction between 'consolidated' and 'transitional' and 'failed' democracies, sometimes even between 'good' and 'defective' democracies, should not be turned into a dogma; and that actually existing, 'consolidated' democracies are in no way blessed with divine immunity from internal corrosion and external weathering. The challenging point is monitory democracy as we have come to know it has no transversal or meta-historical guarantees. Democracy is not a First Principle, which is why it should be regarded as a tender plant that requires a well-watered and nutritious soil of institutions and customs fertilised regularly with good and regular doses of the spiritual food called humility.

Index*

*Warmest thanks to Stuart Rollo for his skilled preparation of the following entries.

Aarhus Convention, 267
Abu Hamid Al-Ghazali, 455
Academi. *See* Blackwater
Adams, Ansel, 131
Adamson, Peter, 298
Adler, Emanuel, 73
Adorno, Theodor, 122, 146
Afghanistan
  US invasion and democracy, 439
Aga Khan Development Network, 125
Aghion, Annie, 360
Ahmad, Irfan, 89
Al-Azmeh, Aziz, 324
Albert, David Z., 310
Albrecht, Glenn A., 268
Alden, Edward, 410
Alexander, Jeffrey C., 225
Al-Ghazali, Abu Hamid, 455
Aliber, Robert, 21
Allen, Woody, 134
Alonso, Sonia, 29, 254, 355, 391
Althusius, Johannes, 184, 327
Ambedkar, B. R., 124
Amnesty International, 68, 71, 125, 167, 177, 295, 403
Amsterdam Treaty of Union, 333
Amundsen, Roald, 348
Anders, Günther, 262
Anheier, Helmut K., 225
Annan, Kofi, 174
Anonymous, 168
Antarctic and Southern Ocean Coalition, 354, 374
Antarctic Treaty, 40, 350, 356–357, 360–361, 363–365, 375
Antarctica, 347
  biosphere, 370
  citizen scientists, 356
  Earth system science, 359
  governance, 40
  monitory democracy, 355
  resources, 373
  sovereignty, 364
  stewardship, 349
  the future of sovereignty, 372
Aquaculture Stewardship Council, 24
Aranda people, 94
Arcadian Law, 43, 390
Archibugi, Daniele, 34, 308
Arendt, Hannah, 145, 180, 185, 198, 203, 217
Ariès, Philippe, 272, 287
Aristotle, 37, 240, 252, 388, 463
  critique of numerical equality, 240
  on citizenship, 270, 321
Arjomand, Amir, 324
Aron, Raymond, 14, 318–319, 427
Asia-Pacific region
  integration, 34
  media consumption and communications patterns, 138

471

Assange, Julian, 169–170
Atatürk, 369
Athens
  imperial democracy, 44
Augé, Marc, 313
Aung San Suu Kyi, 410
Australia
  Aboriginal society, 86, 90
  colonialism in Australia, 11
  democratic monarchists, 80
  early colonisation, 83
  indigenisation, 12
  indigenous peoples, 39, 75
  origins of democracy in Australia, 11
Avaaz.org, 167

Badiou, Alain, 159
Balint, Jennifer, 98
Bangladesh Liberation War, 41
Barber, Benjamin, 308
Barber, Benjamin R., 52
Barnett, Michael N., 73
Barth, Fredrik, 335
Bashir Bashir, 12
Basso, Keith H., 212
Bator, Francis M., 24
Beaver Hills Initiative, 268
Beck, John C., 235
Becker, Carl L., 196
Becker, Gavin de, 423
Beckett, Samuel, 193, 215
Behrendt, Larissa, 88, 94
Belanger, Dian Olson, 356
Benjamin, Walter, 217
Benkler, Yochai, 163
Bennett, W. Lance, 163
Bense, Max, 262
Bentham, Jeremy, 279
Benton, Lauren, 362
Beppe Grillo, 164
Bergh, Albert E., 76
Bergson, Henri, 445
Berkman, Paul Arthur, 356
Berlusconi, Silvio, 15, 157, 457
Bernays, Edward, 146
Berndt, Catherine, 94
Berndt, Ronald, 94
Bertrand, Romain, 9
Best Party
  Iceland, 164
Beuve-Méry, Hubert, 165

Bevir, Mark, 33
Bhachan, Amitabh, 176
Bhutan
  environmental custodianship, 268
Bingham Powell, Jr, G., 51
biosphere, 6, 9
  and civil society, 106, 232
  and fossil fuels, 257
  and quantum. *See* quantum thinking: biosphere
  Antarctic stewardship. *See* Antarctica: stewardship
  Antarctica, 352
  environmental catastrophe, 29, 209, 214, 221, 258
  governance, 265
  green politics, 249
  in indigenous society, 12, 93
  stewardship, 259
  the impact of megaprojects, 208
Bjornlund, Eric C., 116
Black Death, 217
Blackstone, William, 273, 362
Blackwater, 44
Blair, Tony, 19, 187, 442
Blanning, T.C.W., 397
Bluntschli, Johann K., 46
Bly, Nellie, 158
Bobbio, Norberto, 29
Bodenständigkeit., 30
Bodin, Jean, 325, 362
Bohm, David, 314
Bohr, Niels, 359
Bonneuil, Christophe, 249, 255
Boorstin, Daniel, 187
Boorstin, Daniel J., 173
Bourdieu, Pierre, 146
Brady, Anne-Marie, 367
Brandeis, Louis D., 157
Brazil
  national policy conferences, 118
Briquet, Jean Louis, 9
Bronfenbrenner, Urie, 283
Brougham, Lord Henry, 77
Brown, Alexander J., 11, 95
Brown, Tina, 155
Bruno, Giordano, 198
Buchan, Bruce, 81, 83
Buchanan, George, 326
Burke, Edmund, 144, 172
Burma Watch International, 168

Bush, George W., 50, 187, 407, 442, 445, 458
Butler, Judith, 54
Buzan, Barry, 419
Byrd, Richard, 348

California Watch, 168
Calvin, William, 149
Cambers, Andrew, 149
Camp, John M., 385
Campbell, Alastair, 187
campfire democracy. *See* democracy:proto-democracy
Camus, Albert, 123
capitalism
  and civil society, 225
  and democracy, 19, 21
  civic capitalism, 246
  global finance, 24
  predatory capitalism, 22
  the problem of underconsumption, 235
Caplan, Bryan, 21
Carlyle, Thomas, 80, 133, 171–172, 177, 366
Carothers, Thomas, 47, 442
Carr, Mike, 268
Carter, Jimmy, 67, 174
Casales-Riperro, Andreu, 159, 244
Castells, Manuel, 162, 314
Castles, Francis G., 338
catastrophe, 213
  political implications, 216
  prevention, 220
Catherine the Great, 396
Chamfort, Sébastien-Roch Nicolas, 297
Chang, Hao, 10
Chartist movement, 22
Chen Shui-bian, 68, 71
Chen, Xiaobei, 283
Cheneval, Francis, 34, 308
Chesterman, Simon, 407
Chiang Kai-Shek, 63
children, 6
  16th century shift in political perspective, 272
  child labour, 281
  child-citizens, 283, 292
  commercial consumption, 290
  contemporary politicisation of children, 284
  in the political order, 270
  socio-economic improvement, 280
  voting age, 291
  youth subculture, 289

China
  China's rise, 47
  citizenship concept, 323
  colonial sources of democracy, 10
Christiano, Thomas, 316
Churchill, Winston, 88, 296
churnalism, 18, 193
citizen journalism, 18
citizenship, 37
  18th century France, 327
  European citizenship, 37
  in China. *See* China:citizenship concept
  in Islam, 324
  nation-centric, 327
  statist model, 325
Civicus, 225
civil society
  and markets, 230, *See* markets and trade: civil society
  and nonviolence, 416
  and the biosphere. *See* biosphere:and civil society
  conceptual modernisation 18th and 19th centuries, 226
  early conceptions, 26
  failures, 427
  institutions of civil society, 243
Clastres, Pierre, 91
climate change, 304, 350
Clinton, Bill, 198, 403
Clinton, Hillary, 140
Cohen, Jared, 140
Cohen, Michael A., 188
Cohn, Norman, 217
Colaresi, Michael P., 42
Colas, Dominique, 340
Colbert, Stephen, 187
Cole, David, 15
Collier, Paul, 380
colonialism, 8
  and representative democracy, 97
  in Australia. *See* Australia:colonialism in Australia
  in Taiwan, 62
  origins of democracy, 75
  settler societies, 11
Commission for the Conservation of Antarctic Marine Living Resources, 268
communicative abundance, 17, 103, 120, 125, 205
  and democracy, 36

communicative abundance (cont.)
  and post-truth, 131
  and power relations, 127
  and privacy, 151
  facts in communicative abundance, 142
  information overload, 129
  technological features, 162
  the architecture of, 135
complex notion of equality, 238
Confucius, 452
Consumer Financial Protection Bureau, 25
Consumer Protection Act, 25
Convention on Biological Diversity, 267
Cook, Captain James, 82–83
Cooper, Robert, 343
co-operative movement, 22
Copernicus, 2, 198
Coppedge, Michael, 304
Corradi, Juan, 413
Cotton, James, 34
Coughlan, Robert, 359
Couldry, Nick, 173
Crick, Bernard, 222
Croce, Benedetto, 463
Crosby, Alfred W., 400
cross-border self-government, 312
Crossman, Richard, 358
Cuba
  US intervention, 41
Curran, James, 143
Curthoys, Ann, 96, 98
cyber security, 17
cyberspace
  anachronism, 144

Dahl, Robert, 56, 457
Dahl, Robert A., 32, 48, 288, 305, 307, 309
Dahrendorf, Ralf, 332
Dalai Lama, 177, 313
dark money, 29
Darnton, Robert, 150
Dauvergne, Peter, 233
Davenport, Thomas H., 235
Davies, Susanne, 85
de Certeau, Michel, 9
de Correspondent, 204
de Neubourg, C.J., 298
de Sainte Croix, G.E.M., 385
de Tocqueville, Alexis, 78, 116, 238, 242, 254–256, 393, 406
Dean, Malcolm, 199

Delian League, 383
Delumeau, Jean, 216, 418
demarchy, 21
Demeny, Paul, 292
democracy
  20th century spread of democracy, 440
  and christianity, 445
  and empire, 383
  and expertise, 357
  and fear, 413, 418
  and first principles, 444
  and Islam, 452
  and nonviolence, 451
  and the industrial revolution, 254
  and truth, 451
  as a way of life, 5
  banyan democracy, 8
  consequentialist arguments for democracy, 56
  cosmopolitan democracy, 35
  cross-border democracy, 32
  deliberative democracy, 14, 35, 87, 263
  democratic decline, 466
  democratic historicity, 5, 13, 52, 147
  democratisation, 43
  democratisation of information, 147
  electoral democracy, 7
  ethic of democracy, 55
  failure, 14, 16, 24, 217, 236
  financial regulation, 25
  first principles, 456
  foundationalist arguments for democracy, 54
  green politics, 249
  historical materialism and democracy, 103
  kaleidoscopic qualities, 36
  language in democracy, 2, 4, 8, 49
  liberal democracy, 13, 43
  monitory democracy, 468
  nationalism, 394
  non-violent power sharing, 414
  participatory democracy, 14, 52
  polyarchal democracy, 32
  proto-democracy, 86
  representative democracy, 7, 16, 20, 52, 62, 76, 79, 119, 262, 390, 399, 402
  rethinking equality, 236
  sovereignty, 363
  spreading democracy through war, 406

the global spread of democracy, 10
The Humpty Dumpty Principle, 3
universal franchise, 29, 78
vulnerabilities, 22
war and violence in democracy, 40, 121, 379, 409
Western-centrism, 6–7
Democracy Barometer, 129
Democratic Audit network, 129, 168
democratic empires, 44
democratic peace theory, 45, 48, 401, 404
democratic pessimism, 21
democratic sovereignty, 19
Derrida, Jacques, 154, 308, 363, 369
Dershowitz, Alan, 379
Descartes, René, 464
Descola, Philippe, 265
Desmond, William, 433
despotism, 411
Destutt de Tracy, Antoine L. C., 305
de-territorialisation, 36
Deutsch, Karl, 73, 342, 407
Dewey, John, 123, 146, 295
Diamond, Jared, 6, 218, 252
Diamond, Larry, 5, 407
Dickens, Charles, 197, 254, 278
Digital Michelangelo Project, 149
digitization of historical records, 149
Disraeli, Benjamin, 42, 407
Dodd–Frank Wall Street Reform, 25
Dostoevsky, Fyodor, 234
Doumani, George A., 349
Dower, John W., 10
dragon fruit democracy, 9
Droz, Jacques, 397
Dryzek, John S., 263
Dunn, John, 7, 443
Duterte, Rodrigo, 467
Dutton, W. H., 145
Dyer MacCann, Richard, 133

East Asia, 34
Eco, Umberto, 15, 191
Edelman, Murray, 146
Education Act 1880, 281
Edward Green, Jeffrey, 136
Einstein, Albert, 36
Elazar, Daniel J., 305
Electoral Assistance Division of the United Nations, 119

Elias, Norbert, 274, 416, 423
Eliot, George, 111
Eliot, T. S., 51
Ellsberg, Daniel, 211
Ellul, Jacques, 146
Emerson, Ralph Waldo, 171, 176–177
Engels, Friedrich, 227, 231
Entner, Roger, 137
Epimenides of Knossos, 186
equality principle, 27
Erasmus, Desiderius, 275
Estrada, Joseph, 163
European Union
  citizenship, 318, 332
    future prospects, 345
    kaleidoscopic qualities, 329
  de-militarisation, 339
  equality, 336
  European Court of Justice, 37
  European disintegration, 37
  financial regulation, 43
  structure, 38
Evans, Julie, 86, 98
Exxon Valdez, 258
Eyre, Edward John, 85

Facebook, 137, 153
fascism
  as mutation of democracy, 121
  in Taiwan, 63
fear
  and death, 430
  and the media. *See* media:and fear
  as a public problem, 425
  modern categorisation, 433
  overcoming fear, 422
  Post Traumatic Stress Disorder, 435
  the democratisation of fear, 431
  the triangle of fear, 418
Feenstra, Ramón, 159, 164, 244
Fernandez, James W., 210
Ferraris, Maurizio, 154
Ferrero, Guglielmo, 414
Fiege, Mark, 254
Finley, M. I., 460
Finley, Moses, 460
Fish, Stanley, 55
Fitzgerald, John, 323
Five Star Movement, See Beppe Grillo
Flannery, Tim, 264
Flinders, Matthew, 211

Flyvbjerg, Bent, 210, 232
Fogarty, Ellie, 373
Ford, Lisa, 84
Fording, Richard C., 314
Formosan Association for Human Rights, 68
Foster, Charles, 268
Foucault, Michel, 195, 204
France
  early conceptions of citizenship. *See* citizenship:18th century France
  economic inequality, 231
  French Revolution, 395
  French revolutionary wars, 397
  imperial democracy, 44
  inequality, 27
  Napoleonic Wars, 398
  Pacific nuclear testing, 128
Frank, Anne, 288
Frankfurt, Harry G., 196, 200
Fressoz, Jean-Baptiste, 249, 255
Freud, Anna, 286
Freud, Sigmund, 411, 434
Friedman, Thomas L., 140
Friedrich, Carl J., 122, 124
Fujitani, Takashi, 152
Fukushima nuclear meltdown, 215
Fukuyama, Francis, 9, 42, 104, 114, 210, 235, 380, 441
Fullilove v. Klutznick, 240
Fung, Archon, 113, 308, 467
Furet, François, 395

Gadamer, Hans-Georg, 2
Gamson, Joshua, 173
Gandhi, Mahatma, 11, 175, 177, 468
Garlan, Y., 386
Gasset, Ortega y, 53, 212
Geertz, Clifford, 92
Gehrke, Hans-Joachim, 390
Gellner, Ernest, 37, 220
genocide
  of indigenous peoples, 49, 84, 97
Genovese, Ann, 98
Germany
  Pirate Party, 164
Gerring, John, 304
Ginsborg, Paul, 15
Girard, René, 48
Glassman, Ronald, 87
Glassner, Barry, 432
Global Accountability Project, 168

Global Agenda Council on the Role of Civil Society, 225
global federalism, 308
global financial crisis 2008, 25
Global Witness, 167
globalisation
  first wave of globalisation, 10
  sovereignty trilemma, 33
globalisation of fear, 411
Goldstein, Joseph, 286
Goodall, Chris, 267
Goodin, Robert E., 304, 458
Gorbachev, Mikhail, 174
Gore, Al, 174
Goya, Francisco, 229
Great Reform Act of 1832, 83
Greek democracy, 460
  and labour, 252
  and military virtue, 50
  and oligarchy, 76
  and privacy, 154
  assembly democracy, 20, 52
  participatory democracy, 14
  positive justifications, 460
  pre-Athenian, 387
  rivalry and war, 383, 399
  size, 305
Green Belt Movement, 174
green politics, 249
  human custodianship, 265
  political parties, 267
Green, David, 226
Green, Josephine, 144
Greenpeace, 350
Grefe, Christiane, 267
Greffrath, Mathias, 442
Grey, George, 83, 85
Griffith, D.W., 133
Griffiths, Tom, 349
Grimm, Dieter, 114
Grimshaw, Patricia, 86
Grossman, Lawrence K., 140
groupthink, 202
Grüne Akademie, 267
Guaraní people, 117
Guha, Ramachandra, 11
Guizot, François, 79

Habermas, Jürgen, 226, 264, 308
Hall, Charles, 231
Hall, Edward T., 212

Index 477

Hall, G. Stanley, 410
Hall, Peter A., 22, 247
Hall, Stuart, 289
Hallberg, Peter, 327
Hardt, Michael, 226
Hart, Paul 't, 201
Hartley, John, 165, 190
Hassner, Pierre, 427
Havel, Václav, 199, 215, 226
Hawksley, Humphrey, 380
Hazlitt, William, 57
Health and Morals of Apprentices Act 1802, 281
Hearst, William Randolph, 159
Hedge Chris, 173
Hegel, Georg Wilhelm Friedrich, 227, 297, 338, 427
  on family, 276
Heidegger, Martin, 29, 197, 214, 258–259, 261, 264–265
  on mechanisation, 258
Heinrich Böll Foundation, 267
Held, David, 7, 34, 308
Hetherington, Kregg, 117
Hiatt, L. R., 85
Hickman, Martin, 167
High Seas Fisheries Compliance Agreement, 370
Hirschman, Albert, 429
Hirst, John B., 10
Hiskes, Richard P., 29
historical materialism, 253
Hobbes, Thomas, 82, 171, 213, 325, 362, 392, 424, 432
Hobsbawm, Eric, 214
Hobson, Christopher, 41, 406
Hodgson, Marshall G. S., 324
Homer, 253, 384
Hook, Sidney, 123
Hoover, Herbert, 175
Horkheimer, Max, 48, 146
Hortefeux, Brice, 161
Hsiao, Michael, 72
Hsin-liang, Hsu, 66
Human Rights Watch, 125, 167
humility
  and representation, 262
  and the biosphere, 265, 352, 370
  humble government, 80, 237
  humbling democracy, 51, 316, 461, 467
  political virtue, 463–464

Humphreys, David, 312
Huntington, Samuel P., 9, 104, 114–115
Husserl, Edmund, 151
Hutt, John, 83

I Kuan Tao, 64
Iceland
  banking bubble, 202
Ike, Nobutaka, 10
Ikenberry, John, 407
Illpirra people, 93
imaginative thinking, 51
imperial democracies, 409
India
  Bangladesh intervention, 41
  practical outcomes of democracy, 56
indigenisation, 6, 8, 11, 59, 75, 91, 96, 455
  in Australia. See Australia:indigenisation
  in Taiwan, 61, 69
indigenisation of democracy, 8
indigenous peoples, 6, 39, 49, 75
  Aboriginal Australians. See Australia: Aboriginal society
  and restorative justice, 98
  and self-government, 95
  and the biosphere, 268
  as minorities under Westminster principles, 95
  biosphere, 311
  colonialism and representative democracy, 81
  Maori. See New Zealand:Maori society
  North America, 86
  resistance to colonialism, 11
inequality
  economic, 23, 26, 228, 235
  social, 23, 26, 228
Institute for Global Food Security, 24
International Commission of Jurists, 71
international institutions, 31
International Olympic Committee, 117
Internet of things, 144
interwar period, 110
Iraq War 2003, 42, 128
Isocrates, 460
Ivison, Duncan, 81

Jacques, Martin, 48
James, Howard, 337
Janis, Irving, 201

Japan
  colonial sources of democracy, 10
  imperial Japan, 62
Jay, Martin, 185
Jeffers, Susan J., 423
Jefferson, Thomas, 76, 262
Jefferson, Tony, 289
Jones, A. H. M., 460
Jones, Ernest, 434
JPMorgan, 25
Jumblatt, Walid, 442
Juncker, Jean-Claude, 343
Jünger, Friedrich Georg, 262

Kadivar, Mohsen, 453
Kahneman, Daniel, 57, 204
Kanerva, Ilkka, 161
Kant, Immanuel, 180, 327, 396, 404
Kapuściński, Ryszard, 424
Kästner, Erich, 267, 352
Kaul, Nitasha, 11
Keaton, Diane, 134
Keen, Ian, 91
Kelly, Loretta, 94
Kenny, Anthony, 419
Keynes, John Maynard, 25
Keynesian economics, 228
Keyssar, Alexander, 10, 78
Khalaf, Samir, 404
Khan, Aamir, 176
Khanna, Parag, 34, 303
Kierkegaard, Søren, 420
Kim Jong-il, 184
Kim, HeeMin, 314
Kindleberger, Charles P., 21
King, Jr, Martin Luther, 124, 176
Klein, Maury, 235
Kocka, Juergen, 19
Kocka, Jürgen, 20
Koestler, Arthur, 120
Kohl, Helmut, 320
Kolbert, Elizabeth, 233
Kothari, Rajni, 457
Koyré, Alexandre, 18, 180–181, 198
Krizhanich, Iurii, 326
Krugman, Paul, 410
Kuhn, Thomas, 197
Kunai people, 88
Kuomintang, 63
Kymlicka, Will, 12

Laclau, Ernesto, 53
Lane, Robert E., 229
Lange, David, 234
Lapidus, Ira M., 324
Lasswell, Harold D., 146
Latham, Robert, 34
Latour, Bruno, 266, 352, 354
Lavenex, Sandra, 34
Le Goff, Jacques, 301
Le Pen, Marine, 15
Lefebvre, Henri, 307
Lehmann Brothers, 25
Leibfried, Stephan, 338
Lévinas, Emmanuel, 417, 424
Levine, Dan, 152
Liddle, R. William, 11
Lifton, Robert Jay, 358
Lin, Christine L., 66
Lin, Lihyun, 65–66
Linz, Juan J., 62
Lippincott, Benjamin E., 79
Lippmann, Walter, 334
Lipscomb, Andrew A., 76
Lipset, Seymour Martin, 234
Lisbon Treaty, 39, 320, 322, 330
Locke, John, 81, 275
Loraux, Nicole, 383, 460
Lord Byron, 275
Lord Derby, 42, 407
Lord Justice Leveson, 167
Loritja people, 93
Low Countries
  sixteenth century democratic origins, 20
Luther, Martin, 272
Lysias, 460

Maathai, Wangari, 174
Machiavelli, Niccolo, 181, 187, 340, 369, 415
Macintyre, Stuart, 81
Mack, Andrew J.R., 405
Macpherson, C.B., 5, 22, 231, 450
Madison, James, 11, 88, 118
Madsen, Richard, 323
Mahbubani, Kishore, 48
Maier, Charles S., 31, 303
Malcolm, Janet, 154
Malinowski, Bronislaw, 86, 89
Malkin, Benjamin Heath, 274
Malm, Andreas, 254
Malthus, Thomas, 227

managed democracy, 47
  in Russia. *See* Russia:managed democracy
Mandela, Nelson, 174, 179
Mann, Michael, 305, 380
Mann, Thomas, 50, 122–124
Manovich, Lev, 148
Mao Tse-Tung, 53, 63–64, 242
Marcuse, Herbert, 291
Maritain, Jacques, 122, 445
markets and trade
  abolition of, 28
  civil society, 242
  damaging effects on civil society, 230
  market failure, 21, 24, 230, 428
  market instability, 27
  new market dysfunctions, 232
  predatory markets, 226
  re-socialisation of markets, 244
Marshall Plan, 38, 329
Marshall, T.H., 328, 336
Marshall, Thomas H., 22, 247
Maruyama, Masao, 2
Marx, Karl, 22, 227, 231
Marzano, Stefano, 144
Mass Psychology, 2, 21
Mauss, Marcel, 229
May, Theresa, 213
Mayer-Schönberger, Viktor, 156
Mazzini, Giuseppe, 22, 447
McCain, John, 188
McCord, Edward L., 353
McGeough, Paul, 442
McKenna, Mark, 96
McLuhan, Marshall, 135, 141, 173
McNeill, J.R., 251
McNeill, John R., 428
McNulty, Sheila, 410
Mearsheimer, John J., 185
Mebarak, Shakira, 176
Médecins Sans Frontières, 403
media
  and democracy, 16
  and fear, 429
  fear, 417
  in the post-truth era. *See* post-truth:and the media
media decadence, 18
Mediapart, 168
media-saturated societies
  and democracy, 103
  and monitory democracy, 17
  conflict within, 166
  silence in, 211
Mediterranean Action Plan, 268
megaprojects, 207
Mencius, 452
Merkel, Wolfgang, 10, 29, 254, 391
Merlan, Francesca, 91
Metzger, Thomas A., 324
Mexico
  US intervention, 41
Michelson, Albert Abraham, 3
Michelutti, Lucia, 9
military contractors, 43
military technology, 400
Mill, James, 448, 450
Mill, John Stuart, 134, 297, 450
Miller, Alice, 277, 435
Milosević, Slobodan, 423
Mises, Ludwig von, 109
Mitchell, Jessie, 96–97
Mitchell, Timothy, 257
Moffitt, Benjamin, 15, 53
monitory democracy, 13, 104
  'glocalisation', 119
  a universal norm?, 440
  and energy politics, 257
  and human rights, 125
  and inequality, 23
  and media, 17–18
  and peoplehood, 54
  and physical space, 306
  and quantum thinking, 310
  and war, 401
  Antarctica. *See* Antarctica:monitory democracy
  arguments for, 120, 439
  democratic virtues, 463
  de-territorialisation, 316
  innovations, 30
  institutions of monitory democracy, 107
  intellectual roots, 123
  misunderstandings, 113
  networked and viral communications, 131
  populism, 53
  principle, 110
  reasons for monitory democracy, 46
  resistance to monitory democracy, 46
  voluntary public scrutiny by governments, 118

Monnet, Jean, 38, 329
Montaigne, Michel de, 203
Montesquieu, 251, 326, 411–413, 415, 419, 432
Moore, Barrington Jr., 20
Moore's law, 134
Morozov, Evgeny, 143
Morris, Meaghan, 204
Morris, William, 247
Mosley, Max, 155
Mother Teresa, 176
Motte, Standish, 84
Mouffe, Chantal, 48
muckraking, 158
Mueller, Harald, 404
Muir, John, 250
Mulgan, Geoff, 23, 247
Müller, Jan-Werner, 308
Munck, Gerardo L., 106
Murakami, Haruki, 218
Murdoch, Rupert, 167
Murray people, 94
Mururoa Atoll. *See* France:Pacific nuclear testing
Musil, Robert, 5
Muslim world, 452
Myers, Fred R., 92

Nancy, Jean-Luc, 56
nationalism, 38
Navarria, Giovanni, 111–112, 163
Negri, Antonio, 226
Nehru, Jawaharlal, 88, 179
Neuman, W. Russell, 138
Neumann, Franz, 411, 428
Neville, Peter R., 283
New Zealand
  indigenous peoples, 39
  Maori society, 90
News Corporation
  phone-hacking scandal, 167
News of the World, 167, *See* Mosley, Max
Newton, Isaac, 198
Ngarinyerri people, 93
Nichiren Buddhist sect, 64
Nicholas of Cusa, 198
Niebuhr, Reinhold, 123–124
Nielsen, Carl, 37
Nietzsche, Friedrich, 46, 52, 80, 195, 440, 463
Nippert-Eng Christena, 151

Nixon, Richard, 65, 128, 186, 199
Noelle-Neumann, Elisabeth, 160
Nordenskjöld, Otto, 367
Norris, Pippa, 51, 159
Nova, Alessandro, 268, 352
nuclear weapons
  Anti-Ballistic Missile Treaty, 401, 427

O'Neill, John, 246, 283
Obama, Barack, 56, 88, 160, 188, 192
Ober, Josiah, 382
Obinger, Herbert, 338
Octen, J.C., 390
OECD Anti-Bribery Convention, 120
Offe, Claus, 23, 247, 318, 429, 467
Office for Democratic Institutions and Human Rights, 119
Oil and democracy. *See* monitory democracy: and energy politics
Oliver, Jamie, 291
One China Policy, 68
Open Government Platform, 119
Open Rights Group, 156
Organization for Security and Co-operation in Europe, 116, 119
Orton, Joseph, 86
Orwell, George, 123, 238
Ostrom, Elinor, 317
overkill, 399

Paine, Thomas, 80, 227, 447
Paine, Tom, 199
Palestine
  foreign intervention, 41
Palin, Sarah, 188
Pamuk, Orhan, 462
Panek, Elliot, 138
Park, Yong Jin, 138
Parker, Theodore, 444
Parliament Watch, 115
parliamentary democracy, 13, 217
  under threat in the 1940s, 46
Pateman, Carole, 14
Patočka, Jan, 209
Peceny, Mark, 406
Peloponnesian War, 389
Pels, Peter, 9
Pempel, T. J., 34

Pérez-Díaz, Víctor, 229, 241
Pericles, 383–384, 460
Pettit, Philip, 443
Pfaff, William, 343
Philippines
    US intervention, 41
Philips, David, 86
Phillips, Adam, 288
Pickering, Paul, 77
Pierce, Franklin, 175
Piketty, Thomas, 19, 26, 228, 230
Pinochet, Augusto, 361
Pintupi people, 92
Pitjantjatjara people, 88, 92
Pitty, Roderic, 99
Plamenatz, John, 296
Plato, 66, 122, 180–181, 460
Platt, Anthony M., 296
Plutocracy, 23
Podunavac, Milan, 322
Poe, Edgar Allan, 423
Pogrebinschi, Thamy, 118
Pol Pot, 242
Polanyi, Karl, 22, 242–244
political culture, 7
Politifact, 195
Poll Khol, 165
Pomerantsev, Peter, 175
Pomeranz, Kenneth, 254
Popper, Karl, 450
populism, 38, 122
    in managed democracy, 47
    populist leaders, 15
Portugal
    Lisbon Earthquake 1755, 217
post sovereignty, 36
Postero, Nancy Grey, 13
post-truth, 126
    and mass society, 182
    and the media, 188, 205
    bullshit, 200
    gaslighting, 193
    lying, 180
    the distinction between truth and lying, 194
    truthseeking, 203
power
    humbling of arbitrary power, 56
    and children, 294
    and communicative-abundance, 159, 163

and experts, 358
and mega-projects, 208
and political accountability, 19
and the media, 126, 190
and truth, 201
children and power, 270, 273
democratic restraint, 15
humbling of arbitrary power, 199, 347, 467
    Taiwan, 69
imperial power, 11, 44, 383
in human life, 5
in indigenous society, 91, 98
labour power, 243, 252
market power, 230, 241
power relations, 5
power-contesting mechanisms, 16, 34, 103, 106, 112, 118, 266, 355, 462
power-scrutinising mechanisms, 14
the citizen and the state, 325, 327
the privatisation of power, 210
transnational power monitoring, 119, 167, 312, 403, 465
war and violence, 50
power relations, 358
    and media, 127
    in monitory democracy, 109
Priestley, J. B., 123
Pritchard, David, 252, 386
Pritchard, David M., 44, 383
privacy
    private-public distinction, 156
Privacy International, 156
Proudhon, Pierre-Joseph, 28
Przeworski, Adam, 106, 304
Ptolemy, 2
Putin, Vladimir, 47

quantum thinking, 36, 301, 309, 370
    biosphere, 311
    non-linearity, 302

Raaflaub, K.A., 385–386
Raaflaub, Kurt A., 461
Radcliffe-Brown, Alfred R., 91
Radischev, Aleksandr, 327
Rainbow Warrior sinking, 128
Rainbow, Stephen L., 267
Rashomon Effect, 210

Reed, Lou, 289
Reich, Robert B., 23, 247
Reilly, Alexander, 98
Reilly, Benjamin, 11
Reiter, Dan, 405–406
Reporters without Borders, 403
responsibility to protect, 41
Reynolds, Henry, 86
Rice, Condoleezza, 442
Riedel, Manfred, 325
Riesenberg, Peter, 325
Riis, Jacob, 158
Robespierre, Maximilien, 395
Robinson, Eric W., 388
Rodrik, Dani, 33
Rojek, Chris, 173
Romantic Circles, 149
Roosevelt, Franklin D., 121, 185
Roosevelt, Theodore, 178, 255
Roper, Jon, 79
Rorty, Richard, 55, 157, 191, 441, 443, 456
Rosanvallon, Pierre, 10, 27, 231, 237
Rosenberg, Alfred, 122
Rosenthal, Hattie, 430
Ross, Daniel, 380
Rousseau, Jean-Jacques, 135, 176, 236, 276, 305, 318, 327, 391
Rowe, Dorothy, 186
Rowland, F. Sherwood, 220
Rowley, Charles, 98
Royal Bank of Scotland, 25
Rufer, Alfred, 397
Rummel, R.J., 426
Runciman, David, 366
Rush, Benjamin, 433
Russell, Bertrand, 146
Russell, Lord John, 83–84
Russett, Bruce, 48, 404–405
Russett, Bruce M., 387
Russia
  managed democracy, 47
Rwanda
  foreign intervention, 41

Sadiki, Larbi, 11
Sahlins, Marshall, 8, 90
Saint-Amand, Pierre, 48
Salamon, Lester M., 225
Sale, Kirkpatrick, 269
Salzen, Eric A., 419

Sanford James, 425
Saramago, José, 321
Sartori, Giovanni, 15
Sartre, Jean-Paul, 341, 417
Sassen, Saskia, 33–34
Scarry, Elaine, 221
Schaefer, Hans, 389
Schaffer, Frederic, 8
Schama, Simon, 322, 397
Scheps, Leo, 11
Schimmelfennig, Frank, 34, 308
Schlamm, Willi, 24
Schmidt, Eric, 174
Schmidt, Helmut, 174
Schmitt, Carl, 47, 96, 303, 363, 381
Schmitter, Philippe, 38, 330, 339
Schöber, Felix, 66
Schudson, Michael, 18, 104, 118, 189, 205, 334, 359
Schuller, Wolfgang, 387
Schumpeter, Joseph, 109, 231
Scientific Committee on Antarctic Research, 360
Scott, C.P., 165
Sea Shepherd Conservation Society, 354
Segerberg, Alexandra, 163
Sen, Amartya, 441
Senegal
  language in government, 8
Sengupta, Somini, 152
Serbia
  October 2000 revolution, 423
Shakespeare, William, 172, 197
Shirky, Clay, 163
Sieyès, Abbé, 237
Silas Deane affair, 199
Simmel, Georg, 178, 229, 416, 429
Sinclair, Upton, 257
Singer, J. David, 404
Singer, Max, 426
Skinner, Quentin, 82, 321
Small, Melvin, 404
Smith, Adam, 26, 226, 230, 340
Smith, Rogers M., 54
Smith, Tony, 45, 403, 406
socialism
  origins of socialism, 21
Solnit, Albert J., 286
Sommerville, John C., 273
Soskice, David, 22, 247

Soto, Hernando De, 232
Space Hijackers, 168
Spain
  indignados movement, 164
Spears, Britney, 187
Spencer, Diana, 154, 176
Spinoza, Baruch, 463
St Augustine, 274
Stam, Allan C., 405–406
Stanner, W.E.H., 93
state surveillance
  Taiwan, 64
Steffens, Lincoln, 158
Stepan, Alfred, 62
Stephen, James Fitzjames, 294
Stewart, Potter, 168
Stieglitz, Alfred, 131
Stocking, George W., 85
Streeck, Wolfgang, 19, 32, 339
Students for a Democratic Society, 113
Sun Yat-Sen, 452
Surkov, Vladislav, 175, 457
Swain, Shurlee, 86
Syria
  foreign intervention, 41
Syrian Observatory for Human Rights, 168

Taiwan
  White terror, 63
  coming of democracy, 42
  democracy in Taiwan, 61
  democratic characteristics, 9
  Democratic Progressive Party, 66
  democratic transition, 67
  independence movement, 72
  kolonko democracy, 70
  media suppression, 65
  national identity formation, 62
Taiwan Political Prisoner Rescue
  Association, 68
Tallien, Jean Lambert, 327
Tanner, Lindsey, 200
Taplin, George, 93
Tarbell, Ida, 158
Taruskin, Richard, 37
Tassier, Suzanne, 397
Te Urewera Act 2014, 268
Teller, Edward, 359
Teng-hui, Lee, 72
territorial Sovereignty, 7, 32, 62, 304, 307, 362, 392

and monitory democracy, 110
Thailand
  practical outcomes of democracy, 56
Thaksin Shinawatra, 15, 467
Thatcher, Margaret, 333
Thayer, G. Robert, 268
the Elders, 174
the European Citizen, 318
the Treaty of Amsterdam, 322
the Vietnam War
  Gulf of Tonkin incident, 185
Therborn, Goran, 285
Therborn, Göran, 304
Thompson, E.P., 245
Thompson, John B., 145, 151
Thomson, Edward Deas, 85
Thomson, Janice E., 416
Thucydides, 122, 384, 430, 433, 460
Tibet
  Central Tibetan Administration and monitory democracy, 313
Timor Leste
  foreign intervention, 41
Tindemans Report, 320
Tito, Josip Broz, 53
Tormey, Simon, 159
Transparency International, 129, 168
Trechsel, Alexander H., 38, 330
Triggs, Gillian, 364
Trivers, Robert, 209
Truman, Harry, 175, 199
Trump, Donald, 25, 157, 190, 457
Tsurumi, E. Patricia, 62
Tuchman, Gaye, 165
Tully, Mark, 138
Tures, John A., 406
Turner, Graeme, 173
Tutu, Desmond, 176, 178
Twitter, 136, 153
Tyler, Stephen A., 212

Ukraine
  foreign intervention, 41
Uluru-Kata Tjuta National Park, 39
UN Convention on the Rights of the Child, 287
UN Highly Migratory Fish Stocks Agreement, 370

unelected representatives, 170
lionism, 179
United Kingdom
  British colonial governance, 77
  financial regulation, 9
  London Olympics 2012, 209
United Nations
  power structure, 33
United Nations Charter, 125
United Nations Security Council, 65
United States
  Bay of Pigs, 201
  economic inequality, 231
  financial regulation, 25
  foreign interventions, 41, 406
  global order, 403, 426
  imperial democracy, 44, 442
  invasion of Iraq 2003, See Iraq War
  Jeffersonian democracy, 76
  media consumption and communication patterns, 137
  oil boom, 256
  poverty, 27
  recognition of communist China, 65
  September 11 attacks, 410
  war on terror, 40, 342, 379, 410
Universal Declaration of Human Rights, 63, 71, 125
Urbinati, Nadia, 81, 254
Urwin, Derek W., 38, 329
US Foreign Corrupt Practices Act 1977, 120
Utzon, Jørn, 209

Vallès, Jules, 278
van Heerden, C., 144
Vattimo, Gianni, 55, 131, 194
Veblen, Thorstein, 19
Vibert, Frank, 108
Vidal, Gore, 467
Vilar, Emílio Rui, 179
Vogl, Frank, 120
von Bülow, Bernhard, 394
von Clausewitz, Carl, 181
von Hayek, Friedrich, 21, 106, 230, 232
von Humboldt, Wilhelm, 156
Vote Compass, 115

Wadham, Jemma L., 357
Wakabayashi, Masatoshi, 160
Walras, Leon, 233
war and violence in democracy, 48

war on terror. See United States:war on terror
Ward, Alan, 78
Ward, Ivan, 434
Warren, Samuel D., 157
Watergate affair, 128
Watson, Tom, 167
wealth redistribution, 22
Weber, Max, 4, 142, 170, 178, 323, 334
Weber, Paul, 192
Weinberg, Steven, 310
Wen-Chia, Luo, 66, 72
Wernicke, Stephan, 318
Wesley, Susanna, 277
Western decline, 47
Western democracy, 13
Western-centrism, 441
Westphal, Carl, 434
whaling disputes, 368
Whanganui River Te Awa Tupua framework agreement, 39
Whitman, Walt, 111, 241, 469
Wight, Martin, 78
Wijnberg, Rob, 204
WikiLeaks, 16, 127, 168
  'collateral murder' video, 169
Wikipedia, 148
wild thinking, 3, 16, 52, 133
Wildavsky, Aaron, 426
Wilde, Alexander, 12
Wilde, Oscar, 197
Wilders, Geert, 15
Willis, J.W., 85
Wilson, Woodrow, 45, 281
Winnicott, D.W., 429
wise citizens, 130, 203
Wittgenstein, Ludwig, 4, 197, 219, 382, 456
Wolin, Sheldon S., 53, 171
Wolof, 8
Woolf, Stuart, 397
World War, First, 217
World War, Second, 46, 121, 217, 401
  American entry, 185
World Wide Web Consortium, 167
Worsthorne, Peregrine, 189
Wright, Erik Olin, 113, 467
Wu, Rwei-Ren, 10, 62
Wu, Zhuoliu, 61

Xe Services. See Blackwater

Yergin, Daniel, 256
Yolngu people, 93
YouTube, 148

Zagorin, Perez, 195

Zakaria, Fareed, 47
Zamosc, Leon, 13
Zhang, Weiwei, 48
Zielonka, Jan, 37, 39, 319
Zilboorg, Gregory, 431